APPLYING ETHICS

Applying Ethics

A Text with Readings

JEFFREY OLEN
Regis University
Colorado Springs

VINCENT BARRY
Bakersfield College

JULIE C. VAN CAMP
California State University
Long Beach

AUSTRALIA • BRAZIL • CANADA • MEXICO • SINGAPORE
SPAIN • UNITED KINGDOM • UNITED STATES

THOMSON
WADSWORTH

Editor: *Worth Hawes*
Assistant Editors: *Lee McCracken, Barbara Hillaker*
Editorial Assistant: *Patrick Stockstill*
Technology Project Manager: *Julie Aguilar*
Marketing Manager: *Christina Shea*
Marketing Assistant: *Mary Anne Payumo*
Marketing Communications Manager: *Stacey Purviance*
Creative Director: *Rob Hugel*
Executive Art Director: *Maria Epes*
Print Buyer: *Nora Massuda*
Permissions Editor: *Bob Kauser*
Production Service: *Matrix Productions Inc.*
Text Designer: *Lisa Henry*
Copy Editor: *Connie Day*
Cover Designer: *Yvo Riezebos Design*
Cover Image: *Jim Frazier/Images.com/Corbis*
Compositor: *International Typesetting and Composition*
Text and Cover Printer: *West Group*

Printed in the United States of America
1 2 3 4 5 6 7 11 10 09 08 07

Library of Congress Control Number: 2006934778

ISBN-13: 978-0-495-09499-9
ISBN-10: 0-495-09499-4

Thomson Higher Education
10 Davis Drive
Belmont, CA 94002-3098
USA

For more information about our products, contact us at:
Thomson Learning Academic Resource Center 1-800-423-0563
For permission to use material from this text or product, submit a request online at **http://www.thomsonrights.com.**
Any additional questions about permissions can be submitted by e-mail to **thomsonrights@thomson.com.**

To Jane Cullen
—J.O.

To My Students
—J.C.V.C

To Jim Wilson
—V.B.

CONTENTS

shinler
Govier

Nozick

PREFACE

FOR MOST STUDENTS taking applied ethics, it will be their first—and maybe only—philosophy course. They may have thought and argued about such topics as abortion and the death penalty, welfare and affirmative action, but they enter the classroom with little experience in moral philosophy or critical thinking. Nor do they always have a firm handle on the legal, scientific, and other information relevant to the issues they'll be discussing. Throughout the nine editions of *Applying Ethics*, the book's goal has been to meet these students' needs. *Applying Ethics* is, as the subtitle says, a text with readings, providing a variety of features to help students and their instructors approach the most significant moral controversies of the day.

The book contains two distinct parts. Part 1, "Moral Reasoning," provides the philosophical background that many users will find helpful. The first chapter deals with moral reasons and principles, drawing on the views of such philosophers as Aristotle, Kant, Mill, and Rawls. It also includes discussions of ethical relativism and what it means to think morally. The second chapter is an introduction to critical thinking, with particular emphasis on the evaluation of moral arguments.

The chapters in Part 2, "Issues," begin with introductory essays by the book's authors. Each lays out the relevant moral issues and background material. Next come pro and con arguments on the chapter's central dispute, written in colloquial "point–counterpoint" style. After that come four readings, each preceded by head notes summarizing the main points and followed by questions for analysis. And then, to provoke further class discussion, each chapter ends with four Case Presentations.

NEW FEATURES

1. New Chapter 12, "Computer Ethics and the Internet."
2. New case presentations: the cervical cancer vaccine, the *Goodridge* gay marriage decision, and polygamy in Chapter 3; abortion for sex selection in Chapter 4; Terri Schiavo in Chapter 5; stem cell research in Chapter 6; Stanley "Tookie" Williams in Chapter 7; the Geneva Conventions and Guantanamo Bay in Chapter 8; reparations and sexual harassment on "Friends" in Chapter 10.
3. Updates of Chapter 1, including expanded selections from Aristotle and Kant.

4. Updates of Chapter 3, including new case presentations on the cervical cancer vaccine, the *Goodridge* gay marriage decision, and polygamy.
5. Updates of Chapter 4, including a new case presentation on abortion for sex selection.
6. Updates of Chapter 5, including updates on Jack Kevorkian, *Washington v. Glucksberg*, and a new case presentation: "Terri Schiavo: Voluntary Euthanasia or Murder?"
7. Updates of Chapter 6, including new information on stem cell research, two new readings (Bonnie Steinbock, "The Morality of Killing Human Embryos," and Paul Lauritzen, "Stem Cells, Biotechnology, and Human Rights: Implications for a Posthuman Future); two new case presentations on the presidential policy on stem cell research and public reaction to the president's veto of stem cell research funding.
8. Updates of Chapter 7, including updates on the execution of juvenile offenders and DNA evidence, and a new case presentation on Stanley "Tookie" Williams.
9. Updates of Chapter 8, including new readings (Alan Dershowitz, "Make Torture an Option"; David Luban, "Torture and the Ticking Bomb"; David Cole, "National Security State") and a new case presentation on "The Geneva Conventions and Guantanamo Bay."
10. Updates of Chapter 10, including updates on Prop 209, and new case presentations on "Reparations: An Overdue Debt to African Slaves in America?" and "Friendly Sexual Harassment?"
11. Updates of Chapter 11, including both animal rights and environmental ethics.
12. Appendices on "How to Write a Philosophy Paper," "Plagiarism: What It Is, Why It's Wrong, and How to Avoid It," and "How to Do Research and Citation on the Web" are now available on the Wadsworth Web site.
13. Several case presentations and readings from previous editions are now available on the Wadsworth web site.

ACKNOWLEDGMENTS

As a teacher who has used this book for many years, I have long been grateful for the work of Vincent Barry, who produced the first two editions alone, and Jeffrey Olen, who joined him as co-author. Ken King was the Wadsworth philosophy editor for the first four editions, followed by Tammy Goldfield, Peter Adams, Steve Wainwright, and his assistant Lee McCracken. Along with the many helpful suggestions from teachers over the years on successive editions, the following provided special help for this one: Paul Bruno, Assumption College; Matthew Burstein, Southern Methodist University; Jerry Caplan, California Lutheran University; Nancy Slonneger Hancock, Northern Kentucky University; Augustine Yaw Frimpong-Mansoh, California State University, Bakersfield; Dan O'Bryan, Sierra Nevada College; Charles J. Sabatino, Daemen College; Aeon J. Skoble, Bridgewater State College; and Peter Vallentyne, University of Missouri, Columbia.

I have been honored to join such an exceptional team for the eighth and ninth editions and hope this new one lives up to the expectations of our most important readers, our students.

Julie C. Van Camp

PART ONE

Moral Reasoning

CHAPTER ONE

Moral Reasons

WHEN WE ACT, we act for reasons. We eat breakfast because we are hungry or because it gives us the energy we need to get through the morning. We read a book because we want to be entertained or because we want to learn something. We buy a car because it's reliable, fun to drive, or affordable.

At any one time, we might—and usually do—have many reasons to do all sorts of things. Most of what we do we do for more than one reason. We buy a car because it's reliable *and* fun to drive and affordable, and we read a book because it's entertaining *and* informative.

But not all of our relevant reasons support the same course of action when we choose to do something. Often, we find ourselves faced with conflicting reasons, reasons both to do and not to do something. In addition to our reasons *for* eating breakfast, we might have reasons for *not* eating it. We might be in a hurry, or we might be trying to lose weight.

When our reasons lead us in different directions like that, we must decide which direction to take. Although we can make our decision in a purely arbitrary way—by flipping a coin, perhaps—the rational way to proceed is to weigh the conflicting reasons and ask ourselves which of the conflicting reasons are the best reasons. If we are lucky, we will answer the question correctly. That is, we will choose the best thing to do, the right course of action. We will do what we ought to do under the circumstances.

If we are unlucky, we will choose the wrong course of action. We will do what we ought not do.

Of course, whether we choose correctly is not merely a matter of luck. If it were, rational deliberation would be no more trustworthy than the flip of a coin. Whether we choose correctly is also a matter of how well informed we are, how carefully we reason, how accurately we gauge the pros and cons of the alternatives, how exhaustive our deliberations are. Thus, we can minimize the element of luck when buying a car by test-driving various models, by reading reports in *Car and Driver* and *Consumer Reports,* and by giving careful attention to our own needs and preferences. Do we really need a car with this much power? Does appearance matter that much to us? Can we afford all of these options?

We can also minimize the element of luck by making sure that we reason in a reliable way. In the next chapter, we will take a careful look at what makes reasoning reliable. For the rest of this chapter, though, we concentrate on a particular kind of reasoning—moral reasoning.

MORAL REASONING

To reason morally is not to reason in a certain way. Rather, it is to consider certain kinds of reasons—moral reasons. It is to try to arrive at the best moral reasons for acting, to choose the morally right course of action, to do what we morally ought to do.

There are, after all, many different ways in which an action can be right or wrong. An artist who puts the right finishing touches on a painting does what is aesthetically right. An investor who buys and sells stock at the right times does what is financially right. Someone who gives up smoking cigarettes does what is right for her health. And someone who returns a found wallet does what is morally right. In the first case, we have an action supported by the best aesthetic reasons. In the second, one supported by the best financial reasons. In the third, one supported by the best health-related reasons. In the fourth, one supported by the best moral reasons.

Sometimes an action will be right in one way but wrong in another. That is, the best reasons of one kind will support it, while the best reasons of another kind will support something else. Reasons of self-interest, for example, might lead us to conclude that we ought to keep a found wallet. Moral reasons, on the other hand, lead us to conclude that we ought to return it. In cases like that, we must decide which kind of reason is best. We must decide what we ought to do, all things considered.

When we make these all-things-considered judgments, we generally do so based on what matters to us most. Some people are willing to risk their health because they enjoy smoking; others are not. Some people are willing to forego a higher paying job for a more pleasant one; others are not. Some people are willing to set aside their self-interest to do what is morally right; others are not.

Although we generally give people a lot of leeway in determining what most matters to them, we do expect them to give moral reasons high priority. And when the moral stakes are very high, we expect people to give moral reasons top priority. We expect them to realize that the morally right course of action is the best course of action—what they ought to do, all things considered.

These are not unreasonable expectations. If we are to live together in society, we must cooperate with one another. And if we are to cooperate with one another, we must trust one another. And we cannot trust people who treat honesty, good faith, and loyalty lightly.

INDIVIDUAL MORALITY AND SOCIAL MORALITY

Honesty, good faith, and loyalty are important considerations of *individual* morality. When each of us, as individuals, must decide what to do, we must, if we are to decide morally, consider whether we are being honest or dishonest, faithful to our commitments to others or unfaithful to them, loyal to those who deserve our loyalty or disloyal to them. The roles that such considerations play in our lives are crucial to our understanding of ourselves as moral people. And the roles that they play in the lives of others are crucial to our moral judgments of both them and their actions.

Because the topics discussed in Part 2 of this book concern the morality of various kinds of actions, considerations of individual morality will play an important role in those discussions. But so will moral considerations of another kind—*social* morality. In discussing issues such as abortion, we will be concerned not only with whether it is moral for an individual woman to have an abortion in various kinds of circumstances, but also with how society as a whole should deal with abortion.

The two concerns are related, of course, but as we shall see, answering the first does not necessarily settle the second. Rape and armed robbery are obviously immoral, and even rational rapists and armed robbers, we can safely suppose, understand why we require laws forbidding such behavior and why we are perfectly justified in locking up people who disobey them. But no rational person believes that every immoral act should be punishable by imprisonment or even made illegal. Who would want to prosecute everyone who cheats in a "friendly" game of tennis?

Also, we might have good reason to want society to regulate various kinds of behavior that do not violate any considerations of individual morality. Many people feel, for instance, that a mature, psychologically sound adult does nothing immoral by enjoying pornography in the privacy of his or her home, but these same people might also feel that pornography presents serious social dangers and should be curbed or outlawed.

Obviously, what we need are some general principles of social morality to guide us when we ask ourselves how society ought to deal with morally important social issues. And just as obviously, we need some general principles of individual morality to guide us when we ask ourselves how individuals ought to act in particular situations.

But before we take a look at various principles of individual and social morality, we should take a look at another issue, the issue of ethical relativism.

ETHICAL RELATIVISM

Ethical relativism is the view that moral truths are not absolutely true but true relative to a particular society or individual. According to an ethical relativist, whether an action is right or wrong depends on the moral norms of society or the moral commitments of the individual, and no absolute standard exists by which differing rules or commitments can be judged. So what's morally right in one society may be morally wrong in another, and what's morally right for Mary might be morally wrong for John.

As this description suggests, there are two forms of relativism—**cultural relativism** and **individual relativism.** According to the cultural relativist, the rightness or wrongness of an action depends on society's norms. According to the individual relativist, the rightness or wrongness of an action depends on the individual's own commitments.

The appeal of ethical relativism rests on two points. First, different societies often do have different moral norms, and individuals often do have different moral commitments. Second, there seems to be no decisive way to settle moral disputes as there are decisive ways to settle many other kinds of disputes. If two individuals or societies differ radically about right and wrong, there seem to be no tests or experiments we can run to confirm the views of one or the other.

Both kinds of relativism exist in varying degrees. Someone can be a relativist about some matters—sexual morality, for instance—but a nonrelativist about others—slavery, for instance. Someone can also be a cultural relativist about some matters and an individual relativist about others or both a cultural and individual relativist about all moral matters. Relativism can also come in more or less sophisticated versions. In the least sophisticated versions, arguing about abortion, affirmative action, or any other issue we address in Part 2 is like arguing about whether chocolate tastes better than vanilla. In other words, morality is merely a matter of taste or custom; and one taste or custom is as good as another, whether the taste is for slavery or brightly colored clothes, for theft or science fiction. In the more sophisticated versions of relativism, morality is much more complicated; and arguments about the issues in Part 2 concern much more than individual taste or social custom, leading to the conclusion that some tastes or customs are decidedly worse than others.

Relativism is, of course, a controversial view. Opponents argue that variation in moral commitments does not prove that moral truth is relative any more than variation in scientific belief proves that scientific truth is relative. They also argue that the difficulty of deciding moral disputes can be dispelled by a deeper understanding of morality. Although we cannot go through all the arguments for and against the many forms of relativism here, we should note a few points that pertain to the rest of the book.

First of all, even if it turns out that some form of relativism is true, that does not mean we cannot criticize the norms of our society or the moral commitments of others. Morality is not, as the least sophisticated forms of relativism would have it, merely an arbitrary matter of taste, like the preference for vanilla over chocolate, nor is it merely a matter of custom, like Fourth of July fireworks. As will be stressed throughout this book, we have the norms and commitments we do for *reasons,* and because they govern the most important areas of our lives, it is important that we examine these reasons carefully. Perhaps some of our moral commitments rest on false beliefs. Perhaps some rest on outmoded assumptions about what makes for a harmonious or desirable society. Perhaps some are inconsistent with other more deeply held moral commitments, such as fairness. Perhaps we neglected important considerations when we first arrived at some of our moral commitments.

The discovery of such flaws in our moral reasoning has led us to abandon a variety of practices, from racial segregation to involuntary medical treatment. As we shall see, many people feel that similar flaws undercut our justification of other practices—abortion, for instance, or treatment of animals, or capital punishment. And whether we feel that our conceptions of fairness and a desirable society are absolutely valid or only relatively valid, we can—and must, if we are to consider our society a good one—test our practices against them.

PRINCIPLES OF INDIVIDUAL MORALITY

It is easy to think of morality as a system of rules—some telling us not to do certain things, like cheat, lie, break promises, steal, rape, and kill, and others telling us to do certain things, like help others in need, pay our debts, and be loyal to friends and family. But why do we have these rules and not others?

The quick answer is that these are the rules we were taught. And there is no arguing with that answer. Moral rules are the rules accepted by the members of a given society, the rules we agree to follow and expect others to follow, in large part because we were taught to do so. But if we look at morality in only that way, we do both morality and ourselves a disservice. We do morality a disservice by making it look arbitrary. We are in effect saying that we have the moral rules we do because we have the moral rules we do. And we do ourselves a disservice by making ourselves look like mindless followers of arbitrary rules.

But moral rules are not arbitrary. We have the rules we do for good reason. And we are not mindless followers of them. We accept them because we understand that we have them for good reason. And when we feel that reason requires us to change them, we do just that.

Consider one timely example of moral change. Not too long ago, women were expected to live their lives within narrowly defined roles. It was considered their duty to stay home with their children, their obligation to see to various household tasks, and while men might be praised for helping out every now and then, they were not morally required to do so. They were morally required to be the family breadwinner, and women were morally required not to take jobs from other family breadwinners.

All that has changed, of course—or is at least in the process of changing. Many women and an increasing number of men have come to doubt the acceptability of such rules. And what makes them unacceptable is that they are now seen as violating some general moral *principles*—the principle of fairness, most notably. Women do not believe it fair that their lives are so restricted, and many men have come to agree.

What this example shows is that morality is not merely a matter of rules but also of principles—general standards for evaluating conduct, standards that we apply to all behavior and rules.

This point can be made in another way. No moral rule is exceptionless. Sometimes we are morally justified in breaking a promise. Sometimes we are morally justified in failing to help someone in need. Consider how easy it is to find yourself in a situation in which you must break a promise to Mary to help John or must fail to help John to keep your promise to Mary. Unless we allow that the two rules have exceptions and one of them applies here, we are left with a morally immovable object and a morally irresistible force—that is, a morally impossible situation. To resolve the dilemma, we must recognize that one of the rules takes precedence in this particular case and that we are dealing with a legitimate exception to the other. How do we decide which takes precedence? By appealing to some general moral principle.

There is also one more thing that shows the importance of moral principles. The debates of Part 2 of this book are, in part, about what moral rules we should adopt. Should we adopt a rule that forbids us to give terminally ill patients in great pain a lethal injection if they request it? Should we adopt a rule that permits us to do so? Or should we adopt a rule that requires us to do so? Should we adopt a rule forbidding all abortions, some abortions, or no abortions? If suitable answers are to be found, we must appeal to moral principles.

The Principle of Utility

One of the best known general moral principles is closely associated with a number of moral philosophers, most notably the British philosopher John Stuart Mill (1806–1873). It is known as both the **principle of utility** and the **greatest happiness principle.** It tells us to produce the greatest balance of happiness over unhappiness, making sure that we give equal consideration to the happiness and unhappiness of everyone who stands to be affected by our actions.

The principle of utility can be applied in two different ways. The first is to apply it to individual *acts.* How are we to do that? Well, we might ask ourselves every time we act which of the options open to us will maximize happiness, but Mill did not recommend that procedure because it would be much too time consuming. Since we know that lying and stealing and cheating will rarely maximize happiness when everyone is taken equally into account, the sensible thing to do is avoid such behavior without worrying about the principle of utility.

But we sometimes have reason to believe that what usually maximizes happiness might not. Remember the example in which you cannot both keep your promise to Mary and help John. Although keeping promises usually maximizes happiness and helping others usually maximizes happiness, in this case, one will not. That's when Mill tells us to appeal to the principle of utility before we act.

The second way is to apply the principle to *rules* rather than to acts. Following this method, we appeal to the principle of utility only when we are considering which moral rules we should adopt. We ask ourselves which of the alternatives will maximize happiness if generally followed by the members of our society. Would a moral rule permitting mercy killing maximize happiness, or would one forbidding it? Whichever one would, that's the rule we ought to adopt.

The principle of utility is certainly a reasonable moral principle, whether applied to acts or rules. How our behavior affects others should be of moral concern to us. Moreover, we want our moral rules to make our society a good society, and it is hard to argue against the claim that a happy society is better than an unhappy society. So it is not surprising that utilitarian considerations play an important role in the moral reasoning of many individuals. Nor is it surprising that they play an important role in many of the arguments of Part 2.

Still, most people believe that it would be a mistake to make the principle of utility the final arbiter of *all* moral decisions. Suppose Bill borrows $10 from Carol on the condition that he pay her back tomorrow. Doesn't that create an obligation to her? And since it does, does Bill have the moral right to neglect that obligation merely because he can maximize happiness by doing something else with the money?

That's one reason for recognizing limits to the principle. Another is that it is a very demanding principle. Very rarely, after all, do most of us take into equal account everybody's happiness before we act. Often, we think that our own happiness and the happiness of people who most matter to us should take precedence. That's why we sometimes splurge on presents for our families, even though we might create greater happiness by spending our money on the poor instead. Although we might agree that it would be commendable to do otherwise, it hardly seems *wrong* to splurge on the people we love.

Even when applied to rules rather than acts, the principle of utility seems to have its limitations. Although we want our moral rules to create happiness and avoid unhappiness, we don't want them to do only that. We also want them to be fair. And we sometimes find that the principle of utility justifies unfair rules. For example, we can easily imagine rules allowing researchers to experiment on selectively chosen human beings. Such rules might very well create the greatest balance of happiness over unhappiness but still be morally unacceptable—because the chosen few would be involuntary subjects or because they would have to be "sacrificed" during the experiments. Although the medical knowledge gained might benefit the rest of us so enormously that it outweighs the harm to the subjects, it is unfair of us to benefit at their expense in that way.

So the principle of utility cannot be, as Mill thought, the one fundamental moral principle that underlies all of morality. But the effect of our actions and moral rules on the happiness and unhappiness of people remains an important moral consideration all the same.

Fairness

Fairness, we just saw, often plays a crucial role in moral reasoning. But as we shall see in Part 2, it's not always easy to know what the fairest thing to do is. The problem will be especially acute when we discuss affirmative action, an issue in which different but equally important notions of fairness lead to different resolutions. We can't look at all the conceptions of fairness that come into play in moral reasoning here—some are better considered in Part 2 and some in connection with principles of social morality—but we can look at some.

The Golden Rule

Many people take the golden rule to be the best standard of fairness. Certainly, it is a principle that most of us learned very early in our moral education and one that plays a very large role in our moral lives. But applying it is not as simple a matter as most people think.

For most of us, to do unto others as we would have them do unto us is to do much more than we are inclined to do. Even more important, it is to do much more than we think we ought to do. Most of us would be very pleased if utter strangers walked up to us and gave us wads of $100 bills, for example. Yet we do not think that we ought to do the same for others.

The reason we rarely think of such things when we think of the golden rule is that we usually apply it in the context of other moral rules and principles. That is, we don't necessarily think that we ought to act toward others as we would *like* them to act toward us so much as we think that we ought to act toward others as they *ought* to act toward us. If we are to act morally, we must follow the same moral rules in our dealings with others that we expect them to follow in their dealings with us.

When we look at the golden rule that way, we recognize that none of us is a special case. The same moral standards apply to all of us. That is indeed an important thing to recognize if we are to reason morally, but it doesn't always tell us what those standards are.

The negative version of the golden rule gives us more help here. The negative version tells us *not* to treat others as we would *not* have them treat us. That is certainly one reason we find a moral rule allowing experimentation on unwilling subjects morally unacceptable. We would not have somebody experiment on us against our will.

But even the negative version requires a context of other rules and principles for its application because not all of us find the same treatment unacceptable. Consider one common example. Some people prefer to be lied to rather than face unpleasant truths, while others insist on the truth come what may (a fact that physicians are probably most aware of). But that does not mean that the people who don't want to hear the truth should withhold it from those who do.

Respect for Persons

Why shouldn't people who want the truth withheld from them withhold it from others who don't? The answer is simple. In such cases, they should respect the wishes of others. How the other person feels about being lied to matters more than how the would-be liar feels.

More generally, we should always treat other people with respect, and many moral philosophers take **respect for persons** to be *the* fundamental moral principle. The kind of respect they have in mind should not be confused with the kind of respect exemplified by calling people by their appropriate titles. It is a special kind of respect, often called Kantian respect, after the German philosopher Immanuel Kant (1724–1804). Kantian respect is captured by this moral principle: Never use other people merely as a means to your own ends. The reading "Respect for Persons," included here, discusses this in more detail.

Be sure to notice the word "merely" in the principle. It makes a crucial difference, telling us when it is moral to use another person for our own ends and when it is not. It tells us that it is moral to use a bank teller to cash our checks, a waiter to bring our food, a mechanic to fix our cars, and an accountant to prepare our tax forms. Why are they and other like examples moral? Because the people involved are not *merely* serving our own ends. They are serving their own ends as well. They are, among other things, earning their food and rent money.

For an example of using others merely as a means to our own ends, we can return to an earlier one. To experiment on unwilling subjects is a perfect illustration. To do that is to give no consideration to the subjects' ends. It is to treat them as mere things that exist for our own ends, not as persons who have their own ends in life.

Put another way, respect for persons is intimately connected to the recognition that persons are *autonomous* beings. Our behavior is the product of our choices, and our choices are the product of what we take to be the best reasons for acting. And that is what makes us autonomous. We have our own goals and aspirations, we are capable of evaluating and weighing them against one another, we can reject or change them as we see fit, and we can determine how best to achieve those goals and then act accordingly.

To respect persons, then, is to recognize them as autonomous beings and treat them accordingly. It is to recognize that they have their own reasons for acting and to give those reasons the same respect we feel our own reasons warrant from others. And forcing someone to be a subject in a medical experiment is an obvious case of failing to respect his or her autonomy. So is any kind of coercion—from extortion and armed robbery to slavery and murder.

Many other cases are less obvious. Lying is one. When John lies to Maria, he is trying to manipulate her. His goal is to get her to act as he wants her to act, not as she would act if she knew the truth. Withholding information is another. If Maria wants to borrow John's car for purposes he doesn't approve of, she violates Kantian respect by not telling him. She is manipulating him. And the same is true of making commitments we have no intention of honoring.

Does that mean we should never lie, withhold information, or break a promise? Kant thought we should never lie, but we needn't agree with him. Not only do we find white lies permissible, but we also think it right to lie in some cases if there is no other way to prevent someone from doing serious harm. Respect for persons certainly justifies the moral rule "Don't lie," but it needn't lead to the conclusion that lying to save an innocent life isn't a legitimate exception. The important thing about respect for persons is that it cannot justify lying merely for our own convenience or merely to maximize happiness.

If we want to know what does count as a legitimate exception, probably the best thing to do is apply the following test. Imagine that a group of reasonable people is trying to decide what rules they ought to follow and that the rules they pick will include a list of all the exceptions. If it seems likely that they would freely agree to the proposed exception, then we may consider it legitimate.

Many moral philosophers like that test because it manifests Kantian respect. To apply it is to treat others as they would agree to be treated if it were up to them to participate in the making of our moral rules. And to treat them that way is to recognize them as autonomous beings.

Kantian respect is a very powerful notion. It can explain why various kinds of behavior are wrong and why others are right. Also, it is a very reasonable thing to accept as a general moral principle. But many people believe that it's not powerful enough. Since animals are not autonomous beings, it provides no guidelines for our treatment of them. The same can be said about fetuses. Also, Kantian respect seems to permit a variety of practices that many people consider immoral, like homosexuality among consenting adults or giving lethal injections to terminally ill patients who ask for them.

Whether these practices are immoral is, of course, a matter of great controversy, which is why we will look at them in Part 2. Still, the fact that they are controversial shows that many people adhere to other moral principles. Respect for persons may give us an excellent handle on fairness, but like the principle of utility, it may not be our only fundamental moral principle.

Proper Human Excellences

The moral principles we have looked at so far focus on an individual's obligations to others. They provide general guidelines for how we ought to act toward one another. But ethical thought has also paid close attention to another aspect of human life—the human good. Philosophers who pursue this line of thought do not focus on obligations but on character traits and activities that are distinctively human and, when taken together, constitute the good life for human beings. According to this approach to ethics, there are certain excellences uniquely proper to human life, and the full moral life involves the development of these excellences.

Before considering what these excellences might be, let's look at why this line of thought is so appealing. A good place to start is with the ancient Greek philosopher Aristotle (384–322 B.C.E.), included in the readings here. As Aristotle pointed out, human artifacts have distinctive purposes. The purpose of a pen is to write; of a lamp, to give light; of a knife, to cut. And knowing the purpose of any artifact, we also know how to tell whether it is a good or bad one. A knife with a strong blade is better than one with a weak blade. So is a knife with a handle that gives us a sure, comfortable grip better than one with a handle that does not. Thus, a strong blade and a sure, comfortable grip can be called excellences proper to a knife.

Similar remarks hold for human activities—from performing surgery to playing basketball. Each has its own purpose (or purposes), and there are corresponding excellences appropriate to engaging in each of them. Good basketball players are able to shoot, pass, rebound, and make it difficult for opponents to shoot, pass, and rebound; various physical and mental skills, plus proper conditioning, will help them do just those things.

Of course, not all of us are basketball players—or surgeons, welders, attorneys, or lifeguards, for that matter. So the distinctive excellences proper to those roles need not concern us. But some excellences are proper to all of these roles, and those that are, such as concentration and pride in our work, should concern us. Even more important, we are sons or daughters, friends, neighbors, co-workers, and citizens, and we are—or are likely to be—lovers, spouses, parents, and grandparents. And the excellences proper to these roles—loyalty, generosity, honesty, kindness, and the like—are proper to us all. They are, that is, proper human excellences, which are often called **virtues.**

Are there proper human excellences apart from our social roles? Aristotle thought so. He believed that there are natural purposes as well as social purposes. To him, everything in nature has a natural purpose or goal—from the acorn, whose natural purpose is to become an oak tree, to the human being. The human being's natural purpose is ***eudaimonia***, a Greek word usually translated as "happiness" but better understood as total well-being. It is what all of us naturally strive for.

Aristotle believed that a good part of *eudaimonia* is fulfilling our social roles, but far from all of it. We are not, after all, just social animals (or as he put it, political animals). We are also rational animals. Indeed, our ability to reason as we do is, he thought, the trait that best defines us. So an essential part of *eudaimonia* must consist in the proper use of reason. And that means that we must live well-ordered lives, lives not given to extremes. We should not let courage turn to foolhardiness or generosity turn to extravagance. Nor should we let our emotions run away with us. We should display them only when appropriate, and then only to the appropriate degree.

To avoid extremes is the key to what Aristotle called practical wisdom, which is one of the two kinds of wisdom that humans are capable of. The other is the wisdom that comes from contemplating the world in which we live. It is a deep understanding of the world, and like practical wisdom, it too is a proper human excellence. We cannot achieve total well-being without it.

Aristotle's concern with contemplation takes us far from the issues of Part 2, but his other points do have relevance for us. For one thing, many of the issues we'll be discussing relate directly to various social roles and the excellences proper to them. Is it the proper role of healthcare professionals actively and intentionally to bring about the death of a terminally ill patient? To treat a baby born three months premature one way and a fetus of six months another?

These issues also touch on the more general human excellences. Thus, we will consider compassion for the dying, respect for nature, mercy for those convicted of capital crimes, understanding toward pregnant women, and concern for fetuses.

Moreover, virtue and the notion of a well-ordered life play a large role in the discussion of sexual morality. The Catholic thinker Thomas Aquinas (1225–1274) is most important here. Taking his cue from Aristotle's view on purpose in nature, he argued that our sexual organs have as their natural purpose procreation, and any sexual activity that is not open to that end is disordered and immoral. Catholic thinking since Aquinas has continued to emphasize that purpose, but it has also emphasized another proper purpose of human sexuality—the expression of fully human love and dignity. According to this line of thought, sex that is not such an expression, including all sex outside of marriage, is disordered and immoral.

The Catholic position is, of course, highly controversial. So, for that matter, is Aristotle's view that there are natural purposes in addition to social ones. But those controversies are matters for Part 2. For now, the important point is this: Ethical thinking includes consideration of human virtues as well as of obligations to others. And in asking what moral rules to adopt, we must ask ourselves what kind of people we should be and how we should live our lives.

The Will of God

To many people, religious belief provides the final word on moral questions. And because the issues we'll be looking at later have been addressed by religious traditions of all kinds, many people rely on their religious belief for guidance. It is not surprising, then, that much of the popular debate that we find in such places as the letter-to-the-editor sections of local newspapers is filled with appeals to the will of God.

Why give God the final word in these matters? Two possibilities come readily to mind. The first is that God is the ultimate source of morality. God made the universe and put human beings in it for some purpose, and whether we act rightly or wrongly depends on how well we pursue that purpose. In other words, there are both moral laws and physical laws, and God is the author of both.

That was the view of Thomas Aquinas, who referred to the system of divine moral laws as **natural law.** Unlike the conventional laws enacted by legislatures, the natural law, according to Aquinas, is embedded in nature, just as natural purposes are embedded in nature. It is also embedded in human reason. So the natural law is not only the law of God but the law of reason as well. And by turning our reason to moral matters, Aquinas said, we can know such basic moral truths as "Thou shalt not kill" as surely as we know that two plus two equals four.

According to the other possibility, God is not so much the source of morality as the best authority on morality. What makes God the best authority depends on how we think of morality. Some people think of morality as a collection of moral facts, much as they think of science as a collection of scientific facts. And God, being all knowing, knows both kinds of facts. Others think of morality in a different way. To them, the right thing to do is what an ideal observer would consider the best thing to do—an ideal observer being someone who is fully informed about the case at hand and totally impartial. And God alone is in that position.

Reliance on God does raise some problems, though. Can we really be certain what God wants us to do? Different religious traditions do give conflicting answers to various moral questions, and even within any given religious tradition, we can often find conflicting answers. Moreover, we should not forget agnostics and atheists, nor should we forget religious individuals who, for one reason or another, sincerely believe that they must look to their own consciences for the ultimate answers to moral questions.

Such considerations needn't lead to disrespect for religious belief, of course, any more than they need lead to the conclusion that religious people should disregard religious belief when making moral decisions. But they do show the limitations of religious belief for purposes of moral argument.

As we shall see in the next chapter, a good argument goes from statements accepted as true to a conclusion well supported by those statements. If the initial statements are not accepted by our opponents, our arguments will have no force. Also, the better our justification for accepting those initial statements as true, the better the argument. And given the role that faith plays in religious belief, statements about God can have less independent justification than the conclusions they are asked to support.

It is for those reasons, more than antipathy toward religious belief, that moral philosophers addressing a varied audience concentrate on arguments that do not rely on statements about God's will. And it is for the same reasons that this book will do the same.

References to natural law, on the other hand, will appear in Part 2, since philosophers from the time of Aristotle to the present have argued that human behavior can be divided into the natural and unnatural without reliance on the will of God. In Chapter 3, for example, Roger Scruton bases his position on sexual morality on his views on human nature, and J. Gay-Williams argues in Chapter 5 that "mercy" killing violates human nature.

PRINCIPLES OF SOCIAL MORALITY

So far, we have been concerned with how individuals ought to act. Our focus has been on the moral principles that guide individuals when they must determine what they, and others, ought to do.

But we act collectively as well as individually. Most important for our purposes, we act as a municipality, as a state, as a nation. We enact laws, we imprison, fine, and execute people, we enter into treaties and wage war. And collective action, like individual action, can be moral or immoral. Whether it is one or the other, like individual action, depends on how well it is supported by moral principles.

As we shall see, the relevant principles are often the same. Individually and collectively, we should be concerned with human happiness, so the principle of utility is an important principle of social morality. Individually and collectively, we should be concerned with fairness, so respect for persons too is an important principle of social morality. And when we act collectively, we care about what kind of society we should be as much as we care about what kind of individuals we should be when we act individually.

But collective action does pose one special difficulty. When Congress acts, the United States acts, but many U.S. citizens will invariably disagree with how Congress acts, including some members of Congress itself. Their disagreement notwithstanding, they are bound by the acts of Congress. They must pay taxes for purposes they find abhorrent, they must submit to regulations they find offensive, and they must give up freedoms they hold dear—that, or face fine or imprisonment. Governments, even democratic governments like our own, are inherently coercive. That is the special difficulty, and it is why we need additional principles of social morality.

Social Justice

If we ask ourselves what kind of society we should be, the natural answer is this: a just society. Candidates on the campaign trail may disagree on all sorts of issues, but none will speak out in favor of injustice. Many will speak out in favor of positions that others consider unjust, but they will argue in turn that our own positions are the unjust ones. We disagree about what justice requires, but not that we are morally required to be just.

In other words, the issue of social justice—what makes a society a just one—is a very controversial matter. People of good will who share the same principles of individual morality—people who are fair, loyal, honest, faithful, and kind—have great difficulty agreeing on principles of social justice.

That difficulty is due largely to the difficulty noted just before. Government action is coercive action. All of us are in principle against coercion, but we also recognize the occasional need for it. Unfortunately, we don't always recognize it on the same occasions. A look at some important principles of social justice will explain why.

Individual Rights

The Bill of Rights explicitly guarantees us a number of individual freedoms—freedoms of speech, press, religion, and assembly, for example. As part of our Constitution, these guarantees are part of the fundamental law of the land, as are the Bill of Rights' guarantees of a fair trial and its protection against unreasonable search and seizure.

Although these guarantees are set forth in plain enough English, many people of good will disagree about how they should be interpreted. That our guarantee of a free press allows us to criticize government policies is not a matter of controversy. That it allows us to print and sell hard-core pornography is. When such controversies arise, they are settled by the courts, which are the ultimate legal arbiters of how these guarantees are to be understood.

The courts also serve as the ultimate legal arbiters in controversies about implicit constitutional guarantees. The right to privacy, to pick an example that will concern us in Part 2, is not explicitly mentioned in the Bill of Rights or anywhere else in the Constitution. Still, the courts have held that it is a constitutionally protected one.

If enough of us disagree with the courts, we can amend the Constitution. But barring such amendments, the decisions of the courts remain the law of the land. They set the legal limits on what kinds of individual behavior the various levels of government can regulate and on the ways it can regulate them. Even if we doubt that a woman has a moral right to abort a fetus in the early months of her pregnancy, we cannot doubt, as matters now stand, that she has the legal right to do so.

But ought she have that legal right? Ought consenting adults have the legal right to engage in private homosexual acts? Ought we grant pornography the same protections as weekly newsmagazines? What legal rights should we grant? And why?

Natural Rights

One historically important answer to these questions is this: We ought to have the legal right to do whatever we have the natural right to do because no government can justly violate our natural rights. That answer was powerfully advanced by the English philosopher John Locke (1632–1704) and echoed by Thomas Jefferson in the Declaration of Independence. Among its most recent champions was the American philosopher Robert Nozick (1938–2002).

Natural rights are rights that all of us are born with. They belong to us by virtue of the fact that we are human beings, and no one has the right to interfere with our exercise of them. Locke and Nozick list them as life, liberty, and property; Jefferson as life, liberty, and the pursuit of happiness. Because no one can interfere with the exercise of our natural rights, we cannot interfere with anyone else's. And that places the only legitimate limits on our exercise of those rights. Our right to swing our arms, the popular saying has it, stops at someone else's nose. But as long as no one's nose (or property, for that matter) is in the way, we are free to swing.

Even the government, according to natural rights theorists, has no right to interfere. The reason is simple. The government derives its rightful powers from the governed, and the governed cannot transfer to the government any rights they do not have by nature. Since all of us have the right to protect our natural rights, we can transfer the right to protect our lives, liberty, and property to the government. Since none of us has the right to interfere with anyone else's natural rights, we cannot transfer any such right to the government. A just society can have police forces, then, but it cannot tell us what we can and cannot read. It can imprison thieves and rapists, but it cannot imprison its peaceful critics.

These restrictions on government action are more severe than they might at first seem. They leave much behavior—even immoral behavior—free of government interference. The 1964 Civil Rights Act forbidding racial discrimination in privately owned places of public accommodation like theaters and restaurants is, on this view, an unjust law. Since no one has a natural right to enter anyone's property against the owner's wishes, racial exclusion is an exercise of natural property rights that the government cannot interfere with. It goes without saying, then, that this view would not endorse government-mandated affirmative-action programs, one of the topics to be considered in Part 2. Nor would it endorse government payments to the poor, another topic we will consider. Since no one has the natural right to force others to give to the poor, we cannot transfer that right to the government.

Mutual Agreement behind the Veil of Ignorance

Many philosophers are suspicious of natural rights. Where do they come from? How do we get them? Locke and Jefferson thought them God given, but few philosophers today are willing to argue that way. And that leaves the origin of natural rights mysterious at best.

John Rawls (1921–2002), another American philosopher, takes a different approach to individual rights. Instead of saying that a just society is one that protects but does not interfere with natural rights, he says that the individual rights we ought to have are those that a just society would give us.

What is a just society, according to Rawls? A society in which no one has an unfair advantage over others. And how do we ensure that no one has an unfair advantage over others? By adopting fundamental principles of social justice that pass the following test: They must be principles that we would rationally agree upon behind the **veil of ignorance.** And what, finally, is it to be behind the veil of ignorance? It is to know how the principles would shape society but not to know what particular positions each of us would have in that society.

The reason that test would work, Rawls says, is that rational people would not agree to live in any unjust society if they did not know whether they would be the ones who would be unfairly taken advantage of. They would not, for example, be willing to institute slavery if they didn't know whether they'd be slave or master. Anything they would agree to behind the veil of ignorance, therefore, must be just.

What they would agree to are the following two principles:

The Equality Principle Every person has a right to the greatest basic freedom compatible with equal freedom for all. That is, there must be equal freedom for all, and if freedom can be increased without violating that requirement, it must be.

The Difference Principle All social and economic inequalities must meet two requirements. First, they must be to everyone's advantage, including the people at the bottom. It is, for example, to the advantage of everyone that surgeons make more money than unskilled workers. Everyone, including unskilled workers, benefits by having enough surgeons, and financial rewards help guarantee that enough people will pay the cost in time and money of going through medical school. Second, the inequalities must be attached to positions open to all. If surgeons are to be paid more than unskilled workers, then no one can be excluded from becoming a surgeon because of, say, race or sex.

The first principle gives us many freedoms covered by Locke's and Nozick's natural rights, including speech, press, religion, assembly, and more generally, the freedom to do as we please as long as we do not interfere with the rights of others.

The second principle, on the other hand, gives us many individual rights that are not among Locke's and Nozick's natural rights. In doing so, it places some important restrictions on Locke's and Nozick's natural rights—most important, on property rights. For example, the difference principle gives people at the bottom of the social-economic ladder the right to a minimum level of income. If their income falls below that level, the government has the obligation to supplement it with money collected through taxes. And that, from the viewpoint of natural rights advocates, is an unjust restriction on other people's property rights. The government is taking money that they earned so it can help the poor rather than letting them spend it as they see fit.

Equality

Another central principle of social justice is equality. A society in which all citizens are not treated equally can hardly be considered a just one. On that we all agree, just as we all agree that we ought to be a just society. But we do not all agree on what equal treatment requires of us any more than we all agree on what justice requires of us.

Consider equal treatment under the law, for example. To many people, equal treatment under the law is merely a procedural matter. As long as each of us is treated according to the same legal procedures, we are granted equal treatment under the law. Thus, what matters in criminal trials, say, is that all defendants are allowed full exercise of their rights, including their rights to counsel, to subpoena witnesses, to cross-examination, and to a jury of their peers. To others, equal treatment under the law means much more. If, for example, juries are more likely to apply the death penalty in cases where the victim is white than in cases where the victim is black, then equal treatment under the law is denied in capital cases, regardless of procedural guarantees.

Similar difficulties muddle the issue of equal opportunity. To some people, equal opportunity means lack of discrimination: As long as employers and universities choose employees and students on the basis of merit, not on the basis of sex or race, equal opportunity is secured. To others, equal opportunity requires affirmative action. Given the history of oppression against blacks, they argue, mere lack of discrimination cannot secure equal opportunity. Others go even further. Can we really believe, they ask, that the son of a millionaire and the daughter of a welfare recipient begin life with equal advantages? How many of you have enjoyed the same opportunities in life as George W. Bush? Can we really believe that differences in natural endowment make no difference to opportunity? How many of you have enjoyed the same opportunities as Michael Jordan or Julia Roberts?

People who argue that way generally conclude that equal treatment requires equality of results. Given that we cannot start out equally, there can be no real equal opportunity. The just thing to do, then, is see that society's wealth is distributed equally. Or they might reach a variation of that conclusion, arguing instead that the just thing to do is see that society's wealth is distributed according to need. Rawls, as we saw, argues in favor of equal distribution, except when it is in everyone's interest that some people have more. The German philosopher Karl Marx (1818–1883) famously advanced another principle: From each according to his abilities, to each according to his needs.

The General Welfare

The doctrine of natural rights greatly influenced the American Founding Fathers. Its influence appears not only in the Declaration of Independence but also in the Bill of Rights. The preamble to the Constitution shows another concern of the Founding Fathers—the general welfare—which brings us to another important principle of social morality: The different levels of government should promote the general welfare, or as it is often put, the common good, or the public interest.

Thus, we have come to expect our governments to do much in the promotion of the general welfare. We expect public schools and libraries, public funding of highways and medical research, zoning ordinances that guarantee us livable neighborhoods, laws protecting our rivers and air, and much else that is no longer controversial.

Much else that governments do to promote the general welfare is controversial. So is much else that various people propose that our governments do to promote it. Sometimes the controversy is merely over practical considerations, as when we debate whether one policy or another will better increase worker productivity. Often, though, the controversy is over profoundly moral considerations, as when we debate the issues of Part 2 of this book.

One particularly profound moral consideration concerns the general welfare itself. Many people of good will differ over what constitutes the general welfare. Another concerns how far the government can rightly go in promoting it. Many people of good will also differ about the proper limits of government action.

Public Decency and Morality

To most people, the general welfare includes a healthy moral environment. Part of a healthy moral environment is public decency. Some things—like sex between married people—are obviously moral in private but generally considered indecent in public thoroughfares. Other things—like drinking a few Scotches too many—are less obviously moral in private (here reasonable people will differ) and also considered indecent in public thoroughfares. Thus, we have laws against indecent exposure and drunk and disorderly conduct, laws that most people agree promote the general welfare.

More controversially, some people feel that the general welfare requires more and that a healthy moral environment includes more than public decency. They feel that it includes various restrictions on private behavior too. Homosexual acts between consenting adults constitute one area of private behavior that is illegal in many jurisdictions. Another involves pornography. In some jurisdictions, certain films cannot be shown in theaters even if minors are kept out and billboards visible to the passing public are not themselves pornographic.

What principles do proponents of these restrictions appeal to? The following three are most important.

The Principle of Paternalism John Stuart Mill distinguished what he called self-regarding virtues and vices from other-regarding virtues and vices. Gluttony is an example of a self-regarding vice. Although overeating might cause direct harm to ourselves, it does not cause direct harm to others. A propensity to settle disagreements by beating up those who disagree with us, on the other hand, is an other-regarding vice. It does cause direct harm to others.

The legitimacy of laws forbidding assault and battery is not to be disputed. And the same goes for many similar laws involving other-regarding vices. But when we turn to self-regarding vices, the legitimacy of laws involving them is often disputed. People who steal from us, extort money from us, or rape us violate our most cherished rights, and it is the job of government to protect those rights. Gluttons do not violate our rights. Nor do homosexuals or pornography watchers. If homosexuality and pornography viewing are vices (and reasonable people disagree), they do not on the face of it seem to be other-regarding vices.

Some people justify restrictions on such behavior by appealing to a principle of paternalism: Just as parents are justified in preventing their children from harming themselves, so are governments justified in preventing their citizens from harming themselves. And if homosexuality and pornography cause us moral harm, governments should outlaw them. Otherwise, they do not promote the general welfare.

Protecting the Public Morality Mill's distinction between self-regarding and other-regarding vices rests on the presence or absence of direct harm to others.

Many self-regarding vices, though, can and do cause *indirect* harm to others. A glutton can eat himself into a fatal heart attack, for example, and then his wife and children will suffer.

The courts have made similar claims about the indirect harm that can result from homosexuality and pornography. Sometimes, the harm they refer to is moral harm. If society tolerates behavior it considers immoral, that behavior may spread. And that means that people who engage in that behavior may be causing indirect moral harm to others.

Moreover, the indirect moral harm may come to minors as well as adults. Even if pornography is limited by law to adults only, minors will always find a way to view it. Just as legal drinking ages don't prevent minors from drinking their parents' liquor or getting adults to buy it for them, so do laws prohibiting sales of pornography to minors fail to prevent minors from looking at their parents' pornography or getting adults to buy it for them.

Whether or not the behavior does spread to minors, courts have repeatedly held that governments do have a legitimate interest in protecting the public morality, and that their legitimate interest in doing so does justify prohibiting behavior that many of us would consider self-regarding.

Preventing Indirect Social Costs The glutton who eats himself into a fatal heart attack may end up harming more than just his wife and children. His death may have social costs as well, especially if his family is forced to go on welfare. Indeed, many self-regarding vices have social costs. Smoking-related illnesses exact enormous costs in lost work hours, medical care, and insurance premiums. So do injuries resulting from failure to use automobile seat belts.

Much debate over the issues of Part 2 also involves the social costs of private behavior. Many people have expressed concern about the long-term effects of legal tolerance of homosexuality. How will it affect society's family structure? And what changes will that lead to in other areas of society? Will legal recognition of "**civil unions**" among people of the same gender lead to a deterioration of the sanctity of traditional marriage among heterosexuals?

Many other people reject the claim that such considerations can justify restrictions on private behavior. Many more reject the principle of paternalism and the principle of protecting the public morality. To them, such principles of collective action lead to unacceptable limits on individual freedom. Some worry that these principles, carried to their extremes, would lead to the outlawing of everything bad for us, including ice cream and other foods high in cholesterol. Others have even stronger objections. Their concern is that such considerations are in principle unacceptable.

People like Nozick would rule them out on the grounds of natural right. If our natural right to liberty is to count for anything, it must include the right to decide for ourselves what is morally harmful to us. Others would rule them out on different grounds. To them, the basic issue is that we live in a free society. In a free society, the general welfare is not to be advanced at the cost of individual freedoms that cause direct harm to nobody else. The government has an obligation to prevent violence toward women, but in a free society, it should fulfill that obligation by educating its citizens and punishing offenders—not by restricting the legitimate freedoms of nonoffenders.

Pluralism and Freedom

In the previous section, we looked at reasons in favor of government action. It's now time to look at reasons against government action. All can be seen as arguments in favor of individual freedom. They can also be seen as arguments in favor of **pluralism.**

A pluralistic society is a society with many independent centers of power, a society in which no one institution has unlimited power over the others. The more independent and varied the institutions of society are, the more pluralistic the society; the more limits that are placed on the most powerful institution of society, the more pluralistic the society.

In our society, of course, the federal government is the most powerful institution. Among the independent centers of power are the family, the press, religions, business and labor organizations, private (and perhaps even public) universities, and the like. And to the extent that the government allows these other institutions to pursue their own ends in their own ways, the more pluralistic our own society.

Although pluralism is not highly valued in all societies (the People's Republic of China and Iran, for example), it is highly valued in our own. The Founding Fathers, in placing limits on the powers of the federal government, sought to protect pluralism. And the frequent calls we hear to limit governmental interference in matters best left to the family, or the medical professions, or any other institutions are calls to protect or advance pluralism.

Individual Freedom

One reason for valuing pluralism is its close connection to individual freedom. The connection is twofold.

First, to allow institutions to pursue their own ends in their own ways is, more often than not, to allow individuals to pursue their own ends in their own ways. If the government leaves certain areas of concern to the family, it leaves them to individual family members. If it allows research decisions to be made by the scientific community, it allows them to be made by individual scientists. And the less it interferes with media organizations, the less it interferes with individual journalists.

Second, the more independent centers of power there are and the more independent they are permitted to be, the more bulwarks there are against government restrictions on individual freedom. A free press protects the freedoms of all of us, not just of journalists. Independent universities, hospitals, and businesses protect the freedom to choose among varied alternatives of all of us, not just the freedoms of professors, physicians, and managers.

To be sure, independent institutions can also threaten our freedoms. Businesses with monopoly powers, for instance, can greatly restrict our freedom of choice in the marketplace. They can also threaten vital public goods such as clean air and water. So we cannot allow them to be unbridled centers of power, any more than we can allow the government to be one. Nor can we give parents unbridled power over their children or hospitals unbridled power over their patients.

How and where to set these limits fuel many of the controversies of Part 2. Is the joint decision to withhold treatment from defective newborns within the proper bounds of parents and physicians? Should private businesses be free to pursue affirmative action, should they be forced to pursue it, or should they be barred from doing so?

How we answer such questions depends on a number of factors, some specific to each issue and others relating to the general principles we've been examining. Fairness, of course, is an important factor. So is the matter of individual rights. But where fairness should lead us and what rights are at stake are not always clear. What is fair to the minority woman might not be fair to the white male. And the question of what rights we ought to extend to a newborn child or fetus is far from settled.

The general welfare is also an important factor. It can, after all, be harmed by government action as well as advanced by government action. So far, we have looked only at ways in which government action can advance it. But pluralists are equally concerned about the ways government action can harm it.

The Social Utility of Pluralism

For Locke, Jefferson, and Nozick, the individual freedoms that rightfully belong to us are matters of natural right, and they need no further justification than that. For Rawls, the individual freedoms that rightfully belong to us are the ones we would agree to under ideal conditions of fairness. For Mill, the individual freedoms that rightfully belong to us are the ones that will maximize human happiness.

Mill felt very strongly that the only freedom that will not maximize human happiness is the freedom to harm others. He felt that other-regarding vices fall under the legitimate control of governments, but not self-regarding ones. Many of his arguments for this claim center on specific individual freedoms, and it would take us far beyond our purposes here to look at all of them. But two general arguments are very important for us.

The first is one we often hear in political debates: Individuals are in a better position to know what makes them happy than paternalistic governments are. Individuals will make mistakes from time to time, but so will governments. The important point is that individuals will make them less frequently. For one thing, we know ourselves better than our governments know us. For another, each of us is different, and it is extremely unlikely that one judgment about self-regarding behavior made for all individuals in society will promote individual happiness as efficiently as individual judgments made by each of us.

The second deals directly with the link between public morality and the general welfare. According to Mill, the best way to live our lives must always remain an open question. Nobody can now know for certain that particular ways of life are the best ways of life. If we outlaw certain kinds of self-regarding behavior, Mill said, we cut off moral experimentation that might help us discover better ways of life. And even if we can be fairly certain that some ways of life are not good ones, we will not maximize happiness by outlawing them. Bad ways of life may still have some good in them. Also, the rest of us can always learn from bad examples, even if what we learn is only to have greater confidence in the goodness of our own ways of life. A docile citizenry, one that does what it is told rather than what it thinks best, is not a citizenry likely to maximize happiness. Nor, those who agree with Mill might add, are docile hospitals, universities, or media organizations likely to maximize happiness.

SUMMARY AND CONCLUSIONS

We have looked at a variety of general moral principles in this chapter, some primarily concerned with individual morality and others with social morality. In doing so, we have also looked at the most important considerations we can bring to bear when deciding how we should act, whether individually or collectively. Among them are human happiness, fairness, justice, individual rights, equality, individual freedom, and the general welfare.

What conclusions can we draw from our discussions? Perhaps the most obvious conclusion is that moral questions can be very difficult questions. One moral principle can lead us to one answer, while another equally important moral principle can lead us to another answer. Thus, we may very well be stuck with some very hard choices—between respecting individual freedoms and promoting the general welfare, for example. Also, we may very well find that the same moral principle leads us to different answers. In cases like that, we will find ourselves stuck with hard choices of another kind—between being fair to one group or another, for example, or between protecting one individual's rights or another's.

The existence of such moral dilemmas often leads to a kind of moral skepticism, the view that our answers to moral questions are opinions, not knowledge. Whether that view is correct is a much too complicated matter to deal with here. But even if it is correct, it does not mean that we should give up trying to answer moral questions. They remain very important questions. The answers we eventually decide on will have great impact on the kind of society we are and on the lives of all of us who live in it. We have a responsibility to deal with these questions as best we can, even if we cannot be sure that our answers represent knowledge.

And even if our answers are opinions, not all opinions are equal. At the beginning of a baseball season, nobody can know who will win the World Series, but that doesn't mean that we can't distinguish good picks from bad picks. Few of you can know which career choice will work out best for you, but that doesn't mean that any opinion on the matter is as good as any other. Similarly, perhaps none of us can know whether a woman really has a moral right to an abortion or whether justice really requires affirmative action, but that doesn't mean that we can't distinguish better and worse ways of dealing with those issues.

Basing our judgments on moral principle is one thing we must do if we are to deal with these issues well. But we must also do something else. We must make sure that our debates on these issues are thoughtful, careful, and well reasoned. The combination of good moral principles and faulty reasoning guarantees very little. In this chapter, we look at the principles; in the next, we will look at reasoning.

Moral Virtue

ARISTOTLE

The following selection is from Books One and Two of Aristotle's *Nichomachean Ethics.* In Book One, Aristotle argues that the highest human good is *eudaimonia* (total well-being, or

From *The Ethics of Aristotle*, translated by A. K. Thomson, George Allen & Unwin Ltd. Reprinted by permission.

happiness). It is, he says, our only self-sufficient goal and the ultimate goal of all human action. He then argues that human happiness is determined by the proper function of humans, which he defines as "an activity of the soul or a course of action in accordance with reason." Thus, a happy individual is one who lives in accordance with reason, and each individual should develop virtues (character traits or dispositions) that lead to this goal. Because human reason is both practical and intellectual, human virtues come in two kinds, moral and intellectual.

In Book Two, Aristotle turns to a discussion of the moral virtues. After stressing the importance of childhood training and self-discipline in the development of moral virtues, he proceeds to define the nature of moral virtue. Moral virtue is, he concludes, a "mean" between the vices of deficiency and excess; that is, virtue is a form of moderation, a midpoint between two extremes. Courage, for example, is a midpoint between cowardice and foolhardiness. Friendliness is a midpoint between flattery and surliness.

BOOK ONE

Chapter I

It is thought that every activity, artistic or scientific, in fact every deliberate action or pursuit, has for its object the attainment of some good. We may therefore assent to the view which has been expressed that 'the good' is 'that at which all things aim.'[1] Since modes of action involving the practised hand and the instructed brain are numerous, the number of their ends is proportionately large. For instance, the end of medical science is health; of military science, victory; of economic science, wealth. All skills of that kind which come under a single 'faculty'—a skill in making bridles or any other part of a horse's gear comes under the faculty or art of horsemanship, while horsemanship itself and every branch of military practice comes under the art of war, and in like manner other arts and techniques are subordinate to yet others—in all these the ends of the master arts are to be preferred to those of the subordinate skills, for it is the former that provide the motive for pursuing the latter.[2]

Chapter IV

To resume. Since every activity involving some acquired skill or some moral decision aims at some good, what do we take to be the end of politics—what is the supreme good attainable in our actions? Well, so far as the name goes there is pretty general agreement. 'It is happiness,' say both intellectuals and the unsophisticated, meaning by 'happiness' living well or faring well. But when it comes to saying in what happiness consists, opinions differ and the account given by the generality of mankind is not at all like that given by the philosophers. The masses take it to be something plain and tangible, like pleasure or money or social standing. Some maintain that it is one of these, some that it is another, and the same man will change his opinion about it more than once. When he has caught an illness he will say that it is health, and when he is hard up he will say that it is money. Conscious that they are out of their depths in such discussions, most people are impressed by anyone who pontificates and says something that is over their heads. Now it would no doubt be a waste of time to examine all these opinions; enough if we consider those which are most in evidence or have something to be said for them. Among these we shall have to discuss the view held by some that, over and above particular goods like those I have just mentioned, there is another which is good in itself and the cause of whatever goodness there is in all these others....

Chapter V

Let us return from this digression.—There is a general assumption that the manner of a man's life is a clue to what he on reflection regards as the good—in other words happiness. Persons of low tastes (always in the majority) hold that it is pleasure. Accordingly they ask for nothing better than the sort of life which consists in having a good time. (I have in mind the three well-known types of life—that just mentioned, that of the man of affairs, that of the philosophic student.) The utter vulgarity of the herd of men comes out in their preference for the sort of existence a cow leads. Their view would hardly get a respectful hearing, were it not that those who occupy great positions sympathize with a monster of sensuality like Sardanapalus. The gentleman, however, and the man of affairs identify the good with honour, which may fairly be described as the end which men pursue in political or public life. Yet honour is surely too superficial a thing to be the good we are seeking. Honour depends more on those who confer than on him who receives it, and we cannot but feel that the good is something personal and almost inseparable from its possessor. Again, why do men seek honour? Surely in order to confirm the favourable opinion they have formed of themselves. It is at all events by intelligent men who know them personally that they seek to be honoured. And for what? For their moral qualities. The inference is clear; public men prefer virtue to honour. It might therefore seem reasonable to suppose that virtue rather than honour is the end pursued in the life of the public servant. But clearly even virtue cannot be quite the end. It is possible, most people think, to possess virtue while you are asleep, to possess it without acting under its influence during any portion of one's life. Besides, the virtuous man may meet with the most atrocious luck or ill-treatment; and nobody, who was not arguing for argument's sake, would maintain that a man with an existence of that sort was 'happy.'[3] The third type of life is the 'contemplative,' and this we shall discuss later.

As for the life of the business man, it does not give him much freedom of action. Besides, wealth obviously is not the good we seek, for the sole purpose it serves is to provide the means of getting something else. So far as that goes, the ends we have already mentioned would have a better title to be considered the good, for they are desired on their own account. But in fact even their claim must be disallowed. We may say that they have furnished the ground for many arguments, and leave the matter at that.

Chapter VII

From this digression we may return to the good which is the object of our search. What is it? The question must be asked because good seems to vary with the art or pursuit in which it appears. It is one thing in medicine and another in strategy, and so in the other branches of human skill. We must enquire, then, what is the good which is the end common to all of them. Shall we say it is that for the sake of which everything else is done? In medicine this is health, in military science victory, in architecture a building, and so on—different ends in different arts; every consciously directed activity has an end for the sake of which everything that it does is done. This end may be described as its good. Consequently, if there be some one thing which is the end of all things consciously done, this will be the doable good; or, if there be more than one end, then it will be all of these. Thus the ground on which our argument proceeds is shifted, but the conclusion arrived at is the same.

I must try, however, to make my meaning clearer.

In our actions we aim at more ends than one—that seems to be certain—but, since we choose some (wealth, for example, or flutes and tools or instruments generally) as means to something else, it is clear that not all of them are ends in the full sense of the word, whereas the good, that is the supreme good, is surely such an end. Assuming then that there is some one thing which alone is an end beyond which there are no further ends, we may call *that* the good of which we are in search. If there be more than one such final end, the good will be that end which has the highest degree of finality. An object pursued for its own sake possesses a higher degree of finality than one pursued with an eye to something else. A corollary to that is that a thing which is never chosen as a means to some remoter object has a higher degree of finality than things which are chosen both as ends in themselves and as means to such ends. We may conclude, then, that something which is always chosen for its own sake and never for the sake of something else is without qualification a final end.

Now happiness more than anything else appears to be just such an end, for we always choose it for its own sake and never for the sake of some other thing. It is different with honour, pleasure, intelligence and good qualities generally. We choose them indeed for their own sake in the sense that we should be glad to have them irrespective of any advantage which might accrue from them. But we also choose them for the sake of our happiness in the belief that they will be instrumental in promoting that. On the other hand nobody chooses happiness as a means of achieving them or anything else whatsoever than just happiness.

The same conclusion would seem to follow from another consideration. It is a generally accepted view that the final good is self-sufficient. By 'self-sufficient' is meant not what is sufficient for oneself living the life of a solitary but includes parents, wife and children, friends and fellow-citizens in general. For man is a social animal.[4] A self-sufficient thing, then, we take to be one which on its own footing tends to make life desirable and lacking in nothing. And we regard happiness as such a thing. Add to this that we regard it as the most desirable of all things without having it counted in with some other desirable thing. For, if such an addition were possible, clearly we should regard it as more desirable when even the smallest advantage was added to it. For the result would be an increase in the number of advantages, and the larger sum of advantages is preferable to the smaller.

Happiness then, the end to which all our conscious acts are directed, is found to be something final and self-sufficient.

But no doubt people will say, 'To call happiness the highest good is a truism. We want a more distinct account of what it is.' We might arrive at this if we could grasp what is meant by the 'function' of a human being. If we take a flautist or a sculptor or any craftsman—in fact any class of men at all who have some special job or profession—we find that his special talent and excellence comes out in that job, and this is his function. The same thing will be true of man simply as man—that is of course if 'man' does have a function. But is it likely that joiners and shoemakers have certain functions or specialized activities, while man as such has none but has been left by Nature a functionless being? Seeing that eye and hand and foot and every one of our members has some obvious function, must we not believe that in like manner a human being has a function over and above these particular functions? Then what exactly is it? The mere act of living is not peculiar to man—we find it even in the vegetable kingdom—and what we are looking for is something peculiar to him. We must therefore exclude from our definition the life that manifests itself in mere nurture and growth. A step higher should come the life that is confined to experiencing sensations. But that we see is shared by horses, cows and the brute creation as a whole. We are left, then, with a life concerning which we can make two statements. First, it belongs to the rational part of man. Secondly, it finds expression in actions. The rational part may be either active or passive: passive in so far as it follows the dictates of reason, active in so far as it possesses and exercises the power of reasoning. A similar distinction can be drawn within the rational life; that is to say, the reasonable element in it may be active or passive. Let us take it that what we are concerned with here is the reasoning power in action, for it will be generally allowed that when we speak of 'reasoning' we really mean *exercising* our reasoning faculties. (This seems the more correct use of the word.) Now let us assume for the moment the truth of the following propositions. (*a*) The function of a man is the exercise of his non-corporeal faculties or 'soul' in accordance with, or at least not divorced from, a rational principle. (*b*) The function of an individual and of a *good* individual in the same class—a harp player, for example, and a good harp player, and so through the classes—is generically the same, except that we must add superiority in accomplishment to the function, the function of the harp player being merely to play on the harp, while the function of the good harp player is to play on it well. (*c*) The function of man is a certain form of life, namely an activity of the soul exercised in combination with a rational principle or reasonable ground of action. (*d*) The function of a good man is to exert such activity well. (*e*) A function is performed well when performed in accordance with the excellence proper to it.—If these assumptions are granted, we conclude that the good for man is 'an activity of soul in accordance with goodness' or (on the supposition that there may be more than one form of goodness) 'in accordance with the best and most complete form of goodness.'

There is another condition of happiness; it cannot be achieved in less than a complete lifetime. One swallow does not make a summer; neither does one fine day. And one day, or indeed any brief period of felicity, does not make a man entirely and perfectly happy. . . .

BOOK TWO

Chapter I

Virtue, then, is of two kinds, intellectual and moral. Of these the intellectual is in the main indebted to teaching for its production and growth, and this calls for time and experience. Moral goodness, on the other hand, is the child of habit, from which it has got its very name, ethics being derived from *ethos,* "habit," by a slight alteration in the quantity of the *e*. This is an indication that none of the moral virtues is implanted in us by nature, since nothing that nature creates can be taught by habit to change the direction of its development. For instance a stone, the natural tendency of which is to fall down, could never, however often you threw it up in the air, be trained to go in that direction. No more can you train fire to burn downwards. Nothing in fact, if the law of its being is to behave in one way, can be habituated to behave in another. The moral virtues, then, are produced in us neither *by* Nature nor *against* Nature. Nature, indeed, prepares in us the ground for their reception, but their complete formation is the product of habit.

Consider again these powers or faculties with which Nature endows us. We acquire the ability to use them before we do use them. The senses provide us with a good illustration of this truth. We have not acquired the sense of sight from repeated acts of seeing, or the sense of hearing from repeated acts of hearing. It is the other way round. We had these senses before we used them; we did not acquire them as a result of using them. But the moral virtues we do acquire by first exercising them. The same is true of the arts and crafts in general. The craftsman has to learn how to make things, but he learns in the process of making them. So men become builders by building, harp players by playing the harp. By a similar process we become just by performing just actions, temperate by performing temperate actions, brave by performing brave actions. Look at what happens in political societies—it confirms our view. We find legislators seeking to make good men of their fellows by making good behaviour habitual with them. That is the aim of every lawgiver, and when he is unable to carry it out effectively, he is a failure; nay, success or failure in this is what makes the difference between a good constitution and a bad.

Again, the creation and the destruction of any virtue are effected by identical causes and identical means; and this may be said, too, of every art. It is as a result of playing the harp that harpers become good or bad in their art. The same is true of builders and all other craftsmen. Men will become good builders as a result of building well, and bad builders as a result of building badly. Otherwise what would be the use of having anyone to teach a trade? Craftsmen would all be born either good or bad. Now this holds also of the virtues. It is in the course of our dealings with our fellow-men that we become just or unjust. It is our behaviour in a crisis and our habitual reactions to danger that make us brave or cowardly, as it may be. So with our desires and passions. Some men are made temperate and gentle, others profligate and passionate, the former by conducting themselves in one way, the latter by conducting themselves in another, in situations in which their feelings are involved. We may sum it all up in the generalization, "Like activities produce like dispositions." This makes it our duty to see that our activities have the right character, since the differences of quality in them are repeated in the dispositions that follow in their train. So it is a matter of real importance whether our early education confirms us in one set of habits or another. It would be nearer the truth to say that it makes a very great difference indeed, in fact all the difference in the world.

Chapter II

Since the branch of philosophy on which we are at present engaged differs from the others in not being a subject of merely intellectual interest—I mean we are not concerned to know what goodness essentially is, but how we are to become good men, for this alone gives the study its practical value—we must apply our minds to the solution of the problems of conduct. For, as I remarked, it is our actions that determine our dispositions.

Now that when we act we should do so according to the right principle, is common ground and I propose to take it as a basis of discussion.[5] But we must begin with the admission that any theory of conduct must be content with an outline without much precision in details. We noted this when I said at the beginning of our discussion of this part of our subject that the measure of exactness of statement in any field of study must be determined by the nature of the matter studied. Now matters of conduct and considerations of what is to our advantage have no fixity about them any more than matters affecting our health. And if this be true of moral philosophy as a whole, it is still more true that the discussion of particular problems in ethics admits of no exactitude. For they do not fall under any science or professional tradition, but those who are following some line of conduct are forced in every collocation of circumstances to think out for themselves what is suited to these circumstances, just as doctors and navigators have to do in their different *métiers*. We can do no more than give our arguments, inexact as they necessarily are, such support as is available.

Let us begin with the following observation. It is in the nature of moral qualities that they can be destroyed by deficiency on the one hand and excess on the other. We can see this in the instances of bodily health and strength.[6] Physical strength is destroyed by too much and also by too little exercise. Similarly health is ruined by eating and drinking either too much or too little, while it is produced, increased and preserved by taking the right quantity of drink and victuals. Well, it is the same with temperance, courage, and the other virtues. The man who shuns and fears everything and can stand up to nothing becomes a coward. The man who is afraid of nothing at all, but marches up to every danger, becomes foolhardy. In the same way the man who indulges in every pleasure without refraining from a single one becomes incontinent. If, on the other hand, a man behaves like the Boor in comedy and turns his back on every pleasure, he will find his sensibilities becoming blunted. So also temperance and courage are destroyed both by excess and deficiency, and they are kept alive by observance of the mean.

Let us go back to our statement that the virtues are produced and fostered as a result, and by the agency, of actions of the same quality as effect their destruction. It is also true that after the virtues have been formed they find expression in actions of that kind. We may see this in a concrete instance—bodily strength. It results from taking plenty of nourishment and going in for hard training, and it is the strong man who is best fitted to cope with such conditions. So with the virtues. It is by refraining from pleasures that we become temperate, and it is when we have become temperate that we are most able to abstain from pleasures. Or take courage. It is by habituating ourselves to make light of alarming situations and to confront them that we become brave, and it is when we have become brave that we shall be most able to face an alarming situation.

Chapter III

We may use the pleasure (or pain) that accompanies the exercise of our dispositions as an index of how far they have established themselves. A man is temperate who abstaining from bodily pleasures finds this abstinence pleasant; if he finds it irksome, he is intemperate. Again, it is the man who encounters danger gladly, or at least without painful sensations, who is brave; the man who has these sensations is a coward. In a word, moral virtue has to do with pains and pleasures. There are a number of reasons for believing this. (1) Pleasure has a way of making us do what is disgraceful; pain deters us from doing what is right and fine. Hence the importance—I quote Plato—of having been brought up to find pleasure and pain in the right things. True education is just such a training. (2) The virtues operate with actions and emotions, each of which is accompanied by pleasure or pain. This is only another way of saying that virtue has to do with pleasures and pains. (3) Pain is used as an instrument of punishment. For in her remedies Nature works by opposites, and pain can be remedial. (4) When any disposition finds its complete expression it is, as we noted, in dealing with just those things by which it is its nature to be made better or worse, and which constitute the sphere of its operations. (5) Now when men become bad it is under the influence of pleasures and pains when they seek the wrong ones among them, or seek them at the wrong time, or in the wrong manner, or in any of the wrong forms which such offenses may take; and in seeking the wrong pleasures and pains they shun the right. This has led some thinkers to identify the moral virtues with conditions of the soul in which passion is eliminated or reduced to a minimum. But this is to make too absolute a statement—it needs to be qualified by adding that such a condition must be attained "in the right manner and at the right time" together with the other modifying circumstances.

So far, then, we have got this result. Moral goodness is a quality disposing us to act in the best way when we are dealing with pleasures and pains, while vice is one which leads us to act in the worst way when we deal with them.

The point may be brought out more clearly by some other considerations. There are three kinds of things that determine our choice in all our actions—the morally fine, the expedient, the pleasant; the three that we shun—the base, the harmful, the painful. Now in his dealings with all of these it is the good man who is most likely to go right, and the bad man who tends to go wrong, and that most notably in the matter of pleasure. The sensation of pleasure is felt by us in common with all animals, accompanying everything we choose, for even the fine and the expedient have a pleasurable effect upon us. (6) The capacity for experiencing pleasure has grown in us from infancy as part of our general development, and human life, being dyed in grain with it, receives therefrom a colour hard to scrape off. (7) Pleasure and pain are also the standards by which with greater or less strictness we regulate our considered actions. Since to feel pleasure and pain rightly or wrongly is an important factor in human behaviour, it follows that we are primarily concerned with these sensations. (8) Heraclitus says it is hard to fight against anger, but it is harder still to fight against pleasure. Yet to grapple with the harder has always been the business, as of art, so of goodness, success in a task being proportionate to its difficulty. This gives us another reason for believing that morality and statesmanship must concentrate on pleasures and pains, seeing it is the man who deals rightly with them who will be good, and the man who deals with them wrongly who will be bad.

Here, then, are our conclusions. (a) Virtue is concerned with pains and pleasures. (b) The actions which produce virtue are identical in character with those which increase it. (c) These actions differently performed destroy it. (d) The actions which produced it are identical with those in which it finds expression.

Chapter IV

A difficulty, however, may be raised as to what we mean when we say that we must perform just actions if we are to become just, and temperate actions if we are to be temperate. It may be argued that, if I do what is just and temperate, I am just and temperate already, exactly as, if I spell words or play music correctly, I must already be literate or musical. This I take to be a false analogy, even in the arts. It is possible to spell a word right by accident or because somebody tips you the answer. But you will be a scholar only if your spelling is done as a scholar does it, that is thanks to the scholarship in your own mind. Nor will the suggested analogy with the arts bear scrutiny. A work of art is good or bad in itself—let it possess a certain quality, and that is all we ask of it. But virtuous actions are not done in a virtuous—a just or temperate—way merely because *they* have the appropriate quality. The *doer* must be in a certain frame of mind when he does them. Three conditions are involved. (1) The agent must act in full consciousness of what he is doing. (2) He must "will" his action, and will it for its own sake. (3) The act must proceed from a fixed and unchangeable disposition. Now these requirements, if we except mere knowledge, are not counted among the necessary qualifications of an artist. For the acquisition of virtue, on the other hand, knowledge is of little or no value, but the other requirements are of immense, of sovran, importance, since it is the repeated performance of just and temperate actions that produces virtue. Actions, to be sure, are *called* just and temperate when they are such as a just or temperate man would do. But the doer is just or temperate not because he does such things but when he does them in the way of just and temperate persons. It is therefore quite fair to say that a man becomes just by the performance of just, and temperate by the performance of temperate, actions; nor is there the smallest likelihood of a man's becoming good by any other course of conduct. It is not, however, a popular line to take, most men preferring theory to practice under the impression that arguing about morals proves them to be philosophers, and that in this way they will turn out to be fine characters. Herein they resemble invalids, who listen carefully to all the doctor says but do not carry out a single one of his orders. The bodies of such people will never respond to treatment—nor will the souls of such "philosophers."

Chapter V

We now come to the formal definition of virtue. Note first, however, that the human soul is conditioned in three ways. It may have (1) feelings, (2) capacities, (3) dispositions; so virtue must be one of these three. By "feelings" I mean desire, anger, fear, daring, envy, gratification, friendliness, hatred, longing, jealousy, pity and in general all states of mind that are attended by pleasure or pain. By "capacities" I mean those faculties in virtue of which we may be described as capable of the feelings in question—anger, for instance, or pain, or pity. By "dispositions" I mean states of mind in virtue of which we are well or ill disposed in respect of the feelings concerned. We have, for instance, a bad disposition where angry feelings are concerned if we are disposed to become excessively or insufficiently angry, and a good disposition in this respect if we consistently feel the due amount of anger, which comes between these extremes. So with the other feelings.

Now, neither the virtues nor the vices are feelings. We are not spoken of as good or bad in respect of our feelings but of our virtues and vices. Neither are we praised or blamed for the way we feel. A man is not praised for being frightened or angry, nor is he blamed just for being angry; it is for being angry in a particular way. But we *are* praised and blamed for our virtues and vices. Again, feeling angry or frightened is something we can't help, but our virtues are in a manner expressions of our will; at any rate there is an element of will in their formation. Finally, we are said to be "moved" when our feelings are affected, but when it is a question of moral goodness or badness we are not said to be "moved" but to be "disposed" in a particular way. A similar line of reasoning will prove that the virtues and vices are not capacities either. We are not spoken of as good or bad, nor are we praised or blamed, merely because we are *capable* of feeling. Again, what capacities we have, we have by nature; but it is not nature that makes us good or bad. . . . So, if the virtues are neither feelings nor capacities, it remains that they must be dispositions. . . .

Chapter VI

It is not, however, enough to give this account of the *genus* of virtue—that it is a disposition; we must describe its *species*. Let us begin, then, with this proposition. Excellence of whatever kind affects that of which it is the excellence in two ways. (1) It produces a good state in it. (2) It enables it to perform its function well. Take eyesight. The goodness of your eye is not only that which makes your eye good, it is also that which makes it function well. Or take the case of a horse. The goodness of a horse makes him a good horse, but it also makes him good at running, carrying a rider and facing the enemy. Our proposition, then, seems to be true, and it enables us to say that virtue in a man will be the disposition which (a) makes him a good man, (b) enables him to perform his function well. We have already touched on this point, but more light will be thrown upon it if we consider what is the specific nature of virtue.

In anything continuous and divisible it is possible to take the half, or more than the half, or less than the half. Now these parts may be larger, smaller and equal either in relation to the thing divided or in relation to us. The equal part may be described as a mean between too much and too little. By the mean of the thing I understand a point equidistant from the extremes; and this is one and the same for everybody. Let me give an illustration. Ten, let us say, is "many" and two is "few" of something. We get the mean of the thing if we take six;[7] that is, six exceeds and is exceeded by an equal number. This is the rule which gives us the arithmetical mean. But such a method will not give us the mean in relation to ourselves. Let ten pounds of food be a large, and two pounds a small, allowance for an athlete. It does not follow that the trainer will prescribe six pounds. That might be a large or it might be a small allowance for the particular athlete who is to get it. It would be little for Milo but a lot for a man who has just begun his training.[8] It is the same in all walks of life. The man who knows his business avoids both too much and too little. It is the mean he seeks and adopts—not the mean of the thing but the relative mean.

Every form, then, of applied knowledge, when it performs its function well, looks to the mean and works to the standard set by that. It is because people feel this that they apply the *cliché*, "You couldn't add anything to it or take anything from it" to an artistic masterpiece, the implication being that too much and too little alike destroy perfection, while the mean preserves it. Now if this be so, and if it be true, as we say, that good craftsmen work to the standard of the mean, then, since goodness like nature is more exact and of a higher character than any art, it follows that goodness is the quality that hits the mean. By "goodness" I mean goodness of moral character, since it is moral goodness that deals with feelings and actions, and it is in them that we find excess, deficiency and a mean. It is possible, for example, to experience fear, boldness, desire, anger, pity, and pleasures and pains generally, too much or too little or to the right amount. If we feel them too much or too little, we are wrong. But to have these feelings at the right times on the right occasions toward the right people for the right motive and in the right way is to have them in the right measure, that is somewhere between the extremes; and this is what characterizes goodness. The same may be said of the mean and extremes in actions. Now it is in the field of actions and feelings that goodness operates; in them we find excess, deficiency and, between them, the mean, the first two being wrong, the mean right and praised as such.[9] Goodness, then, is a mean condition in the sense that it aims at and hits the mean.

Consider, too, that it is possible to go wrong in more ways than one. (In Pythagorean terminology evil is a form of the Unlimited, good of the Limited.) But there is only one way of being right. That is why going wrong is easy, and going right difficult; it is easy to miss the bull's eye and difficult to hit it. Here, then, is another explanation of why the too much and the too little are connected with evil and the mean with good. As the poet says,

> Goodness is one, evil is multiform.

We may now define virtue as a disposition of the soul in which, when it has to choose among actions and feelings, it observes the mean relative to us, this being determined by such a rule or principle as would take shape in the mind of a man of sense or practical wisdom. We call it a mean condition as lying between two forms of badness, one being excess and the other deficiency; and also for this reason, that, whereas badness either falls short of or exceeds the right measure in feelings and actions, virtue discovers the mean and deliberately chooses it. Thus, looked at from the point of view of its essence as embodied in its definition, virtue no doubt is a mean; judged by the standard of what is right and best, it is an extreme.

But choice of a mean is not possible in every action or every feeling. The very names of some have an immediate connotation of evil. Such are malice, shamelessness, envy among feelings, and among actions adultery, theft, murder. All these and more like them have a bad name as being evil in themselves; it is not merely the excess or deficiency of them that we censure. In their case, then it is impossible to act rightly; whatever we do is wrong. Nor do circumstances make any difference in the rightness or wrongness of them. When a man commits adultery there is no point in asking whether it is with the right woman or at the right time or in the right way, for to do anything like that is simply wrong. It would amount to claiming that there is a mean and excess and defect in unjust or cowardly or intemperate actions. If such a thing were possible, we should find ourselves with a mean quantity of excess, a mean of deficiency, an excess of excess and a deficiency of deficiency. But just as in temperance and justice there can be no mean or excess or deficiency, because the mean in a sense *is* an extreme, so there can be no mean or excess or deficiency in those vicious actions—however done, they are wrong. Putting the matter into general language, we may say that there is no mean in the extremes, and no extreme in the mean, to be observed by anybody.

Chapter VII

But a generalization of this kind is not enough; we must show that our definition fits particular cases. When we are discussing actions particular statements come nearer the heart of the matter, though general statements cover a wider field. The reason is that human behaviour consists in the performance of particular acts, and our theories must be brought into harmony with them.

You see here a diagram of the virtues. Let us take our particular instances from that.

In the section confined to the feelings inspired by danger you will observe that the mean state is "courage." Of those who go to extremes in one direction or the other the man who shows an excess of fearlessness has no name to describe him,[10] the man who exceeds in confidence or daring is called "rash" or "foolhardy," the man who shows an excess of fear and a deficiency of confidence is called a "coward." In the pleasures and pains—though not all pleasures and pains, especially pains—the virtue which observes the mean is "temperance," the excess is the vice of "intemperance." Persons defective in the power to enjoy pleasures are a somewhat rare class, and so have not had a name assigned to them: suppose we call them "unimpressionable." Coming to the giving and acquiring of money, we find that the mean is "liberality," the excess "prodigality," the deficiency "meanness." But here we meet a complication. The prodigal man and the mean man exceed and fall short in opposite ways. The prodigal exceeds in giving and falls short in getting money, whereas the mean man exceeds in getting and falls short in giving it away. Of course this is but a summary account of the matter—a bare outline. But it meets our immediate requirements. Later on these types of character will be more accurately delineated.

But there are other dispositions which declare themselves in the way they deal with money. One is "lordliness" or "magnificence," which differs from liberality in that the lordly man deals in large sums, the liberal man in small. Magnificence is the mean state here, the excess is "bad taste" or "vulgarity," the defect is "shabbiness." These are not the same as the excess and defect on either side of liberality. How they differ is a point which will be discussed later. In the matter of honour the mean is "proper pride," the excess "vanity," the defect "poor-spiritedness." And just as liberality differs, as I said, from magnificence in being concerned with small sums of money, so there is a state related to proper pride in the same way, being concerned with small honours, while pride is concerned with great. For it is possible to aspire to small honours in the right way, or to a greater or less extent than is right. The man who has this aspiration to excess is called "ambitious"; if he does not cherish it enough, he is "unambitious"; but the man who has it to the right extent—that is, strikes the mean—has no special designation. This is true also of the corresponding dispositions with one exception, that of the ambitious man, which is called "ambitiousness." This will explain why each of the extreme characters stakes out a claim in the middle region. Indeed we ourselves call the character between the extremes sometimes "ambitious" and sometimes "unambitious." That is proved by our sometimes praising a man for being ambitious and sometimes for being unambitious. The reason will appear later. In the meantime let us continue our discussion of the remaining virtues and vices, following the method already laid down.

Let us next take anger. Here too we find excess, deficiency and the mean. Hardly one of the states of mind involved has a special name; but, since we call the man who attains the mean in this sphere "gentle," we may call his disposition "gentleness." Of the extremes the man who is angry overmuch may be called "irascible," and his vice "irascibility" while the man who reacts too feebly to anger may be called "poor-spirited" and his disposition "poor-spiritedness."

There are, in addition to those we have named, three other modes of observing the mean which in some ways resemble and in other ways differ from one another. They are all concerned with what we do and say in social intercourse, but they differ in this respect, that one is concerned with truthfulness in such intercourse, the other two with the agreeable, one of these two with the agreeable in amusement, the other with the agreeable element in every relation of life. About these two, then, we must say a word, in order that we may more fully convince ourselves that in all things the mean is to be commended, while the extremes are neither commendable nor right but reprehensible. I am afraid most of these too are nameless; but, as in the other cases, we must try to coin names for them in the interests of clearness and to make it easy to follow the argument. Well then, as regards veracity, the character who aims at the mean may be called "truthful"and what he aims at "truthfulness." Pretending, when it goes too far, is "boastfulness" and the man who shows it is a "boaster" or "braggart." If it takes the form of understatement, the pretense is called "irony" and the man who shows it "ironical." In agreeableness in social amusement the man who hits the mean is "witty" and what characterizes him is "wittiness." The excess is "buffoonery" and the man who exhibits that is a "buffoon." The opposite of the buffoon is the "boor" and his characteristic is "boorishness." In the other sphere of the agreeable—the general business of life—the person who is agreeable in the right way is "friendly" and his disposition "friendliness." The man who makes himself too agreeable, supposing him to have no ulterior object, is "obsequious"; if he has such an object, he is a "flatterer." The man who is deficient in this quality and takes every opportunity of making himself disagreeable may be called "peevish" or "sulky" or "surly."

Even when feelings and emotional states are involved one notes that mean conditions exist. And here also, it would be agreed, we may find one man observing the mean and another going beyond it, for instance the "shamefaced" man, who is put out of countenance by anything. Or a man may fall short here of the due mean. Thus anyone who is deficient in a sense of shame, or has none at all, is called "shameless." The man who avoids both extremes is "modest," and him we praise. For, while modesty is not a form of goodness, it is praised; it and the modest man. Then there is "righteous indignation." This is felt by anyone who strikes the mean between "envy" and "malice," by which last word I mean a pleased feeling at the misfortunes of other people. These are emotions concerned with the pains and pleasures we feel at the fortunes of our neighbours. The man who feels righteous indignation is pained by undeserved good fortune; but the envious man goes beyond that and is pained at anybody's success. The malicious man, on the other hand, is so far from being pained by the misfortunes of another that he is actually tickled by them. . . .

Chapter IX

I have said enough to show that moral excellence is a mean, and I have shown in what sense it is so. It is, namely, a mean between two forms of badness, one of excess and the other of defect, and is so described because it aims at hitting the mean point in feelings and in actions. This makes virtue hard of achievement, because finding the middle point is never easy. It is not everybody, for instance, who can find the center of a circle—that calls for a geometrician. Thus, too, it is easy to fly into a passion—anybody can do that—but to be angry with the right person and to the right extent and at the right time and with the right object and in the right way—that is not easy, and it is not everyone who can do it. This is equally true of giving or spending money. Hence we infer that to do these things properly is rare, laudable and fine. . . .

NOTES

1. It is of course obvious that to a certain extent they do not all aim at the same thing, for in some cases the end will be an activity, in others the product which goes beyond the actual activity. In the arts which aim at results of this kind the results or products are intrinsically superior to the activities.
2. It makes no difference if the ends of the activities are the activities themselves or something over and above these, as in the case of the sciences I have mentioned.
3. I am absolved from a more detailed discussion of this point by the full treatment it has received in current literature.
4. Of course we must draw the line somewhere. For, if we stretch it to include ancestors and descendants and friends' friends, there will be no end to it. But there will be another opportunity of considering this point.
5. There will be an opportunity later of considering what is meant by this formula, in particular what is meant by "the right principle" and how, in its ethical aspect, it is related to the moral virtues.
6. If we are to illustrate the material, it must be by concrete images.
7. $6 - 2 = 10 - 6$
8. What applies to gymnastics applies also to running and wrestling.
9. Being right or successful and being praised are both indicative of excellence.
10. We shall often have to make similar admissions.

QUESTIONS FOR ANALYSIS

1. What is the nature of "happiness"? How much weight should we give to the varying opinions of different people about the nature of happiness?
2. How is happiness different from honour, pleasure, intelligence, and good qualities generally? What does Aristotle mean in claiming that happiness is final and self-sufficient?
3. Do you agree with Aristotle that a complete lifetime is required to achieve happiness?
4. According to Aristotle, moral qualities can be destroyed by both excess and deficiency. What examples does he give? What other examples might he have used?
5. What connections does Aristotle make between virtue and pleasure? What roles do pleasure and pain play in moral education?
6. Whether an action is virtuous, Aristotle says, depends on both the action and the doer's frame of mind. Why? What must the frame of mind be?
7. Why does Aristotle call goodness a mean? In what sense does goodness aim at and hit the mean? Can you think of virtues that are not aptly described as means?

Respect for Persons

IMMANUEL KANT

In these selections from *Foundations of the Metaphysics of Morals,* Immanuel Kant develops his principle of respect for persons. He explains his concept of the categorical imperative, which he contrasts with hypothetical imperatives. Hypothetical imperatives are conditional commands. They are commands we have reason to follow if they serve some desire of ours. According to Kant, all imperatives except the supreme principle of morality are hypothetical. For example, "Be at the theater at eight" is conditional on our desire to see the movie from the beginning. A categorical imperative, on the other hand, is a command that applies to all rational beings *independent* of their desires. It is a command that reason tells us to follow no matter what. Because its authority does not depend on subjective factors, Kant considers it an objective law of reason. Because it applies to all of us, he calls it a universal practical law for all rational beings. And because this universal law has its source in our own capacity to reason, he calls us *legislators* of the universal law.

Though Kant says there is only one categorical imperative, he offers three formulations. The first is "[N]ever act in such a way that I could not also will that my maxim should be a universal law." By maxim, he means the principle on which a person's decision to act is made. To use one of Kant's own examples, someone who borrows money with no intention of repaying it would be acting on the maxim, "Whenever I need money I'll borrow it and promise to repay it though I know I never will." That maxim could never be a universal law, he says, because under those conditions, no one would believe promises any more and the institution of promising would self-destruct.

The third formulation is similar to the first, though Kant does not state it in the form of an imperative. It is "the idea of the will of every rational being as making universal law."

Kant's second formulation is "Act so that you treat humanity, whether in your own person or in that of another, as an end and never as a means only." Human beings, he says, have unconditional worth; that is, we do not consider our own existence to be a means to some further end but we consider it to be an end in itself. Therefore, we should not treat one another merely as a means to some further end. He then discusses the inherent worth and dignity of persons. Because we are subject only to the laws of our own reason, he says, we are autonomous beings. And our autonomy gives us a dignity and worth beyond all price. Because of our priceless dignity and worth, all persons are worthy of respect.

FIRST SECTION

...Nothing in the world—indeed nothing even beyond the world—can possibly be conceived which could be called good without qualification except a GOOD WILL. Intelligence, wit, judgment, and other talents of the mind however they may be named, or courage, resoluteness, and perseverance as qualities of temperament, are doubtless in many respects good and desirable; but they can become extremely bad and harmful if the will, which is to make use of these gifts of nature and which in its special constitution is called character, is not good. It is the same with gifts of fortune. Power, riches, honor, even health, general well-being and the contentment with one's condition which is called happiness make for pride and even arrogance if there is not a good will to correct their influence on the mind and on its principle of action, so as to make it generally fitting to its entire end. It need hardly be mentioned that the sight of a being adorned with no feature of a pure and good will yet enjoying lasting good fortune can never give pleasure to an impartial rational observer. Thus the good will seems to constitute the indispensable condition even of worthiness to be happy....

The good will is not good because of what it effects or accomplishes or because of its competence to achieve some intended end; it is good only because of its willing (i.e., it is good in itself). And, regarded for itself, it is to be esteemed as incomparably higher than anything which could be brought about by it in favor of any inclination or even of the sum total of all inclinations. Even if it should happen that, by a particularly unfortunate fate or by the niggardly provision of a stepmotherly nature, this will should be wholly lacking in power to accomplish its purpose, and if even the greatest effort should not avail it to achieve anything of its end, and if there remained only the good will—not as a mere wish, but as the summoning of all the means in our power—it would sparkle like a jewel all by itself, as something that had its full worth in itself. Usefulness or fruitlessness can neither diminish nor augment this worth. Its usefulness would be only its setting, as it were, so as to enable us to handle it more conveniently in commerce or to attract the attention of those who are not yet connoisseurs, but not to recommend it to those who are experts or to determine its worth....

Thus the moral worth of an action does not lie in the effect which is expected from it or in any principle of action which has to borrow its motive from this expected effect. For all these effects (agreeableness of my own condition, indeed even the promotion of the happiness of others) could be brought about through other causes and would not require the will of a rational being, while the highest and unconditional good can be found only in such a will. Therefore the preeminent good can consist only in the conception of law in itself (which can be present only in a rational being) so far as this conception and not the hoped-for effect is the determining ground of the will. This preeminent good, which we call moral, is already present in the person who acts according to this conception, and we do not have to look for it first in the result.

But what kind of law can that be, the conception of which must determine the will without reference to the expected result? Under this condition alone can the will be called absolutely good without qualification. Since I have robbed the will of all impulses which could come to it from obedience to any law, nothing remains to serve as a principle of the will except universal conformity to law as such. That is, I ought never to act in such a way that I could not also will that my maxim should be a universal law. Strict conformity to law as such (without assuming any particular law applicable to certain actions) serves as the principle of the will, and it must serve as such a principle if duty is not to be a vain delusion and chimerical concept. The common sense of mankind (*gemeine Menschenvernunft*) in its practical judgments is in perfect agreement with this and has this principle constantly in view.

Let the question, for example, be: May I, when in distress, make a promise with the intention not to keep it? I easily distinguish the two meanings which the question can have, viz., whether it is prudent to make a false promise, or whether it conforms to duty. The former can undoubtedly be often the case, though I do see clearly that it is not sufficient merely to escape from the present difficulty by this expedient, but that I must consider whether inconveniences much greater than the present one may not later spring from this lie. Even with all my supposed cunning, the consequences cannot be so easily foreseen. Loss of credit might be far more disadvantageous than the misfortune I am now seeking to avoid, and it is hard to tell whether it might not be more prudent to act according to a universal maxim and to make it a habit not to promise anything without intending to fulfill it. But it is soon clear to me that such a maxim is based only on an apprehensive concern with consequences.

To be truthful from duty, however, is an entirely different thing from being truthful out of fear of untoward consequences, for in the former case the concept of the action itself contains a law for me, while in the latter I must first look about to see what results for me may be connected with it. To deviate from the principle of duty is certainly bad, but to be unfaithful to my maxim of prudence can sometimes be very advantageous to me, though it is certainly safer to abide by it. The shortest but most infallible way to find the answer to the question as to whether a deceitful promise is consistent with duty is to ask myself: would I be content that my maxim of extricating myself from difficulty by a false promise should hold as a universal law for myself as well as for others? And could I say to myself that everyone may make a false promise when he is in a difficulty from which he otherwise cannot escape? Immediately I see that I could will the lie but not a universal law to lie. For with such a law there would be no promises at all, inasmuch as it would be futile to make a pretense of my intention in regard to future actions to those who would not believe this pretense or—if they overhastily did so—would pay me back in my own coin. Thus my maxim would necessarily destroy itself as soon as it was made a universal law.

I do not, therefore, need any penetrating acuteness to discern what I have to do in order that my volition may be morally good. Inexperienced in the course of the world, incapable of being prepared for all its contingencies, I only ask myself: Can I will that my maxim become a universal law? If not, it must be rejected, not because of any disadvantage accruing to myself or even to others, but because it cannot enter as a principle into a possible enactment of universal law, and reason extorts from me an immediate aspect for such legislation. I do not as yet discern on what is grounded (this is a question the philosopher may investigate), but I at least understand that it is an estimation of a worth which far outweighs all the worth of whatever is recommended by the inclinations, and that the necessity that I act from pure respect for the practical law constitutes my duty. To duty every other motive must give place, because duty is the condition of a will good in itself, whose worth transcends everything. . . .

SECOND SECTION

. . . Everything in nature works according to laws. Only a rational being has the capacity of acting according to the *conception* of laws (i.e., according to principles). This capacity is the will. Since reason is required for the derivation of actions from laws, will is nothing less than practical reason. . . .

The conception of an objective principle, so far as it constrains a will, is a command (of reason), and the formula of this command is called an *imperative.*

All imperatives are expressed by an "ought" and thereby indicate the relation of an objective law of reason to a will which is not in its subjective constitution necessarily determined by this law. This relation is that of constraint. Imperatives say that it would be good to do or to refrain from doing something, but they say it to a will which does not always do something simply because the thing is presented to it as good to do. Practical good is what determines the will by means of the conception of reason and hence not by subjective causes but objectively, on grounds which are valid for every rational being as such. It is distinguished from the pleasant, as that which has an influence on the will only by means of a sensation from purely subjective causes, which hold for the senses only of this or that person and not as a principle of reason which holds for everyone. . . .

All imperatives command either *hypothetically* or *categorically.* The former present the practical necessity of a possible action as a means to achieving something else which one desires (or which one may possibly desire). The categorical imperative would be one which presented an action as of itself objectively necessary, without regard to any other end.

Since every practical law presents a possible action as good and thus as necessary for a subject practically determinable by reason, all imperatives are formulas of the determination of action which is necessary by the principle of a will which is in any way good. If the action is good only as a means to something else, the imperative is hypothetical; but if it is thought of as good in itself, and hence as necessary in a will which of itself conforms to reason as the principle of this will, the imperative is categorical....

Finally, there is one imperative which directly commands certain conduct without making its condition some purpose to be reached by it. This imperative is categorical. It concerns not the material of the action and its intended result, but the form and principle from which it originates. What is essentially good in it consists in the mental disposition, the result being what it may. This imperative may be called the imperative of morality....

If I think of a hypothetical imperative as such, I do not know what it will contain until the condition is stated [under which it is an imperative]. But if I think of a categorical imperative, I know immediately what it will contain. For since the imperative contains, besides the law, only the necessity of the maxim of acting in accordance with the law, while the law contains no condition to which it is restricted, nothing remains except the universality of law as such to which the maxim of the action should conform; and this conformity alone is what is represented as necessary by the imperative.

There is, therefore, only one categorical imperative. It is: Act only according to that maxim by which you can at the same time will that it should become a universal law.

Now if all imperatives of duty can be derived from this one imperative as a principle, we can at least show what we understand by the concept of duty and what it means, even though it remain undecided whether that which is called duty is an empty concept or not.

The universality of law according to which effects are produced constitutes what is properly called nature in the most general sense (as to form) (i.e., the existence of things so far as it is determined by universal laws). [By analogy], then, the universal imperative of duty can be expressed as follows: Act as though the maxim of your action were by your will to become a universal law of nature....

...Suppose that there were something the existence of which in itself had absolute worth, something which, as an end in itself, could be a ground of definite laws. In it and only in it could lie the ground of a possible categorical imperative, i.e., of a practical law.

Now, I say, man and, in general, every rational being exists as an end in himself and not merely as a means to be arbitrarily used by this or that will. In all his actions, whether they are directed to himself or to other rational beings, he must always be regarded at the same time as an end. All objects of inclinations have only a conditional worth, for if the inclinations and the needs founded on them did not exist, their object would be without worth. The inclinations themselves as the sources of needs, however, are so lacking in absolute worth that the universal wish of every rational being must be indeed to free himself completely from them. Therefore, the worth of any objects to be obtained by our actions is at all times conditional. Beings whose existence does not depend on our will but on nature, if they are not rational beings, have only a relative worth as means and are therefore called "things"; on the other hand, rational beings are designated "persons" because their nature indicates that they are ends in themselves, i.e., things which may not be used merely as means. Such a being is thus an object of respect and, so far, restricts all [arbitrary] choice. Such beings are not merely subjective ends whose existence as a result of our action has a worth for us, but are objective ends, i.e., beings whose existence in itself is an end. Such an end is one for which no other end can be substituted, to which these beings should serve merely as means. For, without them, nothing of absolute worth could be found, and if all worth is conditional and thus contingent, no supreme practical principle for reason could be found anywhere.

Thus if there is to be a supreme practical principle and a categorical imperative for the human will, it must be one that forms an objective principle of the will from the conception of that which is necessarily an end for everyone because it is an end in itself. Hence this objective principle can serve as a universal practical law. The ground of this principle is: rational nature exists as an end in itself. Man necessarily thinks of his own existence in this way; thus far it is a subjective principle of human actions. Also every other rational being thinks of his existence by means of the same rational ground which holds also for myself; thus it is at the same time an objective principle from which, as a supreme practical ground, it must be possible to derive all laws of the will. The practical imperative, therefore, is the following: Act so that you treat humanity, whether in your own person or in that of another, always as an end and never as a means only. . . .

If we now look back upon all previous attempts which have ever been undertaken to discover the principle of morality, it is not to be wondered at that they all had to fail. Man was seen to be bound to laws by his duty, but it was not seen that he is subject only to his own, yet universal, legislation, and that he is only bound to act in accordance with his own will, which is, however, designed by nature to be a will giving universal laws. For if one thought of him as subject only to a law (whatever it may be), this necessarily implied some interest as a stimulus or compulsion to obedience because the law did not arise from his will. Rather, his will was constrained by something else according to a law to act in a certain way. By this strictly necessary consequence, however, all the labor of finding a supreme ground for duty was irrevocably lost, and one never arrived at duty but only at the necessity of action from a certain interest. This might be his own interest or that of another, but in either case the imperative always had to be conditional and could not at all serve as a moral command. This principle I will call the principle of *autonomy* of the will in contrast to all other principles which I accordingly count under heteronomy.

The concept of each rational being as a being that must regard itself as giving universal law through all the maxims of its will, so that it may judge itself and its actions from this standpoint, leads to a very fruitful concept, namely, that of a *realm of ends.*

By "realm" I understand the systematic union of different rational beings through common laws. Because laws determine ends with regard to their universal validity, if we abstract from the personal difference of rational beings and thus from all content of their private ends, we can think of a whole of all ends in systematic connection, a whole of rational beings as ends in themselves as well as of the particular ends which each may set for himself. This is a realm of ends, which is possible on the aforesaid principles. For all rational beings stand under the law that each of them should treat himself and all others never merely as means but in every case also as an end in himself. Thus there arises a systematic union of rational beings through common objective laws. This is a realm which may be called a realm of ends (certainly only an ideal), because what these laws have in view is just the relation of these beings to each other as ends and means.

A rational being belongs to the realm of ends as a member when he gives universal laws in it while also himself subject to these laws. He belongs to it as sovereign when he, as legislating, is subject to the will of no other. The rational being must regard himself always as legislative in a realm of ends possible through the freedom of the will, whether he belongs to it as member or as sovereign. He cannot maintain the latter position merely through the maxims of his will but only when he is a completely independent being without need and with power adequate to his will.

Morality, therefore, consists in the relation of every action to that legislation through which alone a realm of ends is possible. This legislation, however, must be found in every rational being. It must be able to arise from his will, whose principle then is to take no action according to any maxim which would be inconsistent with its being a universal law and thus to act only so that the will through its maxims could regard itself at the same time as universally lawgiving. If now the maxims do not by their nature already necessarily conform to this objective principle of rational beings as universally lawgiving, the necessity of acting according to that principle is called practical constraint, i.e., duty. Duty pertains not to the sovereign in the realm of ends, but rather to each member, and to each in the same degree.

The practical necessity of acting according to this principle, i.e., duty, does not rest at all on feelings, impulses, and inclinations; it rests merely on the relation of rational beings to one another, in which the will of a rational being must always be regarded as legislative, for otherwise it could not be thought of as an end in itself. Reason, therefore, relates every maxim of the will as giving universal laws to every other will and also to every action toward itself; it does so not for the sake of any other practical motive or future advantage but rather from the idea of the dignity of a rational being who obeys no law except that which he himself also gives.

In the realm of ends everything has either a *price* or a *dignity*. Whatever has a price can be replaced by something else as its equivalent; on the other hand, whatever is above all price, and therefore admits of no equivalent, has a dignity.

That which is related to general human inclinations and needs has a *market price*. That which, without presupposing any need, accords with a certain taste, i.e., with pleasure in the mere purposeless play of our faculties, has an *affective price*. But that which constituted the condition under which alone something can be an end in itself does not have mere relative worth, i.e., a price, but an intrinsic worth, i.e., *dignity*.

Now morality is the condition under which alone a rational being can be an end in itself, because only through it is it possible to be a legislative member in the realm of ends. Thus morality and humanity, so far as it is capable of morality, alone have dignity. Skill and diligence in work have a market value; wit, lively imagination, and humor have an affective price; but fidelity in promises and benevolence on principle (not from instinct) have intrinsic worth. Nature and likewise art contain nothing which could replace their lack, for their worth consists not in effects which flow from them, nor in advantage and utility which they procure; it consists only in intentions, i.e., maxims of the will which are ready to reveal themselves in this manner through actions even though success does not favor them. These actions need no recommendation from any subjective disposition or taste in order that they may be looked upon with immediate favor and satisfaction, nor do they have need of any immediate propensity or feeling directed to them. They exhibit the will which performs them as the object of an immediate respect, since nothing but reason is required in order to impose them on the will. The will is not to be cajoled into them, for this, in the case of duties, would be a contradiction. This esteem lets the worth of such a turn of mind be recognized as dignity and puts it infinitely beyond any price, with which it cannot in the least be brought into competition or comparison without, as it were, violating its holiness.

And what is it that justifies the morally good disposition or virtue in making such lofty claims? It is nothing less than the participation it affords the rational being in giving universal laws. He is thus fitted to be a member in a possible realm of ends to which his own nature already destined him. For, as an end in himself, he is destined to be legislative in the realm of ends, free from all laws of nature and obedient only to those which he himself gives. Accordingly, his maxims can belong to a universal legislation to which he is at the same time also subject. A thing has no worth other than that determined for it by the law. The legislation which determines all worth must therefore have a dignity, i.e., unconditional and incomparable worth. For the esteem which a rational being must have for it, only the word "respect" is a suitable expression. Autonomy is thus the basis of the dignity of both human nature and every rational nature. . . .

QUESTIONS FOR ANALYSIS

1. Why is "good will" considered good without qualification? How is it different from other good things?
2. How is a categorical imperative different from a hypothetical imperative? How do categorical imperatives get their authority? What does Kant mean in saying that all rational beings are "legislators" of universal law?
3. How would Kant evaluate this maxim: "I will keep my promises only when it is my own personal best interest"?
4. What does Kant mean by "absolute worth"? Why do persons, but not things, have absolute worth?
5. What does it mean to treat a person as a thing rather than as an end in itself? What examples can you think of?
6. According to Kant, human autonomy lies in the fact that we are subject to the moral law of our own will, not a moral law from an external source. What does it mean to be subject to a law of our own will? Why does our subjection to it make us autonomous?
7. What is the importance of Kant's distinction between price and dignity? Why does he say that human autonomy is the basis of human dignity?
8. What does Kant mean by a "realm of ends"? What role does the concept play in his moral thought?

Utilitarianism

JOHN STUART MILL

In the following selection from *Utilitarianism,* John Stuart Mill argues that the principle of utility, or the greatest happiness principle—choose the action that creates the greatest happiness for all concerned—is the foundation of all morality. All other moral principles, he says, are "secondary principles," which we adopt because following them will help us maximize happiness. Because he takes the principle of utility to be fundamental, he calls his view utilitarianism.

After defining *happiness* as "pleasure and the absence of pain," Mill distinguishes higher—distinctively human—pleasures from lower—animal—pleasures. The rest of the selection is devoted to defending utilitarianism from various objections, the most notable being that it amounts to expediency and selfishness.

The creed which accepts as the foundation of morals Utility, or the Greatest Happiness Principle, holds that actions are right in proportion as they tend to promote happiness, wrong as they tend to produce the reverse of happiness. By happiness is intended pleasure and the absence of pain; by unhappiness, pain and the privation of pleasure. To give a clear view of the moral standard set up by the theory, much more requires to be said, in particular, what things it includes in the ideas of pain and pleasure and to what extent this is left an open question. But these supplementary explanations do not affect the theory of life on which this theory of morality is grounded—namely, that pleasure and freedom from pain are the only things desirable as ends, and that all desirable things (which are as numerous in the utilitarian as in any other scheme) are desirable either for the pleasure inherent in themselves or as means to the promotion of pleasure and the prevention of pain.

From John Stuart Mill, *Utilitarianism.*

Now, such a theory of life excites in many minds, and among them in some of the most estimable in feeling and purpose, inveterate dislike. To suppose that life has (as they express it) no higher end than pleasure—no better and nobler object of desire and pursuit—they designate as utterly mean and groveling, as a doctrine worthy only of swine, to whom the followers of Epicurus were, at a very early period, contemptuously likened; and modern holders of the doctrine are occasionally made the subject of equally polite comparisons by its German, French, and English assailants.

When thus attacked, the Epicureans have always answered that it is not they, but their accusers who represent human nature in a degrading light, since the accusation supposes human beings to be capable of no pleasures except those of which swine are capable. If this supposition were true, the charge could not be gainsaid, but would then be no longer an imputation; for if the sources of pleasure were precisely the same to human beings and to swine, the rule of life which is good enough for the one would be good enough for the other. The comparison of the Epicurean life to that of beasts is felt as degrading precisely because a beast's pleasures do not satisfy a human being's conceptions of happiness. Human beings have faculties more elevated than the animal appetites and, when once made conscious of them, do not regard anything as happiness which does not include their gratification. I do not, indeed, consider the Epicureans to have been by any means faultless in drawing out their scheme of consequences from the utilitarian principle. To do this in any sufficient manner, many Stoic, as well as Christian, elements require to be included. But there is no known Epicurean theory of life which does not assign to the pleasures of the intellect, of the feelings and imagination, and of the moral sentiments a much higher value as pleasures than to those of mere sensation.

It must be admitted, however, that utilitarian writers in general have placed the superiority of mental over bodily pleasures chiefly in the greater permanency, safety, uncostliness, etc., of the former—that is, in their circumstantial advantages rather than in their intrinsic nature. And on all these points, utilitarians have fully proved their case; but they might have taken the other and, as it may be called, higher ground with entire consistency. It is quite compatible with the principle of utility to recognize the fact that some *kinds* of pleasure are more desirable and more valuable than others. It would be absurd that while, in estimating all other things, quality is considered as well as quantity, the estimation of pleasures should be supposed to depend on quantity alone.

If I am asked what I mean by difference of quality in pleasures or what makes one pleasure more valuable than another, merely as a pleasure, except its being greater in amount, there is but one possible answer. Of two pleasures, if there be one to which all or almost all who have experience of both give a decided preference, irrespective of any feeling of moral obligation to prefer it, that is the more desirable pleasure. If one of the two is, by those who are competently acquainted with both, placed so far above the other that they prefer it, even though knowing it to be attended with a greater amount of discontent, and would not resign it for any quantity of the other pleasure of which their nature is capable, we are justified in ascribing to the preferred enjoyment a superiority in quality so far outweighing quantity as to render it, in comparison, of small account.

Now, it is an unquestionable fact that those who are equally acquainted with and equally capable of appreciating and enjoying both do give a most marked preference to the manner of existence which employs their higher faculties. Few human creatures would consent to be changed into any of the lower animals for a promise of the fullest allowance of a beast's pleasures; no intelligent human being would consent to be a fool, no instructed person would be an ignoramus, no person of feeling and conscience would be selfish and base, even though they should be persuaded that the fool, the dunce, or the rascal is better satisfied with his lot than they are with theirs. They would not resign what they possess more than he for the most complete satisfaction of all the desires which they have in common with him. . . .

I must again repeat what the assailants of utilitarianism seldom have the justice to acknowledge, that the happiness which forms the utilitarian standard of what is right in conduct is not the agent's own happiness, but that of all concerned. As between his own happiness and that of others, utilitarianism requires him to be as strictly impartial as a disinterested and benevolent spectator. In the golden rule of Jesus of Nazareth, we read the complete spirit of the ethics of utility. To do as you would be done by and to love your neighbor as yourself constitute the ideal perfection of utilitarian morality. As the means of making the nearest approach to this ideal, utility would enjoin first that laws and social arrangements should place the happiness, or (as speaking practically it may be called) the interest, of every individual as nearly as possible in harmony with the interest of the whole; and secondly, that education and opinion, which have so vast a power over human character, should so use that power as to establish in the mind of every individual an indissoluble association between his own happiness and the good of the whole—especially between his own happiness and the practice of such modes of conduct, negative and positive, as regard for the universal happiness prescribes, so that not only he may be unable to conceive the possibility of happiness to himself consistently with conduct opposed to the general good, but also that a direct impulse to promote the general good may be in every individual one of the habitual motives of action and the sentiments connected therewith may fill a large and prominent place in every human being's sentient existence. If the impugners of the utilitarian morality represented it to their own minds in this its true character, I know not what recommendation possessed by any other morality they could possibly affirm to be wanting to it, what more beautiful or more exalted developments of human nature any other ethical system can be supposed to foster, or what springs of action, not accessible to the utilitarian, such systems rely on for giving effect to their mandates.

The objectors to utilitarianism cannot always be charged with representing it in a discreditable light. On the contrary, those among them who entertain anything like a just idea of its disinterested character sometimes find fault with its standard as being too high for humanity. They say it is exacting too much to require that people shall always act from the inducement of promoting the general interests of society. But this is to mistake the very meaning of a standard of morals and confound the rule of action with the motive of it. It is the business of ethics to tell us what are our duties or by what test we may know them; but no system of ethics requires that the sole motive of all we do shall be a feeling of duty: on the contrary, ninety-nine hundredths of all our actions are done from other motives, and rightly so done, if the rule of duty does not condemn them. It is the more unjust to utilitarianism that this particular misapprehension should be made a ground of objection to it, inasmuch as utilitarian moralists have gone beyond almost all others in affirming that the motive has nothing to do with the morality of the action, though much with the worth of the agent. He who saves a fellow creature from drowning does what is morally right, whether his motive be duty or the hope of being paid for his trouble; he who betrays the friend that trusts him is guilty of a crime, even if his object be to serve another friend to whom he is under greater obligations. But to speak only of actions done from the motive of duty, and in direct obedience to principle: it is a misapprehension of the utilitarian mode of thought to conceive it as implying that people should fix their minds upon so wide a generality as the world or society at large. The great majority of good actions are intended not for the benefit of the world, but for that of individuals, of which the good of the world is made up; and the thoughts of the most virtuous man need not on these occasions travel beyond the particular persons concerned, except so far as is necessary to assure himself that in benefiting them he is not violating the rights, that is the legitimate and authorized expectations, of anyone else. The multiplication of happiness is, according to the utilitarian ethics, the object of virtue: the occasions on which any person (except one in a thousand) has it in his power to do this on an extended scale, in other words to be a public benefactor, are but exceptional; and on these occasions alone is he called on to consider public utility; in every other case, private utility, the interest or happiness of some few persons, is all he has to attend to. Those alone the influence of whose actions extends to society in general need concern themselves habitually about so large an object. In the case of abstinences, indeed—of things which people forbear to do from moral considerations, though the consequences in the particular case might be beneficial—it would be unworthy of an intelligent agent not to be consciously aware that the action is of a class which, if practiced generally, would be generally injurious, and that this is the ground of the obligation to abstain from it. The amount of regard for the public interest implied in this recognition is no greater than is demanded by every system of morals, for they all enjoin to abstain from whatever is manifestly pernicious to society. . . .

Again, Utility is often summarily stigmatized as an immoral doctrine by giving it the name of Expediency and taking advantage of the popular use of that term to contrast it with Principle. But the Expedient, in the sense in which it is opposed to the Right, generally means that which is expedient for the particular interest of the agent himself, as when a minister sacrifices the interests of his country to keep himself in place. When it means anything better than this, it means that which is expedient for some immediate object, some temporary purpose, but which violates a rule whose observance is expedient in a much higher degree. The Expedient, in this sense, instead of being the same thing as the useful, is a branch of the hurtful.

Thus, it would often be expedient, for the purpose of getting over some momentary embarrassment, or attaining some object immediately useful to ourselves or others, to tell a lie. But inasmuch as the cultivation in ourselves of a sensitive feeling on the subject of veracity is one of the most useful, and the enfeeblement of that feeling one of the most hurtful, things to which our conduct can be instrumental; and inasmuch as any, even unintentional, deviation from truth does that much toward weakening the trustworthiness of human assertion, which is not only the principal support of all present social well-being, but the insufficiency of which does more than any one thing that can be named to keep back civilization, virtue, everything on which human happiness on the largest scale depends—we feel that the violation, for a present advantage, of a rule of such transcendent expediency is not expedient and that he, who for the sake of a convenience to himself or to some other individual, does what depends on him to deprive mankind of the good, and inflict upon them the evil, involved in the greater or less reliance which they can place in each other's word, acts the part of one of their worst enemies.

Yet, that even this rule, sacred as it is, admits of possible exceptions is acknowledged by all moralists, the chief of which is when the withholding of some fact (as of information from a malefactor or of bad news from a person dangerously ill) would save an individual (especially an individual other than oneself) from great and unmerited evil, and when the withholding can only be effected by denial. But in order that the exception may not extend itself beyond the need and may have the least possible effect in weakening reliance on veracity, it ought to be recognized and, if possible, its limits defined; and if the principle of utility is good for anything, it must be good for weighing these conflicting utilities against one another and marking out the region within which one or the other preponderates.

Again, defenders of utility often find themselves called upon to reply to such objections as this—that there is not time, previous to action, for calculating and weighing the effects of any line of conduct on the general happiness. This is exactly as if anyone were to say that it is impossible to guide our conduct by Christianity because there is not time, on every occasion on which anything has to be done, to read through the Old and New Testaments. The answer to the objection is that there has been ample time, namely, the whole past duration of the human species. During all that time, mankind have been learning by experience the tendencies of actions, on which experience all the prudence, as well as all the morality of life, are dependent. People talk as if the commencement of this course of experience had hitherto been put off, and as if, at the moment when some man feels tempted to meddle with the property or life of another, he had to begin considering for the first time whether murder and theft are injurious to human happiness. Even then, I do not think that he would find the question very puzzling; but, at all events, the matter is now done to his hand. It is truly a whimsical supposition that if mankind were agreed in considering utility to be the test of morality, they would remain without any agreement as to what is useful and would take no measures for having their notions on the subject taught to the young and enforced by law and opinion. There is no difficulty in proving any ethical standard whatever to work ill, if we suppose universal idiocy to be conjoined with it; but on any hypothesis short of that, mankind must by this time have acquired positive beliefs as to the effects of some actions on their happiness; and the beliefs which have thus come down are the rules of morality for the multitude, and for the philosopher until he has succeeded in finding better.

That philosophers might easily do this, even now, on many subjects; that the received code of ethics is by no means of divine right; and that mankind have still much to learn as to the effects of actions on the general happiness—I admit, or, rather, earnestly maintain. The corollaries from the principle of utility, like the precepts of every practical art, admit of indefinite improvement, and, in a progressive state of the human mind, their improvement is perpetually going on. But to consider the rules of morality as improvable is one thing; to pass over the intermediate generalizations entirely, and endeavor to test each individual action directly by the first principle, is another. It is a strange notion that the acknowledgment of a first principle is inconsistent with the admission of secondary ones. To inform a traveler respecting the place of his ultimate destination is not to forbid the use of landmarks and direction-posts on the way. The proposition that happiness is the end and aim of morality does not mean that no road ought to be laid down to that goal or that persons going thither should not be advised to take one direction, rather than another. Men really ought to leave off talking a kind of nonsense on this subject, which they would neither talk nor listen to on other matters of practical concernment. Nobody argues that the art of navigation is not founded on astronomy because sailors cannot wait to calculate the Nautical Almanack. Being rational creatures, they go to sea with it ready calculated; and all rational creatures go out upon the sea of life with their minds made up on the common questions of right and wrong, as well as on many of the far more difficult questions of wise and foolish. And this, as long as foresight is a human quality, it is to be presumed they will continue to do. Whatever we adopt as the fundamental principle of morality, we require subordinate principles to apply it by; the impossibility of doing without them, being common to all systems, can afford no argument against any one in particular; but gravely to argue as if no such secondary principles could be had, and as if mankind had remained till now, and always remain, without drawing any general conclusions from the experience of human life, is as high a pitch, I think, as absurdity has ever reached in philosophical controversy.

The remainder of the stock arguments against utilitarianism mostly consist in laying to its charge the common infirmities of human nature and the general difficulties which embarrass conscientious persons in shaping their course through life. We are told that a utilitarian will be apt to make his own particular case an exception to moral rules and, when under temptation, will see a utility in the breach of a rule greater than he will see in its observance. But is utility the only creed which is able to furnish us with excuses for evildoing and means of cheating our own conscience? They are afforded in abundance by all doctrines which recognize as a fact in morals the existence of conflicting considerations, which all doctrines do that have been believed by sane persons. It is not the fault of any creed, but of the complicated nature of human affairs, that rules of conduct cannot be so framed as to require no exceptions and that hardly any kind of action can safely be laid down as either always obligatory or always condemnable. There is no ethical creed which does not temper the rigidity of its laws by giving a certain latitude, under the moral responsibility of the agent, for accommodation to peculiarities of circumstances; and under every creed, at the opening thus made, self-deception and dishonest casuistry get in. There exists no moral system under which there do not arise unequivocal cases of conflicting obligation. These are the real difficulties, the knotty points both in the theory of ethics and in the conscientious guidance of personal conduct. They are overcome practically with greater or with less success according to the intellect and virtue of the individual; but it can hardly be pretended that anyone will be the less qualified for dealing with them from possessing an ultimate standard to which conflicting rights and duties can be referred. If utility is the ultimate source of moral obligations, utility may be invoked to decide between them when their demands are incompatible. Though the application of the standard may be difficult, it is better than none at all: while in other systems the moral laws all claiming independent authority, there is no common umpire entitled to interfere between them; their claims to precedence one over another rest on little better than sophistry, and unless determined, as they generally are, by the unacknowledged influence of considerations of utility, afford a free scope for the action of personal desires and partialities. We must remember that only in these cases of conflict between secondary principles is it requisite that first principles should be appealed to. There is no case of moral obligation in which some secondary principle is not involved; and, if only one, there can seldom be any real doubt which one it is in the mind of any person by whom the principle itself is recognized.

QUESTIONS FOR ANALYSIS

1. How does Mill distinguish higher and lower pleasures? What test does he propose?
2. According to Mill, utilitarianism and the golden rule are both in the same spirit. Why? Do you agree? Why or why not?
3. What is the importance of Mill's distinction between private and public utility? What criticism is it intended to disarm?
4. Mill says that we need appeal directly to the greatest happiness principle only when secondary principles conflict. Why?
5. Mill's ethical view is often called hedonistic because it considers pleasure to be the only good desirable in itself. Can you think of goods that are desirable independent of any pleasure they might give?

The Need for More Than Justice

ANNETTE C. BAIER

In the following essay, Annette C. Baier, professor *emerita* of philosophy at the University of Pittsburgh, provides a contemporary feminist criticism of the ethical tradition that begins with Kant and continues through John Rawls. Baier's starting point is the work of psychologist Carol Gilligan, whose studies suggest that women are more likely than men to adopt an ethics of care in addition to an ethics of Kantian respect. Baier contrasts Gilligan's studies to the earlier studies of psychologist Lawrence Kohlberg. In those studies, Kohlberg concluded that individuals go through various stages of moral development. As young children, they view right and wrong in terms of parental authority. Then they move to a conventional stage, in which right and wrong are determined by the groups they belong to. At the final stages, they move beyond conventional rules to higher moral principle, first utilitarian and then Kantian. According to Gilligan, this model of moral maturity does not reflect the experience of women, who tend to view moral decisions in terms of human interdependence and needs as well as justice and rights.

After comparing these two models of moral maturity, Baier argues that traditional justice-oriented ethics is inadequate. It masks inequalities among people, oversimplifies human relationships, and understates the moral importance of emotions like love. The best moral theory, she concludes, must place care on an equal footing with justice.

In recent decades in North American social and moral philosophy, alongside the development and discussion of widely influential theories of justice, taken as Rawls takes it as the "first virtue of social institutions,"[1] there has been a counter-movement gathering strength, one coming from some interesting sources. For some of the most outspoken of the diverse group who have in a variety of ways been challenging the assumed supremacy of justice among the moral and social virtues are members of those sections of society whom one might have expected to be especially aware of the supreme importance of justice, namely blacks and women. Those who have only recently won recognition of their equal rights, who have only recently seen the correction or partial correction of long-standing racist and sexist injustices to their race and sex, are among the philosophers now suggesting that justice is only one virtue among many, and one that may need the presence of the others in order to deliver its own undenied value. Among these philosophers of the philosophical counterculture, as it were—but an increasingly large counterculture—I include Alasdair MacIntyre,[2] Michael Stocker,[3] Lawrence Blum,[4] Michael Slote,[5] Laurence Thomas,[6] Claudia Card,[7] Alison Jaggar,[8] Susan Wolf[9] and a whole group of men and women, myself included, who have been influenced by the writings of Harvard educational psychologist Carol Gilligan, whose book *In a Different Voice* (Harvard 1982; hereafter D.V.) caused a considerable stir both in the popular press and, more slowly, in the philosophical journals.[10]

Let me say quite clearly at this early point that there is little disagreement that justice is *a* social value of very great importance, and injustice an evil. Nor would those who have worked on theories of justice want to deny that other things matter besides justice. Rawls, for example, incorporates the value of freedom into his account of justice, so that denial of basic freedoms counts as injustice. Rawls also leaves room for a wider theory of the right, of which the theory of justice is just a part. Still, he does claim that justice is the "first" virtue of social institutions, and it is only that claim about priority that I think has been challenged. It is easy to exaggerate the differences of view that exist, and I want to avoid that. The differences are as much in emphasis as in substance, or we can say that they are differences in tone of voice. But these differences do tend to make a difference in approaches to a wide range of topics not just in moral theory but in areas like medical ethics, where the discussion used to be conducted in terms of patients' rights, of informed consent, and so on, but now tends to get conducted in an enlarged moral vocabulary, which draws on what Gilligan calls the ethics of *care* as well as that of *justice*.

For "care" is the new buzz-word. It is not, as Shakespeare's Portia demanded, mercy that is to season justice, but a less authoritarian humanitarian supplement, a felt concern for the good of others and for community with them. The "cold jealous virtue of justice" (Hume) is found to be too cold, and it is "warmer"more communitarian virtues and social ideals that are being called in to supplement it. One might say that liberty and equality are being found inadequate without fraternity, except that "fraternity" will be quite the wrong word, if as Gilligan initially suggested, it is *women* who perceive this value most easily. ("Sorority" will do no better, since it is too exclusive, and English has no gender-neuter word for the mutual concern of siblings.) She has since modified this claim, allowing that there are two perspectives on moral and social issues that we all tend to alternate between, and which are not always easy to combine, one of them what she called the justice perspective, the other the care perspective. It is increasingly obvious that there are many male philosophical spokespersons for the care perspective (Laurence Thomas, Lawrence Blum, Michael Stocker) so that it cannot be the prerogative of women. Nevertheless Gilligan still wants to claim that women are most unlikely to take *only* the justice perspective, as some men are claimed to, at least until some mid-life crisis jolts them into "bifocal" moral vision (see D.V., ch. 6).

Gilligan in her book did not offer any explanatory theory of why there should be any difference between female and male moral outlook, but she did tend to link the naturalness to women of the care perspective with their role as primary caretakers of young children, that is with their parental and specifically maternal role.... Later, both in "The Conquistador and the Dark Continent: Reflections on the Nature of Love" (*Daedalus* [Summer 1984]), and "The Origins of Morality in Early Childhood" (Chicago: University of Chicago Press, 1987), she develops this explanation. She postulates two evils that any infant may become aware of, the evil of detachment or isolation from others whose love one needs, and the evil of relative powerlessness and weakness. Two dimensions of moral development are thereby set—one aimed at achieving satisfying community with others, the other aiming at autonomy or equality of power. The relative predominance of one over the other development will depend both upon the relative salience of the two evils in early childhood, and on early and later reinforcement or discouragement in attempts made to guard against these two evils. This provides the germs of a theory about *why,* given current customs of child-rearing, it should be mainly women who are not content with only the moral outlook that she calls the justice perspective, necessary though that was and is seen by them to have been to their hard won liberation from sexist oppression. They, like the blacks, used the language of rights and justice to change their own social position, but nevertheless see limitations in that language, according to Gilligan's findings as a moral psychologist. She reports the discontent with the individualist more or less Kantian moral framework that dominates Western moral theory and which influenced moral psychologists such as Lawrence Kohlberg,[11] to whose conception of moral maturity she seeks an alternative. Since the target of Gilligan's criticism is the dominant Kantian tradition, and since that has been the target also of moral philosophers as diverse in their own views as Bernard Williams,[12] Alasdair MacIntyre, Philippa Foot,[13] Susan Wolf, Claudia Card, her book is of interest as much for its attempt to articulate an alternative to the Kantian justice perspective as for its implicit raising of the question of male bias in Western moral theory, especially liberal democratic theory. For whether the supposed blind spots of that outlook are due to male bias, or to non-parental bias, or to early traumas of powerlessness or to early resignation to "detachment" from others, we need first to be persuaded that they *are* blind spots before we will have any interest in their cause and cure. Is justice blind to important social values, or at least only one-eyed? What is it that comes into view from the "care perspective" that is not seen from the "justice perspective"?

Gilligan's position here is most easily described by contrasting it with that of Kohlberg, against which she developed it. Kohlberg, influenced by Piaget and the Kantian philosophical tradition as developed by John Rawls, developed a theory about typical moral development which saw it to progress from a pre-conventional level, where what is seen to matter is pleasing or not offending parental authority-figures, through a conventional level in which the child tries to fit in with a group, such as a school community, and conform to its standards and rules, to a post-conventional critical level, in which such conventional rules are subjected to tests, and where those tests are of a Utilitarian, or, eventually, a Kantian sort—namely ones that require respect for each person's individual rational will, or autonomy, and conformity to any implicit social contract such wills are deemed to have made, or to any hypothetical ones they would make if thinking clearly. What was found when Kohlberg's questionnaires (mostly by verbal response to verbally sketched moral dilemmas) were applied to female as well as male subjects, Gilligan reports, is that the girls and women not only scored generally lower than the boys and men, but tended to *revert* to the lower stage of the conventional level even after briefly (usually in adolescence) attaining the post conventional level. Piaget's finding that girls were deficient in "the legal sense" was confirmed.

These results led Gilligan to wonder if there might not be a quite different pattern of development to be discerned, at least in female subjects. She therefore conducted interviews designed to elicit not just how far advanced the subjects were towards an appreciation of the nature and importance of Kantian autonomy, but also to find out what the subjects themselves saw as progress or lack of it, what conceptions of moral maturity they came to possess by the time they were adults. She found that although the Kohlberg version of moral maturity as respect for fellow persons, and for their rights as equals (rights including that of free association), did seem shared by many young men, the women tended to speak in a different voice about morality itself and about moral maturity. To quote Gilligan, "Since the reality of interconnexion is experienced by women as given rather than freely contracted, they arrive at an understanding of life that reflects the limits of autonomy and control. As a result, women's development delineates the path not only to a less violent life but also to a maturity realized by interdependence and taking care" (D.V., 172). She writes that there is evidence that "women perceive and construe social reality differently from men, and that these differences center around experiences of attachment and separation... because women's sense of integrity appears to be intertwined with an ethics of care, so that to see themselves as women is to see themselves in a relationship of connexion, the major changes in women's lives would seem to involve changes in the understanding and activities of care" (D.V., 171). She contrasts this progressive understanding of care, from merely pleasing others to helping and nurturing, with the sort of progression that is involved in Kohlberg's stages, a progression in the understanding, not of mutual care, but of mutual *respect,* where this has its Kantian overtones of distance, even of some fear for the respected, and where personal autonomy and *in*dependence, rather than more satisfactory interdependence, are the paramount values.

This contrast, one cannot but feel, is one which Gilligan might have used the Marxist language of alienation to make. For the main complaint about the Kantian version of a society with its first virtue justice, construed as respect for equal rights to formal goods such as having contracts kept, due process, equal opportunity including opportunity to participate in political activities leading to policy and law-making, to basic liberties of speech, free association and assembly, religious worship, is that none of these goods do much to ensure that the people who have and mutually respect such rights will have any other relationships to one another than the minimal relationship needed to keep such a "civil society" going. They may well be lonely, driven to suicide, apathetic about their work and about participation in political processes, find their lives meaningless and have no wish to leave offspring to face the same meaningless existence. Their rights, and respect for rights, are quite compatible with very great misery, and misery whose causes are not just individual misfortunes and psychic sickness, but social and moral impoverishment....

Let me try to summarize the main differences, as I see them, between on the one hand

Gilligan's version of moral maturity and the sort of social structures that would encourage, express and protect it, and on the other the orthodoxy she sees herself to be challenging. I shall from now on be giving my own interpretation of the significance of her challenges, not merely reporting them.[14] The most obvious point is the challenge to the individualism of the Western tradition, to the fairly entrenched belief in the possibility and desirability of each person pursuing his own good in his own way, constrained only by a minimal formal common good, namely a working legal apparatus that enforces contracts and protects individuals from undue interference by others. Gilligan reminds us that noninterference can, especially for the relatively powerless, such as the very young, amount to neglect, and even between equals can be isolating and alienating. On her less individualist version of individuality, it becomes defined by responses to dependency and to patterns of interconnexion, both chosen and unchosen. It is not something a person *has,* and which she then chooses relationships to suit, but something that develops out of a series of dependencies and interdependencies, and responses to them. This conception of individuality is not flatly at odds with, say, Rawls' Kantian one, but there is at least a difference of tone of voice between speaking as Rawls does of each of us having our own rational life plan, which a just society's moral traffic rules will allow us to follow, and which may or may not include close association with other persons, and speaking as Gilligan does of a satisfactory life as involving "progress of affiliative relationship" (D.V., 170) where "the concept of identity expands to include the experience of interconnexion" (D.V., 173). Rawls can allow that progress to Gilligan-style moral maturity may be *a* rational life plan, but not a moral constraint on every life-pattern. The trouble is that it will not do just to say "let this version of morality be an optional extra. Let us agree on the essential minimum, that is on justice and rights, and let whoever wants to go further and cultivate this more demanding ideal of responsibility and care." For, first, it cannot be satisfactorily cultivated without closer cooperation from others than respect for rights and justice will ensure, and, second, the encouragement of some to cultivate it while others do not could easily lead to exploitation of those who do. It obviously *has* suited some in most societies well enough that others take on the responsibilities of care (for the sick, the helpless, the young) leaving them free to pursue their own less altruistic goods. Volunteer forces of those who accept an ethic of care, operating within a society where the power is exercised and the institutions designed, redesigned, or maintained by those who accept a less communal ethic of minimally constrained self-advancement, will not be the solution. The liberal individualists may be able to "tolerate" the more communally minded, if they keep the liberals' rules, but it is not so clear that the more communally minded can be content with just those rules, not be content to be tolerated and possibly exploited.

For the moral tradition which developed the concept of rights, autonomy and justice is the same tradition that provided "justifications" of the oppression of those whom the primary right-holders depended on to do the sort of work they themselves preferred not to do. The domestic work was left to women and slaves, and the liberal morality for right-holders was surreptitiously supplemented by a different set of demands made on domestic workers. As long as women could be got to assume responsibility for the care of home and children, and to train their children to continue the sexist system, the liberal morality could continue to be the official morality, by turning its eyes away from the contribution made by those it excluded. The long unnoticed moral proletariat were the domestic workers, mostly female. Rights have usually been for the privileged. Talking about laws, and the rights those laws recognize and protect, does not in itself ensure that the group of legislators and rights-holders will not be restricted to some elite. Bills of rights have usually been proclamations of the rights of some in-group, barons, landowners, males, whites, non-foreigners. The "justice perspective," and the legal sense that goes with it, are shadowed by their patriarchal past. What did Kant, the great prophet of autonomy, say in his moral theory about women? He said they were incapable of legislation, not fit to vote, that they needed the guidance of more "rational" males.[15] Autonomy was not for them, only for first class, really rational, persons. It is ironic that Gilligan's original findings in a way confirm Kant's views—it seems that autonomy really may not be for women. Many of them reject that ideal (D.V., 48), and have been found not as good at making rules as are men. But where Kant concludes—"so much the worse for women," we can conclude—"so much the worse for the male fixation on the special skill of drafting legislation, for the bureaucratic mentality of rule worship, and for the male exaggeration of the importance of independence over mutual interdependence."

It is however also true that the moral theories that made the concept of a person's rights central were not just the instruments for excluding some persons, but also the instruments used by those who demanded that more and more persons be included in the favored group. Abolitionists, reformers, women, used the language of rights to assert their claims to inclusion in the group of full members of a community. The tradition of liberal moral theory has in fact developed so as to include the women it had for so long excluded, to include the poor as well as rich, blacks and whites, and so on. Women like Mary Wollstonecraft used the male moral theories to good purpose. So we should not be wholly ungrateful for those male moral theories, for all their objectionable earlier content. They were undoubtedly patriarchal, but they also contained the seeds of the challenge, or antidote, to this patriarchal poison.

But when we transcend the values of the Kantians, we should not forget the facts of history—that those values were the values of the oppressors of women. The Christian church, whose version of the moral law Aquinas codified, in his very legalistic moral theory, still insists on the maleness of the God it worships, and jealously reserves for males all the most powerful positions in its hierarchy. Its patriarchical prejudice is open and avowed. In the secular moral theories of men, the sexist patriarchal prejudice is today often less open, not as blatant as it is in Aquinas, in the later natural law tradition, and in Kant..., but is often still there. No moral theorist today would say that women are unfit to vote, to make laws, or to rule a nation without powerful male advisors (as most queens had), but the old doctrines die hard.... Traces of the old patriarchal poison still remain in even the best contemporary moral theorizing. Few may actually say that women's place is in the home, but there is much muttering, when unemployment figures rise, about how the relatively recent flood of women into the work force complicates the problem, as if it would be a good thing if women just went back home whenever unemployment rises, to leave the available jobs for the men. We still do not really have a wide acceptance of the equal right of women to employment outside the home. Nor do we have wide acceptance of the equal duty of men to perform those domestic tasks which in no way depend on special female anatomy, namely cooking, cleaning, and the care of weaned children. All sorts of stories (maybe true stories), about children's need for one "primary" parent, who must be the mother if the mother breast feeds the child, shore up the unequal division of domestic responsibility between mothers and fathers, wives and husbands. If we are really to transvalue the values of our patriarchal past, we need to rethink all of those assumptions, really test those psychological theories. And how will men ever develop an understanding of the "ethics of care" if they continue to be shielded or kept from that experience of caring for a dependent child, which complements the experience we all have had of being cared for as dependent children? These experiences form the natural background for the development of moral maturity as Gilligan's women saw it.

Exploitation aside, why would women, once liberated, not be content to have their version of morality merely tolerated? Why should they not see themselves as voluntarily, for their own reasons, taking on *more* than the liberal rules demand, while having no quarrel with the content of those rules themselves, nor with their remaining the only ones that are expected to be generally obeyed? To see why, we need to move on to three more differences between the Kantian liberals (usually contractarians) and their critics. These concern the relative weight put on relationships between equals, and the relative weight put on freedom of choice, and on the authority of intellect over emotions. It is a typical feature of the dominant moral theories and traditions... that relationships between equals or those who are deemed equal in some important sense, have been the relations that morality is concerned primarily to regulate. Relationships between those who are clearly unequal in power, such as parents and children, earlier and later generations in relation to one another, states and citizens, doctors and patients, the well and the ill, large states and small states, have had to be shunted to the bottom of the agenda, and then dealt with by some sort of "promotion" of the weaker so that an appearance of virtual equality is achieved. Citizens collectively become equal to states, children are treated as adults-to-be, the ill and dying are treated as continuers of their earlier more potent selves, so that their "rights" could be seen as the rights of equals. This pretense of an equality that is in fact absent may often lead to desirable protection of the weaker, or more dependent. But it somewhat masks the question of what our moral relationships are to those who are our superiors or our inferiors in power. A more realistic acceptance of the fact that we begin as helpless children, that at almost every point of our lives we deal with both the more and the less helpless, that equality of power and interdependency, between two persons or groups, is rare and hard to recognize when it does occur, might lead us to a more direct approach to questions concerning the design of institutions structuring these relationships between unequals (families, schools, hospitals, armies) and of the morality of our dealings with the more and the less powerful....

The recognition of the importance for all parties of relations between those who are and cannot but be unequal, both of these relations in themselves and for their effect on personality formation and so on other relationships, goes along with a recognition of the plain fact that not all morally important relationships can or should be freely chosen. So far I have discussed three reasons women have not to be content to pursue their own values within the framework of the liberal morality. The first was its dubious record. The second was its inattention to relations of inequality or its pretence of equality. The third reason is its exaggeration of the scope of choice, or its inattention to unchosen relations. Showing up the partial myth of equality among actual members of a community, and of the undesirability of trying to pretend that we are treating all of them as equals, tends to go along with an exposure of the companion myth that moral obligations arise from freely *chosen* associations between such equals. Vulnerable future generations do not choose their dependence on earlier generations. The unequal infant does not choose its place in a family or nation, nor is it treated as free to do as it likes until some association is freely entered into. Nor do its parents always choose their parental role, or freely assume their parental responsibilities any more than we choose our power to affect the conditions in which later generations will live. Gilligan's attention to the version of morality and moral maturity found in women, many of whom had faced a choice of whether or not to have an abortion, and who had at some point become mothers, is attention to the perceived inadequacy of the language of rights to help in such choices or to guide them in their parental role. It would not be much of an exaggeration to call the Gilligan "different voice" the voice of the potential parents. The emphasis on care goes with a recognition of the often unchosen nature of the responsibilities of those who give care, both of children who care for their aged or infirm parents, and of parents who care for the children they in fact have. Contract soon ceases to seem the paradigm source of moral obligation once we attend to parental responsibility, and justice as a virtue of social institutions will come to seem at best only first equal with the virtue, whatever its name, that ensures that each new generation is made appropriately welcome and prepared for their adult lives.

... The fourth feature of the Gilligan challenge to liberal orthodoxy is a challenge to its typical *rationalism,* or intellectualism, to its assumption that we need not worry what passions persons have, as long as their rational wills can control them. This Kantian picture of a controlling reason dictating to possibly unruly passions also tends to seem less useful when we are led to consider what sort of person we need to fill the role of parent, or indeed want in any close relationship. It might be important for father figures to have rational control over their violent urges to beat to death the children whose screams enrage them, but more than control of such nasty passions seems needed in the mother or primary parent, or parent-substitute, by most psychological theories. They need to love their children, not just to control their irritation. So the emphasis in Kantian theories on rational control of emotions, rather than on cultivating desirable forms of emotion, is challenged by Gilligan, along with the challenge to the assumption of the centrality of autonomy, or relations between equals, and of freely chosen relations....

It is clear, I think, that the best moral theory has to be a cooperative product of women and men, has to harmonize justice and care. The morality it theorizes about is after all for all persons, for men and for women, and will need their combined insights. As Gilligan said (D.V., 174), what we need now is a "marriage" of the old male and the newly articulated female insights. If she is right about the special moral aptitudes of women, it will most likely be the women who propose the marriage, since they are the ones with more natural empathy, with the better diplomatic skills, the ones more likely to shoulder responsibility and take moral initiative, and the ones who find it easiest to empathize and care about how the other party feels. Then, once there is this union of male and female moral wisdom, we maybe can teach each other the moral skills each gender currently lacks, so that the gender difference in moral outlook that Gilligan found will slowly become less marked.

NOTES

1. John Rawls, *A Theory of Justice* (Cambridge: Harvard University Press, 1971).
2. Alasdair MacIntyre, *After Virtue* (Notre Dame: Notre Dame University Press).
3. Michael Stocker, "The Schizophrenia of Modern Ethical Theories," *Journal of Philosophy* 73, 14, pp. 453–66, and "Agent and Other: Against Ethical Universalism," *Australasian Journal of Philosophy* 54, pp. 206–20.
4. Lawrence Blum, *Friendship, Altruism and Morality* (London: Routledge & Kegan Paul 1980).
5. Michael Slote, *Goods and Virtues* (Oxford: Oxford University Press 1983).
6. Laurence Thomas, "Love and Morality" in *Epistemology and Sociobiology*, James Fetzer, ed. (1985) and "Justice, Happiness and Self Knowledge," *Canadian Journal of Philosophy* (March, 1986). Also "Beliefs and the Motivation to be Just," *American Philosophical Quarterly* 22(4), pp. 347–52.
7. Claudia Card, "Mercy," *Philosophical Review* 81, 1, and "Gender and Moral Luck," [in *Identity Characters, and Morality: Essays in Moral Psychology*, Owen Flanagan, ed. (Cambridge: MIT Press, 1990.)].
8. Alison Jaggar, *Feminist Politics and Human Nature* (London: Rowman and Allenheld 1983).
9. Susan Wolf, "Moral Saints," *Journal of Philosophy* 79 (August, 1982), pp. 419–39.
10. For a helpful survey article see Owen Flanagan and Kathryn Jackson, "Justice, Care & Gender: The Kohlberg-Gilligan Debate Revisited," *Ethics.*
11. Lawrence Kohlberg, *Essays in Moral Development*, vols. I & II (New York: Harper and Row 1981, 1984).
12. Bernard Williams, *Ethics and the Limits of Philosophy* (Cambridge: Cambridge University Press 1985).
13. Philippa Foot, *Virtues and Vices* (Berkeley: University of California Press 1978).
14. I have previously written about the significance of her findings for moral philosophy in "What Do Women Want in a Moral Theory?" *Nous* 19 (March 1985), "Trust and Antitrust," *Ethics* 96 (1986), and in "Hume the Women's Moral Theorist?" in *Women and Moral Theory*, Kittay and Meyers, ed., [Totowa, N.J.: Rowman & Littlefield, 1987].
15. Immanuel Kant, *Metaphysics of Morals*, sec. 46.

QUESTIONS FOR ANALYSIS

1. What does Baier mean by the ethics of care? How does it differ from the ethics of justice?
2. How, according to Baier and Gilligan, do men and women differ in moral development? How do they account for these differences? Why do they think these differences are relevant to moral theory?
3. According to Baier, the ethics of justice is compatible with "great misery" and "social and moral impoverishment." Why? How can the ethics of care correct these problems?
4. Why does Baier find fault with the traditional moral emphasis on equality and freely chosen relationships?
5. Some recent studies have cast doubt on the claim that there are distinctively masculine and feminine perspectives on morality. If correct, do these studies affect Baier's criticisms of the ethics of justice?
6. Does the ethics of justice ignore the experience of women? Why or why not?

CHAPTER TWO

Good Reasoning

- **Arguments**
- **Evaluating Moral Arguments**
- **Summary and Conclusions**

NOT ALL OPINIONS are equal, the first chapter concluded, and we looked at a few examples that seemed to show that some opinions are indeed better than others. However, we did not explain *why* some opinions are better than others.

Of course, given the nature of the examples, explanation might have seemed unnecessary. Let's go back to two of them. If any opinion about the best career for Mary is to be a good one, it must be based on some obvious factors—what she likes to do, what she's good at, availability of jobs, where she would like to live, and so on. Any opinion that ignores these factors is not one that will have much value to her. Similarly, any worthwhile opinion at the beginning of the baseball season regarding the outcome of the World Series must be based on equally obvious factors, like pitching and hitting.

The same can be said about any opinion. If it is to be a good one, it must be well grounded. It must be supported by good reasons. And the better the support, the better the opinion, whether it's a scientific opinion or a moral one, an opinion about what's wrong with your car, or an opinion about what's wrong with something you did. To be sure, an opinion that is not well grounded may turn out to be correct. Even the most ignorant of ignoramuses are right sometimes. But when they are, it is a matter of pure luck. Their opinions are not to be trusted in the future because they are not arrived at in a reliable way.

What makes an opinion well grounded? Well, one obvious consideration is knowledge. The more relevant details we know about a particular matter, the better grounded our opinions will be. Be sure to notice the word *relevant.* It is most important, particularly when we deal with moral problems. In fact, one of the biggest difficulties we will encounter in our dealings with the issues of Part 2 is trying to decide what the relevant details are.

Another thing is logic. A well-supported opinion is logically arrived at. It comes at the end of a reliable pattern of reasoning. Or as philosophers often put it, it is the conclusion of a strong *argument.*

ARGUMENTS

To philosophers, scientists, attorneys, and others who engage in intellectual debate, an **argument** is a collection of statements. One of the statements is the conclusion. The other statements are called *premises, reasons, evidence, supporting statements,* or *grounds*. Whatever we call them, the important point is this: Their purpose is to show that the conclusion is true or that it is reasonable to accept the conclusion as true.

Much of Part 2 will be devoted to arguments for and against various positions. And much of your task in reading Part 2 will be to do your best to evaluate these arguments. That is, you will have to decide whether the arguments for or against particular positions are the better ones. And to do that, you will have to ask yourself a variety of questions: Are the supporting statements true? If so, do they really lend support to the conclusions, or are they irrelevant to the conclusions? Are the patterns of reasoning followed by these arguments reliable ones? Has anything of importance been left out of these arguments?

In the rest of this chapter, we give you some help in answering these questions. But first, we must distinguish two kinds of argument.

Deductive Arguments

Consider the following two sentences:

1. If Clint Eastwood is a bulldog, then he has four legs.
2. Clint Eastwood is a bulldog.

Chances are, you know what comes next:

3. Therefore, Clint Eastwood has four legs.

How did you know that? Not because of anything you know about Clint Eastwood. People may have different opinions about his movies, but all of us agree that he has only two legs. Nor does your knowledge of bulldogs make a difference. Suppose the first sentence had been "If Clint Eastwood is a bulldog, then he has eight legs." Then you would have drawn a different conclusion: "Therefore, Clint Eastwood has eight legs."

What makes the difference is your knowledge of a rule of **deductive logic,** as follows:

1. If A, then B.
2. A.
3. Therefore, B.

That rule is called a **truth-preserving rule.** To say that the rule is truth preserving is to say that whenever you follow it, if the first two statements (called the **premises**) are true, the conclusion will also be true. Truth-preserving rules are also called *valid rules,* and any argument that follows only valid rules is called a **valid deductive argument.**

The notion of a valid deductive argument will prove to be very useful. Even more important is the notion of a **sound deductive argument.** To be sound, an argument must pass two tests: first, it must be valid, and second, all its premises must be true. A valid argument with false premises may or may not have a true conclusion, but the conclusion of a sound argument must be true. In other words, if we can assure ourselves that all the premises of an argument are true, and if we can also assure ourselves that the argument follows only valid deductive rules, then we can assure ourselves that the conclusion must be true.

There are many valid rules of deductive reasoning, far too many to go into here. Fortunately, we do not need to know all of them to decide whether an argument is valid. Instead, we can use a simple method for detecting invalidity. That method is known as the method of **counterexample.** Consider the following argument, which many people mistakenly think is valid:

1. If John took a shower, then he got wet.
2. John didn't take a shower.
3. Therefore, John didn't get wet.

That argument follows this rule:

1. If A, then B.
2. A is not true.
3. Therefore, B is not true.

And we can show that *that* rule is not truth preserving by giving a counterexample to the rule. To do that, we find an argument that has true premises, follows the same rule, but has a false conclusion. If we can do that, the rule is certainly not truth preserving. For instance,

1. If Rin Tin Tin had been a collie, then he'd have been a dog.
2. Rin Tin Tin was not a collie.
3. Therefore, Rin Tin Tin was not a dog.

Here's another example of an invalid argument:

1. Some baseball players are left-handed.
2. Some baseball players are pitchers.
3. Therefore, some pitchers are left-handed.

If you don't believe that the argument is invalid, consider this counterexample:

1. Some animals are human.
2. Some animals are fish.
3. Therefore, some fish are human.

And here, finally, is another:

1. All ravens are black.
2. A dove is not a raven.
3. Therefore, a dove is not black.

And here is a counterexample:

1. All ravens are black.
2. A panther is not a raven.
3. Therefore, a panther is not black.

In each of the preceding cases, we provided a counterexample by constructing an entirely new argument. Sometimes you may find it easier just to ask a few questions about the original argument. Take the argument that concluded that John didn't get wet (because he didn't take a shower). What if he'd taken a bath instead? Or take the argument that concluded that some pitchers are left-handed (because some baseball players are pitchers and some are left-handed). What if all the left-handed players are outfielders? Or take the last one. What if there are black doves?

Fortunately, you will not come upon many invalid arguments in the readings in Part 2. Unfortunately, you *will* come across many invalid arguments in other discussions of the same issues—perhaps even in class discussions—so recognizing one when you see it is an important skill.

What you are more likely to come across in the readings in Part 2 are valid but *unsound* arguments. So you must be careful to ask whether the premises are true when you evaluate the arguments you encounter.

Inductive Arguments

Most ordinary reasoning is not deductive. The supporting statements, if true, do not guarantee the truth of the conclusion. Rather, they establish that it is more reasonable than not to accept the conclusion. That is, they establish that the conclusion is likely to be true. Arguments of that kind are called **inductive arguments.** The supporting statements of inductive arguments are called *reasons, evidence,* or *grounds* instead of premises, and a good inductive argument is called a **warranted argument** instead of a sound one.

When we reason from cause to effect or from effect to cause, we generally reason inductively. If, for example, we hear a loud bang outside, we would most likely conclude that a car had just backfired. Although other explanations are possible—somebody might have shot her neighbor, say—in most neighborhoods, a backfiring car is the most probable one. Since our evidence does admit of other possibilities, though, we cannot say that we reasoned deductively. Similarly, when we put a pot of water on the stove and come back later expecting the water to be boiling, we are also reasoning inductively. Various factors may have kept the water from boiling—the gas might have been turned off, for instance—but more likely than not, the water is boiling.

Most generalizations are also examples of inductive reasoning. We examine a sample taken from a larger population, notice some features shared by a certain percentage of our sample, and then conclude that the same—or nearly the same—pattern occurs in the population at large. Thus, from a sample of green and only green emeralds, we conclude that all emeralds are green, and from a sample of Nielsen families, we conclude that more viewers watch NFL football games than NBA basketball games. These generalizations are reliable, but they are not arrived at by deductive reasoning. Because there is always some probability—however small—that the larger population does not match the sample, such reasoning is inductive.

Although inductive reasoning does not have rules in the same way that deductive reasoning does, we use a variety of criteria to evaluate inductive arguments. For our purposes, the most important are those that concern *causal* generalizations because those are the kinds of arguments that will be most prominent in Part 2.

Consider this argument:

1. John takes two aspirin tablets every day.
2. John never has a cold.
3. Therefore, aspirin prevents colds.

There is much, of course, that is wrong with that argument. Two flaws are most obvious. First, a sample of one is hardly large enough to support a generalization about all human beings. Second, no care has been taken to rule out other explanations of John's good fortune. Thus, the following are important criteria for evaluating causal generalizations. First, the sample must be large enough to support the generalization. Second, it must also be representative of the larger population that's being generalized about.

Third, to help rule out other explanations, there must be a *control group*—another sample as much like the original sample (called the *experimental group*) as possible except that its members are not exposed to the factor being tested. If we are testing to see whether aspirin prevents colds, for example, we will want to study two groups, one that takes aspirin daily and one that does not. Only after the control group and the experimental group have been compared are we entitled to make our causal generalization.

But even then, we must be careful. Statistical links are not the same as causal links. Two factors may be associated without one being the cause of the other. Sneezing and coughing often go together, but one does not cause the other. Rather, both have a common cause—often a flu virus. So even after a statistical link has been established, further experiments may be necessary to establish a causal link.

To be sure, few people are ever in a position to carry out such experiments. For most of us, inductive reasoning is far less formal. We do not have the statistical techniques to evaluate the reliability of our samples, nor do we have the time and money to design and carry out tests on experimental and control groups. That's why we must rely on people who do—scientists—before we can say that a causal generalization has been established. This does not mean, however, that we can't reach reasonable conclusions before science has spoken. We can. Indeed, often we must. But when doing so, we must remember two points.

First, we must keep in mind that the more closely our reasoning resembles the scientist's, the better it is. The more numerous and representative the cases we have to generalize from, the better our evidence and the more reasonable our conclusion. And the more justified we are in ruling out other causes, the more reasonable our conclusion.

Second, no matter how reasonable our conclusion may be, we are not entitled to claim that we've established it. Inductive reasoning, unlike deductive reasoning, cannot be neatly divided into the sound and the unsound. Although it *can* be divided into the warranted and the unwarranted, warrant admits of degrees. One sound deductive argument is as conclusive as another. One warranted inductive argument is not as conclusive as another. Our confidence in our conclusions, then, should be no greater than the degree of our warrant. And as long as our inductive reasoning is informal, our degree of warrant requires a corresponding degree of humility.

Moral Arguments

A familiar position on abortion is that abortion is wrong except to save the life of the mother, and a common justification for that position is that taking an innocent life is wrong except to save a life. Proponents of broad abortion rights, on the other hand, often support their views by claiming that women have the right to control their own bodies as long as they don't harm anyone else. Like all the moral arguments we will come across in Part 2, each proceeds from a general moral principle (the first about taking an innocent life, the second about a woman's rights over her body) to a moral conclusion about a particular issue (the morality of abortion). The best way to examine such arguments is to treat them as abbreviated deductive arguments. We do that by supplying additional premises that make the arguments valid.

Consider the first argument. We are given only one premise:

1. Taking an innocent life is wrong except to save a life.

One premise that must be added is the following:

2. Abortion is the taking of an innocent life.

Together, those premises lead to:

3. Therefore, abortion is wrong except to save a life.

Though that is an important conclusion of the argument, it is only an *intermediate* conclusion. To get to the *final* conclusion, we must add another premise:

4. The only life that can be saved by an abortion is the mother's.

From that premise and the intermediate conclusion, we get the final conclusion:

5. Therefore, abortion is wrong except to save the life of the mother.

Because the preceding argument reaches an intermediate conclusion, it is a two-step argument. Multiple-step arguments are not unusual in moral debates. In fact, the opposing argument, once the missing premises are added, turns out to be a three-step argument because it goes through two intermediate conclusions, one at line three and the other at line five:

1. Women have the right to control their own bodies as long as they don't harm another person.
2. A woman's right to control her body includes the right to have any medical procedure she and her doctor choose.
3. Therefore, a woman has a right to any medical procedure she and her doctor choose as long as it doesn't harm another person.
4. An abortion is a medical procedure.
5. Therefore, a woman has a right to an abortion as long as it doesn't harm another person.
6. An abortion hurts nothing but the fetus, which is not a person.
7. Therefore, women have the right to an abortion.

Both of these arguments are valid, but since they reach opposite conclusions, they cannot both be sound. At least one of them must have at least one false premise. And that is why it is useful for us to treat moral arguments as deductive. If we do so, they become much easier to evaluate. We can lay out opposing arguments in a clear fashion, make sure that we understand the reasoning behind each one, isolate all of the premises, and then examine the premises of each to see whether they are true. The ones with true premises, or with premises more likely to be true, are the ones we should accept.

EVALUATING MORAL ARGUMENTS

Once again, one of your main tasks in dealing with the issues of Part 2 will be to evaluate arguments in favor of opposing positions. As we just saw, that task breaks down into two subtasks. The first is to try to reconstruct each argument as a valid deductive argument. The second is to examine the premises to see if they are true. Let's begin our discussion of these two tasks by looking at an example.

A Sample Evaluation

A common argument in favor of legalized abortion is often put this way: Catholics and fundamentalist Christians have no right to turn their religious beliefs into law. That is a very short argument. If we are to try to turn it into a valid argument, we must ask ourselves what premises are *assumed* by the argument but not explicitly stated by it. That is, we must ask what premises we should *add* to make the argument valid.

One way we can make it valid is by adding only one premise. Then the argument would go like this:

1. Catholics and fundamentalist Christians have no right to turn their religious beliefs into law.
2. That abortions should be banned is a religious belief of Catholics and fundamentalist Christians.
3. Therefore, Catholics and fundamentalist Christians have no right to make abortions illegal.

That is a valid argument, to be sure, but it's not very convincing as it stands. After all, why should we pick on Catholics and fundamentalist Christians? Do Presbyterians have the right to turn their religious beliefs into law? Quakers? Jews? Also, the conclusion is a very weak one. It claims that two groups have no right to make abortion illegal but not that nobody has the right to make abortion illegal.

So let's try another approach.

1. No religious group has the right to turn its religious beliefs into law.
2. Opponents of abortion are trying to turn their religious beliefs into law.
3. Therefore, opponents of abortion have no right to make abortion illegal.

That's a little better. At least it doesn't pick on two religious groups unfairly. Still, the premises are not very plausible. The trouble with the first is that *many* religious beliefs have been turned into law, often rightfully. Religious beliefs against murder, armed robbery, and rape come most readily to mind. The trouble with the second is that many opponents of abortion oppose it for nonreligious reasons. If the argument is to have any force, then, further changes must be made.

For example,

1. If there are no good nonreligious reasons for turning some group's religious beliefs into law, then nobody has the right to turn those beliefs into law.
2. That abortion should be banned is a religious belief of some groups.
3. Therefore, if there are no good nonreligious reasons for making abortion illegal, nobody has the right to make it illegal.
4. There are no good nonreligious reasons for making abortion illegal.
5. Therefore, nobody has the right to make abortion illegal.

Is that much better? Not really. For one thing, item four is not obviously true. Indeed, whether it *is* true is precisely what the debate over abortion is all about. For another thing, what the argument now boils down to is this:

1. If there are no good reasons to make abortion illegal, it should be legal.
2. There are no good reasons to make abortion illegal.
3. Therefore, abortion should be legal.

And that is not much of an argument at all. Granted, it is certainly valid, but until we have an argument in favor of premise two, opponents of abortion have no reason to take it seriously.

Reconstructing Arguments

What we did in the previous section is not nearly as difficult as it might first appear. All it takes is a little common sense plus the knowledge of a few valid rules of deductive logic. And those few rules are also common sense. One, which we already looked at in our Clint Eastwood example, is:

1. If A, then B.
2. A.
3. Therefore, B.

That is a rule that all of you already knew. No doubt you know the others as well. For example,

1. Either John is home or he's at the library.
2. He's not home.
3. Therefore, what?

The answer, obviously, is that he's at the library. And the rule is:

1. A or B.
2. A is not true.
3. Therefore, B.

Here's another:

1. If Mary is home, she's in the den.
2. She's not in the den.
3. Therefore, what?

The answer here is that she's not home. And the rule is:

1. If A, then B.
2. B is not true.
3. Therefore, A is not true.

There are only three others you need to know (and no doubt already know), and they are equally matters of common sense. Examples are:

1. All dogs are mammals.
2. Lassie is a dog.
3. Therefore, Lassie is a mammal.

And:

1. All dogs are mammals.
2. My parrot is not a mammal.
3. Therefore, my parrot is not a dog.

And:

1. No pigs can fly.
2. Robins can fly.
3. Therefore, robins aren't pigs.

And the rules are:

1. All A is B.
2. C is A.
3. Therefore, C is B.

And:

1. All A is B.
2. C is not B.
3. Therefore, C is not A.

And:

1. No A is B.
2. C is B.
3. Therefore, C is not A.

Armed with these common-sense rules, you will be able to turn any logical moral argument into a valid deductive argument. That is, as long as the argument doesn't depend on any invalid rules, you can do what we did in the previous section. For example, we often hear that homosexuality is wrong because it's unnatural. That claim is really an abbreviated argument, as follows:

1. Anything unnatural is morally wrong.
2. Homosexuality is unnatural.
3. Therefore, homosexuality is morally wrong.

Of course, few people actually put it that way. The first premise is generally left unsaid, but common sense tells us that something like the first premise is required if the argument is to be valid. Along the same lines, common sense tells us that something must be added when people claim that capital punishment is wrong because it does not deter crime any better than life imprisonment does. When we add what is needed, we get:

1. If one punishment is more severe than another, it is wrong to impose the more severe one if it is not a better deterrent than the less severe one.
2. Capital punishment is more severe than life imprisonment.
3. Therefore, it is wrong to impose capital punishment if it is not a better deterrent than life imprisonment.
4. Capital punishment is not a better deterrent than life imprisonment.
5. Therefore, it is wrong to impose capital punishment.

How do we know which premises to add? There is no precise formula that anybody can give, but we can provide some general directions. First, we must choose premises that can be used with valid deductive rules. When we look at the claim that homosexuality is wrong because it's unnatural, for instance, we know that the conclusion is "Homosexuality is wrong" and that one premise is "Homosexuality is unnatural." What we need, then, is a premise like "If anything is unnatural, it's wrong," or "All unnatural behavior is wrong."

Second, we must make sure that our added premises are *general* enough to look like real moral principles, not prejudices. That is why we put "anything" and "all unnatural behavior" in the above premises, not "homosexuality" and "all homosexual acts." If we make the premise read "If homosexuality is unnatural, then it's wrong," somebody could justifiably ask us "Why just homosexuality?" That's why we changed "Catholics and fundamentalist Christians" to "religious groups" in an earlier example. In moral arguments, we must appeal to moral principles, and the more general a statement is, the more like a genuine moral principle and the less like an expression of prejudice it is.

Third, we must add *enough* premises to make the argument valid. That requirement is not just a matter of logic. If we are to evaluate an argument adequately, we must be able to examine all of its premises. And if we don't have enough premises to make the argument valid, we are lacking at least one assumed premise.

Fourth, we must use a little **charity,** even if we don't agree with the argument's conclusion. We must allow our opponents the best arguments we can if we are to give them a fair hearing. This means that we must do our best to give them *plausible* premises. A few pages back, for example, we looked at the claim that a woman has the right to an abortion because she has the right to control her own body. One of the premises we added was "A woman's right to control her own body includes the right to have any medical procedure she and her doctor choose." Now that may or may not be true, but it is certainly plausible. On the other hand, the following premise is most certainly not: "A woman's right to control her body includes the right to murder her children." Granted, many abortion foes believe that pro-choice advocates are claiming that, but it is most unfair to make it a premise in their arguments.

Fifth, we must do our best to make sure that the premises we add are *faithful* to the beliefs of the person putting forth the argument. Although we cannot always be sure on this point, there are ways to increase our confidence. If we add a premise that is inconsistent with sentences that appear elsewhere in the reading, we have probably failed. Of course, sometimes people are inconsistent, but if it is possible to read them in a way that makes them consistent, we should do so. (That, of course, is required of us by the principle of charity.)

Also, arguers often give us hints of their broader commitments. In his reading arguing against abortion, for example, John T. Noonan makes it clear that he agrees with much of traditional Catholic theology, although he attempts to rest his arguments on purely secular grounds. We should not supply anti-Catholic premises to Noonan.

Sixth, we must be careful not to beg any questions. To *beg a question* is to assume what you are trying to prove, and a **question-begging argument** is one that contains the conclusion as one of its premises. Sometimes that cannot be helped. If John says that he believes Mary because she's honest, and he knows she's honest because she told him so, and he believed her because she's honest, there is not much we can do to save his argument. On the other hand, we are not forced to beg any questions when reconstructing the pro-choice argument based on a woman's right to control her own body. In that case, we should not add the following:

2. A woman's right to control her body includes the right to do anything moral.
3. Abortions are moral.
4. Therefore, a woman has the right to an abortion.

Although premise three is not precisely the same as the conclusion, it is certainly close enough to qualify as question begging.

Seventh, we must be careful not to *equivocate*. That is, we must not allow the argument to turn on different meanings of the same word. For example, the word *unnatural* can mean either "perverse" or "out of the ordinary." Many things, like writing poetry or skydiving, are unnatural in the second sense of the word but not the first. Anyone who argues that skydiving is out of the ordinary, and therefore unnatural, and therefore perverse is guilty of equivocating. Of course, sometimes the arguments we are trying to reconstruct *will* turn on equivocations. Some arguments against homosexuality, for example, may turn on an equivocation on *natural* much like the one we just looked at. In those cases, we have no choice but to give up. An argument that turns on an equivocation is not a valid one, and we cannot make it valid without creating an entirely different argument.

Examining Premises

Once we have a valid argument before us, we must next ask whether it is a sound argument. The first premises to look at are the general ones because they are most likely to be questionable. Although many statements with words like *all* and *every* and *any* and *no* are true, many others are not.

Consider the general statements that appear in our pro- and anti-abortion arguments, for example. Is it really true that a woman's right to control her own body includes the right to have *any* medical procedure she and her doctor choose? What about experimental procedures that have not been approved for the general public? Or procedures that have been outlawed because they are ineffective or dangerous?

Similarly, is it really true that taking an innocent life is *always* wrong except to save another life? (The word *always* did not appear in the premise of our argument, but as in many general statements, the general word is assumed. With a sentence like "Dogs are mammals," or even "A dog is a mammal," we should understand it as being about all dogs unless we are told otherwise.) Judith Jarvis Thomson, in her defense of abortion that appears in Part 2, doesn't think so, and she provides examples to back up her point.

Thomson's examples are meant to be *counterexamples* to the generalization in the anti-abortion argument, just as the examples of unapproved medical procedures were offered as counterexamples to the generalization in the pro-abortion argument. That is, they are meant to be examples in which the generalization breaks down.

If the proposed counterexamples are genuine counterexamples, we may still be able to save the premise in a slightly altered form. Suppose we grant that a woman does not have the right to an unapproved medical procedure. All we have to do is add the phrase "medically approved" to that premise and other premises in which it is now needed to make the argument valid. The additions will not harm the argument because most abortions are medically approved.

On the other hand, the counterexamples may be decisive. That is, there may be no way to alter the premise without destroying the argument. Whether Thomson's counterexamples are decisive is not for us to decide now, but we can look at another case in which counterexamples are decisive. Take this argument:

1. Lying is wrong.
2. Telling a friend that her ugly baby is cute is lying.
3. Therefore, telling a friend that her ugly baby is cute is wrong.

Most of us agree that white lies are genuine counterexamples to the first premise. Honesty is commendable, but not when it causes our friends great hurt and the lie is an innocuous one. But once we change the first premise to exempt white lies, the argument falls apart.

One way to challenge a general premise, then, is to find a decisive counterexample. Another way is to question the assumptions it rests on. Many people, for example, take issue with premise six of the pro-abortion argument, which says that a fetus is not a person (or no fetus is a person, or all fetuses are not persons). They cannot point to a counterexample that abortion proponents will accept because the view that fetuses are not persons is based on certain assumptions about what it is to be a person—and those assumptions rule out all fetuses. What abortion opponents must do, then, is challenge the assumptions. That is, they must show that the other side is wrong about what it is to be a person and that a proper understanding would show that all or most or some fetuses are persons.

Very often, the challenged assumptions will be moral assumptions. An argument may conclude that something is right because it is justified by the principle of utility, say. Someone who disagrees with the argument, on the other hand, might feel that respect for persons must take precedence in this instance. Another argument may conclude that justice requires us to do one thing, while someone who disagrees might feel that justice requires us to do something else.

Such disagreements are, of course, very hard to settle. They often boil down to what philosophers call conflicting **moral intuitions.** By moral intuition, we do not mean some mysterious sixth sense for divining moral truths. Rather, we mean only a moral conviction arrived at after careful consideration of the relevant facts—a conviction that strikes us as right but not provable. But even though they are not provable, moral intuitions can be challenged, discussed, and even changed on reasonable grounds.

The idea is to think of a variety of cases—some ordinary, some a bit fanciful—and see if consideration of these cases has any effect on our intuitions. What these cases add is new relevant information. Many of our moral intuitions, after all, are based on a small sample of possible cases. Some of them may be generalizations we've arrived at a little too quickly. Often, we can benefit by opening them up to some careful scrutiny. So when you come across arguments that rest on moral assumptions that conflict with your intuitions, it is best to examine both the assumptions and your intuitions as carefully as possible.

Other general statements that require careful scrutiny are **causal generalizations.** Although many causal generalizations are extremely well established—friction causes heat, for example—many others are controversial at best. Among the most controversial are those that some readings in Part 2 rely on—about the deterrent effects of capital punishment or the effects of various social programs on the poor. Most of us have our own opinions on these matters, but more often than not, they are based on what we take to be common sense rather than on well-designed studies.

By well-designed studies, of course, we mean studies with large representative samples and adequate controls. Sometimes such studies exist, but they are inconclusive. Sometimes different studies on the same issue will come to conflicting conclusions. Sometimes they just don't exist. How, then, can we evaluate causal generalizations under such conditions?

First, see how they are supported. Often, they are supported by *analogies.* Many opponents of mercy killing and abortion sometimes draw analogies between those practices and what went on in Nazi death camps. When faced with such analogies, we must ask in what ways they hold up and in what ways they do not. Are there relevant differences that suggest that the compared practices will have different effects? Are there better analogies than the ones being drawn?

Causal claims might also be supported by an argument called the *slippery slope* argument. The idea here is that what at first looks like one small step is just the beginning of a series of small steps that will be difficult or impossible to stop after we've taken the first one. J. Gay-Williams, in a reading included in Part 2, argues that administering lethal injections to pain-wracked terminally ill patients who ask for them is the beginning of such a slippery slope—and that at the bottom we will find ourselves ordering the deaths of undesirables as a matter of social policy.

Whether Gay-Williams is right about that is again something that is not for us to decide here. But as a general rule, we should scrutinize such arguments carefully. Not all slopes are as slippery as they first appear. Perhaps there are very good reasons for taking the first step and very good reasons for not taking the second. Perhaps there are principled reasons for digging in our heels somewhere along the way and nothing to stop us from doing so.

Also, causal generalizations might be "supported" by a kind of *hand waving.* That is, the argument might boil down to a nonargument, something like "Everybody knows that . . . " To be sure, there are many things that everybody *does* know, and things that everybody knows are the best premises for an argument we can find. But we must be careful, especially when dealing with causal generalizations, and even more especially when dealing with causal generalizations about human behavior, to ask whether *anybody,* let alone everybody, really knows that they're true.

Moreover, the mere fact that we don't know that they're false is insufficient support for them. The proper response to ignorance is to try to learn more. If we must decide what to do before we can learn more, we must do the same kind of calculating that's required whenever we try to make a rational decision under conditions of uncertainty. That is, we must ask ourselves what we stand to gain and lose by acting on a belief we don't know to be true. (For an example of this kind of reasoning, see Ernest Van Den Haag's defense of capital punishment in Part 2.)

Finally, causal generalizations might be supported by inductive arguments based on things we *do* know. Because these arguments will not support their conclusions as strongly as well-designed studies can, they must be approached very carefully. At best, they can establish their conclusions as reasonable, perhaps even more reasonable than their competitors, given what we now know. But what we now know, we must remember, is incomplete. That is why well-designed studies are so important. They fill in the many gaps in current knowledge, and once those gaps are filled, we may find that what was once the most reasonable conclusion is false.

Two other kinds of general premises deserve consideration here. These are generalizations about the arguer's supporters and opponents. For example, you may come across the claim that social scientists agree that such and such is true. To make the argument valid, you must add a premise like "Whatever social scientists agree on is true," or the weaker "If social scientists agree on something, we should accept it as true." You might also hear someone argue that you should not accept opponents' arguments because the opponents are untrustworthy for one reason or another. Then you must add a premise like "Arguments by untrustworthy people are unsound."

The first two of these premises appeal to the *authority* of social scientists. Are they true? Not as they now stand. On the other hand, this variation probably is: "If social scientists agree on a generalization about human behavior that is based on strong research, we should accept it as true." Of course, not being social scientists ourselves, we cannot adequately evaluate their research, but if social scientists at respectable universities claim that their agreement is based on strong research, we are certainly justified in believing them. If their agreement is just a widely shared hunch, however, then their authority is lessened. And if their agreement is on a matter other than human behavior—if it is on the best brand of toothpaste, say—then their authority evaporates.

The third of the three premises, about untrustworthy opponents, is an example of an ***ad hominem* argument** (from the Latin phrase for "to the man"). Like appeals to authority, they may or may not be acceptable. The premise at hand is not. Granted, untrustworthy people often do present unsound arguments, but as long as they do present arguments, we should evaluate those arguments, not the arguers. (Even paranoids have enemies, as the saying has it.) On the other hand, when someone offers us nothing better than an unsupported claim rather than an argument, all we can go on is the trustworthiness of the person making the offer.

Trying Alternative Premises

In the previous sections, we saw that we sometimes have to change an argument's premise. Often, the reason is that the premise is questionable or downright false. Why change it rather than just reject the argument? The principle of charity gives us one answer. But we are interested in more than just fairness to our opponents. We are also interested in solving moral problems, and that interest should lead us to consider the strongest arguments possible.

For example, let's return to our argument against capital punishment. The first premise read

1. If one punishment is more severe than another, it is wrong to impose the more severe one if it is not a better deterrent than the less severe one.

There seem to be many counterexamples to that statement. Is the threat of a ten-year prison term a greater deterrent than the threat of a nine-year prison term? Is the threat of life imprisonment a greater deterrent than the threat of a thirty-year prison term? Although we can't be absolutely sure about the answers to these questions, the more plausible answer is no. Still, we see nothing wrong in giving some people thirty-year sentences and others life sentences.

More generally, though, we can say this: Deterrence is not the only consideration in determining a just sentence. Another is our concern to protect other people from individuals convicted of serious crimes. Still another is our feeling that the severity of the punishment should reflect the severity of the crime. Presumably, people who argue against capital punishment on the grounds that it does not deter know that. So we might recast the premise this way:

1. If two punishments equally reflect the severity of the crime and offer equal protection from the convicted criminal, it is wrong to impose the more severe one if it is not a better deterrent.

Notice how this procedure helps us focus on the important issues. By exposing points that the argument takes for granted, it allows us to evaluate them as well as the points it does not take for granted. Now we must add new premises—that life imprisonment protects others from convicted criminals as well as capital punishment protects them, and that life imprisonment reflects the severity of capital crimes as adequately as capital punishment does. And we must then evaluate them.

Moreover, we might want to evaluate the new version of the first premise. Why, we might ask, must punishment *always* reflect the severity of the crime? If we really believe that it must, shouldn't we have even more awful punishments than we now have? If a man brutally rapes and tortures a half dozen women before killing them, does that mean we should subject him to something equally horrible? Or should we recognize instead that there are moral limits to the severity of punishment regardless of other factors, and maybe those limits mean we should stop short of capital punishment?

In short, trying new premises helps us do more than just evaluate arguments. It helps us think clearly and thoroughly about the problems at hand.

Another example also helps show this. Sometimes we should try new premises because the ones we first added are not the only reasonable possibilities. That reason applies to one of the premises in the pro-abortion argument we looked at:

2. A woman's right to control her body includes the right to have any medically approved medical procedure she and her doctor choose.

Perhaps people who defend the right to an abortion on the grounds of a woman's right to control her own body mean something else, like:

3. A woman's right to control her body includes the right not to have her body used for purposes she does not want it used for.

In that case, we get a new intermediate conclusion:

4. A woman has the right not to have her body used for purposes she does not want it used for as long as she does not harm another person.

Then we add this premise:

5. A woman carrying an unwanted fetus is having her body used for purposes she does not want it used for.

And then we get this intermediate conclusion:

6. Therefore, a woman has the right not to carry an unwanted fetus as long as she does not harm another person.

Whether this version or the original version of the argument is sound is, once again, not to be decided here. But looking at both can be important. Judith Jarvis Thomson's article, for example, focuses on the new interpretation of a woman's right to control her own body, not the original one, and it might make an important difference. The reason it might is that Thomson believes a woman has the right not to have her body used in a way she doesn't want it to be used even in some cases where an innocent person *is* harmed, even fatally. Thus, she defends a woman's right to have an abortion without the premise that fetuses are not persons.

Questions of Relevance

Whether a premise is really relevant to the moral issue at hand is, of course, an important matter. Much of the advice for evaluating arguments that we've been looking at has been closely connected to the question of relevance.

Most important has been the advice about supplying and evaluating implicit general premises. If the implicit general premise turns out to be false, that is often because an explicit premise is irrelevant. To pick an obvious example, remember the implicit premise in our sample *ad hominem* argument: Arguments by untrustworthy people are unsound. Any premise that requires a general premise like that is irrelevant. That is why we need not, in general, pay any attention to *ad hominem* arguments. It is also why the arguments we will find in the readings in Part 2 will not depend on many of the emotion-laden phrases we often find in the letters columns of local newspapers, phrases like "bra burners," "Bible thumpers," "secular humanists," "bleeding hearts," and "ultra-rightists."

Irrelevancies that are intended to distract our attention from the real issues are known as **red herrings.** Because red herrings often involve appeals to our emotions, many textbooks caution their readers to be extremely wary of emotional appeals. This is good advice, if not taken too far—especially in moral arguments. When emotion takes us where reason does not, appeals to emotion are certainly out of order. On the other hand, appeals to emotion are unavoidable in moral debate. Any argument in favor of voluntary euthanasia, for example, must appeal to our sympathy for pain-wracked terminally ill patients. Any argument in favor of capital punishment must appeal to our fear and loathing of brutal murderers. Such appeals will be there even if unintended. Important moral issues are emotional ones, and there is no getting around it.

But if we cannot totally separate emotion from moral argument, we can still question particular connections in particular cases. Are our emotions being whipped up by flamboyant language? By questionable claims? By sentimental anecdotes that are unrepresentative of most relevant cases? Is our attention being diverted from relevant facts? From important moral considerations like individual rights and obligations? If so, we are being victimized by red herrings.

We must also take care not to be victimized by another kind of irrelevance—the *straw man.* Sustained arguments for a position usually include criticisms of opposing arguments. If the opposing arguments are faithfully rendered, all is as it should be. But if they are unfaithfully rendered, the arguer is attacking a straw man. And whatever defects the straw man may have, they are irrelevant to what really matters—the opponent's real arguments. So one question you must always be careful to ask is this: Is *that* what the people on the other side are *really* saying?

Fallacies

A **fallacy** is an unreliable means of arguing that does not provide good reason for accepting the argument's conclusion. **Formal fallacies** are invalid deductive rules like those we looked at in the beginning of this chapter. **Informal fallacies,** on the other hand, are a mixed bag of unreliable strategies that people commonly tend to use. In general, informal fallacies arise in arguments that rely on hidden premises that are false or irrelevant or otherwise suspect. Although we did not introduce the term earlier, we did look at various informal fallacies when we discussed how to supply and evaluate missing premises. Here, for convenience, is a list of those informal fallacies with brief definitions and examples.

Ad Hominem Argument

An attack on the opponent rather than the opponent's argument. Name calling and casting doubt on an opponent's character are the most common but not the only forms. For example, to say that men have no rightful say in abortion disputes would be to commit this fallacy. The same goes for saying that a fur seller's arguments against animal rights aren't worth hearing.

Faulty Analogy

A misuse of an **argument by analogy,** which is an argument that two things that are alike in some respects must be alike in other respects. Suppose, for example, someone notes that tigers and hard-core pornography are alike in that both can be harmful to children. This is true, as far as it goes, even if the types of harm are quite different. But if he then goes on to conclude that pornography must be controlled in the same way as tigers—banned from private homes, say—he has carried the analogy too far. For one thing, there are constitutional protections regarding expression but none regarding the ownership of dangerous animals. For another, there are less drastic ways of protecting children from pornography than banning it from private homes.

Questionable Authority

Supporting a conclusion by depending on the judgment of someone who is not a reliable authority on the subject at hand. Citing horror stories from supermarket tabloids to back up a point—unless it's a point about the tabloids themselves, of course—is an obvious example. The same could be said about most postings on Internet bulletin boards or an athlete's paid endorsement of cereal.

Begging the Question

Assuming as a premise what you want to prove. If, for example, someone claims that all opponents of affirmative action are racist and then defends the point by saying, "If they weren't racist, they wouldn't oppose it," that person is begging the question.

Equivocation

Implicit reliance on two different meanings of the same word to reach a conclusion. For example, it's been said on occasion that the preamble to the Declaration of Independence does not apply to women because it says "all men are created equal" rather than "all humans" or "all persons." But the word *men* in the document refers to both male and female humans, not just to males.

Hand Waving

Claiming that something is true (or false) because everyone knows so. A classic case of hand waving is the following: "We don't need evidence to prove that capital punishment is a better deterrent to crime than life imprisonment. Everyone knows it—it's just common sense."

Hasty Generalization

Reaching a general conclusion from a sample that is biased or too small. Some abortion opponents, for example, have argued that women who have abortions suffer great psychological trauma but defend their assertion by pointing to only a few isolated cases.

Appeal to Ignorance

Arguing that a claim is true (or false) because we have no evidence proving otherwise. Arguing that global warming is (or is not) a compelling threat because nobody's proved that it isn't (or is) exemplifies such an appeal.

Post Hoc, Ergo Propter Hoc **("after this, therefore because of this")**

Claiming that one thing is caused by another because it follows the other. Politicians, for example, like to take credit for every good thing that happens after they take office, when it's not always clear that their policies are responsible.

Red Herring

An irrelevant issue introduced to distract attention from the issue at hand. Suppose, for example, someone presents an argument in favor of increasing welfare benefits to families with children, and you respond by saying, "Look at all the babies dying in abortion clinics. If you really cared about children, you'd be doing something about that." However sincere your convictions, you'd be committing this fallacy.

Slippery Slope

Assuming that an action will lead to an unwanted outcome as the result of many small steps that will inevitably follow. Whether such an assumption is a fallacy depends on your justification for making it. For an obvious example of when it would be a fallacy, imagine someone arguing that having sex with someone you don't plan to marry will eventually lead you to become a streetwalker—because it's one small step to having sex with someone you don't love, and another small step to having sex with multiple partners, and another small step to accepting expensive gifts for sex, and another small step to soliciting sex for money on the street.

Straw Man

A distortion of an opponent's actual position. This is a very common tactic that can be found in any controversy that arouses passion. In environmental debates, for example, we often hear it from both sides. Someone will argue that a proposed regulation is too expensive and will be met by the charge that he or she advocates the poisoning of children. Or someone will argue for better protection of endangered species and will be told he or she is saying owls matter more than people.

Although it is useful to keep these fallacies in mind, we should also point out that wrongly accusing an opponent of committing a fallacy can itself be considered a fallacy. For example, the fact that an opponent appeals to an authority does not automatically mean she has committed a fallacy. Many appeals to authority are justified. What matters is whether the alleged authority is a good authority on the topic at hand. Similarly, whether someone commits a fallacy by drawing an analogy depends on how strong the analogy is. For a third example, whether a claim that one thing causes another is a post hoc fallacy depends on the supporting evidence. When tobacco company executives argue that scientists have established only a statistical link between smoking and cancer, not a causal link, they are the ones who commit the fallacy.

SUMMARY AND CONCLUSIONS

In a play by the seventeenth-century French playwright Molière, the main character is delighted to learn that he has been speaking prose for as long as he has been talking. One thing you might have learned during the course of this chapter is that you have been reasoning logically for as long as you have been thinking. But some people speak better prose than others, and some people reason more logically than others. In each case, what often makes the difference is a bit of reflection on what distinguishes good prose or logical reasoning, followed by a little practice.

This chapter has picked out some of the features that distinguish logical reasoning, and it has applied them to various moral arguments. So should you apply them to the moral arguments of Part 2. If you do, you will provide yourself with more than just a little practice. Before we turn to Part 2, though, we should make a few final remarks.

First, don't be intimidated by the task of evaluating arguments. You don't have to write out every argument and then rewrite it every time you think of an alternative missing premise. All you have to do is *think* as you read or listen. And that holds not just for the readings in Part 2 but for any argument you encounter—in a newspaper, a conversation, another course, or anyplace else. Passive reading or listening is never good reading or listening, especially when the writer or speaker is trying to convince you of something.

Second, the techniques for evaluating arguments we have looked at are intended not only for other people's arguments but for our own too. Whenever we arrive at a conclusion, we do so for reasons, and our reasons may be good or bad, better or worse. It is important, then, that we challenge ourselves as well as others.

Third, this is a book in applied ethics, as its title makes clear. Although every textbook is (or at least should be) an exercise in applied logic (as well as applied prose), our basic concern is to come to grips with some important moral problems. And that means you should apply the material in *both* chapters of Part 1 to the material in Part 2. We want our moral conclusions to be based on both our most general moral principles and good reasoning.

Because this chapter has said little about those principles so far, it should close by tying them to what it has said. Each of the sample moral arguments we looked at contained at least one moral principle—about a woman's rights, the taking of innocent life, or the justification of punishment, to mention just three. Some were more general than others, but none was as general as the principle of utility, say, or respect for persons. This does not mean, though, that these most general principles have no important work to do in moral arguments. Why not?

For one thing, the less general principles are based on the most general ones. We accept them because we believe the most general ones require us to accept them. If we think that some kinds of punishment are unjustified, it's because we think them unfair or inconsistent with respect for persons or because we think they will not maximize utility. Also, if we think that there are legitimate exceptions to the less general principles, it's because we think that the most general ones require the exceptions. Thus, we justify white lies, for example, because a principle more general than honesty—the principle of utility, say—requires it. So these most general principles did play an important role in our sample arguments, even though we did not make them explicit.

Sometimes, however, they *must* be made explicit. That happens when a less general principle, or a proposed exception to a less general principle, is controversial. When that does happen, we need an argument for the principle or its proposed exception, and that will take us back to the most general principles. We will have to ask whether any of our most general principles support the controversial premise. If they don't, we can reject it. If they do, then we will have to ask whether any of our other most general principles give a conflicting answer. If they don't do that, we can accept the premise. If they do, we will have to ask which of the conflicting principles should take precedence.

That last question is a particularly difficult one to answer, and moral problems that turn on it are particularly difficult to resolve to everyone's satisfaction. Men and women of good will may, in the end, come to different resolutions because they cannot agree on which principle takes precedence. Not surprisingly, many of the problems of Part 2 turn on precisely that question, which is why they are still with us. But difficult is not the same as impossible, which is why many similar problems are no longer with us.

If we were writing this book thirty years ago, we might have included a chapter on civil disobedience—we might have looked at arguments for and against the view that people have the moral right to protest laws they consider unjust by peacefully and publicly violating those laws. Also, our chapter on discrimination would have been very different. Instead of looking at arguments for and against affirmative action, we might very well have been considering whether private employers have the right to discriminate *against* minorities and women. Today, such chapters would be unthinkable. The extraordinarily powerful moral arguments of people like Martin Luther King, Jr., have made them unthinkable. Perhaps in another thirty years, we will be able to make the same statement about some of the chapters in the book you are now reading.

PART TWO

Issues

CHAPTER THREE

Sexual Morality

- **The Traditional View**
- **The Libertarian View**
- **Treating Sex Differently**
- **Arguments for Sexual Libertarianism**
- **Arguments against Sexual Libertarianism**

ROGER SCRUTON **Sexual Morality**
ALAN H. GOLDMAN **Plain Sex**
MICHAEL LEVIN **Why Homosexuality Is Abnormal**
TIMOTHY F. MURPHY **Homosexuality and Nature**

CASE PRESENTATIONS: • ***Disease v. promiscuity?*** • **Lawrence v. Texas:** ***Private Rights and Public Morality*** • **Goodridge v. Dept. of Public Health:** ***A Right of Gay Marriage*** • ***A Slippery Slope to Polygamy***

DURING THE 1960S and 1970s, the United States was abuzz with talk of the "new morality" and the "sexual revolution." Almost everywhere, people were discussing singles bars, casual sex, one-night stands, open marriage, unwed motherhood, creative divorce, cohabitation, group sex, teen sex, and sexual preference. Traditional sexual morality was breaking or had already broken down.

To traditionalists, the changes were at best disturbing and at worst alarming. They worried about the future of their children, of the family, and of society. What they saw when they looked around was moral decline. To those caught up in the revolution, on the other hand, the changes were liberating. When they looked around, they saw new options, new freedoms, new manners of expression, and fulfillment.

Many of you are likely to take the sexual revolution as much for granted as you take the American Revolution. Some of you may even wonder what all the fuss was about. Others may think of the old morality as quaint. You might ask: Were women really supposed to remain virgins until marriage? Did people really think that living together was immoral? Could a talented and beautiful movie star like Ingrid Bergman really be run out of Hollywood for having an affair with a married man? Did parents and universities really insist on separate dorms for male and female students?

Of course, others of you do not take the new morality for granted. Some of you probably agree totally with the traditionalists, despite the pressures you might feel from your peers. Some of you probably accept parts of the new morality but not others parts. Perhaps you believe in nonmarital sex but feel that the people involved should love each other. Perhaps you find nothing wrong with premarital sex but draw the line at adultery. Perhaps you accept total freedom when it comes to heterosexual sex but believe that homosexuality is immoral.

Such differences show that the victory of the sexual revolution was not total. Moreover, certain trends in today's world suggest that we may be in store for some counterrevolutionary changes. The risk of AIDS and other sexually transmitted diseases seems to be affecting the sexual behavior of both heterosexuals and homosexuals. The large number of teenage pregnancies is also causing doubts about the new morality. And some feminists have begun calling for a "new celibacy."

For these reasons and others, debate about sexual morality continues. The issues involved are many and complex. The best place to start, no doubt, is with the two extreme positions: the traditional and the libertarian.

THE TRADITIONAL VIEW

The traditional view can be put quite simply: All sex outside marriage is wrong. Although people have held the traditional view for a variety of reasons, its most influential line of defense comes from the Roman Catholic church.

As we saw in Part 1, Catholic moral teaching was greatly influenced by Aristotle, the ancient Greek philosopher whose ideas were incorporated into church doctrine by the medieval thinker St. Thomas Aquinas. Four of Aristotle's ideas are particularly important here. First, everything in nature has a purpose. Second, everything in nature has an essential nature—certain features that constitute its defining features. Third, everything in nature has its proper good. Fourth, something's natural purpose, its essential nature, and its proper good are intimately related.

That the Roman Catholic church believes that the natural purpose of sex is reproduction is well known. Equally well known is one consequence that the church draws from that belief—that artificial means of birth control are immoral. Less well known are other, related beliefs that are also directly related to sexual morality. These beliefs are spelled out in the Vatican's 1976 "Declaration on Certain Questions Concerning Sexual Ethics." The full text is available in English on the Vatican's own web site: http://www.vatican.va/

There, the authors stress what they take to be an essential characteristic of human beings—the ability to engage in fully human love, which includes genuine caring, sincerity, respect, commitment, and fidelity. Moreover, the declaration argues, fully human love does not stop at romantic love; it naturally evolves into parental love. That is, true human love is made complete by love for the children produced by that love. These facts about human sexuality are what set it apart from mere animal sexuality. They are also what make it more valuable. Equally important, they are what give human sex and sexual relationships their special dignity.

To engage in sex without love, then, or to engage in sex not open to the possibility of procreation, is to engage in sex that violates our essential nature and dignity. And since to violate our essential nature and dignity is to turn away from the proper human good, to engage in sex without love or sex not open to procreation is to engage in wrongful sex. This does not mean, however, that unmarried sex with love and without contraception is moral in the church's view. Given the changeableness of human desire and commitment, we need added guarantees of sincerity and fidelity. And only marriage can provide those guarantees.

THE LIBERTARIAN VIEW

According to the libertarian view, sex is an activity like any other—tennis, say, or conversation or studying—and what determines whether any sexual act is moral or immoral is no different from what determines whether any other act is moral or immoral. As long as the act involves no dishonesty, exploitation, or coercion, and as long as it does not violate any obligations to others, it is not immoral.

Consider premarital sex. Many things can make it immoral. If John tells Mary that he loves her and wants to take her home to meet his parents and she goes to bed with him as a result, John acts immorally if he doesn't mean what he tells her. If Mary has a venereal disease and does not warn John ahead of time, then she acts immorally. If John tries to coerce Mary into performing sexual acts she dislikes, then he acts immorally. But if neither of them is looking for anything more than a one-night stand, and if neither holds back any important information, and if neither resorts to any coercion or breaks any promise, and if neither violates any obligation to a third person, then neither does anything wrong.

Of course, we are assuming here that both John and Mary are adults. Children are incapable of the kind of informed consent required to ensure that they are not being exploited. But there are other things we need not assume. For example, we need not assume that the adults involved are of different sexes. Whatever holds for John and Mary also holds for John and Bill or for Jane and Mary. Nor need we assume that only *two* adults are involved. Group sex that violates none of our conditions is perfectly acceptable to the libertarian. Furthermore, we need not even assume that John and Mary are not close relatives, like brother and sister. Even incest is acceptable to the libertarian, as long as there is no dishonesty, coercion, or exploitation and as long as reliable means of contraception are used.

Similar remarks hold for adultery. Even though marriage involves the promise of fidelity, husbands and wives are perfectly free to release each other from their vows, just as we are all free to release one another from any other promise. If a married couple agrees that both members would be happier if they could have extramarital affairs, then they are morally free to do so—provided, of course, that they do not keep their marriage a secret from sexual partners who do not wish to have affairs with married people.

Arguments in favor of **sexual libertarianism** are basically of the "why not" sort. Why *shouldn't* sex be treated like any other activity? Why should we consider it moral to play tennis with somebody we don't love but immoral to have sex with somebody we don't love? Why should we consider it moral to eat lunch with somebody of the same sex but immoral to have sex with that very same person? Why should we be permitted to go to a movie purely for pleasure but not have sex purely for pleasure? What's so different about sex that it requires such special rules? Why can't sexual morality be determined by the same general moral principles—the principle of utility, respect for persons, the golden rule, and so forth—that determine right and wrong in the rest of our lives?

TREATING SEX DIFFERENTLY

We have already looked at one answer to the libertarian's questions, the one offered by the Vatican. Not surprisingly, sexual libertarians reject it. Many of their reasons for rejecting it will become apparent throughout this chapter, but for now, let's just mention one. Libertarians generally feel that it is up to each individual to determine his or her own good. Human dignity lies in our capacity to pursue our own good as we see fit—provided we do not interfere with another person's pursuit of his or her own good—not in adhering to any particular sexual morality. Sex between consenting adults is a private matter, and private matters are matters of individual conscience.

Many other answers to the libertarians' arguments focus on the social context of sex. The sex lives of any particular individuals may be private, but the widespread adoption of any particular sexual morality can have far-reaching social ramifications. Let's look at several of these issues.

Venereal Diseases and AIDS

Gonorrhea, syphilis, and other venereal diseases are familiar hazards of sex. Although some can be extremely serious—even fatal—if left untreated, they *are* treatable. Because they are, fear of contracting them rarely interferes with most people's sex lives. When genital herpes burst on the scene in the seventies, however, fear did begin to play a role in many people's sexual decisions. Although not as dangerous as syphilis, herpes is a chronic condition.

In the eighties, a new and far more dangerous threat appeared—AIDS (acquired immune deficiency syndrome). There is no known cure for AIDS, nor has a vaccine been developed to prevent its spread, and that leaves its victims with the hopeless prospect of a protracted, agonizing death and leaves potential victims with a terrifying question mark.

Although there is much controversy over how AIDS is transmitted, five means of transmission are well established: anal sex, vaginal sex, intravenous needles and syringes, blood transfusions, and pregnancy. (Other feared possibilities, like "deep" kissing and eating utensils, have not been established as means of transmitting the disease.) Because of the controversy over transmission of AIDS, there is a corresponding controversy over its potential victims. Historically, the groups facing the highest risk in the United States have been male homosexuals, intravenous drug users, hemophiliacs, the sex partners of members of these three groups, and children of women at risk when pregnant.

AIDS has already taken a terrible toll among the homosexual population. According to the Centers for Disease Control and Prevention, homosexual sex between men still accounted for 47 percent of new HIV/AIDS cases diagnosed in the United States in 2004, the most recent year for which data are available. Heterosexual sex accounted for 33 percent of all new cases in 2004. Females accounted for 27 percent of all new diagnoses in 2004, and 15 percent of those were women aged thirteen to twenty-four years. Injection drug use continues to be a major form of transmission, accounting for one-third of new cases, either from direct transmission through needles or from sex with a drug user. The most rapid rate of increase in infection in recent years has been among young women and women of color. Whether AIDS can or cannot be spread by casual contact and whether all of us or only those of us in high-risk groups need be immediately concerned for our own safety, AIDS does raise serious concerns about sexual morality. Given what we do know, sexual promiscuity—both heterosexual and homosexual—increases the risk of AIDS, not only to ourselves, but to our partners and future children.

At the minimum, then, people who cannot be certain about their sexual partners should engage in "safe" sex. That is, they should use condoms. Even libertarians can agree on that point. Other people go further. Some argue that the threat of AIDS should cause us to return to traditional sexual morality. Others claim that we need not go that far. Perhaps we should retreat from promiscuity, they say, but monogamous relationships among unmarried people can be just as safe as among married people. Still others claim that the threat of AIDS does not even require monogamy, as long as we do not engage in sex with people in high-risk groups.

Threats to the Family

One of the most alarming trends in recent years is the sharp rise in single-parent households. Although different people find different aspects of the trend alarming, one concern is shared by all. Most single parents are women, and single women and their children are often poor. As much as 40 percent of the homeless population in the nation consists of children. Most are with single mothers, although economic difficulties also account for a recent surge in homeless families.

That many single parents are teenagers is another concern shared by all. Whether they are forced to drop out of school or manage to continue their educations, teenage motherhood places a great burden on them, their children, and society.

The causes of single parenthood are complex. Any list of contributing factors would have to include a variety of social conditions, including, most notably, poverty. But nothing can be more evident than this: no sex, no children. Another point is equally evident: the fewer the divorces, the fewer the single parents. And it is these two points that critics of sexual libertarianism stress.

Regarding the first, they say that the spread of the sexual revolution from adults to teenagers was inevitable. When unmarried rock stars and other teen heroes openly live together and have children, when the media are filled with representations of casual sex, how can teenagers not be affected? And given their lack of maturity and responsibility, the normal confusions of adolescence, and various pressures that many teens feel, how could we have expected anything less than an explosion of teen pregnancies?

The connection between the sexual revolution and divorce may seem more tenuous, but to some people, it is no less real. If sex outside marriage is freely available and without moral stigma, if sexual adventure and variety are prized at least as much as monogamy, if love and commitment are no longer seen as natural accompaniments to sex, then marital ties inevitably weaken.

What makes sex different, according to this line of argument, then, is the intimate connection between sexual behavior and the health of the family, plus the social costs that the decline of the family entails. If sexual morality concerned only the individuals involved in any particular sexual act, then perhaps we could treat sex like tennis. But it doesn't, so we can't.

Personal Fulfillment

For those of us with no aspirations to be Pete Sampras or Venus Williams, tennis is little more than an enjoyable game, a pleasant way to get fresh air and exercise, or a welcome opportunity for camaraderie. Even if such things are important to us, and even if tennis is our favorite way to get them, the role of tennis in our lives remains relatively limited.

Can we say the same about sex? Hardly. For one thing, there is a strong biological component to our sexual lives. Thus, both biological and behavioral scientists talk of sex *drives* as well as desires. For another, sexual development cannot be separated from psychological development. How we learn to deal with our sexuality is crucial to the kind of person we become, and our sexual identity is a critical feature of our personal identity. For yet another, our sexual relationships are among the most powerful and influential relationships we can have.

Critics of sexual libertarianism often charge that to treat sex like any other activity is to miss everything that is important about sex and its role in our lives. In particular, it is to ignore its importance to personal growth and fulfillment. Any sexual morality must take account of that fact. Such critics don't necessarily call for a return to traditional morality, but they do insist that we view sex as more than merely a pleasant activity. What we should do is ask ourselves questions like these: Does our sex life contribute to our sense of worth and dignity? Is it consistent with our most important goals in life? Does it reflect the kind of person we most want to be? Is it the sex life of a mature, well-adjusted person? Does it help us develop or maintain the character traits that most matter to us? Does it enhance our lives as much as it might? Does it help us build the kind of relationships we most value?

To ask such questions is to steer a middle course between the sexual traditionalist and the sexual libertarian. The questions are, after all, very much in the spirit of the Vatican declaration. The concerns they raise—fundamental values, personal dignity and fulfillment, the quality of our lives and relationships—are the same. But unlike the authors of the declaration, many people who insist that we ask these questions do not assume that our answers must follow any particular line. In that respect, they are more like the libertarians. For example, they allow that many people engaged in loving homosexual relationships can answer yes to all these questions. So can many unmarried heterosexuals with active sex lives.

People who support this way of treating sex, then, are like the traditionalists in that they do not treat sex like any other activity, but they are like the libertarians in that they make room for a variety of personal decisions about sex.

The Naturalness Argument

Another line of attack against sexual libertarianism also shares certain features with the Vatican declaration. According to this line, sex organs and sexual activity are natural phenomena, and like any other natural phenomenon, they have their own natural manifestations and purposes. In that case, we can distinguish natural from unnatural sex and natural from unnatural use of our sex organs. And since what is natural is moral and what is unnatural is immoral, we can distinguish moral from immoral sex.

Although the Vatican declaration applies this reasoning to a variety of sexual behaviors—masturbation and the use of contraception, for instance, as well as homosexuality—many people confine it to homosexuality alone.

What is it that makes homosexuality unnatural? Various answers are given. Homosexual behavior violates the laws of nature, some people say. Or it is an abnormal occurrence in nature. Or it involves an unnatural use of sex organs.

Libertarian Objections

Many libertarians share some of the concerns we have just looked at. They do not, however, conclude that these concerns justify a retreat from full sexual freedom. Sexual libertarians do not advocate moral irresponsibility, they say, but only sexual freedom. And sexual libertarianism can be just as morally responsible as sexual traditionalism.

Consider the AIDS threat. Certainly, libertarians say, we all have an obligation to avoid behavior that might cause us to become carriers of the virus and pass it on to others. And just as certainly, that obligation involves taking necessary precautions like using condoms when we cannot be sure about our sexual partners. But as long as we do take such necessary precautions, we have no obligation to turn to chastity or heterosexual monogamy.

As for teen pregnancy and single parenthood, sexual libertarians argue that the blame for these problems does not rest with them. As long as they behave responsibly, they cannot be held accountable for the irresponsibility of others. Nor should they be morally required to restrict their sex lives. The solution to such social problems lies in education, easy access to birth control counseling, and social programs to alleviate poverty and hopelessness—not in the restriction of sexual freedom.

Libertarians also point out that about half of all women and children experiencing homelessness are fleeing domestic violence. As many of those relationships were traditional marriages, there must be other explanations for this homelessness and poverty than the availability of sex outside marriage. Perhaps women are less likely now to tolerate domestic violence and instead seek other options.

What about personal fulfillment? Many libertarians might well agree with many of the remarks in that argument, as long as each individual is free to supply his or her own answers to the recommended questions. Others, though, might wonder why sex need be taken so seriously. If Jane is satisfied enough with her life, even though she takes a very casual approach to sex, why should she feel any more pressure to involve herself in any soul searching about sex than about any other aspect of her life? No doubt sex and sexual relationships are very important to many people, but if other people feel differently, who's to say they shouldn't?

Finally, there is the naturalness argument. Here, libertarians remain totally unimpressed. Does homosexuality really violate the laws of nature? No, because *nothing* can violate the laws of nature. Natural laws are not like criminal laws. They describe how the world actually works. They do not tell us how we ought to behave. Everything that happens, then, must be in accord with natural law. Is homosexuality an abnormal occurrence in nature? Perhaps, but that does not make it immoral. After all, great genius, great basketball talent, and great musical ability are even more abnormal, but we prize them when they occur, not condemn them. Does homosexuality involve the unnatural use of our sex organs? Again, perhaps, but how does that differ from using our ears for holding earrings, our eyes for giving playful winks, or our thumbs for hitching rides?

Advocates of **civil unions** for homosexual couples also point out that many of those relationships are as stable as heterosexual marriages, even though the unions are not traditional relationships. These advocates suggest that the values of traditional marriages are highly regarded in these civil unions and should be encouraged, regardless of the sexual preference of the couple. Many of these couples also adopt children who are otherwise difficult to place, including the children of drug addicts and AIDS-infected babies. Thus, they promote traditional family values, even though they are outside the definition of a traditional heterosexual marriage.

ARGUMENTS FOR SEXUAL LIBERTARIANISM

1. ***Sex is a private matter.***

POINT: "Whatever goes on between consenting adults in private is nobody's business but their own, and that holds as much for sex as for anything else. Why should anybody even care whether Mary has fifteen lovers or none, whether Jack prefers sex with Bill to sex with Jane, or whether married couples like to 'swing' with other married couples? Just because you personally disapprove of such things doesn't make them wrong. We all have the right to live our lives as we see fit as long as we don't interfere with the rights of others to live their lives as they see fit. Promiscuous people, homosexuals, and swingers don't tell you how to live your life. Don't tell them how to live theirs."

COUNTERPOINT: "Sex isn't nearly as private as you think. All of society is affected by the sexual revolution you're so fond of. Who do you think has to pick up the tab for all the illegitimate children your libertarianism is giving us? The taxpayers. And who has to pick up the tab for AIDS research? The taxpayers. And who has to live with all the abortion mills, the fear of AIDS, and the worry over how all of this free sex will affect our children? All of us."

2. ***You can't turn the clock back on the sexual revolution.***

POINT: "Whether you approve of what's happened to sexual morality or not, one thing's certain: You can't turn the clock back. Once people get a taste of freedom—sexual or any other kind—they don't want to give it up. Do you really think that sexually active unmarried people are going to turn to celibacy, or that homosexuals are going to deny their sexual identity and pretend to be something they're not, or that married couples who feel that open marriage works better for them than fidelity are going to settle for fidelity? Let's face it. Human nature just doesn't work that way."

COUNTERPOINT: "Maybe not, but that doesn't make the sexual revolution right. The whole point of morality is to curb some of the excesses of human nature, to try to get people to exercise their freedoms responsibly. Besides, nobody expects to turn everything around overnight. The point is to insist that certain behavior is wrong, to make young people understand the proper place of sex in their lives, and to get them to make responsible choices about sex. It'll take some time, but eventually the changes can come."

3. ***Curbing sexual freedom is unfair.***

POINT: "You're neglecting an important point here—fairness. The crux of the issue isn't just that people don't want to turn back the clock but that it's *unfair* to make them turn it back. You're comfortable with your traditional morality, but to other people, it can be a straitjacket. For them, it's impossible to live fulfilling lives under those conditions. The worst victims, of course, would be the homosexuals. What are they supposed to do—live a heterosexual lie or give up sex and love altogether? But they wouldn't be the only victims.

Some people are totally unsuited to marriage. Others are totally unsuited to monogamy. They have as much right to fulfilling sex lives as you do."

COUNTERPOINT: "Nobody has the right to seek fulfillment immorally. And there's nothing unfair about making people turn away from immoral behavior. I'm not denying that traditional sexual morality is more demanding for some people than it is for others, but that doesn't make it any different from any other area of moral concern. Pathological liars and kleptomaniacs have a harder time doing right than the rest of us do, but our sympathy for them can't lead us to approve of their lies and thefts. The same holds for homosexuals. We can sympathize, but we can't condone."

4. ***Traditional sexual morality is hypocritical.***

POINT: "What you're really calling for is a return to hypocrisy. Let's all pretend to be faithful heterosexual monogamists while we do whatever we feel like doing on the sly. Adultery, premarital sex, promiscuity, and homosexuality aren't new, you know. The only thing that's changed is that people are more honest about them now. And that's a change for the good."

COUNTERPOINT: "Adultery, premarital sex, promiscuity, and homosexuality may not be new, but they're sure a lot more prevalent than they used to be. And you can thank your precious honesty for that. Once people start being proud about things like that, once they start going public about them, it has to start affecting other people's behavior. They start thinking, 'If it's good enough for Dick and Jane, maybe I should give it a try.' In other words, a little bit of hypocrisy is a good thing. You don't want armed robbers telling their kids there's nothing wrong with armed robbery, do you? Well, I don't want unwed mothers telling their kids there's nothing wrong with premarital sex."

ARGUMENTS AGAINST SEXUAL LIBERTARIANISM

1. ***Sexual libertarianism undermines public morality.***

POINT: "Morality is like law. Once you encourage disrespect for a particular law, you encourage disrespect for all laws. And once you encourage disrespect for sexual morality, you encourage disrespect for all of morality. That's why it's no surprise that the sexual revolution brought with it an explosion of pornography and abortion. It's also why I wouldn't be surprised to learn that people don't care as much about loyalty and honesty as they used to. After all, a large part of your revolution is that marriage vows don't have to mean anything."

COUNTERPOINT: "Sexual libertarianism isn't about disrespect for morality. It's about moral change. If you want to talk about disrespect for morality, the real culprit is your traditional sexual morality. That's a morality that people won't adhere to, and a morality like that is bound to breed disrespect. And don't confuse sexual libertarianism with disloyalty and dishonesty. A husband and wife who agree that affairs with other people will make their marriage better aren't being disloyal to each other—and they're certainly not being dishonest."

2. ***Sex without love is empty.***

POINT: "One of the biggest problems with your view is that it erases the connection between sex and love. Even you have to admit that sex with someone you love is better than sex with someone you don't love. With someone you love, sex isn't mere empty pleasure. It's communication, it's sharing, it's an expression of affection and care. It *means* something. The sex that you advocate means nothing at all. It's sterile, and it adds nothing of worth to our lives. What you're really doing is reducing human sexuality to animal sexuality. We might as well be rabbits, according to you. But we're not rabbits, and because we're not, loveless sex can't possibly satisfy us or be fulfilling for us."

COUNTERPOINT: "First of all, I'm not advocating any kind of sex. All I'm advocating is people's moral right to engage in the kinds of sex they prefer as long as they don't hurt anyone. Second, who are you to declare that the kind of sex you prefer is the best kind of sex for anyone else? Third, even if you're right—even if loving sex is better than loveless sex—what morally important difference does that make? Some cars are better than others, but there's nothing immoral about driving the inferior ones. Or to pick an even closer analogy, celebrating good news with someone you love is probably better than celebrating good news with someone you don't love, but nobody's going to say you're doing wrong if you do celebrate good news with someone you don't love."

3. ***Sexual libertarianism undermines marriage.***

POINT: "If society adopts your position, we might as well forget about the institution of marriage. Unmarried people will have no good reason to get married because sex will be freely available. Even having children won't count as a good reason any more, as it becomes more and more acceptable to be an unmarried parent. And married people will have little reason to stay married. After all, once marital fidelity goes, there goes the most important bond between husband and wife. And even if some kind of bond remains, how can it stand up against the constant temptations that married people will face? Or the jealousies? Or the insecurities?"

COUNTERPOINT: "Aren't you being a little too cynical? People get married for lots of reasons other than sex, and they stay married because of a variety of bonds and intimacies. I'm not going to deny that sexual libertarianism can have some negative effects on marriage, but I *am* going to deny that the effects are all negative. For one thing, people with sexual experience before marriage are less likely to confuse sex with love, and that makes it less likely that they'll choose their spouses unwisely. For another, they're less likely to feel they've missed something before getting married, and that should help protect them from temptation. And for still another, some marriages actually gain from being open to extramarital affairs. If married people feel the need for sexual variety, the possibility of having an open marriage can remove a reason for divorce."

4. ***Sexual libertarianism is turning society upside down.***

POINT: "Your views have led to a number of crazy consequences. I'm not just talking about such tragedies as teen mothers, but things like the gay rights movement. First we have homosexuals demanding the right to teach in elementary schools, then we have homosexual couples demanding the right to adopt children, then we have them demanding that homosexual 'spouses' be included in family medical plans and the like. I have no idea where all this is ultimately heading, but it's certainly not in the right direction. We can't let children grow up believing that homosexuality is just another lifestyle, and we can't have society treating homosexual relationships like real marriages. No society can survive that."

COUNTERPOINT: "Why not? If homosexuality isn't immoral to begin with, what's wrong with giving homosexuals the same rights as heterosexuals? If you're afraid that we'd end up raising an entire generation of homosexual children, you're just being unrealistic. Besides, you're mixing up two different issues. Whether homosexuality is moral is one thing. Whether homosexual relationships should have the same legal status as heterosexual marriages is another."

Sexual Morality

ROGER SCRUTON

In this essay, taken from Chapter 11 of his book *Sexual Desire,* British philosopher Roger Scruton argues for the traditional view of sexual morality. Earlier in the chapter, he develops a general moral view based on Aristotle's *Nichomachean Ethics.* Among the most important features of his view are the following:

First, morality is a constraint on practical reasoning. That is, morality rejects certain kinds of behavior even though individuals might have many prudent reasons for engaging in them.

Second, the goal of human conduct is *eudaimonia*—happiness, or fulfillment—which requires both physical health and the flourishing of the individual as a rational being. The goal of morality is to develop in the individual the dispositions—**virtues**—that lead to his or her happiness.

Third, the best model of moral reasoning is moral education. In educating our children to develop virtuous dispositions, we are teaching them to be critical of their immediate desires and to desire what is most reasonable to desire so that they will flourish and live fulfilled adult lives. In doing so, we think in terms of general human conditions as well as in terms of the individual conditions of our children. Likewise, in our own moral reasoning, we must ask ourselves not only how to achieve our own individual goals but also what goals we, as human beings, ought to have. In other words, we must think in terms of interpersonal values as well as personal preferences.

In the following selection, he applies this general view to sexual morality.

We must now attempt to apply the Aristotelian strategy to the subject-matter of this book, and ask whether there is such a thing as sexual virtue, and, if so, what is it, and how is it acquired? Clearly, sexual desire, which is an interpersonal attitude with the most far-reaching consequences for those who are joined by it, cannot be morally neutral. On the contrary, it is in the experience of sexual desire that we are most vividly conscious of the distinction between virtuous and vicious impulses, and most vividly aware that, in the choice between them, our happiness is at stake.

The Aristotelian strategy enjoins us to ignore the actual conditions of any particular person's life, and to look only at the permanent features of human nature. We know that people feel sexual desire; that they feel erotic love, which may grow from desire; that they may avoid both these feelings, by dissipation or self-restraint. Is there anything to be said about desire, other than that it falls within the general scope of the virtue of temperance, which enjoins us to desire only what reason approves?

The first, and most important, observation to be made is that the capacity for love in general, and for erotic love in particular, is a virtue. . . . I [have] tried to show that erotic love involves an element of mutual self-enhancement; it generates a sense of the irreplaceable value, both of the other and of the self, and of the activities which bind them. To receive and to give this love is to achieve something of incomparable value in the process of self-fulfillment. It is to gain the most powerful of all interpersonal *guarantees;* in erotic love the subject becomes conscious of the full reality of his personal existence, not only in his own eyes, but in the eyes of another. Everything that he is and values gains sustenance from his love, and every project receives a meaning beyond the moment. All that exists for us as mere hope and hypothesis—the attachment to life and to the body—achieves under the rule of *erōs* the aspect of a radiant certainty. Unlike the cold glances of approval, admiration and pride, the glance of love sees value precisely in that which is the source of anxiety and doubt: in the merely contingent, merely "empirical," existence of the flesh, the existence which we did not choose, but to which we are condemned. It is the answer to man's fallen condition. . . .

To receive erotic love, however, a person must be able to give it: or if he cannot, the love of others will be a torment to him, seeking from him that which he cannot provide, and directing against him the fury of a disappointed right. It is therefore unquestionable that we have reason to acquire the capacity for erotic love, and, if this means bending our sexual impulses in a certain direction, that will be the direction of sexual virtue. Indeed, the argument of the last two chapters has implied that the development of the sexual impulse towards love may be impeded: there are sexual habits which are vicious, precisely in neutralising the capacity for love. The first thing that can be said, therefore, is that we all have reason to avoid those habits and to educate our children not to possess them.

Here it may be objected that not every love is happy, that there are many—Anna Karenina, for example, or Phaedra—whose capacity for love was the cause of their downfall. But we must remind ourselves of the Aristotelian strategy. In establishing that courage or wisdom is a virtue, the Aristotelian does not argue that the possession of these virtues is in every particular circumstance bound to be advantageous. . . .

It is not the particular personal tragedy but the generality of the human condition that determines the basis of sexual morality. Tragedy and loss are the rare but necessary outcomes of a process which we all have reason to undergo. (Indeed, it is part of the point of tragedy that it divorces in our imagination the right and the good from the merely prudential: that it sets the value of life against the value of mere survival.) We wish to know, in advance of any particular experience, which dispositions a person must have if he is successfully to express himself in sexual desire and to be fulfilled in his sexual endeavours. Love is the fulfillment of desire, and therefore love is its *telos.* A life of celibacy may also be fulfilled; but, assuming the general truth that most of us have a powerful, and perhaps overwhelming, urge to make love, it is in our interests to ensure that love—and not some other thing—is made.

Love, I have argued, is prone to jealousy, and the object of jealousy is defined by the thought of the beloved's desire. Because jealousy is one of the greatest of psychical catastrophes, involving the possible ruin of both partners, a morality based in the need for erotic love must forestall and eliminate jealousy. It is in the deepest human interest, therefore, that we form the habit of fidelity. This habit is natural and normal; but it is also easily broken, and the temptation to break it is contained in desire itself—in the element of generality which tempts us always to experiment, to verify, to detach ourselves from that which is too familiar in the interest of excitement and risk. Virtuous desire is faithful; but virtuous desire is also an artefact, made possible by a process of moral education which we do not, in truth, understand in its complexity.

If that observation is correct, a whole section of traditional sexual morality must be upheld. The fulfillment of sexual desire defines the nature of desire: *to telos phuseis estin*. And the nature of desire gives us our standard of normality. There are enormous varieties of human sexual conduct, and of "common-sense" morality: some societies permit or encourage polygamy, others look with indifference upon premarital intercourse, or regard marriage itself as no more than an episode in a relation that pre-exists and perhaps survives it. But no society, and no "common-sense" morality. . . looks with favour upon promiscuity or infidelity, unless influenced by a doctrine of "emancipation" or "liberation" which is dependent for its sense upon the very conventions which it defies. Whatever the institutional forms of human sexual union, and whatever the range of permitted partners, sexual desire is itself inherently "nuptial": it involves concentration upon the embodied existence of the other, leading through tenderness to the "vow" of erotic love. It is a telling observation that the civilisation which has most tolerated the institution of polygamy—the Islamic—has also, in its erotic literature, produced what are perhaps the intensest and most poignant celebrations of monogamous love, precisely through the attempt to capture, not the institution of marriage, but the human datum of desire.[1]

The nuptiality of desire suggests, in its turn, a natural history of desire: a principle of development which defines the "normal course" of sexual education. "Sexual maturity" involves incorporating the sexual impulse into the personality, and so making sexual desire into an expression of the subject himself, even though it is, in the heat of action, a force which also overcomes him. If the Aristotelian approach to these things is as plausible as I think it is, the virtuous habit will also have the character of a "mean": it will involve the disposition to desire what is desirable, despite the competing impulses of animal lust (in which the intentionality of desire may be demolished) and timorous frigidity (in which the sexual impulse is impeded altogether). Education is directed towards the special kind of temperance which shows itself, sometimes as chastity, sometimes as fidelity, sometimes as passionate desire, according to the "right judgement" of the subject. In wanting what is judged to be desirable, the virtuous person wants what may also be loved, and what may therefore be obtained without hurt or humiliation.

Virtue is a matter of degree, rarely attained in its completion, but always admired. Because traditional sexual education has pursued sexual virtue, it is worthwhile summarising its most important features, in order to see the power of the idea that underlies and justifies it.

The most important feature of traditional sexual education is summarised in anthropological language as the "ethic of pollution and taboo."[2] The child was taught to regard his body as sacred, and as subject to pollution by misperception or misuse. The sense of pollution is by no means a trivial side-effect of the "bad sexual encounter": it may involve a penetrating disgust, at oneself, one's body and one's situation, such as is experienced by the victim of rape. Those sentiments—which arise from our "fear of the obscene"—express the tension contained within the experience of embodiment. At any moment we can become "mere body," the self driven from its incarnation, and its habitation ransacked. The most important root idea of personal morality is that I am in my body, not (to borrow Descartes' image) as a pilot in a ship, but as an incarnate self. My body is identical with me, and sexual purity is the precious guarantee of this.

Sexual purity does not forbid desire: it simply ensures the status of desire as an interpersonal feeling. The child who learns "dirty habits" detaches his sex from himself, sets it outside himself as something curious and alien. His fascinated enslavement to the body is also a withering of desire, a scattering of erotic energy and a loss of union with the other. Sexual purity sustains the subject of desire, making him present as a self in the very act which overcomes him.

. . . The purely human redemption which is offered to us in love is dependent, in the last analysis, upon public recognition of the value of chastity, and of the sacrilege involved in a sexual impulse that wanders free from the controlling impulse of respect. The "pollution" of the prostitute is not that she gives herself for money, but that she gives herself to those whom she hates or despises. This is the "wound" of unchastity, which cannot be healed in solitude by the one who suffers it, but only by his acceptance into a social order which confines the sexual impulse to the realm of intimate relations. The chaste person sustains the ideal of sexual innocence, by giving honourable form to chastity as a way of life. Through his example, it becomes not foolish but admirable to ignore the promptings of a desire that brings no intimacy or fulfillment. Chastity is not a private policy, followed by one individual alone for the sake of his peace of mind. It has a wider and more generous significance: it attempts to draw others into complicity, and to sustain a social order that confines the sexual impulse to the personal sphere. . . .

The child was traditionally brought up to achieve sexual fulfillment only *through* chastity, which is the condition which surrounds him on his first entering the adult world—the world of commitments and obligations. At the same time, he was encouraged to ponder certain "ideal objects" of desire. These, presented to him under the aspect of an idealised physical beauty, were never *merely* beautiful, but also endowed with the moral attributes that fitted them for love. This dual inculcation of "pure" habits and "ideal" love might seem, on the face of it, to be unworthy of the name of education. Is it not, rather, like the mere *training* of a horse or a dog, which arbitrarily forbids some things and fosters others, without offering the first hint of a reason why? And is it not the distinguishing mark of education that it engages with the rational nature of its recipient, and does not merely mould him indifferently to his own understanding of the process? Why, in short, is this moral education, rather than a transference into the sexual sphere—as Freud would have it—of those same processes of interdiction that train us to defecate, not in our nappies, but in a porcelain pot?

The answer is clear. The cult of innocence is an attempt to *generate* rational conduct, by incorporating the sexual impulse into the self-activity of the subject. It is an attempt to impede the impulse, until such a time as it may attach itself to the interpersonal project that leads to its fulfillment: the project of union with another person, who is wanted not merely for his body, but for the person who is this body. Innocence is the disposition to avoid sexual encounter, except with the person whom one may fully desire. Children who have lost their innocence have acquired the habit of gratification through the body alone, in a state of partial or truncated desire. Their gratification is detached from the conditions of personal fulfillment and wanders from object to object with no settled tendency to attach itself to any, pursued all the while by a sense of the body's obscene dominion. "Debauching of the innocent" was traditionally regarded as a most serious offence, and one that offered genuine *harm* to the victim. The harm in question was not physical, but moral: the undermining of the process which prepares the child to enter the world of *erōs*. . . .

The personal and the sexual can become divorced in many ways. The task of sexual morality is to unite them, to sustain thereby the intentionality of desire, and to prepare the individual for erotic love. Sexual morality is the morality of embodiment: the posture which strives to unite us with our bodies, precisely in those situations when our bodies are foremost in our thoughts. Without such a morality the human world is subject to a dangerous divide, a gulf between self and body, at the verge of which all our attempts at personal union falter and withdraw. Hence the prime focus of sexual morality is not the attitude to others, but the attitude to one's own body and its uses. Its aim is to safeguard the integrity of our embodiment. Only on that condition, it is thought, can we inculcate either innocence in the young or fidelity in the adult. Such habits are, however, only one part of sexual virtue. Traditional morality has combined its praise of them with a condemnation of other things—in particular of the habits of lust and perversion. And it is not hard to find the reason for these condemnations.

Perversion consists precisely in a diverting of the sexual impulse from its interpersonal goal, or towards some act that is intrinsically destructive of personal relations and of the values that we find in them. The '"dissolution" of the flesh, which the Marquis de Sade regarded as so important an element in the sexual aim, is in fact the dissolution of the soul; the perversions described by de Sade are not so much attempts to destroy the flesh of the victim as to rid his flesh of its personal meaning, to wring out, with the blood, the rival perspective. That is true in one way or another of all perversion, which can be simply described as the habit of finding a sexual release that avoids or abolishes the *other,* obliterating his embodiment with the obscene perception of his body. Perversion is narcissistic, often solipsistic, involving strategies of replacement which are intrinsically destructive of personal feeling. Perversion therefore prepares us for a life without personal fulfillment, in which no human relation achieves foundation in the acceptance of the other, as this acceptance is provided by desire.

Lust may be defined as a genuine sexual desire, from which the goal of erotic love has been excluded, and in which whatever tends towards that goal—tenderness, intimacy, fidelity, dependence—is curtailed or obstructed. There need be nothing perverted in this. Indeed the special case of lust which I have discussed under the title of Don Juanism, in which the project of intimacy is constantly abbreviated by the flight towards another sexual object, provides one of our paradigms of desire. Nevertheless, the traditional condemnation of lust is far from arbitrary, and the associated contrast between lust and love far from a matter of convention. Lust is also a habit, involving the disposition to give way to desire, without regard to any personal relation with the object. (Thus perversions are all forms of lust even though lust is not in itself a perversion.) Naturally, we all feel the promptings of lust, but the rapidity with which sexual acts become sexual habits, and the catastrophic effect of a sexual act which cannot be remembered without shame or humiliation, give us strong reasons to resist them, reasons that Shakespeare captured in these words:

> Th'expence of Spirit in a waste of shame
> Is lust in action, and till action, lust
> Is perjur'd, murdrous, blouddy, full of blame,
> Savage, extreame, rude, cruell, not to trust,
> Injoyd no sooner but dispised straight,
> Past reason hunted, and no sooner had,
> Past reason hated as a swollowed bayt,
> On purpose layd to make the taker mad:
> Mad in pursuit and in possession so,
> Had, having, and in quest to have, extreame,
> A blisse in proofe, and prov'd, a very woe,
> Before a joy proposd, behind, a dreame,
> All this the world well knowes, yet none knowes well
> To shun the heaven that leads men to this hell.

In addition to the condemnation of lust and perversion, however, some part of traditional sexual education can be seen as a kind of sustained war against fantasy. It is undeniable that fantasy can play an important part in all our sexual doings, and even the most passionate and faithful lover may, in the act of love, rehearse to himself other scenes of sexual abandon than the one in which he is engaged. Nevertheless, there is truth in the contrast (familiar, in one version, from the writings of Freud)[3] between fantasy and reality, and in the sense that the first is in some way destructive of the second. Fantasy replaces the real, resistant, objective world with a pliant substitute—and that, indeed, is its purpose. Life in the actual world is difficult and embarrassing. Most of all it is difficult and embarrassing in our confrontation with other people, who, by their very existence, make demands that we may be unable or unwilling to meet. It requires a great force, such as the force of sexual desire, to overcome the embarrassment and self-protection that shield us from the most intimate encounters. It is tempting to take refuge in substitutes, which neither embarrass us nor resist the impulse of our spontaneous cravings. The habit grows, in masturbation, of creating a compliant world of desire, in which unreal objects become the focus of real emotions, and the emotions themselves are rendered incompetent to participate in the building of personal relations. The fantasy blocks the passage to reality, which becomes inaccessible to the will.

Even if the fantasy can be overcome so far as to engage in the act of love with another, a peculiar danger remains. The other becomes veiled in substitutes; he is never fully himself in the act of love; it is never clearly *him* that I desire, or *him* that I possess, but always rather a composite object, a universal body, of which he is but one among a potential infinity of instances. Fantasy fills our thoughts with a sense of the obscene, and the orgasm becomes, not the possession of another, but the expenditure of energy on his depersonalised body. Fantasies are private property, which I can dispose according to my will, with no answerability to the other whom I abuse through them. He, indeed, is of no intrinsic interest to me, and serves merely as my opportunity for self-regarding pleasure. For the fantasist, the ideal partner is indeed the prostitute, who, because she can be purchased, solves at once the moral problem presented by the presence of another at the scene of sexual release.

The connection between fantasy and prostitution is deep and important. The effect of fantasy is to "commodify" the object of desire, and to replace the law of sexual relationship between people with the law of the market. Sex itself can then be seen as a commodity:[4] something that we pursue and obtain in quantifiable form, and which comes in a variety of packages: in the form of a woman or a man; in the form of a film or a dream; in the form of a fetish or an animal. In so far as the sexual act is seen in this way, it seems morally neutral—or, at best, impersonal. Such criticism as may be offered will concern merely the dangers for the individual and his partner of this or that sexual package: for some bring diseases and discomforts of which others are free. The most harmless and hygienic act of all, on this view, is the act of masturbation, stimulated by whatever works of pornography are necessary to prompt the desire for it in the unimaginative. This justification for pornography has, indeed, recently been offered.

As I have already argued, however, fantasy does not exist comfortably with reality. It has a natural tendency to realise itself: to remake the world in its own image. The harmless wanker with the video-machine can at any moment turn into the desperate rapist with a gun. The "reality principle" by which the normal sexual act is regulated is a principle of personal encounter, which enjoins us to respect the other person, and to respect, also, the sanctity of his body, as the tangible expression of another self. The world of fantasy obeys no such rule, and is governed by monstrous myths and illusions which are at war with the human world—the illusions, for example, that women wish to be raped, that children have only to be awakened in order to give and receive the intensest sexual pleasure, that violence is not an affront but an affirmation of a natural right. All such myths, nurtured in fantasy, threaten not merely the consciousness of the man who lives by them, but also the moral structure of his surrounding world. They render the world unsafe for self and other, and cause the subject to look on everyone, not as an end in himself, but as a possible means to his private pleasure. In his world, the sexual encounter has been "fetishised," to use the apt Marxian term,[5] and every other human reality has been poisoned by the sense of the expendability and replaceability of the other.

It is a small step from the preoccupation with sexual virtue, to a condemnation of obscenity and pornography (which is its published form). Obscenity is a direct assault on the sentiment of desire, and therefore on the social order that is based in desire and which has personal love as its goal and fulfillment. There is no doubt that the normal conscience cannot remain neutral towards obscenity, any more than it can remain neutral towards paedophilia and rape (which is not to say that obscenity must also be treated as a *crime*). It is therefore unsurprising that traditional moral education has involved censorship of obscene material, and a severe emphasis on "purity in thought, word and deed"—an emphasis which is now greeted with irony or ridicule.

Traditional sexual education was, despite its exaggerations and imbecilities, truer to human nature than the libertarian culture which has succeeded it. Through considering its wisdom and its shortcomings, we may understand how to resuscitate an idea of sexual virtue, in accordance with the broad requirements of the Aristotelian argument that I have, in this chapter, been presenting. The ideal of virtue remains one of "sexual integrity": of a sexuality that is entirely integrated into the life of personal affection, and in which the self and its responsibility are centrally involved and indissolubly linked to the pleasures and passions of the body.

Traditional sexual morality has therefore been the morality of the body. Libertarian morality, by contrast, has relied almost entirely on a Kantian view of the human subject, as related to his body by no coherent moral tie. Focussing as he does on an idea of purely personal respect, and assigning no distinctive place to the body in our moral endeavour, the Kantian inevitably tends towards permissive morality. No sexual act can be wrong merely by virtue of its physical character, and the ideas of obscenity, pollution and perversion have no obvious application. His attitude to homosexuality is conveniently summarised in this passage from a Quaker pamphlet:

> We see no reason why the physical nature of the sexual act should be the criterion by which the question whether it is moral should be decided. An act which (for example) expresses true affection between two individuals and gives pleasure to them both, does not seem to us to be sinful by reason *alone* of the fact that it is homosexual. The same criteria seem to apply whether a relationship is heterosexual or homosexual.[6]

Such sentiments are the standard offering of the liberal and utilitarian moralities of our time. However much we may sympathise with their conclusions, it is not possible to accept the shallow reasoning that leads up to them. . . .

The reader may be reluctant to follow me in believing that traditional morality is largely justified by the ideal of sexual integrity. But if he accepts the main tenor of my argument, he must surely realise that the ethic of "liberation," far from promising the release of the self from hostile bondage, in fact heralds the dissipation of the self in loveless fantasy: th'expence of Spirit, in a waste of shame.

NOTES

1. Cf. the love poetry of Hafiz, of Omar Khayam, and of the Divan poets; and also the tales of faithful love in the *Thousand and One Nights.*
2. See Mary Douglas, *Implicit Meanings,* London, 1975, and *Purity and Danger,* London, 1966, for a study of the phenomena of disgust and pollution among African tribes.
3. "Formulations Regarding the Two Principles in Mental Functioning" (1911), in *Collected Papers,* tr. J. Riviere, New York, pp. 1924–50, vol. IV.
4. An eccentric and politicised, but frequently perceptive, critique of this "commodification" of sex is contained in Stephen Heath, *The Sexual Fix,* London, 1982.
5. Karl Marx, *Capital,* tr. S. Moore and E. Aveling, ed. F. Engels, London, 1887, vol. I, Part 1, ch. 1, section 4.
6. A. Heron (ed.), *Towards a Quaker View of Sex,* London, 1963, quoted in Ronald Atkinson, *Sexual Morality,* London, 1965, p. 148.

QUESTIONS FOR ANALYSIS

1. According to Scruton, sexual morality must be based on "the permanent features of human nature," not "the conditions of any particular person's life." What permanent features does he mean? Do all humans share them? If so, are they really permanent?
2. Scruton argues that masturbation is a pollution of the body. On what grounds? Do you agree?
3. Scruton bases much of his traditional sexual morality on the need to eliminate jealousy. Why? Do you consider this approach a sound one?
4. What does Scruton mean by "sexual integrity"? Why, in his view, does traditional sexual morality guarantee it and libertarian sexual morality compromise it? Do you think that there are other kinds of sexual integrity ignored by Scruton?
5. Although Scruton does not explicitly condemn homosexuality, he criticizes a common justification for it. Can his arguments in the rest of the essay be used to condemn homosexuality, or can they be used to support at least some homosexual relationships?

Plain Sex

ALAN H. GOLDMAN

In the following selection, Alan Goldman, professor of philosophy at the College of William and Mary, defends the libertarian position. Central to his argument is his rejection of what he calls "means-ends" scrutiny of sex analyses that treat sex as essentially a means to some further end like love, reproduction, or communication. To him, sexual desire is just the desire for contact with another person's body, and the goal sex is the pleasure such contact gives. Sex can also be a means of reproduction or of expressing love, he realizes, but those are extraneous purposes to the act of sex itself.

Given that analysis of sex, he concludes that sexual behavior cannot be morally evaluated by any norms other than those by which we evaluate any other kind of behavior—Kant's principle of respect for persons, for instance. We can distinguish perverted from normal sex, but perversion in this case is just a statistical notion, carrying no moral significance.

I

Several recent articles on sex herald its acceptance as a legitimate topic for analytic philosophers (although it has been a topic in philosophy since Plato). One might have thought conceptual analysis unnecessary in this area; despite the notorious struggles of judges and legislators to define pornography suitably, we all might be expected to know what sex is and to be able to identify at least paradigm sexual desires and activities without much difficulty. Philosophy is nevertheless of relevance here if for no other reason than that the concept of sex remains at the center of moral and social consciousness in our, and perhaps any, society. Before we can get a sensible view of the relation of sex to morality, perversion, social regulation, and marriage, we require a sensible analysis of the concept itself; one which neither understates its animal pleasure nor overstates its importance within a theory or system of value. I say "before," but the order is not quite so clear, for questions in this area, as elsewhere in moral philosophy, are both conceptual and normative at the same time. Our concept of sex will partially determine our moral view of it, but as philosophers we should formulate a concept that will accord with its proper moral status. What we require here, as elsewhere, is "reflective equilibrium," a goal not achieved by traditional and recent analyses together with their moral implications. Because sexual activity, like other natural functions such as eating or exercising, has become imbedded in layers of cultural, moral, and superstitious superstructure, it is hard to conceive it in its simplest terms. But partially for this reason, it is only by thinking about plain sex that we can begin to achieve this conceptual equilibrium.

I shall suggest here that sex continues to be misrepresented in recent writings, at least in philosophical writings, and I shall criticize the predominant form of analysis which I term "means-end analysis." Such conceptions attribute a necessary external goal or purpose to sexual activity, whether it be reproduction, the expression of love, simple communication, or interpersonal awareness. They analyze sexual activity as a means to one of these ends, implying that sexual desire is a desire to reproduce, to love or be loved, or to communicate with others. All definitions of this type suggest false views of the relation of sex to perversion and morality by implying that sex which does not fit one of these models or fulfill one of these functions is in some way deviant or incomplete.

The alternative, simpler analysis with which I will begin is that sexual desire is desire for contact with another person's body and for the pleasure which such contact produces; sexual activity is activity which tends to fulfill such desire of the agent. Whereas Aristotle and Butler were correct in holding that pleasure is normally a byproduct rather than a goal of purposeful action, in the case of sex this is not so clear. The desire for another's body is, principally among other things, the desire for the pleasure that physical contact brings. On the other hand, it is not a desire for a particular sensation detachable from its causal context, a sensation which can be derived in other ways. This definition in terms of the general goal of sexual desire appears preferable to an attempt to more explicitly list or define specific sexual activities, for many activities such as kissing, embracing, massaging, or holding hands may or may not be sexual, depending upon the context and more specifically upon the purposes, needs, or desires into which such activities fit. The generality of the definition also represents a refusal (common in recent psychological texts) to overemphasize orgasm as the goal of sexual desire or genital sex as the only norm of sexual activity (this will be hedged slightly in the discussion of perversion below).

Central to the definition is the fact that the goal of sexual desire and activity is the physical contact itself, rather than something else which this contact might express. By contrast, what I term "means-end analyses" posit ends which I take to be extraneous to plain sex, and they view sex as a means to these ends. Their fault lies not in defining sex in terms of its general goal, but in seeing plain sex as merely a means to other separable ends. I term these "means-end analyses" for convenience, although "means-separable-end analyses," while too cumbersome, might be more fully explanatory. The desire for physical contact with another person is a minimal criterion for (normal) sexual desire, but is both necessary and sufficient to qualify normal desire as sexual. Of course, we may want to express other feelings through sexual acts in various contexts; but without the desire for the physical contact in and for itself, or when it is sought for other reasons, activities in which contact is involved are not predominantly sexual. Furthermore, the desire for physical contact in itself, without the wish to express affection or other feelings through it, is sufficient to render sexual the activity of the agent which fulfills it. Various activities with this goal alone, such as kissing and caressing in certain contexts, qualify as sexual even without the presence of genital symptoms of sexual excitement. The latter are not therefore necessary criteria for sexual activity.

This initial analysis may seem to some either over- or underinclusive. It might seem too broad in leading us to interpret physical contact as sexual desire in activities such as football and other contact sports. In these cases, however, the desire is not for contact with another body per se, it is not directed toward a particular person for that purpose, and it is not the goal of the activity—the goal is winning or exercising or knocking someone down or displaying one's prowess. If the desire is purely for contact with another specific person's body, then to interpret it as sexual does not seem an exaggeration. A slightly more difficult case is that of a baby's desire to be cuddled and our natural response in wanting to cuddle it. In the case of the baby, the desire may be simply for the physical contact, for the pleasure of the caresses. If so, we may characterize this desire, especially in keeping with Freudian theory, as sexual or protosexual. It will differ nevertheless from full-fledged sexual desire in being more amorphous, not directed outward toward another specific person's body. It may also be that what the infant unconsciously desires is not physical contact per se but signs of affection, tenderness, or security, in which case we have further reason for hesitating to characterize its wants as clearly sexual. The intent of our response to the baby is often the showing of affection, not the pure physical contact, so that our definition in terms of action which fulfills sexual desire *on the part of the agent* does not capture such actions, whatever we say of the baby. (If it is intuitive to characterize our response as sexual as well, there is clearly no problem here for my analysis.) The same can be said of signs of affection (or in some cultures polite greeting) among men or women: these certainly need not be homosexual when the intent is only to show friendship, something extrinsic to plain sex although valuable when added to it.

Our definition of sex in terms of the desire for physical contact may appear too narrow in that a person's personality, not merely her or his body, may be sexually attractive to another, and in that looking or conversing in a certain way can be sexual in a given context without bodily contact. Nevertheless, it is not the contents of one's thoughts per se that are sexually appealing, but one's personality as embodied in certain manners of behavior. Furthermore, if a person is sexually attracted by another's personality, he or she will desire not just further conversation, but actual sexual contact. While looking at or conversing with someone can be interpreted as sexual in given contexts it is so when intended as preliminary to, and hence parasitic upon, elemental sexual interest. Voyeurism or viewing a pornographic movie qualifies as a sexual activity, but only as an imaginative substitute for the real thing (otherwise a deviation from the norm as expressed in our definition). The same is true of masturbation as a sexual activity without a partner.

That the initial definition indicates at least an ingredient of sexual desire and activity is too obvious to argue. We all know what sex is, at least in obvious cases, and do not need philosophers to tell us. My preliminary analysis is meant to serve as a contrast to what sex is not, at least, not necessarily. I concentrate upon the physically manifested desire for another's body, and I take as central the immersion in the physical aspect of one's own existence and attention to the physical embodiment of the other. One may derive pleasure in a sex act from expressing certain feelings to one's partner or from awareness of the attitude of one's partner, but sexual desire is essentially desire for physical contact itself: it is a bodily desire for the body of another that dominates our mental life for more or less brief periods. Traditional writings were correct to emphasize the purely physical or animal aspect of sex; they were wrong only in condemning it. This characterization of sex as an intensely pleasurable physical activity and acute physical desire may seem to some to capture only its barest level. But it is worth distinguishing and focusing upon this least common denominator in order to avoid the false views of sexual morality and perversion which emerge from thinking that sex is essentially something else.

II

We may turn then to what sex is not, to the arguments regarding supposed conceptual connections between sex and other activities which it is necessary to conceptually distinguish. The most comprehensible attempt to build an extraneous purpose into the sex act identifies that purpose as reproduction, its primary biological function. While this may be "nature's" purpose, it certainly need not be ours (the analogy with eating, while sometimes overworked, is pertinent here). While this identification may once have had a rational basis which also grounded the identification of the value and morality of sex with that applicable to reproduction and childrearing, the development of contraception rendered the connection weak. Methods of contraception are by now so familiar and so widely used that it is not necessary to dwell upon the changes wrought by these developments in the concept of sex itself and in a rational sexual ethic dependent upon that concept. In the past, the ever present possibility of children rendered the concepts of sex and sexual morality different from those required at present. There may be good reasons, if the presence and care of both mother and father are beneficial to children, for restricting reproduction to marriage. Insofar as society has a legitimate role in protecting children's interests, it may be justified in giving marriage a legal status, although this question is complicated by the fact (among others) that children born to single mothers deserve no penalties. In any case, the point here is simply that these questions are irrelevant at the present time to those regarding the morality of sex and its potential social regulation. (Further connections with marriage will be discussed below.)

It is obvious that the desire for sex is not necessarily a desire to reproduce, that the psychological manifestation has become, if it were not always, distinct from its biological roots. There are many parallels, as previously mentioned, with other natural functions. The pleasures of eating and exercising are to a large extent independent of their roles in nourishment or health (as the junk-food industry discovered with a vengeance). Despite the obvious parallel with sex, there is still a tendency for many to think that sex acts which can be reproductive are, if not more moral or less immoral, at least more natural. These categories of morality and "naturalness," or normality, are not to be identified with each other, as will be argued below, and neither is applicable to sex by virtue of its connection to reproduction. The tendency to identify reproduction as the conceptually connected end of sex is most prevalent now in the pronouncements of the Catholic church. There the assumed analysis is clearly tied to a restrictive sexual morality according to which acts become immoral and unnatural when they are not oriented towards reproduction, a morality which has independent roots in the Christian sexual ethic as it derives from Paul. However, the means-end analysis fails to generate a consistent sexual ethic: homosexual and oral-genital sex is condemned while kissing or caressing, acts equally unlikely to lead in themselves to fertilization, even when properly characterized as sexual according to our definition, are not.

III

Before discussing further relations of means-end analyses to false or inconsistent sexual ethics and concepts of perversion, I turn to other examples of these analyses. One common position views sex as essentially an expression of love or affection between the partners. It is generally recognized that there are other types of love besides sexual, but sex itself is taken as an expression of one type, sometimes termed "romantic" love.[1] Various factors again ought to weaken this identification. First, there are other types of love besides that which it is appropriate to express sexually, and "romantic" love itself can be expressed in many other ways. I am not denying that sex can take on heightened value and meaning when it becomes a vehicle for the expression of feelings of love or tenderness, but so can many other usually mundane activities such as getting up early to make breakfast on Sunday, cleaning the house, and so on. Second, sex itself can be used to communicate many other emotions besides love, and, as I will argue below, can communicate nothing in particular and still be good sex.

On a deeper level, an internal tension is bound to result from an identification of sex, which I have described as a physical-psychological desire, with love as a long-term, deep emotional relationship between two individuals. As this type of relationship, love is permanent, at least in intent, and more or less exclusive. A normal person cannot deeply love more than a few individuals even in a lifetime. We may be suspicious that those who attempt or claim to love many love them weakly if at all. Yet, fleeting sexual desire can arise in relation to a variety of other individuals one finds sexually attractive. It may even be, as some have claimed, that sexual desire in humans naturally seeks variety, while this is obviously false of love. For this reason, monogamous sex, even if justified, almost always represents a sacrifice or the exercise of self-control on the part of the spouses, while monogamous love generally does not. There is no such thing as casual love in the sense in which I intend the term "love." It may occasionally happen that a spouse falls deeply in love with someone else (especially when sex is conceived in terms of love), but this is relatively rare in comparison to passing sexual desires for others; and while the former often indicates a weakness or fault in the marriage relation, the latter does not.

If love is indeed more exclusive in its objects than is sexual desire, this explains why those who view sex as essentially an expression of love would again tend to hold a repressive or restrictive sexual ethic. As in the case of reproduction, there may be good reasons for reserving the total commitment of deep love to the context of marriage and family—the normal personality may not withstand additional divisions of ultimate commitment and allegiance. There is no question that marriage itself is best sustained by a deep relation of love and affection; and even if love is not naturally monogamous, the benefits of family units to children provide additional reason to avoid serious commitments elsewhere which weaken family ties. It can be argued similarly that monogamous sex strengthens families by restricting and at the same time guaranteeing an outlet for sexual desire in marriage. But there is more force to the argument that recognition of a clear distinction between sex and love in society would help avoid disastrous marriages which result from adolescent confusion of the two when sexual desire is mistaken for permanent love, and would weaken damaging jealousies which arise in marriages in relation to passing sexual desires. The love and affection of a sound marriage certainly differs from the adolescent romantic variety, which is often a mere substitute for sex in the context of a repressive sexual ethic.

In fact, the restrictive sexual ethic tied to the means-end analysis in terms of love again has failed to be consistent. At least, it has not been applied consistently, but forms part of the double standard which has curtailed the freedom of women. It is predictable in light of this history that some women would now advocate using sex as another kind of means, as a political weapon or as a way to increase unjustly denied power and freedom. The inconsistency in the sexual ethic typically attached to the sex-love analysis, according to which it has generally been taken with a grain of salt when applied to men, is simply another example of the impossibility of tailoring a plausible moral theory in this area to a conception of sex which builds in conceptually extraneous factors.

I am not suggesting here that sex ought never to be connected with love or that it is not a more significant and valuable activity when it is. Nor am I denying that individuals need love as much as sex and perhaps emotionally need at least one complete relationship which encompasses both. Just as sex can express love and take on heightened significance when it does, so love is often naturally accompanied by an intermittent desire for sex. But again love is accompanied appropriately by desires for other shared activities as well. What makes the desire for sex seem more intimately connected with love is the intimacy which is seen to be a natural feature of mutual sex acts. Like love, sex is held to lay one bare psychologically as well as physically. Sex is unquestionably intimate, but beyond that the psychological toll often attached may be a function of the restrictive sexual ethic itself, rather than a legitimate apology for it. The intimacy involved in love is psychologically consuming in a generally healthy way, while the psychological tolls of sexual relations, often including embarrassment as a correlate of intimacy, are too often the result of artificial sexual ethics and taboos. The intimacy involved in both love and sex is insufficient in any case in light of previous points to render a means-end analysis in these terms appropriate.

IV

In recent articles, Thomas Nagel and Robert Solomon, who recognize that sex is not merely a means to communicate love, nevertheless retain the form of this analysis while broadening it. For Solomon, sex remains a means of communicating (he explicitly uses the metaphor of body language), although the feelings that can be communicated now include, in addition to love and tenderness, domination, dependence, anger, trust, and so on.[2] Nagel does not refer explicitly to communication, but his analysis is similar in that he views sex as a complex form of interpersonal awareness in which desire itself is consciously communicated on several different levels. In sex, according to his analysis, two people are aroused by each other, aware of the other's arousal, and further aroused by this awareness.[3] Such multileveled conscious awareness of one's own and the other's desire is taken as the norm of a sexual relation, and this model is therefore close to that which views sex as a means of interpersonal communication.

Solomon's analysis is beset by the same difficulties as those pointed out in relation to the narrower sex-love concept. Just as love can be communicated by many activities other than sex, which do not therefore become properly analyzed as essentially vehicles of communication (making breakfast, cleaning the house, and so on), the same is true of the other feelings mentioned by Solomon. Domination can be communicated through economic manipulation, trust by a joint savings account. Driving a car can be simultaneously expressing anger, pride, joy, and so on. We may, in fact, communicate or express feelings in anything we do, but this does not make everything we do into language. Driving a car is not to be defined as an automotive means of communication, although with a little ingenuity we might work out an automotive vocabulary (tailgating as an expression of aggression or impatience; beating another car away from a stoplight as expressing domination) to match the vocabulary of "body language." That one can communicate various feelings during sex acts does not make these acts merely or primarily a means of communicating.

More importantly, to analyze sex as a means of communication is to overlook the intrinsic nature and value of the act itself. Sex is not a gesture or series of gestures, in fact not necessarily a means to any other end, but a physical activity intensely pleasurable in itself. When a language is used, the symbols normally have no importance in themselves; they function merely as vehicles for what can be communicated by them. Furthermore skill in the use of language is a technical achievement that must be carefully learned; if better sex is more successful communication by means of a more skillful use of body language, then we had all better be well schooled in the vocabulary and grammar. Solomon's analysis, which uses the language metaphor, suggests the appropriateness of a sex-manual approach, the substitution of a bit of technological prowess for the natural pleasure of the unforced surrender to feeling and desire.

It may be that Solomon's position could be improved by using the analogy of music rather than that of language, as an aesthetic form of communication. Music might be thought of as a form of aesthetic communicating, in which the experience of the "phonemes" themselves is generally pleasing. And listening to music is perhaps more of a sexual experience than having someone talk to you. Yet, it seems to me that insofar as music is aesthetic and pleasing in itself, it is not best conceived as primarily a means for communicating specific feelings. Such an analysis does injustice to aesthetic experience in much the same way as the sex-communication analysis debases sexual experience itself.[4]

For Solomon, sex that is not a totally self-conscious communicative art tends toward vulgarity,[5] whereas I would have thought it the other way around. This is another illustration of the tendency of means-end analyses to condemn what appears perfectly natural or normal sex on my account. Both Solomon and Nagel use their definitions, however, not primarily to stipulate moral norms for sex, as we saw in earlier analyses, but to define norms against which to measure perversion. Once again, neither is capable of generating consistency or reflective equilibrium with our firm intuitions as to what counts as subnormal sex, the problem being that both build factors into their norms which are extraneous to an unromanticized view of normal sexual desire and activity. If perversion represents a breakdown in communication, as Solomon maintains, then any unsuccessful or misunderstood advance should count as perverted. Furthermore, sex between husband and wife married for several years, or between any partners already familiar with each other, would be, if not perverted, nevertheless subnormal or trite and dull, in that the communicative content would be minimal in lacking all novelty. In fact the pleasures of sex need not wear off with familiarity, as they would if dependent upon the communicative content of the feelings. Finally, rather than a release or relief from physical desire through a substitute imaginative outlet, masturbation would become a way of practicing or rehearsing one's technique or vocabulary on oneself, or simply a way of talking to oneself, as Solomon himself says.[6]

Nagel fares no better in the implications of his overintellectualized norm. Spontaneous and heated sex between two familiar partners may well lack the complex conscious multileveled interpersonal awareness of which he speaks without being in the least perverted. The egotistical desire that one's partner be aroused by one's own desire does not seem a primary element of the sexual urge, and during sex acts one may like one's partner to be sometimes active and aroused, sometimes more passive. Just as sex can be more significant when love is communicated, so it can sometimes be heightened by an awareness of the other's desire. But at other times this awareness of an avid desire of one's partner can be merely distracting. The conscious awareness to which Nagel refers may actually impede the immersion in the physical of which I spoke above, just as may concentration upon one's "vocabulary" or technique. Sex is a way of relating to another, but primarily a physical rather than intellectual way. For Nagel, the ultimate in degeneration or perversion would have to be what he calls "mutual epidermal stimulation"[7] without mutual awareness of each other's state of mind. But this sounds like normal, if not ideal, sex to me (perhaps only a minimal description of it). His model certainly seems more appropriate to a sophisticated seduction scene than to the sex act itself,[8] which according to the model would often have to count as a subnormal anticlimax to the intellectual foreplay. While Nagel's account resembles Solomon's means-end analysis of sex, here the sex act itself does not even qualify as a preferred or central means to the end of interpersonal communication.

V

I have now criticized various types of analysis sharing or suggesting a common means-end form. I have suggested that analyses of this form relate to attempts to limit moral or natural sex to that which fulfills some purpose or function extraneous to basic sexual desire. The attempts to brand forms of sex outside the idealized models as immoral or perverted fail to achieve consistency with intuitions that they themselves do not directly question. The reproductive model brands oral-genital sex a deviation, but cannot account for kissing or holding hands; the communication account holds voyeurism to be perverted but cannot accommodate sex acts without much conscious thought or seductive nonphysical foreplay; the sex-love model makes most sexual desire seem degrading or base. The first and last condemn extramarital sex on the sound but irrelevant grounds that reproduction and deep commitment are best confined to family contexts. The romanticization of sex and the confusion of sexual desire with love operate in both directions: sex outside the context of romantic love is repressed; once it is repressed, partners become more difficult to find and sex becomes romanticized further, out of proportion to its real value for the individual.

What all these analyses share in addition to a common form is accordance with and perhaps derivation from the Platonic-Christian moral tradition, according to which the animal or purely physical element of humans is the source of immorality, and plain sex in the sense I defined it is an expression of this element, hence in itself to be condemned. All the analyses examined seem to seek a distance from sexual desire itself in attempting to extend it conceptually beyond the physical. The love and communication analyses seek refinement or intellectualization of the desire; plain physical sex becomes vulgar, and too straightforward sexual encounters without an aura of respectable cerebral communicative content are to be avoided. Solomon explicitly argues that sex cannot be a "mere" appetite, his argument being that if it were, subway exhibitionism and other vulgar forms would be pleasing.[9] This fails to recognize that sexual desire can be focused or selective at the same time as being physical. Lower animals are not attracted by every other member of their species, either. Rancid food forced down one's throat is not pleasing, but that certainly fails to show that hunger is not a physical appetite. Sexual desire lets us know that we are physical beings and, indeed, animals; this is why traditional Platonic morality is so thorough in its condemnation. Means-end analyses continue to reflect this tradition, sometimes unwittingly. They show that in conceptualizing sex it is still difficult, despite years of so-called revolution in this area, to free ourselves from the lingering suspicion that plain sex as physical desire is an expression of our "lower selves," that yielding to our animal natures is subhuman or vulgar.

VI

Having criticized these analyses for the sexual ethics and concepts of perversion they imply, it remains to contrast my account along these lines.

To the question of what morality might be implied by my analysis, the answer is that there are no moral implications whatever. Any analysis of sex which imputes a moral character to sex acts in themselves is wrong for that reason. There is no morality intrinsic to sex, although general moral rules apply to the treatment of others in sex acts as they apply to all human relations. We can speak of a sexual ethic as we can speak of a business ethic, without implying that business in itself is either moral or immoral or that special rules are required to judge business practices which are not derived from rules that apply elsewhere as well. Sex is not in itself a moral category, although like business it invariably places us into relations with others in which moral rules apply. It gives us opportunity to do what is otherwise recognized as wrong, to harm others, deceive them or manipulate them against their wills. Just as the fact that an act is sexual in itself never renders it wrong or adds to its wrongness if it is wrong on other grounds (sexual acts towards minors are wrong on other grounds, as will be argued below), so no wrong act is to be excused because done from a sexual motive. If a "crime of passion" is to be excused, it would have to be on grounds of temporary insanity rather than sexual context (whether insanity does constitute a legitimate excuse for certain actions is too big a topic to argue here). Sexual motives are among others which may become deranged, and the fact that they are sexual has no bearing in itself on the moral character, whether negative or exculpatory, of the actions deriving from them. Whatever might be true of war, it is certainly not the case that all's fair in love or sex.

Our first conclusion regarding morality and sex is therefore that no conduct otherwise immoral should be excused because it is sexual conduct, and nothing in sex is immoral unless condemned by rules which apply elsewhere as well. The last clause requires further clarification. Sexual conduct can be governed by particular rules relating only to sex itself. But these precepts must be implied by general moral rules when these are applied to specific sexual relations or types of conduct. The same is true of rules of fair business, ethical medicine, or courtesy in driving a car. In the latter case, particular acts on the road may be reprehensible, such as tailgating or passing on the right, which seem to bear no resemblance as actions to any outside the context of highway safety. Nevertheless their immorality derives from the fact that they place others in danger, a circumstance which, when avoidable, is to be condemned in any context. This structure of general and specifically applicable rules describes a reasonable sexual ethic as well. To take an extreme case, rape is always a sexual act and it is always immoral. A rule against rape can therefore be considered an obvious part of sexual morality which has no bearing on nonsexual conduct. But the immorality of rape derives from its being an extreme violation of a person's body, of the right not to be humiliated, and of the general moral prohibition against using other persons against their wills, not from the fact that it is a sexual act.

The application elsewhere of general moral rules to sexual conduct is further complicated by the fact that it will be relative to the particular desires and preferences of one's partner (these may be influenced by and hence in some sense include misguided beliefs about sexual morality itself). This means that there will be fewer specific rules in the area of sexual ethics than in other areas of conduct, such as driving cars, where the relativity of preference is irrelevant to the prohibition of objectively dangerous conduct. More reliance will have to be placed upon the general moral rule, which in this area holds simply that the preferences, desires, and interests of one's partner or potential partner ought to be taken into account. This rule is certainly not specifically formulated to govern sexual relations; it is a form of the central principle of morality itself. But when applied to sex, it prohibits certain actions, such as molestation of children, which cannot be categorized as violations of the rule without at the same time being classified as sexual. I believe this last case is the closest we can come to an action which is wrong *because* it is sexual, but even here its wrongness is better characterized as deriving from the detrimental effects such behavior can have on the future emotional and sexual life of the naive victims, and from the fact that such behavior therefore involves manipulation of innocent persons without regard for their interests. Hence, this case also involves violation of a general moral rule which applies elsewhere as well.

Aside from faulty conceptual analyses of sex and the influence of the Platonic moral tradition, there are two more plausible reasons for thinking that there are moral dimensions intrinsic to sex acts per se. The first is that such acts are normally intensely pleasurable. According to a hedonistic, utilitarian moral theory they therefore should be at least prima facie morally right, rather than morally neutral in themselves. To me this seems incorrect and reflects unfavorably on the ethical theory in question. The pleasure intrinsic to sex acts is a good, but not, it seems to me, a good with much positive moral significance. Certainly I can have no duty to pursue such pleasure myself, and while it may be nice to give pleasure of any form to others, there is no ethical requirement to do so, given my right over my own body. The exception relates to the context of sex acts themselves, when one partner derives pleasure from the other and ought to return the favor. This duty to reciprocate takes us out of the domain of hedonistic utilitarianism, however, and into a Kantian moral framework, the central principles of which call for just such reciprocity in human relations. Since independent moral judgments regarding sexual activities constitute one area in which ethical theories are to be tested, these observations indicate here, as I believe others indicate elsewhere, the fertility of the Kantian, as opposed to the utilitarian, principle in reconstructing reasoned moral consciousness.

It may appear from this alternative Kantian viewpoint that sexual acts must be at least prima facie wrong in themselves. This is because they invariably involve at different stages the manipulation of one's partner for one's own pleasure, which might appear to be prohibited on the formulation of Kant's principle which holds that one ought not to treat another as a means to such private ends. A more realistic rendering of this formulation, however, one which recognizes its intended equivalence to the first universalizability principle, admits no such absolute prohibition. Many human relations, most economic transactions for example, involve using other individuals for personal benefit. These relations are immoral only when they are one-sided, when the benefits are not mutual, or when the transactions are not freely and rationally endorsed by all parties. The same holds true of sexual acts. The central principle governing them is the Kantian demand for reciprocity in sexual relations. In order to comply with the principle, one must recognize the subjectivity of one's partner (not merely by being aroused by her or his desire, as Nagel describes). Even in an act which by its nature "objectifies" the other, one recognizes a partner as a subject with demands and desires by yielding to those desires, by allowing oneself to be a sexual object as well, by giving pleasure or ensuring that the pleasures of the acts are mutual. It is this kind of reciprocity which forms the basis for morality in sex, which distinguishes right acts from wrong in this area as in others. (Of course, prior to sex acts one must gauge their effects upon potential partners and take these longer range interests into account.)

VII

I suggested earlier that in addition to generating confusion regarding the rightness or wrongness of sex acts, false conceptual analyses of the means-end form cause confusion about the value of sex to the individual. My account recognizes the satisfaction of desire and the pleasure this brings as the central psychological function of the sex act for the individual. Sex affords us a paradigm of pleasure, but not a cornerstone of value. For most of us it is not only a needed outlet for desire but also the most enjoyable form of recreation we know. Its value is nevertheless easily mistaken by being confused with that of love, when it is taken as essentially an expression of that emotion. Although intense, the pleasures of sex are brief and repetitive rather than cumulative. They give value to the specific acts which generate them, but not the lasting kind of value which enhances one's whole life. The briefness of these pleasures contributes to their intensity (or perhaps their intensity makes them necessarily brief), but it also relegates them to the periphery of most rational plans for the good life.

By contrast, love typically develops over a long term relation; while its pleasures may be less intense and physical, they are of more cumulative value. The importance of love to the individual may well be central in a rational system of value. And it has perhaps an even deeper moral significance relating to the identification with the interests of another person, which broadens one's possible relationships with others as well. Marriage is again important in preserving this relation between adults and children, which seems as important to the adults as it is to the children in broadening concerns which have a tendency to become selfish. Sexual desire, by contrast, is desire for another which is nevertheless essentially self-regarding. Sexual pleasure is certainly a good for the individual, and for many it may be necessary in order for them to function in a reasonably cheerful way. But it bears little relation to those other values just discussed, to which some analyses falsely suggest a conceptual connection.

VIII

While my initial analysis lacks moral implications in itself, as it should, it does suggest by contrast a concept of sexual perversion. Since the concept of perversion is itself a sexual concept, it will always be defined relative to some definition of normal sex; and any conception of the norm will imply a contrary notion of perverse forms. The concept suggested by my account again differs sharply from those implied by the means-end analyses examined above. Perversion does not represent a deviation from the reproductive function (or kissing would be perverted), from a loving relationship (or most sexual desire and many heterosexual acts would be perverted), or from efficiency in communicating (or unsuccessful seduction attempts would be perverted). It is a deviation from a norm, but the norm in question is merely statistical. Of course, not all sexual acts that are statistically unusual are perverted—a three-hour continuous sexual act would be unusual but not necessarily abnormal in the requisite sense. The abnormality in question must relate to the *form of the desire* itself in order to constitute sexual perversion; for example, desire, not for contact with another, but for merely looking, for harming or being harmed, for contact with items of clothing. This concept of sexual abnormality is that suggested by my definition of normal sex in terms of its typical desire. However, not all unusual desires qualify either, only those with the typical physical sexual effects upon the individual who satisfies them. These effects, such as erection in males, were not built into the original definition of sex in terms of sexual desire, for they do not always occur in activities that are properly characterized as sexual, say, kissing for the pleasure of it. But they do seem to bear a closer relation to the definition of activities as perverted. (For those who consider only genital sex sexual, we could build such symptoms into a narrower definition, then speaking of sex in a broad sense as well as "proper" sex.)

Solomon and Nagel disagree with this statistical notion of perversion. For them the concept is evaluative rather than statistical. I do not deny that the term "perverted" is often used evaluatively (and purely emotively for that matter), or that it has a negative connotation for the average speaker. I do deny that we can find a norm, other than that of statistically usual desire, against which all and only activities that properly count as sexual perversions can be contrasted. Perverted sex is simply abnormal sex, and if the norm is not to be an idealized or romanticized extraneous end or purpose, it must express the way human sexual desires usually manifest themselves. Of course not all norms in other areas of discourse need be statistical in this way. Physical health is an example of a relatively clear norm which does not seem to depend upon the numbers of healthy people. But the concept in this case achieves its clarity through the connection of physical health with other clearly desirable physical functions and characteristics, for example, living longer. In the case of sex, that which is statistically abnormal is not necessarily incapacitating in other ways, and yet these abnormal desires with sexual effects upon their subject do count as perverted to the degree to which their objects deviate from usual ones. The connotations of the concept of perversion beyond those connected with abnormality or statistical deviation derive more from the attitudes of those likely to call certain acts perverted than from specifiable features of the acts themselves. These connotations add to the concept of abnormality that of *sub*normality, but there is no norm against which the latter can be measured intelligibly in accord with all and only acts intuitively called perverted.

The only proper evaluative norms relating to sex involve degrees of pleasure in the acts and moral norms, but neither of these scales coincides with statistical degrees of abnormality, according to which perversion is to be measured. The three parameters operate independently (this was implied for the first two when it was held above that the pleasure of sex is a good, but not necessarily a moral good). Perverted sex may be more or less enjoyable to particular individuals than normal sex, and more or less moral, depending upon the particular relations involved. Raping a sheep may be more perverted than raping a woman, but certainly not more condemnable morally.[10] It is nevertheless true that the evaluative connotations attaching to the term "perverted" derive partly from the fact that most people consider perverted sex highly immoral. Many such acts are forbidden by longstanding taboos, and it is sometimes difficult to distinguish what is forbidden from what is immoral. Others, such as sadistic acts, are genuinely immoral, but again not at all because of their connection with sex or abnormality. The principles which condemn these acts would condemn them equally if they were common and nonsexual. It is not true that we properly could continue to consider acts perverted which were found to be very common practice across societies. Such acts, if harmful, might continue to be condemned properly as immoral, but it was just shown that the immorality of an act does not vary with its degree of perversion. If not harmful, common acts previously considered abnormal might continue to be called perverted for a time by the moralistic minority; but the term when applied to such cases would retain only its emotive negative connotation without consistent logical criteria for application. It would represent merely prejudiced moral judgments.

To adequately explain why there is a tendency to so deeply condemn perverted acts would require a treatise in psychology beyond the scope of this paper. Part of the reason undoubtedly relates to the tradition of repressive sexual ethics and false conceptions of sex; another part to the fact that all abnormality seems to disturb and fascinate us at the same time. The former explains why sexual perversion is more abhorrent to many than other forms of abnormality; the latter indicates why we tend to have an emotive and evaluative reaction to perversion in the first place. It may be, as has been suggested according to a Freudian line,[11] that our uneasiness derives from latent desires we are loathe to admit, but this thesis takes us into psychological issues I am not competent to judge. Whatever the psychological explanation, it suffices to point out here that the conceptual connection between perversion and genuine or consistent moral evaluation is spurious and again suggested by misleading means-end idealizations of the concept of sex.

The position I have taken in this paper against those concepts is not totally new. Something similar to it is found in Freud's view of sex, which of course was genuinely revolutionary, and in the body of writings deriving from Freud to the present time. But in his revolt against romanticized and repressive conceptions, Freud went too far—from a refusal to view sex as merely a means to a view of it as the end of all human behavior, although sometimes an elaborately disguised end. This pansexualism led to the thesis (among others) that repression was indeed an inevitable and necessary part of social regulation of any form, a strange consequence of a position that began by opposing the repressive aspects of the means-end view. Perhaps the time finally has arrived when we can achieve a reasonable middle ground in this area, at least in philosophy if not in society.

NOTES

1. Even Bertrand Russell, whose writing in this area was a model of rationality, at least for its period, tends to make this identification and to condemn plain sex in the absence of love: "sex intercourse apart from love has little value, and is to be regarded primarily as experimentation with a view to love." *Marriage and Morals* (New York: Bantam, 1959), p. 87.
2. Robert Solomon, "Sex and Perversion," *Philosophy and Sex,* ed. R. Baker and F. Elliston (Buffalo: Prometheus, 1975).

3. Thomas Nagel, "Sexual Perversion," *The Journal of Philosophy* 66, no. 1 (16 January 1969).
4. Sex might be considered (at least partially) as communication in a very broad sense in the same way as performing ensemble music, in the sense that there is in both ideally a communion or perfectly shared experience with another. This is, however, one possible ideal view whose central feature is not necessary to sexual acts or desire per se. And in emphasizing the communication of specific feelings by means of body language, the analysis under consideration narrows the end to one clearly extrinsic to plain and even good sex.
5. Solomon, pp. 284–285.
6. Ibid., p. 283. One is reminded of Woody Allen's rejoinder to praise of his technique: "I practice a lot when I'm alone."
7. Nagel, p. 15.
8. Janice Moulton made the same point in a paper at the Pacific APA meeting, March 1976.
9. Solomon, p. 285.
10. The example is like one from Sara Ruddick, "Better Sex," *Philosophy and Sex,* p. 96.
11. See Michael Slote, "Inapplicable Concepts and Sexual Perversion," *Philosophy and Sex.*

QUESTIONS FOR ANALYSIS

1. What is the significance of this essay's title?
2. According to Goldman, "We all know what sex is, at least in obvious cases, and we do not need philosophers to tell us." Do you agree? Does his analysis of sex agree with what we all know?
3. In rejecting the view that the purpose of sex is reproduction, Goldman compares sex to eating. What's the point of the comparison? Is it a good one?
4. What contrasts does Goldman draw between love and sexual desire?
5. Why does Goldman believe that perversion is not an evaluative norm against which we can judge sexual behavior?
6. Goldman claims that there is no morality intrinsic to sex. What does he mean by that? What are his reasons for claiming it?
7. In considering various means-ends analyses of sex, has Goldman missed any purpose of sex that you think important?

Why Homosexuality Is Abnormal

MICHAEL LEVIN

In this selection from a much longer essay, Michael Levin, professor of philosophy at City College of New York, defends three positions on homosexuality: that it is abnormal, that it leads to unhappiness, and that it should not be legalized.

In defending the first position, Levin gives an evolutionary definition of the function of a body part: a body part is for a given activity if it helps its host, and if this contribution is how the body part got where it is and stays there. Based on that definition, he concludes that homosexuality involves the misuse of sexual organs and is therefore abnormal. In defending the second position, he argues that homosexuals are in fact less happy than heterosexuals and that there is good evolutionary reason for their relative unhappiness. In defending the third position, he argues that legalization would convey societal approval of homosexuality, which would encourage children to take up a way of life that creates unhappiness.

It is important to note that Levin is not using the unnaturalness argument discussed earlier in this chapter. He does not consider homosexuality immoral in itself, and he explicitly says that the term *abnormal* should not be taken in an evaluative or normative way.

INTRODUCTION

This paper defends the view that homosexuality is abnormal and hence undesirable—not because it is immoral or sinful, or because it weakens society or hampers evolutionary development, but for a purely mechanical reason. It is a misuse of bodily parts. Clear empirical sense attaches to the idea of *the use* of such bodily parts as genitals, the idea that they are *for* something, and consequently to the idea of their misuse. I argue on grounds involving natural selection that misuse of bodily parts can with high probability be connected to unhappiness. I regard these matters as prolegomena to such policy issues as the rights of homosexuals, the rights of those desiring not to associate with homosexuals, and legislation concerning homosexuality, issues which I shall not discuss systematically here. However, I do in the last section draw a seemingly evident corollary from my view that homosexuality is abnormal and likely to lead to unhappiness. . . .

Despite the publicity currently enjoyed by the claim that one's "sexual preference" is nobody's business but one's own, the intuition that there is something unnatural about homosexuality remains vital. The erect penis fits the vagina, and fits it better than any other natural orifice; penis and vagina seem made for each other. This intuition ultimately derives from, or is another way of capturing, the idea that the penis is not *for* inserting into the anus of another man—that so using the penis is not the way it is *supposed*, even *intended*, to be used. Such intuitions may appear to rest on an outmoded teleological view of nature, but recent work in the logic of functional ascription shows how they may be explicated, and justified, in suitable naturalist terms. . . .

ON "FUNCTION" AND ITS COGNATES

To bring into relief the point of the idea that homosexuality involves a misuse of bodily parts, I will begin with an uncontroversial case of misuse, a case in which the clarity of our intuitions is not obscured by the conviction that they are untrustworthy. Mr. Jones pulls all his teeth and strings them around his neck because he thinks his teeth look nice as a necklace. He takes pureéd liquids supplemented by intravenous solutions for nourishment. It is surely natural to say that Jones is misusing his teeth, that he is not using them for what they are for, that indeed the way he is using them is incompatible with what they are for. Pedants might argue that Jones's teeth are no longer part of him and hence that he is not misusing any bodily parts. To them, I offer Mr. Smith, who likes to play "Old MacDonald" on his teeth. So devoted is he to this amusement, in fact, that he never uses his teeth for chewing—like Jones, he takes nourishment intravenously. Now, not only do we find it perfectly plain that Smith and Jones are misusing their teeth, we predict a dim future for them on purely physiological grounds; we expect the muscles of Jones's jaw that are used for—that *are* for—chewing to lose their tone, and we expect this to affect Jones's gums. Those parts of Jones's digestive tract that are for processing solids will also suffer from disuse. The net result will be deteriorating health and perhaps a shortened life. Nor is this all. Human beings enjoy chewing. Not only has natural selection selected in muscles for chewing and favored creatures with such muscles, it has selected in a tendency to find the use of those muscles reinforcing. Creatures who do not enjoy using such parts of their bodies as deteriorate with disuse, will tend to be selected out. Jones, product of natural selection that he is, descended from creatures who at least tended to enjoy the use of such parts. Competitors who didn't simply had fewer descendants. So we expect Jones sooner or later to experience vague yearnings to chew something, just as we find people who take no exercise to experience a general listlessness. Even waiving for now my apparent reification of the evolutionary process, let me emphasize how little anyone is tempted to say "each to his own" about Jones or to regard Jones's disposition of his teeth as simply a deviation from a statistical norm. This sort of case is my paradigm when discussing homosexuality.

The main obstacle to talk of what a process or organic structure is for is that, literally understood, such talk presupposes an agent who intends that structure or process to be used in a certain way. Talk of function derives its primitive meaning from the human use of artifacts, artifacts being for what purposive agents intend them for. Indeed, there is in this primitive context a natural reason for using something for what it is for: to use it otherwise would frustrate the intention of some purposeful agent. Since it now seems clear that our bodily parts were not emplaced by purposeful agency, it is easy to dismiss talk of what they are for as "theologically" based on a faulty theory of how we came to be built as we are, . . .

Until recently, philosophers of science half-countered, half-conceded such doubts by "rationally reconstructing" the locution "structure *S* is for function *F* in organism *O*" as—omitting inessential refinements—"*S*'s doing *F* in *O* is necessary for the integrity or prosperity of *O*," . . . This, the classical analysis, suffers from two weaknesses. First, it quite severs the link stressed earlier between a structure's having a function and the inadvisability of using that structure in a way inconsistent with its function. An organism may not be interested in survival, or prosperity, or the prosperity of some genetically defined group that contains the organism. The classical analysis provides no clue as to why Jones should desist from stringing his teeth on a necklace. It must be supplemented with the premise that survival or fitness are desirable, and however strong the desire to survive may be as a *de facto* motive, there are too many cogent arguments against survival as a basic norm for this supplement to be plausible. . . .

The more decisive second objection to the classical analysis is the existence of clear counter-examples—counter-examples that turn out, on reflection, to be connected to the first objection. An accidentally incurred heart lesion might be necessary for the heart's pumping blood if it is otherwise diseased; but the lesion is not *for* pumping blood. A patient's heartbeat might be the only way his doctor can diagnose a disease that would be fatal if undiagnosed; but the beat of his heart is not *for* diagnosis. Such cases suggest that the classical analysis pays insufficient attention to how structures come to be in organisms and why they persist in reproductive cohorts. In light of this, a more adequate explication . . . runs . . . an organ is for a given activity if the organ's performing that activity helps its host or organisms suitably related to its host, *and* if this contribution is how the organ got and stays where it is. This disqualifies the fortuitous heart lesion and the symptomatic heartbeat, which did not arise or persist by increasing (inclusive) fitness. This definition also distinguishes what something is for from what it may be *used* for on some occasion. Teeth are for chewing—we have teeth because their use in chewing favored the survival of organisms with teeth—whereas Jones is using his teeth for ornamentation. . . .

Nature is interested in making its creatures like what is (inclusively) good for them. A creature that does not enjoy using its teeth for chewing uses them less than does a toothed competitor who enjoys chewing. Since the use of teeth for chewing favors the survival of an individual with teeth, and, other things being equal, traits favorable to the survival of individuals favor survival of the relevant cohort, toothed creatures who do not enjoy chewing tend to get selected out. We today are the filtrate of this process, descendants of creature who like to chew. . . .

And here—to return to the main strand of the argument—is why it is advisable to use your organs for what they are for: you will enjoy it. Jones's behavior is ill-advised not only because of the avertible objective consequences of his defanging himself, but because he will feel that something is missing. Similarly, this is why you should exercise. It is not just that muscles are for running. We have already heard the sceptic's reply to that: "So what? Suppose I don't mind being flabby? Suppose I don't give a hang about what will propagate my genetic cohort?" Rather, running is good because nature made sure people like to run. This is, of course, the prudential "good," not the moral "good"—but I disavowed at the outset the doctrine that misuse of bodily parts is *morally* bad, at least in any narrow sense. You ought to run because running was once necessary for catching food: creatures who did not enjoy running, if there ever were any, caught less food and reproduced less frequently than competitors who enjoyed running. These competitors passed on their appetites along with their muscles *to you*. This is not to say that those who suffer the affective consequences of laziness must recognize them as such, or even be able to identify them against their general background feeling-tone. They may not realize they would feel better if they exercised. They may even doubt it. They may have allowed their muscles to deteriorate beyond the point at which satisfying exercise is possible. For all that, evolution has decreed that a life involving regular exercise is on the whole more enjoyable than a life without. The same holds for every activity that is the purpose of an organ. . . .

APPLICATIONS TO HOMOSEXUALITY

The application of this general picture to homosexuality should be obvious. There can be no reasonable doubt that one of the functions of the penis is to introduce semen into the vagina. It does this, and it has been selected in because it does this. . . . Nature has consequently made this use of the penis rewarding. It is clear enough that any proto-human males who found unrewarding the insertion of penis into vagina have left no descendants. In particular, proto-human males who enjoyed inserting their penises into each other's anuses have left no descendants. This is why homosexuality is abnormal, and why its abnormality counts prudentially against it. Homosexuality is likely to cause unhappiness because it leaves unfulfilled an innate and innately rewarding desire. And should the reader's environmentalism threaten to get the upper hand, let me remind him again of an unproblematic case. Lack of exercise is bad and even abnormal not only because it is unhealthy but also because one feels poorly without regular exercise. Nature made exercise rewarding because, until recently, we had to exercise to survive. Creatures who found running after game unrewarding were eliminated. Laziness leaves unreaped the rewards nature has planted in exercise, even if the lazy man cannot tell this introspectively. If this is a correct description of the place of exercise in human life, it is by the same token a correct description of the place of heterosexuality.

It hardly needs saying, but perhaps I should say it anyway, that this argument concerns tendencies and probabilities. Generalizations about human affairs being notoriously "true by and large and for the most part" only, saying that homosexuals are bound to be less happy than heterosexuals must be understood as short for "Not coincidentally, a larger proportion of homosexuals will be unhappy than a corresponding selection of the heterosexual population." There are, after all, genuinely jolly fat men. To say that laziness leads to adverse affective consequences means that, because of our evolutionary history, the odds are relatively good that a man who takes no exercise will suffer adverse affective consequences. Obviously, some people will get away with misusing their bodily parts. Thus, when evaluating the empirical evidence that bears on this account, it will be pointless to cite cases of well-adjusted homosexuals. I do not say they are non-existent; my claim is that, of biological necessity, they are rare.

My argument might seem to show at most that heterosexual behavior is (self-) reinforcing, not that homosexuality is self-extinguishing—that homosexuals go without the built-in rewards of heterosexuality, but not that homosexuality has a built-in punishment. This distinction, however, is merely verbal. They are two different ways of saying that homosexuals will find their lives less rewarding than will heterosexuals. Even if some line demarcated happiness from unhappiness absolutely, it would be irrelevant if homosexuals were all happily above the line. It is the comparison with the heterosexual life that is at issue. A lazy man might count as happy by some mythic absolute standard, but he is likely to be less happy than someone otherwise like him who exercises. . . .

Talk of what is "in the genes" inevitably provokes the observation that we should not blame homosexuals for their homosexuality if it is "in their genes." True enough. Indeed, since nobody decides what he is going to find sexually arousing, the moral appraisal of sexual object "choice" is entirely absurd. However, so saying is quite consistent with regarding homosexuality as a misfortune, and taking steps—this is being within the realm of the will—to minimize its incidence, especially among children. Calling homosexuality involuntary does not place it outside the scope of evaluation. Victims of sickle cell anemia are not blameworthy, but it is absurd to pretend that there is nothing wrong with them. Homosexual activists are partial to genetic explanations and hostile to Freudian environmentalism in part because they see a genetic cause as exempting homosexuals from blame. But surely people are equally blameless for indelible traits acquired in early childhood. And anyway, a blameless condition may still be worth trying to prevent. . . .

Utilitarians must take the present evolutionary scenario seriously. The utilitarian attitude toward homosexuality usually runs something like this: even if homosexuality is in some sense unnatural, as a matter of brute fact homosexuals take pleasure in sexual contact with members of the same sex. As long as they don't hurt anyone else, homosexuality is as great a good as heterosexuality. But the matter cannot end here. Not even a utilitarian doctor would have words of praise for a degenerative disease that happened to foster a certain kind of pleasure (as sore muscles uniquely conduce to the pleasure of stretching them). A utilitarian doctor would presumably try just as zealously to cure diseases that feel good as less pleasant degenerative diseases. A pleasure causally connected with great distress cannot be treated as just another pleasure to be toted up on the felicific scoreboard. Utilitarians have to reckon with the inevitable consequences of pain-causing pleasure.

Similar remarks apply to the question of whether homosexuality is a "disease." A widely-quoted pronouncement of the American Psychiatric Association runs:

> Surely the time has come for psychiatry to give up the archaic practice of classifying the millions of men and women who accept or prefer homosexual object choices as being, by virtue of that fact alone, mentally ill. The fact that their alternative life-style happens to be out of favor with current cultural conventions must not be a basis in itself for a diagnosis.

Apart from some question-begging turns of phrase, this is right. One's taste for mutual anal intercourse is nothing "in itself" for one's psychiatrist to worry about, any more than a life of indolence is anything "in itself" for one's doctor to worry about. In fact, in itself there is nothing wrong with a broken arm or an occluded artery. The fact that my right ulna is now in two pieces is just a fact of nature, not a "basis for diagnosis." But this condition is a matter for medical science anyway, because it will lead to pain. Permitted to persist, my fracture will provoke increasingly punishing states. So if homosexuality is a reliable sign of present or future misery, it is beside the point that homosexuality is not "by virtue of the that fact alone" a mental illness. . . .

EVIDENCE AND FURTHER CLARIFICATION

I have argued that homosexuality is "abnormal" in both a descriptive and a normative sense because—for evolutionary reasons—homosexuals are bound to be unhappy. In Kantian terms, I have explained how it is possible for homosexuality to be unnatural even if it violates no cosmic purpose or such purposes as we retrospectively impose on nature. What is the evidence for my view? For one thing, by emphasizing homosexual unhappiness, my view explains a ubiquitous fact in a simple way. The fact is the universally acknowledged unhappiness of homosexuals. Even the staunchest defenders of homosexuality admit that, as of now, homosexuals are not happy. . . .

The usual environmentalist explanation for homosexuals' unhappiness is the misunderstanding, contempt and abuse that society heaps on them. But this not only leaves unexplained why society has this attitude, it sins against parsimony by explaining a nearly universal phenomenon in terms of variable circumstances that have, by coincidence, the same upshot. Parsimony urges that we seek the explanation of homosexual unhappiness in the nature of homosexuality itself, as my explanation does. Having to "stay in the closet" may be a great strain, but is does not account for all the miseries that writers on homosexuality say is the homosexual's lot. . . .

It is interesting to reflect on a natural experiment that has gotten under way in the [past] decade. . . . A remarkable change in public opinion, if not private sentiment, has occurred in

America. For whatever reason—the prodding of homosexual activists, the desire not to seem like a fuddy-duddy—various organs of opinion are now hard at work providing a "positive image" for homosexuals. Judges allow homosexuals to adopt their lovers. The Unitarian Church now performs homosexual marriages. Hollywood produces highly sanitized movies like *Making Love* and *Personal Best* about homosexuality. Macmillan strongly urges its authors to show little boys using cosmetics. Homosexuals no longer fear revealing themselves, as is shown by the prevalence of the "clone look." Certain products run advertising obviously directed at the homosexual market. On the societal reaction theory, there ought to be an enormous rise in homosexual happiness. I know of no systematic study to determine if this is so, but anecdotal evidence suggests it may not be. The homosexual press has been just as strident in denouncing pro-homosexual movies as in denouncing Doris Day movies. Especially virulent venereal diseases have very recently appeared in homosexual communities, evidently spread in epidemic proportions by unabating homosexual promiscuity. One selling point for a presumably serious "gay rights" rally in Washington D.C. was an "all-night disco train" from New York to Washington. What is perhaps most salient is that, even if the changed public mood results in decreased homosexual unhappiness, the question remains of why homosexuals in the recent past, who suffered greatly for being homosexuals, persisted in being homosexuals.

But does not my position also predict—contrary to fact—that any sexual activity not aimed at procreation or at least sexual intercourse leads to unhappiness? First, I am not sure this conclusion is contrary to the facts properly understood. It is universally recognized that, for humans and the higher animals, sex is more than the insertion of the penis into the vagina. Foreplay is necessary to prepare the female and, to a lesser extent, the male. Ethologists have studied the elaborate mating rituals of even relatively simple animals. Sexual intercourse must therefore be understood to include the kisses and caresses that necessarily precede copulation, behaviors that nature has made rewarding. What my view does predict is that exclusive preoccupation with behaviors normally preparatory for intercourse is highly correlated with unhappiness. And, so far as I know, psychologists do agree that such preoccupation or "fixation" with, e.g., cunnilingus, is associated with personality traits independently recognized as disorders. In this sense, sexual intercourse really is virtually necessary for well-being. Only if one is antecedently convinced that "nothing is more natural than anything else" will one confound foreplay as a prelude to intercourse with "foreplay" that leads nowhere at all. . . .

ON POLICY ISSUES

Homosexuality is intrinsically bad only in a prudential sense. It makes for unhappiness. However, this does not exempt homosexuality from the larger categories of ethics—rights, duties, liabilities. Deontic categories apply to acts which increase or decrease happiness or expose the helpless to the risk of unhappiness.

If homosexuality is unnatural, legislation which raises the odds that a given child will become homosexual raises the odds that he will be unhappy. The only gap in the syllogism is whether legislation which legitimates, endorses or protects homosexuality does increase the chances that a child will become homosexual. If so, such legislation is *prima facie* objectionable. The question is not whether homosexual elementary school teachers will molest their charges. Pro-homosexual legislation might increase the incidence of homosexuality in subtler ways. If it does, and if the protection of children is a fundamental obligation of society, legislation which legitimates homosexuality is a dereliction of duty. I am reluctant to deploy the language of "children's rights," which usually serves as one more excuse to interfere with the prerogatives of parents. But we do have obligations to our children, and one of them is to protect them from harm. If, as some have suggested, children have a right to protection from a religious education, they surely have a right to protection from homosexuality. So protecting them limits somebody else's freedom, but we are often willing to protect quite obscure children's rights at the expenses of the freedom of others. There is a movement to ban TV commercials for sugar-coated cereals, to protect children from the relatively trivial harm of tooth decay. Such a ban would restrict the freedom of advertisers, and restrict it even though the last clear chance of avoiding the harm, and thus the responsibility, lies with the parents who control the TV set. I cannot see how one can consistently support such legislation and also urge homosexual rights, which risk much graver damage to children in exchange for increased freedom for homosexuals. . . . The right of a homosexual to work for the Fire Department is not a negligible good. Neither is fostering a legal atmosphere in which as many people as possible grow up heterosexual.

It is commonly asserted that legislation granting homosexuals the privilege or right to be firemen endorses not homosexuality, but an expanded conception of human liberation. It is conjectural how sincerely this can be said in a legal order that forbids employers to hire whom they please and demands hours of paperwork for an interstate shipment of hamburger. But in any case legislation "legalizing homosexuality" cannot be neutral. . . . Society cannot grant unaccustomed rights and privileges to homosexuals while remaining neutral about the value of homosexuality. Working from the assumption that society rests on the family and its consequences, the Judaeo-Christian tradition has deemed homosexuality a sin and withheld many privileges from homosexuals. Whether or not such denial was right, for our society to grant these privileges to homosexuals *now* would amount to declaring that it has rethought the matter and decided that homosexuality is not as bad as it had previously supposed. And unless such rethinking is a direct response to new empirical findings about homosexuality, it can only be a revaluing. Someone who suddenly accepts a policy he has previously opposed is open to the same interpretation: he has come to think better of the policy. And if he embraces the policy while knowing that this interpretation will be put on his behavior, and if he knows that others know that he knows they will so interpret it, he is acquiescing in this interpretation. He can be held to have intended, meant, this interpretation. A society that grants privileges to homosexuals while recognizing that, in the light of generally known history, this act can be interpreted as a positive re-evaluation of homosexuality, is signalling that it now thinks homosexuality is all right. Many commentators in the popular press have observed that homosexuals, unlike members of racial minorities, can always "stay in the closet" when applying for jobs. What homosexual rights activists really want, therefore, is not access to jobs but legitimation of their homosexuality. Since this is known, giving them what they want will be seen as conceding their claim to legitimacy. . . .

QUESTIONS FOR ANALYSIS

1. What's the point of Levin's analogy between homosexuality and Smith's treatment of his teeth? Is the analogy a good or a bad one? Why?
2. According to Levin, the misuse of a body part is not in itself morally wrong. Why? Then why does he say that homosexuality should be discouraged by law?
3. What kind of evidence does Levin cite to show that homosexuals are less happy than heterosexuals? How persuasive is it? Why does he reject what he calls the environmentalist explanation of homosexual unhappiness?
4. Levin says, "Calling homosexuality involuntary does not place it outside the scope of evaluation." Why doesn't it? Do you agree?
5. According to Levin, laws legalizing homosexuality can't be morally neutral. Why not? Do you agree?
6. How does Levin's argument resemble the argument from nature? How does it differ from it? Does Levin's argument escape the standard objections to the argument from nature?

Homosexuality and Nature

TIMOTHY F. MURPHY

The following essay by Timothy F. Murphy, professor of philosophy in the Biomedical Sciences College of Medicine, University of Illinois at Chicago, is a rebuttal of Michael Levin's arguments. Evolution cannot, Murphy argues, give us a standard for normal and abnormal behavior, and departures from behavior that once helped a species adapt to its environment may be beneficial today. He also disputes Levin's view that homosexuality in itself is likely to cause unhappiness, first by criticizing Levin's evidence and then by arguing that Levin fails to rule out anti-gay discrimination as the main cause.

Finally, Murphy criticizes Levin's arguments against gay rights. Using the same utilitarian reasoning as Levin, he notes that the happiness of homosexuals will be much enhanced by the removal of discrimination. Even more important, he disputes the claim that gay-rights legislation will turn children into homosexuals; homosexuality may be the result of biology, he says, or of environmental influences too early in life to be affected by the law.

The nature and legitimacy of homosexual behaviour continue to generate considerable controversy. Since 1973, the American Psychiatric Association has formally professed that homosexuality per se is no disease entity,[1] but one may still seek and find practitioners of sexual conversion therapy.[2] While some religious thinkers have become more tolerant of it,[3] others continue to conceptualize homosexuality as a sin of the first order, a sin said to be formally condemned in strong Old and New Testament language. While at present 26 states of the Union do *not* have criminal statutes for private consensual homosexual behaviour, the US Supreme Court recently held that states may criminalize such behaviours if they so choose.

There are many ways used to argue against the moral legitimacy of homosexual behaviour, whether such behaviour is transient or exclusive. Some seek recourse to concepts of sinfulness, diseases or crime in order to flesh out objections. Others appeal to the argument that homosexuality, its religious, medical, and criminal implications apart, is a kind of unnatural aberration which undermines its practitioners' prospects for happiness. I will consider this kind of argument here and contend that such an argument fails to establish that homosexuality is any significant abnormality and that neither its purported abnormality nor the unhappiness said to be associated with such behaviour can constitute a basis for criminalizing consensual homosexual behaviour or for failing to provide equal protections under the law for homosexuals in the area of public housing, service, jobs, and so on. I consider Michael Levin's "Why homosexuality is abnormal" as paradigmatic of the kind of argument I wish to investigate.[4] Although I confine myself to his specific argument and frequently use its language, my position is applicable *a fortiori* to all similar kinds of positions.

THE ARGUMENT FROM NATURE

Levin says homosexuality is abnormal because it involves a misuse of body parts, that there is "clear empirical sense" of that misuse, and that homosexual behaviour is contrary to the evolutionary

From Timothy F. Murphy, "Homosexuality and Nature: happiness and the law at stake," *Journal of Applied Philosophy,* vol. 4, no. 2, 1987.

adaptive order. Homosexual behaviour is abnormal, he says, because it is not the kind of behaviour which brought us to be the kind of physically constituted persons that we are today. Persons who used their penises for *coitus per anum* presumably left no ancestors. (Levin does not accept sociobiological contentions that homosexuality plays a supporting role in adaptive success.) That there are penises and vaginas today is due to the fact that they *were* used for heterosexual coitus, and hence we can infer that heterosexual coitus is indeed what such organs are for. Levin says: "an organ is for a given activity if the organ's performing that activity helps its host or organism suitable related to its host, *and* if this contribution is how the organ got and stays where it is."[5] Homosexual behaviour constitutes, according to this line of thought, an abandonment of certain functions on which species survival depended, and that abandonment is said to imply the loss of naturally occurring rewards selected for by adaptive success. This latter point does not mean that there are *no* compensatory pleasure, for just as the obese person will find gustatory rewards in his or her food, the homosexual who misuses his or her body parts can find *some* compensatory sexual rewards. It is just that the willful overeater or homosexual cannot reap the deepest rewards that nature has provided for in heterosexual usages and achievements.

Despite the effort which Levin takes to show that homosexual behaviour falls outside the behaviour upon which human adaptive success depended, I cannot say that I think this argument is even remotely convincing. Indeed, I believe it to be subject to a damning criticism. Even if it were certainly established that homosexuality was not part of originally adaptive behaviour, I do not see how that conclusion alone could establish the abnormality of homosexuality because there is neither a premise that natural selection has any kind of ultimate normative force nor a premise that human beings are bound to continue to be the kind of things that cosmic accident brought them to be. There is nothing in Levin's argument to sustain a claim that departures from a blind, accidental force of nature, or whatever metaphor of randomness is chosen, must be resisted. Without a logically prior and controlling premise that patterns of adaptive success possess ultimate, normative, force, then it seems that human beings are completely at liberty to dispose of their work, their behaviour, and even such things as their anatomy and physiology as they see fit. H. Tristam Engelhardt has made an argument along similar lines: that we human beings may choose our futures and are in no metaphysically binding sense bound to continue being the kind of persons blind determinants of nature have brought us to be.[6] Violations of a random order of nature carry no inherent penalty for there is no ultimate enforcer, or at least none is specified by this argument. Levin believes that he can show the abnormality of homosexuality without having to show that it violates some cosmic principle, by showing its inherent obstacles to adaptive success. But I think it is because no cosmic principle is invoked that we can judge that adaptive success itself is no binding force. The only guide available for human beings in respect of their lives, sexuality, and future is their will and imagination. Should the entire population of the planet choose to become exclusive homosexuals, for example, leaving the business of reproduction to ectogenesis, I cannot think of a reason *derived from nature* why they should not do so.

Levin's argument, and others like it, ignore the prospects of beneficial departures from the naturally adaptive order. His argument assumes that each departure from our adaptive heritage will be unhappy in result. The argument, too, assumes that *all* behaviour of *all* persons must serve the purpose of adaptation. Clearly, it is possible that some departures from the adaptive order are possible which do not threaten a species survival as a whole. If a species can survive if only a majority of its members use their organs in a particular fashion, then it may enjoy a surplus of adaptive protection even for those who act in wholly non-procreative fashion. Homosexuality, then, might have served some beneficial advantage (as sociobiology asserts) or it may have been (and this is more important for my argument) no impediment to selective adaptation. If this is so, it is hard to see in what sense homosexuality would have to be reckoned as a natural aberration.

Even if one were to accept Levin's suggestions regarding the abnormality of homosexuality with respect to natural selection, it seems to me that his definition of homosexuality is highly problematic. He defines homosexuality behaviourally, i.e. as something one does with one's body, specifically with one's organs. It is *behaviour* which is said to be unnatural. Since there are, after all, self-identified gay men and lesbians who have never had sexual relations with a member of the same (or opposite) sex, this definition seems ill-advised. By their own lights, adolescents and closeted adults see themselves as homosexual, their sexual continence notwithstanding. How is one to understand the nature of their sexual dispositions if there is no overt behaviour? Is their homoerotic desire itself abnormal? Or is only behaviour abnormal? I believe that homosexuality is better defined as primarily a psychic phenomenon and that specific homosexual behaviour is virtually epiphenomenal, merely a matter of what biology makes possible (this claim would also apply to heterosexuality). Most psychiatric texts follow this approach.[7] If one accepts the condition that homosexuality is primarily a psychic phenomenon, and if one wanted to argue its abnormality along the lines Levin has suggested, it would seem that one would have to argue that homoeroticism is somehow a misuse of the brain! There are arguments, of course, that attempt to show homosexuality as a result of some psychic disrepair, but even though these arguments are themselves the matter of much debate, that debate is only about psychical development, not about uses of the brain. It is hard to imagine that one could show homoeroticism as a misuse of the brain.

Finally, it is to be noted that Levin believes that homosexuality may be intuited as abnormal. He says that such an intuition "remains vital."[8] Yet however profoundly felt and however psychologically convincing intuitions may be, still they can be conceptually shallow and more importantly even dead wrong. That is, the appeal to intuition is by itself no guarantee of the accuracy of the intuition, for presumably one would, for purposes of confirmation, have to check the intuition against some other external criterion of justification. I am hard-pressed to see how this intuition of homosexuality's abnormality is to be made available to others who do not already share it. Indeed, arguments from intuition are like issues said to be self-evident: precious little can be said on their behalf, they are either seen or not. Yet Levin seems to assume that the readers of his essay *already* share the intuition. . . .

PROSPECTS FOR HAPPINESS

Levin makes a great deal of the supposed link between homosexuality and unhappiness. One may assume that he would reply to my foregoing remarks by admitting that even if it were true that humans are not bound by any ultimate metaphysical sexual directive, then it would still remain true that prudential cautions obtain against homosexuality and that these cautions are sufficient to ground legal measure designed to minimize the occurrence of homosexuality. "Homosexuality," Levin says, "is likely to cause unhappiness because it leaves unfulfilled an innate and innately rewarding desire,"[9] a desire supposedly ingrained through millennia of evolutionary selection. One might find some happy homosexuals, but Levin believes that such exceptions are inconsequential and do not disable his argument. He does not say that happy homosexuals are non-existent, only that they are rare and that their lives will be inherently less rewarding than those of heterosexuals. Moreover, "Even if some line demarcated happiness from unhappiness absolutely, it would be irrelevant if homosexuals were all happily above that line. It is the comparison with the heterosexual life that is at issue."[10] The happiest persons are practitioners of heterosexuality, therefore, even if, according to Levin, each and every homosexual was, by his or her own admission, happy. But homosexuals are not even proximately happy, Levin says. According to him, awash in the travails of their own self-punishing promiscuity, present-day homosexuals would like to believe that all their ills are the result of an ill-constructed society, that their unhappiness is merely artifactual and in principle eliminable by the appropriate cultural and political accommodations. Levin suggests that this belief is a self-serving rationalization. . . . Happiness has not followed the work of various American organs to provide a positive image of homosexuals, judges allowing homosexuals to adopt their lovers, the Hollywood production of "highly sanitized" movies about homosexuality, publishers urging their authors to show little boys using cosmetics, or advertisers appealing directly to the homosexual market. That there has not been a resultant rise in homosexual happiness is said to be evident from (a) the gay press not liking Hollywood's movies, (b) the appearance of especially virulent diseases in homosexual populations, and (c) gay men needing frivolous enticements to get them to support important political causes on their behalf.[11]

By the way of comment on all this, I would first note that Levin has formulated his position in terms that *in principle* do not admit of refutation. He said that in principle, however happy homosexuals may be, they still cannot be as happy as heterosexuals. Of course, it is possible that a claim is unfalsifiable because the claim is indeed true. On the other hand, I think one would do better to see a definitional fiat being asserted here: human happiness, *true* human happiness is said to be coextensive with the happiness of heterosexual behaviour. By definition there is nothing which could falsify this proposition, *not even* the self-asserted happiness of each and every homosexual person. I believe that this claim is no argument, avoiding as it does any potentially falsifying statement, and that it ought to be rejected as untestable rather than accepted as true by definition. As I have urged above, moreover, I do not believe that the accidental contingency of the primacy of heterosexual sexuality requires that all human happiness be sought there or that, perhaps, other kinds of happiness cannot be engineered.

Secondly, the kind of evidence that Levin uses to establish the unhappiness of homosexuals is altogether anecdotal and trivial.[12] That Hollywood continues to make bad movies, even when their subjects are "sanitized" gay men and lesbians, is no evidence that homosexuality *per se* leads to unhappiness. The existence of viral disease is a major concern of gay men, but it is not because they are gay that it is their concern; it is because these viral diseases happen by accident of fate to affect the gay population. Would one want to argue that heterosexuals qua heterosexuals are somehow intrinsically headed for unhappiness as AIDS expands into that population? Moreover, that homosexuals mix business with pleasure is no argument that they are less serious about their political agenda (let alone unhappier) than others. There is a kind of unfair asymmetry being used here in adducing Levin's evidence. If one uses such issues as he conjures up as evidence of the continuing unhappiness of homosexuals, why couldn't one equally and legitimately use similar evidence against the supposed happiness of heterosexuals? Most wars, for example, are the doing of heterosexuals. Nuclear weapons are their products. Most bad movies are also theirs. Must one infer therefore the continuing unhappiness of heterosexuals and assert prudential cautions against heterosexuality? If Levin's use of anecdotal evidence is acceptable against homosexuals, then it ought to be equally acceptable as an indictment of heterosexuality. Ironically, the case against heterosexuality would probably have to be seen as more damaging.

As for Levin's claims that homosexuals ought to be happier these days than they were in the past, it is probably the case that this is true. Anecdotal evidence may be used here since Levin uses it. The increasing success of gay pride parades ought to be taken as an indicator of some measure of increased homosexual happiness. At the very least persons who participate in them have been freed of the fear of some of the unhappy consequences that could befall them following public identification of their being gay. It is not without significance that in Boston, for example, the 1986 gay pride parade attracted some 25,000–30,000 participants whereas the first parade of 1970 had but 50! Furthermore, the heady increase in the number of gay and lesbian organizations for social, business, and political and support services indicates that homosexuals are not much inclined to wallow in despair over their sexual fate. One could go on in this vein, but I think it is important to consider that a verdict about the happiness of homosexuals would be a one-sided verdict indeed if it were to follow only from the evidence Levin puts forward.

To put specific quarrels about evidence aside, it seems to me that Levin fails almost culpably to imagine what a society would have to be like in order to be free of the oppressive elements which contribute to the putative unhappiness of homosexuals. In order to see the extent to which homosexual unhappiness is caused by social repressions and to what extent it is intrinsic, society would have to be completely free at every significant level of bias against homosexuals. To begin with—let's call this Phase I of the agenda: there should be no gratuitous assumption of heterosexuality in education, politics, advertising, and so on, just as a gender-neutral society would not presume the priority, real and symbolic, of males. For example, in education, texts and films ought to incorporate the experiences of gay men and lesbians. Educational measures should attempt to reduce anti-homosexuality in the same ways and to the same extent they educate against racism. In a society reconstructed along these lines, moreover, there would also have to be no right of access or entitlement possessed by a heterosexual that could be denied to a homosexual. *Only* in such radically restructured society would one be able to see if homosexual unhappiness were immune to social deconstruction. Even if it weren't, one could still argue that homosexuals are not necessarily unhappy but that their happiness requires social protections or accommodations unrequired by heterosexuals. That is, homosexuals might need, as Phase II of the agenda, entitlements which heterosexuals do not in the way, for example, that legally-mandated minority hiring quotas serve other specific populations. Of course, one might want to argue that such entitlements would be anti-democratic and therefore objectionable. This protestation however would not by itself diminish the point being made: that homosexual unhappiness is perhaps adventitious and that the only way of discovering this is to protect homosexuals in their lives, jobs, and interests in ways that are not presently served.

It is unlikely, of course, that the above-described experiment in social reconstruction is in any important sense immediately forthcoming. Nevertheless, that the experiment may be clearly formulated and seen as the definitive test of the social-reaction theory of homosexual unhappiness is sufficient ground to show that Levin's account of the unhappiness of homosexuals is unproved, its adduced evidence merely anecdotal. Even if it were true, I will argue later, since not all human unhappiness is tractable to social interventions, any residual unhappiness that was to survive Phase I and II of our social reformation agenda would still be no evidence against homosexuality.

ISSUES AT LAW

Levin believes that the abnormality of homosexuality and its attendant unhappiness are warrant enough to ground legal enactments against homosexuality and this is a matter of protecting citizens from lives impoverished by the loss of heterosexual rewards. Any legislation therefore that raises the odds that a child will become homosexual ought to be rejected as prima facie objectionable, as a dereliction of the duty of protecting children from the unhappy homosexual selves they might become.[13] The U.S. Supreme Court recently ruled in *Bowers v. Hardwick* that states may enact, if they choose, statutes proscribing private consensual homosexual behaviour since, according to the opinion, there is nothing in the Constitution making such behaviour a fundamental right.[14] Levin's argument would presumably extend further since private consensual homosexual behaviour is socially invisible and unlikely as such to influence persons to become homosexual. Although he does not specifically mention what kinds of laws ought to be called for, or what kinds of laws ought to be rejected, presumably he means denying homosexuals protections in jobs, housing, foster-parenting, and so on. In short, the law would presumably have to serve the function of rendering homosexuality entirely invisible else there would continue to exist subtle promptings to homosexuality by virtue of degree of acceptance extended to it. Levin says he does not believe that this legal scenario would put any undue burden on any actual homosexual since, unlike members of racial minorities, he or she can always stay in the closet while applying for jobs, housing and the like. Therefore to give homosexuals protections they don't really need would have to be interpreted as a *de facto* social legitimation of homosexuality. This implied approval might be causally involved in the production of more homosexuals and therefore ought to be rejected.

I do not believe that this argument is convincing. First of all, the "cause" or "causes" of homosexuality are a matter of continuing controversy. There are metaphysical arguments that homosexuality is the result of some cosmic principle of world ordering; Plato's *Symposium* depicts homosexuals (and heterosexuals) as the result of an angry god's punishment. Biological theories hold homosexuality to be the result of some developmental variance or organismal dysfunction. Genetic theories try to locate the origins of homosexuality at the lowest level of biological causality, the gene. The most numerous kinds of theories are psychosocial theories which see homoeroticism as the result of either original psychical constitution or some developmental influences. Even the briefest perusal of the literature of the "cause" of homosexuality leaves one with the conclusion that the "cause" is an essentially disputed concept.[15] There is not even agreement that homosexuality is a reifiable trait (any more than, say, courage) that can be explained by reference to a universally pre-existing set of conditions.[16] This dispute is important to consider since Levin seems to hold, without justification (at least without explanation), a developmental theory of homosexuality, a theory that homosexuals are made not born. This may or may not be true, but it seems wrong-headed to establish legal policy on the basis of one particular speculative theory of the origins of homosexual behaviour. If homosexuality is primarily a function of biological variance, for example, such laws and forbearances that Levin would see as desirable would have no effect whatever on the production of more homosexuals. Even if the law diligently erased all evidence of homosexual behaviour and persons from public view, one could not automatically assume a reduced number of homosexuals or a decrease in homosexual behaviour. I suspect that most persons are homosexual and become homosexual in ways completely immune to the written or enforced statutes of the various states. Children who never hear a word about homosexuality in their youth nevertheless become homosexuals. Children who walk past homosexual clubs and persons in the streets of certain American cities do not thereby automatically become homosexuals. Would it really be the case that there are more homosexuals spawned in West Virginia because there are no laws against private, consensual homosexual behaviour there than in Virginia where there are such laws?[17] The net result of efforts to criminalize and reduce the visibility of homosexuality then would be to impose burdens on those who are perhaps involuntarily homosexual. At the very least, Levin's theory gratuitously supposes a developmental theory of homosexuality, a theory which has its insistent critics. One should also point out that even if some developmental theory of homosexuality were true, it is not necessarily the case that changing statutes would halt the flow of homosexuals since there may be other pathways to homosexuality. It is also the suspicion of many psychologists that homosexual tendencies are established very early on in childhood, in which case one presumes fairly that statutes criminalizing sodomy and lacks of protection in housing on the basis of sexual orientation have little to do with either ingraining or stifling homosexual dispositions.

If the reason that Levin suggests anti-homosexual measures is to contain human unhappiness, then his argument may be turned on its head. If the reason, or part of the reason that homosexuals are unhappy is because of the existence of certain legally permissible discriminations (or what comes to the same thing: fear of such), then it can certainly be suggested that laws ought to be changed in order to protect and enlarge the happiness of homosexuals, whether their homosexuality is elective or involuntary. In the name of their happiness, they ought to be afforded protections under the law, freedom from fear of prosecution for their private consensual behaviour and freedom to occupy jobs as persons they are, not as the persons others would have them be. The law could further protect them by saving them from blackmailers who would expose their homosexuality to employers, landlords, and so on. It is eminently clear that the law could at least enlarge the happiness of gay men and lesbians in these respects even if it cannot vouchsafe them absolute satisfaction in their lives.

Interestingly enough, even if all the unhappiness said to be associated with being homosexual were not eliminated by a dogged social reconstruction that achieved full parity between homosexuality and heterosexuality, it would still not follow that the law ought to be put to the purpose of eliminating homosexuality (assuming it could). Life, sad to say, is in some of its aspects inherently tragic. For example, in some important ways, law or society could never fully compensate the atheist for the lost rewards of religion. Atheism can discover in the world no incentives to conduct, no promise of the eventual recompense for injustices borne, and no guarantee that the heart's desires will be met.[18] Society might provide such consolations as it can, but it is certainly the case that a certain tragedy antagonistic to human happiness is an irreducible element of atheistic thought. That atheism leads to this measure of unhappiness would certainly not be a reason for instituting social and legal barriers to atheism on the theory that children ought to be glowingly happy (if self-deceived) theists rather than unhappy atheists. Human dignity is not automatically overthrown by a position of atheism; the atheist accepts and honours those satisfactions that are within his or her power. That homosexuality too might lead to a certain amount of unhappiness does not thereby overthrow the dignity of homosexual persons. One realizes merely that the law is no unfailing conduit to human happiness.

Levin's conclusions that legal measures ought to be taken to minimize the possibility that children become themselves the sad new recruits of homosexuality therefore cannot stand. I believe, on the contrary, that the law ought to do what it can to protect homosexuals from socially inflicted unhappiness. Levin's point that to decriminalize homosexual behaviour and to provide legal protections for homosexual persons would be seen as social legitimization of homosexuality (and not just tolerance) is correct. But this is no point over which to despair, for this inference is precisely compatible with the underlying metaphysics of gay activism, that homosexuality is no degrading impoverishment of human life. On the contrary, it has an integrity of its own apart from invidious comparisons with heterosexuality. Therefore, lest society be a political enforcer of sexual ideology, homosexuals ought to be afforded equal standing and protections under the law, and this in the name of serving human happiness.

CONCLUSIONS

Levin has argued that homosexuality is a self-punishing maladaption likely to cause unhappiness since homosexuals do not use their organs for what they are for. Human happiness is said to attend that behaviour which follows out the natural paths plotted by evolutionary selection. As homosexuality has not thus far been shown to have contributed (*pace* sociobiology) to the kind of beings we are today, it may be assumed that homosexual behaviour is abnormal. As such behaviour, too, is linked with unhappiness it is to be rejected as both abnormal and unrewarding. The law ought to follow this conclusion through and reject any inducements to homosexuality.

I have argued against this position on a number of grounds. The most important is this: nature is represented here by Levin as without guiding or controlling force. Therefore, as pathways of evolutionary adaptation are themselves only a matter of metaphysical blind accident, nature lacks normative force and human beings are completely at liberty to dispose of the world, their behaviour, and their bodies as they see fit. One could still try to argue against homosexuality on prudential grounds, on grounds that it causes unhappiness, but I have argued that conclusions from claims about unhappiness are inconclusive because it is not clear how much homosexual unhappiness is adventitious and how much intrinsic. Levin's evidence that such unhappiness is intrinsic is anecdotal evidence of the most unconvincing kind. A complete reconstruction of society such that homosexuality was on a par with heterosexuality would be required in order to distinguish adventitious from intrinsic unhappiness and make the argument conclusive. But even if there were residual unhappiness attaching to homosexuality under socially liberating conditions of this grand experiment, such unhappiness might be likened to the irreducible tragic aspects of atheism: Such an unhappiness is no writ for legal and social measures designed to stem the genesis of either atheists or homosexuals.

On the contrary, rather than using the law as an instrument of enforcing invisibility on homosexuals, the law should, I think, be used to afford what measure of happiness it can. How far the law ought to serve the needs of gay men and lesbians is, of course, a matter of debate. But it seems to follow that at the very least, the law ought to protect gay men and lesbians from unhappiness caused by victimization and social exclusions which it is within the law's power to reject.

NOTES

1. Ronald Bayer (1981) *Homosexuality and American Psychiatry* (New York, Basic Books).
2. Mark Schwartz & William H. Masters (1984) The Masters and Johnson Program for Dissatisfied Homosexual Men, *American Journal of Psychiatry,* 141, pp. 173–181.
3. See some of the selections in Edward Batchelor, Jr. (Ed.) (1980) *Homosexuality and Ethics* (New York, Pilgrim Press).
4. Michael Levin (1985) Why homosexuality is abnormal, *Monist* (Spring) pp. 251–283.
5. Levin, p. 256.
6. See H. Tristam Engelhardt, Jr. (1986) *The Foundations of Bioethics,* pp. 375–387 (New York, OUP).
7. Michael Gelder, Dennis Gath, & Richard Mayou (1983) *Oxford Textbook of Psychiatry,* p. 468 (Oxford, OUP).
8. Levin, p. 251.
9. Levin, p. 261.
10. Levin, p. 262.
11. Levin, pp. 268–269.
12. Levin's reading of the "evidence" is also suspect. At one point he refers to the narrative (1977) *The Sexual Outlaw* (New York, Grove Press), saying that even such a sympathetic observer as John Rechy admits that the immediate cause of homosexual unhappiness is a taste for promiscuity, anonymous encounters, and humiliation. This, I submit, is an embarrassing misrepresentation of Rechy's book, for that book explicitly, insistently, and frequently criticizes the hypocritical, violent sociolegal ethic which Rechy identifies itself as (the?) major cause of homosexual promiscuity and unhappiness. He says, for example: "Imagine the horror of living with that constant fear, those threats. Imagine being forbidden to seek out a sexual partner. Imagine that—and you begin to understand the promiscuous rage of the sexual outlaw" (p. 102).
13. Levin, p. 274.
14. Bowers v. Hardwick, No. pp. 85–140 (30 June, 1986).
15. Irving Bieber, H.J. Dain, P.R. Dince, M.G. Orellich, H.G. Grand, R.H. Grundlach, M.W. Kremer, A.H. Rifkin, C.B. Wilbur & T.B. Bieber (1962) *Homosexuality: a psychoanalytic study* (New York, Basic Books). The introduction to this book reviews critically a number of theories.
16. Douglas Futuyma & Stephen J. Risch (1984) Sexual orientation, sociobiology and evolution, in J.P. DeCecco & M.G. Shively (Eds.) *Bisexual and Homosexual Identities: critical theoretical issues,* pp. 157–168 (New York, Haworth Press).
17. Sodomy laws in US (illus.), *New York Times,* 1 July 1986, p. A19.
18. Ernest Nagel (1965) A defense of atheism, in: P. Edwards & A. Pap *A Modern Introduction to Philosophy,* pp. 460–472, rev. edn (New York, Free Press).

QUESTIONS FOR ANALYSIS

1. Does Murphy refute Levin's argument against gay rights? Why or why not?
2. Murphy criticizes Levin for defining homosexuality as a kind of behavior rather than a disposition. Is this a valid criticism in terms of Levin's argument?
3. How does Murphy rebut Levin's arguments about the relative unhappiness of homosexuals? How persuasive is his rebuttal?
4. According to Murphy, even if it could be shown that homosexuality had no original adaptive value, that wouldn't show that it's abnormal. Why? Do you agree?
5. How would Levin respond to Murphy's criticisms?

CASE PRESENTATION

Disease v. Promiscuity?

On June 29, 2006, the Advisory Committee on Immunization Practices (ACIP) of the Centers for Disease Control announced its recommendation that a new vaccine protecting women from the human papillomavirus (HPV) be given routinely to girls aged eleven to twelve years. It noted that the vaccine was most effective before any sexual activity, which might expose girls and women to the virus. They also recommended that girls and women aged thirteen to twenty-six be given the vaccine.

Scientists have long known that two types of HPV cause 70 percent of all cervical cancer, a disease that causes 3700 deaths each year in the United States. Unlike most cancers, the clear causal link between the virus and the cancer makes this a highly preventable disease with a vaccine against the virus.

It is estimated that at least half of the U.S. adult population has been infected with HPV, the most widespread sexually transmitted disease (STD) in the United States, even though most of those cases will not lead to cervical cancer. Currently, the Pap test provides early-detection testing for adult women, but this test is not readily available to many women, and it detects abnormalities in the cervix after they have already developed. The vaccine would prevent most of those abnormalities from ever developing, but only if the vaccine were administered before any exposure to the virus.

The National Organization for Women notes that women's-health advocates have urged that all girls be vaccinated. The organization Advocates for Youth urges that the vaccine be included in all school vaccination programs, with an "opt-out" option for parents who object to the vaccine for their daughters.

However, representatives of the Family Research Council, a conservative Christian advocacy organization, have expressed concern about the message that vaccination would convey to young girls as a license to engage in premarital sex. The FRC urges abstinence until marriage as the best protection against all sexually transmitted diseases. Although it does not officially object to voluntary vaccination, the FRC opposes making the vaccine mandatory by state and local governments or school boards.

The National Vaccine Information Center also opposes the CDC action, stating that the safety of the vaccine has not been satisfactorily demonstrated. The NVIC was founded in 1982 by parents of children who had been injured by various vaccines.

In July 2006, the Los Angeles Unified School District announced that it would make the vaccine available to female students, but only with parental consent. Families unable to pay the cost will be given free vaccines.

QUESTIONS FOR ANALYSIS

1. Should access to this vaccine be restricted, so as to avoid sending a message to young girls that sex is safe? Should it be available only through private physicians, not public school districts? Should public tax funds be used to pay for this vaccine, when some traditionalists believe it immorally encourages promiscuity?
2. Is vaccination likely to lead to greater promiscuity and to the failure of "abstinence only" education campaigns? Should the government require that everyone receiving the vaccine be urged to practice abstinence as a better form of prevention?
3. Some traditionalists lamented the advent of the birth control pill in the 1960s, maintaining that it removed a strong deterrent to sex outside of marriage—namely, unwanted pregnancies. The advent of incurable and often fatal STDs, such as herpes and HIV/AIDS, led many to restrain their sexual activity for fear of disease, and traditionalists seem to have gathered momentum in this environment for their "abstinence only" message. Although vaccines have not yet been developed for herpes or AIDS, scientists are attempting to develop such vaccines. Would they be likely to encourage more promiscuity, as some fear the HPV vaccine will do? Would it be better for the government to spend more funds on encouragement of abstinence and less on scientific research to develop such vaccines against STDs?

CASE PRESENTATION

Lawrence v. Texas: *Private Rights and Public Morality*

This 2003 U.S. Supreme Court decision overturned the 1986 decision *Bowers v. Hardwick*, which had held that private homosexual conduct among consenting adults was not protected under the U.S. Constitution.

MAJORITY OPINION (WRITTEN BY JUSTICE KENNEDY)

Liberty protects the person from unwarranted government intrusions into a dwelling or other private places. In our tradition the State is not omnipresent in the home. And there are other spheres of our lives and existence, outside the home, where the State should not be a dominant presence. Freedom extends beyond spatial bounds. Liberty presumes an autonomy of self that includes freedom of thought, belief, expression, and certain intimate conduct. The instant case involves liberty of the person both in its spatial and more transcendent dimensions.

The question before the Court is the validity of a Texas statute making it a crime for two persons of the same sex to engage in certain intimate sexual conduct. . . . The applicable state law . . . provides: "A person commits an offense if he engages in deviate sexual intercourse with another individual of the same sex." The statute defines "[d]eviate sexual intercourse" as follows:

"(A) any contact between any part of the genitals of one person and the mouth or anus of another person; or

"(B) the penetration of the genitals or the anus of another person with an object." . . .

We conclude the case should be resolved by determining whether the petitioners were free as adults to engage in the private conduct in the exercise of their liberty under the Due Process Clause of the Fourteenth Amendment to the Constitution. For this inquiry we deem it necessary to reconsider the Court's holding in *Bowers*.

. . . The Court began its substantive discussion in *Bowers* as follows: "The issue presented is whether the Federal Constitution confers a fundamental right upon homosexuals to engage in sodomy and hence invalidates the laws of the many States that still make such conduct illegal and have done so for a very long time.". . . That statement, we now conclude, discloses the Court's own failure to appreciate the extent of the liberty at stake. To say that the issue in *Bowers* was simply the right to engage in certain sexual conduct demeans the claim the individual put forward, just as it would demean a married couple were it to be said marriage is simply about the right to have sexual intercourse. The laws involved in *Bowers* and here are, to be sure, statutes that purport to do no more than prohibit a particular sexual act. Their penalties and purposes, though, have more far-reaching consequences, touching upon the most private human conduct, sexual behavior, and in the most private of places, the home. The statutes do seek to control a personal relationship that, whether or not entitled to formal recognition in the law, is within the liberty of persons to choose without being punished as criminals.

This, as a general rule, should counsel against attempts by the State, or a court, to define the meaning of the relationship or to set its boundaries absent injury to a person or abuse of an institution the law protects. It suffices for us to acknowledge that adults may choose to enter upon this relationship in the confines of their homes and their own private lives and still retain their dignity as free persons. When sexuality finds overt expression in intimate conduct with another person, the conduct can be but one element in a personal bond that is more enduring. The liberty protected by the Constitution allows homosexual persons the right to make this choice.

. . . It must be acknowledged, of course, that the Court in *Bowers* was making the broader point that for centuries there have been powerful voices to condemn homosexual conduct as immoral. The condemnation has been shaped by religious beliefs, conceptions of right and acceptable behavior, and respect for the traditional family. For many persons these are not trivial concerns but profound and deep convictions accepted as ethical and moral principles to which they aspire and which thus determine the course of their lives. These considerations do not answer the question before us, however. The issue is whether the majority may use the power of the State to enforce these views on the whole society through operation of the criminal law. . . .

. . . Equality of treatment and the due process right to demand respect for conduct protected by the substantive guarantee of liberty are linked in important respects, and a decision on the latter point advances both interests. If protected conduct is made criminal and the law which does so remains unexamined for its substantive validity, its stigma might remain even if it were not enforceable as drawn for equal protection reasons. When homosexual conduct is made criminal by the law of the State, that declaration in and of itself is an invitation to subject homosexual persons to discrimination both in the public and in the private spheres. The central holding of *Bowers* has been brought in question by this case, and it should be addressed. Its continuance as precedent demeans the lives of homosexual persons. . . .

. . .*Bowers* was not correct when it was decided, and it is not correct today. It ought not to remain binding precedent. *Bowers v. Hardwick* should be and now is overruled.

The present case does not involve minors. It does not involve persons who might be injured or coerced or who are situated in relationships where consent might not easily be refused. It does not involve public conduct or prostitution. It does not involve whether the government must give formal recognition to any relationship that homosexual persons seek to enter. The case does involve two adults who, with full and mutual consent from each other, engaged in sexual practices common to a homosexual lifestyle. The petitioners are entitled to respect for their private lives. The State cannot demean their existence or control their destiny by making their private sexual conduct a crime. Their right to liberty under the Due Process Clause gives them the full right to engage in their conduct without intervention of the government. . . . The Texas statute furthers no legitimate state interest which can justify its intrusion into the personal and private life of the individual.

Had those who drew and ratified the Due Process Clauses of the Fifth Amendment or the Fourteenth Amendment known the components of liberty in its manifold possibilities, they might have been more specific. They did not presume to have this insight. They knew times can blind us to certain truths and later generations can see that laws once thought necessary and proper in fact serve only to oppress. As the Constitution endures, persons in every generation can invoke its principles in their own search for greater freedom. . . .

Justice Scalia, dissenting

. . .The Texas statute undeniably seeks to further the belief of its citizens that certain forms of sexual behavior are "immoral and unacceptable," . . . the same interest furthered by criminal laws against fornication, bigamy, adultery, adult incest, bestiality, and obscenity. *Bowers* held that this was a legitimate state interest. The Court today reaches the opposite conclusion. The Texas statute, it says, "furthers no legitimate state interest which can justify its intrusion into the personal and private life of the individual," . . . . The Court embraces instead Justice Stevens' declaration in his *Bowers* dissent, that "the fact that the governing majority in a State has traditionally viewed a particular practice as immoral is not a sufficient reason for upholding a law prohibiting the practice," . . . . This effectively decrees the end of all morals legislation. If, as the Court asserts, the promotion of majoritarian sexual morality is not even a legitimate state interest, none of the above-mentioned laws can survive rational-basis review. . . .

One of the most revealing statements in today's opinion is the Court's grim warning that the criminalization of homosexual conduct is "an invitation to subject homosexual persons to discrimination both in the public and in the private spheres." . . . It is clear from this that the Court has taken sides in the culture war, departing from its role of assuring, as neutral observer, that the democratic rules of engagement are observed. Many Americans do not want persons who openly engage in homosexual conduct as partners in their business, as scoutmasters for their children, as teachers in their children's schools, or as boarders in their home. They view this as protecting themselves and their families from a lifestyle that they believe to be immoral and destructive. The Court views it as "discrimination" which it is the function of our judgments to deter. . . .

One of the benefits of leaving regulation of this matter to the people rather than to the courts is that the people, unlike judges, need not carry things to their logical conclusion. The people may feel that their disapprobation of homosexual conduct is strong enough to disallow homosexual marriage, but not strong enough to criminalize private homosexual acts—and may legislate accordingly. The Court today pretends that it possesses a similar freedom of action, so that we need not fear judicial imposition of homosexual marriage, as has recently occurred in Canada (in a decision that the Canadian Government has chosen not to appeal). . . . At the end of its opinion—after having laid waste the foundations of our rational-basis jurisprudence—the Court says that the present case "does not involve whether the government must give formal recognition to any relationship that homosexual persons seek to enter." . . . Do not believe it. . . . Today's opinion dismantles the structure of constitutional law that has permitted a distinction to be made between heterosexual and homosexual unions, insofar as formal recognition in marriage is concerned. If moral disapprobation of homosexual conduct is "no legitimate state interest" for purposes of proscribing that conduct, . . . ; and if, as the Court coos (casting aside all pretense of neutrality), "[w]hen sexuality finds overt expression in intimate conduct with another person, the conduct can be but one element in a personal bond that is more enduring," . . . ; what justification could there possibly be for denying the benefits of marriage to homosexual couples exercising "[t]he liberty protected by the Constitution," . . . Surely not the encouragement of procreation, since the sterile and the elderly are allowed to marry. This case "does not involve" the issue of homosexual marriage only if one entertains the belief that principle and logic have nothing to do with the decisions of this Court. Many will hope that, as the Court comfortingly assures us, this is so. . . .

QUESTIONS FOR ANALYSIS

1. Has the majority opinion struck the right balance between the appropriate roles of the law and of private morality? Is there any immoral behavior that should still be illegal, even if society's concerns originated in moral prohibitions?
2. Under the reasoning of the majority opinion here, should the criminal laws on fornication, bigamy, adultery, adult incest, bestiality, and obscenity also be struck down? If not, what considerations can you cite to support the continuation of those laws?
3. Does Justice Scalia engage in "slippery slope" reasoning?
4. Does the majority opinion provide a compelling basis for eventually holding that homosexual "marriage" is a constitutional right, despite the court's insistence that it has not? Is Justice Scalia right to be concerned that the reasoning of the majority makes it inevitable that homosexual "marriage" will eventually be found to be a constitutional right?
5. How would Levin and Murphy, respectively, critique *Lawrence v. Texas*?

CASE PRESENTATION

Goodridge v. Dept. of Public Health: *A Right of Gay Marriage*

In 2004 the Supreme Court of Massachusetts, in a 4-3 decision, held that homosexuals had the same rights under state law to the benefits of marriage as heterosexuals

MAJORITY OPINION (WRITTEN BY CHIEF JUDGE MARSHALL)

Marriage is a vital social institution. The exclusive commitment of two individuals to each other nurtures love and mutual support; it brings stability to our society. For those who choose to marry, and for their children, marriage provides an abundance of legal, financial, and social benefits. In return it imposes weighty legal, financial, and social obligations. The question before us is whether, consistent with the Massachusetts Constitution, the Commonwealth may deny the protections, benefits, and obligations conferred by civil marriage to two individuals of the same sex who wish to marry. We conclude that it may not. The Massachusetts Constitution affirms the dignity and equality of all individuals. It forbids the creation of second-class citizens. In reaching our conclusion we have given full deference to the arguments made by the Commonwealth. But it has failed to identify any constitutionally adequate reason for denying civil marriage to same-sex couples.

We are mindful that our decision marks a change in the history of our marriage law. Many people hold deep-seated religious, moral, and ethical convictions that marriage should be limited to the union of one man and one woman, and that homosexual conduct is immoral. Many hold equally strong religious, moral, and ethical convictions that same-sex couples are entitled to be married, and that homosexual persons should be treated no differently than their heterosexual neighbors. Neither view answers the question before us. Our concern is with the Massachusetts Constitution as a charter of governance for every person properly within its reach. . . .

Whether the Commonwealth may use its formidable regulatory authority to bar same-sex couples from civil marriage is a question not previously addressed by a Massachusetts appellate court. It is a question the United States Supreme Court left open as a matter of Federal law in Lawrence . . . where it was not an issue. . . . The Massachusetts Constitution is, if anything, more protective of individual liberty and equality than the Federal Constitution; it may demand broader protection for fundamental rights; and it is less tolerant of government intrusion into the protected spheres of private life.

Barred access to the protections, benefits, and obligations of civil marriage, a person who enters into an intimate, exclusive union with another of the same sex is arbitrarily deprived of membership in one of our community's most rewarding and cherished institutions. That exclusion is incompatible with the constitutional principles of respect for individual autonomy and equality under law. . . .

The plaintiffs include business executives, lawyers, an investment banker, educators, therapists, and a computer engineer. Many are active in church, community, and school groups. They have employed such legal means as are available to them—for example, joint adoption, powers of attorney, and joint ownership of real property—to secure aspects of their relationships. Each plaintiff attests a desire to marry his or her partner in order to affirm publicly their commitment to each other and to secure the legal protections and benefits afforded to married couples and their children. . . .

The plaintiffs' claim that the marriage restriction violates the Massachusetts Constitution can be analyzed in two ways. Does it offend the Constitution's guarantees of equality before the law? Or do the liberty and due process provisions of the Massachusetts Constitution secure the plaintiffs' right to marry their chosen partner? In matters implicating marriage, family life, and the upbringing of children, the two constitutional concepts frequently overlap, as they do here. . . .

We begin by considering the nature of civil marriage itself. Simply put, the government creates civil marriage. In Massachusetts, civil marriage is, and since pre-Colonial days has been, precisely what its name implies: a wholly secular institution. . . . No religious ceremony has ever been required to validate a Massachusetts marriage. . . .

Without the right to marry—or more properly, the right to choose to marry—one is excluded from the full range of human experience and denied full protection of the laws for one's "avowed commitment to an intimate and lasting human relationship." . . . Because civil marriage is central to the lives of individuals and the welfare of the community, our laws assiduously protect the individual's right to marry against undue government incursion. . . .

For decades, indeed centuries, in much of this country (including Massachusetts) no lawful marriage was possible between white and black Americans. That long history availed not when the Supreme Court of California held in 1948 that a legislative prohibition against interracial marriage violated the due process and equality guarantees of the Fourteenth Amendment, . . . or when, nineteen years later, the United States Supreme Court also held that a statutory bar to interracial marriage violated the Fourteenth Amendment. . . . As both [decisions] make clear, the right to marry means little if it does not include the right to marry the person of one's choice, subject to appropriate government restrictions in the interests of public health, safety, and welfare. . . .

The individual liberty and equality safeguards of the Massachusetts Constitution protect both "freedom from" unwarranted government intrusion into protected spheres of life and "freedom to" partake in benefits created by the State for the common good. . . . Both freedoms are involved here. Whether and whom to marry, how to express sexual intimacy, and whether and how to establish a family—these are among the most basic of every individual's liberty and due process rights. . . . And central to personal freedom and security is the assurance that the laws will apply equally to persons in similar situations. . . . The liberty interest in choosing whether and whom to marry would be hollow if the Commonwealth could, without sufficient justification, foreclose an individual from freely choosing the person with whom to share an exclusive commitment in the unique institution of civil marriage. . . .

Our laws of civil marriage do not privilege procreative heterosexual intercourse between married people above every other form of adult intimacy and every other means of creating a family. . . . Fertility is not a condition of marriage, nor is it grounds for divorce. People who have never consummated their marriage, and never plan to, may be and stay married. . . . People who cannot stir from their deathbed may marry. . . . While it is certainly true that many, perhaps most, married couples have children together (assisted or unassisted), it is the exclusive and permanent commitment of the marriage partners to one another, not the begetting of children, that is the *sine qua non* of civil marriage. . . .

No one disputes that the plaintiff couples are families, that many are parents, and that the children they are raising, like all children, need and should have the fullest opportunity to grow up in a secure, protected family unit. Similarly, no one disputes that, under the rubric of marriage, the State provides a cornucopia of substantial benefits to married parents and their children. . . .

In this case, we are confronted with an entire, sizeable class of parents raising children who have absolutely no access to civil marriage and its protections because they are forbidden from procuring a marriage license. It cannot be rational under our laws, and indeed it is not permitted, to penalize children by depriving them of State benefits because the State disapproves of their parents' sexual orientation. . . .

An absolute statutory ban on same-sex marriage bears no rational relationship to the goal of economy. First, the department's conclusory generalization—that same-sex couples are less financially dependent on each other than opposite-sex couples—ignores that many same-sex couples, such as many of the plaintiffs in this case, have children and other dependents (here, aged parents) in their care. The department does not contend, nor could it, that these dependents are less needy or deserving than the dependents of married couples. Second, Massachusetts marriage laws do not condition receipt of public and private financial benefits to married individuals on a demonstration of financial dependence on each other; the benefits are available to married couples regardless of whether they mingle their finances or actually depend on each other for support. . . .

We also reject the argument suggested by the department, and elaborated by some amici, that expanding the institution of civil marriage in Massachusetts to include same-sex couples will lead to interstate conflict. We would not presume to dictate how another State should respond to today's decision. But neither should considerations of comity prevent us from according Massachusetts residents the full measure of protection available under the Massachusetts Constitution. The genius of our Federal system is that each State's Constitution has vitality specific to its own traditions, and that, subject to the minimum requirements of the Fourteenth Amendment, each State is free to address difficult issues of individual liberty in the manner its own Constitution demands. . . .

Here, no one argues that striking down the marriage laws is an appropriate form of relief. Eliminating civil marriage would be wholly inconsistent with the Legislature's deep commitment to fostering stable families and would dismantle a vital organizing principle of our society. . . .

We construe civil marriage to mean the voluntary union of two persons as spouses, to the exclusion of all others. This reformulation redresses the plaintiffs' constitutional injury and furthers the aim of marriage to promote stable, exclusive relationships. It advances the two legitimate State interests the department has identified: providing a stable setting for child rearing and conserving State resources. It leaves intact the Legislature's broad discretion to regulate marriage. . . .

We declare that barring an individual from the protections, benefits, and obligations of civil marriage solely because that person would marry a person of the same sex violates the Massachusetts Constitution. We vacate the summary judgment for the department. We remand this case to the Superior Court for entry of judgment consistent with this opinion. Entry of judgment shall be stayed for 180 days to permit the Legislature to take such action as it may deem appropriate in light of this opinion. . . .

Justice Sosman, dissenting, with whom Spina and Cordy join

. . . Reduced to its essence, the court's opinion concludes that, because same-sex couples are now raising children, and withholding the benefits of civil marriage from their union makes it harder for them to raise those children, the State must therefore provide the benefits of civil marriage to same-sex couples just as it does to opposite-sex couples. Of course, many people are raising children outside the confines of traditional marriage, and, by definition, those children are being deprived of the various benefits that would flow if they were being raised in a household with married parents. That does not mean that the Legislature must accord the full benefits of marital status on every household raising children. Rather, the Legislature need only have some rational basis for concluding that, at present, those alternate family structures have not yet been conclusively shown to be the equivalent of the marital family structure that has established itself as a successful one over a period of centuries. People are of course at liberty to raise their children in various family structures, as long as they are not literally harming their children by doing so. . . . That does not mean that the State is required to provide identical forms of encouragement, endorsement, and support to all of the infinite variety of household structures that a free society permits. . . .

Although the Goodrich couple in this decision announced their intention to divorce in July 2006, in the two years after this court decision some 8,000 gay and lesbian couples have reportedly been married in Massachusetts. Efforts began almost immediately in the state to amend the Constitution to ban gay marriage and civil unions. Such state constitutional amendments had been passed in 20 states by 2006 and efforts were under way in almost another 20 states. Courts in several states, including Georgia, New York, and Washington, have upheld bans on gay marriage. At the Federal level, continuing efforts to amend the U.S. Constitution to ban gay marriage have failed to achieve the required three-fourths majority required to pass in both houses of Congress.

QUESTIONS FOR ANALYSIS

1. Arguments against the morality of homosexuality sometimes appeal to the "unnaturalness" of these relationships. Should the inability of gay or lesbian couples to procreate in the traditional way support a prohibition on their marriage or civil union? How should we determine what counts as "natural" for these purposes?
2. Do Levin's arguments against homosexuality effectively defeat the claims of a right to marriage by homosexual couples? Do Murphy's arguments in support of the morality of homosexuality support those claims?
3. Justice Scalia, in his dissent in *Lawrence*, claimed that decision set the groundwork for claims of a right to homosexual marriage in later decisions. Does the *Goodridge* decision here vindicate his worry? Could an argument for a right to homosexual marriage be made without appealing to the principles of *Lawrence*?
4. Should courts always defer to the moral preferences of the majority? Or do they have an obligation to uphold individual civil liberties, even if the rights claimed are unpopular with the majority?

CASE PRESENTATION

A Slippery Slope to Polygamy?

In Justice Scalia's dissent in *Lawrence*, he warned that the majority opinion set the stage for striking down other laws that banned behavior most consider immoral, including bigamy. In the few years since he wrote those words, several legal challenges have been made in Utah to that state's laws prohibiting polygamy, although none has succeeded to date.

The territory of Utah made several unsuccessful attempts to achieve statehood in the nineteenth century, but these attempts were rebuffed, in large measure, because of the practice of polygamy in the Church of Jesus Christ of Latter-Day Saints, the Mormons. LDS doctrine at the time claimed that it was "the duty of male members" of the church to practice polygamy. In 1862, President Abraham Lincoln signed legislation banning bigamy in the territories. The law was upheld in 1879 in a U.S. Supreme Court decision, *Reynolds v. United States*, a decision that has never been overturned. That Court said that a right of religious freedom in the First Amendment to the Constitution did not invalidate the ban on bigamy. The Court noted that polygamy had long been considered an "odious" practice in the Western world, although it was accepted in some areas of Asia and Africa. It also noted approvingly an argument that the real "innocent victims" of polygamy are the "pure-minded women" and "innocent children" who are the "sufferers" of this practice.

Utah finally achieved statehood in 1896, but only after including a ban on polygamy in its state constitution and a policy change by the Mormon church that it no longer advocated polygamy. But even today, break-away groups claiming allegiance to the original Mormon teaching practice polygamy in Utah and other western states. In 2004, a trio sued in Federal court, claiming their rights were violated when the Salt Lake County Clerk denied them a marriage license. The case was dismissed, noting that the *Lawrence* decision protected, at most, the private sexual practices of consenting adults but did not require the state to issue a marriage license. Another case was brought in the Utah State Supreme Court in 2006 challenging the state law prohibiting polygamy and arguing that the *Lawrence* decision should be considered precedent for a liberty right to engage in polygamy.

In March 2006, HBO launched an original series called "Big Love," in which a fictional Salt Lake City businessman in contemporary Utah is a polygamist with three wives. The show includes a disclaimer: "According to a joint report issued by the Utah and Arizona attorney generals' offices, July 2005, 'Approximately 20,000 to 40,000 or more people currently practice polygamy in the United States.' The Mormon Church officially banned the practice of polygamy in 1890." News reports at the time of the premiere indicated considerable concern in Utah that the series would revive old stereotypes about their Church. An anti-polygamy group called "Tapestry Against Polygamy" has argued that the practice exploits women and children, and it helps women in such illegal marriages to escape.

QUESTIONS FOR ANALYSIS

1. Does the reasoning of the Massachusetts Supreme Court granting a right of gay marriage also support a right to polygamous marriage?
2. Can gay marriage be distinguished from polygamous marriage in analyzing human rights to liberty and privacy?
3. Is it possible for women to freely consent to a polygamous marriage with one man? Are women and children the victims of these arrangements, as the *Reynolds* court said over a century ago?
4. Would you support polygamous marriage if both men and women had an equal right to multiple spouses?
5. Is polygamous marriage any more or less "natural" than homosexual marriage? What do you understand "natural" to mean for these purposes?

CHAPTER FOUR

Abortion

- **Biological Background**
- **The Moral Problem**
- **The Ontological Status of the Fetus**
- **The Moral Status of the Fetus**
- **Pro-Life Arguments (against Abortion)**
- **Pro-Choice Arguments (for Abortion)**

JOHN T. NOONAN **An Almost Absolute Value in History**
JUDITH JARVIS THOMSON **A Defense of Abortion**
MARY ANNE WARREN **On the Moral and Legal Status of Abortion**
ROSALIND HURSTHOUSE **Virtue Theory and Abortion**

CASE PRESENTATIONS: ***Conceived in Violence, Born in Hate* • *Death in Pensacola* • *The Fight for Martina Greywind's Baby* • *Sex-Selection Abortions***

JANE ROE WAS an unmarried pregnant woman who wished to have an abortion, an intentional termination of a pregnancy by inducing the loss of the fetus. But Ms. Roe lived in Texas, where statutes forbade abortion except to save the life of the mother. So she went to court to prove that the statutes were unconstitutional.

The three-judge district court ruled that Jane Roe had reason to sue, that the Texas criminal abortion statutes were void on their face, and most important, that the right to choose whether to have children was protected by the right to privacy implicit in several amendments to the U.S. Constitution. Even though the word "privacy" does not appear in the Constitution, the court reasoned that privacy rights they had earlier recognized to use contraception and to permit interracial marriage extended to a right to choose whether or not to have children. Since the district court denied a number of other aspects of the suit, the case went to the U.S. Supreme Court. On January 22, 1973, in the now famous *Roe v. Wade* decision (410 U.S. 113), the Supreme Court affirmed the district court's judgment.

Expressing the views of seven members of the Court, Justice Blackmun pointed out that the right to privacy applies to a woman's decision on whether to terminate her pregnancy but that her right to terminate is not absolute. Her right may be limited by the state's legitimate interests in safeguarding the woman's health, in maintaining proper medical standards, and in protecting human life. Blackmun went on to point out that fetuses are not included within the definition of *person* as used in the Fourteenth Amendment. Most important, he indicated that prior to the end of the first trimester of pregnancy, the state may not interfere with or regulate an attending physician's decision, reached in consultation with the patient, that the patient's pregnancy should be terminated. After the first trimester and until the fetus is viable, the state may regulate the abortion procedure only for the health of the mother. After the fetus becomes viable, the state may prohibit all abortions except those necessary to preserve the health or life of the mother.

In dissenting, Justices White and Rehnquist said that nothing in the language or history of the U.S. Constitution supported the Court's judgment and that the Court had simply manufactured a new constitutional right for pregnant women. The abortion issue, they said, should have been left with the people and the political processes they had devised to govern their affairs.

So for the time being at least, the question of a woman's constitutional right to an abortion has been legally resolved. But the issue is hardly settled. Since the *Roe* decision, a number of anti-abortion movements have surfaced, and many state legislatures have passed restrictive abortion laws, some designed to narrow abortion rights and discourage abortions, others designed to challenge *Roe v. Wade* in the courts in the hope that it will be overturned.

In an important case decided July 3, 1989, *Webster v. Reproductive Health Services* (492 U.S. 490), the U.S. Supreme Court upheld a Missouri law that declared in its preamble that the "life of each human being begins at conception." The Court considered this statement to be only a "value judgment favoring childbirth over abortion" and said they would not rule on its constitutionality or unconstitutionality. The law also requires physicians to conduct viability tests on the fetuses of women twenty weeks pregnant and prohibits the use of public funds, employees, and facilities to perform, assist, or counsel abortions not necessary to save the mother's life. Moreover, four justices indicated a willingness to overturn the *Roe* decision. Since then, the Court has upheld state laws requiring parental consent for abortions on minors.

The Court's most significant decision on abortion since *Webster* was *Planned Parenthood v. Casey* (505 U.S. 833), announced June 29, 1992. The issue in this case was a Pennsylvania law regulating abortions. Although the Court again upheld the right to abortion by a 5 to 4 majority, it also upheld two of the law's restrictions. The first requires a twenty-four hour waiting period following a mandatory presentation intended to dissuade the woman from having an abortion. The second requires teenagers to have the consent of a parent or a judge. Also upheld were two other provisions: one specifying medical emergencies that exempt a woman from the restrictions, the other requiring clinics and doctors to provide the state with statistical reports on abortions performed. One other requirement, that married women first tell their husbands, was struck down as placing an "undue burden" on them.

Also significant was the Court's *Stenberg v. Carhart* decision (530 U.S. 914), announced June 28, 2000. At issue was a Nebraska law banning in all circumstances except to save the woman's life a rare but highly controversial abortion technique called *evacuation and extraction* (D&X). The law did not use that term, however. Instead, it referred to the procedure with the term commonly used by abortion opponents, "partial birth abortion," which the law defined as "deliberately and intentionally delivering into the vagina a living unborn child, or a substantial portion thereof, for the purpose of performing a procedure that the person performing such procedure knows will kill the unborn child." The majority opinion cited two chief reasons for declaring the law unconstitutional. First, the law allowed no exception to preserve the woman's health. Second, the law's definition of "partial birth abortion" was broad enough to cover another abortion procedure, the one most commonly used in the second trimester (*dilation and evacuation,* or D&E). In doing so, it placed an "undue burden on a woman's right to terminate her pregnancy before viability."

Three years after this decision, the U.S. Congress passed, and President George W. Bush signed into law, a Federal ban very similar to the Nebraska ban struck down in the *Carhart* decision. The Federal ban has been struck down by several lower courts. It was considered by the U.S. Supreme Court in fall 2006 (*Gonzales v. Planned Parenthood*), with a decision anticipated no later than June 2007.

In the next section, we will explain these and other abortion procedures. For now, it's enough to say that abortion opponents are drafting new laws prohibiting D&X that are designed to withstand the Court's objections. We should also stress that the fight to overturn *Roe v. Wade,* whether through a constitutional amendment or sympathetic appointments to the Supreme Court, continues. Thus, abortion remains a live and controversial issue, both morally and legally.

Some say an abortion is right if (1) it is therapeutic—that is, if it is necessary to preserve the physical or mental health of the woman; (2) it prevents the birth of a child with a severe disability; or (3) it ends a pregnancy resulting from some criminal act of sexual intercourse. Others say that even therapeutic abortions are immoral. Still others argue that any restrictive abortion legislation is wrong and must be liberalized to allow a woman to have an abortion on demand—that is, at the request of her and her physician, regardless of or even in the absence of reasons. To evaluate such claims, it is helpful to know some biological background and to consider what sort of entities the unborn are and whether they have rights.

BIOLOGICAL BACKGROUND

Because most of the controversy surrounding the abortion issue concerns precisely when a human individual or "person" is considered to exist, it is important to have some background about the development of the human fetus and familiarity with the terms that designate the various developmental stages. Conception or fertilization occurs when a female germ cell, or *ovum,* is penetrated by a male germ cell, or *spermatozoon*. The result is a single cell containing a full genetic code of forty-six chromosomes, called the *zygote*. The zygote then journeys down the fallopian tube, which carries ova from the ovary to the uterus. This passage generally takes two or three days. During the journey, the zygote begins a process of cellular division that increases its size. Occasionally, the zygote ends its journey in the fallopian tube, where it continues to develop. Because the tube is so narrow, such a pregnancy generally must be terminated by surgery.

When the multicell zygote reaches the uterus, it floats free in the intrauterine fluid and develops into what is termed a *blastocyst,* a ball of cells surrounding a fluid-filled cavity. By the end of the second week, the blastocyst implants itself in the uterine wall. From the end of the second week until the end of the eighth week, the unborn entity is termed an *embryo*. In the interim (four to five weeks), organ systems begin to develop, and the embryo takes on distinctly human external features.

The eighth week is important in the biological development and in a discussion of abortion because it is then that brain activity generally becomes detectable. From this point until birth, the embryo is termed a *fetus*, although in common parlance *fetus* is used to designate the unborn entity at whatever stage.

Two other terms that designate events in fetal development are worth noting because they sometimes arise in abortion discussions. One is *quickening*, which refers to when the mother begins to feel the movements of the fetus. This occurs somewhere between the thirteenth and twentieth weeks. The second term is *viability*, the point at which the fetus is capable of surviving outside the womb. The fetus ordinarily reaches viability around the twenty-fourth week. Generally, then, events during pregnancy unfold as follows:

Developmental Timetable

zygote: first through third day

blastocyst: second day through second week

embryo: third week through eighth week

fetus: ninth week until birth

quickening: thirteenth week through twentieth week

viability: around twenty-fourth week

Should the unborn entity be terminated at any point in this timetable, an abortion is said to occur. Thus, *abortion simply refers to the termination of a pregnancy*.

Abortions can happen for a number of reasons. Sometimes the abortion occurs "spontaneously" because of internal biochemical factors or because of an injury to the woman. Such spontaneous abortions are ordinarily termed *miscarriages*. These generally involve no moral issues.

Abortions also can result directly from human intervention, which can occur in a variety of ways. Sometimes it happens very early, as when a woman takes a drug such as the "morning-after pill" to prevent the blastocyst from implanting in the uterine wall.

Subsequent intervention during the first trimester (through the twelfth week) usually takes the form of *vacuum aspiration*. In this procedure, the narrow opening of the uterus, the cervix, is dilated, and a small vacuum tube is inserted into the uterus to evacuate its contents through suction.

The most common abortion procedure after the twelfth week is dilation and evacuation. This procedure also involves dilation of the cervix, but the doctor uses surgical instruments, rather than a vacuum tube, to empty the uterus. How this procedure is performed depends on how advanced the pregnancy is. Up to week fifteen, fetal tissue is easily broken, so a spoon-shaped instrument known as a curette is used to scrape the uterine walls to make sure that no fetal tissue remains. After week fifteen, the fetus is generally too large to pass through the cervix, and its bones, having become more rigid, are less likely to break off. In that case, the evacuation requires that the fetus be dismembered after it has been partially pulled through the cervix.

After week sixteen, at the earliest, two other variants of D&E may be used. In the first, known as *intact D&E*, the skull of the fetus is collapsed by a sharp instrument before the entire fetus is pulled through the cervix. In the second, the position of the fetus is reversed to the breech position (feet first) and the skull is collapsed after the fetal body is pulled through the cervix. This procedure, dilation and extraction, was the one that Nebraska attempted to ban.

Before the widespread use of D&E in second trimester abortions, the most common method in use was *saline injection,* in which salt water is injected into the uterus to induce a miscarriage. The change to D&E came about because it is safer for the woman's health. Similarly, intact D&E is considered safer after the sixteenth week of pregnancy, and in a few rare cases—although there is some dispute among doctors—D&X is considered even safer.

Finally, there is one other form of abortion to consider, *mifepristone,* or RU-486, the abortion pill. Mifepristone works by blocking the action of progesterone, a steroid hormone needed to maintain a pregnancy. Approved first by France and China in 1988, and by thirteen other countries since, it did not receive approval in the United States until September 28, 2000, when the Food and Drug Administration (FDA) declared it safe and effective. Abortion by mifepristone is a three-step process. First, the woman takes the drug in her doctor's office. Second, she returns within thirty-six or forty-eight hours to take another drug, misoprostal, which forces the uterus to contract and expel the fetus. Third, she returns to the doctor's office two weeks later to make sure the pregnancy is terminated and her uterus is free of the fetal tissue.

In approving mifepristone, the FDA issued a number of restrictions. Most important, the drug cannot be used after the seventh week following the woman's last menstrual period. Since most abortions are performed later than that, no one yet knows how common its use will be.

THE MORAL PROBLEM

The key moral problem of abortion is: Under what conditions, if any, is abortion morally justifiable? In answer to this question, three positions are broadly identifiable.

(1) The so-called conservative view holds that abortion is never morally justifiable or, at most, justifiable only when the abortion is necessary to save the mother's life. This view is commonly associated with Roman Catholics, although they are certainly not the only persons who espouse it. (2) The so-called liberal view holds that abortion is always morally justifiable, regardless of the reasons or the time in fetal development. (3) The so-called intermediate or moderate views consider abortion morally acceptable up to a certain point in fetal development and/or claim that some reasons, not all, provide a sufficient justification for abortion.

While there is no consensus on the moral acceptability of abortion, there is agreement that any answer to the question depends on one's view of what sort of entities fetuses are and whether such entities have rights. These two important problems generally are referred to as the ontological and moral status of the fetus.

THE ONTOLOGICAL STATUS OF THE FETUS

In philosophy, the term **ontology** refers to the theory and nature of being and existence. When we speak of the **ontological** status of the fetus, we mean the kind of entity the fetus is. Determining the ontological status of fetuses bears directly on the issue of fetal rights and, subsequently, on permissible treatment of the fetus.

Actually, the problem of ontological status embraces a number of questions, such as: (1) whether the fetus is an individual organism; (2) whether the fetus is biologically a human being; (3) whether the fetus is psychologically a human being; (4) whether the fetus is a person.[1] Presumably, to affirm question two is to attribute more significant status to the fetus than to affirm question one, and to affirm question three is to assign even greater status. To affirm question four, that the fetus is a person, probably is to assign the most significant status to the fetus, although this, as well as the other presumptions, depends on the precise meaning of the concepts involved.

Complicating the question of the fetus's ontological status is the meaning of the expression *human life*. The concept of "human life" can be used in at least two different ways. On the one hand, it can refer to *biological* human life—that is, to a set of biological characteristics that distinguish the human species from other nonhuman species. In this sense, "human life" may be coextensive with "individual organism" as in question one. On the other hand, "human life" may refer to *psychological* human life—that is, to life that is characterized by the properties that are distinctly human. Among these properties might be the abilities to use symbols, to think, and to imagine. Abortion discussions can easily founder when these distinctions are not made. For example, many who would agree that abortion involves the taking of human life in the biological sense would deny that it involves taking human life in the psychological sense. Moreover, they might see nothing immoral about taking life exclusively in the biological sense, although they would consider taking life in the psychological sense morally unacceptable. Thus, they find nothing morally objectionable about abortion. Of course, at the root of this judgment is an assumption about the meaning of *human life*.

Intertwined with one's concept of human life is one's concept of "personhood." The concept of personhood may or may not differ from either the biological or the psychological sense of "human life." Some would argue that to be a person is simply to have the biological and/or psychological properties that make an organism human. However, others would propose additional conditions for personhood, such as consciousness, self-consciousness, rationality, even the capacities for communication and moral judgment. In this view, an entity must satisfy some or all of these criteria, even additional ones, to be a person. Still other theorists would extend the concept of personhood to include properties bestowed by human evaluation, in addition to the factual properties possessed by a person. Thus, they might argue that a person must be the bearer of legal rights and social responsibilities, and must be capable of being assigned moral responsibility, of being praised or blamed.

Clearly, the conditions that one believes are necessary for "person" status directly affect the ontological status of the fetus. For example, if the condition is only of an elementary biological nature, then the fetus can more easily qualify as a person than if the conditions include a list of factual properties. Further, if personhood must be analyzable in terms of properties bestowed by human evaluation, it becomes substantially more difficult for the fetus to qualify as a person.

---

[1] Tom L. Beauchamp and Le Roy Waiters, *Contemporary Issues in Bioethics* (Belmont, Calif.: Dickenson, 1978), p. 188.

In the final analysis, the ontological status of fetuses remains an open issue. But some viewpoint ultimately underpins any position on the morality of abortion. Whether conservative, liberal, or moderate, one must be prepared eventually to defend one's view of the ontological status of fetuses.

When Ontological Status Is Attained

Further complicating the problem of the ontological status is the question of when in fetal development the fetus gains full ontological status. Whether one claims the fetus is an individual organism, a biological human being, a psychological human being, or a full-fledged person, one must specify at what point in its biological development the fetus attains this status. It is one thing to say what status the fetus has; it is another to say *when* it has attained such status. A judgment about when the fetus has the status bears as directly on abortion views as does a judgment of the status itself.

We can identify a number of positions on when status is attained. An extreme conservative position would argue that the fetus has full ontological status from conception; at the time of conception, the fetus must be regarded as an individual person. In direct contrast to this view is the extreme liberal position, which holds that the fetus never achieves ontological status.

Viewing these as polar positions, we can identify a cluster of moderate views that fall between them. In every instance, the moderate view tries to pinpoint full ontological status somewhere between conception and birth. For example, some draw the line when brain activity is first present; others draw it at quickening; still others draw the line at viability.

Continuing progress in medicine has made these determinations increasingly difficult. With extraordinary medical support, very premature infants can be kept alive, challenging traditional views of what counts as viability. Some believe viability should be measured by an ability to live outside the womb without any medical intervention. Others believe newborn infants meet the test of viability even with the support of incubators, transfusions, and increasingly sophisticated medical assistance.

Medical advances have also challenged our definition of death, the cessation of the life of a person. Where cessation of a heartbeat once counted as death, the advent of heart transplants and mechanical hearts forced a change. Persons are now considered legally dead when all brain wave activity ceases. Some moderate abortion advocates suggest that the start of brain activity in a fetus should be the decisive point at which the fetus becomes a person and thus has the rights of persons. But there is disagreement about the extent of brain activity that would be required for such a test of personhood. And abortion foes say that the potential of a fetus for the development of brain activity—something a deceased person no longer has—makes the end of the life of a person irrelevant for determining the start of the life of a person.

THE MORAL STATUS OF THE FETUS

The issue of moral status of the fetus is generally, but not always, discussed in terms of the fetus's rights. What rights, if any, does it have? Any position on abortion must at some point address this question, and all seriously argued positions do, at least by implication.

Various views on the moral status of the fetus are currently circulating. Each view can be associated with one or another of the views on the fetus's ontological status. For example, claiming that the fetus has full ontological status at conception, the extreme conservative view also holds that it has full moral status at the same stage. From the moment of conception on, the unborn entity enjoys the same rights we attribute to any adult human. In this view, abortion would be a case of denying the unborn the right to life. Therefore, abortion could never be undertaken without reasons sufficient to override the unborn's claim to life. In other words, only conditions that would justify the killing of an adult human—for example, self-defense—would morally justify an abortion.

Liberals similarly derive their view of moral status from their theory of ontological status. The extreme liberal view would deny the fetus any moral status. In this view, abortion is not considered comparable to killing an adult person. Indeed, abortion may be viewed as removing a mass of organic material, not unlike an appendectomy. Its removal raises no serious moral problems. A somewhat less liberal view, while granting the fetus ontological status as being biologically human, claims it is not human in any significant moral sense and thus has no significant rights.

Likewise, moderates would assign moral status to the fetus at the point that the entity attained full ontological status. If brain activity is taken as the point of ontological status, for example, then abortions conducted before that time would not raise serious moral questions; those conducted subsequent to that development would. Currently, viability seems to be an especially popular point at which to assign ontological status. And so, many moderate theorists today insist that abortion raises significant moral questions only *after* the fetus has attained viability. This view is reflected in some of the opinions delivered in the *Roe v. Wade* case.

It is important to note that granting the fetus moral status does not at all deny moral status to the woman. Indeed, the question of whose rights should take precedence when a conflict develops raises thorny questions, especially for conservatives and moderates. For example, while granting the fetus full moral status, some conservatives nonetheless approve of therapeutic abortions—abortions performed to save the woman's life or to correct some life-threatening condition. These are often viewed as cases of self-defense or justifiable homicide. Since self-defense and justifiable homicide commonly are considered acceptable grounds for killing an adult person, they are also taken as moral justification for killing a fetus. But other conservatives disapprove of even therapeutic abortions.

Similarly, while moderates grant the fetus moral status at some point in development, they too must arbitrate cases of conflicting rights. They must determine just what conditions are sufficient for allowing the woman's right to override the fetus's right to life. Here the whole gamut of conditions involving the pregnancy must be evaluated, including rape, incest, fetal deformity, and of course, physical or psychological harm to the woman.

Moral Implications

Determining the moral status of the fetus, then, is directly related to determining when the fetus is actually a human. There is no question that even at the zygote stage, and from then on, the fetus is at least potentially human (until it becomes actually so). At whatever point it becomes human, we face a set of serious moral issues regarding abortion, among which are

1. Does the fetus have a right to be carried to full term?
2. Under what circumstances, if ever, can we take an innocent human life?
3. Is any other right more important than the right to life—for example, the woman's right to privacy, the woman's right not to be forced to carry a child that will make it impossible for her to have children in the future, or the woman's right not to carry the child of her rapist or her father or brother?
4. If the woman's life is in danger because of the pregnancy, how do we decide whose right prevails?

If, as is the case at present, we can't agree at what point the fetus becomes fully human, we're confronted with another set of problems.

1. Can we morally disregard the possibility that the fetus may be actually human (or may not)? If we do, does that imply, at best, an indifference to an important moral value? And is not such an attitude of not caring about a moral value itself morally questionable at least?
2. Can we ever act morally on a doubt—for example, a doubt about our obligation, the morally relevant facts, the morally correct means? How are we to resolve our doubt?
3. If reasonable people in the country hold irreconcilable moral and religious views on an issue such as abortion, is it appropriate for the government to "take sides" by forcing everyone to accept one of those views, whether through legislation or court decisions?

PRO-LIFE ARGUMENTS (AGAINST ABORTION)

1. *Abortion is murder.*

POINT: "The simple fact of the matter is that abortion is murder. What you call a 'fetus' is an unborn baby, a human being, and an abortion is nothing but the deliberate killing of that human being."

COUNTERPOINT: "Murder is the deliberate killing of a human person, and though a fetus is certainly a human *something,* it's hardly a person. In the earliest stages, it's nothing but a mass of cells. Even in later stages, when it begins to biologically resemble a human person, it still doesn't have anything remotely resembling a human life. It has no hopes, no plans, no concept of self, no stake in its own future. Sentimentalize it all you like, you still can't put a fetus ahead of the woman who carries it."

2. *Abortion sets a dangerous precedent.*

POINT: "Anything that leads to disrespect for human life is wrong. Anything that leads to a casual attitude toward human life is wrong. Whatever else you say about abortion, it certainly leads to disrespect for and a casual attitude toward human life. And that doesn't just hold for abortions of convenience or for sex selection. It holds for therapeutic abortions and abortions of deformed fetuses as well. Once we decide that some human lives can be destroyed because they're inconvenient or not worth living, what's to stop us from killing individuals with severe disabilities, dysfunctions, senility, and mentally illness?"

COUNTERPOINT: "Abortion has been legal in this country for more than two decades, and we haven't started to slide down any slippery slopes because of it yet. To the contrary, in 1990 Congress passed, and the president signed, a landmark civil rights act for individuals with handicaps. We both know that abortion is a distinct issue from the treatment of various groups in society, and each has to be decided on its own merits."

3. ***Abortion involves psychological risks to the woman.***

POINT: "A woman and the child she's carrying are as close to each other as any two humans can get. And I don't just mean biologically close but emotionally and psychologically close as well. Just ask any mother. A woman who intentionally harms her unborn child violates the deepest levels of her unconscious needs and desires, and she's bound to pay a psychological price for it. Plenty already have, as both psychologists and women who've had abortions can tell you."

COUNTERPOINT: "Many women, maybe even most, do want to carry their fetuses to term. And no doubt there are some women who do carry emotional scars from their abortions. But the vast majority of women who had abortions seem to have come through them quite well. The psychological portrait you paint of women and the deepest levels of their unconscious is nothing but a stereotype. And your desire to protect them from their considered decisions concerning what's best for them is insulting paternalism."

4. ***Alternatives to abortion are available.***

POINT: "You abortion rights advocates make it sound as though abortion is the only alternative to rearing an unwanted child. But it's not. Countless couples and individuals are dying to have children but can't. Because of all the abortion mills throughout the country, many of them can't even adopt a healthy infant. So adoption is one alternative to abortion. Even in cases of infants with severe deformities, there are alternatives. If no one wants to adopt them, there are plenty of agencies and institutions to take care of them."

COUNTERPOINT: "Why should a woman be treated as a breeding animal for childless couples? The mere fact that other people want her child doesn't mean she has to face the health risks and discomforts of pregnancy for them. It's her body, after all. Besides, the anguish of giving up a child carried to term can be much worse than aborting a fetus. And as for infants with severe deformities, what kind of favor are you doing them by sentencing them to miserable lives in institutions?"

5. ***Women must be responsible for their sexual activity.***

POINT: "No woman *has* to get pregnant. There are plenty of readily available contraceptives on the market. If a woman doesn't take advantage of them, it's her own fault and she has to take responsibility for her carelessness. To condone abortion is to condone her own irresponsibility. Even worse, it's to condone the killing of innocent life as an after-the-fact form of birth control."

COUNTERPOINT: "First of all, no form of birth control is 100 percent effective, except abstinence. To say that every unwanted pregnancy is the result of carelessness is like saying that every driver struck by another car is at fault. But even if the woman was careless, that doesn't affect her right to have an abortion any more than careless driving affects the driver's right to medical treatment. To deny her that right is to engage in vindictiveness, not to uphold any principle of responsibility."

PRO-CHOICE ARGUMENTS (FOR ABORTION)

1. ***Women have rights over their own bodies.***

POINT: "An unwanted pregnancy is an invasion of the woman's body, and to force a woman to carry a fetus to term is to force her to use her body for purposes she doesn't want to use it for. So the real issue here is whether women have the right to control their own bodies, whether they have the right to avail themselves of a simple, safe medical procedure to allow themselves to live their lives as they choose. Clearly the answer has to be yes. It's as fundamental a right as I can think of."

COUNTERPOINT: "No right is absolute. My right to swing my fist stops at your nose. My right to say whatever I please stops at yelling "fire!" in a crowded theater. Similarly, a woman's right to control her own body stops at taking the life of her unborn child. All your talk of 'invasion' and 'simple medical procedures' obscures the plain fact that once a woman conceives a child she's responsible for it. And that responsibility overrides her right to control her own body."

2. ***Unwanted pregnancies carry physical and emotional burdens.***

POINT: "Pregnancy isn't easy for women. Apart from the morning sickness, the back pains, the pain of childbirth, and a host of other discomforts in normal pregnancies, the possibility of unforeseen complications poses a real risk to their physical health and sometimes even their lives. To demand that a woman face all that in an unwanted pregnancy is to demand too much. And the unreasonable demands don't even stop there. Unwanted pregnancies carry emotional burdens as well as physical ones. Pregnancy can be a significant interruption in a woman's life, and motherhood can bring a serious disruption of her hopes and plans. Reproductive freedom isn't just a slogan. It's a matter of allowing a woman to control her own destiny."

COUNTERPOINT: "Yes, pregnancy can be difficult, and though I don't want to sound unsympathetic to pregnant women, I still have to insist that the woman isn't the only one involved here. Against the back pains, hemorrhoids, and varicose veins you have to balance the life of her child, which has to count for more. And as for the disruption of her hopes and plans, nobody says she has to rear the child. Don't forget—there's always adoption. The only place you may have a point is when it comes to serious risk to the woman's life. But to justify abortion for *every* woman on the grounds that she *might* face that risk is preposterous. Modern medicine has come too far for that."

3. ***The alternative to legal abortion is back alley abortion.***

POINT: "You may think that the burdens of unwanted pregnancy are minor, but many women don't. If safe, legal abortions aren't available to them, they'll resort to unsafe, illegal abortions. And if the past is any guide, that means serious infections in many cases and in some cases even death, especially for poor women who won't be able to afford anything but back alley abortions."

COUNTERPOINT: "Now you're confusing the issue. Whatever problems there may be in enforcing abortion laws is one issue. Whether abortion is moral or immoral is another. Enforcement problems might provide a reason not to ban abortions, but they certainly don't make abortions morally right. Then again, enforcement problems don't even provide a very good reason against banning abortions. As unfortunate as back alley abortions are for both the mothers and their unborn children, legalization encourages abortions; and if they're banned, there will be fewer of them."

4. ***The woman counts more than the fetus.***

POINT: "Everything you say is based on a single assumption—that the fetus counts as much as or even more than the woman. But that can't be true. A woman is a full-fledged person. She has real desires and fears, real aspirations and memories. She's connected to the world through her family and friends. She cares about her life and her future. At the very most, a fetus has only the potential for all that. And though I'm not saying the fetus's potential counts for nothing, I am saying an actual full human life out in the world has to count more than a potential full human life in the womb."

COUNTERPOINT: "Your distinction between an actual human life and a potential one just doesn't hold up. The difference between the mother and her unborn child isn't a matter of kind but of degree. Human life begins at conception. At that moment, we don't have a potential human life but a developing one. And who's to say that the more developed human life counts for more than the less developed one? If a woman doesn't count more than a ten-year-old, and if neither counts more than a two-year-old, why should any one of them count more than an unborn human life?"

An Almost Absolute Value in History

JOHN T. NOONAN

Like many authors on the subject of abortion, John T. Noonan, a judge on the U.S. Court of Appeals for the 9th Circuit, locates the central issue in the ontological status of the fetus. In his essay, Noonan assigns the fetus full ontological status at the moment of conception.

Noonan not only puts this view in the context of traditional Christian theology, but he also tests its strength compared with the other distinctions of ontological status that are commonly made: viability, experience, quickening, attitude of parents, and social visibility. Noonan shows why he thinks each of these distinctions is unsound.

From John T. Noonan, "An Almost Absolute Value in History," in *Morality of Abortion: Legal and Historical Perspectives*, ed. John T. Noonan (Cambridge, Mass: Harvard University Press, 1970). Reprinted by permission of the author.

In addition to the unique problems that each of these distinctions has, Noonan believes that they share one overriding problem: They are distinctions that appear to be arbitrary. Noonan feels that if distinctions leading to moral judgments are not to appear arbitrary, they should relate to some real difference in probabilities. He argues that his position passes this test because it recognizes the fact that 80 percent of the zygotes formed will develop into new beings. For Noonan, this probability is a most compelling reason for granting the conceptus (fetus) full ontological status.

In short, conception is the decisive moment of humanization, for it is then that the fetus receives the genetic code of the parents. These arguments lead Noonan to condemn abortion, except in cases of self-defense.

The most fundamental question involved in the long history of thought on abortion is: How do you determine the humanity of a being? To phrase the question that way is to put in comprehensive humanistic terms what the theologians either dealt with as an explicitly theological question under the heading of "ensoulment" or dealt with implicitly in their treatment of abortion. The Christian position as it originated did not depend on a narrow theological or philosophical concept. It had no relation to theories of infant baptism. It appealed to no special theory of instantaneous ensoulment. It took the world's view on ensoulment as that view changed from Aristotle to Zacchia. There was, indeed, theological influence affecting the theory of ensoulment finally adopted, and, of course, ensoulment itself was a theological concept, so that the position was always explained in theological terms. But the theological notion of ensoulment could easily be translated into humanistic language by substituting "human" for "rational soul"; the problem of knowing when a man is a man is common to theology and humanism.

If one steps outside the specific categories used by the theologians, the answer they gave can be analyzed as a refusal to discriminate among human beings on the basis of their varying potentialities. Once conceived, the being was recognized as man because he had man's potential. The criterion for humanity, thus, was simple and all-embracing: If you are conceived by human parents, you are human.

The strength of this position may be tested by a review of some of the other distinctions offered in the contemporary controversy over legalizing abortion. Perhaps the most popular distinction is in terms of viability. Before an age of so many months, the fetus is not viable, that is, it cannot be removed from the mother's womb and live apart from her. To that extent, the life of the fetus is absolutely dependent on the life of the mother. This dependence is made the basis of denying recognition to its humanity.

There are difficulties with this distinction. One is that the perfection of artificial incubation may make the fetus viable at any time: It may be removed and artificially sustained. Experiments with animals already show that such a procedure is possible. This hypothetical extreme case relates to an actual difficulty: there is considerable elasticity to the idea of viability. Mere length of life is not an exact measure. The viability of the fetus depends on the extent of its anatomical and functional development. The weight and length of the fetus are better guides to the state of its development than age, but weight and length vary. Moreover, different racial groups have different ages at which their fetuses are viable. Some evidence, for example, suggests that Negro fetuses mature more quickly than white fetuses. If viability is the norm, the standard would vary with race and with many individual circumstances.

The most important objection to this approach is that dependence is not ended by viability. The fetus is still absolutely dependent on someone's care in order to continue existence; indeed a child of one or three or even five years of age is absolutely dependent on another's care for existence; uncared for, the older fetus or the younger child will die as surely as the early fetus detached from the mother. The unsubstantial lessening in dependence at viability does not seem to signify any special acquisition of humanity.

A second distinction has been attempted in terms of experience. A being who has had experience, has lived and suffered, who possesses memories, is more human than one who has not. Humanity depends on formation by experience. The fetus is thus "unformed" in the most basic human sense.

This distinction is not serviceable for the embryo which is already experiencing and reacting. The embryo is responsive to touch after eight weeks and at least at that point is experiencing. At an earlier stage the zygote is certainly alive and responding to its environment. The distinction may also be challenged by the rare case where aphasia has erased adult memory: Has it erased humanity? More fundamentally, this distinction leaves even the older fetus or the younger child to be treated as an unformed inhuman thing. Finally, it is not clear why experience as such confers humanity. It could be argued that certain central experiences such as loving or learning are necessary to make a man human. But then human beings who have failed to love or to learn might be excluded from the class called man.

A third distinction is made by appeal to the sentiments of adults. If a fetus dies, the grief of the parents is not the grief they would have for a living child. The fetus is an unnamed "it" till birth, and is not perceived as personality until at least the fourth month of existence, when movements in the womb manifest a vigorous presence demanding joyful recognition by the parents.

Yet feeling is notoriously an unsure guide to the humanity of others. Many groups of humans have had difficulty in feeling that persons of another tongue, color, religion, sex, are as human as they. Apart from reactions to alien groups, we mourn the loss of a ten-year-old boy more than the loss of his one-day-old brother or his 90-year-old grandfather. The difference felt and the grief expressed vary with the potentialities extinguished, or the experience wiped out; they do not seem to point to any substantial difference in the humanity of baby, boy, or grandfather.

Distinctions are also made in terms of sensation by the parents. The embryo is felt within the womb only after about the fourth month. The embryo is seen only at birth. What can be neither seen nor felt is different from what is tangible. If the fetus cannot be seen or touched at all, it cannot be perceived as man.

Yet experience shows that sight is even more untrustworthy than feeling in determining humanity. By sight, color became an appropriate index for saying who was a man, and the evil of racial discrimination was given foundation. Nor can touch provide the test; a being confined by sickness, "out of touch" with others, does not thereby seem to lose his humanity. To the extent that touch still has appeal as a criterion, it appears to be a survival of the old English idea of "quickening"—a possible mistranslation of the Latin *animatus* used in the canon law. To that extent, touch as a criterion seems to be dependent on the Aristotelian notion of ensoulment, and to fall when this notion is discarded.

Finally, a distinction is sought in social visibility. The fetus is not socially perceived as human. It cannot communicate with others. Thus, both subjectively and objectively, it is not a member of society. As moral rules are rules for the behavior of members of society to each other, they cannot be made for behavior toward what is not yet a member. Excluded from the society of men, the fetus is excluded from the humanity of men.

By force of the argument from the consequences, this distinction is to be rejected. It is more subtle than that founded on an appeal to physical sensation, but it is equally dangerous in its implications. If humanity depends on social recognition, individuals or whole groups may be dehumanized by being denied any status in their society. Such a fate is fictionally portrayed in *1984* and has actually been the lot of many men in many societies. In the Roman empire, for example, condemnation to slavery meant the practical denial of most human rights; in the Chinese Communist world, landlords have been classified as enemies of the people and so treated as nonpersons by the state. Humanity does not depend on social recognition, though often the failure of society to recognize the prisoner, the alien, the heterodox as human has led to the destruction of human beings. Anyone conceived by a man and a woman is human. Recognition of this condition by society follows a real event in the objective order, however imperfect and halting the recognition. Any attempt to limit humanity to exclude some group runs the risk of furnishing authority and precedent for excluding other groups in the name of the consciousness or perception of the controlling group in the society.

A philosopher may reject the appeal to the humanity of the fetus because he views "humanity" as a secular view of the soul and because he doubts the existence of anything real and objective which can be identified as humanity. One answer to such a philosopher is to ask how he reasons about moral questions without supposing that there is a sense in which he and the others of whom he speaks are human. Whatever group is taken as the society which determines who may be killed is thereby taken as human. A second answer is to ask if he does not believe that there is a right and wrong way of deciding moral questions. If there is such a difference, experience may be appealed to: To decide who is human on the basis of the sentiment of a given society has led to consequences which rational men would characterize as monstrous.

The rejection of the attempted distinctions based on viability and visibility, experience and feeling, may be buttressed by the following considerations: Moral judgments often rest on distinctions, but if the distinctions are not to appear arbitrary fiat, they should relate to some real difference in probabilities. There is a kind of continuity in all life, but the earlier stages of the elements of human life possess tiny probabilities of development. Consider, for example, the spermatozoa in any normal ejaculate: There are about 200,000,000 in any single ejaculate, of which one has a chance of developing into a zygote. Consider the oocytes which may become ova: There are 100,000 to 1,000,000 oocytes in a female infant, of which a maximum of 390 are ovulated. But once spermatozoon and ovum meet and the conceptus is formed, such studies as have been made show that roughly in only 20 percent of the cases will spontaneous abortion occur. In other words, the chances are about 4 out of 5 that this new being will develop. At this stage in the life of the being there is a sharp shift in probabilities, an immense jump in potentialities. To make a distinction between the rights of spermatozoa and the rights of the fertilized ovum is to respond to an enormous shift in possibilities. For about twenty days after conception, the egg may split to form twins or combine with another egg to form a chimera, but the probability of either event happening is very small.

It may be asked, What does a change in biological probabilities have to do with establishing humanity? The argument from probabilities is not aimed at establishing humanity but at establishing an objective discontinuity which may be taken into account in moral discourse. As life itself is a matter of probabilities, as most moral reasoning is an estimate of probabilities, so it seems in accord with the structure of reality and the nature of moral thought to found a moral judgment on the change in probabilities at conception. The appeal to probabilities is the most commonsensical of arguments; to a greater or smaller degree all of us base our actions on probabilities, and in morals, as in law, prudence and negligence are often measured by the account one has taken of the probabilities. If the chance is 200,000,000 to 1 that the movement in the bushes into which you shoot is a man's, I doubt if many persons would hold you careless in shooting; but if the chances are 4 out of 5 that the movement is a human being's, few would acquit you of blame. Would the argument be different if only one out of ten children conceived came to term? Of course this argument would be different. This argument is an appeal to probabilities that actually exist, not to any and all states of affairs which may be imagined.

The probabilities as they do exist do not show the humanity of the embryo in the sense of a demonstration in logic any more than the probabilities of the movement in the bush being a man demonstrate beyond all doubt that the being is a man. The appeal is a "buttressing" consideration, showing the plausibility of the standard adopted. The argument focuses on the decisional factor in any moral judgment and assumes that part of the business of a moralist is drawing lines. One evidence of the nonarbitrary character of the line drawn is the difference of probabilities on either side of it. If a spermatozoon is destroyed, one destroys a being which had a chance of far less than 1 in 200 million of developing into a reasonable being, possessed of the genetic code, a heart and other organs, and capable of pain. If a fetus is destroyed, one destroys a being already possessed of the genetic code, organs, and sensitivity to pain, and one which had an 80 percent chance of developing further into a baby, outside the womb, who, in time, would reason.

The positive argument for conception as the decisive moment of humanization is that at conception the new being receives the genetic code. It is this genetic information which determines his characteristics, which is the biological carrier of the possibility of human wisdom, which makes him a self-evolving being. A being with a human genetic code is man.

This review of current controversy over the humanity of the fetus emphasizes what a fundamental question the theologians resolved in asserting the inviolability of the fetus. To regard the fetus as possessed of equal rights with other humans was not, however, to decide every case where abortion might be employed. It did decide the case where the argument was that the fetus should be aborted for its own good. To say a being was human was to say it had a destiny to decide for itself which could not be taken from it by another man's decision. But human beings with equal rights often come in conflict with each other, and some decision must be made as to whose claims are to prevail. Cases of conflict involving the fetus are different only in two respects: the total inability of the fetus to speak for itself and the fact that the right of the fetus regularly at stake is the right to life itself.

The approach taken by the theologians to these conflicts was articulated in terms of "direct" and "indirect." Again, to look at what they were doing from outside their categories, they may be said to have been drawing lines or "balancing values." "Direct" and "indirect" are spatial metaphors: "line drawing" is another. "To weigh" or "to balance" values is a metaphor of a more complicated mathematical sort hinting at the process which goes on in moral judgments. All the metaphors suggest that, in the moral judgments made, comparisons were necessary, that no value completely controlled. The principle of double effect was no doctrine fallen from heaven, but a method of analysis appropriate where two relative values were being compared. In Catholic moral theology, as it developed, life even of the innocent was not taken as an absolute. Judgments on acts affecting life issued from a process of weighing. In the weighing, the fetus was always given a value greater than zero, always a value separate and independent from its parents. This valuation was crucial and fundamental in all Christian thought on the subject and marked it off from any approach which considered that only the parents' interests needed to be considered.

Even with the fetus weighed as human, one interest could be weighed as equal or superior: that of the mother in her own life. The casuists between 1450 and 1895 were willing to weigh this interest as superior. Since 1895, that interest was given decisive weight only in the two special cases of the cancerous uterus and the ectopic pregnancy. In both of these cases the fetus itself had little chance of survival even if the abortion were not performed. As the balance was once struck in favor of the mother whenever her life was endangered, it could be so struck again. The balance reached between 1895 and 1930 attempted prudentially and pastorally to forestall a multitude of exceptions for interests less than life.

The perception of the humanity of the fetus and the weighing of fetal rights against other human rights constituted the work of the moral analysts. But what spirit animated their abstract judgments? For the Christian community it was the injunction of Scripture to love your neighbor as yourself. The fetus as human was a neighbor; his life had parity with one's own. The commandment gave life to what otherwise would have been only rational calculation.

The commandment could be put in humanistic as well as theological terms: Do not injure your fellow man without reason. In these terms, once the humanity of the fetus is perceived, abortion is never right except in self-defense. When life must be taken to save life, reason alone cannot say that a mother must prefer a child's life to her own. With this exception, now of great rarity, abortion violates the rational humanist tenet of the equality of human lives.

For Christians the commandment to love had received a special imprint in that the exemplar proposed of love was the love of the Lord for his disciples. In the light given by this example, self-sacrifice carried to the point of death seemed in the extreme situations not without meaning. In the less extreme cases, preference for one's own interests to the life of another seemed to express cruelty or selfishness irreconcilable with the demands of love.

QUESTIONS FOR ANALYSIS

1. Do you agree that considering the unborn a person from the moment of conception poses fewer problems than any of the alternative views?
2. What problems does Noonan see in distinctions based on: (a) viability, (b) experience, (c) feelings of adults, (d) social visibility?
3. Explain how Noonan used "biological probabilities" to buttress his view of the unborn as a person from the moment of conception. Is his argument persuasive?
4. On what grounds does Noonan object to abortion?
5. Is it accurate to say that Noonan finds abortion always impermissible?

A Defense of Abortion

JUDITH JARVIS THOMSON

Philosopher Judith Jarvis Thomson, Massachusetts Institute of Technology, wrote this essay in 1971. It has since become a classic in the literature of abortion.

What makes her treatment of the pro-choice position unique is that it begins by conceding, for the sake of argument, that the fetus is a person from the moment of conception. This concession is significant because, as Thomson points out, most opposition to abortion builds on the assumption that the fetus has person status and rights from the moment of conception.

Thomson focuses her essay on an important question: Granted that the fetus is a person from the moment of conception, does it necessarily follow that abortion is always wrong? She thinks not. Relying primarily on a series of analogies, she attacks the argument that the immorality of abortion is entailed by the premise that asserts the person status of the fetus.

Toward the end of her essay, Thomson admits that anti-abortionists might object that the immorality of abortion follows not so much from the fact that the fetus is a person as from the special relationship between the fetus and the mother. Thus, anti-abortionists claim that the fetus is a person for whom the woman has a unique kind of responsibility because she is the mother.

In responding to this claim, Thomson argues that we have no responsibility for another person unless we have assumed it. If parents do not take any birth control measures, if they

From Judith Jarvis Thomson, "A Defense of Abortion." *Philosophy & Public Affairs*, 1, no. 1 (Fall 1971). Ms. Thomson acknowledges her indebtedness to James Thomson for discussion, criticism, and many helpful suggestions.

do not elect an abortion, if they choose to take the child home with them from the hospital, then certainly, they have a responsibility to and for the child. For they then have assumed responsibility, implicitly and explicitly, in all their actions. But if a couple has taken measures to prevent conception, this implies quite the opposite of any "special responsibility" for the unintended and unwanted fetus. Thus, in Thomson's view, the woman has no special responsibility to the fetus simply because of a biological relationship.

Ironically, as Thomson points out, many pro-choice advocates object to her argument for a couple of reasons. First, while Thomson argues that abortion is not impermissible, she does not think it is always permissible. There may be times, for example, when carrying the child to term requires only minimal inconvenience; in such cases, the woman would be required by "Minimally Decent Samaritanism" to have the child. Those supporting abortion on demand object to such a limitation of choice.

Second, while Thomson, like act utilitarians, would sanction some acts of abortion, she is not arguing for the right to kill the unborn child. That is, removing a nonviable fetus from the mother's body and thereby guaranteeing its death is not the same as removing a viable fetus from the mother's body and then killing it. In Thomson's view, the former may be permissible; the latter never is. Again, some pro-choice advocates object to this limitation of choice.

Most opposition to abortion relies on the premise that the fetus is a human being, a person, from the moment of conception. The premise is argued for, but, as I think, not well. Take, for example, the most common argument. We are asked to notice that the development of a human being from conception through birth into childhood is continuous; then it is said that to draw a line, to choose a point in this development and say "before this point the thing is not a person, after this point it is a person" is to make an arbitrary choice, a choice for which in the nature of things no good reason can be given. It is concluded that the fetus is, or anyway that we had better say it is, a person from the moment of conception. But this conclusion does not follow. Similar things might be said about the development of an acorn into an oak tree, and it does not follow that acorns are oak trees, or that we had better say they are. Arguments of this form are sometimes called "slippery slope arguments"—the phrase is perhaps self-explanatory—and it is dismaying that opponents of abortion rely on them so heavily and uncritically.

I am inclined to agree, however, that the prospects for "drawing a line" in the development of the fetus look dim. I am inclined to think also that we shall probably have to agree that the fetus has already become a human person well before birth. Indeed, it comes as a surprise when one first learns how early in its life it begins to acquire human characteristics. By the tenth week, for example, it already has a face, arms and legs, fingers and toes; it has internal organs, and brain activity is detectable.[1] On the other hand, I think that the premise is false, that the fetus is not a person from the moment of conception. A newly fertilized ovum, a newly implanted clump of cells, is no more a person than an acorn is an oak tree. But I shall not discuss any of this. For it seems to me to be of great interest to ask what happens if, for the sake of argument, we allow the premise. How, precisely, are we supposed to get from there to the conclusion that abortion is morally impermissible? Opponents of abortion commonly spend most of their time establishing that the fetus is a person, and hardly any time explaining the step from there to the impermissibility of abortion. Perhaps they think the step too simple and obvious to require much comment. Or perhaps instead they are simply being economical in argument. Many of those who defend abortion rely on the premise that the fetus is not a person, but only a bit of tissue that will become a person at birth; and why pay out more arguments than you have to? Whatever the explanation, I suggest that the step they take is neither easy nor obvious, that it calls for closer examination than it is commonly given, and that when we do give it this closer examination we shall feel inclined to reject it.

I propose, then, that we grant that the fetus is a person from the moment of conception. How does the argument go from here? Something like this, I take it. Every person has a right to life. So the fetus has a right to life. No doubt the mother has a right to decide what shall happen in and to her body; everyone would grant that. But surely a person's right to life is stronger and more stringent than the mother's right to decide what happens in and to her body, and so outweighs it. So the fetus may not be killed; an abortion may not be performed.

It sounds plausible. But now let me ask you to imagine this. You wake up in the morning and find yourself back to back in bed with an unconscious violinist. A famous unconscious violinist. He has been found to have a fatal kidney ailment, and the Society of Music Lovers has canvassed all the available medical records and found that you alone have the right blood type to help. They have therefore kidnapped you, and last night the violinist's circulatory system was plugged into yours, so that your kidneys can be used to extract poisons from his blood as well as your own. The director of the hospital now tells you, "Look, we're sorry the Society of Music Lovers did this to you—we would never have permitted it if we had known. But still, they did it, and the violinist now is plugged into you. To unplug you would be to kill him. But never mind, it's only for nine months. By then he will have recovered from his ailment, and can safely be unplugged from you." Is it morally incumbent on you to accede to this situation? No doubt it would be very nice of you if you did, a great kindness. But do you *have* to accede to it? What if it were not nine months, but nine years? Or longer still? What if the director of the hospital says, "Tough luck, I agree, but you've now got to stay in bed, with the violinist plugged into you, for the rest of your life. Because remember this. All persons have a right to life, and violinists are persons. Granted you have a right to decide what happens in and to your body, but a person's right to life outweighs your right to decide what happens in and to your body. So you cannot ever be unplugged from him." I imagine you would regard this as outrageous, which suggests that something really is wrong with that plausible-sounding argument I mentioned a moment ago.

In this case, of course, you were kidnapped; you didn't volunteer for the operation that plugged the violinist into your kidneys. Can those who oppose abortion on the ground I mentioned make an exception for a pregnancy due to rape? Certainly. They can say that persons have a right to life only if they didn't come into existence because of rape; or they can say that all persons have a right to life, but that some have less of a right to life than others, in particular, that those who came into existence because of rape have less. But these statements have a rather unpleasant sound. Surely the question of whether you have a right to life at all, or how much of it you have, shouldn't turn on the question of whether or not you are the product of a rape. And in fact the people who oppose abortion on the ground I mentioned do not make this distinction, and hence do not make an exception in the case of rape.

Nor do they make an exception for a case in which the mother has to spend the nine months of her pregnancy in bed. They would agree that would be a great pity, and hard on the mother; but all the same, all persons have a right to life, the fetus is a person, and so on. I suspect, in fact, that they would not make an exception for a case in which, miraculously enough, the pregnancy went on for nine years, or even the rest of the mother's life.

Some won't even make an exception for a case in which continuation of the pregnancy is likely to shorten the mother's life; they regard abortion as impermissible even to save the mother's life. Such cases are nowadays very rare, and many opponents of abortion do not accept this extreme view. All the same, it is a good place to begin: A number of points of interest come out in respect to it.

1. Let us call the view that abortion is impermissible even to save the mother's life "the extreme view." I want to suggest first that it does not issue from the argument I mentioned earlier without the addition of some fairly powerful premises. Suppose a woman has become pregnant, and now learns that she has a cardiac condition such that she will die if she carries the baby to term. What may be done for her? The fetus, being a person, has a right to life, but as the mother is a person too, so has she a right to life. Presumably they have an equal right to life. How is it supposed to come out that an abortion may not be performed? If mother and child have an equal right to life, shouldn't we perhaps flip a coin? Or should we add to the mother's right to life her right to decide what happens in and to her body, which everybody seems to be ready to grant—the sum of her rights now outweighing the fetus' right to life?

The most familiar argument here is the following. We are told that performing the abortion would be directly killing[2] the child, whereas doing nothing would not be killing the mother, but only letting her die. Moreover, in killing the child, one would be killing an innocent person, for the child has committed no crime, and is not aiming at his mother's death. And then there are a variety of ways in which this might be continued. (1) But as directly killing an innocent person is always and absolutely impermissible, an abortion may not be performed. Or, (2) as directly killing an innocent person is murder, and murder is always and absolutely impermissible, an abortion may not be performed.[3] Or, (3) as one's duty to refrain from directly killing an innocent person is more stringent than one's duty to keep a person from dying, an abortion may not be performed. Or, (4) if one's only options are directly killing an innocent person or letting a person die, one must prefer letting the person die, and thus an abortion may not be performed.[4]

Some people seem to have thought that these are not further premises which must be added if the conclusion is to be reached, but that they follow from the very fact that an innocent person has a right to life.[5] But this seems to me to be a mistake, and perhaps the simplest way to show this is to bring out that while we must certainly grant that innocent persons have a right to life, the theses in (1) through (4) are all false. Take (2), for example. If directly killing an innocent person is murder, and thus is impermissible, then the mother's directly killing the innocent person inside her is murder, and thus is impermissible. But it cannot seriously be thought to be murder if the mother performs an abortion on herself to save her life. It cannot seriously be said that she *must* refrain, that she *must* sit passively by and wait for her death. Let us look again at the case of you and the violinist. There you are, in bed with the violinist, and the director of the hospital says to you, "It's all most distressing, and I deeply sympathize, but you see this is putting an additional strain on your kidneys, and you'll be dead within the month. But you *have* to stay where you are all the same. Because unplugging you would be directly killing an innocent violinist, and that's murder, and that's impermissible." If anything in the world is true, it is that you do not commit murder, you do not do what is impermissible, if you reach around to your back and unplug yourself from that violinist to save your life.

The main focus of attention in writings on abortion has been on what a third party may or may not do in answer to a request from a woman for an abortion. This is in a way understandable. Things being as they are, there isn't much a woman can safely do to abort herself. So the question asked is what a third party may do, and what the mother may do, if it is mentioned at all, is deduced, almost as an afterthought, from what it is concluded that third parties may do. But it seems to me that to treat the matter in this way is to refuse to grant to the mother that very status of person which is so firmly insisted on for the fetus. For we cannot simply read off what a person may do from what a third party may do. Suppose you find yourself trapped in a tiny house with a growing child. I mean a very tiny house, and a rapidly growing child—you are already up against the wall of the house and in a few minutes you'll be crushed to death. The child on the other hand won't be crushed to death; if nothing is done to stop him from growing he'll be hurt, but in the end he'll simply burst open the house and walk out a free man. Now I could well understand it if a bystander were to say, "There's nothing we can do for you. We cannot choose between your life and his, we cannot be the ones to decide who is to live, we cannot intervene." But it cannot be concluded that you too can do nothing, that you cannot attack it to save your life. However innocent the child may be, you do not have to wait passively while it crushes you to death. Perhaps a pregnant woman is vaguely felt to have the status of house, to which we don't allow the right of self-defense. But if the woman houses the child, it should be remembered that she is a person who houses it.

I should perhaps stop to say explicitly that I am not claiming that people have a right to do anything whatever to save their lives. I think, rather, that there are drastic limits to the right of self defense. If someone threatens you with death unless you torture someone else to death, I think you have not the right, even to save your life, to do so. But the case under consideration here is very different. In our case there are only two people involved, one whose life is threatened, and one who threatens it. Both are innocent: The one who is threatened is not threatened because of any fault, the one who threatens does not threaten because of any fault. For this reason we may feel that we bystanders cannot intervene. But the person threatened can.

In sum, a woman surely can defend her life against the threat to it posed by the unborn child, even if doing so involves its death. And this shows not merely that the theses in (1) through (4) are false; it shows also that the extreme view of abortion is false, and so we need not canvass any other possible ways of arriving at it from the argument I mentioned at the outset.

2. The extreme view could of course be weakened to say that while abortion is permissible to save the mother's life, it may not be performed by a third party, but only by the mother herself. But this cannot be right either. For what we have to keep in mind is that the mother and the unborn child are not like two tenants in a small house which has, by an unfortunate mistake, been rented to both: The mother *owns* the house. The fact that she does adds to the offensiveness of deducing that the mother can do nothing from the supposition that third parties can do nothing. But it does more than this: It casts a bright light on the supposition that third parties can do nothing. Certainly it lets us see that a third party who says "I cannot choose between you" is fooling himself if he thinks this is impartiality. If Jones has found and fastened on a certain coat, which he needs to keep him from freezing, but which Smith also needs to keep him from freezing, then it is not impartiality that says "I cannot choose between you" when Smith owns the coat. Women have said again and again "This body is *my* body!" and they have reason to feel angry, reason to feel that it has been like shouting into the wind. Smith, after all, is hardly likely to bless us if we say to him, "Of course it's your coat, anybody would grant that it is. But no one may choose between you and Jones who is to have it."

We should really ask what it is that says "no one may choose" in the face of the fact that the body that houses the child is the mother's body. It may be simply a failure to appreciate this fact. But it may be something more interesting, namely the sense that one has a right to refuse to lay hands on people, even where it would be just and fair to do so, even where justice seems to require that somebody do so. Thus justice might call for somebody to get Smith's coat back from Jones, and yet you have a right to refuse to be the one to lay hands on Jones, a right to refuse to do physical violence to him. This, I think, must be granted. But then what should be said is not "no one may choose," but only "*I* cannot choose," and indeed not even this, but "*I* will not *act*," leaving it open that somebody else can or should, and in particular that anyone in a position of authority, with the job of securing people's rights, both can and should. So this is no difficulty. I have not been arguing that any given third party must accede to the mother's request that he perform an abortion to save her life, but only that he may.

I suppose that in some views of human life the mother's body is only on loan to her, the loan not being one which gives her any prior claim to it. One who held this view might well think it impartiality to say "I cannot choose." But I shall simply ignore this possibility. My own view is that if a human being has any just, prior claim to anything at all, he has a just, prior claim to his own body. And perhaps this needn't be argued for here anyway, since, as I mentioned, the arguments against abortion we are looking at do grant that the woman has a right to decide what happens in and to her body.

But although they do grant it, I have tried to show that they do not take seriously what is done in granting it. I suggest the same thing will reappear even more clearly when we turn away from cases in which the mother's life is at stake, and attend, as I propose we now do, to the vastly more common cases in which a woman wants an abortion for some less weighty reason than preserving her own life.

3. Where the mother's life is not at stake, the argument I mentioned at the outset seems to have a much stronger pull. "Everyone has a right to life, so the unborn person has a right to life." And isn't the child's right to life weightier than anything other than the mother's own right to life, which she might put forward as ground for an abortion?

This argument treats the right to life as if it were unproblematic. It is not, and this seems to me to be precisely the source of the mistake.

For we should now, at long last, ask what it comes to, to have a right to life. In some views having a right to life includes having a right to be given at least the bare minimum one needs for continued life. But suppose that what in fact is the bare minimum a man needs for continued life is something he has no right at all to be given? If I am sick unto death, and the only thing that will save my life is the touch of Henry Fonda's cool hand on my fevered brow, then all the same, I have no right to be given the touch of Henry Fonda's cool hand on my fevered brow. It would be frightfully nice of him to fly in from the West Coast to provide it. It would be less nice, though no doubt well meant, if my friends flew out to the West Coast and carried Henry Fonda back with them. But I have no right at all against anybody that he should do this for me. Or again, to return to the story I told earlier, the fact that for continued life that violinist needs the continued use of your kidneys does not establish that he has a right to be given the continued use of your kidneys. He certainly has no right against you that *you* should give him continued use of your kidneys. For nobody has any right to use your kidneys unless you give him such a right; and nobody has the right against you that you shall give him this right—if you do allow him to go on using your kidneys, this is a kindness on your part, and not something he can claim from you as his due. Nor has he any right against anybody else that *they* should give him continued use of your kidneys. Certainly he had no right against the Society of Music Lovers that they should plug him into you in the first place. And if you now start to unplug yourself, having learned that you will otherwise have to spend nine years in bed with him, there is nobody in the world who must try to prevent you, in order to see to it that he is given something he has a right to be given.

Some people are rather stricter about the right to life. In their view, it does not include the right to be given anything, but amounts to, and only to, the right not to be killed by anybody. But here a related difficulty arises. If everybody is to refrain from killing that violinist, then everybody must refrain from doing a great many different sorts of things. Everybody must refrain from slitting his throat, everybody must refrain from shooting him and everybody must refrain from unplugging you from him. But does he have a right against everybody that they shall refrain from unplugging you from him? To refrain from doing this is to allow him to continue to use your kidneys. It could be argued that he has a right against us that we should allow him to continue to use your kidneys. That is, while he had no right against us that we should give him the use of your kidneys, it might be argued that he anyway has a right against us that we shall not now intervene and deprive him of the use of your kidneys. I shall come back to third-party interventions later. But certainly the violinist has no right against you that *you* shall allow him to continue to use your kidneys. As I said, if you do allow him to use them, it is a kindness on your part, and not something you owe him.

The difficulty I point to here is not peculiar to the right of life. It reappears in connection with all the other natural rights; and it is something which an adequate account of rights must deal with. For present purposes it is enough just to draw attention to it. But I would stress that I am not arguing that people do not have a right to life—quite to the contrary, it seems to me that the primary control we must place on the acceptability of an account of rights is that it should turn out in that account to be a truth that all persons have a right to life. I am arguing only that having a right to life does not guarantee having either a right to be given the use of or a right to be allowed continued use of another person's body—even if one needs it for life itself. So the right to life will not serve the opponents of abortion in the very simple and clear way in which they seem to have thought it would.

4. There is another way to bring out the difficulty. In the most ordinary sort of case, to deprive someone of what he has a right to is to treat him unjustly. Suppose a boy and his small brother are jointly given a box of chocolates for Christmas. If the older boy takes the box and refuses to give his brother any of the chocolates, he is unjust to him, for the brother has been given a right to half of them. But suppose that, having learned that otherwise it means nine years in bed with that violinist, you unplug yourself from him. You surely are not being unjust to him, for you gave him no right to use your kidneys, and no one else can have given him any such right. But we have to notice that in unplugging yourself, you are killing him; and violinists, like everybody else, have a right to life, and thus in the view we were considering just now, the right not to be killed. So here you do what he supposedly has a right you shall not do, but you do not act unjustly to him in doing it.

The emendation which may be made at this point is this: The right to life consists not in the right not to be killed, but rather in the right not to be killed unjustly. This runs a risk of circularity, but never mind: It would enable us to square the fact that the violinist has a right to life with the fact that you do not act unjustly toward him in unplugging yourself, thereby killing him. For if you do not kill him unjustly, you do not violate his right to life, and so it is no wonder you do him no injustice.

But if this emendation is accepted, the gap in the argument against abortion stares us plainly in the face: It is by no means enough to show that the fetus is a person, and to remind us that all persons have a right to life—we need to be shown also that killing the fetus violates its right to life, that abortion is unjust killing. And is it?

I suppose we may take it as a datum that in the case of pregnancy due to rape the mother has not given the unborn person a right to the use of her body for food and shelter. Indeed, in what pregnancy should it be supposed that the mother has given the unborn person such a right? It is not as if there were unborn persons drifting about the world, to whom a woman who wants a child says "I invite you in."

But it might be argued that there are other ways one can have acquired a right to the use of another person's body than by having been invited to use it by that person. Suppose a woman voluntarily indulges in intercourse, knowing of the chance it will issue in pregnancy, and then she does become pregnant; is she not in part responsible for the presence, in fact the very existence, of the unborn person inside? No doubt she did not invite it in. But doesn't her partial responsibility for its being there itself give it a right to the use of her body?[6] If so, then her aborting it would be more like the boy's taking away the chocolates, and less like your unplugging yourself from the violinist—doing so would be depriving it of what it does have a right to, and thus would be doing it an injustice.

And then, too, it might be asked whether or not she can kill it even to save her own life: If she voluntarily called it into existence, how can she now kill it, even in self-defense?

The first thing to be said about this is that it is something new. Opponents of abortion have been so concerned to make out the independence of the fetus, in order to establish that it has a right to life, just as its mother does, that they have tended to overlook the possible support they might gain from making out that the fetus is *dependent* on the mother, in order to establish that she has a special kind of responsibility for it, a responsibility that gives it rights against her which are not possessed by any independent person—such as an ailing violinist who is a stranger to her.

On the other hand, this argument would give the unborn person a right to its mother's body only if her pregnancy resulted from a voluntary act, undertaken in full knowledge of the chance a pregnancy might result from it. It would leave out entirely the unborn person whose existence is due to rape. Pending the availability of some further argument, then, we would be left with the conclusion that unborn persons whose existence is due to rape have no right to the use of their mothers' bodies, and thus that aborting them is not depriving them of anything they have a right to and hence is not unjust killing.

And we should also notice that it is not at all plain that this argument really does go even as far as it purports to. For there are cases and cases, and the details make a difference. If the room is stuffy, and I therefore open a window to air it, and a burglar climbs in, it would be absurd to say, "Ah, now he can stay, she's given him a right to the use of her house—for she is partially responsible for his presence there, having voluntarily done what enabled him to get in, in full knowledge that there are such things as burglars, and that burglars burgle." It would be still more absurd to say this if I had had bars installed outside my windows, precisely to prevent burglars from getting in, and a burglar got in only because of a defect in the bars. It remains equally absurd if we imagine it is not a burglar who climbs in, but an innocent person who blunders or falls in. Again, suppose it were like this: Peopleseeds drift about in the air like pollen, and if you open your windows, one may drift in and take root in your carpets or upholstery. You don't want children, so you fix up your windows with fine mesh screens, the very best you can buy. As can happen, however, and on very, very rare occasions does happen, one of the screens is defective; and a seed drifts in and takes root. Does the personplant who now develops have a right to the use of your house? Surely not—despite the fact that you voluntarily opened your windows, you knowingly kept carpets and upholstered furniture, and you knew that screens were sometimes defective. Someone may argue that you are responsible for its rooting, that it does have a right to your house, because after all you could have lived out your life with bare floors and furniture, or with sealed windows and doors. But this won't do—for by the same token anyone can avoid a pregnancy due to rape by having a hysterectomy, or anyway by never leaving home without a (reliable) army.

It seems to me that the argument we are looking at can establish at most that there are *some* cases in which the unborn person has a right to the use of its mother's body, and therefore *some* cases in which abortion is unjust killing. There is room for much discussion and argument as to precisely which, if any. But I think we should sidestep this issue and leave it open, for at any rate the argument certainly does not establish that all abortion is unjust killing.

5. There is room for yet another argument here, however. We surely must grant that there may be cases in which it would be morally indecent to detach a person from your body at the cost of his life. Suppose you learn that what the violinist needs is not nine years of your life, but only one hour: All you need do to save his life is spend one hour in that bed with him. Suppose also that letting him use your kidneys for that one hour would not affect your health in the slightest. Admittedly you were kidnapped. Admittedly you did not give anyone permission to plug him into you. Nevertheless it seems to me plain you *ought* to allow him to use your kidneys for that hour—it would be indecent to refuse.

Again, suppose pregnancy lasted only an hour, and constituted no threat to life or death [sic]. And suppose that a woman becomes pregnant as a result of rape. Admittedly she did not voluntarily do anything to bring about the existence of a child. Admittedly she did nothing at all which would give the unborn person a right to the use of her body. All the same it might well be said, as in the newly emended violinist story, that she *ought* to allow it to remain for that hour that it would be indecent in her to refuse.

Now some people are inclined to use the term "right" in such a way that it follows from the fact that you ought to allow a person to use your body for the hour he needs, that he has a right to use your body for the hour he needs, even though he has not been given that right by any person or act. They may say that it follows also that if you refuse, you act unjustly toward him. This use of the term is perhaps so common that it cannot be called wrong; nevertheless it seems to me to be an unfortunate loosening of what we would do better to keep a tight rein on. Suppose that box of chocolates I mentioned earlier had not been given to both boys jointly, but was given only to the older boy. There he sits, stolidly eating his way through the box, his small brother watching enviously. Here we are likely to say "You ought not to be so mean. You ought to give your brother some of those chocolates." My own view is that it just does not follow from the truth of this that the brother has any right to any of the chocolates. If the boy refuses to give his brother any, he is greedy, stingy, callous—but not unjust. I suppose that the people I have in mind will say it does follow that the brother has a right to some of the chocolates, and thus that the boy does act unjustly if he refuses to give his brother any. But the effect of saying this is to obscure what we should keep distinct, namely the difference between the boy's refusal in this case and the boy's refusal in the earlier case, in which the box was given to both boys jointly, and in which the small brother thus had what was from any point of view clear title to half.

A further objection to so using the term "right" that from the fact that A ought to do a thing for B, it follows that B has a right against A that A do it for him, is that it is going to make the question of whether or not a man has a right to a thing turn on how easy it is to provide him with it; and this seems not merely unfortunate, but morally unacceptable. Take the case of Henry Fonda again. I said earlier that I had no right to the touch of his cool hand on my fevered brow, even though I needed it to save my life. I said it would be frightfully nice of him to fly in from the West Coast to provide me with it, but that I had no right against him that he should do so. But suppose he isn't on the West Coast. Suppose he has only to walk across the room, place a hand briefly on my brow—and lo, my life is saved. Then surely he ought to do it, it would be indecent to refuse. Is it to be said, "Ah, well, it follows that in this case she has a right to the touch of his hand on her brow, and so it would be an unjustice in him to refuse"? So that I have a right to it when it is easy for him to provide it, though no right when it's hard? It's rather a shocking idea that anyone's rights should fade away and disappear as it gets harder and harder to accord them to him.

So my own view is that even though you ought to let the violinist use your kidneys for the one hour he needs, we should not conclude that he has a right to do so—we should say that if you refuse, you are, like the boy who owns all the chocolates and will give none away, self-centered and callous, indecent in fact, but not unjust. And similarly, that even supposing a case in which a woman pregnant due to rape ought to allow the unborn person to use her body for the hour he needs, we should not conclude that he has a right to do so; we should conclude that she is self-centered, callous, indecent, but not unjust, if she refuses. The complaints are no less grave; they are just different. However, there is no need to insist on this point. If anyone does wish to deduce "he has a right" from "you ought," then all the same he must surely grant that there are cases in which it is not morally required of you that you allow that violinist to use your kidneys, and in which he does not have a right to use them, and in which you do not do him an injustice if you refuse. And so also for mother and unborn child. Except in such cases as the unborn person has a right to demand it—and we were leaving open the possibility that there may be such cases—nobody is morally *required* to make large sacrifices, of health, of all other interests and concerns, of all other duties and commitments, for nine years, or even for nine months, in order to keep another person alive.

6. We have in fact to distinguish between the two kinds of Samaritan: the Good Samaritan and what we might call the Minimally Decent Samaritan. The story of the Good Samaritan, you will remember, goes like this:

> A certain man went down from Jerusalem to Jericho, and fell among thieves, which stripped him of his raiment, and wounded him, and departed, leaving him half dead.
>
> And by chance there came down a certain priest that way; and when he saw him, he passed by on the other side.
>
> And likewise a Levite, when he was at the place, came and looked on him, and passed by on the other side.
>
> But a certain Samaritan, as he journeyed, came where he was; and when he saw him he had compassion on him.
>
> And went to him, and bound up his wounds, pouring in oil and wine, and set him on his own beast, and brought him to an inn, and took care of him.
>
> And on the morrow, when he departed, he took out two pence, and gave them to the host, and said unto him, "Take care of him; and whatsoever thou spendest more, when I come again, I will repay thee."
>
> (Luke 10:30–35)

The Good Samaritan went out of his way, at some cost to himself, to help one in need of it. We are not told what the options were, that is, whether or not the priest and the Levite could have helped by doing less than the Good Samaritan did, but assuming they could have, then the fact they did nothing at all shows they were not even Minimally Decent Samaritans, not because they were not Samaritans, but because they were not even minimally decent.

These things are a matter of degree, of course, but there is a difference, and it comes out perhaps most clearly in the story of Kitty Genovese, who, as you will remember, was murdered while thirty-eight people watched or listened, and did nothing at all to help her. A Good Samaritan would have rushed out to give direct assistance against the murderer. Or perhaps we had better allow that it would have been a Splendid Samaritan who did this, on the ground that it would have involved a risk of death for himself. But the thirty-eight not only did not do this, they did not even trouble to pick up a phone to call the police. Minimally Decent Samaritanism would call for doing at least that, and their not having done it was monstrous.

After telling the story of the Good Samaritan, Jesus said, "Go, and do thou likewise." Perhaps he meant that we are morally required to act as the Good Samaritan did. Perhaps he was urging people to do more than is morally required of them. At all events it seems plain that it was not morally required of any of the thirty-eight that he rush out to give direct assistance at the risk of his own life, and that it is not morally required of anyone that he give long stretches of his life—nine years or nine months—to sustaining the life of a person who has no special right (we were leaving open the possibility of this) to demand it.

Indeed, with one rather striking class of exceptions, no one in any country in the world is *legally* required to do anywhere near as much as this for anyone else. The class of exceptions is obvious. My main concern here is not the state of the law in respect to abortion, but it is worth drawing attention to the fact that in no state in this country is any man compelled by law to be even a Minimally Decent Samaritan to any person; there is no law under which charges could be brought against the thirty-eight who stood by while Kitty Genovese died. By contrast, in most states in this country women are compelled by law to be not merely Minimally Decent Samaritans, but Good Samaritans to unborn persons inside them. This doesn't by itself settle anything one way or the other, because it may well be argued that there should be laws in this country—as there are in many European countries—compelling at least Minimally Decent Samaritanism.[7] But it does show that there is a gross injustice in the existing state of the law. And it shows also that the groups currently working against liberalization of abortion laws, in fact working toward having it declared unconstitutional for a state to permit abortion, had better start working for the adoption of Good Samaritan laws generally, or earn the charge that they are acting in bad faith.

I should think, myself, that Minimally Decent Samaritan laws would be one thing, Good Samaritan laws quite another, and in fact highly improper. But we are not here concerned with the law. What we should ask is not whether anybody should be compelled by law to be a Good Samaritan, but whether we must accede to a situation in which somebody is being compelled—by nature, perhaps—to be a Good Samaritan. We have, in other words, to look now at third-party interventions. I have been arguing that no person is morally required to make large sacrifices to sustain the life of another who has no right to demand them, and this even where the sacrifices do not include life itself; we are not morally required to be Good Samaritans or anyway Very Good Samaritans to one another. But what if a man cannot extricate himself from such a situation? What if he appeals to us to extricate him? It seems to me plain that there are cases in which we can, cases in which a Good Samaritan would extricate him. There you are, you were kidnapped, and nine years in bed with that violinist lie ahead of you. You have your own life to lead. You are sorry, but you simply cannot see giving up so much of your life to the sustaining of his. You cannot extricate yourself, and ask us to do so. I should have thought that—in light of his having no right to the use of your body—it was obvious that we do not have to accede to your being forced to give up so much. We can do what you ask. There is no injustice to the violinist in our doing so.

7. Following the lead of the opponents of abortion, I have throughout been speaking of the fetus merely as a person, and what I have been asking is whether or not the argument we began with, which proceeds only from the fetus' being a person, really does establish its conclusion. I have argued that it does not.

But of course there are arguments and arguments, and it may be said that I have simply fastened on the wrong one. It may be said that what is important is not merely the fact that the fetus is a person, but that it is a person for whom the woman has a special kind of responsibility issuing from the fact that she is its mother. And it might be argued that all my analogies are therefore irrelevant—for you do not have that special kind of responsibility for that violinist, Henry Fonda does not have that special kind of responsibility for me. And our attention might be drawn to the fact that men and women both *are* compelled by law to provide support for their children.

I have in effect dealt (briefly) with this argument in section 4 above; but a (still briefer) recapitulation now may be in order. Surely we do not have any such "special responsibility" for a person unless we have assumed it, explicitly or implicitly. If a set of parents do not try to prevent pregnancy, do not obtain an abortion, but rather take it home with them, then they have assumed responsibility for it, they have given it rights, and they cannot *now* withdraw support from it at the cost of its life because they now find it difficult to go on providing for it. But if they have taken all reasonable precautions against having a child, they do not simply by virtue of their biological relationship to the child who comes into existence have a special responsibility for it. They may wish to assume responsibility for it, or they may not wish to. And I am suggesting that if assuming responsibility for it would require large sacrifices, then they may refuse. A Good Samaritan would not refuse—or anyway, a Splendid Samaritan, if the sacrifices that had to be made were enormous. But then so would a Good Samaritan assume responsibility for that violinist; so would Henry Fonda, if he is a Good Samaritan, fly in from the West Coast and assume responsibility for me.

8. My argument will be found unsatisfactory on two counts by many of those who want to regard abortion as morally permissible. First, while I do argue that abortion is not impermissible, I do not argue that it is always

permissible. There may well be cases in which carrying the child to term requires only Minimally Decent Samaritanism of the mother, and this is a standard we must not fall below. I am inclined to think it a merit of my account precisely that it does *not* give a general yes or a general no. It allows for and supports our sense that, for example, a sick and desperately frightened fourteen-year-old schoolgirl, pregnant due to rape, may of course choose abortion, and that any law which rules this out is an insane law. And it also allows for and supports our sense that in other cases resort to abortion is even positively indecent. It would be indecent in the woman to request an abortion, and indecent in a doctor to perform it, if she is in her seventh month, and wants the abortion just to avoid the nuisance of postponing a trip abroad. The very fact that the arguments I have been drawing attention to treat all cases of abortion, or even all cases of abortion in which the mother's life is not at stake, as morally on a par ought to have made them suspect at the outset.

Secondly, while I am arguing for the permissibility of abortion in some cases, I am not arguing for the right to secure the death of the unborn child. It is easy to confuse these two things in that up to a certain point in the life of the fetus it is not able to survive outside the mother's body; hence removing it from her body guarantees its death. But they are importantly different. I have argued that you are not morally required to spend nine months in bed, sustaining the life of that violinist; but to say this is by no means to say that if, when you unplug yourself, there is a miracle and he survives, you then have a right to turn around and slit his throat. You may detach yourself even if this costs him his life; you have no right to be guaranteed his death, by some other means, if unplugging yourself does not kill him. There are some people who will feel dissatisfied by this feature of my argument. A woman may be utterly devastated by the thought of a child, a bit of herself, put out for adoption and never seen or heard of again. She may therefore want not merely that the child be detached from her, but more, that it die. Some opponents of abortion are inclined to regard this as beneath contempt—thereby showing insensitivity to what is surely a powerful source of despair. All the same, I agree that the desire for the child's death is not one which anybody may gratify, should it turn out to be possible to detach the child alive.

At this place, however, it should be remembered that we have only been pretending throughout that the fetus is a human being from the moment of conception. A very early abortion is surely not the killing of a person, and so is not dealt with by anything I have said here.

NOTES

1. Daniel Callahan, *Abortion: Law, Choice and Morality* (New York, 1970), p. 373. This book gives a fascinating survey of the available information on abortion. The Jewish tradition in David M. Feldman, *Birth Control in Jewish Law* (New York, 1963), part 5; the Catholic tradition in John T. Noonan, Jr., "An Almost Absolute Value in History" in *The Morality of Abortion*, ed. John T. Noonan, Jr. (Cambridge, Mass., 1970).
2. The term "direct" in the arguments I refer to is a technical one. Roughly, what is meant by "direct killing" is either killing as an end in itself, or killing as a means to some end, for example, the end of saving someone else's life. See note 5 on the next page, for an example of its use.
3. *Cf. Encyclical Letter of Pope Pius XI on Christian Marriage*, St. Paul Editions (Boston, n.d.), p. 32: "However much we may pity the mother whose health and even life is gravely imperiled in the performance of the duty allotted to her by nature, nevertheless what could ever be a sufficient reason for excusing in any way the direct murder of the innocent? This is precisely what we are dealing with here." Noonan (*The Morality of Abortion*, p. 43) reads this as follows: "What cause can ever avail to excuse in any way the direct killing of the innocent? For it is a question of that."
4. The thesis in (4) is in an interesting way weaker than those in (1), (2), and (3): They rule out abortion even in cases in which both mother *and* child will die if the abortion is not performed. By contrast, one who held the view expressed in

(4) could consistently say that one needn't prefer letting two persons die to killing one.

5. Cf. the following passage from Pius XII, *Address to the Italian Catholic Society of Midwives:* "The baby in the maternal breast has the right to life immediately from God.—Hence there is no man, no human authority, no science, no medical, eugenic, social, economic or moral 'indication' which can establish or grant a valid juridical ground for a direct deliberate disposition of an innocent human life, that is a disposition which looks to its destruction either as an end or as a means to another end perhaps in itself not illicit.—The baby, still not born, is a man in the same degree and for the same reason as the mother" (quoted in Noonan, *The Morality of Abortion*, p. 45).
6. The need for a discussion of this argument was brought home to me by members of the Society for Ethical and Legal Philosophy, to whom this paper was originally presented.
7. For a discussion of the difficulties involved, and a survey of the European experience with such laws, see *The Good Samaritan and the Law*, ed. James M. Ratcliffe (New York, 1966).

QUESTIONS FOR ANALYSIS

1. Does the belief that abortion is always impermissible necessarily result from the argument that the unborn is a person from the moment of conception? If not, what additional premises are necessary?
2. Why does Thomson conclude that "a woman surely can defend her life against the threat to it posed by the unborn child, even if doing so involves its death"?
3. How does Thomson answer the claim that the fetus's right to life weighs more (in the moral sense) than anything other than the mother's own right to life?
4. Does Thomson feel that there may be cases in which it would be wrong for a woman to have an abortion? Explain.
5. Distinguish between a "Good Samaritan" and a "Minimally Decent Samaritan."

On the Moral and Legal Status of Abortion

MARY ANNE WARREN

In the following defense of the extreme liberal position on abortion, Mary Anne Warren, professor *emerita* of philosophy, San Francisco State University, challenges both John T. Noonan and Judith Jarvis Thomson. Against Thomson, she argues that the ontological status of the fetus is crucial to any discussion of the morality of abortion. If the fetus is a person with full moral rights, there are many situations—more than Thomson allows—in which abortion is not morally justified. Thomson's example of a woman involuntarily tied to a famous violinist to save his life has little in common with most pregnancies, she argues. It justifies abortion in the case of rape but not in the normal case of unwanted pregnancy, in which the woman bears at least some responsibility for her plight.

Against Noonan, she argues that the fetus is not a person. Her argument relies on a distinction between two senses of "human," the biological sense and the moral sense. Noonan shows that a fetus is human in the former sense but not the latter. And Warren argues, the fetus is not human in the moral sense. To support this claim, she gives five criteria for being a person and argues that the fetus meets none of them. She also argues that being a potential person does not give the fetus rights against the rights of the woman carrying it.

In a postscript added after publication, Warren addresses the issue of infanticide. Her arguments in favor of abortion rights do not support a right to kill newborn babies.

We will be concerned with both the moral status of abortion, which for our purposes we may define as the act which a woman performs in voluntarily terminating, or allowing another person to terminate, her pregnancy, and the legal status which is appropriate for this act. I will argue that, while it is not possible to produce a satisfactory defense of a woman's right to obtain an abortion without showing that a fetus is not a human being, in the morally relevant sense of that term, we ought not to conclude that the difficulties involved in determining whether or not a fetus is human make it impossible to produce any satisfactory solution to the problem of the moral status of abortion. For it is possible to show that, on the basis of intuitions which we may expect even the opponents of abortion to share, a fetus is not a person, and hence not the sort of entity to which it is proper to ascribe full moral rights.

Of course, while some philosophers would deny the possibility of any such proof,[1] others will deny that there is any need for it, since the moral permissibility of abortion appears to them to be too obvious to require proof. But the inadequacy of this attitude should be evident from the fact that both the friends and the foes of abortion consider their position to be morally self-evident. Because pro-abortionists have never adequately come to grips with the conceptual issues surrounding abortion, most, if not all, of the arguments which they advance in opposition to laws restricting access to abortion fail to refute or even weaken the traditional antiabortion argument, i.e., that a fetus is a human being, and therefore abortion is murder.

These arguments are typically of one of two sorts. Either they point to the terrible side effects of the restrictive laws, e.g., the deaths due to illegal abortions, and the fact that it is poor women who suffer the most as a result of these laws, or else they state that to deny a woman access to abortion is to deprive her of her right to control her own body. Unfortunately, however, the fact that restricting access to abortion has tragic side effects does not, in itself, show that the restrictions are unjustified, since murder is wrong regardless of the consequences of prohibiting it; and the appeal to the right to control one's body, which is generally construed as a property right, is at best a rather feeble argument for the permissibility of abortion. Mere ownership does not give me the right to kill innocent people whom I find on my property, and indeed I am apt to be held responsible if such people injure themselves while on my property. It is equally unclear that I have any moral right to expel an innocent person from my property when I know that doing so will result in his death.

Furthermore, it is probably inappropriate to describe a woman's body as her property, since it seems natural to hold that a person is something distinct from her property, but not from her body. Even those who would object to the identification of a person with his body, or with the conjunction of his body and his mind, must admit that it would be very odd to describe, say, breaking a leg, as damaging one's property, and much more appropriate to describe it as injuring one*self*. Thus it is probably a mistake to argue that the right to obtain an abortion is in any way derived from the right to own and regulate property.

But however we wish to construe the right to abortion, we cannot hope to convince those who consider abortion a form of murder of the existence of any such right unless we are able to produce a clear and convincing refutation of the traditional antiabortion argument, and this has not, to my knowledge, been done. With respect to the two most vital issues which that argument involves, i.e., the humanity of the fetus and its implication for the moral status of abortion, confusion has prevailed on both sides of the dispute.

Thus, both pro-abortionists and antiabortionists have tended to abstract the question of whether abortion is wrong to that of whether it is wrong to destroy a fetus, just as though the rights of another person were not necessarily involved. This mistaken abstraction has led to the almost universal assumption that if a fetus is a human being, with a right to life, then it follows immediately that abortion is wrong (except perhaps when necessary to save the woman's life), and that it ought to be prohibited. It has also been generally assumed that unless the question about the status of the fetus is answered, the moral status of abortion cannot possibly be determined. . . . John Noonan is correct in saying that "the fundamental question in the long history of abortion is, How do you determine the humanity of a being?"[2] He summarizes his own antiabortion argument, which is a version of the official position of the Catholic Church, as follows:

> . . . it is wrong to kill humans, however poor, weak, defenseless, and lacking in opportunity to develop their potential they may be. It is therefore morally wrong to kill Biafrans. Similarly, it is morally wrong to kill embryos.[3]

Noonan bases his claim that fetuses are human upon what he calls the theologians' criterion of humanity: that whoever is conceived of human beings is human. But although he argues at length for the appropriateness of this criterion, he never questions the assumption that if a fetus is human then abortion is wrong for exactly the same reason that murder is wrong.

Judith Thomson is, in fact, the only writer I am aware of who has seriously questioned this assumption; she has argued that, even if we grant the antiabortionist his claim that a fetus is a human being, with the same right to life as any other human being, we can still demonstrate that, in at least some and perhaps most cases, a woman is under no moral obligation to complete an unwanted pregnancy.[4] Her argument is worth examining, since if it holds up it may enable us to establish the moral permissibility of abortion without becoming involved in problems about what entitles an entity to be considered human, and accorded full moral rights. To be able to do this would be a great gain in the power and simplicity of the proabortion position, since, although I will argue that these problems can be solved at least as decisively as can any other moral problem, we should certainly be pleased to be able to avoid having to solve them as part of the justification of abortion.

On the other hand, even if Thomson's argument does not hold up, her insight, i.e., that it requires *argument* to show that if fetuses are human then abortion is properly classified as murder, is an extremely valuable one. The assumption she attacks is particularly invidious, for it amounts to the decision that it is appropriate, in deciding the moral status of abortion, to leave the rights of the pregnant woman out of consideration entirely, except possibly when her life is threatened. Obviously, this will not do; determining what moral rights, if any, a fetus possesses is only the first step in determining the moral status of abortion. Step two, which is at least equally essential, is finding a just solution to the conflict between whatever rights the fetus may have, and the rights of the woman who is unwillingly pregnant. While the historical error has been to pay far too little attention to the second step, Ms. Thomson's suggestion is that if we look at the second step first we may find that a woman has a right to obtain an abortion *regardless* of what rights the fetus has.

Our own inquiry will also have two stages. In Section I, we will consider whether or not it is possible to establish that abortion is morally permissible even on the assumption that a fetus is an entity with a full-fledged right to life. I will argue that in fact this cannot be established, at least not with the conclusiveness which is essential to our hopes of convincing those who are skeptical about the morality of abortion, and that we therefore cannot avoid dealing with the question of whether or not a fetus really does have the same right to life as a (more fully developed) human being.

In Section II, I will propose an answer to this question, namely, that a fetus cannot be considered a member of the moral community, the set of beings with full and equal moral rights, for the simple reason that it is not a person, and that it is personhood, and not genetic humanity, i.e., humanity as defined by Noonan, which is the basis for membership in this community. I will argue that a fetus, whatever its stage of development, satisfies none of the basic criteria of personhood, and is not even enough *like* a person to be accorded even some of the same rights on the basis of this resemblance. Nor, as we will see, is a fetus's *potential* personhood a threat to the morality of abortion, since, whatever the rights of potential people may be, they are invariably overridden in any conflict with the moral rights of actual people.

I

We turn now to Professor Thomson's case for the claim that even if a fetus has full moral rights, abortion is still morally permissible, at least sometimes, and for some reasons other than to save the woman's life. Her argument is based upon a clever, but I think faulty, analogy. She asks us to picture ourselves waking up one day, in bed with a famous violinist. Imagine that you have been kidnapped, and your bloodstream hooked up to that of the violinist, who happens to have an ailment which will certainly kill him unless he is permitted to share your kidneys for a period of nine months. No one else can save him, since you alone have the right type of blood. He will be unconscious all that time, and you will have to stay in bed with him, but after the nine months are over he may be unplugged, completely cured, that is, provided that you have cooperated.

Now then, she continues, what are your obligations in this situation? The antiabortionist, if he is consistent, will have to say that you are obligated to stay in bed with the violinist: for all people have a right to life, and violinists are people, and therefore it would be murder for you to disconnect yourself from him and let him die. But this is outrageous, and so there must be something wrong with the same argument when it is applied to abortion. It would certainly be commendable of you to agree to save the violinist, but it is absurd to suggest that your refusal to do so would be murder. His right to life does not obligate you to do whatever is required to keep him alive; nor does it justify anyone else in forcing you to do so. A law which required you to stay in bed with the violinist would clearly be an unjust law, since it is no proper function of the law to force unwilling people to make huge sacrifices for the sake of other people toward whom they have no such prior obligation.

Thomson concludes that, if this analogy is an apt one, then we can grant the antiabortionist his claim that a fetus is a human being, and still hold that it is at least sometimes the case that a pregnant woman has the right to refuse to be a Good Samaritan towards the fetus, i.e., to obtain an abortion. For there is a great gap between the claim that X has a right to life, and the claim that Y is obligated to do whatever is necessary to keep X alive, let alone that he ought to be forced to do so. It is Y's duty to keep X alive only if he has somehow contracted a *special* obligation to do so; and a woman who is unwillingly pregnant, e.g., who was raped, has done nothing which obligates her to make the enormous sacrifice which is necessary to preserve the conceptus.

This argument is initially quite plausible, and in the extreme case of pregnancy due to rape is probably conclusive. Difficulties arise, however, when we try to specify more exactly the range of cases in which abortion is clearly justifiable even on the assumption that the fetus is human. Professor Thomson considers it a virtue of her argument that it does not enable us to conclude that abortion is *always* permissible. It would, she says, be "indecent" for a woman in her seventh month to obtain an abortion just to avoid having to postpone a trip to Europe. On the other hand, her argument enables us to see that "a sick and desperately frightened schoolgirl pregnant due to rape may *of course* choose abortion, and that any law which rules this out is an insane law" (p. 65). So far, so good; but what are we to say about the woman who becomes pregnant not through rape but as a result of her own carelessness, or because of contraceptive failure, or who gets pregnant intentionally and then changes her mind about wanting a child? With respect to such cases, the violinist analogy is of much less use to the defender of the woman's right to obtain an abortion.

Indeed, the choice of a pregnancy due to rape, as an example of a case in which abortion is permissible even if a fetus is considered a human being, is extremely significant; for it is only in the case of pregnancy due to rape that the woman's situation is adequately analogous to the violinist case for our intuitions about the latter to transfer convincingly. The crucial difference between a pregnancy due to rape and the *normal* case of an unwanted pregnancy is that in the normal case we cannot claim that the woman is in no way responsible for her predicament; she could have remained chaste, or taken her pills more faithfully, or abstained on dangerous days, and so on. If, on the other hand, you are kidnapped by strangers, and hooked up to a strange violinist, then you are free of any shred of responsibility for the situation, on the basis of which it could be argued that you are obligated to keep the violinist alive. Only when her pregnancy is due to rape is a woman clearly just as nonresponsible.[5]

Consequently, there is room for the anti-abortionist to argue that in the normal case of unwanted pregnancy a woman has, by her own actions, assumed responsibility for the fetus. For if X behaves in a way which he could have avoided, and which he knows involves, let us say, a 1 percent chance of bringing into existence a human being, with a right to life, and does so knowing that if this should happen then that human being will perish unless X does certain things to keep him alive, then it is by no means clear that when it does happen X is free of any obligation to what he knew in advance would be required to keep that human being alive.

The plausibility of such an argument is enough to show that the Thomson analogy can provide a clear and persuasive defense of a woman's right to obtain an abortion only with respect to those cases in which the woman is in no way responsible for her pregnancy, e.g., where it is due to rape. In all other cases, we would almost certainly conclude that it was necessary to look carefully at the particular circumstances in order to determine the extent of the woman's responsibility, and hence the extent of her obligation. This is an extremely unsatisfactory outcome, from the viewpoint of the opponents of restrictive abortion laws, most of whom are convinced that a woman has a right to obtain an abortion regardless of how and why she got pregnant.

Of course a supporter of the violinist analogy might point out that it is absurd to suggest that forgetting her pill one day might be sufficient to obligate a woman to complete an unwanted pregnancy. And indeed it *is* absurd to suggest this. As we will see, the moral right to obtain an abortion is not in the least dependent upon the extent to which the woman is responsible for her pregnancy. But unfortunately, once we allow the assumption that a fetus has full moral rights, we cannot avoid taking this absurd suggestion seriously. Perhaps we can make this point more clear by altering the violinist story just enough to make it more analogous to a normal unwanted pregnancy and less to a pregnancy due to rape, and then seeing whether it is still obvious that you are not obligated to stay in bed with the fellow.

Suppose, then, that violinists are peculiarly prone to the sort of illness the only cure for which is the use of someone else's bloodstream for nine months, and that because of this there has been formed a society of music lovers who agree that whenever a violinist is stricken they will draw lots and the loser will, by some means, be made the one and only person capable of saving him. Now then, would you be obligated to cooperate in curing the violinist if you had voluntarily joined this society, knowing the possible consequences, and then your name had been drawn and you had been kidnapped? Admittedly, you did not promise ahead of time that you would, but you did deliberately place yourself in a position in which it might happen that a human life would be lost if you did not. Surely this is at least a prima facie reason for supposing that you have an obligation to stay in bed with the violinist. Suppose that you had gotten your name drawn deliberately; surely *that* would be quite a strong reason for thinking that you had such an obligation.

It might be suggested that there is one important disanalogy between the modified violinist case and the case of an unwanted pregnancy, which makes the woman's responsibility significantly less, namely, the fact that the fetus *comes into existence* as the result of the woman's actions. This fact might give her a right to refuse to keep it alive, whereas she would not have had this right had it existed previously, independently, and then as a result of her actions become dependent upon her for its survival.

My own intuition, however, is that X has no more right to bring into existence, either deliberately or as a foreseeable result of actions he could have avoided, a being with full moral rights (Y), and then refuse to do what he knew beforehand would be required to keep that being alive, than he has to enter into an agreement with an existing person, whereby he may be called upon to save that person's life, and then refuse to do so when so called upon. Thus, X's responsibility for Y's existence does not seem to lessen his obligation to keep Y alive, if he is also responsible for Y's being in a situation in which only he can save him.

Whether or not this intuition is entirely correct, it brings us back once again to the conclusion that once we allow the assumption that a fetus has full moral rights it becomes an extremely complex and difficult question whether and when abortion is justifiable. Thus the Thomson analogy cannot help us produce a clear and persuasive proof of the moral permissibility of abortion. Nor will the opponents of the restrictive laws thank us for anything less; for their conviction (for the most part) is that abortion is obviously *not* a morally serious and extremely unfortunate, even though sometimes justified, act comparable to killing in self-defense or to letting the violinist die, but rather is closer to being a morally neutral act, like cutting one's hair.

The basis of this conviction, I believe, is the realization that a fetus is not a person, and thus does not have a full-fledged right to life. Perhaps the reason why this claim has been so inadequately defended is that it seems self-evident to those who accept it. And so it is, insofar as it follows from what I take to be perfectly obvious claims about the nature of personhood and about the proper grounds for ascribing moral rights, claims which ought, indeed, to be obvious to both the friends and foes of abortion. Nevertheless, it is worth examining these claims, and showing how they demonstrate the moral innocuousness of abortion, since this apparently has not been adequately done before.

II

The question which we must answer in order to produce a satisfactory solution to the problem of the moral status of abortion is this: How are we to define the moral community, the set of beings with full and equal moral rights, such that we can decide whether a human fetus is a member of this community or not? What sort of entity, exactly, has the inalienable rights to life, liberty, and the pursuit of happiness? Jefferson attributed these rights to all *men,* and it may or may not be fair to suggest that he intended to attribute them *only* to men. Perhaps he ought to have attributed them to all human beings. If so, then we arrive, first, at Noonan's problem of defining what makes a being human, and, second, at the equally vital question which Noonan does not consider; namely, What reason is there for identifying the moral community with the set of all human beings, in whatever way we have chosen to define that term?

1. On the Definition of "Human"

One reason why this vital second question is so frequently overlooked in the debate over the moral status of abortion is that the term "human" has two distinct, but not often distinguished, senses. This fact results in a slide of meaning, which serves to conceal the fallaciousness of the traditional argument that since (1) it is wrong to kill innocent human beings, and (2) fetuses are innocent human beings, then (3) it is wrong to kill fetuses. For if "human" is used in the same sense in both (1) and (2) then, whichever of the two senses is meant, one of these premises is question-begging. And if it is used in two different senses then of course the conclusion doesn't follow.

Thus, (1) is a self-evident moral truth,[6] and avoids begging the question about abortion only if "human being" is used to mean something like "a full-fledged member of the moral community." (It may or may not also be meant to refer exclusively to members of the species *Homo Sapiens.*) *We may call this the moral* sense of "human." It is not to be confused with what we will call the *genetic* sense, i.e., the sense in which *any* member of the species is a human being, and no member of any other species could be. If (1) is acceptable only if the moral sense is intended, (2) is non-question-begging only if what is intended is the genetic sense.

In "Deciding Who Is Human," Noonan argues for the classification of fetuses with human beings by pointing to the presence of the full genetic code, and the potential capacity for rational thought (p. 135). It is clear that what he needs to show, for his version of the traditional argument to be valid, is that fetuses are human in the moral sense, the sense in which it is analytically true that all human beings have full moral rights. But, in the absence of any argument showing that whatever is genetically human is also morally human, and he gives none, nothing more than genetic humanity can be demonstrated by the presence of the human genetic code. And, as we will see, the *potential* capacity for rational thought can at most show that an entity has the potential for *becoming* human in the moral sense.

2. Defining the Moral Community

Can it be established that genetic humanity is sufficient for moral humanity? I think that there are very good reasons for not defining the moral community in this way. I would like to suggest an alternative way of defining the moral community, which I will argue for only to the extent of explaining why it is, or should be, self-evident. The suggestion is simply that the moral community consists of all and only *people,* rather than all and only human beings;[7] and probably the best way of demonstrating its self-evidence is by considering the concept of personhood, to see what sorts of entity are and are not persons, and what the decision that a being is or is not a person implies about its moral rights.

What characteristics entitle an entity to be considered a person? This is obviously not the place to attempt a complete analysis of the concept of personhood, but we do not need such a fully adequate analysis just to determine whether and why a fetus is or isn't a person. All we need is a rough and approximate list of the most basic criteria of personhood, and some idea of which, or how many, of these an entity must satisfy in order to properly be considered a person.

In searching for such criteria, it is useful to look beyond the set of people with whom we are acquainted, and ask how we would decide whether a totally alien being was a person or not. (For we have no right to assume that genetic humanity is necessary for personhood.) Imagine a space traveler who lands on an unknown planet and encounters a race of beings utterly unlike any he has ever seen or heard of. If he wants to be sure of behaving morally toward these beings, he has to somehow decide whether they are people, and hence have full moral rights, or whether they are the sort of thing which he need not feel guilty about treating as, for example, a source of food.

How should he go about making this decision? If he has some anthropological background, he might look for such things as religion, art, and the manufacturing of tools, weapons, or shelters, since these factors have been used to distinguish our human from our prehuman ancestors, in what seems to be closer to the moral than the genetic sense of "human." And no doubt he would be right to consider the presence of such factors as good evidence that the alien beings were people, and morally human. It would, however, be overly anthropocentric of him to take the absence of these things as adequate evidence that they were not, since we can imagine people who have progressed beyond, or evolved without ever developing, these cultural characteristics.

I suggest that the traits which are most central to the concept of personhood, or humanity in the moral sense, are, very roughly, the following:

1. consciousness (of objects and events external and/or internal to the being), and in particular the capacity to feel pain;
2. reasoning (the *developed* capacity to solve new and relatively complex problems);
3. self-motivated activity (activity which is relatively independent of either genetic or direct external control);
4. the capacity to communicate, by whatever means, messages of an indefinite variety of types, that is, not just with an indefinite number of possible contents, but on indefinitely many possible topics;
5. the presence of self-concepts, and self-awareness, either individual or racial, or both.

Admittedly, there are apt to be a great many problems involved in formulating precise definitions of these criteria, let alone in developing universally valid behavioral criteria for deciding when they apply. But I will assume that both we and our explorer know approximately what (1)–(5) mean, and that he is also able to determine whether or not they apply. How, then, should he use his findings to decide whether or not the alien beings are people? We needn't suppose that an entity must have *all* of these attributes to be properly considered a person; (1) and (2) alone may well be sufficient for personhood, and quite probably (1)–(3) are sufficient. Neither do we need to insist that any one of these criteria is *necessary* for personhood, although once again (1) and (2) look like fairly good candidates for necessary conditions, as does (3), if "activity" is construed so as to include the activity of reasoning.

All we need to claim, to demonstrate that a fetus is not a person, is that any being which satisfies *none* of (1)–(5) is certainly not a person. I consider this claim to be so obvious that I think anyone who denied it, and claimed that a being which satisfied none of (1)–(5) was a person all the same, would thereby demonstrate that he had no notion at all of what a person is—perhaps because he had confused the concept of a person with that of genetic humanity. If the opponents of abortion were to deny the appropriateness of these five criteria, I do not know what further arguments would convince them. We would probably have to admit that our conceptual schemes are indeed irreconcilably different, and that our dispute could not be settled objectively.

I do not expect this to happen, however, since I think that the concept of a person is one which is very nearly universal (to people), and that it is common to both pro-abortionists and antiabortionists, even though neither group has fully realized the relevance of this concept to the resolution of their dispute. Furthermore, I think that on reflection even the antiabortionists ought to agree not only that (1)–(5) are central to the concept of personhood, but also that it is apart of this concept that all and only people have full moral rights. The concept of a person is in part a moral concept; once we have admitted that X is a person we have recognized, even if we have not agreed to respect, X's right to be treated as a member of the moral community. It is true that the claim that X is a *human being* is more commonly voiced as part of an appeal to treat X decently than is the claim that X is a person, but this is either because "human being" is here used in the sense which implies personhood, or because the genetic and moral senses of "human" have been confused.

Note if (1)–(5) are indeed the primary criteria of personhood, then it is clear that genetic humanity is neither necessary nor sufficient for establishing that an entity is a person. Some human beings are not people, and there may be people who are not human beings. A man or woman whose consciousness has been permanently obliterated but who remains alive is a human being which is no longer a person; defective human beings, with no appreciable mental capacity, are not and presumably never will be people; and a fetus is a human being which is not yet a person, and which therefore cannot coherently be said to have full moral rights. Citizens of the next century should be prepared to recognize highly advanced, self-aware robots or computers, should such be developed, and intelligent inhabitants of other worlds, should such be found, as people in the fullest sense, and to respect their moral rights. But to ascribe full moral rights to an entity which is not a person is as absurd as to ascribe moral obligations and responsibilities to such an entity.

3. Fetal Development and the Right to Life

Two problems arise in the application of these suggestions for the definition of the moral community to the determination of the precise moral status of a human fetus. Given that the paradigm example of a person is a normal adult human being, then (1) How like this paradigm, in particular how far advanced since conception, does a human being need to be before it begins to have a right to life by virtue, not of being fully a person as of yet, but of being *like* a person? and (2) To what extent, if any, does the fact that a fetus has the *potential* for becoming a person endow it with some of the same rights? Each of these questions requires some comment.

In answering the first question, we need not attempt a detailed consideration of the moral rights of organisms which are not developed enough, aware enough, intelligent enough, etc., to be considered people, but which resemble people in some respects. It does seem reasonable to suggest that the more like a person, in the relevant respects, a being is, the stronger is the case for regarding it as having a right to life, and indeed the stronger its right to life is. Thus we ought to take seriously the suggestion that, insofar as "the human individual develops biologically in a continuous fashion . . . the rights of a human person might develop in the same way."[8] But we must keep in mind that the attributes which are relevant in determining whether or not an entity is enough like a person to be regarded as having some of the same moral rights are no different from those which are relevant to determining whether or not it is a fully a person—i.e., are no different from (1)–(5)—and that being genetically human, or having recognizably human facial and other physical features, or detectable brain activity, or the capacity to survive outside the uterus, is simply not among these relevant attributes.

Thus it is clear that even though a seven- or eight-month fetus has features which make it apt to arouse in us almost the same powerful protective instinct as is commonly aroused by a small infant, nevertheless it is not significantly more personlike than is a very small embryo. It is *somewhat* more personlike; it can apparently feel and respond to pain, and it may even have a rudimentary form of consciousness, insofar as its brain is quite active. Nevertheless, it seems safe to say that it is not fully conscious, in the way that an infant of a few months is, and that it cannot reason, or communicate messages of indefinitely many sorts, does not engage in self-motivated activity, and has no self-awareness. Thus, in the *relevant* respects, a fetus, even a fully developed one, is considerably less personlike than is the average mature mammal, indeed the average fish. And I think that a rational person must conclude that if the right to life of a fetus is to be based upon its resemblance to a person, then it cannot be said to have any more right to life than, let us say, a newborn guppy (which also seems to be capable of feeling pain), and that right of that magnitude could never override a woman's right to obtain an abortion, at any stage of her pregnancy.

There may, of course, be other arguments in favor of placing legal limits upon the stage of pregnancy in which an abortion may be performed. Given the relative safety of the new techniques of artificially inducing labor during the third trimester, the danger to the woman's life or health is no longer such an argument. Neither is the fact that people tend to respond to the thought of abortion in the later stages of pregnancy with emotional repulsion, since mere emotional responses cannot take the place of moral reasoning in determining what ought to be permitted. Nor, finally, is the frequently heard argument that legalizing abortion, especially late in the pregnancy, may erode the level of respect for human life, leading, perhaps, to an increase in unjustified euthanasia and other crimes. For this threat, if it is a threat, can be better met by educating people to the kinds of moral distinctions which we are making here than by limiting access to abortion (which limitation may, in its disregard for the rights of women, be just as damaging to the level of respect for human rights).

Thus, since the fact that even a fully developed fetus is not personlike enough to have any significant right to life on the basis of its person-likeness shows that no legal restrictions upon the stage of pregnancy in which an abortion may be performed can be justified on the grounds that we should protect the rights of the older fetus; and since there is no other apparent justification for such restrictions, we may conclude that they are entirely unjustified. Whether or not it would be *indecent* (whatever that means) for a woman in her seventh month to obtain an abortion just to avoid having to postpone a trip to Europe, it would not, in itself, be *immoral*, and therefore it ought to be permitted.

4. Potential Personhood and Right to Life

We have seen that a fetus does not resemble a person in any way which can support the claim that it has even some of the same rights. But what about its *potential*, the fact that if nurtured and allowed to develop naturally it will very probably become a person? Doesn't that alone give it at least some right to life? It is hard to deny that the fact that an entity is a potential person is a strong prima facie reason for not destroying it; but we need not conclude from this that a potential person has a right to life, by virtue of that potential. It may be that our feeling that it is better, other things being equal, not to destroy a potential person is better explained by the fact that potential people are still (felt to be) an invaluable resource, not to be lightly squandered. Surely, if every speck of dust were a potential person, we would be much less apt to conclude that every potential person has a right to become actual.

Still, we do not need to insist that a potential person has no right to life whatever. There may well be something immoral, and not just imprudent, about wantonly destroying potential people, when doing so isn't necessary to protect anyone's rights. But even if a potential person does have some prima facie right to life, such a right could not possibly outweigh the right of a woman to obtain an abortion, since the rights of any actual person invariably outweigh those of any potential person, whenever the two conflict. Since this may not be immediately obvious in the case of a human fetus, let us look at another case.

Suppose that our space explorer falls into the hand of an alien culture, whose scientists decide to create a few hundred thousand or more human beings, by breaking his body into its component cells, and using these to create fully developed human beings, with, of course, his genetic code. We may imagine that each of these newly created men will have all of the original man's abilities, skills, knowledge, and so on, and also have an individual self-concept, in short that each of them will be a bona fide (though hardly unique) person. Imagine that the whole project will take only seconds, and that its chances of success are extremely high, and that our explorer knows all of this, and also knows that these people will be treated fairly. I maintain that in such a situation he would have every right to escape if he could, and thus to deprive all of these potential people of their potential lives; for his right to life outweighs all of theirs together, in spite of the fact that they are all genetically human, all innocent, and all have a very high probability of becoming people very soon, if only he refrains from acting.

Indeed, I think he would have a right to escape even if it were not his life which the alien scientists planned to take, but only a year of his freedom, or indeed, only a day. Nor would he be obligated to stay if he had gotten captured (thus bringing all these people-potentials into existence) because of his own carelessness, or even if he had done so deliberately, knowing the consequences. Regardless of how he got captured, he is not morally obligated to remain in captivity for *any* period of time for the sake of permitting any number of potential people to come into actuality, so great is the margin by which one actual person's right to liberty outweighs whatever right to life even a hundred thousand potential people have. And it seems reasonable to conclude that the rights of a woman will outweigh by a similar margin whatever right to life a fetus may have by virtue of its potential personhood.

Thus, neither a fetus's resemblance to a person, nor its potential for becoming a person provides any basis whatever for the claim that it has any significant right to life. Consequently, a woman's right to protect her health, happiness, freedom, and even her life,[9] by terminating an unwanted pregnancy, will always override whatever right to life may be appropriate to ascribe to a fetus, even a fully developed one. And thus, in the absence of any overwhelming social need for every possible child, the laws which restrict the right to obtain an abortion, or limit the period of pregnancy during which an abortion may be performed, are a wholly unjustified violation of a woman's most basic moral and constitutional rights.[10] . . . .

POSTSCRIPT ON INFANTICIDE

Since the publication of this article, many people have written to point out that my argument appears to justify not only abortion, but infanticide as well. For a newborn infant is not significantly more personlike than an advanced fetus, and consequently it would seem that if the destruction of the latter is permissible so too must be that of the former. Inasmuch as most people, regardless of how they feel about the morality of abortion, consider infanticide a form of murder, this might appear to represent a serious flaw in my argument.

Now, if I am right in holding that it is only people who have a full-fledged right to life, and who can be murdered, and if the criteria of personhood are as I have described them, then it obviously follows that killing newborn infants isn't murder. It does *not* follow, however, that infanticide is permissible, for two reasons. In the first place, it would be wrong, at least in this country and in this period of history, and other things being equal, to kill a newborn infant, because even if its parents do not want it and would not suffer from its destruction, there are other people who would like to have it, and would, in all probability, be deprived of a great deal of pleasure by its destruction. Thus, infanticide is wrong for reasons analogous to those which make it wrong to wantonly destroy natural resources, or great works of art.

Second, most people, at least in this country, value infants and would much prefer that they be preserved, even if foster parents are not immediately available. Most of us would rather be taxed to support orphanages than allow unwanted infants to be destroyed. So long as there are people who want an infant preserved, and who are willing and able to provide the means of caring for it, under reasonably humane conditions, it is, *ceteris parabis,* wrong to destroy it.

But, it might be replied, if this argument shows that infanticide is wrong, at least at this time and in this country, doesn't it also show that abortion is wrong? After all, many people value fetuses, are disturbed by their destruction, and would much prefer that they be preserved, even at some cost to themselves. Furthermore, as a potential source of pleasure to some foster family, a fetus is just as valuable as an infant. There is, however, a crucial difference between the two cases: so long as the fetus is unborn, its preservation, contrary to the wishes of the pregnant woman, violates her rights to freedom, happiness, and self-determination. Her rights override the rights of those who would like the fetus preserved, just as if someone's life or limb is threatened by a wild animal, his right to protect himself by destroying the animal overrides the rights of those who would prefer that the animal not be harmed.

The minute the infant is born, however, its preservation no longer violates any of its mother's rights, even if she wants it destroyed, because she is free to put it up for adoption. Consequently, while the moment of birth does not mark any sharp discontinuity in the degree to which an infant possesses the right to life, it does mark the end of its mother's right to determine its fate. Indeed, if abortion could be performed without killing the fetus, she would never possess the right to have the fetus destroyed, for the same reasons that she has no right to have an infant destroyed.

On the other hand, it follows from my argument that when an unwanted or defective infant is born into a society which cannot afford and/or is not willing to care for it, then its destruction is permissible. This conclusion will, no doubt, strike many people as heartless and immoral; but remember that the very existence of people who feel this way, and who are willing and able to provide care for unwanted infants, is reason enough to conclude that they should be preserved.

NOTES

1. For example, Roger Wertheimer, who in "Understanding the Abortion Argument" (*Philosophy and Public Affairs,* 1, no. 1 [Fall, 1971], 67–95,) argues that the problem of the moral status of abortion is insoluble, in that the dispute over the status of the fetus is not a question of fact at all, but only a question of how one responds to the facts.
2. John Noonan, "Abortion and the Catholic Church: A Summary History," *Natural Law Forum,* 12 (1967); 125.
3. John Noonan, "Deciding Who Is Human," *Natural Law Forum,* 13 (1968), 134.
4. "A Defense of Abortion."
5. We may safely ignore the fact that she might have avoided getting raped, e.g., by carrying a gun, since by similar means you might likewise have avoided getting kidnapped, and in neither case does the victim's failure to take all possible precautions against a highly unlikely event (as opposed to reasonable precautions against a rather likely event) mean that he is morally responsible for what happens.
6. Of course, the principle that it is (always) wrong to kill innocent human beings is in need of many other modifications, e.g., that it may be permissible to do so to save a greater number of other innocent human beings, but we may safely ignore these complications here.
7. From here on, we will use "human" to mean genetically human, since the moral sense seems closely connected to, and perhaps derived from, the assumption that genetic humanity is sufficient for membership in the moral community.
8. Thomas L. Hayes, "A Biological View," *Commonweal,* 85 (March 17, 1967), 677–78; quoted by Daniel Callahan, in *Abortion, Law, Choice, and Morality* (London: Macmillan & Co., 1970).
9. That is, insofar as the death rate, for the woman, is higher for childbirth than for early abortion.
10. My thanks to the following people, who were kind enough to read and criticize an earlier version of this paper: Herbert Gold, Gene Glass, Anne Lauterbach, Judith Thomson, Mary Mothersill, and Timothy Binkley.

QUESTIONS FOR ANALYSIS

1. Is Warren's objection to Thomson's analogy of the woman tied up against her will well taken?
2. According to Warren, Noonan makes no case for the position that whatever is genetically human is morally human. Do you agree? If so, what kind of case can be made?
3. Why does Warren discount the claim that being a potential person gives the fetus rights against the mother?
4. Because the fetus has no rights against the woman carrying it, Warren says, there is nothing immoral about having a late-term abortion in order to take a European vacation. Is this step warranted? Are there moral considerations she neglects?
5. Warren likens the moral reasons for not killing an infant to the moral reasons for not destroying a work of art. How persuasive is this analogy?
6. Do you agree with Warren's criteria for being human in the moral sense?

Virtue Theory and Abortion

ROSALIND HURSTHOUSE

The following selection comes from the second part of an essay by Rosalind Hursthouse, professor of philosophy, University of Auckland, New Zealand. The first part, omitted here, is a general discussion of virtue theory, which she bases on Aristotle. Virtue theory, she says there, is concerned with human flourishing (*eudaimonia,* or living well), and she defines a virtue as "a character trait a human being needs to flourish or live well." She also defines a virtuous agent as a person "who has and exercises virtues" and defines a right action as "what a virtuous agent would do in the circumstances."

In the section reprinted here, she applies virtue theory to the abortion debate. Her concern is the morality of abortion, not whether abortion should be legal, and she examines a number of circumstances in which a pregnant woman might consider having one. In each case, she asks whether a virtuous woman would decide to have it. Basic to her answer are two points: Aborting a fetus is a matter that must be taken seriously, and being a parent constitutes, in part, a flourishing human life.

As everyone knows, the morality of abortion is commonly discussed in relation to just two considerations: first, and predominantly, the status of the fetus and whether or not it is the sort of thing that may or may not be innocuously or justifiably killed; and second, and less predominantly (when, that is, the discussion concerns the *morality* of abortion rather than the question of permissible legislation in a just society), women's rights. If one thinks within this familiar framework, one may well be puzzled about what virtue theory, as such, could contribute. Some people assume the discussion will be conducted solely in terms of what the virtuous agent would or would not do. . . . Others assume that only justice, or at most justice and charity,[1] will be applied to the issue, generating a discussion very similar to Judith Jarvis Thomson's.[2]

Now if this is the way the virtue theorist's discussion of abortion is imagined to be, no wonder people think little of it. It seems obvious in advance that in any such discussion there must be either a great deal of extremely tendentious application of the virtue terms *just, charitable,* and so on or a lot of rhetorical appeal to "this is what only the virtuous agent knows." But these are caricatures; they fail to appreciate the way in which virtue theory quite transforms the discussion of abortion by dismissing the two familiar dominating considerations as, in a way, fundamentally irrelevant. In what way or ways, I hope to make both clear and plausible.

Let us first consider women's rights. Let me emphasize again that we are discussing the *morality* of abortion, not the rights and wrongs of laws prohibiting or permitting it. If we suppose that women do have a moral right to do as they choose with their own bodies, or, more particularly, to terminate their pregnancies, then it may well follow that a *law* forbidding abortion would be unjust. Indeed, even if they have no such right, such a law might be, as things stand at the moment, unjust, or impractical, or inhumane: on this issue I have nothing to say in this article. But, putting all questions about the justice or injustice of laws to one side, and supposing only that women have such a moral right, *nothing* follows from this supposition about the morality of abortion, according to virtue theory, once it is noted (quite generally, not with particular reference to abortion) that in exercising a moral right I can do something cruel, or callous, or selfish, light-minded, self-righteous, stupid, inconsiderate, disloyal, dishonest—that is, act viciously.[3] Love and friendship do not survive their parties' constantly insisting on their rights, nor do people live well when they think that getting what they have a right to is of preeminent importance; they harm others, and they harm themselves. So whether women have a moral right to terminate their pregnancies is irrelevant within virtue theory, for it is irrelevant to the question "In having an abortion in these circumstances, would the agent be acting virtuously or viciously or neither?"

What about the consideration of the status of the fetus—what can virtue theory say about that? One might say that this issue is not in the province of any moral theory; it is a metaphysical question, and an extremely difficult one at that. Must virtue theory then wait upon metaphysics to come up with the answer?

At first sight it might seem so. For virtue is said to involve knowledge, and part of this knowledge consists in having the *right* attitude to things. "Right" here does not just mean "morally right" or "proper" or "nice" in the modern sense; it means "accurate, true." One cannot have the right or correct attitude to something if the attitude is based on or involves false beliefs. And this suggests that if the status of the fetus is relevant to the rightness or wrongness of abortion, its status must be known, as a truth, to the fully wise and virtuous person.

But the sort of wisdom that the fully virtuous person has is not supposed to be recondite; it does not call for fancy philosophical sophistication, and it does not depend upon, let alone wait upon, the discoveries of academic philosophers.[4] And this entails the following, rather startling, conclusion: that the status of the fetus—that issue over which so much ink has been spilt—is, according to virtue theory, simply not relevant to the rightness or wrongness of abortion (within, that is, a secular morality).

Or rather, since that is clearly too radical a conclusion, it is in a sense relevant, but only in the sense that the familiar biological facts are relevant. By "the familiar biological facts" I mean the facts that most human societies are and have been familiar with—that, standardly (but not invariably), pregnancy occurs as the result of sexual intercourse, that it lasts about nine months, during which time the fetus grows and develops, that standardly it terminates in the birth of a living baby, and that this is how we all come to be.

It might be thought that this distinction—between the familiar biological facts and the status of the fetus—is a distinction without a difference. But this is not so. To attach relevance to the status of the fetus, in the sense in which virtue theory claims it is not relevant, is to be gripped by the conviction that we must go beyond the familiar biological facts, deriving some sort of conclusion from them, such as that the fetus has rights, or is not a person, or something similar. It is also to believe that this exhausts the relevance of the familiar biological facts, that all they are relevant to is the status of the fetus and whether or not it is the sort of thing that may or may not be killed.

These convictions, I suspect, are rooted in the desire to solve the problem of abortion by getting it to fall under some general rule such as "You ought not to kill anything with the right to life but may kill anything else." But they have resulted in what should surely strike any nonphilosopher as a most bizarre aspect of nearly all the current philosophical literature on abortion, namely, that, far from treating abortion as a unique moral problem, markedly unlike any other, nearly everything written on the status of the fetus and its bearing on the abortion issue would be consistent with the human reproductive facts (to say nothing of family life) being totally different from what they are. Imagine that you are an alien extraterrestrial anthropologist who does not know that the human race is roughly 50 percent female and 50 percent male, or that our only (natural) form of reproduction involves heterosexual intercourse, viviparous birth, and the female's (and only the female's) being pregnant for nine months, or that females are capable of childbearing from late childhood to late middle age, or that childbearing is painful, dangerous, and emotionally charged—do you think you would pick up these facts from the hundreds of articles written on the status of the fetus? I am quite sure you would not. And that, I think, shows that the current philosophical literature on abortion has got badly out of touch with reality.

Now if we are using virtue theory, our first question is not "What do the familiar biological facts show—what can be derived from them about the status of the fetus?" but "How do these facts figure in the practical reasoning, actions and passions, thoughts and reactions, of the virtuous and the nonvirtuous? What is the mark of having the right attitude to these facts and what manifests having the wrong attitude to them?" This immediately makes essentially relevant not only all the facts about human reproduction I mentioned above, but a whole range of facts about our emotions in relation to them as well. I mean such facts as that human parents, both male and female, tend to care passionately about their offspring, and that family relationships are among the deepest and strongest in our lives—and, significantly, among the longest-lasting.

These facts make it obvious that pregnancy is not just one among many other physical conditions; and hence that anyone who genuinely believes that an abortion is comparable to a haircut or an appendectomy is mistaken.[5] The fact that the premature termination of a pregnancy is, in some sense, the cutting off of a new human life, and thereby, like the procreation of a new human life, connects with all our thoughts about human life and death, parenthood, and family relationships, must make it a serious matter. To disregard this fact about it, to think of abortion as nothing but the killing of something that does not matter, or as nothing but the exercise of some right or rights one has, or as the incidental means to some desirable state of affairs, is to do something callous and light-minded, the sort of thing that no virtuous and wise person would do. It is to have the wrong attitude not only to fetuses, but more generally to human life and death, parenthood, and family relationships.

Although I say that the facts make this obvious, I know that this is one of my tendentious points. In partial support of it I note that even the most dedicated proponents of the view that deliberate abortion is just like an appendectomy or haircut rarely hold the same view of spontaneous abortion, that is, miscarriage. It is not so tendentious of me to claim that to react to people's grief over miscarriage by saying, or even thinking, "What a fuss about nothing!" would be callous and light-minded, whereas to try to laugh someone out of grief over an appendectomy scar or a botched haircut would not be. It is hard to give this point due prominence within act-centered theories, for the inconsistency is an inconsistency in attitude about the seriousness of loss of life, not in beliefs about which acts are right or wrong. Moreover, an act-centered theorist may say, "Well, there is nothing wrong with *thinking* 'What a fuss about nothing!' as long as you do not say it and hurt the person who is grieving. And besides, we cannot be held responsible for our thoughts, only for the intentional actions they give rise to." But the character traits that virtue theory emphasizes are not simply dispositions to intentional actions, but a seamless disposition to certain actions and passions, thoughts and reactions.

To say that the cutting off of a human life is always a matter of some seriousness, at any stage, is not to deny the relevance of gradual fetal development. Notwithstanding the well-worn point that clear boundary lines cannot be drawn, our emotions and attitudes regarding the fetus do change as it develops, and again when it is born, and indeed further as the baby grows. Abortion for shallow reasons in the later stages is much more shocking than abortion for the same reasons in the early stages in a way that matches the fact that deep grief over miscarriage in the later stages is more appropriate than it is over miscarriage in the earlier stages (when, that is, the grief is solely about the loss of *this* child, not about, as might be the case, the loss of one's only hope of having a child or of having one's husband's child). Imagine (or recall) a woman who already has children; she had not intended to have more, but finds herself unexpectedly pregnant. Though contrary to her plans, the pregnancy, once established as a fact, is welcomed—and then she loses the embryo almost immediately. If this were bemoaned as a tragedy, it would, I think, be a misapplication of the concept of what is tragic. But it may still properly be mourned as a loss. The grief is expressed in such terms as "I shall always wonder how she or he would have turned out" or "When I look at the others, I shall think, 'How different their lives would have been if this other one had been part of them.' " It would, I take it, be callous and light-minded to say, or think, "Well, she has already *got* four children, what's the problem?"; it would be neither, nor arrogantly intrusive in the case of a close friend, to try to correct prolonged mourning by saying, "I know it's sad, but it's not a tragedy; rejoice in the ones you have." The application of *tragic* becomes more appropriate as the fetus grows, for the mere fact that one has lived with it for longer, conscious of its existence, makes a difference. To shrug off an early abortion is understandable just because it is very hard to be fully conscious of the fetus's existence in the early stages and hence hard to appreciate that an early abortion is the destruction of life. It is particularly hard for the young and inexperienced to appreciate this, because appreciation of it usually comes only with experience.

I do not mean "with the experience of having an abortion" (though that may be part of it) but, quite generally, "with the experience of life." Many women who have borne children contrast their later pregnancies with their first successful one, saying that in the later ones they were conscious of a new life growing in them from very early on. And, more generally, as one reaches the age at which the next generation is coming up close behind one, the counterfactuals "If I, or she, had had an abortion, Alice, or Bob, would not have been born" acquire a significant application, which casts a new light on the conditionals. "If I or Alice have an abortion then some Caroline or Bill will not be born."

The fact that pregnancy is not just one among many physical conditions does not mean that one can never regard it in that light without manifesting a vice. When women are in very poor physical health, or worn out from childbearing, or forced to do very physically demanding jobs, then they cannot be described as self-indulgent, callous, irresponsible, or light-minded if they seek abortions mainly with a view to avoiding pregnancy as the physical condition that it is. To go through with a pregnancy when one is utterly exhausted, or when one's job consists of crawling along tunnels hauling coal, as many women in the nineteenth century were obliged to do, is perhaps heroic, but people who do not achieve heroism are not necessarily vicious. That they can view the pregnancy only as nine months of misery, followed by hours if not days of agony and exhaustion, and abortion only as the blessed escape from this prospect, is entirely understandable and does not manifest any lack of serious respect for human life or a shallow attitude to Motherhood. What it does show is that something is terribly amiss in the conditions of their lives, which make it so hard to recognize pregnancy and childbearing as the good that they can be....

The foregoing discussion, insofar as it emphasizes the right attitude to human life and death, parallels to a certain extent those standard discussions of abortion that concentrate on it solely as an issue of killing. But it does not, as those discussions do, gloss over the fact, emphasized by those who discuss the morality of abortion in terms of women's rights, that abortion, wildly unlike any other form of killing, is the termination of a pregnancy, which is a condition of a woman's body and results in *her* having a child if it is not aborted. This fact is given due recognition not by appeal to women's rights but by emphasizing the relevance of the familiar biological and psychological facts and their connection with having the right attitude to parenthood and family relationships. But it may well be thought that failing to bring in women's rights still leaves some important aspects of the problem of abortion untouched.

Speaking in terms of women's rights, people sometimes say things like, "Well, it's her life you're talking about too, you know; she's got a right to her own life, her own happiness." And the discussion stops there. But in the context of virtue theory, given that we are particularly concerned with what constitutes a good human life, with what true happiness or *eudaimonia* is, this is no place to stop. We go on to ask, "And is this life of hers a good one? Is she living well?"

If we are to go on to talk about good human lives, in the context of abortion, we have to bring in our thoughts about the value of love and family life, and our proper emotional development through a natural life cycle. The familiar facts support the view that parenthood in general, and motherhood and childbearing in particular, are intrinsically worthwhile, are among the things that can be correctly thought to be partially constitutive of a flourishing human life.[6] If this is right, then a woman who opts for not being a mother (at all, or again, or now) by opting for abortion may thereby be manifesting a flawed grasp of what her life should be, and be about—a grasp that is childish, or grossly materialistic, or shortsighted, or shallow.

I said "*may* thereby": this need not be so. Consider, for instance, a woman who has already had several children and fears that to have another will seriously affect her capacity to be a good mother to the ones she has—she does not show a lack of appreciation of the intrinsic value of being a parent by opting for abortion. Nor does a woman who has been a good mother and is approaching the age at which she may be looking forward to being a good grandmother. Nor does a woman who discovers that her pregnancy may well kill her, and opts for abortion.... Nor, necessarily, does a woman who has decided to lead a life centered around some other worthwhile activity or activities with which motherhood would compete.

People who are childless by choice are sometimes described as "irresponsible," or "selfish," or "refusing to grow up," or "not knowing what life is about." But one can hold that having children is intrinsically worthwhile without endorsing this, for we are, after all, in the happy position of there being more worthwhile things to do than can be fitted into one lifetime. Parenthood, and motherhood in particular, even if granted to be intrinsically worthwhile, undoubtedly take up a lot of one's adult life, leaving no room for some other worthwhile pursuits. But some women who choose abortion rather than have their first child, and some men who encourage their partners to choose abortion, are not avoiding parenthood for the sake of other worthwhile pursuits, but for the worthless one of "having a good time," or for the pursuit of some false vision of the ideals of freedom or self-realization. And some others who say "I am not ready for parenthood yet" are making some sort of mistake about the extent to which one can manipulate the circumstances of one's life so as to make it fulfill some dream that one has. Perhaps one's dream is to have two perfect children; a girl and a boy, within a perfect marriage, in financially secure circumstances, with an interesting job of one's own. But to care too much about that dream, to demand of life that it give it to one and act accordingly, may be both greedy and foolish, and is to run the risk of missing out on happiness entirely. Not only may fate make the dream impossible, or destroy it, but one's own attachment to it may make it impossible. Good marriages, and the most promising children, can be destroyed by just one adult's excessive demand for perfection.

Once again, this is not to deny that girls may quite properly say "I am not ready for motherhood yet," especially in our society, and, far from manifesting irresponsibility or light-mindedness, show an appropriate modesty or humility, or a fearfulness that does not amount to cowardice. However, even when the decision to have an abortion is the right decision—one that does not itself fall under a vice-related term and thereby one that the perfectly virtuous could recommend—it does not follow that there is no sense in which having the abortion is wrong, or guilt inappropriate. For, by virtue of the fact that a human life has been cut short, some evil has probably been brought about,[7] and that circumstances make the decision to bring about some evil the right decision will be a ground for guilt if getting into those circumstances in the first place itself manifested a flaw in character.

What "gets one into those circumstances" in the case of abortion is, except in the case of rape, one's sexual activity and one's choices, or the lack of them, about one's sexual partner and about contraception. The virtuous woman (which here of course does not mean simply "chaste woman" but "woman with the virtues") has such character traits as strength, independence, resoluteness, decisiveness, self-confidence, responsibility, serious-mindedness, and self-determination—and no one, I think, could deny that many women become pregnant in circumstances in which they cannot welcome or cannot face the thought of having *this* child precisely because they lack one or some of these character traits. So even in the cases where the decision to have an abortion is the right one, it can still be the reflection of a moral failing—not because the decision itself is weak or cowardly or irresolute or irresponsible or light-minded, but because lack of the requisite opposite of these failings landed one in the circumstances in the first place. Hence the common universalized claim that guilt and remorse are never appropriate emotions about an abortion is denied. They may be appropriate, and appropriately inculcated, even when the decision was the right one.

Another motivation for bringing women's rights into the discussion may be to attempt to correct the implication, carried by the killing-centered approach, that insofar as abortion is wrong, it is a wrong that only women do, or at least (given the preponderance of male doctors) that only women instigate. I do not myself believe that we can thus escape the fact that nature bears harder on women than it does on men,[8] but virtue theory can certainly correct many of the injustices that the emphasis on women's rights is rightly concerned about. With very little amendment, everything that has been said above applies to boys and men too. Although the abortion decision is, in a natural sense, the woman's decision, proper to her, boys and men are often party to it, for well or ill, and even when they are not, they are bound to have been party to the circumstances that brought it up. No less than girls and women, boys and men can, in their actions, manifest self-centeredness, callousness, and light-mindedness about life and parenthood in relation to abortion. They can be self-centered or courageous about the possibility of disability in their offspring; they need to reflect on their sexual activity and their choices, or lack of them, about their sexual partner and contraception; they need to grow up and take responsibility for their own actions and life in relation to fatherhood. If it is true, as I maintain, that insofar as motherhood is intrinsically worthwhile, being a mother is an important purpose in women's lives, being a father (rather than a mere generator) is an important purpose in men's lives as well, and it is adolescent of men to turn a blind eye to this and pretend that they have many more important things to do....

NOTES

1. It seems likely that some people have been misled by Foot's discussion of euthanasia (through no fault of hers) into thinking that a virtue theorist's discussion of terminating human life will be conducted exclusively in terms of justice and charity (and the corresponding vice terms) (Philippa Foot, "Euthanasia," *Philosophy & Public Affairs* 6, no. 2 [Winter 1977]: 85–112). But the act-category *euthanasia* is a very special one, at least as defined in her article, since such an act must be done "for the sake of the one who is to die." Building a virtuous motivation into the specification of the act in this way immediately rules out the application of many other vice terms.
2. Judith Jarvis Thomson, "A Defense of Abortion," *Philosophy & Public Affairs* 1, no. 1 (Fall 1971): 47–66. One could indeed regard this article as proto-virtue theory (no doubt to the surprise of the author) if the concepts of callousness and kindness were allowed more weight.
3. One possible qualification: if one ties the concept of justice very closely to rights, then if women do have a moral right to terminate their pregnancies it *may* follow that in doing so they do not act unjustly. (Cf. Thomson, "A Defense of Abortion.") But it is debatable whether even that much follows.
4. This is an assumption of virtue theory, and I do not attempt to defend it here. An adequate discussion of it would require a separate article, since, although most moral philosophers would be chary of claiming that intellectual sophistication is a necessary condition of moral wisdom or virtue, most of us, from Plato onward, tend to write as if this were so. Sorting out which claims about moral knowledge are committed to this kind of elitism and which can, albeit with difficulty, be reconciled with the idea that moral knowledge can be acquired by anyone who really wants it would be a major task.
5. Mary Anne Warren, in "On the Moral and Legal Status of Abortion," *Monist* 57 (1973), sec. 1, says of the opponents of restrictive laws governing abortion that "their conviction (for the most part) is that abortion is not a *morally* serious and extremely unfortunate, even though sometimes justified, act, comparable to killing in self-defense or to letting the violinist die, but rather is closer to being a *morally neutral* act, like cutting one's hair" (italics mine). I would like to think that no one *genuinely* believes this. But certainly in discussion, particularly when arguing against restrictive

laws or the suggestion that remorse over abortion might be appropriate, I have found that some people *say* they believe it (and often cite Warren's article, albeit inaccurately, despite its age). Those who allow that it is morally serious, and far from morally neutral, have to argue against restrictive laws, or the appropriateness of remorse, on a very different ground from that laid down by the premise "The fetus is just part of the woman's body (and she has a right to determine what happens to her body and should not feel guilt about anything she does to it)."

6. I take this as a premise here, but argue for it in some detail in my *Beginning Lives* (Oxford: Basil Blackwell, 1987). In this connection I also discuss adoption and the sense in which it may be regarded as "second best," and the difficult question of whether the good of parenthood may properly be sought, or indeed bought, by surrogacy.
7. I say "some evil has probably been brought about" on the ground that (human) life is (usually) a good and hence (human) death usually an evil. The exceptions would be (a) where death is actually a good or a benefit, because the baby that would come to be if the life were not cut short would be better off dead than alive, and (b) where death, though not a good, is not an evil either, because the life that would be led (e.g., in a state of permanent coma) would not be a good. (See Foot, "Euthanasia.")
8. I discuss this point at greater length in *Beginning Lives*.

QUESTIONS FOR ANALYSIS

1. Why does Hursthouse think a woman's rights have no bearing on the morality of abortion?
2. What, according to Hursthouse, is the significance of the fetus's status to virtue theory? Why?
3. How does Hursthouse defend her claim that the early termination of a pregnancy is always a serious matter? Do you agree? What about her claim that parenthood helps to constitute human flourishing?
4. What virtues and vices does Hursthouse consider in her essay? Which do you consider the most relevant?
5. Hursthouse says that current philosophical writing about abortion is "out of touch with reality." Why? Would you say the same thing about the other selections in this chapter? How would their authors respond?
6. According to Hursthouse, a woman who finds herself with an unwanted pregnancy lacks one or more virtues. Which virtues does she have in mind? Do you agree?
7. Does virtue theory help to shed light on the abortion debate?

CASE PRESENTATION

Conceived in Violence, Born in Hate[1]

Shortly after returning home, a twenty-seven-year-old mother was gagged, tied up, and raped by a 220-pound guard from a nearby Air Force base who had forced his way into her home. The woman received medical treatment at a hospital and from her own physician. Nevertheless, the episode had left her pregnant.

Not wanting the child, the woman sought an abortion. Although the state's abortion law was, at the time (1955), one of the least restrictive, no hospital in her state would permit her to have an abortion.

Unable to afford to travel abroad for a legal abortion, the woman and her husband were left with two choices: a clandestine illegal abortion or having the baby. Deeply religious and law abiding, the couple chose to carry the baby to term.

During her pregnancy, the woman admitted to hating the fetus she was carrying and to eagerly awaiting the time she would be rid of it. "Thus the child, conceived in violence and born in hatred, came into the world."[2]

[1] Reported in Burton M. Leiser, *Liberty, Justice, and Morals: Contemporary Value Conflicts* (New York: Macmillan, 1973), p. 96.

[2] Leiser, *Liberty, Justice, and Morals,* p. 96.

QUESTIONS FOR ANALYSIS

1. Do you think abortion should or should not be legal in cases such as this?
2. The traditional Roman Catholic position on abortion rests on the assumption that the unborn is a person from conception. Since the fetus is an innocent person, even when a pregnancy is due to rape or incest, the fetus may not be held accountable and made to suffer through its death. According to Roman Catholicism, then, a *direct* abortion is never morally justifiable. (Although the fetus may never be deliberately killed, it may be allowed to die as a consequence of an action that is intended to save the life of the mother, such as the removal of a malignant uterus.) By this account, an abortion in the preceding case would be immoral. Evaluate this position.
3. Christian moralist Joseph Fletcher has written: "No unwanted and unintended baby should ever be born."[3] Do you think such a rule would produce the greatest social benefit?
4. Do you think Rawls's first principle of social justice has any relevance to the abortion issue?

CASE PRESENTATION

Death in Pensacola

Paul J. Hill was a former Presbyterian minister who had been divested by the Orthodox Presbyterian Church. Among the reasons for his divestiture were his many quarrels with the church over abortion. Hill was strongly anti-abortion, the church moderately pro-choice. After his divestiture, he moved to Pensacola, Florida, where he became active in the pro-life movement, founding a group he called Defensive Action and leading protests at the city's two abortion clinics. One of those clinics made front-page headlines throughout the country in March 1993, when abortion doctor David Gunn was shot and killed outside it by an anti-abortion assailant. The killing, in turn, made Hill a national figure. Appearing on such talk shows as *Donahue* and *Sonya Live,* he approved of the murder as biblically justified homicide and advocated more of the same. Then, in July of the following year, he apparently put his theology into practice. Shot dead outside the city's other abortion clinic were Dr. John Britton and clinic volunteer James Barrett. Barrett's wife, June, also a volunteer, survived her wounds. Prosecutors charged Hill with the shootings the following day.

As newspaper reports over the following days made clear, Barrett was an improbable martyr for the pro-choice movement. Unlike Dr. Gunn, who had been an abortion rights advocate, he personally opposed abortions and frequently tried to discourage his patients from having them. Still, in the face of death threats and considerable harassment, he continued to work at the clinic. He wore a bullet-proof vest to and from the clinic as a precaution but refused offers of police protection.

Operation Rescue and other pro-life groups denounced the killings. President Clinton ordered federal marshalls to stand guard at abortion clinics throughout the country three days after the killings occurred. During Dr. Britton's funeral, a small group of abortion opponents demonstrated outside the church. Said one demonstrator, "May he rot in hell."

Paul Hill was executed by the state of Florida on September 3, 2003. His last words before his death included, "If you believe abortion is a lethal force, you should oppose the force and do what you have to do to stop it."

QUESTIONS FOR ANALYSIS

1. Many abortion rights activists blame anti-abortion rhetoric for contributing to violence at clinics, even if the rhetoric comes from peaceful protestors. The rhetoric they have in mind includes calling abortion doctors murderers and comparing abortion to the Nazi holocaust of the Jews. Do you agree?

[3]Joseph Fletcher, *Situation Ethics: The New Morality* (Philadelphia: Westminster Press, 1966), p. 39.

2. Hill and other extreme abortion foes consider abortion the moral equivalent of killing schoolchildren. What do you consider the proper level of protest for people who genuinely feel that way? What steps do you think they can justifiably take to prevent abortions?
3. The year 1994 saw the introduction of three significant legal obstacles to anti-abortion demonstrators. In one, the U.S. Supreme Court ruled that clinics can sue groups like Operation Rescue, which systematically attempt to shut clinics down, under the federal racketeering law. In another, the Court ruled that restricting peaceful demonstrators to a distance from which they cannot block access to a clinic is constitutional. In the third, Congress passed the Access to Clinic Entrances Act, making interference with a woman's right to enter a clinic a federal crime. Do such measures unfairly restrict free speech and assembly rights? Should tougher measures be enacted? Do abortion opponents have the moral right to defy the restrictions as an act of civil disobedience?
4. During the 1992 Democratic Convention in New York City that nominated Bill Clinton for president, abortion foe Harley David Belew was arrested after trying to give the nominee a plastic bag containing a fetus. In Oslo, Norway, almost two years later, thieves stole the famous Edvard Munch painting, *The Scream,* from the National Art Museum and offered to return it if the national television station aired *The Silent Scream,* an anti-abortion film. (Though the station refused, the painting was recovered.) Are such novel but illegal protests justifiable?

CASE PRESENTATION

The Fight for Martina Greywind's Baby

By the young age of twenty-eight years, Martina Greywind had already carried and delivered six children. All had been taken away from her on the grounds that she was an unfit mother. Now she was again pregnant. She was also a penniless street person and a paint-fume addict.

While serving a brief sentence in a Fargo, North Dakota, jail for sniffing paint, she met a group of prisoners doing time for an altogether different offense. Members of an anti-abortion organization called Lambs of Christ, they had come to Fargo to shut down the state's only abortion clinic. Greywind told them of her pregnancy and her plans for abortion. Seeking to change her mind, they made this offer: If she did not abort, they would give her $10,000 plus food and shelter and medical care. Greywind went ahead with the abortion anyway, after the Lamb of Christ members found five couples who were willing to adopt her baby.

Why did she reject the offer? According to those who made it, she was coerced by local prosecutors. Because her paint sniffing had continued during the pregnancy, she faced charges of reckless endangerment of a fetus; the only way to get the charges dropped was to abort. They supported their accusation by claiming she told them in jail that she didn't want the abortion. Greywind did not comment on the claim.

After the abortion, the Lamb of Christ members made another accusation. The state, they said, had violated a state law prohibiting the use of public funds for abortions when it drove Greywind in a state vehicle from a mental hospital to the clinic, a distance of 100 miles.

QUESTIONS FOR ANALYSIS

1. Should Greywind have had the abortion?
2. Abortion rights activists try to frame the abortion debate as a matter of choice. Did Greywind have a real choice or was she coerced?
3. Do laws against reckless endangerment of a fetus promote abortion?
4. Were the Lambs of Christ members trying to help Greywind or merely using her in their anti-abortion crusade?

CASE PRESENTATION

Sex-Selection Abortions

The availability in recent decades of ultrasound technology makes it possible to identify the sex of a fetus in the early months of a pregnancy. The sex can be identified with near certainty at twenty weeks, though some technicians claim reliable identification as early as eleven weeks in the pregnancy. Newer, more invasive genetic testing can identify the sex of the fetus even earlier.

One result is the now-widespread practice of aborting fetuses of a gender undesirable in the minds of the parents. In the nation of India, even though using ultrasound for this purpose was made illegal in 1994, no criminal charges have been reported for violation of this law. Public health experts note that in 2001, only 927 females per 1,000 males were born in India, reflecting the widespread preference for sons. Daughters are considered a liability, for example, because of the requirement that when they marry, their parents provide a dowry to the husband and his family.

Sex-selection abortions also appear to be common in China, where the population control programs of the government limit each couple to one child, and parents typically prefer a son to a daughter. After decades of this practice, one consequence is the difficulty men have in finding a wife, as the proportion of women in the population declines. Although some provinces in China have attempted to ban this use of abortions, their efforts appear no more successful than similar laws in India.

In 2006, the British government proposed banning sex-selection abortions, in the absence of any compelling medical justification, such as the health or life of the mother or serious genetic defects in the fetus. No such ban has been adopted in the United States, but groups that oppose abortion per se have become interested in this sort of ban as a way to limit abortions further. The American Society for Reproductive Medicine (ASRM) has noted that sex-selection procedures might reinforce gender bias in society and encourage other forms of genetic engineering to produce so-called designer babies. The President's Council on Bioethics has reviewed issues in sex-selection abortion but has not offered any formal recommendation either that it be supported or that it be restricted.

One challenge in moral reasoning is whether a pregnant woman should have to give a reason for an abortion that others find morally acceptable, so long as she otherwise conforms with the law. The principle of moral autonomy in medicine suggests that each patient, including a pregnant woman, should be able to make her own decisions in seeking or refusing a medical procedure, regardless of whether others consider those decisions appropriate.

Feminist philosopher Mary V. Rorty, a clinical professor at the Stanford Center for Biomedical Ethics, has noted the dilemma here for feminists. Whereas they might applaud autonomy for women in deciding whether to have an abortion, they also are alarmed at the devaluation of the worth of women reflected in the practice of aborting female fetuses in preference for male children.

QUESTIONS FOR ANALYSIS

1. Assuming an abortion otherwise complies with American law, is it ethical for a woman to terminate a pregnancy simply because she does not like the sex of the fetus? Should she have to defend this decision to someone else, perhaps a medical review board, before the abortion would be performed?
2. If the British ban on sex-selection abortions were adopted in the United States, might this be a slippery slope toward banning other elective abortions or requiring approval by a medical review board for the reasons for the abortion? Should women have to give a reason why they want an abortion? Who should decide what constitutes a "good" reason and what a "bad" reason? Would such a review process threaten the autonomy of women to make their own decisions concerning abortion? Would such review constitute an "undue burden" on women, which the U.S. Supreme Court has

recognized as an unconstitutional barrier to abortion rights?

3. Some disability rights advocates are alarmed that it is permissible in this country to abort a child because prenatal testing determines that it will be born with serious physical defects, such as Down's syndrome. These advocates believe the practice devalues living persons with those conditions. Should feminists be alarmed that sex-selection abortions that terminate female fetuses devalue the status of women in the society?

Euthanasia

- **Personhood**
- **Death**
- **Ordinary vs. Extraordinary Treatment**
- **Killing vs. Allowing to Die**
- **Meaning of *Euthanasia:* Narrow vs. Broad Interpretations**
- **Voluntary vs. Nonvoluntary Euthanasia**
- **Assisted Suicide**
- **The Right to Refuse Treatment**
- **Defective Newborns**
- **Arguments for Voluntary (Active) Euthanasia**
- **Arguments against Voluntary (Active) Euthanasia**

J. GAY-WILLIAMS **The Wrongfulness of Euthanasia**
JAMES RACHELS **Active and Passive Euthanasia**
PHILIPPA FOOT **Euthanasia**
RICHARD BRANDT **A Moral Principle about Killing**

CASE PRESENTATIONS: *"I Did It Because I Loved My Son"* • *"A Choice Central to Personal Dignity"* • *Legalized Assisted Suicide and Decriminalized Euthanasia* • *Terri Schiavo: Voluntary Euthanasia or Murder?*

THE CASE OF KAREN ANN Quinlan has probably done more than any other in recent decades to rivet public attention on the legal and moral aspects of euthanasia, which generally refers to the act of painlessly putting to death a person suffering from a terminal or incurable disease or condition. On the night of April 15, 1975, for reasons still unclear, Karen Ann Quinlan ceased breathing for at least two fifteen-minute periods. Failing to respond to mouth-to-mouth resuscitation by friends, she was taken by ambulance to Newton Memorial Hospital in New Jersey. She had a temperature of 100 degrees, her pupils were unreactive, and she did not respond even to deep pain. Physicians who examined her characterized Karen as being in a "chronic, persistent, vegetative state," and later it was judged that no form of treatment could restore her to cognitive life. Her father, Joseph Quinlan, asked to be appointed her legal guardian with the expressed purpose of discontinuing the use of the respirator by which Karen was being sustained. Eventually, the Supreme Court of New Jersey granted the request. The respirator was turned off. However, Karen Ann Quinlan remained alive but comatose until June 11, 1985, when she died at the age of thirty-one. Although widely publicized, the Quinlan case is by no means the only one that has raised questions concerning euthanasia.

In fact, improvements in biomedical technology have made euthanasia an issue that more and more individuals and institutions must confront and that society must address. Respirators, artificial kidneys, intravenous feeding, new drugs—all have made it possible to sustain an individual's life artificially—that is, long after the individual has lost the capacity to sustain life independently. In cases like Quinlan's, individuals have fallen into a state of irreversible coma, what some health professionals term a vegetative state. In other instances, such as after severe accidents or with congenital brain disease, the individual's consciousness has been so dulled and the personality has so deteriorated that he or she lacks the capacity for development and growth. In still other cases, such as with terminal cancer, individuals vacillate between agonizing pain and a drug-induced stupor, with no possibility of ever again enjoying life. Not too long ago, "nature would have taken its course"; such patients would have died. Today, we have the technological capacity to keep them alive artificially. Should we? Or at least in some instances, are we justified in not doing this and even obliged not to?

As with abortion, euthanasia raises two basic moral issues that must be distinguished. The first deals with the morality of euthanasia itself; the second concerns the morality of euthanasia legislation. We consider both issues in this chapter.

Before discussing the arguments related to these issues, we must clarify a number of concepts central to euthanasia. Among them are the meanings of *personhood* and *death,* the difference between "ordinary" and "extraordinary" treatment, the distinctions between "killing" and "allowing to die," the various meanings of *euthanasia,* and the difference between "voluntary" and "nonvoluntary" euthanasia.

PERSONHOOD

The question of personhood bears as much on euthanasia as on abortion debates. What conditions should be used as the criteria of personhood? Can an entity be considered a **person** merely because it possesses certain biological properties? Or should other factors be introduced, such as consciousness, self-consciousness, rationality, and the capacities for communication and moral judgment? If personhood is just an elementary biological matter, then patients like Karen Ann Quinlan can qualify as persons more easily than if personhood depends on a complex list of psychosocial factors.

In part, the significance of the personhood issue lies in the assignment of basic patient rights; once the criteria for personhood are established, those qualifying presumably enjoy the same general rights as any other patient. Conversely, for those who do not qualify and have no reasonable chance of ever qualifying, the rights issue is far less problematic. This doesn't mean that a death decision necessarily follows when an entity is determined to be a nonperson. But it does mean that whatever may be inherently objectionable about allowing or causing a person to die dissolves because the entity is no longer a person. So the concept of personhood bears directly on a death decision.

DEATH

Related to personhood is the conceptual issue of death. To get some idea of the complexities enshrouding the concept of death, consider this episode, which is based on an actual case.[1]

A terrible auto accident has occurred. One of the cars was occupied by a husband and wife. Authorities on the scene pronounce the man dead and rush the unconscious woman to a hospital, where she spends the next seventeen days in a coma due to severe brain damage. On the morning of the eighteenth day, she dies. Some time afterward, a relative contesting the couple's estate claims that the two people died simultaneously. Did they?

Not too long ago, legal and medical experts would have said yes. But when this case went to the Supreme Court of Arkansas in 1958, the court ruled that since the woman was breathing after the accident, she was alive, even though unconscious. The court relied on the time-honored definition of death as "the cessation of life; the ceasing to exist; defined by physicians as a total stoppage of the circulation of blood and a cessation of the animal and vital functions consequent thereon, such as respiration, pulsation, etc."[2] By this definition, death occurs if and only if there is a total cessation of respiration and blood flow.

Using heart-lung functioning as a criterion for death served well enough until recent developments in biomedical technology made it questionable. One of these developments is the increasing and widespread use of devices that can sustain respiration and heartbeat indefinitely, even when there is no brain activity. If the traditional heart-lung criterion is applied in cases like the preceding, then these individuals are technically still alive. Yet to many—including relatives of the comatose and those who must treat them—such people are, for all intents and purposes, dead.

To address these concerns, a model statute for determination of death was proposed in 1981 by the National Conference of Commissioners on Uniform State Laws, in consultation with the American Medical Association and the American Bar Association. The uniform statute, which has been adopted by twenty-five states, is as follows:

> An Individual who has sustained either (1) irreversible cessation of circulatory and respiratory functions, or (2) irreversible cessation of all functions of the entire brain, including the brain stem, is dead. A determination of death must be made in accordance with accepted medical standards.

Another development that has cast doubt on the traditional definition of death is the need for still-viable organs in transplant surgery. In general, a transplant is most successful if the organs are removed immediately after death. Thus, there is intense pressure on transplant teams to harvest organs as soon as possible. The moral implications of this pressure are serious, as we'll see shortly.

But these developments are only part of what makes the whole issue of defining death so nettlesome. Also relevant are three distinct categories of concerns that can

---

[1] *Smith v. Smith*, 229 Arkansas 579, 3175. W. 2d. 275 (1958).
[2] *Black's Law Dictionary*, 4th ed. (St. Paul, Minn.: West Publishing), 1951, p. 488.

be identified in any discussion of death: the philosophical, the physiological, and the methodical.

Philosophical Concerns

The philosophical level refers to one's basic concept of death, which inevitably springs from some view of what it means to be human. For example, if we believe it is the capacity to think and reason that makes one a human, we will likely associate the loss of personhood with the loss of rationality. If we consider consciousness as the defining characteristic, we will be more inclined to consider a person to have lost that status when a number of characteristics such as the capacities to remember, enjoy, worry, and will are gone. Although the absence of rational or experimental capacities would not necessarily define death, it would dispose us toward such a definition, since we are already disposed to accept the absence of personhood in the absence of those criteria. So there is interplay between our concepts of personhood and death.

Physiological Concerns

These concerns are related to the functioning of specific body systems or organs. The traditional physiological standard for recognizing death has been irreversible loss of circulatory and respiratory functions. This was the so-called "common law" definition of "death" used in the 1958 Arkansas decision and *Black's Law Dictionary*. The more recent uniform statute includes that definition but also includes a standard focused on the central nervous system—the brain and spinal cord. Specifically, these standards are the irreversible loss of reflex activity mediated through the brain or spinal cord, electrical activity in the cerebral neocortex, and/or cerebral blood flow. Whether traditional or recent, these physiological standards can be used individually or in combination. The significance of the physiological category in death decisions is that a patient declared alive by one set of criteria might be ruled dead by another. If a patient is considered dead, obviously euthanasia becomes academic; if the person is considered alive, euthanasia is a real concern.

Methodical Concerns

This category refers to specific means for determining physiological standards. The method used to determine traditional heart-lung standards has been taking the pulse or reading an electrocardiogram or both. For the central nervous system, electroencephalographs can be used to measure electrical activity in the neocortex, and radioactive tracers can be injected into the circulatory system for detecting cerebral blood flow.

Moral Implications

What makes defining death so important in discussions of euthanasia and the general study of bioethics is the interplay between definitional and moral considerations. To illustrate, suppose an attacker has clubbed a woman into a comatose condition. She is rushed to a hospital, is determined to have suffered profound and irreversible brain damage, and is put on an artificial respirator. Efforts to identify her fail. As the team tending her debates whether to remove her from the respirator, one member, using one of the brain-death criteria, claims she is already dead. Therefore, withdrawing the respirator poses no special problems. Another member demurs. Using the heart-lung criterion, she insists that the woman is still alive and that the team has an obligation to sustain her life. What ought the team do?

One answer is, let the law decide. But some states lack an adequate definition of death. Complicating matters, some states allow either of the two alternative definitions. And even where the law is decisive, moral problems remain about the rightness of the standard itself. Beyond this, even when the law sanctions a brain-death criterion, as it now does in most states, it does not compel health professionals or anyone else to implement it. So although brain-death law may legally protect health professionals, it does not obligate them to act. Health professionals, presumably in consultation with others, must still wrestle with moral decisions in cases of irreversible coma.

Then there is the phenomenon of organ transplants, which promises to become of even greater concern as technology and techniques improve. A number of interests are identifiable in such cases. First, there are the interests of recipients, whose welfare depends on the availability of organs. Then there are the interests of health teams, who are obliged to provide adequate healthcare, which may include appropriate quality organs. There are also the interests of the donors, who may fear that their organs will be pirated prior to death or that their own healthcare providers will perform less than adequately in trying to sustain their lives. Moreover, there are the obligations of health teams to guard donors against physical violations as well as the psychological threat of violations and to guard themselves against developing a cannibalistic image. And finally, society at large must be watchful that the rights of its citizens to protection are not flouted, while at the same time ensuring that its ill citizens are not denied needed medical care and treatment, which may involve transplants.

ORDINARY VS. EXTRAORDINARY TREATMENT

A third issue that arises in euthanasia discussions involves the concept of ordinary as opposed to extraordinary treatment, terms used to differentiate two broad categories of medical intervention. Although the terms are often applied facilely, they elude hard-and-fast definition.

Moralist Paul Ramsey, for one, has applied *ordinary* to all medicines, treatments, and surgical procedures that offer a reasonable hope of benefit to the patient but do not involve excessive pain, expense, or other inconveniences. In contrast, he has identified *extraordinary* as measures that are unusual, extremely difficult, dangerous, inordinately expensive, or that offer no reasonable hope of benefit to the patient.[3]

Such descriptions are useful and probably find widespread acceptance. But they do raise questions. An obvious one concerns the concepts used to define *ordinary* and *extraordinary*. What can be considered "reasonable hope of benefit to the patient"? What measures qualify as "unusual"? Ramsey mentions cost, but some would claim that cost has no place in a moral calculation. And then there is always the question of whether these criteria should be used individually or in combination; if in combination, what is the proper mix? Furthermore, patient idiosyncrasies inevitably influence a determination of ordinary and extraordinary in a particular case. For example, the use of antibiotics for a pneumonia patient undoubtedly qualifies as

---

[3]Paul Ramsey, *The Patient as Person* (New Haven, Conn.: Yale University Press, 1970), pp. 122–123.

ordinary treatment. But does it remain ordinary treatment when the patient with pneumonia happens to have terminal cancer with metastasis to the brain and liver? The institutional setting can also affect evaluations of what constitutes ordinary and extraordinary: What is extraordinary treatment in a small community hospital could be ordinary in a large teaching hospital.[4]

The significance of trying to pin down these two concepts is that euthanasia arguments often rely on them to distinguish the permissible from the impermissible act of euthanasia. Most moralists, both religious and secular, argue that health professionals should provide ordinary treatment for the moribund but not extraordinary, which may be withheld or never started. Others insist that health professionals initiate extraordinary measures. Indeed, the medical profession itself makes similar operational distinctions in making death decisions.

KILLING VS. ALLOWING TO DIE

A fourth conceptual issue that we should try to clarify is what some consider to be the difference between killing a person and allowing a person to die. Presumably, "killing" a person refers to a definite action taken to end someone's life, as in the case of the physician who, out of mercy, injects a terminally ill patient with air or a lethal dose of a medication. Killing is an act of commission. In contrast, "allowing to die" presumably is an act of omission, whereby the steps needed to preserve someone's life simply are not taken. For example, a doctor, again out of mercy, fails to give an injection of antibiotics to a terminally ill patient who has contracted pneumonia. As a result of this omission, the patient dies.

Those making this distinction, such as the American Medical Association (AMA), say that the distinction is reasonable because in ordinary language and everyday life we distinguish between causing someone harm and permitting the harm to happen to them. If, in cases of euthanasia, the distinction is not made between killing and allowing to die, we lose the important distinction between causing someone harm and permitting that harm to happen.

Proponents also claim that the distinction acknowledges cases in which additional curative treatment would serve no purpose and in fact would interfere with a person's natural death. It recognizes that medical science will not initiate or sustain extraordinary means to preserve the life of a dying patient when such means would obviously serve no useful purpose for the patient or the patient's family.

Finally, some argue that the distinction is important in determining causation of death and ultimate responsibility. In instances where the patient dies following nontreatment, the proximate cause of death is the patient's disease, not the treatment or the person who did not provide it. If we fail to differentiate between killing and allowing to die, we blur this distinction. If allowing to die is subsumed under the category of euthanasia, then the nontreatment is the cause of the death, not the disease.

Not everyone, however, agrees that the distinction is a logical one. Some argue that withholding extraordinary treatment or suspending heroic measures in terminal cases is tantamount to the intentional termination of the life of one human being by

---

[4]See A. J. Davis and M. A. Aroskar, *Ethical Dilemmas and Nursing Practice* (New York: Appleton-Century-Crofts, 1978), p. 117.

another; that is, it is an act of killing. Thus, they claim that no logical distinction can be made between killing and allowing to die.

Whether or not the distinction between the two can be sustained logically is only one question raised by the killing vs. letting die debate. Another is the moral relevance of such a distinction. Even if the distinction is logical, does it have any bearing on the rightness or wrongness of acts commonly termed *euthanasia?*

On the one hand, for those making the distinction, allowing a patient to die under carefully circumscribed conditions could be moral. On the other hand, they seemingly would regard the killing of a patient, even out of mercy, an immoral act. But those opposing the killing–letting die distinction would not necessarily accept the close connection between killing a dying patient and an immoral act. For them, while killing is generally wrong, in some cases it may be the right thing to do. What determines the morality of killing a patient, what is of moral relevance and importance, is not the manner of causing the death but the circumstances in which the death is caused.

In summary, those distinguishing killing from allowing to die claim that the distinction is logically and morally relevant. Generally, they would condemn any act of killing a patient, while recognizing that some acts of allowing a patient to die may be moral (as, for example, in cases where life is being preserved heroically and death is imminent). In contrast are those who hold that the killing-letting die distinction is not logical and that allowing to die is in effect killing. They claim that killing a patient may be morally justifiable depending on the circumstances and not the manner in which the death is caused. The debate that surrounds the killing vs. allowing to die question is basic to the very meaning of euthanasia, a fifth conceptual issue that needs clarification.

MEANING OF *EUTHANASIA:* NARROW VS. BROAD INTERPRETATIONS

Construing euthanasia (from the Greek, meaning "good or happy death") narrowly, some philosophers have taken it to be the equivalent of killing. Since allowing someone to die does not involve killing, allowing to die would not actually be an act of euthanasia at all. By this account, then, there are acts of allowing to die, which may be moral, and acts of euthanasia, which are always wrong.

Other philosophers interpret the meaning of **euthanasia** more broadly. For them, euthanasia includes not only acts of killing but also acts of allowing to die. In other words, euthanasia can take an active or passive form. **Active** (sometimes termed positive) **euthanasia** refers to the act of painlessly putting to death persons suffering from incurable conditions or diseases. Injecting a lethal dosage of medication into a terminally ill patient would constitute active euthanasia. **Passive euthanasia,** in contrast, refers to any act of allowing a patient to die. Not providing a terminally ill patient the needed antibiotics to survive pneumonia would be an example of passive euthanasia.

It is tempting to view the debate between the narrow and the broad interpretations of euthanasia largely in terms of semantics. While the meaning of euthanasia certainly is a factor in the disagreement, the issue involves more than mere word definition.

One side, the narrow interpretation, considers killing a patient always morally wrong. Since euthanasia, by this definition, is killing a patient, euthanasia is always morally wrong. But allowing a patient to die does not involve killing a patient. Therefore, allowing a patient to die does not fall under the moral prohibition that euthanasia does; allowing a patient to die may be morally right.

The other side, the broad interpretation, considers acts of allowing patients to die acts of euthanasia, albeit passive euthanasia. They argue that if euthanasia is wrong, then so is allowing patients to die (since it is a form of euthanasia). But if allowing patients to die is not wrong, then euthanasia is not always wrong. Generally, those favoring the broad interpretation in fact claim that allowing patients to die is not always wrong and that euthanasia, therefore, may be morally justifiable. With the possible moral justifiability of euthanasia established, it is conceivable that acts of active euthanasia, as well as passive, may be moral. What determines their morality are the conditions under which the death is caused and not the manner in which it is caused. It's within these broad interpretations that the most problematic cases of death decisions fall—including the Quinlan case.

VOLUNTARY VS. NONVOLUNTARY EUTHANASIA

In addition to the preceding, there is another conceptual issue that arises in discussions of euthanasia. It concerns the difference between voluntary and nonvoluntary decisions about death.

Voluntary decisions about death refer to cases in which a competent adult patient requests or gives informed consent to a particular course of medical treatment or nontreatment. Generally speaking, informed consent exists when patients can understand what they are agreeing to and voluntarily choose it. Voluntary decisions also include cases in which persons take their own lives either directly or by refusing treatment and cases where patients deputize others to act in their behalf. For example, a woman who is terminally ill instructs her husband and family not to permit antibiotic treatment should she contract pneumonia or not to use artificial support systems should she lapse into a coma and be unable to speak for herself. Similarly, a man requests that he be given a lethal injection after an industrial explosion has left him with third-degree burns over most of his body and no real hope of recovery. For a decision about death to be voluntary, the individual must give explicit consent.

A nonvoluntary decision about death refers to cases in which the decision is not made by the person who is to die. Such cases would include situations where, because of age, mental impairment, or unconsciousness, patients are not competent to give informed consent to life-or-death decisions and where others make the decisions for them. For example, suppose that as a result of an automobile accident, a man suffers massive and irreparable brain damage, falls into unconsciousness, and can be maintained only by artificial means. Should he regain consciousness, he would likely be little more than a vegetable. Given this prognosis, the man's family, in consultation with his physicians, decides to suspend artificial life-sustaining means and allows him to die.

In actual situations, the difference between voluntary and nonvoluntary decisions about death is not always clear. For example, take the case of a man who has heard his mother say that she would never want to be kept alive with "machines and pumps and tubes." Now that she is in fact being kept alive that way and is unable to express a life-or-death decision, the man is not sure that his mother actually would choose to be allowed to die. Similarly, a doctor might not be certain that the tormented cries of a stomach-cancer patient to be "put out of my misery" are an expression of informed consent or of profound pain and momentary despair.

The voluntary–nonvoluntary distinction is relevant to both the narrow and the broad interpretations of the meaning of euthanasia. Each interpretation seemingly distinguishes four kinds of death decisions in which the voluntary–nonvoluntary distinction plays a part. Thus, the narrow interpretation recognizes cases of

1. **Voluntary euthanasia**
2. Nonvoluntary euthanasia
3. Voluntary allowing to die
4. Nonvoluntary allowing to die

By this account, the first two generally are considered immoral; instances of the second two may be moral under carefully circumscribed conditions.

Recognizing no logical or morally relevant distinction between euthanasia and allowing to die, the broad interpretation allows four forms of euthanasia:

1. Voluntary active euthanasia
2. Nonvoluntary active euthanasia
3. Voluntary passive euthanasia
4. Nonvoluntary passive euthanasia

By this account, any of these types of euthanasia may be morally justifiable under carefully circumscribed conditions.

The narrow and the broad interpretations differ sharply in their moral judgment of *deliberate* acts taken to end or shorten a patient's life—that is, acts that the narrow interpretation terms voluntary or nonvoluntary euthanasia and that the broad interpretation terms voluntary or nonvoluntary *active* euthanasia. Generally, the narrow interpretation considers such acts always morally repugnant; the broad interpretation views them as being morally justifiable under carefully circumscribed conditions.

Some discussions of euthanasia distinguish nonvoluntary euthanasia from involuntary euthanasia. Nonvoluntary in these discussions is limited to euthanasia in which the patient is not able now to make a meaningful decision about euthanasia but has previously made preferences clear to a caretaker or family member, usually through a **living will** or directive. **Involuntary euthanasia** involves a decision made by someone else that the person's life should end, even though that person has never made these preferences known to anyone. This might be a decision by a hospital ethics committee that the person should be euthanized, even though no such wishes were ever expressed by that person. In the discussion here, **nonvoluntary euthanasia** includes all situations where the decision for euthanasia is made by someone other than the patient, whether or not that patient had previously expressed a preference for this course of action.

ASSISTED SUICIDE

Closely related to the issue of euthanasia is that of **assisted suicide,** which has become one of the most debated moral and legal issues of recent years. Most of the debate centers on *physician*-assisted suicide—whether to allow doctors to assist terminally ill patients in taking their own lives, usually by prescribing a lethal dose of drugs. For all the similarities between assisted suicide and voluntary active euthanasia, there is one crucial if subtle difference: In the former, the physician does not directly cause the patient's death but enables the patient to choose the time and circumstances of his or her own death. Because of this difference, proponents of physician-assisted suicide see it as a moral solution to the problem posed by the suffering of the terminally ill. If the terminally ill have the right to end their suffering, which proponents feel they do, then they also have the right to seek their doctors' assistance. Opponents counter that the terminally ill have no right to take their own lives and that assisting in suicide is not the proper role of physicians.

The debate was sparked by Dr. Jack Kevorkian and his "suicide machine," an invention of his that enables patients to give themselves lethal injections. The Michigan doctor first provided the device in 1990 to a woman who suffered from Alzheimer's disease. Because Michigan had no law forbidding assisted suicide at the time, he was not charged. But then, after assisting in the suicides of two other women the following year, he was charged with two counts of murder, both of which a judge dismissed. These dismissals led the state's legislature to enact a temporary ban on assisted suicide. Undeterred, Kevorkian continued to make his machine available, and he was consequently charged with violating the new law. On May 3, 1994, a jury acquitted him. After the temporary ban expired, the State attempted to prosecute him for several assisted suicides, but either juries acquitted him or judges declared mistrials and charges were dropped. Another Michigan state law banning physician-assisted suicide went into effect in 1998. During an episode of "60 Minutes" on CBS, Kevorkian was shown giving a lethal injection to Thomas Youk, who had Lou Gehrig's disease. A few days later, Michigan authorities charged Kevorkian with murder. He was convicted in April 1999 and sentenced to ten to twenty-five years in prison, with eligibility for parole after six years. In July 2006, the Michigan governor ordered a medical evaluation of Kevorkian. He has requested that his sentence be commuted, claiming to have less than a year to live because he has hepatitis C and diabetes. Kevorkian, who was seventy-eight years old in 2006, now claims he assisted in at least 130 deaths.

Kervorkian's persistence and legal troubles generated enormous attention and controversy, which quickly turned to action as voters in various states petitioned for ballot initiatives either to allow assisted suicide or to ban it. In states with existing legislation banning the practice, terminally ill patients went to court asking that the laws be declared unconstitutional. In June 1997, the U.S. Supreme Court upheld the constitutionality of two state laws, Washington's and New York's, that ban assisted suicide (*Washington v. Glucksberg* and *Vacco v. Quill*). Then in October of that year, the Court refused to hear a challenge to an Oregon law—this one passed by voters in a 1994 ballot initiative—that legalizes assisted suicide. After a legal challenge, Oregon voters passed another ballot initiative permitting assisting suicide in 1997. In the first eight years under the Oregon Death with Dignity Act (from 1998 to 2006), 246 assisted suicides had been reported to the State.

In 2002, efforts by the U.S. Department of Justice to prosecute doctors who participated in Oregon's assisted suicide program were halted by a federal court. The U.S. Supreme Court rejected a challenge to the Oregon law by the U.S. Justice Department in January 2005, in a 6-3 decision (*Gonzales v. Oregon*).

So far, attempts to pass a ban on assisted suicide by the U.S. Congress have failed. Thus, the issue is left to the states for now. The terminally ill have no constitutional right to commit suicide, but states may allow them to do so with the assistance of their doctors.

THE RIGHT TO REFUSE TREATMENT

Though the right to refuse medical treatment has long been widely recognized, and though many state courts (as in the Karen Ann Quinlan case) have upheld the right of family members to refuse life-preserving treatment, it was not until the summer of 1990 that the U.S. Supreme Court, in *Cruzan v. Missouri Health Services,* recognized the right of a competent patient to refuse life-preserving medical treatment, including artificial (nonoral) delivery of nutrition and water. The court also ruled that when the patient is not competent to make the decision, it may be made by a surrogate acting according to the patient's wishes.

Thus, the court established a constitutional basis for voluntary passive euthanasia (or allowing to die) in some cases. But the court also ruled that states may require clear and convincing evidence that the surrogate is in fact acting in accordance with the patient's wishes. The case was returned to the Missouri trial court to hear additional evidence of her intent. This court held that there was sufficient clear and convincing evidence to remove the feeding tube, which was done on December 14, 1990. She died eleven days later.

One consequence of the ruling is the legal validity of *living wills,* documents that direct physicians not to apply artificial means of preserving life. A model living will, Directive to Physicians, was created by the California legislature in 1977 as part of the state's Natural Death Act (see Figure 1). Living wills have long been advocated by many Americans, including those who advocate not only the right to refuse treatment but also a broader right, the right to die, which also includes the right to voluntary active euthanasia. That broader right has not been recognized by the courts, and most current controversy surrounding euthanasia concerns whether it should be.

DEFECTIVE NEWBORNS

The legal and moral questions of refusing treatment become more complicated in cases of newborns with defects, babies born with serious birth defects, such as Tay-Sachs, a fatal degenerative disease; Down's syndrome, which manifests itself in mental retardation and various physical abnormalities; and duodenal atresia, in which the upper part of the small intestine, the duodenum, is closed off, therefore preventing the passage and digestion of food. (Although duodenal atresia can usually be treated through surgery, it often is accompanied by other serious birth defects.)

One complication concerns the treatment in question. Allowing defective newborns to die often includes the withholding of ordinary treatment, such as simple nourishment. Another concerns the defects themselves. Although some birth defects, such as anencephalus (the partial or total absence of the brain), guarantee a life in a vegetative state, children with others, such as Down's syndrome, often lead meaningful, if limited, lives.

It is possible to identify three broad positions on the moral acceptability of allowing defective newborns to die. Underpinning each are controversial value assumptions.

The first and most permissive position is that allowing seriously defective newborns to die is morally permissible not only when there is no significant potential for meaningful human existence but also when the emotional or financial hardship of caring for the child would place a grave burden on the family. Adherents to this view argue their case on the grounds that newborns are not yet persons, which, as we saw in Chapter 4, is a controversial assumption.

DIRECTIVE TO PHYSICIANS

Directive made this _____ day of _________________ (month, year).

I, _____________________________ being of sound mind, willfully and voluntarily make known my desire that my life shall not be artificially prolonged under the circumstances set forth below, do hereby declare:

1. If at any time I should have an incurable injury, disease, or illness certified to be a terminal condition by two physicians, and where the application of life-sustaining procedures would serve only to artificially prolong the moment of my death and where my physician determines that my death is imminent whether or not life-sustaining procedures are utilized, I direct that such procedures be withheld or withdrawn, and that I be permitted to die naturally.

2. In the absence of my ability to give directions regarding the use of such life-sustaining procedures, it is my intention that this directive shall be honored by my family and physician(s) as the final expression of my legal right to refuse medical or surgical treatment and accept the consequences from such refusal.

3. If I have been diagnosed as pregnant and that diagnosis is known to my physician, this directive shall have no force or effect during the course of my pregnancy.

4. I have been diagnosed and notified at least 14 days ago as having a terminal condition by ____, M.D., whose address is _______________________________ and whose telephone number is _________________. I understand that if I have not filled in the physician's name and address, it shall be presumed that I did not have a terminal condition when I made out this directive.

5. This directive shall have no force or effect five years from the date filled in above.

6. I understand the full import of this directive and I am emotionally and mentally competent to make this directive.

Signed_____________________________

City, County and State of Residence_____________________________

The declarant has been personally known to me and I believe him or her to be of sound mind.

Witness_____________________________

Witness_____________________________

FIGURE 5.1 Model Living Well (California Natural Death Act)

The second position is that it is permissible only if there is no significant potential for meaningful human existence. Clearly implied here is a quality-of-life judgment, which often elicits debate. Should we make such judgments? And if so, what should count as a meaningful human existence? The degree of retardation associated with Down's syndrome, for example, can vary widely. At what point can we separate a meaningful from a meaningless human existence?

The third position asserts that it is never morally permissible to allow a defective newborn to die. Stated more cautiously, it is never moral to withhold from a defective newborn any treatment that would be provided to a normal one. The clear implication here is that the defective infant has full personhood and must be treated accordingly. Just as clearly, this view rejects any quality-of-life or cost factors in determining the acceptability of allowing a defective infant to die. Like the other positions, this one is fraught with debatable value judgments, and in cases of duodenal atresia, it ignores that normal infants would not require corrective surgery to digest food.

It is quite apparent, then, that whether cases involve defective newborns or adults who are terminally ill, the central moral question concerns the acceptability of a death decision and subsequent action. But there are additional moral problems relating to death decisions in the institutional setting that are worth considering.

ARGUMENTS FOR VOLUNTARY (ACTIVE) EUTHANASIA

1. ***Individuals have the right to decide about their own lives and deaths.***

   POINT: "What more basic right is there than the right of terminally ill patients to control the circumstances of their own deaths? To decide whether they'll spend their last days in great pain or not, hooked up to machines or not, conscious or not, drugged to a stupor or not? If they wish to spare themselves the agony of a drawn-out death and their families the agony of watching them go through it, who are we to deny them the right to do so?"

   COUNTERPOINT: "What you're really saying is that all of us have the right to commit suicide. But we don't have that right and we shouldn't have it. It's one thing to say that we have the right to refuse medical treatment, but it's quite another to say that we have the right to decide when our lives are no longer bearable and then end them. If we follow your reasoning, we'd also have to say that the nonterminally ill have the right to determine the circumstances of their death too. After all, we're all going to die some day anyway."

2. ***Denying terminally ill patients the right to die is unfair and cruel.***

   POINT: "We allow terminally ill patients to refuse life-preserving treatment out of compassion. We allow them to refuse to be hooked up to respirators or intravenous feeding tubes, to refuse treatment for pneumonia. But what can be crueler than to let suffering cancer patients starve to death or wait for pneumonia when we can end their misery immediately? Besides, denying suffering patients the right to active euthanasia isn't fair to those who aren't on life support. Why should they be denied the right to die when it's not denied to those who are on life support?"

   COUNTERPOINT: "The issue isn't the right to die but the right to refuse extraordinary means of treatment, the right of all patients, including the terminally ill, to decide that further medical treatment won't benefit them. There's also another issue at stake, the role of healthcare professionals. When they disconnect life-support systems, they're respecting the autonomy of their patients. If they give them lethal injections, they'll be committing an act of deliberately killing a fellow human being. Everyone feels compassion for these patients, but you can't justify everything in the name of compassion."

3. ***The golden rule requires that we allow active euthanasia for terminally ill patients.***

   POINT: "The simplest way to put the matter is like this: If you were in a terminal cancer ward and found the suffering to be more than you could bear, you'd want your doctor to give you a lethal injection if you asked for it, wouldn't you? Then how can you justify not allowing the same for others? It's a straightforward application of the golden rule. Do unto others as you would have them do unto you."

   COUNTERPOINT: "For all I know, I might end up exactly as you describe, but that still doesn't change anything. Just because we *want* someone to do something for us doesn't mean that we have the *right* to have it done. And it certainly doesn't mean that others have the obligation or even the right to do it. The golden rule applies only to moral actions, and neither suicide nor deliberate killing is moral."

4. ***People have a right to die with dignity.***

POINT: "Not everyone wants to spend his or her last days lying in a hospital bed wasting away to something hardly recognizable as a human being, let alone his or her former self. To constantly fight horrible pain, to be hooked up to an intravenous machine that supplies painkilling narcotics, to drift up and back between a dream state and reality, not to recognize family and friends, to waste away to nothing while dying of dehydration or starvation—to some people that's an unacceptable affront to their dignity. Out of respect for the dignity of others, we allow them to *live* with dignity. Why not allow them to *die* with dignity?"

COUNTERPOINT: "The phrase 'death with dignity' makes perfect sense when we're talking about allowing people to die a natural death instead of being kept alive against their will by artificial means. But you're talking about avoiding natural death instead of facing it. And there's nothing undignified about facing a natural death."

ARGUMENTS AGAINST VOLUNTARY (ACTIVE) EUTHANASIA

1. ***Active euthanasia is the deliberate taking of a human life.***

POINT: "The deliberate killing of a human being is wrong, pure and simple, whether the person wants to die or not. And calling it 'euthanasia' doesn't change the fact that what we're talking about is the deliberate taking of a human life."

COUNTERPOINT: "Certainly, under normal circumstances, taking a human life is wrong, but we're not talking about normal circumstances. The circumstances here involve terminally ill patients who can't bear their pointless suffering. If we're willing to disconnect the life-support systems of such patients if they request it, we should be willing to give them lethal injections if they request it. In both cases, the intention is the same—to respect their wish to be put out of their misery."

2. ***We can't be sure consent is voluntary.***

POINT: "We can't ever be sure consent is voluntary. In fact, the circumstances surrounding most terminally ill patients make voluntary consent impossible. Either they're in terrible pain or they're drugged. In any case, they can't be thinking clearly enough to understand the full impact of what they're consenting to. And that hardly counts as rational free choice."

COUNTERPOINT: "Maybe not, but suppose the patient requests to be euthanized before he or she reaches that point. Or suppose the family feels the patient really wants the lethal injection. We disconnect life-support systems from patients who are no longer capable of giving informed consent in those circumstances. Why not give them lethal injections in the same circumstances?"

3. ***Allowing active euthanasia will lead to abuses.***

POINT: "Killing terminally ill patients who ask for it is a dangerous step. Once you accept the principle of the right to die, what stops you from extending it to the nonterminally ill? Does an athlete who becomes a quadriplegic have the right to be put out of his misery? Someone suffering from chronic depression? Severe arthritis? Alzheimer's disease? And what happens when people like that don't request lethal injections but their families do? Are we to 'euthanize' them too?"

COUNTERPOINT: "I'm not advocating a general right to die, just the right of terminally ill patients to choose the way they die. To suggest that complying with a terminally ill cancer patient's request for a lethal injection will lead to the kind of abuses you mention is to confuse distinct and separate issues. Certainly, nobody's calling for nonvoluntary euthanasia."

4. ***There's always the possibility of mistaken diagnosis, a new cure, or spontaneous remission.***

POINT: "The judgment that a patient is terminally ill isn't always the last word, you know. The diagnosis may be mistaken, a new cure may come along, and cancer patients have been known to go into spontaneous remission. But death is the last word. Once you've killed a patient, he or she is beyond all hope. How would you feel if a wonder drug turned up the next day or if the doctors discovered their diagnosis was wrong?"

COUNTERPOINT: "The judgment that a patient is terminally ill may not always be the last word, but it usually is. Despite what you say, many patients are already beyond hope. No new cure is going to come along in time to save people after cancer has metastasized throughout their bodies. And to hope for spontaneous remission or mistaken diagnosis at that point is absurd. Besides, everything you say holds for passive as well as active euthanasia. When a terminally ill cancer patient comes down with pneumonia, few, if any, people are willing to treat the pneumonia in hopes of finding a wonder drug for cancer. To do so would be outright cruelty. And that's what denying a lethal injection to a patient without pneumonia amounts to—outright cruelty."

The Wrongfulness of Euthanasia

J. GAY-WILLIAMS

In this essay, professor of philosophy J. Gay-Williams defines euthanasia as intentionally taking the life of a person suffering from some illness or injury from which recovery cannot reasonably be expected. While rejecting *voluntary* euthanasia as a *name* for actions that are usually designated by the phrase, Gay-Williams seems to approve of the actions themselves. He argues that euthanasia as intentional killing goes against natural law because it violates the natural inclination to preserve life. Furthermore, in Gay-Williams's view, both self-interest and possible practical effects of euthanasia provide reasons for rejecting it.

My impression is that euthanasia—the idea, if not the practice—is slowly gaining acceptance within our society. Cynics might attribute this to an increasing tendency to devalue human life, but I do not believe this is the major factor. The acceptance is much more likely to be the result of unthinking sympathy and benevolence. Well-publicized, tragic stories like that of Karen Quinlan elicit from us deep feelings of compassion. We think to ourselves, "She and her family would be better off if she were dead." It is an easy step from this very human response to the view that if someone (and others) would be better off dead, then it must be all right to kill that person.[1] Although I respect the compassion that leads to this conclusion, I believe the conclusion is wrong. I want to show that euthanasia is wrong. It is inherently wrong, but it is also wrong judged from the standpoints of self-interest and of practical effects.

Before presenting my arguments to support this claim, it would be well to define "euthanasia." An essential aspect of euthanasia is that it involves taking a human life, either one's own or that of another. Also, the person whose life is taken must be someone who is believed to be suffering from some disease or injury from which recovery cannot reasonably be expected. Finally, the action must be deliberate and intentional. Thus, euthanasia is intentionally taking the life of a presumably hopeless person. Whether the life is one's own or that of another, the taking of it is still euthanasia.

It is important to be clear about the deliberate and intentional aspect of the killing. If a hopeless person is given an injection of the wrong drug by mistake and this causes his death, this is wrongful killing but not euthanasia. The killing cannot be the result of accident. Furthermore, if the person is given an injection of a drug that is believed to be necessary to treat his disease or better his condition and the person dies as a result, then this is neither wrongful killing nor euthanasia. The intention was to make the patient well, not kill him. Similarly, when a patient's condition is such that it is not reasonable to hope that any medical procedures or treatments will save his life, a failure to implement the procedures or treatments is not euthanasia. If the person dies, this will be as a result of his injuries or disease and not because of his failure to receive treatment.

The failure to continue treatment after it has been realized that the patient has little chance of benefitting from it has been characterized by some as "passive euthanasia." This phrase is misleading and mistaken.[2] In such cases, the person involved is not killed (the first essential aspect of euthanasia), nor is the death of the person intended by the withholding of additional treatment (the third essential aspect of euthanasia). The aim may be to spare the person additional and unjustifiable pain, to save him from the indignities of hopeless manipulations, and to avoid increasing the financial and emotional burden on his family. When I buy a pencil it is so that I can use it to write, not to contribute to an increase in the gross national product. This may be the unintended consequence of my action, but it is not the aim of my action. So it is with failing to continue the treatment of a dying person. I intend his death no more than I intend to reduce the GNP by not using medical supplies. His is an unintended dying, and so-called "passive euthanasia" is not euthanasia at all.

1. THE ARGUMENT FROM NATURE

Every human being has a natural inclination to continue living. Our reflexes and responses fit us to fight attackers, flee wild animals, and dodge out of the way of trucks. In our daily lives we exercise the caution and care necessary to protect ourselves. Our bodies are similarly structured for survival right down to the molecular level. When we are cut, our capillaries seal shut, our blood clots, and fibrogen is produced to start the process of healing the wound. When we are invaded by bacteria, antibodies are produced to fight against the alien organisms, and their remains are swept out of the body by special cells designed for clean-up work.

Euthanasia does violence to this natural goal of survival. It is literally acting against nature because all the processes of nature are bent towards the end of bodily survival. Euthanasia defeats these subtle mechanisms in a way that, in a particular case, disease and injury might not.

It is possible, but not necessary, to make an appeal to revealed religion in this connection.[3] Man as trustee of his body acts against God, its rightful possessor, when he takes his own life. He also violates the commandment to hold life sacred and never to take it without just and compelling cause. But since this appeal will persuade only those who are prepared to accept that religion has access to revealed truths, I shall not employ this line of argument.

It is enough, I believe, to recognize that the organization of the human body and our patterns of behavioral responses make the continuation of life a natural goal. By reason alone, then, we can recognize that euthanasia sets us against our own nature.[4] Furthermore, in doing so, euthanasia does violence to our dignity. Our dignity comes from seeking our ends. When one of our goals is survival, and actions are taken that eliminate that goal, then our natural dignity suffers. Unlike animals, we are conscious through reason of our nature and our ends. Euthanasia involves acting as if this dual nature—inclination towards survival and awareness of this as an end—did not exist. Thus, euthanasia denies our basic human character and requires that we regard ourselves or others as something less than fully human.

2. THE ARGUMENT FROM SELF-INTEREST

The above arguments are, I believe, sufficient to show that euthanasia is inherently wrong. But there are reasons for considering it wrong when judged by standards other than reason. Because death is final and irreversible, euthanasia contains within it the possibility that we will work against our own interest if we practice it or allow it to be practiced on us.

Contemporary medicine has high standards of excellence and a proven record of accomplishment, but it does not possess perfect and complete knowledge. A mistaken diagnosis is possible, and so is a mistaken prognosis. Consequently, we may believe that we are dying of a disease when, as a matter of fact, we may not be. We may think that we have no hope of recovery when, as a matter of fact, our chances are quite good. In such circumstances, if euthanasia were permitted, we would die needlessly. Death is final and the chance of error too great to approve the practice of euthanasia.

Also, there is always the possibility that an experimental procedure or a hitherto untried technique will pull us through. We should at least keep this option open, but euthanasia closes it off. Furthermore, spontaneous remission does occur in many cases. For no apparent reason, a patient simply recovers when those all around him, including his physicians, expected him to die. Euthanasia would just guarantee their expectations and leave no room for the "miraculous" recoveries that frequently occur.

Finally, knowing that we can take our life at any time (or ask another to take it) might well incline us to give up too easily. The will to live is strong in all of us, but it can be weakened by pain and suffering and feelings of hopelessness. If during a bad time we allow ourselves to be killed, we never have a chance to reconsider. Recovery from a serious illness requires that we fight for it, and anything that weakens our determination by suggesting that there is an easy way out is ultimately against our own interest. Also, we may be inclined towards euthanasia because of our concern for others. If we see our sickness and suffering as an emotional and financial burden on our family, we may feel that to leave our life is to make their lives easier.[5] The very presence of the possibility of euthanasia may keep us from surviving when we might.

3. THE ARGUMENT FROM PRACTICAL EFFECTS

Doctors and nurses are, for the most part, totally committed to saving lives. A life lost is, for them, almost a personal failure, an insult to their skills and knowledge. Euthanasia as a practice might well alter this. It could have a corrupting influence so that in any case that is severe doctors and nurses might not try hard enough to save the patient. They might decide that the patient would simply be "better off dead" and take the steps necessary to make that come about. This attitude could then carry over to their dealings with patients less seriously ill. The result would be an overall decline in the quality of medical care.

Finally, euthanasia as a policy is a slippery slope. A person apparently hopelessly ill may be allowed to take his own life. Then he may be permitted to deputize others to do it for him should he no longer be able to act. The judgment of others then becomes the ruling factor. Already at this point euthanasia is not personal and voluntary, for others are acting "on behalf of" the patient as they see fit. This may well incline them to act on behalf of other patients who have not authorized them to exercise their judgment. It is only a short step, then, from voluntary euthanasia (self-inflicted or authorized), to directed euthanasia administered to a patient who has given no authorization, to involuntary euthanasia conducted as part of a social policy.[6] Recently many psychiatrists and sociologists have argued that we define as "mental illness" those forms of behavior that we disapprove of.[7] This gives us license then to lock up those who display the behavior. The category of the "hopelessly ill" provides the possibility of even worse abuse. Embedded in a social policy, it would give society or its representatives the authority to eliminate all those who might be considered too "ill" to function normally any longer. The dangers of euthanasia are too great to all to run the risk of approving it in any form. The first slippery step may well lead to a serious and harmful fall.

I hope that I have succeeded in showing why the benevolence that inclines us to give approval of euthanasia is misplaced. Euthanasia is inherently wrong because it violates the nature and dignity of human beings. But even those who are not convinced by this must be persuaded that the potential personal and social dangers inherent in euthanasia are sufficient to forbid our approving it either as a personal practice or as a public policy.

Suffering is surely a terrible thing, and we have a clear duty to comfort those in need and to ease their suffering when we can. But suffering is also a natural part of life with values for the individual and for others that we should not overlook. We may legitimately seek for others and for ourselves an easeful death, as Arthur Dyck has pointed out.[8] Euthanasia, however, is not just an easeful death. It is a wrongful death. Euthanasia is not just dying. It is killing.

NOTES

1. For a sophisticated defense of this position see Philippa Foot, "Euthanasia," *Philosophy & Public Affairs,* vol. 6 (1977), pp. 85–112. Foot does not endorse the radical conclusion that euthanasia, voluntary and involuntary, is always right.
2. James Rachels rejects the distinction between active and passive euthanasia as morally irrelevant in his "Active and Passive Euthanasia," *New England Journal of Medicine,* vol. 292, pp. 78–80. But see the criticism by Foot, pp. 100–103.
3. For a defense of this view see J. V. Sullivan, "The Immorality of Euthanasia," in *Beneficent Euthanasia,* ed. Marvin Kohl (Buffalo, New York: Prometheus Books, 1975), pp. 34–44.
4. This point is made by Ray V. McIntyre in "Voluntary Euthanasia: The Ultimate Perversion," *Medical Counterpoint,* vol. 2, 26–29.
5. See McIntyre, p. 28.

6. See Sullivan, "Immorality of Euthanasia," pp. 34–44, for a fuller argument in support of this view.
7. See, for example, Thomas S. Szasz, *The Myth of Mental Illness,* rev. ed. (New York: Harper & Row, 1974).
8. Arthur Dyck, "Beneficent Euthanasia and Benemortasia," in Kohl, op. cit., pp. 117–129.

QUESTIONS FOR ANALYSIS

1. Why doesn't Gay-Williams consider "passive euthanasia" an act of euthanasia? Do you agree with his distinction?
2. Would it be accurate to say that Gay-Williams applies both religious and nonreligious interpretations to argue against euthanasia? Explain.
3. State his arguments from self-interest.
4. State his arguments from practical effects. Which moral principle or type of ethical theory does this reflect?
5. What critical inquiries, if any, would you make about the author's arguments against euthanasia?
6. Can Gay-Williams's arguments be equally applied against passive euthanasia?

Active and Passive Euthanasia

JAMES RACHELS

The traditional view that there is an important moral difference between active and passive euthanasia is one that was endorsed by J. Gay-Williams in the preceding essay. Active euthanasia involves killing and passive euthanasia letting die, and this fact has led many physicians and philosophers to reject active euthanasia as morally wrong, even while approving of passive euthanasia.

In this essay, professor of philosophy James Rachels (1941–2003) challenges both the use and moral significance of this distinction for several reasons. First, active euthanasia is in many cases more humane than passive. Second, the conventional doctrine leads to decisions concerning life and death on irrelevant grounds. Third, the doctrine rests on a distinction between killing and letting die that itself has no moral significance. Fourth, the most common arguments in favor of the doctrine are invalid. Therefore, in Rachels's view, the American Medical Association's policy statement endorsing the active–passive distinction is unwise.

The distinction between active and passive euthanasia is thought to be crucial for medical ethics. The idea is that it is permissible, at least in some cases, to withhold treatment and allow a patient to die, but it is never permissible to take any direct action designed to kill the patient. This doctrine seems to be accepted by most doctors, and it is endorsed in a statement adopted by the House of Delegates of the American Medical Association on December 4, 1973:

> The intentional termination of the life of one human being by another—mercy killing—is contrary to that for which the medical profession stands and is contrary to the policy of the American Medical Association. The cessation of the employment of extraordinary means to prolong

From James Rachels. "Active and Passive Euthanasia," *New England Journal of Medicine,* 292 (January 9, 1975), 78–80. Reprinted by permission of the publisher.

> the life of the body when there is irrefutable evidence that biological death is imminent is the decision of the patient and/or his immediate family. The advice and judgment of the physician should be freely available to the patient and/or his immediate family.

However, a strong case can be made against this doctrine. In what follows I will set out some of the relevant arguments, and urge doctors to reconsider their views on this matter.

To begin with a familiar type of situation, a patient who is dying of incurable cancer of the throat is in terrible pain, which can no longer be satisfactorily alleviated. He is certain to die within a few days, even if present treatment is continued, but he does not want to go on living for those days since the pain is unbearable. So he asks the doctor for an end to it, and his family joins in the request.

Suppose the doctor agrees to withhold treatment, as the conventional doctrine says he may. The justification for his doing so is that the patient is in terrible agony, and since he is going to die anyway, it would be wrong to prolong his suffering needlessly. But now notice this. If one simply withholds treatment, it may take the patient longer to die, and so he may suffer more than he would if more direct action were taken and a lethal injection given. This fact provides strong reason for thinking that, once the initial decision not to prolong his agony has been made, active euthanasia is actually preferable to passive euthanasia, rather than the reverse. To say otherwise is to endorse the option that leads to more suffering rather than less, and is contrary to the humanitarian impulse that prompts the decision not to prolong his life in the first place.

Part of my point is that the process of being "allowed to die" can be relatively slow and painful, whereas being given a lethal injection is relatively quick and painless. Let me give a different sort of example. In the United States about one in 600 babies is born with Down's syndrome. Most of these babies are otherwise healthy—that is, with only the usual pediatric care, they will proceed to an otherwise normal infancy. Some, however, are born with congenital defects such as intestinal obstructions that require operations if they are to live. Sometimes, the patients and the doctor will decide not to operate, and let the infant die. Anthony Shaw describes what happens then:

> . . .When surgery is denied [the doctor] must try to keep the infant from suffering while natural forces sap the baby's life away. As a surgeon whose natural inclination is to use the scalpel to fight off death, standing by and watching a salvageable baby die is the most emotionally exhausting experience I know. It is easy at a conference, in a theoretical discussion, to decide that such infants should be allowed to die. It is altogether different to stand by in the nursery and watch as dehydration and infection wither a tiny being over hours and days. This is a terrible ordeal for me and the hospital staff—much more so than for the parents who never set foot in the nursery.[1]

I can understand why some people are opposed to all euthanasia, and insist that such infants must be allowed to live. I think I can also understand why other people favor destroying these babies quickly and painlessly. But why should anyone favor letting "dehydration and infection wither a tiny being over hours and days"? The doctrine that says that a baby may be allowed to dehydrate and wither, but may not be given an injection that would end its life without suffering, seems so patently cruel as to require no further refutation. The strong language is not intended to offend, but only to put the point in the clearest possible way.

My second argument is that the conventional doctrine leads to decisions concerning life and death made on irrelevant grounds.

Consider again the case of the infants with Down's syndrome who need operations for congenital defects unrelated to the syndrome to live. Sometimes, there is no operation, and the baby dies, but when there is no such defect, the baby lives on. Now, an operation such as that to remove an intestinal obstruction is not prohibitively difficult. The reason why such operations are not performed in these cases is, clearly, that the child has Down's syndrome and the parents and the doctor judge that because of that fact it is better for the child to die.

But notice that this situation is absurd, no matter what view one takes of the lives and potentials of such babies. If the life of such an infant is worth preserving, what does it matter if it needs a simple operation? Or, if one thinks it better that such a baby should not live on, what difference does it make that it happens to have an unobstructed intestinal tract? In either case, the matter of life and death is being decided on irrelevant grounds. It is the Down's syndrome, and not the intestines, that is the issue. The matter should be decided, if at all, on that basis, and not be allowed to depend on the essentially irrelevant question of whether the intestinal tract is blocked.

What makes this situation possible, of course, is the idea that when there is an intestinal blockage, one can "let the baby die," but when there is no such defect there is nothing that can be done, for one must not "kill" it. The fact that this idea leads to such results as deciding life or death on irrelevant grounds is another good reason why the doctrine should be rejected.

One reason why so many people think that there is an important moral difference between active and passive euthanasia is that they think killing someone is morally worse than letting someone die. But is it? Is killing, in itself, worse than letting die? To investigate this issue, two cases may be considered that are exactly alike except that one involves killing whereas the other involves letting someone die. Then, it can be asked whether this difference makes any difference to the moral assessments. It is important that the cases be exactly alike, except for this one difference, since otherwise one cannot be confident that it is this difference and not some other that accounts for any variation in the assessments of the two cases. So, let us consider this pair of cases:

In the first, Smith stands to gain a large inheritance if anything should happen to his six-year-old cousin. One evening while the child is taking his bath, Smith sneaks into the bathroom and drowns the child, and then arranges things so that it will look like an accident.

In the second, Jones also stands to gain if anything should happen to his six-year-old cousin. Like Smith, Jones sneaks in planning to drown the child in his bath. However, just as he enters the bathroom Jones sees the child slip and hit his head, and fall face down in the water. Jones is delighted; he stands by, ready to push the child's head back under if it is necessary, but it is not necessary. With only a little thrashing about, the child drowns all by himself, "accidentally" as Jones watches and does nothing.

Now Smith killed the child, whereas Jones "merely" let the child die. That is the only difference between them. Did either man behave better, from a moral point of view? If the difference between killing and letting die were in itself a morally important matter, one should say that Jones's behavior was less reprehensible than Smith's. But does one really want to say that? I think not. In the first place, both men acted from the same motive, personal gain, and both had exactly the same end in view when they acted. It may be inferred from Smith's conduct that he is a bad man, although that judgment may be withdrawn or modified if certain further facts are learned about him—for example, that he is mentally deranged. But would not the very same thing be inferred about Jones from his conduct? And would not the same further considerations also be relevant to any modification of this judgment? Moreover, suppose Jones pleaded, in his own defense, "After all, I didn't do anything except just stand there and watch the child drown. I didn't kill him; I only let him die." Again, if letting die were in itself less bad than killing, this defense should have at least some weight. But it does not. Such a "defense" can only be regarded as a grotesque perversion of moral reasoning. Morally speaking, it is no defense at all.

Now, it may be pointed out, quite properly, that the cases of euthanasia with which doctors are concerned are not like this at all. They do not involve personal gain or the destruction of normal healthy children. Doctors are concerned only with cases in which the patient's life is of no further use to him, or in which the patient's life has become or will soon become a terrible burden. However, the point is the same in these cases: The bare difference between killing and letting die does not, in itself, make a moral difference. If a doctor lets a patient die, for humane reasons, he is in the same moral position as if he had given the patient a lethal injection for humane reasons. If his decision was wrong—if, for example, the patient's illness was in fact curable—the decision would be equally regrettable no matter which method was used to carry it out. And if the doctor's decision was the right one, the method used is not in itself important.

The AMA policy statement isolates the crucial issue very well: The crucial issue is "the intentional termination of the life of one human being by another." But after identifying this issue, and forbidding "mercy killing," the statement goes on to deny that the cessation of treatment is the intentional termination of a life. This is where the mistake comes in, for what is the cessation of treatment, in these circumstances, if it is not "the intentional termination of the life of one human being by another"? Of course it is exactly that, and if it were not, there would be no point to it.

Many people will find this judgment hard to accept. One reason, I think, is that it is very easy to conflate the question of whether killing is, in itself, worse than letting die, with the very different question of whether most actual cases of killing are more reprehensible than most actual cases of letting die. Most actual cases of killing are clearly terrible (think, for example, of all the murders reported in the newspapers), and one hears of such cases everyday. On the other hand, one hardly ever hears of a case of letting die, except for the actions of doctors who are motivated by humanitarian reasons. So one learns to think of killing in a much worse light than of letting die. But this does not mean that there is something about killing that makes it in itself worse than letting die, for it is not the bare difference between killing and letting die that makes the difference in these cases. Rather, the other factors—the murderer's motive of personal gain, for example, contrasted with the doctor's humanitarian motivation—account for different reactions to the different cases.

I have argued that killing is not in itself any worse than letting die; if my contention is right, it follows that active euthanasia is not any worse than passive euthanasia. What arguments can be given on the other side? The most common, I believe, is the following:

"The important difference between active and passive euthanasia is that in passive euthanasia, the doctor does not do anything to bring about the patient's death. The doctor does nothing, and the patient dies of whatever ills already afflict him. In active euthanasia, however, the doctor does something to bring about the patient's death: He kills him. The doctor who gives the patient with cancer a lethal injection has himself caused his patient's death; whereas if he merely ceases treatment, the cancer is the cause of death."

A number of points need to be made here. The first is that it is not exactly correct to say that in passive euthanasia the doctor does nothing, for he does do one thing that is very important: He lets the patient die. "Letting someone die" is certainly different, in some respects, from other types of action—mainly in that it is a kind of action that one may perform by way of not performing certain other actions. For example, one may let a patient die by way of not giving medication, just as one may insult someone by way of not shaking his hand. But for any purpose of moral assessment, it is a type of action nonetheless. The decision to let a patient die is subject to moral appraisal in the same way that a decision to kill him would be subject to moral appraisal: It may be assessed as wise or unwise, compassionate or sadistic, right or wrong. If a doctor deliberately let a patient die who was suffering from a routinely curable illness, the doctor would certainly be to blame for what he had done, just as he would be to blame if he had needlessly killed the patient. Charges against him would then be appropriate. If so, it would be no defense at all for him to insist that he didn't "do anything." He would have done something very serious indeed, for he let his patient die.

Fixing the cause of death may be very important from a legal point of view, for it may determine whether criminal charges are brought against the doctor. But I do not think that this notion can be used to show a moral difference between active and passive euthanasia. The reason why it is considered bad to be the cause of someone's death is that death is regarded as a great evil—and so it is. However, if it has been decided that euthanasia—even passive euthanasia—is desirable in a given case, it has also been decided that in this instance death is no greater an evil than the patient's continued existence. And if this is true, the usual reason for not wanting to be the cause of someone's death simply does not apply.

Finally, doctors may think that all of this is only of academic interest—the sort of thing that philosophers may worry about but that has no practical bearing on their own work. After all, doctors must be concerned about the legal consequences of what they do, and active euthanasia is clearly forbidden by the law. But even so, doctors should also be concerned with the fact that the law is forcing upon them a moral doctrine that may well be indefensible, and has a considerable effect on their practices. Of course, most doctors are not now in the position of being coerced in this matter, for they do not regard themselves as merely going along with what the law requires. Rather, in statements such as the AMA policy statement that I have quoted, they are endorsing this doctrine as a central point of medical ethics. In that statement, active euthanasia is condemned not merely as illegal but as "contrary to that for which the medical profession stands," whereas passive euthanasia is approved. However, the preceding considerations suggest that there is really no moral difference between the two, considered in themselves (there may be important moral differences in some cases in their consequences, but, as I pointed out, these differences may make active euthanasia, and not passive euthanasia, the morally preferable option). So, whereas doctors may have to discriminate between active and passive euthanasia to satisfy the law, they should not do any more than that. In particular, they should not give the distinction any added authority and weight by writing it into official statements of medical ethics.

NOTES

1. A. Shaw, "Doctor, Do We Have a Choice?" *The New York Times Magazine*, January 30, 1972, p. 54.

QUESTIONS FOR ANALYSIS

1. Early in his essay, Rachels sets up a familiar situation involving a throat-cancer patient. What is the point of the example? Do you think that suspending pain-relieving drugs is what people generally understand by "withholding treatment"?
2. Explain, through Rachels's own example of the infant with Down syndrome, why he thinks the distinction between active and passive euthanasia leads to life-or-death decisions made on irrelevant grounds.
3. Do you agree with Rachels that the cessation of treatment is tantamount to the intentional termination of life?
4. Rachels claims that killing is not necessarily any worse than allowing a person to die. What are the implications of this claim for the morality of active euthanasia?
5. Rachels believes it is inaccurate and misleading to say that a doctor who allows a patient to die does "nothing" to cause the death. Do you agree?

Euthanasia

PHILIPPA FOOT

Philippa Foot, Griffin Professor *Emerita* of Philosophy at UCLA, as part of her general concerns in this essay, develops a distinction between active and passive euthanasia by using the notion of a "right to life." She disagrees with Rachels, who criticizes the distinction between active and passive as morally irrelevant and inhumane in application. In contrast, Foot offers cases to show the value of making and using the distinction.

The basic issue Foot considers, however, is whether one is ever morally justified in killing people for their own good. Replying, Foot examines the idea of "ordinary human life" and explores the question of when someone's life might be regarded as not worth living any longer. She doesn't believe that it's legitimate for us to decide that for someone else. In her view, everyone has a right to life in the sense she specifies; it is what a person wants that counts. Thus, even if someone would be better off dead, if that person wants to live, we aren't justified in killing him or her. In short, Foot cannot support nonvoluntary active euthanasia. Furthermore, if a person both wants to live and has a right to medical treatment, then involuntary passive euthanasia isn't justified either.

But what of cases involving those whose wishes we don't know—for example, patients in a comatose state? Foot argues that taking the lives of such people would infringe their rights. So she rejects nonvoluntary active euthanasia in these cases. But she does concede that there are cases in which the comatose, were they able, would not want to be kept alive artificially. This leads her to conclude that nonvoluntary passive euthanasia may be sometimes morally permissible.

Although Foot does endorse both forms of voluntary euthanasia (active and passive) as morally legitimate, she doesn't believe that we have a duty to kill people who have decided their lives are no longer worth living. For Foot, the explicit consent by such people merely guarantees that we would not be infringing their right to life by following their wishes.

The widely used *Shorter Oxford English Dictionary* gives three meanings for the word "euthanasia": the first, "a quiet and easy death"; the second, "the means of procuring this"; and the third, "the action of inducing a quiet and easy death." It is a curious fact that no one of the three gives an adequate definition of the word as it is usually understood. For "euthanasia" means much more than a quiet and easy death, or the means of procuring it, or the action of inducing it. The definition specifies only the manner of the death, and if this were all that was implied, a murderer, careful to drug his victim, could claim that his act was an act of euthanasia. We find this ridiculous because we take it for granted that in euthanasia it is death itself, not just the manner of death, that must be kind to the one who dies.

To see how important it is that "euthanasia" should not be used as the dictionary definition allows it to be used, merely to signify that a death was quiet and easy, one has only to remember that Hitler's "euthanasia" program traded on this ambiguity. Under this program, planned before the War but brought into full operation by a decree of 1 September 1939, some 275,000 people were gassed in centers which were to be a model for those in which Jews were later exterminated. Anyone in a state institution could be sent to the gas chambers if it was considered that he could not be "rehabilitated" for useful work. As Dr. Leo Alexander reports, relying on the testimony of a neuropathologist who received 500 brains from one of the killing centers,

> In Germany the exterminations included the mentally defective, psychotics (particularly schizophrenics), epileptics and patients suffering from infirmities of old age and from various organic neurological disorders such as infantile paralysis, Parkinsonism, multiple sclerosis and brain tumors. . . . In truth, all those unable to work and considered nonrehabilitable were killed.[1]

These people were killed because they were "useless" and "a burden on society"; only the manner of their deaths could be thought of as relatively easy and quiet.

Let us insist, then, that when we talk about euthanasia we are talking about a death understood as a good or happy event for the one who dies. This stipulation follows etymology, but is itself not exactly in line with current usage, which would be captured by the condition that the death should *not* be an evil rather than that it *should* be a good. That this is how people talk is shown by the fact that the case of Karen Ann Quinlan and others in a state of permanent coma is often discussed under the heading of "euthanasia." Perhaps it is not too late to object to the use of the word "euthanasia" in this sense. Apart from the break with the Greek origins of the word, there are other unfortunate aspects of this extension of the term. For if we say that the death must be supposed to be a good to the subject, we can also specify that it shall be for his sake that an act of euthanasia is performed. If we say merely that death shall not be an evil to him, we cannot stipulate that benefiting him shall be the motive where euthanasia is in question. Given the importance of the question, For whose sake are we acting? it is good to have a definition of euthanasia which brings under this heading only cases of opting for death for the sake of the one who dies. Perhaps what is most important is to say either that euthanasia is to be for the good of the subject or at least that death is to be no evil to him, thus refusing to talk Hitler's language. However, in this paper it is the first condition that will be understood, with the additional proviso that by an act of euthanasia we mean one of inducing or otherwise opting for death for the sake of the one who is to die.

A few lesser points need to be cleared up. In the first place it must be said that the word "act" is not to be taken to exclude omission; we shall speak of an act of euthanasia when someone is deliberately allowed to die, for his own good, and not only when positive measures are taken to see that he does. The very general idea we want is that of a choice of action or inaction directed at another man's death and causally effective in the sense that, in conjunction with actual circumstances, it is a sufficient condition of death. Of complications such as overdetermination, it will not be necessary to speak.

A second, and definitely minor, point about the definition of an act of euthanasia concerns the question of fact versus belief. It has already been implied that one who performs an act of euthanasia thinks that death will be merciful for the subject since we have said that it is on account of this thought that the act is done. But is it enough that he acts with this thought, or must things actually be as he thinks them to be? If one man kills another, or allows him to die, thinking that he is in the last stages of a terrible disease, though in fact he could have been cured, is this an act of euthanasia or not? Nothing much seems to hang on our decision about this. The same condition has got to enter into the definition whether as an element in reality or only as an element in the agent's belief. And however we define an act of euthanasia, culpability or justifiability will be the same: if a man acts through ignorance, his ignorance may be culpable or it may not.[2]

These are relatively easy problems to solve, but one that is dauntingly difficult has been passed over in this discussion of the definition, and must now be faced. It is easy to say, as if this raised no problems, that an act of euthanasia is by definition one aiming at the *good* of the one whose death is in question, and that it is *for his sake* that his death is desired. But how is this to be explained? Presumably we are thinking of some evil already with him or to come on him if he continues to live, and death is thought of as a release from this evil. But this cannot be enough. Most people's lives contain evils such as grief or pain, but we do not therefore think that death would be a blessing to them. On the contrary, life is generally supposed to be a good even for someone who is unusually unhappy or frustrated. How is it that one can ever wish for death for the sake of the one who is to die? This difficult question is central to the discussion of euthanasia, and we shall literally not know what we are talking about if we ask whether acts of euthanasia defined as we have defined them are ever morally permissible without first understanding better the reason for saying that life is a good, and the possibility that it is not always so.

If a man should save my life he would be my benefactor. In normal circumstances this is plainly true; but does one always benefit another in saving his life? It seems certain that he does not. Suppose, for instance, that a man were being tortured to death and was given a drug that lengthened his sufferings; this would not be a benefit but the reverse. Or suppose that in a ghetto in Nazi Germany a doctor saved the life of someone threatened by disease, but that the man once cured was transported to an extermination camp; the doctor might wish for the sake of the patient that he had died of the disease. Nor would a longer stretch of life always be a benefit to the person who was given it. Comparing Hitler's camps with those of Stalin, Dmitri Panin observes that in the latter the method of extermination was made worse by agonies that could stretch out over months.

> Death from a bullet would have been bliss compared with what many millions had to endure while dying of hunger. The kind of death to which they were condemned has nothing to equal it in treachery and sadism.[3]

These examples show that to save or prolong a man's life is not always to do him a service: it may be better for him if he dies earlier rather than later. It must therefore be agreed that while life is normally a benefit to the one who has it, this is not always so.

The judgment is often fairly easy to make—that life is or is not a good to someone—but the basis for it is very hard to find. When life is said to be a benefit or a good, on what grounds is the assertion made?

The difficulty is underestimated if it is supposed that the problem arises from the fact that one who is dead has nothing, so that the good someone gets from being alive cannot be compared with the amount he would otherwise have had. For why should this particular comparison be necessary? Surely it would be enough if one could say whether or not someone whose life was prolonged had more good than evil in the extra stretch of time. Such estimates are not always possible, but frequently they are; we say, for example, "He was very happy in those last years," or, "He had little but unhappiness then." If the balance of good and evil determined whether life was a good to someone, we would expect to find a correlation in the judgments. In fact, of course, we find nothing of the kind. First, a man who has no doubt that existence is a good to him may have no idea about the balance of happiness and unhappiness in his life, or of any other positive and negative factors that may be suggested. So the supposed criteria are not always operating where the judgment is made. And secondly, the application of the criteria gives an answer that is often wrong. Many people have more evil than good in their lives; we do not, however, conclude that we would do these people no service by rescuing them from death.

To get around this last difficulty Thomas Nagel has suggested that experience itself is a good which must be brought in to balance accounts.

> . . . life is worth living even when the bad elements of experience are plentiful, and the good ones too meager to outweigh the bad ones on their own. The additional positive weight is supplied by experience itself, rather than by any of its contents.[4]

This seems implausible because if experience itself is a good it must be so even when what we experience is wholly bad, as in being tortured to death. How should one decide how much to count for this experiencing; and why count anything at all?

Others have tried to solve the problem by arguing that it is a man's desire for life that makes us call life a good: if he wants to live, then anyone who prolongs his life does him a benefit. Yet someone may cling to life where we would say confidently that it would be better for him if he died, and he may admit it too. Speaking of those same conditions in which, as he said, a bullet would have been merciful, Panin writes,

> I should like to pass on my observations concerning the absence of suicides under the extremely severe conditions of our concentration camps. The more that life became desperate, the more a prisoner seemed determined to hold on to it.[5]

One might try to explain this by saying that hope was the ground of this wish to survive for further days and months in the camp. But there is nothing unintelligible in the idea that a man might cling to life though he knew those facts about his future which would make any charitable man wish that he might die.

The problem remains, and it is hard to know where to look for a solution. Is there a conceptual connection between *life* and *good*? Because life is not always a good we are apt to reject this idea, and to think that it must be a contingent fact that life is usually a good, as it is a contingent matter that legacies are usually a benefit, if they are. Yet it seems not to be a contingent matter that to save someone's life is ordinarily to benefit him. The problem is to find where the conceptual connection lies.

It may be good tactics to forget for a time that it is euthanasia we are discussing and to see how *life* and *good* are connected in the case of living beings other than men. Even plants have things done to them that are harmful or beneficial, and what does them good must be related in some way to their living and dying. Let us therefore consider plants and animals, and then come back to human beings. At least we shall get away from the temptation to think that the connection between life and benefit must everywhere be a matter of happiness and unhappiness or of pleasure and pain; the idea being absurd in the case of animals and impossible even to formulate for plants.

In case anyone thinks that the concept of the beneficial applies only in a secondary or analogical way to plants, he should be reminded that we speak quite straightforwardly in saying, for instance, that a certain amount of sunlight is beneficial to most plants. What is in question here is the habitat in which plants of particular species flourish, but we can also talk, in a slightly different way, of what does them good, where there is some suggestion of improvement or remedy. What has the beneficial to do with sustaining life? It is tempting to answer, "everything," thinking that a healthy condition just is the one apt to secure survival. In fact, however, what is beneficial to a plant may have to do with reproduction rather than the survival of the individual member of the species. Nevertheless there is a plain connection between the beneficial and the life-sustaining even for the individual plant; if something makes it better able to survive in conditions normal for that species, it is ipso facto good for it. We need go no further, and could go no further, in explaining why a certain environment or treatment is good for a plant than to show how it helps this plant to survive.[6]

This connection between the life-sustaining and the beneficial is reasonably unproblematic, and there is nothing fanciful or zoomorphic in speaking of benefiting or doing good to plants. A connection with its survival can make something beneficial to a plant. But this is not, of course, to say that we count life as a good to a plant. We may save its life by giving it what is beneficial; we do not benefit it by saving its life.

A more ramified concept of benefit is used in speaking of animal life. New things can be said, such as that an animal is better or worse off for something that happened, or that it was a good or bad thing for it that it did happen. And new things count as benefit. In the first place, there is comfort, which often is, but need not be, related to health. When loosening a collar which is too tight for a dog we can say, "That will be better for it." So we see that the words "better for it" have two different meanings which we mark when necessary by a difference of emphasis, saying "better *for* it" when health is involved. And secondly, an animal can be benefited by having its life saved. "Could you do anything for it?" can be answered by, "Yes, I managed to save its life." Sometimes we may understand this, just as we would for a plant, to mean that we had checked some disease. But we can also do something for an animal by scaring away its predator. If we do this, it is a good thing for the animal that we did, unless of course it immediately meets a more unpleasant end by some other means. Similarly, on the bad side, an animal may be worse off for our intervention, and this is not because it pines or suffers but simply because it gets killed.

The problem that vexes us when we think about euthanasia comes on the scene at this point. For if we can do something for an animal—can benefit it—by relieving its suffering but also by saving its life, where does the greater benefit come when only death will end pain? It seemed that life was a good in its own right; yet pain seemed to be an evil with equal status and could therefore make life not a good after all. Is it only life without pain that is a good when animals are concerned? This does not seem a crazy suggestion when we are thinking of animals, since unlike human beings they do not have suffering as part of their normal life. But it is perhaps the idea of ordinary life that matters here. We would not say that we had done anything for an animal if we had merely kept it alive, either in an unconscious state or in a condition where, though conscious, it was unable to operate in an ordinary way; and the fact is that animals in severe and continuous pain simply do not operate normally. So we do not, on the whole, have the option of doing the animal good by saving its life though the life would be a life of pain. No doubt there are borderline cases, but that is no problem. We are not trying to make new judgments possible, but rather to find the principle of the ones we do make.

When we reach human life, the problems seem even more troublesome. For now we must take quite new things into account, such as the subject's own view of his life. It is arguable that this places extra constraints on the solution: might it not be counted as a necessary condition of life's being a good to a man that he should see it as such? Is there not some difficulty about the idea that a benefit might be done to him by saving or prolonging his life even though he himself wished for death? Of course he might have a quite mistaken view of his own prospects, but let us ignore this and think only of cases where it is life as he knows it that is in question. Can we think that the prolonging of this life would be a benefit to him even though he would rather have it end than continue? It seems that this cannot be ruled out. That there is no simple incompatibility between life as a good and the wish for death is shown by the possibility that a man should wish himself dead, not for his own sake, but for the sake of someone else. And if we try to amend the thesis to say that life cannot be a good to one who wishes *for his own sake* that he should die, we find the crucial concept slipping through our fingers. As Bishop Butler pointed out long ago, not all ends are either benevolent or self-interested. Does a man wish for death for his own sake in the relevant sense if, for instance, he wishes to revenge himself on another by his death? Or what if he is proud and refuses to stomach dependence or incapacity even though there are many good things left in life for him? The truth seems to be that the wish for death is sometimes compatible with life's being a good and sometimes not, which is possible because the description "wishing for death" is one covering diverse states of mind from that of the determined suicide, pathologically depressed, to that of one who is surprised to find that the thought of a fatal accident is viewed with relief. On the one hand, a man may see his life as a burden but go about his business in a more or less ordinary way; on the other hand, the wish for death may take the form of a rejection of everything that is in life, as it does in severe depression. It seems reasonable to say that life is not a good to one permanently in the latter state, and we must return to this topic later on.

When are we to say that life is a good or a benefit to a man? The dilemma that faces us is this. If we say that life as such is a good, we find ourselves refuted by the examples given at the beginning of this discussion. We therefore incline to think that it is as bringing good things that life is a good, where it is a good. But if life is a good only because it is the condition of good things, why is it not equally an evil when it brings bad things? And how can it be a good even when it brings more evil than good?

It should be noted that the problem has here been formulated in terms of the balance of good and evil, not that of happiness and unhappiness, and that it is not to be solved by the denial (which may be reasonable enough) that unhappiness is the only evil or happiness the only good. In this paper no view has been expressed about the nature of goods other than life itself. The point is that on any view of the goods and evils that life can contain, it seems that a life with more evil than good could still itself be a good.

It may be useful to review the judgments with which our theory must square. Do we think that life can be a good to one who suffers a lot of pain? Clearly we do. What about severely handicapped people; can life be a good to them? Clearly it can be, for even if someone is almost completely paralyzed, perhaps living in an iron lung, perhaps able to move things only by means of a tube held between his lips, we do not rule him out of order if he says that some benefactor saved his life. Nor is it different with mental handicap. There are many fairly severely handicapped people—such as those with Down's Syndrome (Mongolism)—for whom a simple affectionate life is possible. What about senility? Does this break the normal connection between life and good? Here we must surely distinguish between forms of senility. Some forms leave a life which we count someone as better off having than not having, so that a doctor who prolonged it would benefit the person concerned. With some kinds of senility this is, however, no longer true. There are some in geriatric wards who are barely conscious, though they can move a little and swallow food put into their mouths. To prolong such a state, whether in the old or in the very severely mentally handicapped, is not to do them a service or confer a benefit. But of course it need not be the reverse: only if there is suffering would one wish for the sake of the patient that he should die.

It seems, therefore, that merely being alive even without suffering is not a good, and that we must make a distinction similar to that which we made when animals were our topic. But how is the line to be drawn in the case of men? What is to count as ordinary human life in the relevant sense? If it were only the very senile or very ill who were to be said not to have this life, it might seem right to describe it in terms of *operation*. But it will be hard to find the sense in which the men described by Panin were not operating, given that they dragged themselves out to the forest to work. What is it about the life that the prisoners were living that makes us put it on the other side of the dividing line from that of some severely ill or suffering patients, and from most of the physically or mentally handicapped? It is not that they were in captivity, for life in captivity can certainly be a good. Nor is it merely the unusual nature of their life. In some ways the prisoners were living more as other men do than the patient in an iron lung.

The suggested solution to the problem is, then, that there is a certain conceptual connection between *life* and *good* in the case of human beings as in that of animals and even plants. Here, as there, however, it is not the mere state of being alive that can determine, or itself count as, a good, but rather life coming up to some standard of normality. It was argued that it is as part of ordinary life that the elements of good that a man may have are relevant to the question of whether saving his life counts as benefiting him. Ordinary human lives, even very hard lives, contain a minimum of basic goods, but when these are absent the idea of life is no longer linked to that of good. And since it is in this way that the elements of good contained in a man's life are relevant to the question of whether he is benefited if his life is preserved, there is no reason why it should be the balance of good and evil that counts.

It should be added that evils are relevant in one way when, as in the examples discussed above, they destroy the possibility of ordinary goods, but in a different way when they invade a life from which the goods are already absent for a different reason. So, for instance, the connection between *life* and *good* may be broken because consciousness has sunk to a very low level, as in extreme senility or severe brain damage. In itself this kind of life seems to be neither good nor evil, but if suffering sets in, one would hope for a speedy end.

The idea we need seems to be that of life which is ordinary human life in the following respect—that it contains a minimum of basic human goods. What is ordinary in human life—even in very hard lives—is that a man is not driven to work far beyond his capacity; that he has the support of a family or community; that he can more or less satisfy his hunger; that he has hopes for the future; that he can lie down to rest at night. Such things were denied to the men in the Vyatlag camps described by Panin;

not even rest at night was allowed them when they were tormented by bed-bugs, by noise and stench, and by routines such as body-searches and bath-parades—arranged for the night time so that work norms would not be reduced. Disease too can so take over a man's life that the normal human goods disappear. When a patient is so overwhelmed by pain or nausea that he cannot eat with pleasure, if he can eat at all, and is out of the reach of even the most loving voice, he no longer has ordinary human life in the sense in which the words are used here. And we may now pick up a thread from an earlier part of the discussion by remarking that crippling depression can destroy the enjoyment of ordinary goods as effectively as external circumstances can remove them.

This, admittedly inadequate, discussion of the sense in which life is normally a good, and of the reasons why it may not be so in some particular case, completes the account of what euthanasia is here taken to be. An act of euthanasia, whether literally act or rather omission, is attributed to an agent who opts for the death of another because in his case life seems to be an evil rather than a good. The question now to be asked is whether acts of euthanasia are ever justifiable. But there are two topics here rather than one. For it is one thing to say that some acts of euthanasia considered only in themselves and their results are morally unobjectionable, and another to say that it would be all right to legalize them. Perhaps the practice of euthanasia would allow too many abuses, and perhaps there would be too many mistakes. Moreover, the practice might have very important and highly undesirable side effects, because it is unlikely that we could change our principles about the treatment of the old and the ill without changing fundamental emotional attitudes and social relations. The topics must, therefore, be treated separately. In the next part of the discussion, nothing will be said about the social consequences and possible abuses of the practice of euthanasia, but only about acts of euthanasia considered in themselves.

What we want to know is whether acts of euthanasia, defined as we have defined them, are ever morally permissible. To be more accurate, we want to know whether it is ever sufficient justification of the choice of death for another that death can be counted a benefit rather than harm, and that this is why the choice is made.

It will be impossible to get a clear view of the area to which this topic belongs without first marking the distinct grounds on which objection may lie when one man opts for the death of another. There are two different virtues whose requirements are, in general, contrary to such actions. An unjustified act of killing, or allowing to die, is contrary to justice or to charity, or to both virtues, and the moral failings are distinct. Justice has to do with what men *owe* each other in the way of noninterference and positive service. When used in this wide sense, which has its history in the doctrine of the cardinal virtues, justice is not especially connected with, for instance, law courts but with the whole area of rights, and duties corresponding to rights. Thus murder is one form of injustice, dishonesty another, and wrongful failure to keep contracts a third; chicanery in a law court or defrauding someone of his inheritance are simply other cases of injustice. Justice as such is not directly linked to the good of another, and may require that something be rendered to him even where it will do him harm, as Hume pointed out when he remarked that a debt must be paid even to a profligate debauchee who "would rather receive harm than benefit from large possessions."[7] Charity, on the other hand, is the virtue which attaches us to the good of others. An act of charity is in question only where something is not demanded by justice, but a lack of charity and of justice can be shown where a man is denied something which he both needs and has a right to; both charity and justice demand that widows and orphans are not defrauded, and the man who cheats them is neither charitable nor just.

It is easy to see that the two grounds of objection to inducing death are distinct. A murder is an act of injustice. A culpable failure to come to the aid of someone whose life is threatened is normally contrary, not to justice, but to charity. But where one man is under contract, explicit or implicit, to come to the aid of another, injustice too will be shown. Thus injustice may be involved either in an act or an omission, and the same is true of a lack of charity; charity may demand that someone be aided, but also that an unkind word not be spoken.

The distinction between charity and justice will turn out to be of the first importance when voluntary and nonvoluntary euthanasia are distinguished later on. This is because of the connection between justice and rights, and something should now be said about this. I believe it is true to say that wherever a man acts unjustly he has infringed a right, since justice has to do with whatever a man is owed, and whatever he is owed is his as a matter of right. Something should therefore be said about the different kinds of rights. The distinction commonly made is between having a right in the sense of having a liberty, and having a "claim-right" or "right of recipience."[8] The best way to understand such a distinction seems to be as follows. To say that a man has a right in the sense of a liberty is to say that no one can demand that he do not do the thing which he has a right to do. The fact that he has a right to do it consists in the fact that a certain kind of objection does not lie against his doing it. Thus a man has a right in this sense to walk down a public street or park his car in a public parking space. It does not follow that no one else may prevent him from doing so. If for some reason I want a certain man not to park in a certain place I may lawfully park there myself or get my friends to do so, thus preventing him from doing what he has a right (in the sense of a liberty) to do. It is different, however, with a claim-right. This is the kind of right which I have in addition to a liberty when, for example, I have a private parking space; now others have duties in the way of noninterference, as in this case, or of service, as in the case where my claim-right is to goods or services promised to me. Sometimes one of these rights gives other people the duty of securing to me that to which I have a right, but at other times their duty is merely to refrain from interference. If a fall of snow blocks my private parking space, there is normally no obligation for anyone else to clear it away. Claim-rights generate duties; sometimes these duties are duties of noninterference; sometimes they are duties of service. If your right gives me the duty not to interfere with you, I have "no right" to do it; similarly, if your right gives me the duty to provide something for you, I have "no right" to refuse to do it. What *I* lack is the right which is a liberty; I am not "at liberty" to interfere with you or to refuse the service.

Where in this picture does the right to life belong? No doubt people have the right to live in the sense of a liberty, but what is important is the cluster of claim-rights brought together under the title of the right to life. The chief of these is, of course, the right to be free from interferences that threaten life. If other people aim their guns at us or try to pour poison into our drink we can, to put it mildly, demand that they desist. And then there are the services we can claim from doctors, health officers, bodyguards, and firemen; the rights that depend on contract or public arrangement. Perhaps there is no particular point in saying that the duties these people owe us belong to the right to life; we might as well say that all the services owed to anyone by tailors, dressmakers, and couturiers belong to a right called the right to be elegant. But contracts such as those understood in the patient–doctor relationship come in an important way when we are discussing the rights and wrongs of euthanasia, and are therefore mentioned here.

Do people have the right to what they need in order to survive, apart from the right conferred by special contracts into which other people have entered for the supplying of these necessities? Do people in the underdeveloped countries in which starvation is rife have the right to the food they so evidently lack? Joel Feinberg, discussing this question, suggests that they should be said to have "a claim," distinguishing this from a "valid claim," which gives a claim-right.

> The manifesto writers on the other side who seem to identify needs, or at least basic needs, with what they call "human rights," are more properly described, I think, as urging upon the world community the moral principle that *all* basic human needs ought to be recognized as *claims* (in the customary *prima facie* sense) worthy of sympathy

> and serious consideration right now, even though, in many cases, they cannot yet plausibly be treated as *valid* claims, that is, as grounds of any other people's duties. This way of talking avoids the anomaly of ascribing to all human beings now, even those in pre-industrial societies, such "economic and social rights" as "periodic holidays with pay."[9]

This seems reasonable, though we notice that there are some actual rights to service which are not based on anything like a contract, as for instance the right that children have to support from their parents and parents to support from their children in old age, though both sets of rights are to some extent dependent on existing social arrangements.

Let us now ask how the right to life affects the morality of acts of euthanasia. Are such acts sometimes or always ruled out by the right to life? This is certainly a possibility; for although an act of euthanasia is, by our definition, a matter of opting for death for the good of the one who is to die, there is, as we noted earlier, no direct connection between that to which a man has a right and that which is for his good. It is true that men have the right only to the kind of thing that is, in general, a good: we do not think that people have the right to garbage or polluted air. Nevertheless, a man may have the right to something which he himself would be better off without; where rights exist, it is a man's will that counts, not his or anyone else's estimate of benefit or harm. So the duties complementary to the right to life—the general duty of noninterference and the duty of service incurred by certain persons—are not affected by the quality of a man's life or by his prospects. Even if it is true that he would be, as we say, "better off dead," so long as he wants to live this does not justify us in killing him and may not justify us in deliberately allowing him to die. All of us have the duty of noninterference, and some of us may have the duty to sustain his life. Suppose, for example, that a retreating army has to leave behind wounded or exhausted soldiers in the wastes of an arid or snowbound land where the only prospect is death by starvation or at the hands of an enemy notoriously cruel. It has often been the practice to accord a merciful bullet to men in such desperate straits. But suppose that one of them demands that he should be left alive? It seems clear that his comrades have no right to kill him, though it is a quite different question as to whether they should give him a life-prolonging drug. The right to life can sometimes give a duty of positive service, but does not do so here. What it does give is the right to be left alone.

Interestingly enough, we have arrived by way of a consideration of the right to life at the distinction normally labeled "active" versus "passive" euthanasia, and often thought to be irrelevant to the moral issue.[10] Once it is seen that the right to life is a distinct ground of objection to certain acts of euthanasia, and that this right creates a duty of noninterference more widespread than the duties of care, there can be no doubt about the relevance of the distinction between passive and active euthanasia. Where everyone may have the duty to leave someone alone, it may be that no one has the duty to maintain his life, or that only some people do.

Where then do the boundaries of the "active" and "passive" lie? In some ways the words are themselves misleading, because they suggest the difference between act and omission which is not quite what we want. Certainly the act of shooting someone is the kind of thing we were talking about under the heading of "interference" and omitting to give him a drug a case of refusing care. But the act of turning off a respirator should surely be thought of as no different from the decision not to start it; if doctors had decided that a patient should be allowed to die, either course of action might follow, and both should be counted as passive rather than active euthanasia if euthanasia were in question. The point seems to be that interference in a course of treatment is not the same as other interference in a man's life, and particularly if the same body of people are responsible for the treatment and for its discontinuance. In such a case we could speak of the disconnecting of the apparatus as killing the man, or of the hospital as allowing him to die. By and large, it is the act of killing that is ruled out under the heading of noninterference, but not in every case.

Doctors commonly recognize this distinction, and the grounds on which some philosophers have denied it seem untenable. James Rachels, for instance, believes that if the difference between active and passive is relevant anywhere, it should be relevant everywhere, and he has pointed to an example in which it seems to make no difference which is done. If someone saw a child drowning in a bath it would seem just as bad to let it drown as to push its head under water.[11] If "it makes no difference" means that one act would be as iniquitous as the other, this is true. It is not that killing is *worse* than allowing to die, but that the two are contrary to distinct virtues, which gives the possibility that in some circumstances one is impermissible and the other permissible. In the circumstances invented by Rachels, both are wicked: it is contrary to justice to push the child's head under the water—something one has no right to do. To leave it to drown is not contrary to justice, but it is a particularly glaring example of lack of charity. Here it makes no practical difference because the requirements of justice and charity coincide; but in the case of the retreating army they did not: charity would have required that the wounded soldier be killed had not justice required that he be left alive.[12] In such a case it makes all the difference whether a man opts for the death of another in a positive action, or whether he allows him to die. An analogy with the right to property will make the point clear. If a man owns something, he has the right to it even when its possession does him harm, and we have no right to take it from him. But if one day it should blow away, maybe nothing requires us to get it back for him; we could not deprive him of it, but we may allow it to go. This is not to deny that it will often be an unfriendly act or one based on an arrogant judgment when we refuse to do what he wants. Nevertheless, we would be within our rights, and it might be that no moral objection of any kind would lie against our refusal.

It is important to emphasize that a man's rights may stand between us and the action we would dearly like to take for his sake. They may, of course, also prevent action which we would like to take for the sake of others, as when it might be tempting to kill one man to save several. But it is interesting that the limits of allowable interference, however uncertain, seem stricter in the first case than the second. Perhaps there are no cases in which it would be all right to kill a man against his will *for his own sake* unless they could equally well be described as cases of allowing him to die, as in the example of turning off the respirator. However, there are circumstances, even if these are very rare, in which one man's life would justifiably be sacrificed to save others, and "killing" would be the only description of what was being done. For instance, a vehicle which had gone out of control might be steered from a path on which it would kill more than one man to a path on which it would kill one.[13] But it would not be permissible to steer a vehicle towards someone in order to kill him, against his will, for his own good. An analogy with property rights illustrates the point. One may not destroy a man's property against his will on the grounds that he would be better off without it; there are, however, circumstances in which it could be destroyed for the sake of others. If his house is liable to fall and kill him, that is his affair; it might, however, without injustice be destroyed to stop the spread of a fire.

We see then that the distinction between active and passive, important as it is elsewhere, has a special importance in the area of euthanasia. It should also be clear why James Rachels' other argument, that it is often "more humane" to kill than to allow to die, does not show that the distinction between active and passive euthanasia is morally irrelevant. It might be "more humane" in this sense to deprive a man of the property that brings evils on him, or to refuse to pay what is owed to Hume's profligate debauchee; but if we say this we must admit that an act which is "more humane" than its alternative may be morally objectionable because it infringes rights.

So far we have said very little about the right to service as opposed to the right to noninterference, though it was agreed that both might be brought under the heading of "the right to life." What about the duty to preserve life that may belong to special classes of persons such as bodyguards, firemen, or doctors? Unlike the general public, they are not within their rights if they merely refrain from interfering and do not try to sustain life. The subject's claim-rights are twofold as far as they are concerned, and passive as well as active euthanasia may be ruled out here if it is against his will. This is not to say that he has the right to any and every service needed to save or prolong his life; the rights of other people set limits to what may be demanded, both because they have the right not to be interfered with and because they may have a competing right to services. Furthermore, one must inquire just what the contract or implicit agreement amounts to in each case. Firemen and bodyguards presumably have a duty which is simply to preserve life, within the limits of justice to others and of reasonableness to themselves. With doctors it may, however, be different, since their duty relates not only to preserving life but also to the relief of suffering. It is not clear what a doctor's duties are to his patient if life can be prolonged only at the cost of suffering or suffering relieved only by measures that shorten life. George Fletcher has argued that what the doctor is under contract to do depends on what is generally done, because this is what a patient will reasonably expect.[14] This seems right. If procedures are part of normal medical practice, then it seems that the patient can demand them however much it may be against his interest to do so. Once again, it is not a matter of what is "most humane."

That the patient's right to life may set limits to permissible acts of euthanasia seems undeniable. If he does not want to die, no one has the right to practice active euthanasia on him, and passive euthanasia may also be ruled out where he has a right to the services of doctors or others.

Perhaps few will deny what has so far been said about the impermissibility of acts of euthanasia simply because we have so far spoken about the case of one who positively wants to live, and about his rights, whereas those who advocate euthanasia are usually thinking either about those who wish to die or about those whose wishes cannot be ascertained either because they cannot properly be said to have wishes or because, for one reason or another, we are unable to form a reliable estimate of what they are. The question that must now be asked is whether the latter type of case, where euthanasia though not involuntary would again be nonvoluntary, is different from the one discussed so far. Would we have the right to kill someone for his own good so long as we had no idea that he positively wished to live? And what about the life-prolonging duties of doctors in the same circumstances? This is a very difficult problem. On the one hand, it seems ridiculous to suppose that a man's right to life is something which generates duties only where he has signaled that he wants to live; as a borrower does indeed have a duty to return something lent on indefinite loan only if the lender indicates that he wants it back. On the other hand, it might be argued that there is something illogical about the idea that a right has been infringed if someone incapable of saying whether he wants it or not is deprived of something that is doing him harm rather than good. Yet on the analogy of property we would say that a right has been infringed. Only if someone had earlier told us that in such circumstances he would not want to keep the thing could we think that his right had been waived. Perhaps if we could make confident judgments about what anyone in such circumstances would wish, or what he would have wished beforehand had he considered the matter, we could agree to consider the right to life as "dormant," needing to be asserted if the normal duties were to remain. But as things are, we cannot make any such assumption; we simply do not know what most people would want, or would have wanted, us to do unless they tell us. This is certainly the case so far as active measures to end life are concerned. Possibly it is different, or will become different, in the matter of being kept alive, so general is the feeling against using sophisticated procedures on moribund patients, and so much is this dreaded by people who are old or terminally ill. Once again the distinction between active and passive euthanasia has come on the scene, but this time because most people's attitudes to the two are so different. It is just possible that we might presume, in the absence of specific evidence, that someone would not wish, beyond a certain point, to be kept alive; it is certainly not possible to assume that he would wish to be killed.

In the last paragraph we have begun to broach the topic of voluntary euthanasia, and this we must now discuss. What is to be said about the case in which there is no doubt about someone's wish to die: either he has told us beforehand that he would wish it in circumstances such as he is now in, and has shown no sign of a change of mind, or else he tells us now, being in possession of his faculties and of a steady mind. We should surely say that the objections previously urged against acts of euthanasia, which it must be remembered were all on the ground of rights, had disappeared. It does not seem that one would infringe someone's right to life in killing him with his permission and in fact at his request. Why should someone not be able to waive his right to life, or rather, as would be more likely to happen, to cancel some of the duties of noninterference that this right entails? (He is more likely to say that he should be killed by this man at this time in this manner, than to say that anyone may kill him at any time and in any way.) Similarly, someone may give permission for the destruction of his property, and request it. The important thing is that he gives a critical permission, and it seems that this is enough to cancel the duty normally associated with the right. If someone gives you permission to destroy his property, it can no longer be said that you have no right to do so, and I do not see why it should not be the case with taking a man's life. An objection might be made on the ground that only God has the right to take life, but in this paper religious as opposed to moral arguments are being left aside. Religion apart, there seems to be no case to be made out for an infringement of rights if a man who wishes to die is allowed to die or even killed. But of course it does not follow that there is no moral objection to it. Even with property, which is after all a relatively small matter, one might be wrong to destroy what one had the right to destroy. For, apart from its value to other people, it might be valuable to the man who wanted it destroyed, and charity might require us to hold our hand where justice did not.

Let us review the conclusion of this part of the argument, which has been about euthanasia and the right to life. It has been argued that from this side come stringent restrictions on the acts of euthanasia that could be morally permissible. Active nonvoluntary euthanasia is ruled out by that part of the right to life which creates the duty of noninterference, though passive nonvoluntary euthanasia is not ruled out, except where the right to life-preserving action has been created by some special condition such as a contract between a man and his doctor, and it is not always certain just what such a contract involves. Voluntary euthanasia is another matter: as the preceding paragraph suggested, no right is infringed if a man is allowed to die or even killed at his own request.

Turning now to the other objection that normally holds against inducing the death of another, that it is against charity, or benevolence, we must tell a very different story. Charity is the virtue that gives attachment to the good of others, and because life is normally a good, charity normally demands that it should be saved or prolonged. But as we so defined an act of euthanasia that it seeks a man's death for his own sake—for his good—charity will normally speak in favor of it. This is not, of course, to say that charity can require an act of euthanasia which justice forbids, but if an act of euthanasia is not contrary to justice—that is, it does not infringe rights—charity will rather be in its favor than against.

Once more the distinction between nonvoluntary and voluntary euthanasia must be considered. Could it ever be compatible with charity to seek a man's death although he wanted to live, or at least had not let us know that he wanted to die? It has been argued that in such circumstances active euthanasia would infringe his right to life, but passive euthanasia would not do so, unless he had some special right to life-preserving service from the one who allowed him to die. What would charity dictate? Obviously when a man wants to live there is a presumption that he will be benefited if his life is prolonged, and if it is so the question of euthanasia does not arise. But it is, on the other hand, possible that he wants to live where it would be better for him to die: perhaps he does not realize the desperate situation he is in, or perhaps he is afraid of dying. So, in spite of a very proper resistance to refusing to go along with a man's own wishes in the matter of life and death, someone might justifiably refuse to prolong the life even of someone who asked him to prolong it, as in the case of refusing to give the wounded soldier a drug that would keep him alive to meet a terrible end. And it is even more obvious that charity does not always dictate that life should be prolonged where a man's own wishes, hypothetical or actual, are not known.

So much for the relation of charity to nonvoluntary passive euthanasia, which was not, like nonvoluntary active euthanasia, ruled out by the right to life. Let us now ask what charity has to say about voluntary euthanasia, both active and passive. It was suggested in the discussion of justice that if of sound mind and steady desire, a man might give others the *right* to allow him to die or even to kill him, where otherwise this would be ruled out. But it was pointed out that this would not settle the question of whether the act was morally permissible, and it is this that we must now consider. Could not charity speak against what justice allowed? Indeed it might do so. For while the fact that a man wants to die suggests that his life is wretched, and while his rejection of life may itself tend to take the good out of the things he might have enjoyed, nevertheless his wish to die might here be opposed for his own sake just as it might be if suicide were in question. Perhaps there is hope that his mental condition will improve. Perhaps he is mistaken in thinking his disease incurable. Perhaps he wants to die for the sake of someone else on whom he feels he is a burden, and we are not ready to accept this sacrifice whether for ourselves or others. In such cases, and there will surely be many of them, it could not be for his own sake that we will him or allow him to die, and therefore euthanasia as defined in this paper would not be in question. But this is not to deny that there could be acts of voluntary euthanasia both passive and active against which neither justice nor charity would speak.

We have now considered the morality of euthanasia both voluntary and nonvoluntary, and active and passive. The conclusion has been that nonvoluntary active euthanasia (roughly, killing a man against his will or without his consent) is never justified; that is to say, that a man's being killed for his own good never justifies the act unless he himself has consented to it. A man's rights are infringed by such an action, and it is therefore contrary to justice. However, all the other combinations, nonvoluntary passive euthanasia, voluntary active euthanasia, and voluntary passive euthanasia, are sometimes compatible with both justice and charity. But the strong condition carried in the definition of euthanasia adopted in this paper must not be forgotten; an act of euthanasia as here understood is one whose purpose is to benefit the one who dies.

In the light of this discussion let us look at our present practices. Are they good or are they bad? And what changes might be made, thinking now not only of the morality of particular acts of euthanasia but also of the indirect effects of instituting different practices, of the abuses to which they might be subject and of the changes that might come about if euthanasia became a recognized part of the social scene.

The first thing to notice is that it is wrong to ask whether we should introduce the practice of euthanasia as if it were not something we already had. In fact we do have it. For instance, it is common, where the medical prognosis is very bad, for doctors to recommend against measures to prolong life, and particularly where a process of degeneration producing one medical emergency after another has already set in. If these doctors are not certainly within their legal rights, this is something that is apt to come as a surprise to them as to the general public. It is also obvious that euthanasia is often practiced where old people are concerned. If someone very old and soon to die is attacked by a disease that makes his life wretched, doctors do not always come in with life-prolonging drugs. Perhaps poor patients are more fortunate in this respect than rich patients, being more often left to die in peace; but it is in any case a well-recognized piece of medical practice, which is a form of euthanasia.

No doubt the case of infants with mental or physical defects will be suggested as another example of the practice of euthanasia as we already have it, since such infants are sometimes deliberately allowed to die. That they are deliberately allowed to die is certain; children with severe spina bifida malformations are not always operated on even where it is thought that without the operation they will die; and even in the case of children with Down's Syndrome who have intestinal obstructions, the relatively simple operation that would make it possible to feed them is sometimes not performed.[15] Whether this is euthanasia in our sense or only as the Nazis understood it is another matter. We must ask the crucial question, "Is it for the sake of the child himself that the doctors and parents choose his death?" In some cases the answer may really be yes, and, what is more important, it may really be true that the kind of life which is a good is not possible or likely for this child, and that there is little but suffering and frustration in store for him.[16] But this must presuppose that the medical prognosis is wretchedly bad, as it may be for some spina bifida children. With children who are born with Down's Syndrome it is, however, quite different. Most of these are able to live on for quite a time in a reasonably contented way, remaining like children all their lives but capable of affectionate relationships and able to play games and perform simple tasks. The fact is, of course, that the doctors who recommend against lifesaving procedures for handicapped infants are usually thinking not of them but rather of their parents and of other children in the family or of the "burden on society" if the children survive. So it is not for their sake but to avoid trouble to others that they are allowed to die. When brought out into the open this seems unacceptable: at least we do not easily accept the principle that adults who need special care should be counted too burdensome to be kept alive. It must in any case be insisted that if children with Down's Syndrome are deliberately allowed to die this is not a matter of euthanasia except in Hitler's sense. And for our children, since we scruple to gas them, not even the manner of their death is "quiet and easy"; when not treated for an intestinal obstruction a baby simply starves to death. Perhaps some will take this as an argument for allowing active euthanasia, in which case they will be in the company of an S.S. man stationed in the Warthgenau who sent Eichmann a memorandum telling him that "Jews in the coming winter could no longer be fed" and submitting for his consideration a proposal as to whether "it would not be the most humane solution to kill those Jews who were incapable of work through some quicker means."[17] If we say we are *unable* to look after children with handicaps, we are no more telling the truth than was the S.S. man who said that the Jews could not be fed.

Nevertheless, if it is ever right to allow deformed children to die because life will be a misery to them, or not to take measures to prolong for a little the life of a newborn baby whose life cannot extend beyond a few months of intense medical intervention, there is a genuine problem about active as opposed to passive euthanasia. There are well-known cases in which the medical staff has looked on wretchedly while an infant died slowly from starvation and dehydration because they did not feel able to give a lethal injection. According to the principles discussed in the earlier part of this paper they would indeed have had no right to give it, since an infant cannot ask that it should be done. The only possible solution—supposing that voluntary active euthanasia were to be legalized—would be to appoint guardians to act on the infant's behalf. In a different climate of opinion this might not be dangerous, but at present, when people so readily assume that the life of a handicapped baby is of no value, one would be loath to support it.

Finally, on the subject of handicapped children, another word should be said about those with severe mental defects. For them too it might sometimes be right to say that one would wish for death for their sake. But not even severe mental handicap automatically brings a child within the scope even of a possible act of euthanasia. If the level of consciousness is low enough it could not be said that life is a good to them, any more than in the case of those suffering from extreme senility. Nevertheless, if they do not suffer it will not be an act of euthanasia by which someone opts for their death. Perhaps charity does not demand that strenuous measures are taken to keep people in this state alive, but euthanasia does not come into the matter, any more than it does when someone is, like Karen Ann Quinlan, in a state of permanent coma. Much could be said about this last case. It might even be suggested that in the case of unconsciousness this "life" is not the life to which "the right to life" refers. But that is not our topic here.

What we must consider, even if only briefly, is the possibility that euthanasia, genuine euthanasia, and not contrary to the requirements of justice or charity, should be legalized over a wider area. Here we are up against the really serious problem of abuse. Many people want, and want very badly, to be rid of their elderly relatives and even of their ailing husbands or wives. Would any safeguards ever be able to stop them describing as euthanasia what was really for their own benefit? And would it be possible to prevent the occurrence of acts which were genuinely acts of euthanasia but morally impermissible because infringing the rights of a patient who wished to live?

Perhaps the furthest we should go is to encourage patients to make their own contracts with a doctor by making it known whether they wish him to prolong their life in case of painful terminal illness or of incapacity. A document such as the Living Will seems eminently sensible, and should surely be allowed to give a doctor following the previously expressed wishes of the patient immunity from legal proceedings by relatives.[18] Legalizing active euthanasia is, however, another matter. Apart from the special repugnance doctors feel towards the idea of a lethal injection, it may be of the very greatest importance to keep a psychological barrier up against killing. Moreover, it is active euthanasia which is the most liable to abuse. Hitler would not have been able to kill 275,000 people in his "euthanasia" program if he had had to wait for them to need life-saving treatment. But there are other objections to active euthanasia, even voluntary active euthanasia. In the first place, it would be hard to devise procedures that would protect people from being persuaded into giving their consent. And secondly, the possibility of active voluntary euthanasia might change the social scene in ways that would be very bad. As things are, people do, by and large, expect to be looked after if they are old or ill. This is one of the good things that we have, but we might lose it, and be much worse off without it. It might come to be expected that someone likely to need a lot of looking after should call for the doctor and demand his own death. Something comparable could be good in an extremely poverty-stricken community where the children genuinely suffered from lack of food; but in rich societies such as ours it would surely be a spiritual disaster. Such possibilities should make us very wary of supporting large measures of euthanasia, even where moral principle applied to the individual act does not rule it out.

NOTES

I would like to thank Derek Parfit and the editors of *Philosophy & Public Affairs* for their very helpful comments.

1. Leo Alexander, "Medical Science under Dictatorship," *New England Journal of Medicine,* 14 July 1949, p. 40.
2. For a discussion of culpable and nonculpable ignorance see Thomas Aquinas, *Summa Theologica,* First Part of the Second Part, Question 6, article 8, and Question 19, articles 5 and 6.
3. Dmitri Panin, *The Notebooks of Sologdin* (London, 1976), pp. 66–67.
4. Thomas Nagel, "Death," in James Rachels, ed., *Moral Problems* (New York, 1971), p. 362.
5. Panin, *Sologdin,* p. 85.
6. Yet some detail needs to be filled in to explain why we should not say that a scarecrow is beneficial to the plants it protects. Perhaps what is beneficial must either be a feature of the plant itself, such as protective prickles, or else must work on the plant directly, such as a line of trees which give it shade.
7. David Hume, *Treatise,* Book III, Part II, Section 1.
8. See, for example, D. D. Raphael, "Human Rights Old and New," in D. D. Raphael, ed., *Political Theory and the Rights of Man* (London, 1967), and Joel Feinberg, "The Nature and Value of Rights," *The Journal of Value Inquiry* 4, no. 4 (Winter 1970): pp. 243–257. Reprinted in Samuel

Gorovitz, ed., *Moral Problems in Medicine* (Englewood Cliffs, New Jersey, 1976).

9. Feinberg, "Human Rights," *Moral Problems in Medicine,* p. 465.
10. See, for example, James Rachels, "Active and Passive Euthanasia," *New England Journal of Medicine* 292, no. 2 (9 Jan. 1975): pp. 78–80.
11. Ibid.
12. It is not, however, that justice and charity conflict. A man does not lack charity because he refrains from an act of injustice which would have been for someone's good.
13. For a discussion of such questions, see my article "The Problem of Abortion and the Doctrine of Double Effect," *Oxford Review,* no. 5 (1967); reprinted in Rachels, *Moral Problems,* and Gorovitz, *Moral Problems in Medicine.*
14. George Fletcher, "Legal Aspects of the Decision not to Prolong Life," *Journal of the American Medical Association* 203, no. 1 (1 Jan. 1968): pp. 119–122. Reprinted in Gorovitz.
15. I have been told this by a pediatrician in a well-known medical center in the United States. It is confirmed by Anthony M. Shaw and Iris A. Shaw, "Dilemma of Informed Consent in Children," *The New England Journal of Medicine* 289, no. 17 (25 Oct. 1973): pp. 885–890. Reprinted in Gorovitz.
16. It must be remembered, however, that many of the social miseries of spina bifida children could be avoided. Professor R. B. Zachary is surely right to insist on this. See, for example, "Ethical and Social Aspects of Spina Bifida," *The Lancet,* 3 Aug. 1968, pp. 274–276. Reprinted in Gorovitz.
17. Quoted by Hannah Arendt, *Eichmann in Jerusalem* (London 1963), p. 90.
18. Details of this document are to be found in J. A. Behnke and Sissela Bok, eds., *The Dilemmas of Euthanasia* (New York, 1975), and in A. B. Downing, ed., *Euthanasia and the Right to Life: The Case for Voluntary Euthanasia* (London, 1969).

QUESTIONS FOR ANALYSIS

1. What does Foot mean by "right to life," and how does she use this notion to distinguish between active and passive euthanasia?
2. Under what conditions might a person's life be regarded as no longer worth living?
3. Why does Foot believe it is not legitimate for us to decide when someone else's life is no longer worth living?
4. Which forms of euthanasia does Foot regard as legitimate and which illegitimate? Cite her reasons.
5. Why does Foot believe we don't have a duty to kill a person who has decided his or her life is no longer worth living?

A Moral Principle about Killing

RICHARD BRANDT

The preceding writers, either explicitly or implicitly, dealt with the moral principle "It is morally wrong to kill innocent human beings." In this essay, philosopher Richard Brandt (1910–1997) observes that this principle is really more useful in determining blame than for guiding us in making decisions. Brandt thinks a more appropriate principle can be based on the presumed obligation not to kill any human being except in justifiable self-defense—unless we have an even stronger moral obligation to do something that cannot be done without killing. In Brandt's view, that other overriding obligation is not to cause injury to another.

This article first appeared in the book *Beneficent Euthanasia,* ed. Marvin Kohl (Buffalo, N.Y.: Prometheus Books, 1975). Reprinted by permission of the publisher.

Brandt is distinguishing, then, between killing and causing injury, so that not every act of killing is an act of injury. After citing examples of what he believes are noninjurious killings and specifying conditions under which an act is noninjurious, Brandt argues that a person in irreversible coma is "beyond injury." If such a person has left instructions that his or her life should be ended, then, in Brandt's view, we are under a *prima facie* obligation to do so. In the absence of explicit instructions, we may attempt to determine what the person's wishes likely would be and carry them out. Of course, if a person has left instructions to be maintained under any circumstances, then we have an obligation to respect that preference.

Throughout the essay, Brandt uses the term "*prima facie* duty" or "obligation," which he has borrowed from the English philosopher William David Ross. *Prima facie* means "at first sight" or "on the surface." Accordingly, a *prima facie* duty is one that dictates what I should do when other relevant factors aren't considered. For example, I have a *prima facie* duty not to lie in every case in which lying is possible. Likewise, I have a *prima facie* duty to prevent the needless suffering of others. In other words, all things being equal, this is what I ought to try to do.

In this essay, Brandt is taking issue with the commonplace view that killing a person is something that is *prima facie* wrong in itself. In his view, killing is wrong *only if* and *because* it is an injury to someone, or *if* and *because* it runs counter to the person's known preference. In short, Brandt believes that a principle about the *prima facie* wrongness of killing derives from principles about when we are *prima facie* obligated not to injure and when we are *prima facie* obligated to respect a person's wishes.

One of the Ten Commandments states: "Thou shalt not kill." The commandment does not supply an object for the verb, but the traditional Catholic view has been that the proper object of the verb is "innocent human beings" (except in cases of extreme necessity), where "innocent" is taken to exclude persons convicted of a capital crime or engaged in an unjust assault aimed at killing, such as members of the armed forces of a country prosecuting an unjust war. Thus construed, the prohibition is taken to extend to suicide and abortion. (There is a qualification: that we are not to count cases in which the death is not wanted for itself or intended as a *means* to a goal that is wanted for itself, provided that in either case the aim of the act is the avoidance of some evil greater than the death of the person.) Can this view that all killing of innocent human beings is morally wrong be defended, and if not, what alternative principle can be?

This question is one the ground rules for answering which are far from a matter of agreement. I should myself be content if a principle were identified that could be shown to be one that would be included in any moral system that rational and benevolent persons would support for a society in which they expected to live. Apparently others would not be so content; so in what follows I shall simply aim to make some observations that I hope will identify a principle with which the consciences of intelligent people will be comfortable. I believe the rough principle I will suggest is also one that would belong to the moral system rational and benevolent people would want for their society.

Let us begin by reflecting on what it is to kill. The first thing to notice is that *kill* is a biological term. For example, a weed may be killed by being sprayed with a chemical. The verb *kill* involves essentially the broad notion of death—the change from the state of being biologically alive to the state of being dead. It is beyond my powers to give any general characterization of this transition, and it may be impossible to give one. If there is one, it is one that human beings, flies, and ferns all share; and to kill is in some sense to bring that transition about. The next thing to notice is that at least human beings do not live forever, and hence killing a human being at a given time must be construed as *advancing the date* of its death, or as *shortening its life*. Thus it may be brought about that the termination of the life of a person occurs at the time t instead of at the time $t + k$. Killing is thus shortening the span of organic life of something.

There is a third thing to notice about *kill*. It is a term of causal agency and has roots in the legal tradition. As such, it involves complications. For instance, suppose I push a boulder down a mountainside, aiming it at a person *X* and it indeed strikes *X*, and he is dead after impact and not before (and not from a coincidental heart attack); in that case we would say that I killed *X*. On the other hand, suppose I tell *Y* that *X* is in bed with *Y*'s wife, and *Y* hurries to the scene, discovers them, and shoots *X* to death; in that case, although the unfolding of events from my action may be as much a matter of causal law as the path of the boulder, we should not say that I killed *X*. Fortunately, for the purpose of principles of the morally right, we can sidestep such complications. For suppose I am choosing whether to do *A* or *B* (where one or the other of these "acts" may be construed as essentially *inaction*—for example, *not* doing what I know is the one thing that will *prevent* someone's death); then it is enough if I know, or have reason to think it highly probable, that were I to do *A*, a state of the world including the death of some person or persons would ensue, whereas were I to do *B*, a state of the world of some specified different sort would ensue. If a moral principle will tell me in this case whether I am to do *A* or *B*, that is all I need. It could be that a moral principle would tell me that I am absolutely never to perform any action *A*, such that were I to do it the death of some innocent human being would ensue, provided there is some alternative action I might perform, such that were I to do it no such death would ensue.

It is helpful, I think, to reformulate the traditional Catholic view in a way that preserves the spirit and intent of that view (although some philosophers would disagree with this assessment) and at the same time avoids some conceptions that are both vague and more appropriate to a principle about when a person is morally blameworthy for doing something than to a principle about what a person ought morally to do. The terminology I use goes back, in philosophical literature, to a phrase introduced by W. D. Ross, but the conception is quite familiar. The alternative proposal is that there is a *strong prima facie obligation* not to kill any human being except in justifiable self-defense; in the sense (of prima facie) that it is morally *wrong* to kill any human being except in justifiable self-defense *unless* there is an even stronger prima facie moral obligation to do something that cannot be done without killing. (The term *innocent* can now be omitted, since if a person is not innocent, there may be a stronger moral obligation that can only be discharged by killing him; and this change is to the good since it is not obvious that we have no prima facie obligation to avoid killing people even if they are not innocent.) This formulation has the result that sometimes, to decide what is morally right, we have to compare the stringencies of conflicting moral obligations—and that is an elusive business; but the other formulation either conceals the same problem by putting it in another place, or else leads to objectionable implications. (Consider one implication of the traditional formulation for a party of spelunkers in a cave by the oceanside. It is found that a rising tide is bringing water into the cave and all will be drowned unless they escape at once. Unfortunately, the first man to try to squeeze through the exit is fat and gets wedged inextricably in the opening, with his head inside the cave. Somebody in the party has a stick of dynamite. Either they blast the fat man out, killing him, or all of them, including him, will drown. The traditional formulation leads to the conclusion that all must drown.)

Let us then consider the principle: "There is a strong prima facie moral obligation not to kill any human being except in justifiable self-defense." I do not believe we want to accept this principle without further qualification; indeed, its status seems not to be that of a basic principle at all, but derivative from some more-basic principles. W. D. Ross listed what he thought were the main basic prima facie moral obligations; it is noteworthy that he listed a prima facie duty not to *cause injury*, but he did not include an obligation not to kill. Presumably this was no oversight. He might have thought that killing a human being is always an injury, so that the additional listing of an obligation not to kill would be redundant; but he might also have thought that killing is sometimes not an injury and that it is prima facie obligatory not to kill only when, and because, so doing would injure a sentient being.

What might be a noninjurious killing? If I come upon a cat that has been mangled but not quite killed by several dogs and is writhing in pain, and I pull myself together and put it out of its misery, I have killed the cat but surely not *injured* it. I do not injure something by relieving its pain. If someone is being tortured and roasted to death and I know he wishes nothing more than a merciful termination of life, I have not injured him if I shoot him; I have done him a favor. In general, it seems I have not injured a person if I treat him in a way in which he would want me to treat him if he were fully rational, or in a way to which he would be indifferent if he were fully rational. (I do not think that terminating the life of a human fetus in the third month is an injury; I admit this view requires discussion.[1])

Consider another type of killing that is not an injury. Consider the case of a human being who has become unconscious and will not, it is known, regain consciousness. He is in a hospital and is being kept alive only through expensive supportive measures. Is there a strong prima facie moral obligation not to withdraw these measures and not to take positive steps to terminate his life? It seems obvious that if he is on the only kidney machine and its use could *save* the life of another person, who could lead a normal life after temporary use, it would be wrong not to take him off. Is there an obligation to continue, or not to terminate, if there is no countering obligation? I would think not, with an exception to be mentioned; and this coincides with the fact that he is *beyond* injury. There is also not an obligation *not* to preserve his life, say, in order to have his organs available for use when they are needed.

There seems, however, to be another morally relevant consideration in such a case—knowledge of the patient's own wishes when he was conscious and in possession of his faculties. Suppose he had feared such an eventuality and prepared a sworn statement requesting his doctor to terminate his life at once in such circumstances. Now, if it is morally obligatory to some degree to carry out a person's wishes for disposal of his body and possessions after his death, it would seem to be equally morally obligatory to respect his wishes in case he becomes a "vegetable." In the event of the existence of such a document, I would think that if he can no longer be injured we are free to withdraw life-sustaining measures and also to take positive steps to terminate life—and are even morally bound, prima facie, to do so. (If, however, the patient had prepared a document directing that his body be preserved alive as long as possible in such circumstances, then there would be a prima facie obligation *not* to cease life-sustaining measures and not to terminate. It would seem obvious, however, that such an obligation would fall far short of giving the patient the right to continued use of a kidney machine when its use by another could save that person's life.) Some persons would not hesitate to discontinue life-sustaining procedures in such a situation, but would balk at more positive measures. But the hesitation to use more positive procedures, which veterinarians employ frequently with animals, is surely nothing but squeamishness; if a person is in the state described, there can be no injury to him in positive termination more than or less than that in allowing him to wither by withdrawing life-supportive procedures.

If I am right in my analysis of this case, we must phrase our basic principle about killing in such a way as to take into account (1) whether the killing would be an injury and (2) the person's own wishes and directives. And perhaps, more important, any moral principle about killing must be viewed simply as an implicate of more basic principles about these matters.

Let us look for corroboration of this proposal to how we feel about another type of case, one in which termination would be of positive benefit to the agent. Let us suppose that a patient has a terminal illness and is in severe pain, subject only to brief remissions, with no prospect of any event that could make his life good, either in the short or long term. It might seem that here, with the patient in severe pain, at least life-supportive measures should be discontinued, or positive termination adopted. But I do not think we would accept this inference, for in this situation the patient, let us suppose, has his preferences and is able to express them. The patient may have strong religious convictions and prefer to go on living despite the pain; if so, surely there is a prima facie moral obligation not positively to terminate his life. Even if, as seemingly in this case, the situation is one in which it would be *rational* for the agent, from the point of view of his own welfare, to direct the termination of his life,[2] it seems that if he (irrationally) does the opposite, there is a prima facie moral obligation not to terminate and some prima facie obligation to sustain it. Evidently a person's own expressed wishes have moral force. (I believe, however, that we think a person's expressed wishes have *less* moral force when we think the wishes are irrational.)

What is the effect, in this case, if the patient himself expresses a preference for termination and would, if he were given the means, terminate his own existence? Is there a prima facie obligation to sustain his life—and pain—against his will? Surely not. Or is there an obligation *not* to take positive measures to terminate his life immediately, thereby saving the patient much discomfort? Again, surely not. What possible reason could be offered to justify the claim that the answer is affirmative, beyond theological ones about God's will and our being bound to stay alive at His pleasure? The only argument I can think of is that there is some consideration of public policy, to the effect that a recognition of such moral permission might lead to abuses or to some other detriment to society in the long run. Such an argument does seem weak.

It might be questioned whether a patient's request should be honored, if made at a time when he is in pain, on the grounds that it is not rational. (The physician may be in a position to see, however, that the patient is quite right about his prospects and that his personal welfare would be maximized by termination.) It might also be questioned whether a patient's formal declaration, written earlier, requesting termination if he were ever in his present circumstances should be honored, on the grounds that at the earlier time he did not know what it would be like to be in his present situation. It would seem odd, however, if *no* circumstances are identifiable in which a patient's request for termination is deemed to have moral force, when his request *not* to terminate is thought morally weighty in the same circumstances even when this request is clearly irrational. I think we may ignore such arguments and hold that, in a situation in which it is rational for a person to choose termination of his life, his expressed wish is morally definitive and removes both the obligation to sustain life and the obligation not to terminate.

Indeed, there is a question whether or not in these circumstances a physician has not a moral obligation at least to withdraw life-supporting measures, and perhaps positively to terminate life. At least there seems to be a general moral obligation to render assistance when a person is in need, when it can be given at small cost to oneself, and when it is requested. The obligation is the stronger when one happens to be the only person in a position to receive such a request or to know about the situation. Furthermore, the physician has acquired a special obligation if there has been a long-standing personal relationship with the patient—just as a friend or relative has special obligations. But since we are discussing not the possible obligation to terminate but the obligation *not* to terminate, I shall not pursue this issue.

The patient's own expression of preference or consent, then, seems to be weighty. But suppose he is unable to express his preference; suppose that his terminal disease not only causes him great pain but has attacked his brain in such a way that he is incapable of thought and of rational speech. May the physician, then, after consultation, take matters into his own hands? We often think we know what is best for another, but we think one person should not make decisions for another. Just as we must respect the decision of a person who has decided after careful reflection that he wants to commit suicide, so we must not take the liberty of deciding to bring another's life to a close contrary to his wishes. So what may be done? Must a person suffer simply because he cannot express consent? There is evidence that can be gathered about what conclusions a person would draw if he were in a state to draw and express them. The patient's friends will have some recollection of things he has said in the past, of his values and general ethical views. Just as we can have good reason to think, for example, that he would vote Democratic if voting for president in a certain year, so we can have good reason to think he would take a certain stand about the termination of his own life in various circumstances. We can know of some persons who because of their religious views would want to keep on living until natural processes bring their lives to a close. About others we can know that they decidedly would not take this view. We can also know what would be the *rational* choice for them to make, and our knowledge of this can be *evidence* about what they would request if they were able. There are, of course, practical complications in the mechanics of a review board of some kind making a determination of this sort, but they are hardly insurmountable.

I wish to consider one other type of case, that of a person who, say, has had a stroke and is leading, and for some time can continue to lead, a life that is comfortable but one on a very low level, *and* who has antecedently requested that his life be terminated if he comes, incurably, into such a situation. May he then be terminated? In this case, unlike the others, there are probably ongoing pleasant experiences, perhaps on the level of some animals, that seem to be a good thing. One can hardly say that *injury* is being done such a person by keeping him alive; and one might say that some slight injury is being done him by terminating his existence. There is a real problem here. Can the (slight) goodness of these experiences stand against the weight of an earlier firm declaration requesting that life be terminated in a situation of hopeless senility? There is no *injury* in keeping the person alive despite his request, but there seems something *indecent* about keeping a mind alive after a severe stroke, when we know quite well that, could he have anticipated it, his own action would have been to terminate his life. I think that the person's own request should be honored; it should be if a person's expressed preferences have as much moral weight as I think they should have.

What general conclusions are warranted by the preceding discussion? I shall emphasize two. First, there is a prima facie obligation *not* to terminate a person's existence when this would injure him (except in cases of self-defense or of senility of a person whose known wish is to be terminated in such a condition) *or* if he wishes not to be terminated. Second, there is *not* a prima facie obligation not to terminate when there would be *no* injury, or when there would be a positive benefit (release from pain) in so doing, provided the patient has not declared himself otherwise or there is evidence that his wishes are to that effect. Obviously there are two things that are decisive for the morality of terminating a person's life: whether so doing would be an *injury* and whether it conforms to what is known of his *preferences.*

I remarked at the outset that I would be content with some moral principles if it could be made out that rational persons would want those principles incorporated in the consciences of a group among whom they were to live. It is obvious why rational persons would want these principles. They would want injury avoided both because they would not wish others to injure them and because, if they are benevolent, they would not wish others injured. Moreover, they would want weight given to a person's own known preferences. Rational people do want the decision about the termination of their lives, where that is possible; for they would be uncomfortable if they thought it possible that others would be free to terminate their lives without consent. The threat of serious illness is bad enough without that prospect. On the other hand, this discomfort would be removed if they knew that termination would not be undertaken on their behalf without their explicit consent, except after a careful inquiry had been made, both into whether termination would constitute an injury and whether they would request termination under the circumstances if they were in a position to do so.

If I am right in all this, then it appears that killing a person is not something that is just prima facie wrong *in itself*; it is wrong roughly only if and because it is an *injury* of someone, or if and because it is contrary to the *known preferences* of someone. It would seem that a principle about the prima facie wrongness of killing is *derivative* from principles about when we are prima facie obligated not to injure and when we are prima facie obligated to respect a person's wishes, at least about what happens to his own body. I do not, however, have any suggestions for a general statement of principles of this latter sort.

NOTES

1. See my "The Morality of Abortion" in *The Monist,* 56 (1972), pp. 503–26; and, in revised form, in *Abortion: Pro and Con,* ed. R. L. Perkins (General Learning Press, 1975).
2. See my "The Morality and Rationality of Suicide," in James Rachels, ed., *Moral Problems* (Harper & Row, 1975); and, in revised form, in E. S. Shneidman, ed., *Suicidology: Current Developments* (Grune & Stratton, 1976).

QUESTIONS FOR ANALYSIS

1. Under what conditions, according to Brandt, can one person be said to injure another?
2. Give an example of killing that causes injury and of killing that doesn't.
3. How do we determine what a comatose person's wishes are if the person has left no directions about terminating his or her life?
4. According to Brandt, under what conditions are we *prima facie* obligated not to terminate a person's existence? Under what conditions is there no at such *prima facie* obligation?
5. Explain the significance (with respect to mercy deaths) of Brandt's deriving a principle about the *prima facie* wrongness of killing from principles about when we are *prima facie* obligated not to injure and when we are *prima facie* obligated to respect a person's wishes.
6. Would you say that Brandt's analysis is consistent or inconsistent with a Kantian view of the morality of euthanasia? (To answer this question, you of course should first try to apply Kant's ethics to the problem of euthanasia. Under what conditions, if ever, do you think Kant would approve of a mercy death?)

CASE PRESENTATION

"I Did It Because I Loved My Son"

In early May 1989, Rudolfo Linares visited his son Samuel in a Chicago hospital, where the fifteen-month-old boy, partially brain dead, lay connected to a respirator. Samuel's coma had begun nine months earlier, when he'd suffocated after swallowing an uninflated balloon at a birthday party.

Along with his wife, Tamara, Rudolfo had been pleading with hospital officials to disconnect the respirator, but always to no avail. Once, in December, he disconnected it himself, but security officers reconnected it. After that, he decided to hire a lawyer to challenge the hospital in court.

Apparently, Rudolfo was growing impatient with the legal process. On this visit to the hospital, he brought a hand gun, which he used to hold off nurses, doctors, and police officers as he disconnected the respirator and held his son in his arms. Crying all the while, he sat with his son for a full forty minutes, long after hospital instruments showed that he was dead.

"I did it because I loved my son," he said.

Prosecutors immediately charged Linares with first-degree murder, but following a storm of national publicity, charges were dropped.

QUESTIONS FOR ANALYSIS

1. Who should decide whether to "pull the plug" in cases like this one: the parents, the attending physician, a hospital committee, or the courts?
2. In its *Cruzan* decision, the U.S. Supreme Court ruled that states can forbid family members to refuse treatment of an incompetent patient without clear evidence that the patient, if competent, would refuse it. Should its ruling apply to patients who, like Samuel, never were competent?
3. Suppose the patient in this case had been an adult who had never expressed an opinion about refusing or accepting treatment in such circumstances. Would his family have the moral right to refuse treatment for him?
4. If hospital officials refuse to stop treatment, do family members have the moral right to take matters into their own hands, as Rudolfo Linares did?

CASE PRESENTATION

"A Choice Central to Personal Dignity"

It was the first time a law banning assisted suicide had come before a federal judge. The setting was the U.S. District Court in Seattle. The federal judge was Judge Barbara Rothstein. Three terminally ill patients seeking assistance in ending their lives, along with five doctors and an organization named Compassion in Dying, were challenging a Washington State law that forbade them to do so. Judge Rothstein's decision came May 3, 1994: The Washington law, which had been on the books for 140 years, was unconstitutional.

As noteworthy as the ruling itself was the reasoning behind it. In declaring the law in violation of the Fourteenth Amendment, Judge Rothstein cited the Supreme Court's *Planned Parenthood v. Casey* decision, which upheld a woman's right to abortion. "Like the abortion decision," she wrote, "the decision of a terminally ill patient to end his or her life 'involves the most intimate and personal choice a person can make in a lifetime,' and constitutes a 'choice central to personal dignity and autonomy.'" Drawing on these similarities, she concluded that "The suffering of a terminally ill person cannot be deemed . . . any less deserving of protection from unwarranted governmental interference than that of a pregnant woman."

For one of the patients, a cancer victim who had already died, the ruling came too late. The other two were now free to seek help. And Compassion in Dying, which for two years had been referring terminally ill patients to doctors for prescription drugs they could take to end their lives, was now free to act more openly. In a front-page story two days after the ruling, *The New York Times* quoted Ralph Mero, the group's director and a Unitarian minister, as follows: "Today, every time I pick up the phone, there are three more people on voice mail asking for help." The report also quoted a statement by the Roman Catholic Bishops of Washington, who said of the ruling, "It undermines the moral integrity of the medical profession, whose duty is to heal and comfort, not kill. And it tramples on our conviction that life, no matter how feeble or impaired, is a sacred gift from God."

The state appealed the decision, and three years later, in *Washington v. Glucksberg,* the U.S. Supreme Court ruled the law constitutional. The Supreme Court reached this conclusion by rejecting the claim that committing suicide was a fundamental liberty interest. It noted that the state of Washington had an "unqualified interest in the preservation of life" and also an interest in "the integrity and ethics of the medical profession." The Court was also concerned about undue coercion of vulnerable groups, especially the poor, elderly, and disabled. It also expressed concern about starting down the slippery slope from assisted suicide to voluntary and even involuntary euthanasia. The Court did, however, state that the debate about assisted suicide could continue, as it was then continuing in Oregon and elsewhere. Although the Court did not find a right to assisted suicide, neither did it say anything that would prohibit a state from passing its own laws to permit assisted suicide. To date, however, Oregon is the only state that has.

QUESTIONS FOR ANALYSIS

1. Do you agree with Judge Rothstein's analogy between the decision of a pregnant woman to abort and a terminally ill patient to take his or her own life?
2. In their statement, the bishops claimed that a physician's duty is "to heal and comfort, not kill." When healing is impossible, what kind of comfort does the patient deserve? Does it include prescribing lethal drugs when asked?
3. The American Medical Association reaffirmed in 2005 its policy that "physician-assisted suicide is fundamentally inconsistent with the physician's professional role." This policy, which has been praised by the National Right to Life Committee, is consistent with the concern expressed by the Supreme Court that finding a right of assisted suicide might challenge the integrity of the medical profession. The AMA urges physicians to focus on more effective treatment of pain and hospice care "to alleviate the physical and emotional suffering that dying patients experience." Is this recommendation sufficient to address the concerns of the patients bringing this case? Should patients have a right of autonomy to make the decision of assisted suicide, so long as they can obtain the services of a willing physician?
4. To address the slippery slope concern, why could not the Supreme Court simply have insisted on "clear and convincing evidence" of the patient's intent, as it did in the *Cruzan* case in 1990? If that standard was sufficient for voluntary euthanasia, why isn't it sufficient for assisted suicide? Is a patient in extreme pain at the end of life capable of giving meaningful consent to assisted suicide?

CASE PRESENTATION

Legalized Assisted Suicide and Decriminalized Euthanasia

Fewer than three years after the U.S. Supreme Court provided a constitutional basis for voluntary passive euthanasia, one European country took a much bolder step. By a vote of 91 to 45, the parliament of the Netherlands decriminalized active euthanasia and doctor-assisted suicide under a set of strict conditions. As reported by the Associated Press, these conditions are:

Voluntary Nature. The request for euthanasia must be made "entirely of the patient's own free will" and not under pressure from others.

Weighing Alternatives. The patient must be well informed and must be able to consider the alternatives.

Certain Decision. The patient must have a "lasting longing for death." Requests made on impulse or based on a temporary depression cannot be considered.

Unacceptable Suffering. "The patient must experience his or her suffering as perpetual, unbearable and hopeless." The physician must be reasonably able to conclude that the suffering experienced is unbearable.

Consultation. The doctor must consult at least one colleague who has faced the question of euthanasia before.

Reporting. A documented written report must be drawn up stating the history of the patient's illness and declaring that the rules have been met.

The vote followed what *The New York Times* called "two decades of tormented national debate." It also followed a significant increase in doctor-reported cases of active euthanasia and assisted suicide from 1990 to 1992. According to the *Times,* Dutch legal and medical experts attributed the increase to "more open discussion of the issue and a clearer agreement on the rules that protect doctors from prosecution."

Soon after the measure passed, many observers expected the Dutch parliament to go even further by legalizing active euthanasia and assisted suicide by physicians, and in 2000, that's exactly what the parliament did. The significance of that step is twofold. First, it means that Dutch physicians who help their patients die are no longer technically committing a crime.

Second, these physicians are no longer accountable to a prosecutor but to a panel of medical, legal, and ethical experts.

In 1994, as we have seen, voters in Oregon took a similar step when they passed a ballot initiative legalizing doctor-assisted suicide. That measure too contains restrictions. Among the most important are these: (1) the means of assistance are limited to a prescription for a lethal dose of medication to be taken orally; (2) two doctors must determine that the patient has six months or less to live; (3) the patient must be of sound mind; (4) the patient's request must be made in writing; (5) the prescription must be written no less than fifteen days after the request; (6) the patient, not the doctor, must administer the pills.

QUESTIONS FOR ANALYSIS

1. The Dutch rules are obviously intended to prevent abuses. Are they sufficiently strict and clear? Do any of the rules seem too vague? Do any need to be made more precise?
2. As reported by the *Times*, a Dutch study found that in 1992 doctors ended the lives of a thousand patients "without an explicit recent request." In most cases, the *Times* reported, "the patient had only days or hours to live, was often in great pain, and was either in a coma or not fully conscious. In more than half the cases the patient had either talked about euthanasia to the doctor or others." Do these findings support J. Gay-Williams's contention that active euthanasia is a slippery slope? Will the new Dutch rules prevent such sliding in the future?
3. Nowhere do the rules say that a patient must be suffering from a terminal illness or that death must be near. Should either condition be added?
4. After the vote, one pro-life Dutch physician declared, "Today the Netherlands abolished the Hippocratic Oath." Do you agree?
5. In many areas of moral controversy—for instance, drugs and prostitution—the Netherlands has pursued a more liberal social policy than the United States. Do you think the Dutch rules for euthanasia and assisted suicide are appropriate for the United States?
6. One forceful opponent of the Oregon measure is the American Medical Association, which argues that doctors cannot reliably determine that a patient has six months or less to live. Is this a serious flaw in the law?
7. The Oregon requirement that the patient, not the doctor, administer the pills is meant to ensure that the patient's death results from suicide, not euthanasia. Is this distinction morally significant?

CASE PRESENTATION

Terri Schiavo: Voluntary Euthanasia or Murder?

On February 25, 1990, a few months before the U.S. Supreme Court announced its decision in the Nancy Cruzan case, a Florida woman named Teresa Shiavo suffered cardiac arrest and never regained consciousness. She required constant care in nursing homes and received food and hydration through tubes. In 1998 her husband Michael petitioned a Florida court to authorize termination of the life support procedures, a petition opposed by Shiavo's parents.

After a trial in 2000, the court determined by clear and convincing evidence, the standard set in the *Cruzan* decision, that she would choose to cease life-prolonging procedures if she were competent to make that decision. The court also concluded that she was in a "persistent vegetative state" with no chance of recovery, the same condition that other courts had found for Nancy Cruzan and Karen Quinlan. The parents in the Cruzan and Quinlan cases had petitioned to remove life support; in the Schiavo case, the parents opposed this removal. But otherwise, the Schiavo case was remarkably like the Cruzan case in its legal reasoning and in the physical condition of the patient. The involvement in this case of the Florida legislature and then of the U.S. Congress and the president turned the Schiavo case into a *cause célèbre* in the public eye.

The feeding tube was removed for the first time on April 24, 2001, but after another court challenge from the parents, it was reinserted two days later. After numerous court fights, it was removed a second time on October 15, 2003. Six days later, the Florida legislature passed legislation authorizing the governor to issue an executive order to reinsert the feeding tube, which was done immediately.

In 2004, the Supreme Court of Florida struck down this Florida legislation as an unconstitutional violation of the separation of powers that recognizes three branches of government—the executive, the legislative, and the judicial. The legislation, the Court said, improperly reversed a final judgment of the Florida court, and the executive order improperly delegated legislative authority to the governor. After more legal challenges from the parents, the feeding tube was removed a third time on March 18, 2005.

Three Republican members of Congress, Senate Majority Leader Bill Frist, Senator Rick Santorum, and House Majority Leader Tom Delay, then issued congressional subpoenas to both Michael and Terri Schiavo demanding that they testify before Congress, a move to force reinsertion of the feeding tube, but a Florida judge refused to let the subpoenas interfere with the Florida order.

On March 20, 2005, which was Palm Sunday, the Senate (with only three members present) passed a bill that transferred jurisdiction over the Schiavo case to the federal courts, in an attempt to remove it from the Florida courts that had ordered removal of the feeding tube. The House of Representatives passed the bill at 12:41 a.m. on March 21. President Bush signed the bill at 1:11 a.m., after flying on Air Force One to Washington from his home in Crawford, Texas, specifically to sign the bill. He issued a statement saying, "I will continue to stand on the side of those defending life for all Americans, including those with disabilities."

Although this federal law gave the federal courts authority to review the case again, all declined to hear it, including the U.S. Supreme Court. After a last-minute flurry of legal attempts to take custody of Schiavo from the hospice, she died on March 31, 2005.

Numerous public opinion polls were taken after these events. They tended to show that solid majorities (well over 50 percent), believed it was proper to have the tube removed and that even more (ranging from 70 to 80 percent in most polls) thought it had been inappropriate for Congress to intervene in this case.

QUESTIONS FOR ANALYSIS

1. Terri Schiavo had no living will to indicate her preferences for treatment. The Florida courts consistently accepted the testimony of several witnesses, including her husband, that she had made statements before the incident indicating that she would not want to be kept alive in such a condition. The parents claimed that, as a devout Roman Catholic, she would not want to violate the Church's teachings on euthanasia by refusing nutrition and hydration. Do you find this evidence satisfactory for making such an important decision? Have you made statements to friends that might be used as evidence if you were to be in Schiavo's condition? Have you prepared a living will to make your preferences clear?
2. The cost of flying Air Force One to Washington is estimated at $34,000 an hour. Critics complained that President Bush could have had someone fly the bill to him in Texas for signing, but his communications director at the time said that the president was concerned that a delay of even a few hours might endanger Schiavo's life. Was this an appropriate use of the taxpayer's money? Were the actions of the Congress and the president consistent with other stated goals of restricting the role of the federal judiciary, respecting states' rights, and promoting the sanctity of marriage? Were they justifiable as a way to send a strong public message of opposition to euthanasia to the American public? Should the Congress pass a law making voluntary-euthanasia a crime when it involves patients in the condition of Schiavo or Cruzan, perhaps by requiring a legally valid living will before feeding tubes or respirators could be removed?
3. Public supporters of Schiavo's parents said they (the supporters) were opposing euthanasia because they supported a "culture of life." Is this opposition to euthanasia consistent with support for capital punishment?

4. Was Schiavo's death an active or a passive euthanasia? Was the removal of the feeding tube an "act" that makes this euthanasia active? Was being allowed to starve and dehydrate to death passive? If Schiavo's husband had refused to give consent to insert the feeding tube the night of her injury, would that have been considered active or passive euthanasia? Once the decision was made to remove the feeding tube, would it have been more humane to simply give Schiavo a lethal injection, rather than lingering for almost two weeks as she starved to death? What might James Rachels have said about this alternative?

CHAPTER SIX

Human Cloning and Stem Cell Research

- **How Cloning Works: A Brief History**
- **Why Clone Humans?**
- **Moral and Legal Issues**
- **Stem Cell Research**
- **Arguments against Human Cloning**
- **Arguments for Human Cloning**

THE 1990S BROUGHT a number of astonishing technological developments, many of them highly controversial. Perhaps the most controversial came from the field of biotechnology, and among them, none created more controversy than the birth of a lamb named Dolly. By all outward appearances a perfectly ordinary lamb, she was the product of the first successful cloning of an adult mammal. Ian Wilmut, who headed the team of Scottish scientists that produced her, announced the feat in 1997, and a staple of fiction suddenly loomed as an imminent reality: the successful cloning of an adult human being.

Not surprisingly, people began talking in earnest about the dangers and promises this startling development raised, whether—as in the book and movie versions of *The Boys from Brazil*—it was the mass production of Hitler clones in a fanatical attempt to resurrect the Third Reich or maybe a U.S. Olympic basketball team composed entirely of Michael Jordan clones. And in the face of such possibilities came a raft of questions: Should the technology be made available when scientists are able to extend it to human beings? If so, to whom? And what kinds of legal restrictions, if any, should we place on its availability? More generally, is there something fundamentally immoral and frightening about human cloning, or is it—like sperm donorship, in vitro fertilization, or surrogate motherhood—a benign form of reproductive technology that individuals have a moral and legal right to use?

A number of national governments took the lead in this discussion. In the United States, for example, President Bill Clinton placed an immediate ban on all federal funding for attempts to clone humans. He also asked the National Bioethics Advisory Commission (NBAC) to issue a report within ninety days on the legal and ethical issues that surround human cloning. The resulting document, citing both safety concerns and moral concerns, called for a continuation of the president's ban. It also called on Congress to pass legislation banning all attempts to clone human beings, whether in clinical settings or research settings. The proposed legislation should, the report added, contain a "sunset clause," which would cause the ban to expire within three to five years; at some time before that point, the status of cloning technology and the ethical and social issues involved should be reevaluated.

President George W. Bush has repeatedly called for a complete ban on cloning, saying, "We must not create life to destroy life. Human beings are not research material to be used in a cruel and reckless experiment." Although the House of Representatives passed the Human Cloning Prohibition Act several years ago, it was never adopted in the Senate. The Human Cloning Ban and Stem Cell Research Protection Act of 2005 was introduced in both the House and the Senate, and it passed in July 2006, after a long delay in Senate passage. On July 19, 2006, President Bush vetoed it because of his objections to stem cell research, and Congress did not have the two-thirds vote necessary to override the veto.

Because of the safety concerns, many have supported the proposed bans, even if they did not have ethical qualms about cloning for purposes of medical research. But many of those safety concerns are being overcome. In fact, as we'll see in the next section, one of the most serious safety problems has already been overcome. The moral concerns, however, which are the subject of this chapter, will no doubt continue long after. Stem cell research involves a different set of procedures and issues, but some of the moral and legal questions are shared with human cloning. When do we become "persons" with moral rights? How can we define our personal identities in this new world of scientific technology?

HOW CLONING WORKS: A BRIEF HISTORY

A **clone** is an exact genetic copy of a molecule, cell, plant, or animal.[1] Though the term is a relatively recent one, the phenomenon itself is as old as the simplest forms of life; whenever single-celled organisms like bacteria reproduce by cell division, the resultant cells are natural clones of the originals. In the laboratory, the cloning of molecules and cells has been a routine part of molecular biology for decades, as when scientists regularly clone DNA fragments in recombinant DNA technology (popularly known as "genetic engineering"). Outside the laboratory, the cloning

[1]This definition and much of what follows in this section are adapted from the second chapter of the NBAC report, *Cloning Human Beings,* U.S. Government, Washington, D.C, 1997.

of plants—a more complex form of cloning—has been a commonplace in ordinary households for a much longer time; whenever we take a cutting of a plant, place it in water, and grow a complete new plant from it, we produce a clone of the original plant.

Animal cloning too has been around a long time. At one end of the animal kingdom—with such invertebrates as worms, for example—an organism can be divided into two parts, and each will regenerate itself into a full genetic duplicate of the original. At the other end, we have the phenomenon of identical human twins, the result of separated embryos in the womb. In both cases, we have examples of natural animal cloning.

In the laboratory, scientists have been successfully cloning animals since the early 1980s, using a technique known as *nuclear transplantation cloning*. In its earliest form, this technique involved removing the nucleus from an unfertilized egg and replacing it with the nucleus of a somatic cell from an embryo. (A **somatic cell** is any cell other than a sperm or an egg, both of which are known as **germ cells.**) The product of the transplant, an embryo, is then implanted into a female for normal gestation.

The significance of Dolly is that the somatic cell used in the transplant came from an adult animal rather than from an embryo. And what makes that difference so important is this: As cells develop and divide after fertilization, they *differentiate* into specific tissues—muscle and bone, for example. That's why embryo cells were used in the earlier cases of cloning—because they had not yet differentiated. Mature cells, on the other hand, are cells that have differentiated, and before Dolly came along, scientists didn't know if the genes of these cells could be reprogrammed to an undifferentiated state. Previous attempts had provided discouraging results. In one series of experiments, in which the nuclei of adult frog skin cells replaced the nuclei of frog eggs, only 4 percent of the embryos resulted in tadpoles, and none of the tadpoles developed into an adult frog. In another series, using cells from adult mice, no successes occurred. With the successful cloning of Dolly, however, it seemed that mature cells could indeed be reprogrammed.

Even so, some doubts remained. The lingering uncertainty centered on the source of the cells that Wilmut's team had used for the transplant: the udder of a six-year-old female sheep in the late stages of pregnancy. Breasts of pregnant mammals grow much larger in the late stages of pregnancy, and a cell taken from one may be quite unusual in a relevant way. As the scientist Stephen J. Gould put it:

> some mammary cells, though technically adult, may remain unusually labile or even 'embryo-like' and thus able to proliferate rapidly to produce new breast tissue at an appropriate stage of pregnancy. Consequently, we may only be able to clone only from unusual adult cells with effectively embryonic potential and not from any stray cheek cell, hair follicle, or drop of blood that happens to fall in the clutches of a mad Xeroxer.[2]

This uncertainty was resolved almost three years later, when scientists at the University of Connecticut at Storrs and the Prefectural Cattle Breeding Development Institute in Japan announced that they had cloned four calves from cells scraped

---

[2]"Dolly's Fashion and Louis's Passion," *Natural History* vol. 106, no. 5 (June 1997): p. 21.

from the ear of a bull—cells without, to use Gould's term, "effectively embryonic potential." This development was significant for another reason as well: the number of successful clones. (Dolly had been a single success among a large number of failures. Of 277 fusions between cell and egg, only twenty-nine became embryos; of those twenty-nine, which Wilmut's team implanted into ewes, only the embryo that produced Dolly resulted in a pregnancy.) Adding to these advances, the same team announced weeks later that it had successfully cloned one of the original clones.

The next major step in animal cloning came in April 2000, when a serious obstacle, particularly important for the prospect of human cloning, was overcome. That obstacle first came to light after an examination of Dolly's chromosomes. The tips of her chromosomes, called *telomeres,* were shorter than those of a sheep produced by sexual reproduction. What was troubling about the finding is that telomeres grow shorter each time a cell divides. So the younger the animal in normal cases, the longer the telomeres; the older the animal, the shorter the telomeres. The implication, then, was that Dolly would not live as long as a sheep conceived through sexual reproduction. And the resulting implication for the ethics of human cloning was obvious. Clearly, most people thought, it would be immoral to produce a human being in that way if he or she could not live a normal human life span. But then scientists at a Massachusetts company called Advanced Cell Technology, who had produced six cloned calves, announced that the telomeres of all the clones were not shorter than normal. To the team's surprise, they were actually longer than normal, suggesting that the calves would have an unusually long life span. So one of the most prominent of the safety issues seems no longer a problem. Others, however, remain, including the dangers of genetic mutation to the clone and other biological damage.

WHY CLONE HUMANS?

Although modern cloning technology is still too young to ensure the safe cloning of humans, many researchers think that eventually it can and will be done. When scientists have the technology to accomplish something, the common line of reasoning goes, they will use it. Besides, even if most scientists oppose its use—and even if its use is outlawed in most corners of the world—all it takes is one millionaire persistent enough to find one scientist willing to clone him. But before we discuss whether scientists ought to use this technology, we should first discuss why anyone would want to.

Some reasons have nothing to do with the aim of producing a fully developed human being. For instance, many scientists (including those at Advanced Cell Technology) see great hope in using cloning to create replacement tissue—spare parts, you might say—for humans. This is not, as some have feared, a matter of keeping a mindless clone in a closet to be "harvested" for parts when needed but of producing an embryo that can be used to generate an organ for transplant. Being an exact genetic match with the host, the organ would not be rejected. For another example, cloning not aimed at producing a fully developed human being would almost certainly bring great gains in scientific knowledge—concerning cell division, say, or genetic differentiation.

But why use cloning for human reproduction? The most obvious reasons concern couples in which one or both partners are infertile. For at least some of them, cloning might be a welcome reproductive technology, a new technique for producing genetic offspring. Similarly, there are cases in which sexual reproduction carries the risk of passing on an inheritable disease, most commonly when both parties carry the same regressive gene for the disease. Also, many homosexuals see cloning as an opportunity for homosexual couples to have children. True, in all these cases, the couples have other options—adoption or sperm donorship, for example—but they may also want their children to be genetically related to at least one of them without having to introduce the genes of some unwanted third party.

Another reason is suggested by the case of Abe and Mary Ayala, a California couple who conceived a child in 1989—seventeen years after the birth of their second and presumed last child—in the hope of providing a compatible bone marrow donor for their leukemia-stricken daughter. Although the child did prove to be a compatible donor, they had no guarantee of success. With the availability of cloning, parents in similar situations could be certain of success, since the clone would be an exact genetic match of the recipient. Then there are those couples who have lost a child in a car accident, say, and want their next child to be as much like the first as possible—a later identical twin of the lost child—or couples who may want a later identical twin of someone else dear to them, such as a parent, a grandparent, or a sibling.

Still other reasons have been given for wanting to clone human beings, some more or less fanciful than others. We may want to pass on specific traits of specific people with the hope of producing another Jordan, Mozart, Gandhi, or Martin Luther King. Or vanity may be a factor in the case of people who want to see a world inhabited by genetic copies of themselves. In other cases, the motivation may be curiosity. How, some may wonder, would they (or some other individual) have turned out if born and reared in another time and environment? Pushing this kind of reasoning even further, we can imagine scientists who specialize in twin research wanting to create clones as subjects in controlled experiments.

MORAL AND LEGAL ISSUES

No doubt many of you find yourselves uncomfortable with at least some of these possibilities, maybe even repulsed by them. And in some cases, the discomfort is fully justified. Consider the last possibility we mentioned, creating clones for experimentation. Given that human clones would have claim to all the rights of any other human being, it would clearly be immoral to experiment on them without their consent. But what about the moral status of human cloning itself?

Perhaps the most important question to ask here is whether people have the moral and legal right to reproduce by any safe means available, including cloning, which may be considered a form of asexual reproduction. Do we have a fundamental right to choose whether and how to reproduce? Notwithstanding the importance of this question, how we answer it will not settle the matter by itself. Even our most fundamental rights are not absolute. Some other factor may override them. That's why we have libel laws, for example, which limit our fundamental right to free expression. Furthermore, someone might grant that we do have a fundamental right to reproduce but deny that cloning is a form of reproduction. Many critics of human cloning say just that. To them, cloning is better described as replication or manufacturing, and they insist that we do not have a right to manufacture human beings.

What if we decide that reproduction is not a fundamental right? We might still say that our general right to freedom allows us the right to take advantage of human cloning. After all, we claim all sorts of rights that are not fundamental as long as there's no rational basis for restricting them. For example, no one would claim a fundamental right to wear socks of a particular color, but what rational basis could there be for banning brown, blue, or white socks?

Other moral issues concern the possible psychological effects of human cloning. Various commentators have wondered how the later twin will feel about his or her worth and future. Will clones feel that their right to their own identity has been infringed upon? Will they feel that their futures are foreclosed, that the limitations they see in their earlier twins, whether physical or mental, unfairly narrow their own choices in life? Will they wonder if they are loved for themselves instead of being valued as a copy of someone else, that they are merely replacements for the previous twins who were really loved? And at least in the earliest cases of human clones, will they feel like freaks?

These questions concern the psychological effects on the later twins. Other questions concern the effects on humanity as a whole. How will the availability of cloning affect humankind's understanding of itself? Will we come to see people as fundamentally different once we know they can be manufactured as well as sexually conceived? Will our view of the role that sex plays in our lives fundamentally change? Will we no longer view individual humans as unique and irreplaceable?

Beyond all that, there are more practical concerns. If, for example, cloning becomes prevalent, what will that do to the genetic diversity of the human species? Or for another example, what if scientists make multiple clones of a great artist, scientist, or moral or political leader? Do we really want some "mad Xeroxer" to produce a run of thirty or more Mozarts, Einsteins, or Kings? Or to return to the fears raised by *The Boys from Brazil*, a run of thirty or more Hitlers?

Another practical issue concerns family relationships. If a woman bears her husband's clone, is he the father to the son she bears, his twin brother, or is he both? And is she both the mother of her child and his sister-in-law? Or suppose instead that she bears her own clone. Is she both mother and twin sister to the child? Then there are cases in which the cell donor is a third party—a relative, say, or some unrelated genius. As an earlier twin, would he or she be the clone's sibling? Related to these questions are questions of legal rights and responsibilities. If the donor is a third party, what responsibilities does he have for his later twin? And what rightful claims does the clone have against his earlier twin?

These last questions raise another concern about human cloning. Once cloning is made available, it will be easy to clone humans without their consent. All it will take is one stray cell, easily obtainable without the person's knowledge or consent. Many of us, presumably, will not want to be cloned. Do we have the right not to be? And if so, how can the right be enforced?

Still other moral issues are familiar from debates surrounding other topics in this book. Just as critics of homosexuality argue that homosexual behavior is immoral because it's unnatural, many opponents of human cloning claim the same about it. Unlike other forms of reproductive technology, such as in vitro fertilization, cloning takes us out of the realm of sex altogether, and that difference, opponents say, presents a fundamental break with natural reproduction. Two other issues arise from the abortion debates. To those who feel that a human embryo is a person, a morally significant being with the right to life, creating a human embryo for scientific research or the generation of organs for transplant is every bit as wrong as abortion. In both cases, they say, a human life is being destroyed. Cloning proponents, on the other hand, argue that the constitutional right to privacy comes into play here. Just as a woman's right to privacy guarantees her right to terminate a pregnancy, so does it guarantee her the right to reproduce by cloning.

STEM CELL RESEARCH

Many have heard of stem cell research because of the highly visible lobbying efforts by such people as the late Christopher Reeve, who had been paralyzed in a riding accident; Michael J. Fox, the film and television star fighting Parkinson's disease; Nancy Reagan, wife of the late President Reagan who died of Alzheimer's; and Mary Tyler Moore, the film and television star who has shared with the public her struggle with diabetes. Public opinion polls in 2006 generally showed that about two-thirds of Americans support stem cell research, as well as federal funding of that research.

The ethical issues presented by stem cell research overlap the debate over cloning, as well as other biomedical issues, especially abortion. But the issues are sufficiently distinct that many people (such as Senator Orrin Hatch, a conservative Republican from Utah) believe they can consistently oppose cloning and abortion while supporting embryonic stem cell research.

Unfortunately, these issues are sometimes blurred in the public debate, and the confusion was exacerbated by a scandal involving a leading South Korean scientist, Hwang Woo-suk, who had been hailed as a pioneer of cloning. In 2004, he announced what he claimed were breakthroughs in creating stem cells for research by cloning human embryos. A year later, he claimed that he had made stem cell lines suitable for biomedical research from the skin cells of eleven people. In December 2005, however, a whistleblower at his lab claimed that the research had been faked, a conclusion later confirmed by a panel of distinguished academic researchers. In March 2006, Hwang was fired from his university, and several researchers on his team received various punishments, including suspension and pay cuts. In May 2006, Hwang was charged by the South Korean government with fraud, embezzlement, and bioethics violations. Supporters of stem cell research have responded by emphasizing the importance of ethical guidelines and effective peer oversight of this type of research in the future.

Two types of stem cell research are at issue in the United States. Research using adult stem cells is widely supported, but the promise of this approach is highly debatable. The White House press office has stated that "a variety of therapeutic treatments for diseases" has been developed from adult stem cells, but this claim is widely disputed. The National Institutes of Health reports that adult stem cells in blood have been used successfully in bone marrow transplants. While embryonic stem cells can differentiate into an almost unlimited range of organs, the adult stem cells are limited to the type of organ or tissue in which they originated, which significantly limits their potential.

Embryonic stem cell research thus seems to have greater potential for finding cures for debilitating diseases, but it also raises important ethical issues. The proposal under most serious consideration would use only the 400,000 embryos that have been created during in vitro fertilization (IVF), which would otherwise be discarded anyway. Strict ethical guidelines would prohibit payment to anyone for providing these embryos, and permission would be required from the persons providing the genetic material that had created the embryos. Specifically, the only ones used would be blastocysts, which are fertilized human eggs from the second day through the second week. (See "Biological Background" in the unit on abortion for more information about these stages.) Although these blastocysts theoretically could be implanted in a woman and produce a living child, fewer than 200 such children have been produced this way. Furthermore, many blastocysts deteriorate during the freezing process and could never be used in this manner.

Critics of this type of stem cell research believe that the blatocyst is a person from the moment of conception, even in the IVF procedure and even though it has never been implanted in a womb where it might develop. Thus, these critics argue, embryonic stem cell research amounts to murder, at least to the strongest opponents. Supporters note that these blastocysts are going to be discarded anyway and would be better used to support medical research that might result in cures for the living who suffer from debilitating conditions, from spinal cord injury to Parkinson's. If critics truly believe this research is immoral, supporters ask, why don't they take steps to make IVF procedures illegal, so as to stop the destruction of hundreds of thousands of blastocysts that are routinely discarded by these fertility clinics? As recently as June 2006, the Vatican reaffirmed its opposition to all IVF (along with its opposition to contraception, abortion, and same-sex marriage), but opponents of embryonic stem cell research in the U.S. Congress have not proposed any such ban on IVF procedures.

Another dimension to this debate is whether federal funding is appropriate. Critics say that their tax dollars should not be used to support a practice they find immoral. If this is a sufficient reason to prohibit all federal funding, supporters say, then is it acceptable to use federal funds to carry out the death penalty when a substantial portion of the American public believes to be it immoral? In this system of government, majority rules in the expenditure of funds, even if many taxpayers find certain expenditures immoral.

As of 2006, five state governments (California, Connecticut, Illinois, Maryland, and New Jersey) had adopted plans to use state funds to support stem cell research. Supporters of this research point out, however, that substantial federal funding is necessary to explore the potential of this type of research effectively. Supporters also express concern that the leading scientists in this area might migrate to countries in Europe and Asia that *are* funding this research, resulting in a serious scientific "brain drain" in this country and loss of the technological potential if and when treatments for disease are found.

ARGUMENTS AGAINST HUMAN CLONING

1. ***Cloning is unfair to the clone.***

POINT: "Imagine what it would be like to be a clone, especially if the person you were cloned from were still alive. Your whole life would be laid out before you. You'd be able to see yourself as an adult, what you'll look like, what you'll be capable of doing and won't be capable of doing, the aches and pains and diseases you'll suffer from, the personality quirks you and others will have to put up with. And you'd know you could never grow up to be all sorts of things you might want to be because you'd see that the person you were cloned from is not capable of any of them. And that's just not fair to the clone. Every human being has a right to an open future."

COUNTERPOINT: "Sorry, but I don't see any unfairness here. First of all, we'd be two different people, just as identical twins are two different people. Genetic makeup isn't everything, you know. How we age, what abilities we have, our health and our personalities depend as much on our environment and choices as they do on our genes. Second, if there are some biological limits on what I can be and do in life, then I might as well know about them in advance. Self-knowledge is good, right? Then why not have it as soon as I can?"

2. ***Cloning is dangerous.***

POINT: "But what about the dangers of cloning? If there were ever something open to the worst kinds of abuse, this is it. Think about some mad scientist intent on producing an army of clones of some ruthless killer or some other mad scientist producing a bunch of human research subjects. And think about all the people who'd be tempted to clone themselves for all the wrong reasons—out of vanity, maybe, or the desire for spare parts. And even without the abuses, there's a host of other dangers. Most important, the more popular cloning becomes, the more we'll have clones of clones of clones of clones, and once that happens, the human race will lose much of its genetic diversity. We'll be like those interbred strains of lab mice used for medical experiments."

COUNTERPOINT: "You can make up horror stories about any new technology, but that doesn't mean they'll come true. And as for people cloning themselves for the wrong reasons, so what? People have children the old-fashioned way for all sorts of reasons, many of them selfish, and nobody's trying to put an end to that. And you can't really believe cloning will come even close to driving out the old-fashioned way of making babies. People *like* the old-fashioned way. I can't imagine them giving it up. Cloning will be like all the other forms of reproductive technology—there for people who need it, but not a replacement for normal sexual reproduction."

3. ***Cloning is repugnant.***

POINT: "Doesn't the idea of human cloning make you even just a little bit sick? It should, because it's repugnant, unnatural, disgusting. What we're talking about here is children with only one biological parent, children being the genetic twins of one of their parents or maybe even some stranger, children created not by a sperm and an egg but by a cheek cell nucleus and an egg. That's just not the way things ought to be."

COUNTERPOINT: "Maybe you find it repugnant, but I don't. A clone is nothing but a later identical twin, and there's nothing repugnant about it. Besides, your repugnance is morally irrelevant in any case. Personally, I find a lot of things repugnant—certain kinds of movies and music, for example—but that doesn't give me the right to deny them to others."

ARGUMENTS FOR HUMAN CLONING

1. *People have a right to reproduce.*

POINT: "Both morally and legally, we have the right to reproduce. Except under the most extreme situations, you wouldn't countenance forced sterilization, would you? Of course not. Nor would you countenance forced abortion, or deny sperm donorship to a woman married to an infertile man, or the opportunity to find a surrogate mother for a woman who can't bear a child herself. So how can you deny anyone the option of cloning, which is just another form of reproductive technology?"

COUNTERPOINT: "Cloning is not just another form of reproductive technology. In fact, it's not reproduction at all, but a means of manufacturing humans, even of mass manufacturing them. No one has the right to do that. And even if you could convince me that cloning is a form of reproduction, I'd still say it's wrong because of the dangers it poses to both the clone and society."

2. *Cloning offers many benefits to individuals.*

POINT: "First of all, you're wrong about the dangers. But even more important, you're ignoring all the benefits cloning offers—to infertile couples, couples in which both the man and the woman carry a recessive gene for the same illness, and to gay couples too, and to couples who have lost a child and would dearly love its identical twin. Not only that, but cloning can also guarantee successful matches for life-saving transplants. How can anyone be against that?"

COUNTERPOINT: "There are alternatives to cloning, you know—sperm donorship, surrogate motherhood, adoption. Nobody has to resort to cloning to have a child. And even the last benefit you mentioned, cloning to ensure successful matches for transplants, won't be necessary. Scientists are already at work on using cloning technology to generate organs without having to bring the embryo to term, and it won't be long before they're successful. As for cloning a dead child, that's just sick. It's one thing to want another one, but to manufacture an exact replica of the dead one? How do you think the clone would feel about that?"

3. *Cloning offers many benefits to society.*

POINT: "But what about the benefits to society? I'm thinking about two in particular. First, think of all we can learn about the respective contributions of our genes and environment to our personalities, intelligence, and skills. Research on identical twins has been of some help here, but there just aren't that many of them, and cloning can give us more twins to study. Second, there are the advantages we can get by cloning great people from a variety of fields—scientists, political leaders, artists, athletes. Wouldn't it be great to have clones of Jonas Salk working on vaccines for diseases like AIDS?"

COUNTERPOINT: "Now you're getting into *Brave New World* territory, manufacturing people to serve some preset purpose or other—scientific research or the mass production of great people. Besides, you already admitted that our choices and the environment play a big role in shaping who we are. What makes you think a Salk clone would have any interest in searching for an AIDS vaccine?"

The Wisdom of Repugnance

LEON R. KASS

Leon R. Kass was appointed chairman of the President's Council on Bioethics by President George W. Bush in 2001. In this excerpt from a longer essay, Kass lays out a broad case against human cloning and calls for an absolute ban on it. Taking his cue from the repugnance that many people feel at the prospect of making exact human genetic copies, he argues that this repugnance reveals the deeper immorality of the technology: its violation of human individuality, its transformation of the role that sex plays in our lives, its confounding of family relationships and their moral ties, and its transformation of "begetting" into "making."

In arguing his case, Kass criticizes three perspectives on cloning that its proponents have taken. The first, the technological perspective, sees cloning as a harmless extension of current reproductive technologies. The second, the liberal perspective, sees cloning in the context of human rights and liberties. The third, the meliorist perspective, sees cloning as a way to improve human beings through advances in health and the elimination of genetic defects. All three, he argues, neglect the profound differences that the availability of cloning would bring about.

Offensive, grotesque, revolting, repugnant, and *repulsive*—those are the words most commonly heard regarding the prospect of human cloning. Such reactions come both from the man or woman in the street and from the intellectuals, from believers and atheists, from humanists and scientists. Even Dolly's creator has said he "would find it offensive" to clone a human being.

People are repelled by many aspects of human cloning. They recoil from the prospect of mass production of human beings, with large clones of look-alikes, compromised in their individuality; the idea of father-son or mother-daughter twins; the bizarre prospects of a woman's giving birth to and rearing a genetic copy of herself, her spouse, or even her deceased father or mother; the grotesqueness of conceiving a child as an exact replacement for another who has died; the utilitarian creation of embryonic genetic duplicates of oneself, to be frozen away or created when necessary, in case of need for homologous tissues or organs for transplantation; the narcissism of those who would clone themselves and the arrogance of others who think they know who deserves to be cloned or which genotype any child-to-be should be thrilled to receive; the Frankensteinian hubris to create human life and increasingly to control its destiny; man playing God. Almost no one finds any of the suggested reasons for human cloning compelling; almost everyone anticipates its possible misuses and abuses. Moreover, many people feel oppressed by the sense that there is probably nothing we can do to prevent it from happening. That makes the prospect all the more revolting.

Revulsion is not an argument; and some of yesterday's repugnances are today calmly accepted—though, one must add, not always for the better. In crucial cases, however, repugnance is the emotional expression of deep wisdom, beyond reason's power fully to articulate it. Can anyone really give an argument fully adequate to the horror which is father-daughter incest (even with consent), or having sex with

From Leon R. Kass, "The Wisdom of Repugnance," from Leon R. Kass and James Q. Wilson, *The Ethics of Human Cloning,* pp. 17–59. Reprinted with the permission of the American Enterprise Institute for Public Policy Research, Washington, D.C.

animals, or mutilating a corpse, or eating human flesh, or raping or murdering another human being? Would anybody's failure to give full rational justification for his revulsion at those practices make that revulsion ethically suspect? Not at all. On the contrary, we are suspicious of those who think that they can rationalize away our horror, say, by trying to explain the enormity of incest with arguments only about the genetic risks of inbreeding.

The repugnance at human cloning belongs in that category. We are repelled by the prospect of cloning human beings not because of the strangeness or novelty of the undertaking, but because we intuit and feel, immediately and without argument, the violation of things that we rightfully hold dear. Repugnance, here as elsewhere, revolts against the excesses of human willfulness, warning us not to transgress what is unspeakably profound. Indeed, in this age in which everything is held to be permissible so long as it is freely done, in which our given human nature no longer commands respect, in which our bodies are regarded as mere instruments of our autonomous rational wills, repugnance may be the only voice left that speaks up to defend the central core of our humanity. Shallow are the souls that have forgotten how to shudder.

The goods protected by repugnance are generally overlooked by our customary ways of approaching all new biomedical technologies. The way we evaluate cloning ethically will in fact be shaped by how we characterize it descriptively, by the context into which we place it, and by the perspective from which we view it. The first task for ethics is proper description. And here is where our failure begins.

Typically, cloning is discussed in one or more of three familiar contexts, which one might call the technological, the liberal, and the meliorist. Under the first, cloning will be seen as an extension of existing techniques for assisting reproduction and determining the genetic makeup of children. Like them, cloning is to be regarded as a neutral technique, with no inherent meaning or goodness, but subject to multiple uses, some good, some bad. The morality of cloning thus depends absolutely on the goodness or badness of the motives and intentions of the cloners. As one bioethicist defender of cloning puts it, "The ethics must be judged [only] by the way the parents nurture and rear their resulting child and whether they bestow the same love and affection on a child brought into existence by a technique of assisted reproduction as they would on a child born in the usual way."

The liberal (or libertarian or liberationist) perspective sets cloning in the context of rights, freedoms, and personal empowerment. Cloning is just a new option for exercising an individual's right to reproduce or to have the kind of child that he wants. Alternatively, cloning enhances our liberation (especially women's liberation) from the confines of nature, the vagaries of chance, or the necessity for sexual mating. Indeed, it liberates women from the need for men altogether, for the process requires only eggs, nuclei, and (for the time being) uteri—plus, of course, a healthy dose of our (allegedly "masculine") manipulative science that likes to do all those things to mother nature and nature's mothers. For those who hold this outlook, the only moral restraints on cloning are adequately informed consent and the avoidance of bodily harm. If no one is cloned without her consent, and if the clonant is not physically damaged, then the liberal conditions for licit, hence moral, conduct are met. Worries that go beyond violating the will or maiming the body are dismissed as "symbolic"—which is to say, unreal.

The meliorist perspective embraces valetudinarians and also eugenicists. The latter were formerly more vocal in those discussions, but they are now generally happy to see their goals advanced under the less threatening banners of freedom and technological growth. These people see in cloning a new prospect for improving human beings—minimally, by ensuring the perpetuation of healthy individuals by avoiding the risks of genetic disease inherent in the lottery of sex, and maximally, by producing "optimum babies," preserving outstanding genetic material, and (with the help of soon-to-come techniques for precise genetic engineering) enhancing inborn human capacities on many fronts. Here the morality of cloning as a means is justified solely by the excellence of the end, that is, by the outstanding traits of individuals cloned—beauty, or brawn, or brains.

These three approaches, all quintessentially American and all perfectly fine in their places, are sorely wanting as approaches to human procreation. It is, to say the least, grossly distorting to view the wondrous mysteries of birth, renewal, and individuality, and the deep meaning of parent-child relations, largely through the lens of our reductive science and its potent technologies. Similarly, considering reproduction (and the intimate relation of family life!) primarily under the political-legal, adversarial, and individualistic notion of rights can only undermine the private yet fundamentally social, cooperative, and duty-laden character of child-bearing, child-rearing, and their bond to the covenant of marriage. Seeking to escape entirely from nature (to satisfy a natural desire or a natural right to reproduce!) is self-contradictory in theory and self-alienating in practice. For we are erotic beings only because we are embodied beings and not merely intellects and wills unfortunately imprisoned in our bodies. And, though health and fitness are clearly great goods, there is something deeply disquieting in looking on our prospective children as artful products perfectible by genetic engineering, increasingly held to our willfully imposed designs, specifications, and margins of tolerable error.

The technical, liberal, and meliorist approaches all ignore the deeper anthropological, social, and indeed, ontological meanings of bringing forth a new life. To this more fitting and profound point of view cloning shows itself to be a major violation of our given nature as embodied, gendered, and engendering beings—and of the social relations built on this natural ground. Once this perspective is recognized, the ethical judgment on cloning can no longer be reduced to a matter of motives and intentions, rights and freedoms, benefits and harms, or even means and ends. It must be regarded primarily as a matter of meaning: Is cloning a fulfillment of human begetting and belonging? Or is cloning rather, as I contend, their pollution and perversion? To pollution and perversion the fitting response can only be horror and revulsion; and conversely, generalized horror and revulsion are prima facie evidence of foulness and violation. The burden of moral argument must fall entirely on those who want to declare the widespread repugnances of humankind to be mere timidity or superstition.

Yet repugnance need not stand naked before the bar of reason. The wisdom of our horror at human cloning can be partially articulated, even if this is finally one of those instances about which the heart has its reasons that reason cannot entirely know.

THE PROFUNDITY OF SEX

To see cloning in its proper context, we must begin not, as I did before, with laboratory technique, but with the anthropology—natural and social—of sexual reproduction.

Sexual reproduction—by which I mean the generation of new life from (exactly) two complementary elements, one female, one male, (usually) through coitus—is established (if that is the right term) not by human decision, culture, or tradition, but by nature; it is the natural way of all mammalian reproduction. By nature, each child has two complementary biological progenitors. Each child thus stems from and unites exactly two lineages. In natural generation, moreover, the precise genetic constitution of the resulting offspring is determined by a combination of nature and chance, not by human design: each human child shares the common natural human species genotype, each child is genetically (equally) kin to each (both) parent(s), yet each child is also genetically unique.

Those biological truths about our origins foretell deep truths about our identity and about our human condition altogether. Every one of us is at once equally human, equally enmeshed in a particular familial nexus of origin, and equally individuated in our trajectory from birth to death—and, if all goes well, equally capable (despite our mortality) of participating, with a complementary other, in the very same renewal of such human possibility through procreation. Though less momentous than our common humanity, our genetic individuality is not humanly trivial. It shows itself forth in our distinctive appearance through which we are everywhere recognized; it is revealed in our "signature" marks of fingerprints and our self-recognizing immune system; it symbolizes and foreshadows exactly the unique, never-to-be repeated character of each human life.

Human societies virtually everywhere have structured child-rearing responsibilities and systems of identity and relationship on the bases of those deep natural facts of begetting. The mysterious yet ubiquitous "love of one's own" is everywhere culturally exploited, to make sure that children are not just produced but well cared for and to create for everyone clear ties of meaning, belonging, and obligation. But it is wrong to treat such naturally rooted social practices as mere cultural constructs (like left- or right-driving, or like burying or cremating the dead) that we can alter with little human cost. What would kinship be without its clear natural grounding? And what would identity be without kinship? We must resist those who have begun to refer to sexual reproduction as the "traditional method of reproduction," who would have us regard as merely traditional, and by implication arbitrary, what is in truth not only natural but most certainly profound.

Asexual reproduction which produces "single-parent" offspring, is a radical departure from the natural human way, confounding all normal understandings of father, mother, sibling, and grandparent and all moral relations tied thereto. It becomes even more of a radical departure when the resulting offspring is a clone derived not from an embryo, but from a mature adult to whom the clone would be an identical twin; and when the process occurs not by natural accident (as in natural twinning), but by deliberate human design and manipulations; and when the child's (or children's) genetic constitution is preselected by the parent(s) (or scientists). Accordingly, as we shall see, cloning is vulnerable to three kinds of concerns and objections, related to these three points: cloning threatens confusion of identity and individuality, even in small-scale cloning; cloning represents a giant step (though not the first one) toward transforming procreation into manufacture, that is, toward the increasing depersonalization of the process of generation and, increasingly, toward the "production" of human children as artifacts, products of human will and design (what others have called the problem of "commodification " of new life); and cloning—like other forms of eugenic engineering of the next generation—represents a form of despotism of the cloners over the cloned, and thus (even in benevolent cases) represents a blatant violation of the inner meaning of parent-child relations, of what it means to have a child, of what it means to say yes to our own demise and "replacement."

Before turning to those specific ethical objections, let me test my claim of the profundity of the natural way by taking up a challenge recently posed by a friend. What if the given natural human way of reproduction were asexual, and we now had to deal with a new technological innovation—artificially induced sexual dimorphism and the fusing of complementary gametes—whose inventors argued that sexual reproduction promised all sorts of advantages, including hybrid vigor and the creation of greatly increased individuality? Would one then be forced to defend natural asexuality because it was natural? Could one claim that it carried deep human meaning?

The response to that challenge broaches the ontological meaning of sexual reproduction. For it is impossible, I submit, for there to have been human life—or even higher forms of animal life—in the absence of sexuality and sexual reproduction. We find asexual reproduction only in the lowest forms of life; bacteria, algae, fungi, some lower invertebrates. Sexuality brings with it a new and enriched relationship to the world. Only sexual animals can seek and find complementary others with whom to pursue a goal that transcends their own existence. For a sexual being, the world is no longer an indifferent and largely homogeneous *otherness*, in part edible, in part dangerous. It also contains some very special and related and complementary beings, of the same kind but of opposite sex, toward whom one reaches out with special interest and intensity. In higher birds and mammals, the outward gaze keeps a lookout not only for food and predators, but also for prospective mates; the beholding of the many-splendored world is suffused with desire for union—the animal antecedent of human eros and the germ of sociality. Not by accident is the human animal both the sexiest animal—whose females do not go into heat but are receptive throughout the estrous cycle and whose males must therefore have greater sexual appetite and energy to reproduce successfully—and also the most aspiring, the most social, the most open, and the most intelligent animal.

The soul-elevating power of sexuality is, at bottom, rooted in its strange connection to mortality, which it simultaneously accepts and tries to over come. Asexual reproduction may be seen as a continuation of the activity of self-preservation. When one organism buds or divides to become two, the original being is (doubly) preserved, and nothing dies. Sexuality, by contrast, means perishability and serves replacement; the two that come together to generate one soon will die. Sexual desire, in human beings as in animals, thus serves an end that is partly hidden from, and finally at odds with, the self-serving individual. Whether we know it or not, when we are sexually active we are voting with our genitalia for our own demise. The salmon swimming upstream to spawn and die tell the universal story: sex is bound up with death, to which it holds a partial answer in procreation.

The salmon and the other animals evince that truth blindly. Only the human being can understand what it means. As we learn so powerfully from the story of the Garden of Eden, our humanization is coincident with sexual self-consciousness, with the recognition of our sexual nakedness and all that it implies: shame at our needy incompleteness, unruly self-division, and finitude; awe before the eternal; hope in the self-transcending possibilities of children and a relationship to the divine. In the sexually self-conscious animal, sexual desire can become eros, lust can become love. Sexual desire humanly regarded is thus sublimated into erotic longing for wholeness, completion, and immortality, which drives us knowingly into the embrace and its generative fruit—as well as into all the higher human possibilities of deed, speech, and song.

Through children, a good common to both husband and wife, male and female achieve some genuine unification (beyond the mere sexual "union," which fails to do so). The two become one through sharing generous (not needy) love for that third being as good. Flesh of their flesh, the child is the parents' own commingled being externalized and given a separate and persisting existence. Unification is enhanced also by their commingled work of rearing. Providing an opening to the future beyond the grave, carrying not only our seed but also our names, our ways, and our hopes that they will surpass us in goodness and happiness, children are a testament to the possibility of transcendence. Gender duality and sexual desire, which first draws our love upward and outside of ourselves, finally provide for the partial overcoming of the confinement and limitation of perishable embodiment altogether.

Human procreation, in sum, is not simply an activity of our rational wills. It is a more complete activity precisely because it engages us bodily, erotically, and spiritually as well as rationally. There is wisdom in the mystery of nature that has joined the pleasure of sex, the inarticulate longing for union, the communication of the loving embrace, and the deep-seated and only partly articulate desire for children in the very activity by which we continue the chain of human existence and participate in the renewal of human possibility. Whether or not we know it, the severing of procreation from sex, love, and intimacy is inherently dehumanizing, no matter how good the product.

We are now ready for the more specific objections to cloning.

THE PERVERSITIES OF CLONING

First, an important if formal objection: Any attempt to clone a human being would constitute an unethical experiment upon the resulting child-to-be. As the animal experiments (frog and sheep) indicate, there are grave risks of mishaps and deformities. Moreover, because of what cloning means, one cannot presume a future cloned child's consent to be a clone, even a healthy one. Thus, ethically speaking, we cannot even get to know whether or not human cloning is feasible.

I understand, of course, the philosophical difficulty of trying to compare a life with defects against nonexistence. Several bioethicists, proud of their philosophical cleverness, use that conundrum to embarrass claims that one can injure a child in its conception, precisely because it is only thanks to that complained-of conception that the child is alive to complain. But common sense tells us that we have no reason to fear such philosophisms. For we surely know that people can harm and even maim children in the very act of conceiving them, say, by paternal transmission of the AIDS virus, maternal transmission of heroin dependence, or, arguably, even by bringing them into being as bastards or with no capacity or willingness to look after them properly. And we believe that to do that intentionally, or even negligently, is inexcusable and clearly unethical.

The objection about the impossibility of presuming consent may even go beyond the obvious and sufficient point that a clonant, were he subsequently to be asked, could rightly resent having been made a clone. At issue are not just benefits and harms, but doubts about the very independence needed to give proper (even retroactive) consent, that is, not just the capacity to choose but the disposition and ability to choose freely and well. It is not at all clear to what extent a clone will fully be a moral agent. For, as we shall see, in the very fact of cloning, and especially of rearing him *as a clone*, his makers subvert the cloned child's independence, beginning with that aspect that comes from knowing that one was an unbidden surprise, a gift, to the world, rather than the designed result of someone's artful project.

Cloning creates serious issues of identity and individuality. The cloned person may experience concerns about his distinctive identity not only because he will be in genotype and appearance identical to another human being, but, in this case, because he may also be twin to the person who is his "father" or "mother"—if one can still call them that. What would be the psychic burdens of being the "child" or "parent" of your twin? The cloned individual, moreover, will be saddled with a genotype that has already lived. He will not be fully a surprise to the world. People are likely always to compare his performance in life with that of his alter ego. True, his nurture and his circumstance in life will be different; genotype is not exactly destiny. Still, one must also expect parental and other efforts to shape that new life after the original—or at least to view the child with the original version always firmly in mind. Why else did they clone from the star basketball player, mathematician, and beauty queen—or even dear old dad—in the first place?

Since the birth of Dolly, there has been a fair amount of doublespeak on the matter of genetic identity. Experts have rushed in to reassure the public that the clone would in no way be the same person or have any confusions about his identity: as previously noted, they are pleased to point out that the clone of Mel Gibson would not be Mel Gibson. Fair enough. But one is shortchanging the truth by emphasizing the additional importance of the intrauterine environment, rearing, and social setting: genotype obviously matters plenty. That, after all, is the only reason to clone, whether human beings or sheep. The odds that clones of Wilt Chamberlain will play in the NBA are, I submit, infinitely greater than they are for clones of Robert Reich.

Curiously, this conclusion is supported, inadvertently, by the one ethical sticking point insisted on by friends of cloning: no cloning without the donor's consent. Though an orthodox liberal objection, it is in fact quite puzzling when it comes from people (such as Ruth Macklin) who also insist that genotype is not identity or individuality and who deny that a child could reasonably complain about being made a genetic copy. If the clone of Mel Gibson would not be Mel Gibson, why should Mel Gibson have grounds to object that someone had been made his clone? We already allow researchers to use blood and tissue samples for research purposes of no benefit to their sources: my falling hair, my expectorations, my urine, and even my biopsied tissues are "not me" and not mine.

Courts have held that the profit gained from uses to which scientists put my discarded tissues do not legally belong to me. Why, then, no cloning without consent—including, I assume, no cloning from the body of someone who just died? What harm is done the donor, if genotype is "not me"? Truth to tell, the only powerful justification for objecting is that genotype really does have something to do with identity, and everybody knows it. If not, on what basis could Michael Jordan object that someone cloned "him," say, from cells taken from a "lost" scraped-off piece of his skin? The insistence on donor consent unwittingly reveals the problem of identity in all cloning.

Genetic distinctiveness not only symbolizes the uniqueness of each human life and the independence of its parents that each human child rightfully attains. It can also be an important support for living a worthy and dignified life. Such arguments apply with great force to any large-scale replication of human individuals. But they are sufficient, in my view, to rebut even the first attempts to clone a human being. One must never forget that these are human beings upon whom our eugenic or merely playful fantasies are to be enacted.

Troubled psychic identity (distinctiveness), based on all-too-evident genetic identity (sameness), will be made much worse by the utter confusion of social identity and kinship ties. For, as already noted, cloning radically confounds lineage and social relations, for "offspring" as for "parents." As bioethicist James Nelson has pointed out, a female child cloned from her "mother" might develop a desire for a relationship to her "father" and might understandably seek out the father of her "mother," who is after all also her biological twin sister. Would "grandpa," who thought his paternal duties concluded, be pleased to discover that the clonant looked to him for paternal attention and support?

Social identity and social ties of relationship and responsibility are widely connected to, and supported by, biological kinship. Social taboos on incest (and adultery) everywhere serve to keep clear who is related to whom (and especially which child belongs to which parents), as well as to avoid confounding the social identity of parent-and-child (or brother-and-sister) with the social identity of lovers, spouses, and coparents. True, social identity is altered by adoption (but as a matter of the best interest of already living children: we do not deliberately produce children for adoption). True, artificial insemination and in vitro fertilization with donor sperm, or whole embryo donation, are in some way forms of "pre-natal adoption"—a not altogether unproblematic practice. Even here, though, there is in each case (as in all sexual reproduction) a known male source of sperm and a known single female source of egg—a genetic father and a genetic mother—should anyone care to know (as adopted children often do) who is genetically related to whom.

In the case of cloning, however, there is but one "parent." The usually sad situation of the "single-parent child" is here deliberately planned, and with a vengeance. In the case of self-cloning, the "offspring" is, in addition, one's twin; and so the dreaded result of incest—to be parent to one's sibling—is here brought about deliberately, albeit without any act of coitus. Moreover, all other relationships will be confounded. What will *father, grandfather, aunt, cousin,* and *sister* mean? Who will bear what ties and what burdens? What sort of social identity will someone have with one whole side—"father's" or "mother's"—necessarily excluded? It is no answer to say that our society, with its high incidence of divorce, remarriage, adoption, extramarital child-bearing, and the rest, already confounds lineage and confuses kinship and responsibility for children (and everyone else), unless one also wants to argue that this is, for children, a preferable state of affairs.

Human cloning would also represent a giant step toward turning begetting into making, procreation into manufacture (literally, something "handmade"), a process already begun with in vitro fertilization and genetic testing of embryos. With cloning, not only is the process in hand, but the total genetic blueprint of the cloned individual is selected and determined by the human artisans. To be sure, subsequent development will take place according to natural processes; and the resulting children will still be recognizably human. But we here would be taking a major step into making man himself simply another one of the man-made things. Human nature becomes merely the last part of nature to succumb to the technological project, which turns all of nature into raw material at human disposal, to be homogenized by our rationalized technique according to the subjective prejudices of the day.

How does begetting differ from making? In natural procreation, human beings come together, complementarily male and female, to give existence to another being who is formed, exactly as we were, *by what we are:* living, hence perishable, hence aspiringly erotic, human beings. In clonal reproduction, by contrast, and in the more advanced forms of manufacture to which it leads, we give existence to a being not by what we are but by what we intend and design. As with any product of our making, no matter how excellent, the artificer stands above it, not as an equal but as a superior, transcending it by his will and creative prowess. Scientists who clone animals make it perfectly clear that they are engaged in instrumental making; the animals are, from the start, designed as means to serve rational human purposes. In human cloning scientists and prospective "parents" would be adopting the same technocratic mentality to human children: human children would be their artifacts.

Such an arrangement is profoundly dehumanizing, no matter how good the product. Mass-scale cloning of the same individual makes the point vividly; but the violation of human equality, freedom, and dignity is present even in a single planned clone. And procreation dehumanized into manufacture is further degraded by commodification, a virtually inescapable result of allowing baby-making to proceed under the banner of commerce. Genetic and reproductive biotechnology companies are already growth industries, but they will go into commercial orbit once the Human Genome Project nears completion. Supply will create enormous demand. Even before the capacity for human cloning arrives, established companies will have invested in the harvesting of eggs from ovaries obtained at autopsy or through ovarian surgery, practiced embryonic genetic alteration, and initiated the stockpiling of prospective donor tissues. Through the rental of surrogate-womb services and through the buying and selling of tissues and embryos, priced according to the merit of the donor, the commodification of nascent human life will be unstoppable.

Finally, and perhaps most important, the practice of human cloning by nuclear transfer—like other anticipated forms of genetic engineering of the next generation—would enshrine and aggravate a profound and mischievous misunderstanding of the meaning of having children and of the parent-child relationship. When a couple now chooses to procreate, the partners are saying yes to the emergence of new life in its novelty, saying yes not only to having a child but also, tacitly, to having whatever child the child turns out to be. In accepting our finitude and opening ourselves to our replacement, we are tacitly confessing the limits of our control. In this ubiquitous way of nature, embracing the future by procreating means precisely that we are relinquishing our grip, in the very activity of taking up our own share in what we hope will be the immortality of human life and the human species. This means that our children are not *our* children: they are not our property, not our possessions. Neither are they supposed to live our lives for us, or anyone else's life but their own. To be sure, we seek to guide them on their way, imparting to them not just life but nurturing, love, and a way of life; to be sure, they bear our hopes that they will live fine and flourishing lives, enabling us in small measure to transcend our own limitations. Still, their genetic distinctiveness and independence are the natural foreshadowing of the deep truth that they have their own and never-before-enacted life to live. They are sprung from a past, but they take an uncharted course into the future.

Much harm is already done by parents who try to live vicariously through their children. Children are sometimes compelled to fulfill the broken dreams of unhappy parents; John Doe, Jr., or John Doe III is under the burden of having to live up to his forebear's name. Still, if most parents have hopes for their children, cloning parents will have expectations. In cloning, such overbearing parents take at the start a decisive step that contradicts the entire meaning of the open and forward-looking nature of parent-child relations. The child is given a genotype that has already lived, with full expectation that the blueprint of a past life ought to be controlling of the life that is to come. Cloning is inherently despotic, for it seeks to make one's children (or someone else's children) after one's own image (or an image of one's choosing) and their future according to one's will. In some cases the despotism may be mild and benevolent. In other cases it will be mischievous and downright tyrannical. But despotism—the control of another through one's will—it inevitably will be.

MEETING SOME OBJECTIONS

The defenders of cloning, of course, are not wittingly friends of despotism. Indeed, they regard themselves mainly as friends of freedom: the freedom of individuals to reproduce, the freedom of scientists and inventors to discover and devise and to foster "progress" in genetic knowledge and technique. They want large-scale cloning only for animals, but they wish to preserve cloning as a human option for exercising our "right to reproduce"—our right to have children, and children with" desirable genes." As law professor John Robertson points out, under our "right to reproduce" we already practice early forms of unnatural, artificial, and extramarital reproduction, and we already practice early forms of eugenic choice. For that reason, he argues, cloning is no big deal.

We have here a perfect example of the logic of the slippery slope, and the slippery way in which it already works in that area. Only a few years ago, slippery-slope arguments were advanced to oppose artificial insemination and in vitro fertilization using unrelated sperm donors. Principles used to justify those practices, it was said, will be used to justify more artificial and more eugenic practices, including cloning. Not so, the defenders retorted, since we can make the necessary distinctions. And now, without even a gesture at making the necessary distinctions, the continuity of practice is held by itself to be justificatory.

The principle of reproductive freedom as currently enunciated by the proponents of cloning logically embraces the ethical acceptability of sliding down the entire rest of the slope—to producing children ectogenetically from sperm to term (should it become feasible) and to producing children whose entire genetic makeup will be the product of parental eugenic planning and choice. If reproductive freedom means the right to have a child of one's own choosing, by whatever means, it knows and accepts no limits.

But, far from being legitimated by a "right to reproduce," the emergence of techniques of assisted reproduction and genetic engineering should compel us to reconsider the meaning and limits of such a putative right. In truth, a "right to reproduce" has always been a peculiar and problematic notion. Rights generally belong to individuals, but this is a right that (before cloning) no one can exercise alone. Does the right then inhere only in couples? Only in married couples? Is it a (woman's) right to carry or deliver or a right (of one or more parents) to nurture and rear? Is it a right to have your own biological child? Is it a right only to attempt reproduction or a right also to succeed? Is it a right to acquire the baby of one's choice?

The assertion of a negative "right to reproduce" certainly makes sense when it claims protection against state interference with procreative liberty, say, through a program of compulsory sterilization. But surely it cannot be the basis of a tort claim against nature, to be made good by technology, should free efforts at natural procreation fail. Some insist that the right to reproduce embraces also the right against state interference with the free use of all technological means to obtain a child. Yet such a position cannot be sustained: for reasons having to do with the means employed, any community may rightfully prohibit surrogate pregnancy, polygamy, or the sale of babies to infertile couples without violating anyone's basic human "right to reproduce." When the exercise of a previously innocuous freedom now involves or impinges on troublesome practices that the original freedom never was intended to reach, the general presumption of liberty needs to be reconsidered.

We do indeed already practice negative eugenic selection, through genetic screening and prenatal diagnosis. Yet our practices are governed by a norm of health. We seek to prevent the birth of children who suffer from known (serious) genetic diseases. When and if gene therapy becomes possible, such diseases could then be treated, in utero or even before implantation. I have no ethical objection in principle to such a practice (though I have some practical worries), precisely because it serves the medical goal of healing existing individuals. But therapy, to be therapy, implies not only an existing "patient." It also implies a norm of health. In this respect, even germline gene "therapy," though practiced not on a human being but on egg and sperm, is less radical than cloning, which is in no way therapeutic. But once one blurs the distinction between health promotion and genetic enhancement, between so-called negative and positive eugenics, one opens the door to all future eugenic designs. "To make sure that a child will be healthy and have good chances in life": that is Robertson's principle, and, owing to its latter clause, it is an utterly elastic principle, with no boundaries. Being over eight feet tall will likely produce some very good chances in life, and so will having the looks of Marilyn Monroe, and so will a genius-level intelligence.

Proponents want us to believe that there are legitimate uses of cloning that can be distinguished from illegitimate uses, but by their own principles no such limits can be found. (Nor could any such limits be enforced in practice.) Reproductive freedom, as they understand it, is governed solely by the subjective wishes of the parents-to-be (plus the avoidance of bodily harm to the child). The sentimentally appealing case of the childless married couple is, on those grounds, indistinguishable from the case of an individual (married or not) who would like to clone someone famous or talented, living or dead. Further, the principle here endorsed justifies not only cloning but, indeed, all future artificial attempts to create (manufacture) "perfect" babies.

A concrete example will show how, in practice no less than in principle, the so-called innocent case will merge with, or even turn into, the more troubling ones. In practice, the eager parent-to-be will necessarily be subject to the tyranny of expertise. Consider an infertile married couple, she lacking eggs or he lacking sperm, that wants a child of their (genetic) own and proposes to clone either husband or wife. The scientist-physician (who is also coowner of the cloning company) points out the likely difficulties: A cloned child is not really their (genetic) child, but the child of only *one* of them; that imbalance may produce strains on the marriage; the child might suffer identity confusion; there is a risk of perpetuating the cause of sterility. The scientist-physician also points out the advantages of choosing a donor nucleus. Far better than a child of their own would be a child of their own choosing. Touting his own expertise in selecting healthy and talented donors, the doctor presents the couple with his latest catalog containing the pictures, the health records, and the accomplishments of his stable of cloning donors, samples of whose tissues are in his deep freeze. Why not, dearly beloved, a more perfect baby?

The "perfect baby," of course, is the project not of the infertility doctors, but of the eugenic scientists and their supporters. For them, the paramount right is not the so-called right to reproduce but what biologist Bentley Glass called, a quarter of a century ago, "the right of every child to be born with a sound physical and mental constitution, based on a sound genotype . . . the inalienable right to a sound heritage." But to secure that right and to achieve the requisite quality control over new human life, human conception and gestation will need to be brought fully into the bright light of the laboratory, beneath which the child-to-be can be fertilized, nourished, pruned, weeded, watched, inspected, prodded, pinched, cajoled, injected, tested, rated, graded, approved, stamped, wrapped, sealed, and delivered. There is no other way to produce the perfect baby.

Yet we are urged by proponents of cloning to forget about the science fiction scenarios of laboratory manufacture and multiple-copied clones and to focus only on the homely cases of infertile couples exercising their reproductive rights. But why, if the single cases are so innocent, should multiplying their performance be so off-putting? (Similarly, why do others object to people's making money from that practice if the practice itself is perfectly acceptable?) When we follow the sound ethical principle of universalizing our choice—would it be right if everyone cloned a Wilt Chamberlain (with his consent, of course)? would it be right if everyone decided to practice asexual reproduction?—we discover what is wrong with such seemingly innocent cases. The so-called science fiction cases make vivid the meaning of what looks to us, mistakenly, to be benign.

Though I recognize certain continuities between cloning and, say, in vitro fertilization, I believe that cloning differs in essential and important ways. Yet those who disagree should be reminded that the "continuity" argument cuts both ways. Sometimes we establish bad precedents and discover that they were bad only when we follow their inexorable logic to places we never meant to go. Can the defenders of cloning show us today how, on their principles, we shall be able to see producing babies ("perfect babies") entirely in the laboratory or exercising full control over their genotypes (including so-called enhancement) as ethically different, in any essential way, from present forms of assisted reproduction? Or are they willing to admit, despite their attachment to the principle of continuity, that the complete obliteration of "mother" or "father," the complete depersonalization of procreation, the complete manufacture of human beings, and the complete genetic control of one generation over the next would be ethically problematic and essentially different from current forms of assisted reproduction? If so, where and how will they draw the line, and why? I draw it at cloning, for all the reasons given.

BAN THE CLONING OF HUMANS

What, then, should we do? We should declare that human cloning is unethical in itself and dangerous in its likely consequences. In so doing, we shall have the backing of the overwhelming majority of our fellow Americans, of the human race, and (I believe) of most practicing scientists. Next, we should do all that we can to prevent the cloning of human beings. We should do that by means of an international legal ban if possible and by a unilateral national ban at a minimum. Scientists may secretly undertake to violate such a law, but they will be deterred by not being able to stand up proudly to claim the credit for their technological bravado and success. Such a ban on clonal baby-making, moreover, will not harm the progress of basic genetic science and technology. On the contrary, it will reassure the public that scientists are happy to proceed without violating the deep ethical norms and intuitions of the human community.

That still leaves the vexed question about laboratory research using early embryonic human clones, specially created only for such research purposes, with no intention to implant them into a uterus. There is no question that such research holds great promise for gaining fundamental knowledge about normal (and abnormal) differentiation and for developing tissue lines for transplantation that might be used, say, in treating leukemia or in repairing brain or spinal cord injuries—to mention just a few of the conceivable benefits. Still, unrestricted clonal embryo research will surely make the production of living human clones much more likely. Once the genies put the cloned embryos into the bottles, who can strictly control where they go, especially in the absence of legal prohibitions against implanting them to produce a child?

I appreciate the potentially great gains in scientific knowledge and medical treatment available from embryo research, especially with cloned embryos. At the same time, I have serious reservations about creating human embryos for the sole purpose of experimentation. There is something deeply repugnant and fundamentally transgressive about such a utilitarian treatment of prospective human life. Such total, shameless exploitation is worse, in my opinion, than the "mere" destruction of nascent life. But I see no added objections, as a matter of principle, to creating and using *cloned* early embryos for research purposes, beyond the objections that I might raise to doing so with embryos produced sexually.

And yet, as a matter of policy and prudence, any opponent of the manufacture of cloned humans must, I think, in the end oppose also the creating of cloned human embryos. Frozen embryonic clones (belonging to whom?) can be shuttled around without detection. Commercial ventures in human cloning will be developed without adequate oversight. To build a fence around the law, prudence dictates that one oppose—for that reason alone—all production of cloned human embryos, even for research purposes. We should allow all cloning research on animals to go forward, but the only defensible barrier we can erect against the slippery slide, I suspect, is to insist on the inviolable distinction between animal and human cloning.

Some readers and certainly most scientists will not accept such prudent restraints, since they desire the benefits of research. They will prefer, even in fear and trembling, to allow human embryo cloning research to go forward.

Very well. Let us test them. If the scientists want to be taken seriously on ethical grounds, they must at the very least agree that embryonic research may proceed if and only if it is preceded by an absolute and effective ban on all attempts to implant into a uterus a cloned human embryo (cloned from an adult) to produce a living child. Absolutely no permission for the former without the latter.

The National Bioethics Advisory Commission's recommendations regarding these matters were a step in the right direction, but a step made limpingly and without adequate support. To its credit, the commission has indeed called for federal legislation to prevent anyone from attempting to create a child through cloning. That was, frankly, more than I expected. But the *moral basis* for the commission's opposition to cloning is, sadly, much less than expected and needed, and the ban it urges is to be only temporary. Trying to clone a human being, says the commission, is "morally unacceptable" "*at this time*" because the technique has not been perfected to the point of safe usage. In other words, once it becomes readily feasible to clone a human being, with little risk of bodily harm to the resulting child, the commission has offered not one agreed- upon reason to object. Indeed, anticipating such improvements in technique, the commission insists that "it is critical" that any legislative ban on baby-making through cloning "should include a sunset clause to ensure that Congress will review the issue after a specified time period (three to five years) to decide whether the prohibition continues to be needed." Although it identifies other ethical concerns (beyond the issue of safety), that blue-ribbon ethics commission takes no stand on any of them! It says only that those issues "require much more widespread and careful public deliberation *before this technology may be used*"—not to decide *whether* the technology *should* be used. Relativistically, the commission wants to ensure only that such ethical and social issues be regularly reviewed "in light of public understandings at that time." This is hardly the sort of opposition to cloning that could be made the basis of any lasting prohibition.

Almost as worrisome, the report is silent on the vexed question of creating cloned human embryos for use in research. Silence is, of course, not an endorsement, but neither is it opposition. Given the currently existing ban on the use of federal funds for any research that involves creating human embryos for experimentation, the commission may have preferred to avoid needless controversy by addressing that issue. Besides, those commissioners (no doubt a big majority) who favor proceeding with cloned embryo research have in fact gained their goal precisely by silence: Both the moratorium on federal funding and the legislative ban called for by the commission are confined *solely* to attempts to *create a child* through cloning. The commission knows well how vigorously and rapidly embryo research is progressing in the private sector, and the commission surely understands that its silence on the subject—along with Congress's—means that the creation of human embryonic clones will proceed and perhaps is already proceeding in private or commercial laboratories. Indeed, the report expects and tacitly welcomes such human embryo research: for by what other means shall we arrive at the expected improvements in human cloning technology that would require the recommended periodic reconsideration of any legislative ban?

In the end, the report of the commission turns out to be a moral and (despite its best efforts) a practical failure. Morally, this ethics commission has waffled on the main ethical question by refusing to declare the production of human clones unethical (or ethical). Practically, the moratorium and ban on baby-making that it calls for, while welcome as temporary restraints, have not been given the justification needed to provide a solid and lasting protection against the production of cloned human beings. To the contrary, the commission's weak ethical stance may be said to undermine even its limited call for restraint. Do we really need a federal law solely to protect unborn babies from bodily harm?

Opponents of cloning need therefore to be vigilant. They should press for legislation to *permanently* prohibit baby-making through cloning, and they should take steps to make such a prohibition effective.

The proposal for such a legislative ban is without American precedent, at least in technological matters, though the British and others have banned cloning of human beings, and we ourselves ban incest, polygamy, and other forms of "reproductive freedom." Needless to say, working out the details of such a ban, especially a global one, would be tricky, what with the need to develop appropriate sanctions for violators. Perhaps such a ban will prove ineffective; perhaps it will eventually be shown to have been a mistake. But it would at least place the burden of practical proof where it belongs: on the proponents of this horror, requiring them to show very clearly what great social or medical good can be had only by the cloning of human beings.

We Americans have lived by, and prospered under, a rosy optimism about scientific and technological progress. The technological imperative—if it can be done, it must be done—has probably served us well, though we should admit that there is no accurate method for weighing benefits and harms. Even when, as in the cases of environmental pollution, urban decay, or the lingering deaths that are the unintended byproducts of medical success, we recognize the unwelcome outcomes of technological advance, we remain confident in our ability to fix all the "bad" consequences—usually by means of still newer and better technologies. How successful we can continue to be in such post hoc repairing is at least an open question. But there is very good reason for shifting the paradigm around, at least regarding those technological interventions into the human body and mind that will surely effect fundamental (and likely irreversible) changes in human nature, basic human relationships, and what it means to be a human being. Here we surely should not be willing to risk everything in the naïve hope that, should things go wrong, we can later set them right.

The president's call for a moratorium on human cloning has given us an important opportunity. In a truly unprecedented way, we can strike a blow for the human control of the technological project, for wisdom, prudence, and human dignity. The prospect of human cloning, so repulsive to contemplate, is the occasion for deciding whether we shall be slaves of unregulated progress, and ultimately its artifacts, or whether we shall remain free human beings who guide our technique toward the enhancement of human dignity. If we are to seize the occasion, we must, as the late Paul Ramsey wrote,

> raise the ethical questions with a serious and not a frivolous conscience. A man of frivolous conscience announces that there are ethical quandaries ahead that we must urgently consider before the future catches up with us. By this he often means that we need to devise a new ethics that will provide the rationalization for doing in the future what men are bound to do because of new actions and interventions science will have made possible. In contrast a man of serious conscience means to say in raising urgent ethical questions that there may be some things that men should never do. The good things that men do can be made complete only by the things they refuse to do.

QUESTIONS FOR ANALYSIS

1. Kass writes that the "technical, liberal, and meliorist approaches all ignore the deeper anthropological, social, and indeed, ontological meanings of bringing forth a new life." What are these deeper meanings, and why does he think those approaches ignore them?
2. According to Kass, cloning "represents a form of despotism." Why? Is he right? Why or why not?
3. Why does Kass believe that higher forms of animal life would have been impossible without sexual reproduction? What role does this belief play in his criticism of cloning?
4. According to Kass, cloning "creates serious issues of identity and individuality." What are those issues? How serious do you think they are?
5. When discussing the view that our right to reproductive freedom guarantees the right to clone, Kass calls it "a perfect example of the logic of the slippery slope." Why? Do you agree?
6. Although he concedes that research on early embryonic clones holds great promise, Kass believes that such research should be banned. Why? Do you think his reasons adequately support his belief?
7. Is cloning more rightly thought of as reproduction or manufacture?

Moral Status of Cloning Humans

MICHAEL TOOLEY

The following selection by Michael Tooley, a professor of philosophy at the University of Colorado, is the second part of a longer essay. The first part examines the safety issues of human cloning and concludes that a temporary legal ban on cloning to produce humans is fully justified. The second part examines the moral issues and reaches two major conclusions: (1) there is nothing intrinsically immoral about human cloning, and (2) it promises to be very beneficial for society.

Along the way, Tooley addresses many of the moral issues raised by cloning's opponents, from the possible psychological harm to clones to the fears raised by what he calls *Brave New World* scenarios, and he finds none of them compelling. In fact, he even argues that there is nothing morally wrong with using cloning to produce "mindless organ banks" to be harvested for transplants. Since these clones would not be persons, he contends, using them that way would not violate respect for persons.

IS IT INTRINSICALLY WRONG TO PRODUCE A PERSON BY CLONING?

Let us now turn to the question of whether the use of cloning to produce a person is, in principle, morally acceptable or not. In this section, I shall focus on the question of whether cloning, so used, is intrinsically wrong. Then, in a later section, I shall consider whether cloning to produce persons necessarily has consequences that render it morally wrong.

How might one attempt to argue that the production of persons via cloning is intrinsically wrong? Here it seems to me that Dan Brock is right when he suggests that there are basically

From *Human Cloning*, James M. Humber and Robert F. Almeder (Totowa, N.J.: Humanities Press, 1998), pp. 77–100.

two lines of argument that deserve examination.[1] First, there is an argument that appeals to what might initially be described as the right of a person to be a unique individual, but which, in the end, must be characterized instead as the right of a person to a genetically unique nature. Second, there is an argument that appeals to the idea that a person has a right to a future that is, in a certain sense, open.

Does a Person Have a Right to a Genetically Unique Nature?

Many people feel that being a unique individual is important, and the basic thrust of this first attempt to show that cloning is intrinsically wrong involves the idea that the uniqueness of individuals would be in some way impaired by cloning. In response, I think that one might very well question whether uniqueness is important. If, for example, it turned out that there was, perhaps on some distant planet, an individual that was qualitatively identical to oneself, down to the last detail, both physical and psychological, would that really make one's own life less valuable, less worth living?

In thinking about this issue, it may be important to distinguish two different cases: first, the case in which the two lives are qualitatively identical because of the operation of deterministic causal laws; second, the case in which it just happens that both individuals are always in similar situations in which they freely decide upon the same actions, have the same thoughts and feelings, and so on. The second of these scenarios, I suggest, is not troubling. The first, on the other hand, may be. But if it is, is it because there is a person who is qualitatively indistinguishable from oneself, or, rather, because one's life is totally determined?

I am inclined to question, accordingly, the perhaps rather widely held view that uniqueness is an important part of the value of one's life. Fortunately, however, one need not settle that issue in the present context, since cloning does not, of course, produce a person who is qualitatively indistinguishable from the individual who has been cloned, for, as is shown by the case of identical twins, two individuals with the same genetic makeup, even if raised within the same family at the same time, will differ in many respects, because of the different events that make up their life histories.

How great are those differences? The result of one study was as follows:

> On average, our questionnaires show that the personality traits of identical twins have a 50 percent correlation. The traits of fraternal twins, by contrast, have a correlation of 25 percent, non-twin siblings a correlation of 11 percent and strangers a correlation of close to zero.[2]

Consequently, the personality traits of an individual and his or her clone should, on average, exhibit no more that a 50 percent correlation, and presumably, the correlation will generally be even less, given that an individual and his or her clone will typically be raised at different times, and in generations that may differ quite substantially in terms of basic beliefs and fundamental values.

The present argument, accordingly, if it is to have any chance, must shift from an appeal to the claim that a person has a right to absolute uniqueness to an appeal to the very different claim that a person has a right to a genetically unique nature. How, then, does the argument fare when reformulated in that way?

An initial point worth noticing is that any appeal to a claimed right to a genetically unique nature poses a difficulty for a theist: if there is such a right, why has God created a world where identical twins can arise? But there are, of course, many features of the world that are rather surprising, if our world is one that was created by an omnipotent, omniscient, and morally perfect person, and so the theist who appeals to a right to a genetically unique nature may simply reply that the presence of twins is just another facet of the general problem of evil.

How can one approach the question of whether persons have a right to a genetically unique nature? Some writers, I think, are content to rest with a burden of proof approach. Here the idea is that, although it may be the case that many people do think that being a unique individual, in the sense of not being qualitatively identical with anyone else, is an important part of what is valuable about being a person, the idea that persons have a right to a genetically unique identity is one that, by contrast, has been introduced only recently, and so those who advance the latter claim really need to offer some reasons for thinking that it is true.

There are, however, other ways of approaching this question that involve offering positive arguments against the claim. One possibility for example, is to appeal to the intuitions that one has upon reflection. Thus, one can consider the case of identical twins, and ask oneself whether, upon reflection, one thinks that it would be prima facie wrong to reproduce if one somehow knew that doing so would result in identical twins. I think it would be surprising if many people felt that this was so.

Another way of approaching the issue is by appealing to some plausible general theory of rights. Thus, for example, I am inclined to think that rights exist when there are serious, self-regarding interests that deserve to be protected. If some such view is correct, then one can approach the question of whether persons have a right to a genetically unique nature by asking whether one has some serious, self-regarding interest that would be impaired if one were a clone. Is the latter the case? The initial reason for thinking that it is not is that the existence of a clone does not seem to impinge on a person in the same way in which being prevented from performing some action that harms no one, or being tortured, or being killed, does: A distant clone might have no impact at all upon one's life.

In response, it might be argued that, while the mere existence of a clone need have no impact on, and so need not impair in any way, one's self-regarding interests, the situation might be very different if one knew of the existence of the clone, since that knowledge might, for example, be damaging to one's sense of individuality. But why should this be so, given that individuals can differ greatly, although sharing the same genetic makeup? It seems to me that if the knowledge that a clone of oneself exists were disturbing to one, this would probably be because of the presence of some relevant, false belief, such as a belief in genetic determinism. But if this is so, then the question arises as to whether rights exist when the interests that they protect are ones that will be harmed only if the potential subjects of the harm have certain false, and presumably irrational, beliefs. My own feeling is that the responsibility for such harm is properly assigned to the individual who has acquired the irrational beliefs whose presence is necessary if there is to be any harm. Consequently, it seems to me that the actions of others should not be constrained in order to prevent such harm from occurring, and thus that there is no right that is violated in such a case.

A third way of thinking about this question of whether there is a right to a genetically unique nature is to consider a scenario in which individuals with the same genetic makeup are very common indeed, and to consider whether such a world would, for example, be inferior to the present world. Imagine, for example, that it is the year 4004 B.C.E., and that God is contemplating creating human beings. He has already considered the idea of letting humans come into being via evolution, but has rejected that plan on the grounds that a lottery approach to such a vital matter as bringing humans into existence hardly seems appropriate. He also considers creating an original human pair that are genetically distinct, and who will then give rise to humans who will be genetically quite diverse. Upon reflection, however, that idea also seems flawed, since the random shuffling of genes will result in individuals who may be physically impaired, or disposed to unpleasant diseases, such as cancer, that will cause them enormous suffering and lead to premature deaths. In the end, accordingly, the Creator decides upon a genetic constitution with the following two properties. First, it will not lead to serious physical handicaps and diseases, and it will allow an individual, who makes wise choices, to grow in mind and spirit. Second, all of the genes involve identical alleles. God then creates one person with that genetic makeup—call her Eve—and a second individual, Adam, whose only genetic difference is that he has one X chromosome, and one Y chromosome, where Eve has two X chromosomes. The upshot will then be that when Adam and Eve reproduce, they will breed true, because of the fact that they have, aside from the one difference, the same genetic makeup, with identical alleles for every inherited character, and so all of their descendants will be genetically identical to either Adam or Eve.

How would such a world compare with the actual world? If one were choosing from behind the Rawlsian veil of ignorance, would it be rational to prefer the actual world, or the alternative world? This is not, perhaps, an easy question. But it is clear that there would be some significant pluses associated with the alternative world. First, unlike the actual world, one would be assured of a genetic makeup that would be free of dispositions to various unwelcome and life-shortening diseases, or to other debilitating conditions such as depression, schizophrenia, and so on. Secondly, inherited traits would be distributed in a perfectly equitable fashion, and no one would start out, as is the case in the actual world, severely disadvantaged, and facing an enormous uphill battle. Third, aside from the differences between men and women, everyone would be physically the same, and so people would differ only with regard to the quality of their "souls", and thus one would have a world in which judgments of people might well have a less superficial basis than is often the case in the actual world. So there would seem to be some serious reasons for preferring the alternative world over the actual world.

The third advantage just mentioned also points, of course, to an obvious practical drawback of the alternative world: knowing who was who would be a rather more difficult matter than it is in the actual world. But this problem can be dealt with by variants on the above scenario. One variant, for example, would involve having identity of genetic makeup, except regarding the genes that determine the appearance of face and hair. Then one would be able to identify individuals in just the way that one typically does in the actual world. This change would mean, of course, that one was no longer considering an alternative world in which there was widespread identity with respect to genetic makeup. Nevertheless, if this other alternative world would be preferable to the actual world, I think that it still provides an argument against the view that individuals have a right to a unique genetic makeup. For, first of all, the preferability of this other alternative world strongly suggests that genetic difference, rather than being desirable in itself, is valuable only to the extent that it is needed to facilitate the easy identification of people. Second, is it plausible to hold that, although genetic uniqueness is crucial, a very high degree of genetic similarity is not? But in the alternative world we are considering here, the degree of genetic similarity between any two individuals would be extraordinarily high. Third, the alternative world is one in which the genes that determine the initial structure of one's brain are not merely very similar, but absolutely the same in all individuals. But, then, can one plausibly hold that genetic uniqueness is morally crucial, while conceding that a world in which individuals do not differ regarding the genes that determine the initial nature of their brains might be better than the actual world?

These three considerations, I suggest, provide good reasons for holding that one cannot plausibly maintain that individuals have a right to a genetically unique nature, without also holding that the actual world is to be preferred to the alternative world just described. The identification problem can, however, also be addressed without shifting to a world where people differ genetically, since one could instead suppose that a different mechanism for identifying other people is built into human beings. God could, for example, incorporate special circuitry into the human brain, which broadcasts both one's name and appropriate identifying information about one, and which picks up the information that is broadcast by other humans within one's perceptual field. The information is then checked against a memory bank containing information about everyone one knows, and if it turns out that one is in perceptual contact with some person with whom one is acquainted, and if one would like to know who the person in question is, one would automatically find oneself in possession of the relevant information.

The result would be a world where all individuals will have exactly the same genetic makeup, aside from an X and a Y chromosome, and all of the attractive features of the original alternative world would be present, without there being any problem of determining who was who. One can then ask how this world compares with the actual world, and whether, in particular, the fact that all people in this alternative world would have essentially the same genetic makeup really seems to be, upon reflection, a reason for preferring the actual world.

The Open Future Argument

Dan Brock mentions a second argument for the view that cloning that aims at producing persons is intrinsically wrong.[3] The argument, which is based upon ideas put forward by Joel Feinberg, who speaks of a right to an open future,[4] and by Hans Jonas, who refers to a right to ignorance of a certain sort,[5] is essentially as follows. One's genetic makeup may very well determine to some extent the possibilities that lie open to one, and so it may constrain the course of one's future life. If there is no one with the same genetic makeup, or if there is such a person, but one is unaware of the fact, or, finally, if there is such a person, but the person is either one's contemporary, or someone who is younger, then one will not be able to observe the course of the life of someone with the same genetic makeup as oneself. But what if one does know of a genetically identical person whose life precedes one's own? Then one could have knowledge that one might well view as showing that certain possibilities were not really open to one, and so one would have less of a sense of being able to choose the course of one's life.

To see why this argument is unsound, one needs to ask about the reasoning that might be involved if someone, observing the earlier life of someone with the same genetic makeup, concludes that his or her own life is subject to certain constraints. One possibility is that one may have observed someone striving very hard, over a long period of time, to achieve some goal and failing to get anywhere near it. Perhaps the earlier, genetically identical individual wanted to be the first person to run the marathon in under two hours, and after several hears of intense and well-designed training, attention to diet, and so one, never got below two and one-half hours. One would then surely be justified in viewing that particular goal as not really open to one. But would that knowledge be a bad thing, as Jonas seems to be suggesting? I would think that, on the contrary, such knowledge would be valuable, since it would make it easier for one to choose goals that one could successfully pursue.

A very different possibility is that one might observe the course of the life of the genetically identical individual, and conclude that no life significantly different from that life could really be open to one. Then one would certainly feel that one's life was constrained to a very unwelcome extent. But in drawing the conclusion that one's life could not be significantly different from that of the other individual, one would be drawing a conclusion for which there is not only no evidence, but one that there is excellent evidence against: The lives of identical twins demonstrate that very different lives indeed are possible, given the same genetic makeup.

In short, the idea that information about the life of a person genetically identical to oneself would provide grounds for concluding that only a narrow range of alternatives was open to one would only be justified if genetic determinism, or a close approximation thereto, was correct. But nothing like genetic determinism is true. This second argument for the view that cloning with the goal of producing persons is intrinsically wrong is, accordingly, unsound.

CONSIDERATIONS IN SUPPORT OF THE CLONING OF PERSONS

Whether it is desirable to produce persons by cloning depends, as we noticed earlier, upon the outcome of an issue that is not yet decided: the aging question. Here, however, I shall simply assume that it will become possible to clone an adult individual in such a way that one winds up with a cell whose chromosomes have full-length telomeres, so that the individual who results will have a normal life expectancy. Given that assumption, I want to argue that there are a number of important benefits that may result from the cloning of humans that is done with the goal of producing persons.

In setting out what I take to be benefits of cloning, I shall not address possible objections. These will be discussed, instead, under "Objections to the Cloning of Humans."

Scientific Knowledge: Psychology and the Heredity-vs-Environment Issue

A crucial theoretical task for psychology is the construction of a satisfactory theory that will explain the acquisition of traits of character, and central to the development of such a theory is information about the extent to which various traits are inherited, or alternatively, dependent on aspects of the environment that are controllable, or, finally, dependent on factors, either in the brain or in the environment, that have a chancy quality. But such knowledge is not just theoretically crucial to psychology. Knowledge of the contributions that are, and are not, made to the individual's development by his or her genetic makeup, by the environment in which he or she is raised, and by chance events, will enable one to develop approaches to child rearing that will increase the likelihood that one can raise people with desirable traits, people who will have a better chance of realizing their potentials, and of leading happy and satisfying lives. So this knowledge is not merely of great theoretical interest: it is also potentially very beneficial to society.

In the attempt to construct an adequate theory of human development, the study of identical twins has been very important, and has generated considerable information on the nature/nurture issue. But adequate theories still seem rather remote. Cloning would provide a powerful way of speeding up scientific progress in this area, since society could produce a number of individuals with the same genetic makeup, and then choose adoptive parents who would provide those individuals with good, but significantly different environments, in which to mature.

Cloning to Benefit Society

One very familiar suggestion is that one might benefit mankind by cloning individuals who have made very significant contributions to society. In the form in which it is usually put, when it is assumed that, if, for example, one had been able to clone Albert Einstein, the result would be an individual who would also make some very significant contribution to science, the suggestion is surely unsound. In the first place, whether an individual will do highly creative work surely depends on traits whose acquisitions is a matter of the environment in which the individual is raised, rather than on being determined simply by his or her genetic makeup. But could it not be argued in response that one could control the environment as well, raising a clone of Einstein, for example, in an environment that was as close as possible to the sort of environment in which Einstein was raised? That, of course, might prove difficult. But even if it could be done, it is not clear that it would be sufficient, because there is a second point that can be made here, namely, that great creative achievements may depend on things that are to some extent accidental, and whose occurrence is not ensured by the combination of a certain genetic makeup and a certain general sort of environment. Many great mathematicians, for example, have developed an intense interest in numbers at an early age. Is there good reason to think that, had one been able to clone Carl Friedrich Gauss, and reared that person in an environment similar to Gauss's, that person would have developed a similar interest in numbers, and gone on to achieve great things in mathematics? Or is it likely that a clone of Einstein, raised in an environment similar to that in which Einstein was raised, would have wondered, as Einstein did, what the world would look like if one could travel as fast as light, and then gone on to reflect on the issues that fascinated Einstein, and that led ultimately to the development of revolutionary theories in physics?

I think that there are, then, some serious problems with the present suggestion in the form in which it is usually put. On the other hand, I am not convinced that a slightly more modest version cannot be sustained. Consider, for example, the Polgar sisters. There we have a case in which the father of three girls succeeded in creating an environment in which all three of his daughters became very strong chess players, and one of them, Judit Polgar, is now the strongest female chess player who has ever lived. Is it not reasonable to think that if one were to make a number of clones of Judit Polgar, and then raise them in an environment very similar to that in which the Polgar sisters were raised, the result would be a number of very strong chess players?

More generally, I think it is clear that there is a strong hereditary basis for intelligence,[6] and I also believe that there is good reason for thinking that other traits that may play a crucial role in creativity, such as extreme persistence, determination, and confidence in one's own abilities, are such as are likely to be produced by the right combination of heredity and environment. So, although the chance that the clone of an outstandingly creative individual will also achieve very great things is perhaps, at least in many areas, not especially high, I think that there is reason for thinking that, given an appropriate environment, the result will be an individual who is likely to accomplish things that may benefit society in significant ways.

Happier and Healthier Individuals

A third benefit of cloning is that it should make it possible to increase the likelihood that the person that one is bringing into existence will enjoy a healthy and happy life. For, to the extent that one's genetic constitution has a bearing on how long one is likely to live, on what diseases, both physical and mental, one is likely to suffer from, and on whether one will have traits of character or temperament that make for happiness, or for unhappiness, by cloning a person who has enjoyed a very long life, who has remained mentally alert, and not fallen prey to Alzheimer's disease, who has not suffered from cancer, arthritis, heart attacks, stroke, high blood pressure, and so on, and who has exhibited no tendencies to depression, or schizophrenia, and so on, one is increasing the chances that the individual that one is producing will also enjoy a healthy and happy life.

More Satisfying Childrearing: Individuals with Desired Traits

Many couples would prefer to raise children who possess certain traits. In some cases they may want children who have a certain physical appearance. In other cases, they might like to have children who have the physical abilities that would enable them to have a better chance of performing at a high level in certain physical activities. Or they might prefer to have children who would have the intellectual capabilities that would enable them to enjoy mathematics or science. Or they might prefer to have children who possess traits that would enable them to engage in, and enjoy, various aesthetic pursuits. Some of the traits that people might like their children to have presumably have a very strong hereditary basis; others are such as a child, given both the relevant genes, and the right environment, would be very likely to acquire. To the extent that the traits in question fall into either of these categories, the production of children via cloning would enable more couples to raise children with traits that they judge to be desirable.

More Satisfying Childrearing: Using Self-Knowledge

There is a second way in which cloning could make childrearing more satisfying, and it emerges if one looks back on one's own childhood. Most people, when they do this, remember things that they think were good, and other things that they think would have been better if they had been different. In some cases, of course, one's views may be unsound, and it may be that some of the things that one's parents did, and which one did not like, actually had good effects on one's development. On the whole, however, it seems plausible that most people have reasonably sound views on which features of the way in which they were raised had good effects overall, and which did not.

The idea, then, is that if a couple raises a child who is a clone of one of the parents, the knowledge that the relevant parent has of the way in which he or she was raised can be used to bring up the child in a way that fits better with the individual psychology of the child. In addition, given the greater psychological similarity that will exist between the child and one of his parents in such a case, the relevant parent will better be able, at any point, to appreciate how things look from the child's point of view. So it would seem that there is a good chance both that such a couple will find childrearing a more rewarding experience, and that the child will have a happier childhood through being better understood.

Infertility

Since the successful cloning that resulted in Dolly, at least one person has expressed the intention of pushing ahead with the idea of using cloning to help infertile couples. For reasons that emerged under the second heading, "Cloning in the Present Context", the idea that cloning should be so used in the near future seems morally very problematic. In principle, however, the general idea would seem to have considerable merit. One advantage, for example, as Dan Brock and others have pointed out, is that "cloning would allow women who have no ova or men who have no sperm to produce an offspring that is biologically related to them."[7] Another advantage, also noted by Brock, is that "embryos might be cloned, either by nuclear transfer or embryo splitting, in order to increase the number of embryos for implantations and improve the chances of successful conception."[8]

Children for Homosexual Couples

Many people, especially in the United States, believe that homosexuality is deeply wrong, and that homosexuals should not be allowed either to marry or to raise children. These opinions, however, would be rejected, I think, by most philosophers, who would hold, on the contrary, that homosexuality is not morally wrong, and that homosexuals should be allowed both to marry, and to raise children. Assume, for the sake of the present discussion, that the latter views are correct. Then, as Philip Kitcher and others have noted, cloning would seem to be a promising method of providing a homosexual couple with children that they could raise, since, in the case of a gay couple, each child could be a clone of one person; in the case of a lesbian couple, every child could, in a sense, be biologically connected with both people:

> A lesbian couple wishes to have a child. Because they would like the child to be biologically connected to each of them, they request that a cell nucleus from one of them be inserted into an egg from the other, and that the embryo be implanted in the uterus of the woman who donated the egg.[9]

Cloning to Save Lives

A final possibility is suggested by the well-known case of the Ayala parents in California, who decided to have another child in the hope, which turned out to be justified, that the resulting child would be able to donate bone marrow for a transplant operation that would save the life of their teenage daughter, who was suffering from leukemia. If cloning had been possible at the time, a course of action would have been available to them that unlike having another child in the normal way, would not have been chancy: If they could have cloned the child who was ill, a tissue match would have been certain.

OBJECTIONS TO THE CLONING OF HUMANS

The Cloning of Mindless Organ Banks

Certain objections to the cloning of humans to produce mindless human organisms that would serve as a source of organs for others are perfectly intelligible. If someone objects to this idea on the grounds that one is destroying a person, the concern that is being expressed here is both completely clear and serious. The same is true if the objection is, instead, that such cloning is seriously wrong, since, in preventing a human organism from developing a functioning brain, one is depriving an immaterial soul associated with the organism in question of the possibility of experiencing life in this world. And, finally, the same is also true if someone holds that such cloning would be wrong, because it involves the destruction of an active potentiality for personhood.

The problem with these objections, accordingly, is not that they are in any way incoherent. Nor is it the case that the points raised are unimportant. The problem is simply that all of these objections are, in the end, unsound, for reasons that emerged earlier. Thus, the problem with the first objection is that there are excellent reasons for holding that human embryos do not possess those capacities, such as the capacity for thought and self-consciousness, that something must have, at some point, if it is to be a person. The problem with the second objection is that there are strong reasons for holding that the ontological basis for the capacities involved in consciousness, self-consciousness, thought, and other mental processes resides in the human brain, and not in any immaterial soul. Finally, the problem with the third objection lies in the assumption that the destruction of an active potentiality for personhood is morally wrong, for that claim is, on the one hand, unsupported by any satisfactory argument, and, on the other hand, exposed to decisive objections, one of which was set out earlier.

Often, however, it seems that people who would agree that the above objections are unsound, and who, moreover, do not view abortion as morally problematic, still express uneasiness about the idea of producing mindless human organ banks. Such uneasiness is rarely articulated, however, and it usually takes the form simply of describing the idea of mindless organ banks as a ghoulish scenario. This sort of dismissal of the use of cloning to produce organ banks is very puzzling. For what we are considering here is a way in which lives can be saved, and so, if one rejects this use of cloning, one is urging a course of action that will result in the deaths of innocent people. To do this on the grounds that mindless organ banks strike one as ghoulish seems morally irresponsible in the extreme: If this use of cloning is to be rejected, serious moral argument is called for.

The Cloning of Humans to Produce Persons

Violation of Rights Objections

Some people oppose cloning that is done with the goal of producing a person, on the grounds that such cloning involves a violation of some right of the person who is produced. The most important versions of this first sort of objection are those considered earlier, namely, that there is a violation either of a person's right to be a unique individual, or, more accurately, to be a genetically unique individual, or, alternatively, of a person's right to enjoy an open future that is not constrained by knowledge of the course of the life of some individual with the same genetic makeup. But for the reasons set out earlier, neither of these objections is sound.

Brave New World Style Objections

Next, there is a type of objection that is not frequently encountered in scholarly discussions, but which is rather common in the popular press, and which involves scenarios in which human beings are cloned in large numbers to serve as slaves, or as enthusiastic soldiers in a dictator's army. Such scenarios, however, do not seem very plausible. Is it really at all likely that, were cloning to become available, society would decide that its rejection of slavery had really been a mistake? Or that a dictator who was unable to conscript a satisfactory army from the existing citizens would be able to induce people to undertake a massive cloning program, in order that, 18 years or so down the line, he would finally have the army he had always wanted?

Psychological Distress

This objection is closely related to the earlier, violation of rights objections, because the idea is that, even if cloning does not violate a person's right to be a unique individual, or to have a unique genetic makeup, or to have an open and unconstrained future, nevertheless, people who are clones may feel that their uniqueness is compromised, or that their future is constrained, and this may cause substantial psychological harm and suffering.

There are two reasons for rejecting this objection as unsound. The first arises once one asks what one is to say about the beliefs in question, that is, the belief that one's uniqueness is compromised by the existence of a clone, and the belief that one's future is constrained if one has knowledge of the existence of a clone. Both beliefs are, as we have seen, false. But, in addition, it also seems clear that such beliefs would be, in general, irrational, since it is hard to see what grounds one could have for accepting either belief, other than something like genetic determinism, against which, as we saw earlier, there is conclusive evidence.

Once it is noted that the feelings that may give rise to psychological distress are irrational, one can appeal to the point that I made earlier, when we considered the question of whether knowledge of the existence of a clone might, for example, be damaging to one's sense of individuality, and whether, if this were so, such damage would be grounds for holding that there was a corresponding right that would be violated by cloning. What I argued at that point was that harm to an individual that arises because the individual has an irrational belief has a different moral status from harm that is not dependent on the presence of an irrational belief, and that, in particular, the possibility of the former sort of harm should not be taken as morally constraining others. The responsibility for such harm should, instead, be assigned to the individual who has the irrational belief, and the only obligation that falls on others is to point out to the person in question why the belief is an irrational one.

The second reason why the present objection cannot be sustained is also connected with the fact that the feelings in question are irrational, since the irrationality of the feelings means that they would not be likely to persist for very long, once cloning had become a familiar occurrence. For example, suppose that John feels that he is no longer a unique individual, or that his future is constrained, given that he is a clone of some other individual. Mary may also be a clone of some individual, and she may point out to John that she is very different from the person with whom she is genetically identical, and that she has not been constrained by the way the other person lived her life. Will John then persist in his irrational belief? This does not really seem very likely. If so, any distress that is produced will not be such as is likely to persist for any significant period of time.

Failing to Treat Individuals as Ends in Themselves

A fourth objection is directed, not against the cloning of persons in general, but against certain cases, such as those in which parents clone a child who is suffering from some life-threatening condition, in order to produce another child who will be able to save the first child's life. The thrust of this objection is that such cases involve a failure to view individuals as ends in themselves. Thus Philip Kitcher, referring to such cases, says that "a lingering concern remains," and he goes on to ask whether such scenarios "can be reconciled with Kant's injunction to 'treat humanity, whether in your own person or in the person of another, always at the same time as an end and never simply as a means.'"[10]

What is one to say about this objection? It may be important to be explicit about what sacrifices the child who is being produced is going to have to make to save his or her sibling. When I set out this sort of case under the subheading "Cloning to Save Lives," I assumed that what was involved was a bone marrow transplant. Kitcher, in his formulation, assumes that it will be a kidney transplant. I think that one might well be inclined to take different views of these two cases, given that, in the kidney donation case, but not the bone marrow case, the donor is making a sacrifice that may have unhappy consequences for that person in the future.

To avoid this complicated factor, let us concentrate, then, on the bone marrow case. In such a case, would there be a violation of Kant's injunction? There could be, if the parents were to abandon, or not really care for the one child, once he or she had provided bone marrow to save the life of the other child. But this, surely, would be a very unlikely occurrence. After all, the history of the human race is mostly the history of unplanned children, often born into situations in which the parents were anything but well off, and yet, typically, those children were deeply loved by their parents.

In short, though this sort of case is, by hypothesis, one in which the parents decide to have a child with a goal in mind that has nothing to do with the well being of that child, this is no reason for supposing that they are therefore likely to treat that child merely as a means, and not also as an end in itself. Indeed, surely there is good reason to think, on the contrary, that such a child will be raised in no less loving a way than is normally the case.

Interfering with Personal Autonomy

The final objection that I shall consider is also one that has been advanced by Philip Kitcher, and he puts it as follows: "If the cloning of human beings is undertaken in the hope of generating a particular kind of person, then cloning is morally repugnant. The repugnance arises not because cloning involves biological tinkering but because it interferes with human autonomy."[11]

This objection would not apply to all of the cases that I mentioned in "Considerations in Support of the Cloning of Persons" as ones in which the cloning of a person would be justified. It does, however, apply to many of them. Is the objection sound? I cannot see that it is. First, notice that, in some cases, when one's goal is to produce "a particular kind of person," what one is aiming at is simply a person who will have certain potentialities. Parents might, for example, want to have children who are capable of enjoying intellectual pursuits. The possession of the relevant capacities does not force the children to spend their lives engaged in such pursuits, and so it is hard to see how cloning that is directed at that goal would interfere with human autonomy.

Second, consider cases in which the goal is not to produce a person who will be *capable* of doing a wider range of things, but an individual who will be *disposed* in certain directions. Perhaps it is this sort of case that Kitcher has in mind when he speaks of interfering with human autonomy. But is it really morally problematic to attempt to create persons who will be disposed in certain directions, and not in others? To answer this question, one needs to consider concrete cases, such as the sorts of cases that I mentioned earlier. Is it morally wrong, for example, to attempt to produce, via cloning, individuals who will, because of their genetic makeup, be disposed not to suffer from conditions that may cause considerable pain, such as arthritis, or from life-threatening diseases, such as cancer, high blood pressure, strokes, and heart attacks? Or to attempt to produce individuals who will have a cheerful temperament, or who will not be disposed to depression, to anxiety, to schizophrenia, or to Alzheimer's disease?

It seems unlikely that Kitcher, or others, would want to say that attempting to produce individuals who will be constitutionally disposed in the ways just indicated is a case of interfering with human autonomy. But then, what are the traits that are such that attempting to create a person with those traits is a case of interfering with human autonomy? Perhaps Kitcher, when he speaks about creating a particular kind of person, is thinking not just of any properties that persons have, but, more narrowly, of such things as personality traits, or traits of character, or having certain interests? But again one can ask whether there is anything morally problematic about attempting to create persons with such properties. Some personality traits are desirable, and parents typically encourage their children to develop those traits. Some character traits are virtues, and others are vices, and both parents and society attempt to encourage the acquisition of the former, and to discourage the acquisition of the latter. Finally, many interests, such as music, art, mathematics, science, games, physical activities, can add greatly to the quality of one's life, and once again, parents typically expose their children to relevant activities, and help their children to achieve levels of proficiency that will enable them to enjoy those pursuits.

The upshot is that, if cloning that aimed at producing people who would be more likely to possess various personality traits, or traits of character, or who would be more likely to have certain interests, was wrong because it was a case of interfering with personal autonomy, then the childrearing practices of almost all parents would stand condemned on precisely the same grounds. But such a claim, surely, is deeply counterintuitive.

In addition, however, one need not rest content with an appeal to intuitions here. The same conclusion follows on many high-order moral theories. Suppose, for example, that one is once again behind the Rawlsian veil of ignorance, and that one is deciding among societies that differ regarding their approaches to the rearing of children. Would it be rational to choose a society in which parents did not attempt to encourage their children to develop personality traits that would contribute to the latters' happiness? Or a society in which parents did not attempt to instill in their children a disposition to act in ways that are morally right? Or one in which parents made no attempt to develop various interests in their children? It is, I suggest, hard to see how such a choice could be a rational one, given that one would be opting, it would seem, for a society in which one would be likely to have a life that, on average, would be less worth living.

I conclude, therefore, that, contrary to what Philip Kitcher has claimed, it is not true that most cloning scenarios are morally repugnant, and that, in particular, there is, in general, nothing morally problematic about aiming at creating a child with specific attributes.

CONCLUSION

In this essay, I have distinguished between two very different cases involving the cloning of a human being—one that aims at the production of mindless human organisms that are to serve as organ banks for the people who are cloned, and another that aims at the creation of persons. Regarding the former, the objections that can be advanced are just the objections that can be directed against abortion, and, for reasons that I briefly outlined above, those objections can be shown to be unsound.

Very different objections arise in the case of cloning whose aim is the production of persons. Concerning this second sort of cloning, I argued that it is important to distinguish between the question of whether such cloning is, in principle, morally acceptable, and whether it is acceptable at the present time. Regarding the latter question, I argued that the present use of cloning to produce persons would be morally problematic. By contrast, concerning the question of whether such cloning is in principle morally acceptable, I argued, first, that such cloning is not intrinsically wrong; second, that there are a number of reasons why the cloning of persons would be desirable; and, third, that the objections that have been directed against such cloning cannot be sustained.

My overall conclusion, in short, is that the cloning of human beings, both to produce mindless organ banks, and to produce persons, is both morally acceptable, in principle, and potentially very beneficial for society.

NOTES

1. Brock, D.W. (1998) Cloning human beings: an assessment of the ethical issues pro and con, in *Clones and Clones,* Nussbaum, M. C. and Sunstein, C. R. , eds., Norton, New York. *See* the section entitled "Would the use of human cloning violate important human rights?"
2. Bouchard, T.J. Jr. (1997) Whenever the twain shall meet. *The Sciences* 37, 52–57.
3. Brock, D. in the section entitled "Would the use of human cloning violate important human rights?"
4. Feinberg, J. (1980) The child's right to an open future, in *Whose Child? Children's Rights, Parental Authority, and State Power,* Aiken, W. and LaFollette, H., eds., Rowan and Littlefield, Totowa, NJ.
5. Jonas, H. (1974) *Philosophical Essay: From Ancient Creed to Technological Man,* Prentice-Hall, Englewood Cliffs, NJ.
6. *See*, for example, the discussion of this issue in Bouchard, pp. 55, 56.
7. Brock, D., in the subsection entitled "Human cloning would be a new means to relieve the infertility some persons now experience."
8. *Ibid.*
9. Kitcher, P. (1998) Whose self is it, anyway? *The Sciences* 37, 58–62. It should be noted that, although Kitcher mentions this idea as initially attractive, in the end he concludes that it is problematic, for a reason that will be considered in the subsection "The Cloning of Humans to Produce Persons."
10. *Ibid.*, p. 61.
11. *Ibid.*, p. 61.

QUESTIONS FOR ANALYSIS

1. Tooley asks us to compare the world as it is to an imaginary world in which God decided to make Adam and Eve genetically identical except for the Y chromosome. What is the point of this thought experiment?
2. What benefits does Tooley think cloning would bring? Are they equally beneficial?
3. Does Tooley adequately rebut the objections to human cloning? Why or why not?
4. Do you agree with Tooley that there is nothing immoral about creating mindless human clones as organ banks?
5. Although Tooley addresses many of the objections that Kass raises against human cloning, he fails to address others. Do you think that adequate rebuttals are available to them?

The Morality of Killing Human Embryos

BONNIE STEINBOCK

Bonnie Steinbock, a professor of philosophy at SUNY Albany and a fellow of the Hastings Center, specializes in applied ethics, especially issues of reproduction and genetics. Here she examines several ethical perspectives on the moral status of the embryos used in stem cell research. Drawing on the extensive examination of these issues in the dialogue about the morality of abortion, she concludes that the embryos used in research lack moral status and thus may be used ethically for this purpose, so long as ethical guidelines are respected and the research is only for important purposes.

Embryonic stem cell research is morally and politically controversial because the process of deriving the embryonic stem (ES) cells kills embryos. If embryos are, as some would claim, human beings like you and me, then ES cell research is clearly impermissible. If, on the other hand, the blastocysts from which embryonic stem cells are derived are not yet human beings, but rather microscopic balls of undifferentiated cells, as others maintain, then ES cell research is probably morally permissible. Whether the research can be justified depends on such issues as its cost, chance of success, and numbers likely to benefit. But this is an issue for any research project, not just ES cell research. What makes the debate over ES cell research controversial is that it, like the debate over abortion, raises "questions that politicians cannot settle: when does human life begin, and what is the moral status of the human embryo?"[1] This paper looks at several theories of moral status and their implications for embryo research.

When we ask whether a being has moral status, we are asking whether it counts or matters from the moral point of view; whether it must be considered in our moral deliberations. It seems obvious that not everything has moral status. We are not required to consider the impact of our moral decisions on mere things—for example, ordinary rocks. It seems equally obvious that paradigmatic people—people like you and me—do have moral status. In fact, most people take it for granted that even if moral status isn't limited to people (that animals count, for example) human beings count for more. To express this in Kantian terms, humanity has a dignity and worth which separates humankind from the

Bonnie Steinbock, "The Morality of Killing Human Embryos," *The Journal of Law, Medicine & Ethics* 34:1 (Spring 2006), pp. 26–34.

rest of creation. Because this view is commonplace in moral thinking and in the law, we can call it the common-sense view of moral status.

THE COMMON-SENSE VIEW: THE BIOLOGICAL HUMANITY CRITERION

The common-sense view of moral status is derived from the Judeo-Christian traditional which teaches that only human beings are created in God's image, and therefore human beings alone have this special moral status. In addition, this special moral status belongs to all human beings, regardless of race, ethnicity, nationality, or gender. We are all God's children. Compared to views that limit moral status to members of one's own group or tribe, the Judeo-Christian view is quite progressive. Theoretically (though often not in reality), it prohibits the enslaving or killing of other human beings, simply because they are "outsiders." The secular version of this view bases the unique moral status of humanity on a biological category—membership in the species *homo sapiens.*

The biological humanity criterion of moral status states that all and only human beings, members of our species, have full moral status. But even those who agree on the criterion may differ on this question: when does a human being come into existence? Sometimes this is put in a different way: when does human *life* begin? But this question, familiar from the abortion debate, poses the issue in a misleading way, because every cell in your body is both human (possessed of a human genome) and alive. Human gametes (ova and sperm) are alive, and sperm even swim. So the question, "When does human life begin?" is better understood as asking, "when does an individual human organism come into existence?"

One answer is that a human organism comes into existence at conception. Those who hold the conception view adopt the biological humanity criterion of moral status, which says that all and only human organisms have full moral status. In addition, they believe that a human organism exists at the moment of conception. Indeed, they usually hold that this is a plain matter of biological fact.

However, this is dubious, as there are biological reasons to think that the unique human organism begins to exist only some time after the beginning of fertilization. Fertilization or conception does not occur at a precise moment. It is a process taking place over hours, even days. The process of conception is not completed until syngamy, when the chromosomes from the egg and the sperm have merged, some time after the sperm has penetrated the egg. However, even syngamy may not mark the beginning of a human organism. Ron Green points out,

> biologists usually describe the cells of an organism has having the full range of cellular structure including a single cell nucleus that contains DNA within its own nuclear membrane. But at syngamy the zygote has no definitive nuclear membrane . . . A distinctive diploid cell nucleus does not make its appearance until the two-cell stage, after the zygote undergoes its first cell division . . . [2]

Moreover, in the early stages of an embryo's life, many of its cells, or blastomers, remain "totipotent." This means that each blastomere, is undifferentiated and remains capable, if properly manipulated, of developing into a full human being. One kind of cloning—called embryo splitting or blastomere separation—is accomplished in this way. Embryo splitting also occurs naturally in the case of identical twins (or triplets). Green comments, "if biological humanness starts with the appearance of a unique diploid genome, twins and triplets are living evidence that the early embryo is not yet one human being, but a community of possibly different individuals held together by a gelatinous memberane."[3] He goes on to quote an embryology text as saying, "a genetically unique but non-individuated embryo has yet to acquire determinate individuality, a stable human identity."[4] In this view, a genuine human organism begins to exist only after twinning is no longer possible: at the beginning of gastrulation when the primitive streak (the precursor of the nervous system) forms. In a pregnancy, gastrulation coincides with implantation, the imbedding of the embryo in the uterus, which occurs about fourteen days after fertilization.

The debate over when a human organism comes into existence occurs within the context of the biological humanity criterion. However, the criterion itself has been challenged.

THE PERSON VIEW

In her classic article, "On the Moral and Legal Status of Abortion,"[5] Mary Anne Warren argues that the conservative view on abortion rests on a confusion between two distinct senses of "human being." One sense is biological or genetic. It refers to the species to which an entity belongs. Human fetuses are unquestionably human in the biological sense. However, it does not follow from their genetic humanity that they are human in the other sense, the moral sense, which refers to their moral status and rights. Why should a biological category confer a special moral status? The belief that humanness does imply such a status and rights (human rights) stems from a failure to distinguish between the two senses. To avoid this confusion, Warren suggests that we reserve the term "human" for the biological or genetic sense, and use the term "person" to refer to beings who are full-fledged members of the moral community, possessed of moral rights—in particular, the right to life. This enables us to avoid begging the question in the abortion debate, for it remains an open question whether a human fetus is a person with a right to life.

Why not base moral status and moral rights on species membership? After all, all the persons we know are, in fact, members of the species *homo sapiens*. Why not use species membership as a marker for moral personhood? The reason is the arbitrariness of limiting moral status to genetic human beings. This can be seen if we imagine coming across an extraterrestrial like the eponymous character in the movie, *E.T.* If we were deciding what it would be morally permissible to do to him—say, put him in a zoo, or make him into hamburger—surely the question would not be decided by the number of chromosomes in his cells (if he even had chromosomes). His not being a member of the species *homo sapiens* would not determine his moral status. It seems likely that we would regard him as a person—a non-human person—with all the rights of any one of us.

The example of *E.T.* is meant to show that biological humanity isn't a necessary condition of full moral status. Instead, moral status is based on certain psychological characteristics, such as sentience, consciousness, self-consciousness, the ability to use language, rationality and moral agency. These characteristics are typical of members of our species, but not necessarily limited to them, as the example of *E.T.* is intended to show. Moreover, there seem to be members of our species who lack these person-making characteristics, such as anencephalic babies and patients in persistent vegetative states. They are biologically human, but not persons, and thus do not have the moral status reserved to persons.

An objection made to the person view is that, without an account of the moral relevance of person-making characteristics, it is as arbitrary as a theory based on species membership. Why should moral status and moral rights be limited to sentient, self-conscious, language-using, rational agents? Moreover, depending on how many person-making characteristics are needed for full moral status and rights, the person view appears to exclude those human beings who, due to severe developmental disabilities or mental illness or senility, or even infancy, do not have the capacity to reason or use language. It is hard to accept that human beings in these categories—who are often members of our own families—are not moral persons, with the same moral status and rights as the rest of us. Advocates of the biological humanity criterion maintain that any criterion other than genetic humanity will have this fatal flaw.

The challenge, then, is to construct a theory of moral status that is neither arbitrary (like the biological humanity criterion) nor unduly restrictive (like the person view). Moreover, the view should explain the moral relevance of its criterion for moral status.

THE INTEREST VIEW[6]

The interest view bases moral status on the possession of interests. The view derives from Joel Feinberg's "interest principle,"[7] which was intended to answer the question, what kinds of beings can logically have rights? Feinberg suggests that the answer comes from the purpose or function of rights, which is to protect the interests of the being alleged to have the rights. He usefully analogizes having an interest in something to having a "stake" in it. I am better off if the things in which I have a stake, such as my health, my career, my assets, my family flourish or prosper. Their flourishing is in my interest. Feinberg writes:

> One's interests, then, taken as a miscellaneous collection, consist of all those things in which one has a stake, whereas one's interest in the singular, one's personal interest or self-interest, consists in the harmonious advancement of one's interests in the plural. These interests.... are distinguishable components of a person's well-being: he flourishes or languishes as they flourish or languish. What promotes them is to his advantage or *in his interest;* what thwarts them is to his detriment or *against his interest.*[8]

This is not to claim a one-to-one connection between what a person desires and what is in his self-interests. I can take an interest in something (like junk food) that is not in my interest; and something can be in my interest but not be something I take an interest in (like exercise). But the reason exercise is in my interest, and junk food is not, is that exercise promotes other goals and desires of mine, such as staying healthy and alive, and eating junk food does not. If I had no desires, goals, or preferences at all, nothing would be in my interest.

Unless a being has interests and a welfare of its own, it makes no sense to ascribe rights to it. Feinberg's insight about the logical conditions of having rights can be applied more generally to having moral status. To have moral status is to count or matter, from the moral point of view. If a being has moral status, then its interests must be considered when we engage in moral deliberation. If a being has no interests, its interests cannot be considered. So the possession of interests is a necessary condition of having moral status, and I would argue that it is also a sufficient condition. That is, if a being has interests, there is no justification for ignoring those interests when making moral decisions. (It is a separate question how much weight to accord to the interests of different beings, that is, whether there are other factors that give some beings a higher moral status than others.)

The Feinbergian account of having interests as having stakes in things suggests a conceptual link between interests and consciousness. Only conscious beings—beings with some sort of mental life, however rudimentary—can have wants; only beings with wants can have a stake in anything; only beings that can have a stake in something can have interests of their own. Non-conscious beings, whether mere things (like cars and rocks and works of art) or living things without nervous systems (like plants), have no interests of their own. This is not to say that they cannot be cared for or neglected; repaired or destroyed; nourished or killed. It is rather to say that it does not matter to non-conscious beings what we do to them. We can preserve their existence, and even promote their welfare in the sense of making them better entities of a certain kind. For example, we can fertilize the roses so that they grow vigorously and bloom; we can bring in the can for regular service so that it runs beautifully. However, we cannot do these things out of concern for what matters to them, because nothing matters to them. They do not have a stake in anything, including their own existence. For this reason, I maintain that they, unlike conscious beings, do not have a welfare or sake of their own.

Some will object that we cannot base moral status on consciousness unless we have a definition of consciousness, but there does not seem to be any satisfactory, non-circular definition. Acknowledging the problem, David Boonin says, "It is tempting to say that to be conscious is to be aware of something, for example, but then awareness will surely have to be defined in terms of being in a conscious state."[9] What follows from the absence of a definition of consciousness? Not much, Boonin argues. It is not as if we had no idea what consciousness is. He writes:

> As Nagel famously put it, using an expression that has since become ubiquitous in discussions of the subject, "an organism has conscious mental states if and only if there is something that it is like to *be* that organism—something it is like for the

> organism." Even if this does not constitute a definition of consciousness, you do know what I am talking about when I refer to the fact that there is something that it is like to be you when you see a clear blue sky, hear a shrill scream, feel a sharp prick, or a cold wind, or a burning itch. And this is enough to make clear what is meant by the claim that there is a morally relevant difference between an organism that is conscious in this sense and an organism that is not.[10]

The morally relevant difference between conscious and non-consciousness beings is that conscious beings have interests and a welfare of their own, compounded out of those interests. Non-conscious beings do not have either of these things.

Sentience is only one form of conscious awareness, but it is a very important one. If a being is sentient, that is, it can experience treatment as painful, it has at least one interest: the interest in not experiencing pain. The fact that a being can suffer gives us a reason to treat it in certain ways, and not in other ways. It matters to sentient beings what one does to them, and this is why they have moral claims on us. To take a homely example, it is fine if a child plucks the petals off a daisy while saying "He loves me, he loves me not." It is not fine if the child recites the rhyme while pulling the legs off an insect, or the feathers off a (trapped) bird.

IMPLICATIONS OF THE INTEREST VIEW FOR EMBRYOS

Embryos are not mere things. They are alive and, under certain conditions, have the potential to become beings with interests—indeed, to become people, like you and me. But their potential to become persons does not give them the moral status or the rights of actual persons. Early embryos, indeed early-gestation fetuses, have no consciousness, no awareness, no experiences of any kind, even the most rudimentary. Without even the precursor of a nervous system, pre-implantation embryos cannot possibly have any kind of consciousness. Without consciousness, they cannot have desires; without desires, they cannot have interests. It is not wrong to kill embryos because it doesn't matter to an embryo whether it is killed or goes on living. Its continued existence is clearly not something an embryo takes an interest in, because it is impossible for a non-conscious non-sentient being to take an interest in anything. More importantly, the interest view maintains that continued existence is not in the interests of a non-sentient fetus. For continued existence to be in its interests, it would have to have a welfare of its own, compounded out of all of its interests taken together. Lacking interests, embryos do not have a welfare of their own. In this respect, they are like gametes. Gametes are alive and human, but this is not sufficient for moral status. To have moral status is to be the kind of being whose interests and welfare we moral agents are required to consider. Without interests, there is nothing to consider. This is not to say that there might not be other reasons, including moral reasons, to protect non-interested beings. It is to say that these reasons cannot stem from their own interests or welfare, since they have none. Indeed, on a plausible conception of harming as setting back a being's interests, it follows that killing non-interested beings does not harm them.[11] If this sounds odd, it is because, for *us,* being killed is ordinarily the greatest of harms. But that is because we have interests, and in particular, an interest in continuing to exist. However, if a being has no interests, death is not a harm to it, any more than being destroyed is a harm to an automobile.

Of course, embryos differ from automobiles in one very significant way: embryos are living beings with the potential to develop into human persons, just like you or me, if they are not killed. In a now-classic article, Don Marquis argues that it is wrong to kill fetuses for the very same reason that it is wrong to kill you or me: because doing so deprives them (and us) of our valuable futures. In the next section, I will assess the Valuable Futures argument and its implications for the morality of killing embryos.

MARQUIS AND THE VALUABLE FUTURES ARGUMENT

According to Marquis, both sides of the abortion debate have insurmountable problems. What is needed is a fresh start, an account of why killing is wrong in the paradigm cases in which everyone would agree that it is wrong—namely, the killing of adult human beings, like you or me. Killing adult human beings is *prima facie* wrong because killing them deprives them of their future. Marquis writes:

> The loss of one's life is one of the greatest losses one can suffer. The loss of one's life deprives one of all the experiences, activities, projects, and enjoyments that would otherwise have constituted one's future. Therefore, killing someone is wrong, primarily because the killing inflicts (one of) the greatest possible losses on the victim . . . . When I am killed, I am deprived both of what I now value which would have been part of my future personal life, but also what would come to value. Therefore, when I die, I am deprived of all of the value of my future. Inflicting this loss on me is ultimately what makes killing me wrong. This being the case, it would seem that what makes killing *any* adult human being *prima facie* seriously wrong is the loss of his or her future.[12]

But exactly the same is true of killing a human fetus, and so abortion is, *prima facie,* wrong. *Prima facie* because killing is wrong only if it deprives the one killed of a "valuable future" or a "future-like-ours" (FLO, as it has come to be referred to). Thus, the valuable futures argument does not imply that it is wrong to kill someone in a persistent vegetative state (PVS) because someone in PVS no longer has a valuable future. It's also consistent with voluntary euthanasia, because persons who are severely and incurably ill and who face a future of pain and despair and who wish to die will not have suffered a loss if they are killed, because the future of which they are deprived is not considered by them to be a valuable one. Equally, the aborting of fetuses with defects so severe as to prevent them having FLO might be justifiable on Marquis's account. How severe would the disabling condition have to be to make abortion morally permissible? Is it only lethal conditions (such as Tay-Sachs disease) which deprive fetuses of FLO? Or could non-lethal conditions, such as mental retardation, deprive a fetus of FLO, and thus justify abortion? Marquis does not address these sorts of questions, indeed, does not provide an account of "just what it is about my future or the futures of other adult human beings which make it wrong to kill us."[13] His aim is, rather, to show that abortion is in general a grave wrong. For most fetuses clearly do have valuable futures. If they are not aborted, they will come to have lives they will value and enjoy, just as you and I value and enjoy our lives. Therefore, abortion is seriously wrong for the same reason that killing an innocent adult human being is seriously wrong: it deprives the victim of his or her valuable future.

On the interest view, the killing of non-sentient beings is not seriously wrong because non-sentient beings are not deprived of anything they want or have a stake in by being killed. Marquis thinks that this reveals a fundamental flaw in the interest view, or indeed in any sentience- or desire-based view. First, it seems to imply that it is not wrong to kill someone in a reversible coma or even in deep and dreamless sleep. Such a person is not now conscious or sentient. If we explain the wrongness of killing him by appealing to his future conscious states, then it seems that it is equally wrong to kill a pre-conscious fetus, who will become conscious and sentient in the natural course of events, if it is not aborted. Either the interest view entails that it is morally permissible to kill temporarily comatose adults, in which case it cannot be the right view of moral status, or it must concede that it is wrong to kill fetuses, in which case it cannot be the basis for a defense of abortion. By contrast, the FLO account can explain the wrongness of killing temporarily unconscious adults; this deprives them of their valuable futures.

Second, Marquis argues, the interest view cannot explain why it is wrong to kill someone who is conscious and sentient, but who does not want to go on living. If it is the desire to go on living that makes killing someone seriously wrong, then presumably it is not wrong to kill someone who does not have the desire to go on living, due to (treatable) depression. But of course, Marquis argues, it *is* wrong, and the FLO account can explain why. A person can have a valuable future, even if, due to depression, he does not now have the desire to go on living.

It would be seriously wrong to kill him and thereby to deprive him of that valuable future. (Presumably it would not be wrong to kill someone whose depression was untreatable and who faced "a future of pain and despair." At least, it would not wrong the person killed, though Marquis leaves it open that there might be other reasons why killing him would be wrong.)

The interest view is not vulnerable to these alleged counter-examples. The difference between a fetus and a temporarily comatose adult (TCA) is that a TCA has desires, including a desire to go on living, that make it seriously wrong to kill him. The same is not true of an embryo or first-trimester fetus, which has no desires at all.[14] Admittedly, a TCA does not have any conscious desires. But even while he is unconscious, he still has desires, just as he still has beliefs. David Boonin points out that not all of our beliefs are ones of which we are consciously aware: they are not all occurrent beliefs. To illustrate the dispositional nature of many of our beliefs, Boonin gives the following example. Ten minutes ago you probably were not consciously aware of believing that a triangle has three sides. Yet if I were to ask you, "how many sides does a triangle have?" you would be disposed to answer, "three." That is why it is a dispositional belief. Nevertheless, it is one of your beliefs, a belief you already have. As Boonin puts it, "you do not lose all of your beliefs each time you go to bed and then acquire a new and identical set of beliefs each time you wake up. You retain your beliefs as dispositional beliefs and occasionally have some or others as occurrent beliefs."[15]

Similarly, if you desire not to be killed, you continue to have that desire dispositionally while you are in a reversible coma. On the basis of this desire, we can ascribe to you an interest in continued existence, an interest that exerts a moral claim on the rest of us not to kill you while you are temporarily comatose. But the same cannot be said of a being, like an embryo, that has never been conscious and so has no desires, occurrent or dispositional, and hence no interests.

In a forthcoming article, "Abortion Revisited," Marquis writes, "Boonin's account of and defense of a dispositional desire strategy for dealing with the alleged temporarily unconscious adult counterexample to the present desire view seems reasonable."[16] I take this to mean that Marquis now agrees that the alleged counter-example of the temporarily comatose adult is not a problem for desire- or sentience-based accounts. But what about someone who has no desire, occurrent or dispositional, to go on living, due to severe but temporary depression? Can the interest view explain why it would be seriously wrong to kill such a person without at the same time implying that it would be seriously wrong to kill a fetus?

Boonin responds by arguing that sometimes we need to correct a person's actual desires because, due to various distorting conditions, they do not represent what the individual really wants. He writes, "... in many cases in which we believe that the present desires of others are morally significant, we distinguish between the actual content of the desire that a person has given her actual circumstances and the content the desire she actually has *would* have had if the actual desire had been formed under more ideal circumstances."[17] In the case of the depressed person who does not want to live, it is the depression that makes him unable to think clearly and unable to enjoy his life. When he comes out of the depression, life will seem to him to be worth living again. So of course it would be seriously wrong to kill him while he is in the depressed state. As Boonin puts it, "...when someone's desires are such that they would very strongly desire that you not do something to them were they able to reflect more clearly on the question, then that counts as a very strong moral reason not to do it."[18]

Marquis thinks that the case of the depressed person ("Hans" in Boonin's example) and the fetus are analogous. If what makes killing Hans seriously wrong is that Hans would want to go on living if he were able to think clearly, then why can't we say that what makes killing the fetus wrong is that it would want to go on living, if it could think about it. This is not like saying that a rock would want to go on living if it could think about it, because unlike a rock, a fetus has a future of value, that is, a life that it will value in the future. In this respect, the fetus is just like Hans. And so Marquis writes, "Fetuses are quite different. Hypothetical desires can be attributed as easily to fetuses as to Hans."[19] However, fetuses do not have distorted desires, which need correcting in order to perceive what they really want. Preconscious fetuses do not have desires at all. It seems to me one thing to ascribe an ideal or hypothetical desire to a person whose desires have been distorted, and quite another to ascribe hypothetical desires to a being incapable of having any desires. In any event, I am not sure how much Marquis wants or needs to base his argument on the ascription of hypothetical desires to fetuses, as he has a different argument, which is not dependent on the existence of such desires. He suggests that we can "...attribute interests to a presently insentient being in virtue of its well-being at some future sentient stage of its natural history."[20] In other words, although the fetus is now unconscious and has no desires, it can still have an interest in its future, in the sense that its future is *in* its interest. The motivation for this claim is the view of the fetus as just one stage in a person's natural history. If my life and my future existence are something I value, then it is rational for me to be glad that I was not killed at an earlier stage, for example, when I was a fetus. My valuable future is its valuable future. Having that future (that is, not being killed) is as much in its interest as it is in mine. Or rather, not being killed is as much in my interest when I was a fetus as it is in my interest now.

MCMAHAN'S MIND ESSENTIALISM

So the next question is, was I ever a fetus? That may seem indisputable, given the biological facts. Everyone, surely, started life as a zygote, which developed into an embryo, which became a fetus, and then was born as a baby. However, this is exactly what Jeff McMahan wants to deny. He writes,

> ...even if we grant that a new human organism begins to exist at conception, it follows from this fact that we began to exist at conception only if we are human organisms...if I am a human organism, I began to exist when this organism did. But the assumption that I am numerically identical with the organism with which (to put it as neutrally as possible) I coexist is hardly uncontroversial.[21]

McMahan thinks that the most plausible account of what I essentially am is an embodied consciousness. And if that's the case, then I never existed as a nonconscious fetus. I came into existence when my organism began to be conscious—sometime between 20 and 28 weeks of gestation.[22] Summarizing McMahan's position, David DeGrazia writes,

> ...the thesis of mind essentialism implies that early fetuses, lacking minds, cannot become minded beings, since it asserts that anything that is ever minded is always minded. Thus, early abortions do not kill beings with significant moral status, making these abortions "relevantly like contraception and wholly unlike the killing of a person." The Valuable Futures Argument therefore trips on the mistaken assumption that the early fetus will develop into a minded being. Because it will not, the early fetus does not *have* a valuable future.[23]

McMahan's theory provides a neat response to Marquis—but only if one accepts his mind essentialism, and the idea that the preconscious fetus cannot develop into a conscious fetus, much less a person like you or me. That seems to me to fly in the face of the facts. It seems much more plausible to say that I was once a child, and before that an infant, and before that a fetus. Boonin, commenting on the pictures in his office of his son, Eli, at various stages after birth, says, "through all of the remarkable changes that these pictures preserve, he remains unmistakably the same little boy." He also has another picture of Eli taken 24 weeks before his birth. Boonin writes, "there is no doubt in my mind that this picture, too, shows that same little boy at a very early stage in his physical development."[24] McMahan would have to say that the sonogram is a picture of Eli's organism at a very early stage, but it is not a picture of Eli. I would say (and I assume Boonin would agree) that I am my organism, although this is not all that I am. However, to posit a "me" that is distinct from my physical self seems implausible, and the wrong way to defend abortion. Rather, I would say that when I was a fetus, it would have been permissible to abort me, because had I been aborted before I became conscious and sentient, it would not have mattered to me. It would have made no more difference to me than preventing my conception. So while I agree with Marquis that I was once a fetus, I deny that when I was a fetus, I had an interest or a stake in my valuable future. I think that when I was a mindless fetus, I had no interests at all.

IMPLICATIONS FOR BLASTOCYSTS

I began this paper with the question whether it is seriously wrong to kill embryos at the blastocyst stage. I want to suggest now that even if Marquis is right about the morality of abortion—that it's wrong to kill fetuses because they have valuable futures it is not plausible to claim that pre-implantation embryos do. For unlike a fetus, an extracorporeal embryo is not developing into someone with a valuable future. Left alone (that is, not aborted), the fetus will (most likely) develop into someone with a valuable future. But the same is just not true of an embryo, whether left-over from IVF or deliberately created for research. Left alone, an extracorporeal embryo will just die. That's not much of a valuable future.

It might be argued that the blastocyst *could* be implanted into a uterus, where it too would develop into a baby, and thus it has, hypothetically, a valuable future. Of course, this is true only of viable embryos. Non-viable embryos—embryos incapable of further development—cannot have valuable futures. Presumably, even on Marquis's view, it would be morally permissible to use non-viable embryos left over from infertility treatment in embryo research (although I do not know if the stem cells derived from non-viable embryos could be used in treating disease should ES cell therapies ever be develop).

Most opponents of ES cell research make no distinction between embryos created by IVF and embryos created by cloning. However, on the Valuable Futures approach, there might be a considerable difference. We know that it is possible, under some set of conditions, for an IVF embryo to develop into a baby. Over 35,000 babies were born in the Untied States alone in 2000 (ASRM/SART Registry 2004). By contrast, biologist Rudof Jaenisch maintains that "a cloned embryo has little, if any, potential to develop into a normal human being." He explains:

> By circumventing the normal processes of gametogenesis and fertilization, nuclear cloning prevents the proper reprogramming of the clone's genome ... which is a prerequisite for the development of an embryo into a normal organism. It is unlikely that these biologic barriers to normal development can be overcome in the foreseeable future.[25]

Jaenisch hastens to point out that the embryonic stem cells derived from a cloned embryo are functionally indistinguishable from those derived from IVF embryos, making them equally useful as a source for ES cells in research or therapy.

The chance a human embryo has of developing into a normal human being is irrelevant from the perspective of the biological humanity criterion. What matters for moral status is that the embryo is a human organism (although, as we have seen, there is considerable debate about when a human organism comes into existence). On this criterion, the moral status of the embryo is determined by its genetic humanity, not what it can or cannot develop into. Marquis, however, explicitly rejects the genetic humanity criterion, because it is hard to see why a merely biological category should make a moral difference. Clearly, he is sympathetic to this objection expressed by pro-choicers: "why, it is asked, is it any more reasonable to base a moral conclusion on the number of chromosomes in one's cells than on the color of one's skin?"[26] By contrast, on the Valuable Futures approach, the developmental potential of an embryo makes all the difference in the world, since if a cloned embryo cannot develop into someone like you or me, it cannot have FLO. Killing it does not deprive it of its valuable future, and therefore, presumably, is not seriously wrong.

This has interesting implications for the "created/spare" distinction, appealed to by the National Bioethics Advisory Commission (NBAC) in its report, *Cloning Human Beings*. According to NBAC, it would be wrong to create embryos solely for the purpose of research; to do so would be inconsistent with the respect due to embryos as a form of human life. However, it would be ethically permissible to use embryos created for reproductive purposes, which are no longer needed (so-called "spare" embryos), since these embryos would be discarded anyway. President Bush considered this argument in his August 6, 2001 address to the nation, but ultimately rejected it. He maintained that it was impermissible to kill any embryos, even those that would be discarded anyway. On the valuable futures approach, it appears that the created/spare distinction has moral relevance, though precisely opposite to that claimed by NBAC. Whereas NBAC argued that only spare embryos can be ethically used (and destroyed) in research, in the valuable futures approach, it would be morally acceptable to use cloned human embryos as sources of stem cells since they lack FLO, but unacceptable to use embryos discarded after fertility treatment, since they have FLO. They have FLO because they could be used to make babies, even if their creators do not wish to use them for this purpose. This is a rather starting implication of the Valuable Futures argument. The claim that it is morally better to use cloned embryos rather than embryos left over from infertility treatment is not one that I have seen anywhere in the Valuable Futures literature.

My own view is that we should reject the created/spare distinction, although not for the reason President Bush gave. I think that it is permissible to use human embryos in research that kills them because embryos lack moral status. In my view, it makes no difference what the source of the embryos is, whether they are created by IVF or cloned; whether they are created specifically for research purposes or are left over from infertility treatment. However, I do not think it is permissible to use embryos for frivolous or trivial purposes. I maintain that respect for human life requires that human embryos be used for morally important purposes, but that is a topic for another paper.[27]

NOTES

1. S. G. Stolberg, "Controversy Reignites Over Stem Cells and Clones," *New York Times,* December 18, 2001, at F1.
2. R. M. Green, *The Human Embryo Research Debates* (New York: Oxford University Press, 2001): at p. 28.
3. *Id.*, at p. 29.
4. See also J. A. Robertson, *Children of Choice: Freedom and the New Reproductive Technologies* (Princeton: Princeton University Press, 1994): at 251, note 13: "...recent studies suggest that a new genome is not expressed until the four-to eight-cell stage of development." See Braude, Bolton, and Moore, "Human Gene Expression First Occurs Between the Four and Eight-Cell Stage of Preimplantation Development," *Nature* 332 (1998): at p. 459, 460.
5. M. Warren, "On the Moral and Legal Status of Abortion," *The Monist* 57, no. 1, (1973): pp. 43–61. Warren's views have changed since 1973, and her current views on moral status are given in her book, *Moral Status.* Nevertheless, her earlier article is an excellent statement of the person view, a view that many people continue to hold.
6. I develop the interest view in Chapter 1 of my book, *Life Before Birth: The Moral and Legal Status of Embryos and Fetuses* (New York: Oxford University Press, 1992).
7. J. Feinberg, "The Rights of Animals and Unborn Generations," in William. T. Blackstone, ed., *Philosophy & Environmental Crisis* (Athens: University of Georgia Press, 1974).
8. J. Feinberg, *Harm to Others* (New York: Oxford University Press, 1984.): at p. 34.
9. D. Boonin, *A Defense of Abortion* (Cambridge: Cambridge University Press, 2003): at p. 102.
10. *Id.,* at pp. 102–103, citing T. Nagel, "What is it like to be a Bat?" in T. Nagel, *Mortal Questions* (Cambridge: Cambridge University Press, 1979): at p. 166.
11. Some philosophers apparently reject the idea that harming involves the setting back or thwarting of a being's interests. See, for example, E. Harman, "The Potentiality Problem," *Philosophical Studies* 114(2003): pp. 173–198. Harman thinks

that it is obvious that beings without moral status can be harmed, and gives the following example: The deprivation of light harms a weed. However, the reason why I maintain that a weed is not harmed when it killed is not that weeds lack moral status. Rather, it is that I agree with Feinberg that harming involves the setting back or thwarting of interests. Since weeds (or prize orchids, for that matter) do not have interests, they cannot be harmed, though they can be killed. To show that this is wrong, one would need to give an alternate account of harming, something Harman does not do.

12. D. Marquis, "Why Abortion is Immoral," *The Journal of Philosophy* 86, no. 4(1989): pp. 183–202, at pp. 189–190.
13. *Id.,* at p. 191.
14. In *Life Before Birth,* I argued that sentience was unlikely until well into the second trimester. "Pain perception requires more than brain waves. It is involves the development of neural pathways and particular cortical and subcortical centers, as well as neurochemical systems associated with pain transmission. In light of this, it seems extremely unlikely that a first-trimester fetus could be sentient," B. Steinbock, *supra* note 6, at 189. This is consistent with moral recent findings of researchers on fetal pain. Vivette Glober and Nicholas Fisk write, "To experience anything, including pain, the subject needs to be conscious, and current evidence suggests that this involves activity in the cerebral cortex and possibly the thalamus. We do not know for sure when or even if the fetus becomes conscious. However, temporary thalamocortical connections start to form at about 17 weeks and become established from 26 weeks. It seems very likely that a fetus can feel pain from that stage." V. Glover and N. Fisk, *British Medical Journal* 313 (1996): 796. For this reason, Glover and Fisk suggest that more attention should be paid to pain relief during labor and delivery for the baby as well as the mother, and that safe methods of administering analgesia to the fetus in late terminations (after 20 weeks) should be developed. At the same time, in an interview with the BBC, Dr. Glover stressed that it is incredibly unlikely that a first-trimester fetus can feel pain because there is no linking to the brain at all. Editor, "Abortion Causes Foetal Pain," *BBC News, at* <(http://news.bbc.co.uk/1/hi/health/900848.stm> (last visited December 6, 2005).
15. D. Boonin, *A Defense of Abortion* (Cambridge: Cambridge University Press, 2003): at 65–66.
16. D. Marquis, "Abortion Revisited," in B. Steinbock, ed., *The Oxford Handbook of Bioethics* (Oxford: Oxford University Press, forthcoming).
17. Boonin, *supra* note 15, at 70.
18. *Id.,* at p. 76.
19. Marquis, *supra* note 16.
20. D. Marquis, "Justifying the Rights of Pregnancy: The Interest View," Review of Bonnie Steinbock," Life Before Birth," *Criminal Justice Ethics* 13, no. 1 (1994): pp. 67–81, at 72.
21. J. McMahan, *The Ethics of Killing: Problems at the Margins of Life* (New York: Oxford University Press, 2002): at p. 4.
22. Or as early as 17 weeks, if Glover and Fisk are right, *supra* note 14.
23. D. DeGrazia, "Identity, Killing, and the Boundaries of Our Existence," *Philosophy & Public Affairs* 31, no. 4 (2003): pp. 413–442, at p. 427.
24. Boonin, *supra* note 15, at xiv.
25. R. Jaenisch, "Human Cloning–The Science and Ethics of Nuclear Transplantation," *New England Journal of Medicine* 351, no. 27 (2004): pp. 2787–2791.
26. D. Marquis, *supra* note 12, at p. 186.
27. See B. Steinbock, "Respect for Human Embryos," in P. Lauritzen, ed., *Cloning and the Future of Human Embryo Research* (New York: Oxford University Press, 2001). See also B. Steinbock, "Moral Status, Moral Value, and Human Embryos: Implications for Stem Cell Research," in B. Steinbock, ed., *The Oxford Handbook of Bioethics* (Oxford: Oxford University Press, forthcoming).

QUESTIONS FOR ANALYSIS

1. Some defenders of embryonic stem cell research argue that because most of the frozen blastocysts will be discarded anyway, it is not unethical to use them in scientific research. Of the various positions on the status of embryos surveyed in Steinbock's article, which would be supportive of this position and why? The "common-sense view," as Steinbock calls it? Warren's "person

view"? Feinberg's "interest principle" The "valuable futures" argument advanced by Marquis? McMahan's "mind essentialism"?
2. How does Steinbock distinguish between the moral status of IVF embryos and embryos created by cloning? Is medical research on cloned embryos less problematic ethically than research on IVF embryos, under her analysis?
3. Steinbock suggests that destroying embryos is justified for "morally important" purposes, but not for "frivolous or trivial" ones. What might be examples of those different purposes? Should this distinction be imposed on the decision to have an abortion? That is, should a woman have to prove that her reasons were not "frivolous or trivial" before she could get an abortion?

Stem Cells, Biotechnology, and Human Rights: Implications for a Posthuman Future

PAUL LAURITZEN

Professor of religious studies and director of the Program in Applied Ethics at John Carroll University in Cleveland, Paul Lauritzen has written extensively on biomedical ethics. Here he expresses concern about research on both embryonic stem cells and adult stem cells. He believes that the debate has been cast too narrowly by all sides in the same terms used in the abortion debate. Instead, we should focus on the broader implications of the morality of the commodification of human lives.

> *. . . the final stage is come when man by eugenics, by prenatal conditioning, and by an education and propaganda based on perfect applied psychology, has obtained full control over himself. Human nature will be the last part of nature to surrender to man.*
>
> —C.S. LEWIS, *The Abolition of Man*

> *This sudden shift from a belief in Nurture, in the form of social conditioning, to Nature, in the form of genetics and brain physiology is the great intellectual event, to borrow Nietzsche's term, of the late twentieth century.*
>
> —TOM WOLFE, *Hooking Up*

I begin with passages from this unlikely pair of authors because, although they represent somewhat different times, differ in temperament, and differ extravagantly in personal style, they share an imaginative capacity to envision the possible consequences of modern technology. The technology that occasioned Lewis's reflections—"the aeroplane, the wireless, and the contraceptive"—may now seem quaint, but the warning he sounded about turning humans into artifacts was eerily prescient. Similarly, although he does not directly take up stem cell research, Tom Wolfe's reflections on brain imaging technology, neuropharmacology, and genomics are worth noting in relation to the future of stem cell research. In his inimitable way, Wolf summarizes one view of the implications of this technology in the title of the essay from which the above passage comes. "Sorry," he says, "but your soul just died."

The point of beginning with Lewis and Wolfe is not that I share their dire predictions about the fate to which they believe technology propels us; instead, I begin with these writers because they invite use to take an expansive view of technology. I believe that a broader perspective is needed in

Paul Lauritzen, "Stem Cells, Biotechnology, and Human Rights: Implications for a Posthuman Future," *Hastings Center Report* 35:2 (March–April 2005): 25–33.

the ongoing public debate over stem cell research and that such a perspective is in fact beginning to emerge.[1] This is not to say that the traditional analysis that has framed much of the debate—analysis of autonomy, informed consent, and commodification, for example—is unhelpful; far from it. Nevertheless, much of the debate about stem cell research has focused on the enormously divisive issue of embryo status. Indeed, the debate about stem cell research seems almost choreographed, the steps all too familiar from the dance of abortion politics. The upshot is that much of the stem cell debate has been too narrowly focused and is repetitive and rigid.[2] For that reason, I urge that we consider stem cell research together with other forms of biogenetic research and therapy. Among other things, shifting the frame of reference in this way would require us to attend much more carefully to issues raised by adult stem cell work. Thus, instead of beginning with a question about embryo status, let us start with a question that has not typically been asked: Is adult stem cell work as unproblematic as it is often assumed to be?

Francis Collins's testimony before the President's Council on Bioethics in December 2002 suggests why this may be a productive question. Collins was asked to speak about "genetic enhancements: current and future prospects," and what he said about pre-implantation genetic screening is instructive. He noted that we are now able to screen both gametes and embryos, but because gamete screening is currently limited to sorting sperm for sex selection, he did not discuss it at length. He did, however, offer an interesting observation. Focusing on gametes, he says, is useful because it "isolates you away from some of the other compelling arguments about moral status of the embryo and allows a sort of cleaner discussion about what are the social goods or evils associated with broad alterations in the sex ratio and inequities in access to that technology."[3] In other words, the ethical issues raised by pre-implantation genetic screening are not limited to those brought about by the destruction of embryos required by PGD; indeed, screening gametes also raises serious moral issues, ones that might be eclipsed if we focus exclusively on embryos.

Might we not make a similar claim about embryonic and adult stem cell research? Adult stem cell research is often thought to sidestep some of the issues raised by work on embryonic stem cell, but in fact, does it not raise many of the most pressing issues surrounding embryonic stem cell research, only in a somewhat cleaner and more direct form?

I believe it does, and that we need to attend to a whole range of issues related to embodiment, species boundaries, and human nature that are raised by recent developments in what Bruce Jennings has referred to as the "regime of biopower."[4] I will discuss two broad concerns posed by stem cell research and related biotechnological interventions. The first has to do with the prospect of transforming the contours of human life in fairly dramatic ways. The second has to do with our attitudes toward the natural world. As we move to change the meaning of human embodiment in fundamental ways, including the possibility of eroding species boundaries, we need to ask whether we are prepared to reduce the entire natural world to the status of an artifact. These concerns raise questions about the meaning of human rights in a posthuman future.

EMBODIMENT, HUMAN RIGHTS AND HUMAN NATURE

To get a sense of what kinds of issues arise when we consider changing the contours of human existence, consider the notion that there is a species-typical pattern for human life that gives a determinate shape to our lives, a shape that has normative significance. On this view, there is a natural "trajectory" to human life, a natural ebb and flow from conception to death, that has implications for developing moral and political positions across a range of social issues, from reproductive technology to physician-assisted suicide. Yet stem cell research appears to challenge the idea of a natural trajectory to human life.

For example, Catherine Waldby and Susan Squier argue that the derivation of stem cells from early embryos demonstrates that embryos do not have one developmental trajectory.

According to Waldby and Squier, stem cell research reveals the plasticity of early embryonic material, and in doing so demonstrates "*the perfect contingency* of any relationship between embryo and person, [and] the non-teleological nature of the embryo's developmental pathways." Indeed, they say, this research shows "that the embryo's life is not proto-human, and that the biology and biography of human life cannot be read backwards into its moments of orgin."[5] This claim may at first appear to be about embryo status, but Waldby and Squier mean to imply much more. In effect, they reject the notion that there is a meaningful trajectory to human life. What was killed when stem cells were first derived from the inner cell mass of a blastocyst, they say, was not a person, but a "biographical idea of human life, where the narrative arc that describes identity across time has been extended to include the earliest moments of ontogeny."[6]

That much more is at stake here than whether embryos are persons is clear if we attend to those who subscribe to the notion of a trajectory of a human life. Gilbert Meilaender, for example, has argued that our attitudes toward death and dying are shaped by our conception of what it means to have a life.[7] Indeed, according to Meilaender, two views of what it means to have a life and to be a person have been at war with each other over the past thirty years, and these views underwrite sharply different positions on practically every bioethical issue. On Meilaender's view, having a life means precisely that one is following a trajectory that traces a "natural pattern" that "moves through youth and adulthood toward old age and, finally, decline and death."[8] As he puts it, "to have a life is to be *terra animata*, a living body whose natural history has a trajectory."[9] Although Meilaender develops the notion of a natural trajectory primarily to address the issue of euthanasia, not stem cell research, talk of "natural history," "natural pattern," and "natural trajectory" is also relevant to stem cell research and related technologies. These new biotechnologies might fundamentally change our views about how and even whether a human life is constrained by the natural aging process. The question these biotechnologies raise, then, is whether such a change should be resisted.

There is little doubt that Meilaender would resist significant alteration of the natural trajectory, and other members of the President's Council on Bioethics, prominently Leon Kass and Francis Fukuyama, have raised similar concerns. But while those who oppose biotechnological interventions that may change the shape of the human life cycle are sometimes lumped together as "life cycle traditionalists," it is important to note that changing the trajectory of a life raises two distinct concerns.

The first is a more or less straightforward concern about the social consequences of altering the human life cycle. This concern is nicely illustrated by Francis Fukuyama's discussion of the social implications of dramatically lengthening the human life span in his book *Our Posthuman Future*. Suppose, he says, that regenerative medicine realizes its promise and the average life span expands from seventy to 110 years or more. What social dislocations can we expect? To explore this question, Fukuyama divides an aging cohort into two categories: the first category comprises people age sixty-five up to eighty-five; the second category is age eighty-five and older. The consequences of greatly expanding membership in these categories should give us pause, Fukuyama concludes, even if older people are much more vigorous than they are today.

"For virtually all of human history up to the present," he writes,

> people's lives and identities were bound up either with reproduction—that is, having families and raising children—or with earning the resources to support themselves and their families. Family and work both enmesh individuals in a web of social obligations over which they frequently have little control and which are a source of struggle and anxiety, but also of tremendous satisfaction. Learning to meet those social obligations is a source of both morality and character.
>
> People in Categories I and II, by contrast, will have a much more attenuated relationship to both family and work. They will be beyond reproductive years, with links primarily to ancestors and descendants. Some in Category I may choose to work, but the obligation to work and

> the kinds of mandatory social ties that work engenders will be replaced largely by a host of elective occupations. Those in Category II will not reproduce, not work, and indeed will see a flow of resources and obligation moving one way: toward them.[10]

Other possible negative consequences include a growing burden on the environment due to overpopulation, a prolongation of adolescent immaturity, increased burdens on an already strained health care system, and other social costs.[11]

The second concern is often expressed in terms of a threat to human identity or what it means to be human, and although this concern frequently has a consequentialist cast, it comes in a largely non-consequentialist form as well. Walter Glannon has developed the most interesting form of the identity argument. According to Glannon, one direct consequence of significantly increasing the human lifespan would be to attenuate the relationship among past, present, and future mental states of a self and thus undermine the psychological grounds of personal identity. Since a sense of psychological connectedness between the present and the future is necessary to ground future-oriented desires, the inevitable erosion of a sense of connectedness that would come with a much longer life would, paradoxically, result in the extinction of the desire for a longer life. Without a reasonably strong sense of psychological connectedness to some future self, one would have little reason to take an interest in the potential projects of that person.

In Glannon's formulation, there would be biological continuity between a present and distant future self, but psychological discontinuity: "there would be a divergence of our biology from our psychology."[12] Strictly speaking, it would be more accurate (and also more helpful) to say that a new biology would result in a new psychology. And, in fact, such a formulation is more consistent with Glannon's analysis, one aspect of which involves examining the formation-storage-retrieval process by which the brain maintains the equilibrium between remembering and forgetting that is critical to psychological unity. Discussing the function of activator and blocker CREB (cyclic AMP response element binary protein), Glannon writes:

> The function of this protein suggests that the requisite unity between these states can hold only for a limited period of time. Anticipation cannot extend so far into the future that it undermines memory of the past. By the same token, there cannot be so much stored memory of past events that it comes at the expense of our ability to anticipate and plan for the future. A break in this equilibrium would . . . undermine our ability to sustain long-term projects by breaking the unity of forward- and backward-looking attitudes necessary to ground these projects.[13]

In effect, the problem with increasing the lifespan is not that it causes psychology and biology to part company. Rather, changing the biology of human aging would profoundly change human psychology.

On one level, then, Glannon's concern about using stem cell therapies to significantly increase the human lifespan is a consequentialist worry about the psychological effects on humans of dissociating the present from the distant past or remote future. According to Glannon, we cannot rationally desire to lengthen the human life span because doing so would have disastrous consequences for our ability to undertake projects, accept responsibility for our past or future actions, or indeed, even care very much about "our" future. Notice, however, that there is a corollary to Glannon's maxim, as reformulated. If a new biology gives rise to a new psychology, it also gives rise to a new ethics. Or to put the point negatively, a new biology threatens our existing ethical commitments.

It is this kind of thought that animates the opposition of the life cycle traditionalists to biotechnologies that might alter the trajectory of a human life. When Leon Kass says that "many human goods . . . are inseparable from our aging bodies, from our living in time, and from the natural life cycle," he has this worry in mind.[14] It is also a central concern of *Our Posthuman Future*. Fukuyama suggests that we can grasp the threat biotechnology poses by noting pervasiveness in modern moral discourse of the language of human rights, which is effectively the only available vocabulary for discussing human goods or ends. The most persuasive account of human rights, however, is framed in relation to the notion of a stable human nature.[15] According to Fukuyama, neither a religious conception of rights nor a positivist conception is viable. But once we recognize the relationship between human rights and human nature, we can give a very precise sense to the worry that we may be heading toward a posthuman future. The fear is that biotechnology will change the species-typical characteristics shared by all humans. If that happens, and if rights are tied to a conception of human nature that is in turn rooted in a biological reality, then biotechnology threatens the very basis of human morality as we know it.

Perhaps the life cycle traditionalists put more weight on the notion of human nature than it can reasonably bear. Still, the connection between a relatively stable set of natural capacities and the claims of human rights is important. Indeed, the sharp social and political disagreements between the life cycle traditionalists and more left-leaning theorists can lead us to overlook a shared commitment to the importance of identifying a stable set of natural human capacities. For example, although Martha Nussbaum is suspicious of the language of human nature because she thinks it has been misused to defend oppressive social structures, her work both on the human capacity for care and compassion and on basic conditions of human flourishing relies centrally on the notion of natural human capacities that give rise to basic human rights.

In a recent article, "Compassion & Terror," Nussbaum discusses Euripides' play *Trojan Women,* and explores the poet's sympathetic imagining of the fate of Trojan women and children in the course of developing her own reflections on the conditions and limits of a compassionate vision.[16] Although she is ultimately concerned about engendering such a vision for Americans in the face of terror—and particularly compassion for innocent women and children far from our shores—her analysis is also thought provoking in light of the future of biomedicine.

Nussbaum notes that compassion requires a series of judgments involving another person's suffering or lack of well-being. We must judge that someone has been harmed, that the harm is serious, and that it was not deserved. Moreover, says Nussbaum, the Western tradition has stressed what could be called the "judgment of similar possibilities." In other words, "we have compassion only insofar as we believe that the suffering person shares vulnerabilities and possibilities with us."[17]

Surely, just about every person's catalog of human vulnerabilities includes illness, old age, and death. Yet arguably stem cell research may significantly transform the "human" experience of illness and death, at least for some. If stem cell therapies were to erode the notion of human nature, such as by blurring species boundaries, might they not also erode some basic moral sensibilities? Mary Midgley, for example, has argued that the notions of both human nature and human rights are importantly tied to membership in our species because rights are "supposed to guarantee the kind of life that all specimens of *Homo sapiens* need."[18]

Although Nussbaum avoids the language of human nature, it is precisely this sort of point that she highlights when she argues that compassion requires the belief that others share vulnerabilities and possibilities with us. Indeed, like Midgley, Nussbaum ties the notion of universal human rights to important human functions and capabilities. The basic idea, she says, is to ask what constitutes the characteristic activities of human beings: "What does the human being do, characteristically, as such—and not, say, as a member of a particular group, or a particular local community?"[19] Nussbaum notes that this inquiry proceeds by examining characteristic human activities in a wide variety of settings, and that comparing and contrasting human activities with the activities of non-human animals is helpful. So, too, is using myths and stories to compare humans and the gods. Such an inquiry, Nussbaum insists, helps us define limits that derive from membership in the natural world. Given the way that talk about "human nature" has been used in the past to exclude groups from full membership in the human moral community, there are good reasons to be careful about it. Nevertheless, unless we maintain some sense of nature that is not culturally constructed, we have no meaningful grounds for complaining about the lack of humane treatment of others.[20]

Indeed, although Nussbaum is exquisitely attentive to the wide variety of cultural interpretations of what it means to be human, she insists that a universal notion of human rights cannot be grounded unless one attends to human biology. Nussbaum's account of the human is neither ahistorical nor a priori; it is linked to an "empirical study of a species-specific form of life."[21] She begins her account of central human capabilities with the body:

> We live all our lives in bodies of a certain sort, whose possibilities and vulnerabilities do not as such belong to one human society rather than another. These bodies, similar far more than dissimilar (given the enormous range of possibilities) are our homes, so to speak, opening certain options and denying others, giving us certain needs and also certain possibilities for excellence. The fact that any given human being might have lived anywhere and belonged to any culture is a great part of what grounds our mutual recognitions; this fact, in turn, has a great deal to do with the general humanness of the body, its great distinctness from other bodies. The experience of the body is culturally shaped, to be sure; the importance we ascribe to its various functions is also culturally shaped. But the body itself, not culturally variant in its nutritional and other related requirements, sets limits on what can be experienced and valued, ensuring a great deal of overlap.[22]

Nussbaum's work is suggestive in another way, for she also notes how anxiety about our embodied existence, and the vulnerability that bodily existence entails, may be a profound impediment to compassion. I cannot do justice to the richness of Nussbaum's account of the emotional obstacles to compassion, but one aspect of her argument is worth noting here. In addition to analyzing the emotion of compassion, Nussbaum examines shame and digust.[23] Drawing on psychological studies of these emotions, she notes that both appear to concern a sense of vulnerability that arises from the fact that we are embodied beings. A sense of inadequacy may lead to the emotion of disgust, for example, which in turn serves to distance the self from its own vulnerabilities.

The problem with this emotional dynamic is the almost universal human tendency to project features of disgust outward, onto others, as a way of shoring up one's own sense of stability and power. "Throughout history," says Nussbaum, "certain disgust properties—sliminess, bad smell, stickiness, decay, foulness—have repeatedly and monotonously been associated with, indeed projected onto, groups by reference to whom privileged groups seek to define their superior human status."[24] Whether it is Jews, women, homosexuals, untouchables, or blacks who have been labeled and treated as disgusting, the underlying anxiety appears to be "the intolerance of humanity in oneself."[25]

Of course, once we label the other as disgusting, it is difficult to see the shared vulnerability that underwrites compassion. That is why social hierarchies based on class, race, religion, ethnicity, or gender are such impediments to compassion: they lead one group to see itself as vastly superior to another group and thus erode the possibility of seeing the common humanity of the other. In such a situation, compassion easily withers. Here, then we see the danger to which Nussbaum's work draws our attention. To the degree that applications of stem cell research may erode a sense of common humanity, and to the degree that such applications may promote a social hierarchy rooted in genetics, they run the risk of blocking compassion and advancing intolerance.

Nussbaum's work identifying the judgments that underwrite compassion and tying a universalist account of rights to common human function and capabilities highlights what may be at stake with stem cell research and with a growing list of biotechnological developments that appear to destabilize the concept of human nature. It suggests why we need to think carefully about the social implications of a situation in which some humans have access to these technologies while other humans do not. At the very least, what Paul Rabinow describes as the biologicaliztion of identity around genetics (rather than gender and race), combined with the possibility of manipulating genetic identity for those with the money or power to do so, does not bode well for securing widespread compassion across economic or technological divides. Even more important, however, is the recognition that the very notion of human rights may ultimately rest on the idea (and what, until recently, has always been the reality) of a natural, relatively stable human condition.

THE NATURAL WORLD AND INSTRUMENTALIZATION

A second, related worry is suggested by C.S. Lewis's warning about our unchecked hubris in seeking utter control over nature. It is not only human nature that we might destabilize, but the concept of "nature" generally and the appropriate treatment of any sentient life. Moreover, given how politically charged the concept of "human nature" is, we might do well, at least initially, to think about challenges to "human nature" by attending to views about "nature" generally, or the "nature" of non-human animals, or both.

These matters are not easily considered from within the typical frame of bioethics. Because the conceptual tools available in bioethics are not well suited to the task, I wish instead to turn to the cultural space that contemporary art provides for moral reflection on social issues posed by definitions of nature.

Patricia Piccinini has explored the issues raised by contemporary biotechnology in her sculptures, photographs, and video installations.[26] Piccinini's exhibition, "Call of the Wild," which appeared at the Museum of Contemporary Art in Sidney, Australia, is like much of her work in that it demonstrates "an interest in the human form and its potential for manipulation and enhancement through bio-technological intervention."[27] Also, like her other work, this exhibition explores the relationship between human and non-human animals as it is mediated by biotechnology. One of the works in the exhibition, "Protein Lattice," is designed to provoke discussion about the possibility of using non-human animals to grow tissue and organs for transplant to humans. It takes as its point of departure the effort to grow human ears on a three-dimensional protein lattice on the back of mice. The installation is quite complex, involving television monitors on which the viewer sees rats trapped in a maze. At the same time, large images of young digitally enhanced human female models are juxtaposed with rats that have human ears on their backs. The rats surround some of the models; others serve as perches for the rats. In another work, "Still Life with Stem Cells," Piccinini presents a young girl playing with a disturbing but still oddly attractive collection of tissue and organs sculpted to look like human flesh and intended to be seen as tissue grown from stem cells.

Although Piccinini's work should certainly be taken on its own aesthetic terms, it is illuminating to think about her work in light of Kass's defense of the "wisdom of repugnance." The images in her art are simultaneously beautiful and repulsive. Indeed, the artist makes clear her own ambivalence about biotechnology and sees her work partly as a vehicle for reflecting on how human manipulation of "nature" is both inspirational and frightening.[28] Jason Scott Robert and Françoise Baylis have recently insisted that if claims about repugnance are to have moral force, then "the intuitions captured by the 'yuck' response must be clarified."[29] One strategy for seeking clarification would be to catalog our reactions to work such as Piccinini's and explore those reactions in a sustained way. For example, the contrast between the beautiful models and the ugly rodents in "Protein Lattice" invites reflection on our views of beauty in relation to what we find repulsive. Why do we recoil from hairless mice with ears gown on their backs, but not from models with breast and lip implants? Why are the mice deemed "unnatural" and repulsive, but not the contestants of the television show "Extreme Makeover," whose bodies are arguably more "unnatural" than those of the mice? Addressing questions of this sort would be a start toward the clarification Robert and Baylis seek.

Or consider the issue of crossing species boundaries as it has been depicted and explored in the "transgenic art" of Eduardo Kac.[30] Several years ago, Kac made national and international headlines with a public art installation that included "Alba, the GFP Bunny." Alba was an albino rabbit that had been genetically modified by the insertion of a gene from a jellyfish that gave it a green fluorescent protein (GPF), causing it to glow green under certain light. Transgenic art, said Kac, is "a new art form based on the use of genetic engineering to transfer natural or synthetic genes to an organism, to create unique living beings."[31]

Many people were outraged at Kac's creation, and many dismissed his work as a publicity stunt, but in fact, part of the point of the Alba project was to generate a public conversation on the cultural and ethical implications of genetic engineering. According to Kac, "the creation of a chimerical animal forces us to examine notions of normalcy, heterogeneity, purity, hybridity and otherness."[32] Kac's work invites us to reflect on the implications of turning nonhuman animals into artifacts. To be sure, we have been doing that for a very long time. Still, it is worth asking whether creating unique living beings for our amusement or philosophical edification is morally justifiable.

That sort of question may be raised regularly in the literature on animal rights, but it is rarely asked in mainstream bioethics literature. Yet Peter Singer and others are surely right that non-human animals have natural capacities and needs and that they suffer when those capacities are thwarted and their needs go unmet. If we fail to notice this suffering, one reason is that we have ceased thinking of non-human animals as sentient beings and instead see them as machine-like. We thus fail to respect non-human animals precisely because we strip them of any determinate nature that might constrain our actions.

The significance of this point to stem cell research is that it may help us to see the reductionism of much contemporary research that understands the humans body simply as material to be manipulated. Think, for example, of the metaphors that have dominated genomic research—the genome as a book or library, the mapping of the genome as conquering a wilderness—and how these metaphors encourage us to think of the body, to borrow Courtney Campbell's words, as "an exploitable natural resource whose contents are of more interest than the integrity of the whole."[33] Arguably we have lost any sense of the "integrity of the whole" in our disregard for non-human animals, and we may now be losing it about humans as well.[34]

MERE "NATURE"

Despite the overwhelming preoccupation with questions of embryo status, ultimately the fundamental question raised by stem cell research is not about the embryo. Instead, it is about the future toward which biotechnology beckons us. Most succinctly, the question is: Does contemporary biotechnology, including or perhaps especially stem cell research, open the door to a post human future? Waldby and Squier raise this question explicitly when they discuss the combination of genetic engineering and stem cell therapy. They suggest that xenotransplanation forces us to confront the prospect of transgressing species boundaries.[35] When a graft involves genetically engineered stem cells from another species, questions are raised not just about the ontological status of the graft recipient, but about the illnesses to which the biomedical technology is responding. Even the line between veterinary and human medicine may be called into question. "Stream cell technologies," Waldby and Squier write, "thus challenge both the temporal and spatial boundaries of human life, both our biography and our biological niche."[36]

Regrettably, with some notable exceptions, the ethical debate about steam cell research has not taken up in a sustained way what it would mean to pursue stem cell therapies that might significantly undermine the notion of a natural human life or erode the boundary between human and non-human species.[37] Since the status of the embryo has received so much attention, questions about the implications of pursuing adult stem cell research have not been systematically asked or answered. Given the potential for alleviating human suffering embedded in the prospects of stem cell research, it is not surprising that there appears to be widespread and largely uncritical acceptance of adult stem cell work. Nevertheless, if the promise of stem cell research is as revolutionary as is often claimed, we are going to need a much more expansive discussion of both embryonic and adult stem cell work than we have had.

I began this article with a passage from C.S. Lewis's essay "The Abolition of Man," and I end with another. Lewis writes:

> Now I take it that when we understand a thing analytically and then dominate and use it for our own convenience we reduce it to the level of "Nature" in the sense that we suspend our judgments of value about it, ignore its final cause (if any), and treat it in terms of quantity. The repression of elements in what would otherwise be our total reaction to it is sometimes very noticeable and even painful: something has to be overcome before we can cut up a dead man or a live animal in a dissecting room.[38]

Although it is perhaps justifiable to reduce the world of nature to *mere* nature, I am inclined to agree with Lewis that something is lost when we do so. Re-reading "The Abolition of Man" in the context of debates about stem cell research, I was struck by the fact that the sort of dynamic Lewis describes in his essay is very close to that recorded in Jonathan Glover's impressive work, *Humanity: A Moral History of the Twentieth Century.*[39] Glover writes that "Human responses are the core of the humanity which contrasts with inhumanity. They are widely distributed, but to identify them with humanity is only partly an empirical claim. It remains also partly an aspiration." As Glover powerfully argues, morality must be rooted in human needs and values, and these needs and values are both rooted in "human nature" and grounded in human aspiration.

As we wrestle with issues of stem cell research, we ought to be conscious of what is at stake in the possibility of redefining either our natures or our aspirations, for as Glover makes clear, the inhumanity of humans is frightening and all too familiar.

ACKNOWLEDGMENT

This essay is a substantially revised version of the report I prepared for the President's Council on Bioethics on recent literature on the ethics of stem cell research. A number of people either helped with the preparation of the report or provided feedback on an earlier draft of this work. Thanks to Christa Adams, Diana Fritz Cates, William Fitz Patrick, James L. Lissemore, Charlie Ponyik, Mary Jane Ponyik, Kristie Varga, Lisa Wells, Lee Zwanziger, and the ethics writers' group at John Carroll University. I am also grateful to the members of the President's Council for their comments on the report.

NOTES

1. See E. Parens and L.P. Knowles, "Reprogenetics and Public Policy: Reflections and Recommendations," *Hastings Center Report,* Special Supplement, 33, no. 4 (2003). See also the report of the President's Council on Bioethics, *Reproduction and Responsibility: The Regulation of New Biotechnologies,* which explores "the intersection of the technologies of assisted reproduction, human genomic knowledge and techniques, and human embryo research" (Washington, D.C.: President's Council on Bioethics, 2004).
2. For exceptions to this generalization, see R. R. Faden et al., "Public Stem Cell Banks: Considerations of Justice in Stem Cell Research and Therapy," *Hastings Center Report 33,* no. 6 (2003): pp. 13–27; H. Bok, K. E. Schill, and R. R. Faden, "Justice. Ethnicity, and Stem-Cell Banks," *The Lancet* vol. 364 (July 2004): pp. 118–21.
3. "Testimony before the Presidents Council on Bioethics" (December 13, 2002). Available at: http:/www.bioethics.gov/transcripts/dec02/session5.html.
4. Jennings defines the regime of biopower as the effort to make or remake the world in the realm of the biological. In relation to medicine, it refers to technologies that promise (or have delivered) significant interventions on the human body. See B. Jennings, "The Liberalism of Life: Bioethics in the Face of Biopower," *Raritan* 22, no. 4 (spring, 2003): pp. 133–46. On the theme of understanding life forms as manufactured products, see S. Krimsky, *Biotechnics and Society: The Rise of Industrial Genetics* (New York: Praeger, 1991).
5. C. Waldby and S. Squler, "Ontogeny, Ontology, and Phylogeny: Embryonic Life and Stem Cell Technologies," *Configurations* 11, no. 1 (2003): 33. See also S. Squier, *Liminal Lives: Imagining the Human at the Frontiers of Biomedicine* (Durham, N.C.: Duke University Press, 2004).

6. Ibid, p. 36.
7. G. Meilaender, "*Terra as animate:* On Having a Life," *Hastings Center Report* 23, no. 4 (1993): pp. 25–32.
8. Ibid., p. 29.
9. Ibid., p. 31.
10. F. Fukuyama, *Our Posthuman Future* (New York: Farrar, Strous and Giroux, 2002), pp. 70–71.
11. See W. Glannon, "Extending the Human Life Span," *The Journal of Medicine and Philosophy* 27, no. 3 (2002): pp. 339–54.
12. W. Glannon, "Identity, Prudential Concern, and Extended Lives," *Bioethics* 13, no. 3 (2002): p. 276.
13. Ibid., pp. 279–80.
14. L. Kass, "Ageless Bodies, Happy Souls," *The New Atlantis* 1 (2003): p. 12.
15. For an account of human rights that disputes this claim, see M. Ignatieff, "Human Rights as Idolatry," in *Human Rights as Politics and Idolatry,* ed. A. Gutman (Princeton, N.J.: Princeton University Press, 2001)
16. M.C. Nussbaum, "Compassion and Terror," *Daedalus* 128, no. 4 (2003): pp. 10–26.
17. Ibid., 16. Diana Fritz Cates has criticized Nussbaum's account of compassion, particularly Nussbaum's insistence that compassion requires the judgment that the person suffers undeservedly. Cates notes that this condition is sharply at odds with the understanding of compassion in some Buddhist and Christian traditions. D.F. Cates, "Conceiving Emotions: Martha Nussbaum's Upheavals of Thought," *Journal of Religious Ethics* 31 (2003): pp. 325–41. Shared possibilities/vulnerabilities can still be crucial, however. Nussbaum offers a subtly different account of the importance of shared vulnerabilities in *Upheavals of Thought* (New York: Cambridge University Press, 2001). See especially pp. 315–21. Thanks to Tom Schubeck for pressing me on this point.
18. M. Midgley, "Biotechnology and Monstrosity: Why We Should Pay Attention to the 'Yuk Factor,'" *Hastings Center Report* 30, no. 5 (2000): 9. See also M. Midgley, *Animals and Why They Matter* (Athens, Ga: University of Georgia Press, 1983).
19. M.C. Nussbaum, "Human Capabilities, Female Human Beings," in *Women, Culture, and Development: A Study of Human Capabilities,* ed. M.C. Nussbaum and J. Glover (Oxford, U.K.: Clarendon Press, 1995), 72.
20. K. Soper, *What Is Nature? Culture, Politics and the Non-Human* (Cambridge, Ma.: Blackwell, 1995).
21. Ibid., p. 75.
22. Ibid., p. 76.
23. Nussbaum, *Upheavals of Thought.* See also M.C. Nussbaum, 'Secret Sewers of Vice': Disgust, Bodies, and the Law," in *The Passion of Law,* ed. S. Bandes (New York: New York University Press, 1999).
24. Nussbaum, *Upheavals of Thought,* 347.
25. Ibid., p. 350.
26. http://www.patriciapiccinini.net/, accessed December 30, 2004.
27. See R. Kent, "Fast Forward: Accelerated Evolution." Available at: http://www.patriciapiccinini.net/.
28. P. Piccinini, "Artist Statement" (1999). Available at: http://ww.patricia piccinini.net//, accessed December 30, 2004.
29. J.S. Robert and F. Baylis, "Crossing Species Boundaries," *American Journal of Bioethics* 3, no. 3 (2003): pp. 1–13.
30. For a very interesting study of nonhuman animals in postmodern art, see S. Baker, *The Postmodern Animal* (London, U.K.: Reaktion Books, 2000).
31. "GFP Bunny," July 16, 2004, http://www.ekac.org/gfpbuny.html#gfpbunnyanchor, accessed December 30, 2004.
32. E. Kac, "GFP Bunny." For a discussion of Kac's work, see *The Eighth Day: The Transgenic Art of Eduardo Kac,* ed. S. Britton and D. Collins (Tempe, Ariz.: Arizona State University, 2003).
33. C. Campbell, "Source or Resource? Human Embryo Research as an Ethical Issue," in *Cloning and the Future of Human Embryo Research,* ed. P. Lauritzen (New York: Oxford University Press, 2001), p. 44.
34. W.S. Merwin captured the danger of this kind of reductionism in a poem entitled, "Dog": "Whatever he was to guard/Is gone. Besides, his glazed eyes/Fixed heavily ahead stare beyond you/Noticing nothing; he does not see you. But wrong:/Look again: it is through you/that he looks, and the danger of his eyes/Is that in them you are not there..." in *Green with Beasts* (London, U.K.: Hart-Davis, 1956).
35. Although he is not discussing stem cell research explicitly, Paul Rabinow's discussion of technological change during the last two decades is helpful. P. Rabinow, *French DNA: Trouble in Purgatory* (Chicago, III.: The University of Chicago Press, 1999), 13. See also L. Sharp, "The Commodification of the Body and Its Parts," *Annual Review of Anthropology* 29 (2000): pp. 287–328.

36. Waldby and Squier, "Ontogeny, Ontology, and Phylogeny," p. 46.
37. Donna Haraway has argued that concerns about boundary crossing are reminiscent of racial and immigration discourses of an earlier era. "In the appeal to intrinsic natures," she writes, "I detect a mystification of kind and purity akin to the doctrines of white racial hegemony and U.S. national integrity and purpose." ("Mice into Wormholes," in *Cyborgs and Citadels,* ed. G.L. Downey and J. Dumit (Santa Fe, N.M.: School of America Research Press, 1997), p. 218).
38. C.S. Lewis, "The Abolition of Man," *The Abolition of Man* (New York: Macmillan, 1947), p. 81.
39. J. Glover, *Humanity: A Moral History of the Twentieth Century* (New Haven, Conn.: Yale University Press, 1999).

QUESTIONS FOR ANALYSIS

1. What does Lauritzen mean by "a meaningful trajectory to human life"? How does he believe this is altered by stem cell research of any kind? Does every improvement in medicine, nutrition, and living conditions that extends our life span alter this trajectory? How, if at all, is stem cell research different in kind, not just in degree, from the long history of improvements in human health and longevity?
2. In what way does our understanding of human rights depend on a "natural, relatively stable human condition"? How can we revise our notion of human rights to recognize genetic alterations increasingly possible through science?
3. Lauritzen laments that contemporary scientific research considers the human body "simply as material to be manipulated." In what other ways *should* we consider the human body? Do artistic creations and literary metaphors assist us in thinking more expansively about the nature of human life? How should we think about ourselves, other than as "material to be manipulated"?
4. What might a "posthuman future" be like? Assuming it might someday be possible to cross species boundaries, what would you consider your ideal form of existence?

CASE PRESENTATION

Recommendations of the President's Council on Bioethics[1]

For the past five years, the prospect of human cloning has been the subject of considerable public attention and sharp moral debate, both in the United States and around the world. Since the announcement in February 1997 of the first successful cloning of a mammal (Dolly the sheep), several other species of mammals have been cloned. Although a cloned human child has yet to be born, and although the animal experiments have had low rates of success, the production of functioning mammalian cloned offspring suggests that the eventual cloning of humans must be considered a serious possibility.

In November 2001, American researchers claimed to have produced the first cloned human embryos, though they reportedly reached only a six-cell stage before they stopped dividing and died. In addition, several fertility specialists, both here and abroad, have announced their intention to clone human beings. The United States Congress has twice taken up the matter, in 1998 and again in 2001–2002, with the House of Representatives in July 2001 passing a strict ban on all human cloning, including the production of cloned human embryos. As of this writing, several cloning-related bills are under consideration in the Senate. Many other nations have banned human cloning, and the United Nations is considering an international convention on the subject...

PUBLIC POLICY OPTIONS

The Council recognizes the challenges and risks of moving from moral assessment to public policy. Reflections on the "social contract" between science

[1]This is excerpted from the executive summary of the Council's report, *Human Cloning and Human Dignity: An Ethical Inquiry,* Washington U.S. Government, 2002. Other chapters in the report include discussions of the historical, scientific, and ethical issues surrounding cloning. The full text is available on the Web: http://www.bioethics.gov/reports/cloningreport/index.html

and society highlight both the importance of scientific freedom and the need for boundaries. We note that other countries often treat human cloning in the context of a broad area of biomedical technology, at the intersection of reproductive technology, embryo research, and genetics, while the public policy debate in the United States has treated cloning largely on its own. We recognize the special difficulty in formulating sound public policy in this area, given that the two ethically distinct matters—cloning-to-produce-children and cloning-for-biomedical-research—will be mutually affected or implicated in any attempts to legislate about either. Nevertheless, our ethical and policy analysis leads us to the conclusion that some deliberate public policy at the federal level is needed in the area of human cloning.

We reviewed the following seven possible policy options and considered their relative strengths and weaknesses: (1) Professional self-regulation but no federal legislative action ("self-regulation"); (2) A ban on cloning-to-produce-children, with neither endorsement nor restriction of cloning-for-biomedical-research ("ban plus silence"); (3) A ban on cloning-to-produce-children, with regulation of the use of cloned embryos for biomedical research ("ban plus regulation"); (4) Governmental regulation, with no legislative prohibitions ("regulation of both"); (5) A ban on all human cloning, whether to produce children or for biomedical research ("ban on both"); (6) A ban on cloning-to-produce-children, with a moratorium or temporary ban on cloning-for-biomedical-research ("ban plus moratorium"); or (7) A moratorium or temporary ban on all human cloning, whether to produce children or for biomedical research ("moratorium on both").

THE COUNCIL'S POLICY RECOMMENDATIONS

Having considered the benefits and drawbacks of each of these options, and taken into account our discussions and reflections throughout this report, the Council recommends two possible policy alternatives, each supported by a portion of the Members.

Majority Recommendation: Ten Members of the Council recommend a ban on cloning-to-produce-children combined with a four-year moratorium on cloning-for-biomedical-research. We also call for a federal review of current and projected practices of human embryo research, pre-implantation genetic diagnosis, genetic modification of human embryos and gametes, and related matters, with a view to recommending and shaping ethically sound policies for the entire field. Speaking only for ourselves, those of us who support this recommendation do so for some or all of the following reasons:

• By permanently banning cloning-to-produce-children, this policy gives force to the strong ethical verdict against cloning-to-produce-children, unanimous in this Council (and in Congress) and widely supported by the American people. And by enacting a four-year moratorium on the creation of cloned embryos, it establishes an additional safeguard not afforded by policies that would allow the production of cloned embryos to proceed without delay.

• It calls for and provides time for further democratic deliberation about cloning-for-biomedical research, a subject about which the nation is divided and where there remains great uncertainty. A national discourse on this subject has not yet taken place in full, and a moratorium, by making it impossible for either side to cling to the status-quo, would force both to make their full case before the public. By banning all cloning for a time, it allows us to seek moral consensus on whether or not we should cross a major moral boundary (creating nascent cloned human life solely for research) and prevents our crossing it without deliberate decision. It would afford time for scientific evidence, now sorely lacking, to be gathered—from animal models and other avenues of human research—that might give us a better sense of whether cloning-for-biomedical-research would work as promised, and whether other morally nonproblematic approaches might be available. It would promote a fuller and better-informed public debate. And it would show respect for the deep moral concerns of the large number of Americans who have serious ethical objections to this research.

• Some of us hold that cloning-for-biomedical-research can never be ethically pursued, and endorse a moratorium to enable us to continue to make our case in a democratic way. Others of us support the moratorium because it would provide the time and incentive required to develop a system of national regulation that might come into use if, at the end of the four-year period, the moratorium were not reinstated or made permanent. Such a system could not be developed overnight, and therefore even those who support the research but want it regulated should see that at the very least a pause is required. In the absence of a moratorium, few proponents of the research would have much incentive to institute an effective regulatory system. Moreover, the very process of proposing such regulations would clarify the moral and prudential judgments involved in deciding whether and how to proceed with this research.

• A moratorium on cloning-for-biomedical-research would enable us to consider this activity in the larger context of research and technology in the areas of developmental biology, embryo research, and genetics, and to pursue a more comprehensive federal regulatory system for setting and executing policy in the entire area.

• Finally, we believe that a moratorium, rather than a lasting ban, signals a high regard for the value of biomedical research and an enduring concern for patients and families whose suffering such research may help alleviate. It would reaffirm the principle that science can progress while upholding the community's moral norms, and would therefore reaffirm the community's moral support for science and biomedical technology.

The decision before us is of great importance. Creating cloned embryos for any purpose requires crossing a major moral boundary, with grave risks and likely harms, and once we cross it there will be no turning back. Our society should take the time to make a judgment that is well-informed and morally sound, respectful of strongly held views, and representative of the priorities and principles of the American people. We believe this ban-plus-moratorium proposal offers the best means of achieving these goals. . . .

Minority Recommendation: Seven Members of the Council recommend a ban on cloning-to-produce-children, with regulation of the use of cloned embryos for biomedical research. Speaking only for ourselves, those of us who support this recommendation do so for some or all of the following reasons:

• By permanently banning cloning-to-produce-children, this policy gives force to the strong ethical verdict against cloning-to-produce-children, unanimous in this Council (and in Congress) and widely supported by the American people. We believe that a ban on the transfer of cloned embryos to a woman's uterus would be a sufficient and effective legal safeguard against the practice.

• It approves cloning-for-biomedical-research and permits it to proceed without substantial delay. This is the most important advantage of this proposal. The research shows great promise, and its actual value can only be determined by allowing it to go forward now. Regardless of how much time we allow it, no amount of experimentation with animal models can provide the needed understanding of human diseases. The special benefits from working with stem cells from cloned human embryos cannot be obtained using embryos obtained by IVF. We believe this research could provide relief to millions of Americans, and that the government should therefore support it, within sensible limits imposed by regulation.

• It would establish, as a condition of proceeding, the necessary regulatory protections to avoid abuses and misuses of cloned embryos. These regulations might touch on the secure handling of embryos, licensing and prior review of research projects, the protection of egg donors, and the provision of equal access to benefits.

• Some of us also believe that mechanisms to regulate cloning-for-biomedical-research should be part of a larger regulatory program governing all research involving human embryos, and that the federal government should initiate a review of present and projected practices of human embryo research, with the aim of establishing reasonable policies on the matter.

Permitting cloning-for-biomedical-research now, while governing it through a prudent and sensible regulatory regime, is the most appropriate way to allow important research to proceed while insuring that abuses are prevented. We believe that the legitimate concerns about human cloning expressed throughout this report are sufficiently addressed by this ban-plus-regulation proposal, and that the nation should affirm and support the responsible effort to find treatments and cures that might help many who are suffering . . .

QUESTIONS FOR ANALYSIS

1. All members of the council agree on recommending a permanent ban on cloning-to-produce-children. Are there developments in medical research that might someday justify permitting such cloning? Are the ethical concerns about cloning-to-produce-children sufficiently strong that no scientific advances would ever justify permitting such cloning?
2. A majority of the council recommends a four-year moratorium on cloning-for-biomedical-research to allow the nation time for further deliberation on the moral issues presented by such research. What additional ethical issues should be examined in an effort to reach the moral consensus sought by these council members? As some of these members state that they do not believe cloning-for-biomedical-research can ever be ethically pursued, is this recommendation just a stalling tactic?
3. A minority of the council recommends allowing cloning-for-biomedical-research immediately, with appropriate government regulation to avoid abuses and misuses of cloned embryos. Why is this group of council members eager to permit this research? Would government regulation be sufficient to protect against possible abuses and overcome the ethical concerns of the majority?

CASE PRESENTATION

A Birth to Save a Life

When Louise Brown, the world's first "test-tube" baby, was born in Oldham, England, she and her parents became instant international celebrities. But that was back in 1978, an entirely different era in terms of reproductive technology. Today, by contrast, in vitro fertilization is an everyday aid in helping women to conceive, not just in the industrialized West but also in such countries as Egypt, Malaysia, and Pakistan. Whether the sperm comes from the woman's husband or an anonymous donor, it is routinely joined with her egg in a laboratory, and just as routinely the newly formed embryo is implanted in the woman's womb. Rarely do these procedures make news.

But the *Washington Post* found one such case newsworthy when it reported in October 2000 that Adam Nash, a test-tube baby, had been conceived and born to save his sister's life. The sister, six-year-old Molly Nash, was born with Franconi anemia, an inherited disease that prevents the production of bone marrow cells. Children who suffer from the condition usually die from leukemia or some other complication by the age of seven, and Molly had already developed a blood condition her doctors called "pre-leukemia." The only effective treatment for Franconi anemia is a successful cell transplant.

Unlike Louise's conception, Adam's involved another, more recent technique as well: preimplantation genetic diagnosis, which allows scientists to examine the genes of an embryo before it's implanted in the womb. Fifteen embryos were created for the Nashes, and researchers at Illinois Masonic Medical Center tested each of them for two genetic traits. First, it had to be free of Franconi anemia; second, it had to be a perfect match for Molly. Two embryos passed, one was implanted, and on August 29, 2000, Adam was born in a Denver hospital, where doctors painlessly removed the needed donor cells from his umbilical cord. A month later, they were introduced into his sister's bloodstream. According to the director of medical genetics at the center that performed the tests, Molly had an 85 to 90 percent chance of being free of the disease. And in an article that appeared in *The New York Times* the following day, the doctor who performed the transplant said that Molly's blood tests had already begun to improve.

What made the story newsworthy was the Nashes' reason for using preimplantation genetic diagnosis. In previous cases, it had been used to select genes that were best for the health of the future child. In this case, it was used for Molly's benefit. That makes Adam's conception and birth the first case in which modern reproductive technology and genetic testing combined to create a suitable donor for a transplant. It will not, however, be the last. Before the story was even reported, ten other families had begun preparing for the same procedure.

Despite the procedure's promise for such families, the articles in both newspapers raised identical ethical questions. As bioethicist Jeffrey P. Kahn told the *Times,* "We've crossed the line that we really never crossed before, selecting based on characteristics that are not best for the child being born, but for somebody else." Dr. Kahn also posed a moral dilemma that goes well beyond the technologies used for the Nashes: "Nobody wants babies to be born strictly for the parts they could create, but by the same token, I don't think we're willing as a society to ask people why they're having children and to say, 'That's not a good enough reason.'"

The other ethical question concerns "designer" babies. "You could say it's like buying a new car, where you decide which package of accessories you want," said Dr. Kahn, this time speaking to the *Post.* "I suppose it's only because we don't yet have the tests that we're not having parents asking for embryos without a predisposition to homosexuality or for kids who will grow to more than six feet tall."

QUESTIONS FOR ANALYSIS

1. Is it morally wrong to create a child for "parts," as the Nashes did? Would it be wrong to use cloning for the same purpose?
2. Are there good and bad reasons for having children? For using reproductive technologies or the genetic testing of embryos? If so, what distinguishes the good from the bad? How closely does the distinction parallel the distinction between good and bad reasons for creating a clone?
3. What, if any, moral concerns does the prospect of choosing embryos for a variety of traits—beauty, say, or athletic ability—raise? How close are they to the moral concerns raised by cloning?
4. Earlier in this chapter, we discussed the case of Abe and Mary Ayala, who conceived and bore a child to provide a compatible donor for their leukemia-stricken daughter. Do you see any important difference between what they did and what the Nashes did?
5. For whatever reasons the Nashes and Ayalas conceived their youngest children, they ended up loving them as much as their other children. Does that make the reasons irrelevant?

CASE PRESENTATION

Presidential Policy

In November 1998, a group of scientists led by James Thomson, at the University of Wisconsin, announced that they had created a line of stem cells out of human embryos a few days after in vitro fertilization. A panel of experts at the National Institutes of Health then developed policies for the funding of research on these embryonic stem cells. Among the requirements were that the embryos had been donated by a couple for research after fertility treatments and were no longer needed by that couple. Before these policies could be implemented, however, George W. Bush became president and came under considerable pressure to ban such research completely. He announced his policy in a televised speech on August 9, 2001. Following are excerpts from that speech:

> . . . The issue of research involving stem cells derived from human embryos is increasingly the subject of a national debate and dinner table discussions. The issue is confronted every day in laboratories as scientists ponder the ethical ramifications of their work. It is agonized over by parents and many couples as they try to have children, or to save children already born.
>
> The issue is debated within the church, with people of different faiths, even many of the same faith coming to different conclusions. Many people are finding that the more they know about stem cell research, the less certain they are about the right ethical and moral conclusions.
>
> My administration must decide whether to allow federal funds, your tax dollars, to be used for scientific research on stem cells derived from human embryos. A large number of these embryos already exist. They are the product of a process called in vitro fertilization, which helps so many couples conceive children. When

doctors match sperm and egg to create life outside the womb, they usually produce more embryos than are planted in the mother. Once a couple successfully has children, or if they are unsuccessful, the additional embryos remain frozen in laboratories.

Some will not survive during long storage; others are destroyed. A number have been donated to science and used to create privately funded stem cell lines. And a few have been implanted in an adoptive mother and born, and are today healthy children.

Based on preliminary work that has been privately funded, scientists believe further research using stem cells offers great promise that could help improve the lives of those who suffer from many terrible diseases—from juvenile diabetes to Alzheimer's, from Parkinson's to spinal cord injuries. And while scientists admit they are not yet certain, they believe stem cells derived from embryos have unique potential.

You should also know that stem cells can be derived from sources other than embryos—from adult cells, from umbilical cords that are discarded after babies are born, from human placenta. And many scientists feel research on these types of stem cells is also promising. Many patients suffering from a range of diseases are already being helped with treatments developed from adult stem cells.

However, most scientists, at least today, believe that research on embryonic stem cells offers the most promise because these cells have the potential to develop in all of the tissues in the body.

Scientists further believe that rapid progress in this research will come only with federal funds. Federal dollars help attract the best and brightest scientists. They ensure new discoveries are widely shared at the largest number of research facilities and that the research is directed toward the greatest public good.

The United States has a long and proud record of leading the world toward advances in science and medicine that improve human life. And the United States has a long and proud record of upholding the highest standards of ethics as we expand the limits of science and knowledge. Research on embryonic stem cells raises profound ethical questions, because extracting the stem cell destroys the embryo, and thus destroys its potential for life. Like a snowflake, each of these embryos is unique, with the unique genetic potential of an individual human being.

As I thought through this issue, I kept returning to two fundamental questions: First, are these frozen embryos human life and, therefore, something precious to be protected? And second, if they're going to be destroyed anyway, shouldn't they be used for a greater good, for research that has the potential to save and improve other lives?

I've asked those questions and others of scientists, scholars, bioethicists, religious leaders, doctors, researchers, members of Congress, my Cabinet, and my friends. I have read heartfelt letters from many Americans. I have given this issue a great deal of thought, prayer, and considerable reflection. And I have found widespread disagreement.

On the first issue, are these embryos human life—well, one researcher told me he believes this five-day-old cluster of cells is not an embryo, not yet an individual, but a pre-embryo. He argued that it has the potential for life, but it is not a life because it cannot develop on its own.

An ethicist dismissed that as a callous attempt at rationalization. Make no mistake, he told me, that cluster of cells is the same way you and I, and all the rest of us, started our lives. One goes with a heavy heart if we use these, he said, because we are dealing with the seeds of the next generation.

And to the other crucial question—if these are going to be destroyed anyway, why not use them for good purpose—I also found different answers. Many argue these embryos are by-products of a process that helps create life, and we should allow couples to donate them to science so they can be used for good purpose instead of wasting their potential. Others will argue there's no such thing as excess life, and the fact that a living being is going to die does not justify experimenting on it or exploiting it as a natural resource.

At its core, this issue forces us to confront fundamental questions about the beginnings of life and the ends of science. It lies at a difficult moral intersection, juxtaposing the need to protect life in all its phases with the prospect of saving and improving life in all its stages.

As the discoveries of modern science create tremendous hope, they also lay vast ethical mine fields. As the genius of science extends the horizons of what we can do, we increasingly confront complex questions about what we should do. We have arrived at that brave new world that seemed so distant in 1932, when Aldous Huxley wrote about human beings created in test tubes in what he called a "hatchery."

In recent weeks, we learned that scientists have created human embryos in test tubes solely to experiment on them. This is deeply troubling, and a warning sign that should prompt all of us to think through these issues very carefully.

Embryonic stem cell research is at the leading edge of a series of moral hazards. The initial stem cell researcher was at first reluctant to begin his research, fearing it might be used for human cloning. Scientists have already cloned a sheep. Researchers are telling us the next step could be to clone human beings to create individual designer stem cells, essentially to grow another you, to be available in case you need another heart or lung or liver.

I strongly oppose human cloning, as do most Americans. We recoil at the idea of growing human beings for spare body parts, or creating life for our convenience. And while we must devote enormous energy to conquering disease, it is equally important that we pay attention to the moral concerns raised by the new frontier of human embryo stem cell research. Even the most noble ends do not justify any means.

My position on these issues is shaped by deeply held beliefs. I'm a strong supporter of science and technology, and believe they have the potential for incredible good—to improve lives, to save life, to conquer disease. Research offers hope that millions of our loved ones may be cured of a disease and rid of their suffering. I have friends whose children suffer from juvenile diabetes. Nancy Reagan has written me about President Reagan's struggle with Alzheimer's. My own family has confronted the tragedy of childhood leukemia. And, like all Americans, I have great hope for cures.

I also believe human life is a sacred gift from our Creator. I worry about a culture that devalues life, and believe as your president I have an important obligation to foster and encourage respect for life in America and throughout the world. And while we're all hopeful about the potential of this research, no one can be certain that the science will live up to the hope it has generated.

Eight years ago, scientists believed fetal tissue research offered great hope for cures and treatments, yet the progress to date has not lived up to initial expectations. Embryonic stem cell research offers both great promise and great peril. So I have decided we must proceed with great care.

As a result of private research, more than sixty genetically diverse stem cell lines already exist. They were created from embryos that have already been destroyed, and they have the ability to regenerate themselves indefinitely, creating ongoing opportunities for research. I have concluded that we should allow federal funds to be used for research on these existing stem cell lines, where the life-and-death decision has already been made.

Leading scientists tell me research on these sixty lines has great promise that could lead to breakthrough therapies and cures. This allows us to explore the promise and potential of stem cell research without crossing a fundamental moral line by providing taxpayer funding that would sanction or encourage further destruction of human embryos that have at least the potential for life.

I also believe that great scientific progress can be made through aggressive federal funding of research on umbilical cord placenta, adult and animal stem cells which do not involve the same moral dilemma. This year, your government will spend $250 million on this important research.

I will also name a President's Council to monitor stem cell research, to recommend appropriate guidelines and regulations, and to consider all of the medical and ethical ramifications of biomedical innovation. This council will consist of leading scientists, doctors, ethicists, lawyers, theologians and others, and will be chaired by Dr. Leon Kass, a leading biomedical ethicist from the University of Chicago.

This council will keep us apprised of new developments and give our nation a forum to continue to discuss and evaluate these important issues. As we go forward, I hope we will always be guided by both intellect and heart, by both our capabilities and our conscience.

I have made this decision with great care, and I pray it is the right one....

QUESTIONS FOR ANALYSIS

1. The president's position relies on the view that embryos are persons with moral status from the moment of fertilization of an egg, even if it was done for in vitro fertilization (IVF) and even though the embryo would be discarded anyway. Of the various theories presented in Steinbock's article here, which would support his position and which might be used to challenge his view?
2. The president rejects utilitarian or consequentialist reasoning that the research should be carried out because of the potential for discovering cures for serious diseases. Identify the passages where he considers this approach, and indicate whether he has presented a compelling argument for rejecting it.
3. Scientists determined after this statement that the claim that sixty stem cell lines were in existence was problematic. Most had been mixed with blood products from rodents, making their usefulness for research doubtful. The

strongest opponents of stem cell research objected to using even these existing lines, because doing so implicitly condoned what they considered the taking of human life. Examine the president's statements on the use of these existing lines. Has he justified their use adequately? Has he provided sufficient basis for continuing scientific research with his claim of the availability of sixty existing lines?

4. If the president believes the embryos have moral status, should he have proposed legislation banning IVF because it inevitably produces excess embryos that are later discarded? Why do you think he has never proposed such a ban?

CASE PRESENTATION

Snowflakes in Summer

For the five years after President Bush announced his policy, intense lobbying efforts tried to get him to change his policy. Nancy Reagan, widow of President Reagan, who had died of Alzheimer's in 2004, was a visible and vocal supporter of embryonic stem cell research. In a public letter dated May 1, 2006, to Senator Orrin Hatch, a conservative Republican from Utah who opposed abortion, she lamented that efforts in the Congress to pass the Stem Cell Research Enhancement Act, which would approve such research with federal funds, had been delayed. She wrote:

> Thank you for your continued commitment to helping the millions of Americans who suffer from devastating and disabling diseases. Your support has given so much hope to so many. It has been nearly a year since the United State House of Representatives first approved the stem cell legislation that would open the research so we could fully unleash its promise. For those who are waiting every day for scientific progress to help their loved ones, the wait for United State Senate action has been very difficult and hard to comprehend.

When Senator Hatch announced his support for the Stem Cell Research Enhancement Act, along with a bipartisan group of Senators, he noted that he was "strongly pro-life" but said, "The fact is, I have never believed that life begins in a Petri dish." He stressed instead the importance of the potential results of the research in treating devastating diseases. The Senate passed the bill and forwarded it to the president for signature.

In a public letter on July 18, 2006, Michael J. Fox, the well-known actor who himself suffers from Parkinson's disease, urged the president to sign the bill. He noted:

> Embryonic stem cell research transforms embryos already marked for destruction into potentially lifesaving research. I can think of no better affirmation of the culture of life.

On July 19, 2006, the president vetoed the Human Cloning Ban and Stem Cell Research Protection Act of 2005, which had been passed by the U.S. Congress after lengthy delays. It was the first veto of his presidency. Congress did not have the necessary two-thirds vote to override the veto. Following are excerpts from his veto statement that day, delivered at a public ceremony to which he had invited several children born from adopted embryos (sometimes called "snowflake" children).

> . . . Like all Americans, I believe our nation must vigorously pursue the tremendous possibility that science offers to cure disease and improve the lives of millions. We have opportunities to discover cures and treatments that were unthinkable generations ago. Some scientists believe that one source of these cures might be embryonic stem cell research. Embryonic stem cells have the ability to grow into specialized adult tissues, and this may give them the potential to replace damaged or defective cells or body parts and treat a variety of diseases.
>
> Yet we must also remember that embryonic stem cells come from human embryos that are destroyed for their cells. Each of these human embryos is a unique human life with inherent dignity and matchless value. We see that value in the children who are with us today. Each of these children began his or her life as a frozen embryo that was created for in vitro fertilization, but remained unused after the fertility treatments were complete. Each of these children was adopted while still an embryo, and has been blessed with the chance to grow up in a loving family.

These boys and girls are not spare parts. They remind us of what is lost when embryos are destroyed in the name of research. They remind us that we all begin our lives as a small collection of cells. And they remind us that in our zeal for new treatments and cures, America must never abandon our fundamental morals. . . .

As science brings us ever closer to unlocking the secrets of human biology, it also offers temptations to manipulate human life and violate human dignity. Our conscience and history as a nation demand that we resist this temptation. America was founded on the principle that we are all created equal, and endowed by our Creator with the right to life. We can advance the cause of science while upholding this founding promise. We can harness the promise of technology without becoming slaves to technology. And we can ensure that science serves the cause of humanity instead of the other way around. . .

QUESTIONS FOR ANALYSIS

1. Nancy Reagan relies entirely on the consequentialist justification of finding treatments for serious diseases and does not address the moral status of the embryos. Is this sufficient to support this research, regardless of the moral status of the embryos?
2. Does Senator Hatch adequately address the claim that the embryos are persons with moral status in support of his view that this research is ethical?
3. Michael J. Fox uses the now-familiar reference to a "culture of life." Does support for this research better promote that culture? Or is it better promoted by the President's position?
4. After the veto, Senator Arlen Specter, a Republican who himself suffers from Hodgkin's lymphoma, a form of cancer, noted that only 128 embryos had been adopted and observed that the remaining 400,000 unneeded embryos would better be used for research than thrown away, an option denied Federal funding with the President's veto. Senator Tom Harkin, a Democrat, complained that, if the President really believes that destroying unused embryos is murder, why does he allow it to continue? Is the President hypocritical in not insisting on murder charges for everyone who produces an excess embryo which is later destroyed?

CHAPTER SEVEN

Capital Punishment

- **The Nature and Definition of Punishment**
- **The Moral Acceptability of Punishment**
- **Aims of Punishment**
- ***Retentionist* and *Abolitionist* Defined**
- **Capital Punishment as Deterrent**
- **Abolitionist Arguments (against Capital Punishment)**
- **Retentionist Arguments (for Capital Punishment)**

JOHN STUART MILL **Speech in Favor of Capital Punishment**
SIDNEY HOOK **The Death Sentence**
ERNEST VAN DEN HAAG **On Deterrence and the Death Penalty**
HUGO ADAM BEDAU **Capital Punishment and Social Defense**

CASE PRESENTATION: ***J. D. Autry: Death in Texas • Karla Faye Tucker and Stanley "Tookie" Williams: Rehabilitation on Death Row? • A Failed Experiment? • Warren McClesky***

LATE ON THE NIGHT of October 4, 1983, in Huntsville, Texas, convicted killer J. D. Autry was taken from his death-row cell in the penitentiary and strapped to a wheeled cot. Intravenous tubes were connected to both arms, ready to administer a dose of poison.

Outside, a crowd shouted "Kill him, kill him, kill him!" whenever television lights were turned on.

In Washington, Supreme Court Justice Byron White waited for a last-minute application for a stay of execution. The application, written on three sheets of a yellow pad, made a new argument related to another case due to be heard by the Court. Shortly after midnight, White granted the stay. The intravenous tubes were disconnected, the straps unbuckled. Autry was returned to his cell. Only in March of 1984 was the execution carried out.

The U.S. Supreme Court decision that paved the way for Autry's execution was *Gregg v. Georgia* (1976). In an earlier decision, *Furman v. Georgia* (1972), the Court had ruled that capital punishment as then administered was cruel and unusual punishment and therefore unconstitutional. The issue in that case was *standardless discretion*—the freedom of a jury (or in some cases, a judge) to use its own discretion in determining a sentence without explicit legal standards to guide its decision. In their attempts to get around the decision, some states passed laws making the death penalty mandatory for certain crimes, while others enacted legal standards to guide the discretion of the sentencing jury or judge. In *Woodson v. North Carolina* (1976), the Supreme Court ruled laws of the first type unconstitutional. In *Gregg v. Georgia,* it upheld laws of the second type for the crime of murder.

Since that decision, capital punishment has withstood another major legal challenge—*McClesky v. Kemp* (1987). In that case, the Supreme Court ruled against Warren McClesky, a black man who had been sentenced to death for killing a white policeman. McClesky argued that the imposition of the death penalty was unconstitutionally affected by racial bias, and in support of his claim, he offered studies showing that convicted killers of white victims were more likely to receive the death penalty than were convicted killers of black victims. Although the Court did not dispute the studies, it rejected his argument. With almost 1,900 convicted killers waiting on death row, the constitutionality of the death penalty was upheld by a 5 to 4 majority.

The application of the death penalty has been narrowed, however. In 2002, in *Atkins v. Virginia,* the U.S. Supreme Court held that execution of people with mental retardation violated the constitutional protection against cruel and unusual punishment. This decision reversed a 1989 decision, *Perry v. Lynaugh,* which said that executing mentally retarded individuals did not violate the Constitution. In the *Atkins* decision, the Court said that executing people mentally retarded does not meet the deterrent nor the retributive purpose of the death penalty. They also noted a growing national consensus that executing mentally retarded people is wrong. Of the thirty-eight states that permit capital punishment, eighteen had banned execution of mentally retarded people.

In 2005, the U.S. Supreme Court, in a 5-4 decision, abolished capital punishment for juvenile offenders in *Roper v. Simmons.* Twenty states had permitted the death penalty for offenders younger than eighteen. The decision canceled the sentences for seventy-two other juveniles then on death row, including twenty-nine awaiting execution in Texas. As recently as 1989, the Court had upheld the death penalty for offenders who were at least sixteen. In announcing the decision, Justice Anthony Kennedy said it reflected "evolving standards of decency that mark the progress of a maturing society." The dissenters said that such policies should be left to the discretion of state legislatures.

Scientific developments, especially DNA testing, have further complicated public debate over the appropriateness of the death penalty. In 2000, the governor of Illinois announced a moratorium on executions, as DNA testing had shown that thirteen people on death row were innocent. Maryland instituted a temporary moratorium, but it was lifted in 2003. Congress passed the Innocence Protection Act of 2004 to help pay the costs of post-conviction DNA testing. Since the advent of DNA testing of evidence, over 100 prisoners on death row have been freed when the tests proved they were innocent.

Although support for the death penalty has declined slightly in the United States, recent polls indicate that more than half the population still supports it. More than 1000 prisoners have been executed since the 1976 *Gregg v. Georgia* decision. Internationally, however, support for capital punishment has been steadily declining. It has been abolished in Canada, Mexico, Russia, South Africa, and most industrialized nations. Amnesty International claims that more than half the nations in the world have abolished the death penalty in law or in practice. Nearly all the executions on the planet are carried out by four nations: China, Iran, Saudi Arabia, and the United States.

The death penalty is a form of punishment. Consequently, one's view of the morality of the death penalty usually is influenced by one's view of punishment generally. So the specific moral question under discussion in this chapter is: Is capital punishment ever a justifiable form of punishment?

THE NATURE AND DEFINITION OF PUNISHMENT

Generally, philosophers discuss punishment in terms of five elements. For something to be punishment, it must (1) involve pain, (2) be administered for an offense against a law or rule, (3) be administered to someone who has been judged guilty of an offense, (4) be imposed by someone other than the offender, and (5) be imposed by rightful authority. Whether a punishment is commensurate with an offense, whether it is fair and equitable—these are very important moral and legal questions. But they must be distinguished from the question of what punishment is.

1. ***Punishment must involve pain, harm, or some other consequence normally considered unpleasant.*** For example, if convicted robbers were sentenced to "five to twenty" in a Beverly Hills country club, this would not be considered punishment, since ordinarily it would not involve pain or other unpleasant consequences (unless the robbers had to pick up the tab). If they were sentenced to have their hands cut off, this could constitute punishment, though draconian by many people's standards.

2. ***The punishment must be administered for an offense against a law or rule.*** While punishment involves pain, obviously not all pain involves punishment. If robbers break into your house and steal your stereo, they are not "punishing" you, even though their action satisfies element one. Although it caused you pain, their action is not taken to punish an offense against a law or rule. However, should the robbers subsequently be sent to prison for the crime, then that action would be administered for breaking a law and thus satisfy element two.

3. ***The punishment must be administered to someone who has been judged guilty of an offense.*** Suppose the robbers are apprehended and imprisoned, although never judged guilty of the robbery. This would not be considered punishment. However, if they are imprisoned after their conviction for stealing your stereo, then they are being punished.

4. ***The punishment must be imposed by someone other than the offender.*** It is true that people sometimes speak of "punishing themselves" for a transgression. This, however, is not punishment in the strict sense but a self-imposed act of atonement. Suffering from a twinge of conscience as they listen to the latest Willie Nelson album on your stereo, the robbers decide to "punish" themselves by listening to Robert Goulet, whom they detest, for two hours each day for a year. Properly speaking, this would not be punishment, although it might qualify as masochism.

5. ***The punishment must be imposed by rightful authority.*** In a strictly legal sense, "rightful authority" would be that constituted by a legal system against whom

the offense is committed. In the case of the robbers, "rightful authority" would likely be a court judge and jury. In a less legal sense, the authority might be a parent, a teacher, or some official who has a right to harm a person in a particular way for having done something or failed to do something.

These five elements, then, generally constitute the nature of punishment. Combining them produces a useful definition of punishment. Thus, a punishment is harm inflicted by a rightful authority on a person who has been judged to have violated a law or rule.[1]

THE MORAL ACCEPTABILITY OF PUNISHMENT

Is punishment ever morally acceptable? This may seem a foolish question to ask, because it is hard to imagine society functioning without an established legal system of punishment. In fact, philosophers generally agree that punishment is morally acceptable. They, like most others, view punishment as a part of the rule and law necessary to minimize the occurrence of forbidden acts. In short, law without punishment is toothless.

Still, there are people who do not share this view. They argue that society should be restructured so that a legal system of punishment is unnecessary. Just how this can or should be done remains problematic. The method most often proposed involves some form of therapeutic treatment or behavior modification for antisocial behavior rather than a traditional form of punishment. Among the most morally controversial procedures for modifying undesirable social behavior are those associated with some startling advances in biomedicine. Such cases rarely can be resolved by a simple appeal to the individual's right to obtain appropriate treatment on request, and they are even less likely to be resolved by an appeal to society's right to order such treatment.

Consider one case provided by a leading research scientist in the field, Dr. J. R. Delgado. A number of years ago, Delgado recalls, an attractive twenty-four-year-old woman of average intelligence and education and a long record of arrests for disorderly conduct approached him and his associates. The patient explained that she had been repeatedly involved in bar brawls in which she would entice men to fight over her. Having spent a number of years in jail and mental institutions, the woman expressed a strong desire but inability to change her behavior. Because past psychological therapy had proved ineffective, both she and her mother urgently requested that some sort of brain surgery be performed to control her antisocial and destructive behavior. As Delgado said: "They asked specifically that electrodes be implanted to orient a possible electrocoagulation of a limited cerebral area; and if that wasn't possible, they wanted a lobotomy."[2]

At that time, medical knowledge could not determine whether such procedures could help resolve the woman's problem, so the physicians rejected surgical intervention. When Delgado and his colleagues explained their decision to the woman and her mother, the two reacted with disappointment and anxiety: "What is the future? Only jail or the hospital?"[3]

---

[1]See Burton M. Leiser, *Liberty, Justice, and Morals* (New York: Macmillan, 1973), pp. 195–197.
[2]J. R. Delgado, *Physical Control of the Mind: Toward a Psycho-Civilized Society* (New York: Harper & Row, 1969), p. 85.
[3]Ibid.

What is the future, indeed? The day could very well come when such therapeutic treatment renders traditional kinds of punishment obsolete, perhaps barbaric. But even then, pressing moral questions will remain concerning society's right to alter an individual's personality against his or her will. For now, most agree that punishment is a morally acceptable practice. What they do not agree on, however, is the aim of punishment.

AIMS OF PUNISHMENT

The aims of punishment can be divided into two categories: (1) in terms of giving people what they deserve or (2) in terms of its desirable consequences. The first category includes retributive theories of punishment; the second includes preventive, deterrent, and reformative theories.

Retribution

The term **retribution** refers to punishment given in return for some wrong done. This view of punishment holds that we should punish people simply because they deserve it. Traditionally, retributive theorists have considered punishment a principle of justice, often referred to as retributory justice, whereby offenders are made to suffer in kind for the harm they have caused others. Arguments in favor of capital punishment commonly make this point.

But another version of retribution associates punishment not with revenge but with respect for persons, both noncriminals and criminals. Proponents of this theory argue that robbers, for example, like everyone else in society, ought to live under the same limitations of freedom. When robbers steal your stereo, they are taking unfair advantage of you, disrupting the balance of equal limitations. When the state subsequently punishes them, the punishment is viewed as an attempt to restore this disrupted balance, to reaffirm society's commitment to fair treatment for all. This version of retribution focuses on the noncriminal generally and the victim in particular, claiming that respect for the parties who abide by society's limitations requires punishment of those who flout those limitations.

The other side of the respect–retribution theory concerns respect for the offender. Proponents of retribution sometimes argue that failure to punish is tantamount to treating offenders with disrespect because it denies them autonomy and responsibility for their actions. Showing respect entails giving people what they deserve, whether that be reward or punishment. To deny praise to a deserving person is disrespectful. By the same token, to deny punishment to a deserving person is equally disrespectful. Both views of respect–retribution can be used in defense of capital punishment.

Prevention

The prevention view of punishment holds that we should punish to ensure that offenders do not repeat their offense and so further injure society.Thus, robbers should be punished, perhaps imprisoned, so that they will not steal anything else. Prevention is one of the most common justifications for capital punishment.

Deterrence

The **deterrence** view holds that we should punish to discourage others from committing similar offenses. Like the prevention theory, it aims to minimize the crime rate. Thus, when other potential thieves see that the robber has been punished for the crime, they will be less likely to steal. Deterrence is perhaps the most common argument made on behalf of capital punishment and thus is the one that those against capital punishment often focus on. For the moment, we will simply observe that if a punishment is to function effectively as a deterrent, it must be severe enough to be undesirable, and just as important, it must be known and certain. Thus, potential offenders must be aware of the kind and severity of the punishment that awaits them, and they must be convinced that they will receive it if they commit the offense.

Reform

The reform theory holds that one should punish to induce people to conform to standards of behavior they have tended to ignore or violate. The idea is that people will emerge from punishment better than they were before, insofar as they will be less likely to breach conventional standards of behavior.

Although rehabilitation often accompanies reform, the aims of each are different. Rehabilitation aims not to punish but to offer the offenders opportunities to find a useful place in society on release from prison. Modern penal institutions attempt to accomplish this goal by providing various recreational, educational, and vocational services for prisoners.

It's important to keep in mind that the aforementioned aims of punishment are not mutually exclusive. It's possible for more than one purpose of punishment to be morally legitimate. In fact, perhaps all four, in varying degrees, might be called for.

RETENTIONIST AND *ABOLITIONIST* DEFINED

Having briefly examined some aspects of punishment, including its nature and definition, its moral acceptability, and its aims, let us now turn to the particular form of punishment that is the topic of this chapter: capital punishment. The central moral question that concerns us is: Is capital punishment ever a justifiable form of punishment?

Those who support retaining or reinstituting capital punishment can be termed **retentionists.** Retentionists are not agreed that all the arguments supporting capital punishment are acceptable or on the conditions under which capital punishment should be imposed. But they do agree that capital punishment is at least sometimes morally justifiable. Those who oppose capital punishment are commonly termed **abolitionists.** Like retentionists, abolitionists disagree among themselves about which arguments against capital punishment are acceptable. But all abolitionists share the belief that capital punishment is never morally justifiable.

One common argument enlisted by both retentionists and abolitionists concerns capital punishment as a deterrent. As we'll see, retentionists sometimes claim that capital punishment deters potential murderers and therefore should be kept. For their part, some abolitionists claim that capital punishment does not serve as a deterrent and offer this—usually with other reasons—for abolishing the death penalty. Because the deterrent argument figures so prominently in capital punishment debates, we should inspect it before beginning this chapter's dialogues.

CAPITAL PUNISHMENT AS DETERRENT

Does capital punishment succeed in deterring potential murderers? At first glance, the answer seems to be a resounding yes. After all, virtually everyone seems deterred from lawbreaking by relatively mild intimidation—for example, being towed away for illegal parking or losing one's driver's license for recklessness. How much more, common sense suggests, must potential murderers be intimidated by the threat of their own death at the executioner's hand. In this instance, however, common sense misleads by failing to recognize that murderers differ from the rest of us in important respects.

First, there's the large category of murderers who kill in a fit of rage or passion. A barroom brawl escalates and one man kills another; in a gang fight, a member of one group kills a member of another, perhaps to save face or avenge a harm; in a family quarrel, a person kills a relative when things get out of hand. The list goes on and on. Such murders, of which there are many, are committed not with forethought of the consequences but in a moment of white-hot anger. Hence, not even the death penalty is likely to deter these murderers. (In fact, in instances of gang killings, it might have the opposite effect: In risking their own lives at the hands of the state, killers might feel they're proving their mettle or giving ultimate evidence of gang loyalty.)

Then there's the category of so-called professional criminals, those who deliberately calculate when, where, and how to commit crimes. It's not at all clear that this type of criminal is deterred by the death penalty. In fact, if professional criminals perceive the likely punishment for nonhomicidal crimes (e.g., robbery, burglary, rape, and so forth) as overly severe, they might be encouraged to kill their victims and witnesses rather than risk getting caught: Killing these people greatly increases the criminals' chances of getting away with their crimes, and so they may not in the least be deterred by the threat of the death penalty.

Besides these kinds of potential murderers are those who seemingly have a death wish. The annals of psychiatry are replete with cases of people so emotionally disturbed that they kill to win the death penalty and end their tortured existence. In effect, their murderous acts are expressions of suicidal impulses. Since they lack the nerve to kill themselves, they want someone else to do it for them—in this case, the state.

But what about cases of so-called normal, nonsuicidal persons who carefully weigh the risks before killing? Are these potential murderers deterred by the death penalty? Even here, the deterrent effect of capital punishment is by no means obvious or certain. What's required is a determination of how many, if any, calculating potential murderers (a small class to begin with) who are not deterred by the threat of life imprisonment would be deterred by the threat of death. Even if such a determination is possible, it's not obvious or certain that there would be any such people at all or much more than a small number annually.

A further complication in assessing the death penalty as deterrent relates not to factual questions such as the preceding but to the moral and legal costs of deterrence. Some claim there's a basic incompatibility between the deterrent efficacy of the death penalty and due process, which refers to a constitutionally guaranteed, specific, systematic procedure of appeal. The death penalty can be deterrent, the argument goes, only if due process is sacrificed. Conversely, due process can govern the inflicting of capital punishment but at the cost of deterrence. When human life is at issue—as of course it is in capital punishment cases—the courts have been understandably scrupulous in reviewing cases for error and ensuring that basic rights have been respected. The consequences of this process of rigorous judicial review are quite apparent: increasing delays of execution, an ever-increasing percentage of those convicted who are never executed, and large numbers of convictions overturned. When fully exercised, the right of appeal can lead to costly, protracted litigation, in which a criminal's fate may hinge as much on the quality of legal representation as on any other factor. Given the delay between murder and the death penalty, and the uncertainty that a death sentence will ever be carried out, one wonders about the death penalty's deterrent effect. On the other hand, to ensure swiftness and certainty mocks one of the most cherished ideals of our system of justice: due process.

Currently, the consensus among social scientists is that no statistical studies on the deterrent effect of capital punishment yield a conclusive answer. We simply don't know whether the threat of death deters people from killing. Given this picture, some argue that since there is a moral presumption against the taking of life, the burden of proving capital punishment is a deterrent should fall on those who advocate the taking of life in the form of capital punishment. But by the same token, one could contend that abolitionists should bear the burden of proof: Since we don't know for sure whether the death penalty is a deterrent, we should give the benefit of doubt to the lives of potential victims of murderers rather than to the murderers. This tack is especially forceful when applied to measures intended to reserve the death penalty for the intentional killings of law enforcement agents and others who need special protection, which they might get from the threat of the death penalty.

ABOLITIONIST ARGUMENTS (AGAINST CAPITAL PUNISHMENT)

1. ***Every human life has dignity and worth.***

   POINT: "Capital punishment is nothing more than legalized cold-blooded murder. Whatever crime a person has committed, he or she is still a human being, and every human life has inherent dignity and worth. Don't get me wrong—I'm not advocating leniency toward vicious murderers. We have to protect ourselves from them, and we have to send a clear signal to other would-be murderers that society will not tolerate heinous crime. But life imprisonment without the possibility of parole is sufficient punishment and deterrent. To strap a fellow human being into a chair and give a lethal dose of gas, a lethal jolt of electricity, or a lethal injection is unworthy of a civilized society. Capital punishment should have gone the way of legalized torture and mutilation years ago. It too is 'cruel and unusual punishment,' and like them it's morally unacceptable in today's world."

   COUNTERPOINT: "I have no quarrel with a general commitment to respect for human life, but imposing the death penalty on depraved murderers who have no respect for human life themselves is the strongest commitment to that principle a society can make. First-degree murder is the ultimate crime, and anyone who commits it deserves to pay the ultimate price. As for capital punishment being 'cruel and unusual' in today's world, whether a punishment falls into that category depends on prevailing moral standards. And as long as democratically elected legislatures are willing to enact it and citizen juries are willing to impose it, it can hardly be considered cruel and unusual."

2. ***Capital punishment is imposed with class and racial bias.***

   POINT: "Statistics show two very disturbing facts about the way capital punishment is imposed in our society. First, the poor, the underprivileged, and members of minority groups are far more likely to be executed than the rich, the influential, and whites. Second, the death penalty is far more likely to be imposed when the victim is white than when the victim is the member of a minority group. Regardless of your high-minded principles, capital punishment shows at best a respect for affluent white life, not human life in general. Because its implementation is patently discriminatory and therefore unjust, it must be stopped."

COUNTERPOINT: "Though the bias you mention is indeed unjust, it's irrelevant to the morality of capital punishment. After all, the same charges have often been made against our criminal justice systems in general. Of course, such bias should be rooted out wherever it exists; and of course, comparable crimes should bring the same punishment. But whether capital punishment is justified for the worst of crimes is one issue. Whether it's currently implemented in a justifiable way is another."

3. *The innocent may die.*

POINT: "The innocent are often convicted of crimes. As tragic as that is when the sentence is a prison term, the tragedy is far worse when the sentence is death. In the former case, society can at least make *some* reparation for time unjustly served, but no fact is more obvious than the fact that nothing can be done for the dead. To execute even one innocent person is inexcusable, and there's no way in the world that we can rule that possibility out without abolishing the death penalty."

COUNTERPOINT: "I can't deny that the execution of an innocent human being is a terrible tragedy. Nor can I deny that the possibility will always be there. That's why we require such safeguards as the automatic right of appeal after capital convictions. But given these safeguards, the possibility remains extremely slim. And as unfortunate as that slim risk is, like many other unfortunate risks, it's one worth taking. The thousands of murders committed in the United States each year require us to take it."

4. *Capital punishment compromises the judicial system.*

POINT: "Capital punishment compromises our judicial system in two ways. First, though the point of capital punishment is to present a tough stance against crime, it sometimes has the opposite effect. Juries have been known to strain the evidence to convict defendants of lesser charges—or even to acquit them—when a conviction of first-degree murder carries a mandatory death sentence. Second, cases of capital punishment invariably involve years of costly appeals. Not only does that delay justice, but it also subjects the victims' families, as well as the convicts', to years of cruel and unusual punishment."

COUNTERPOINT: "Again, the problem isn't capital punishment itself but the way it's implemented. And again, the answer is to improve the judicial system, not to abolish the death penalty. We need greater care in jury selection and a more efficient appeals process. What we don't need is to keep vicious murderers alive as wards of the state."

RETENTIONIST ARGUMENTS (FOR CAPITAL PUNISHMENT)

1. ***Capital punishment deters crime.***

POINT: "Simple common sense tells us that capital punishment is a more powerful deterrent against crime than prison. The more severe the punishment, the greater the risk to the would-be criminal; and the greater the risk, the more reason not to commit the crime. I'm not saying that every would-be killer is rational enough to weigh the pros and cons before deciding whether to kill, but it certainly stands to reason that some are. And as long as that's true, capital punishment serves its purpose—saving innocent lives."

COUNTERPOINT: "Regardless of what your common sense tells you, the statistics offer no support. There just isn't any conclusive evidence that the death penalty is a more powerful deterrent than prison. Besides, my common sense doesn't agree with yours. Mine tells me that very few murderers follow any kind of rational weighing of pros and cons. And in the rare cases when they do, the murderer isn't thinking that a life sentence won't be too high a price to pay. It's far more likely that the murderer doesn't expect to get caught in the first place."

2. ***Capital punishment keeps the convicted murderer from killing again.***

POINT: "Capital punishment guarantees at least one thing. We don't have to worry that an executed murderer will kill again. Even if every murderer sentenced to imprisonment for life without possibility of parole never leaves prison alive, which is highly doubtful, we still have to worry about murders committed in prison. The rest of society may be protected from these killers, but prison guards and fellow inmates aren't. Don't forget: Since they're already serving the maximum sentence, they have nothing to fear from killing again."

COUNTERPOINT: "The truth of the matter is that convicted murderers rarely do kill again, whether in prison or in society after release or parole. Since we can never know which ones will kill again, we'd have to execute hundreds who wouldn't just to prevent one who would. Clearly, that can't be just. We might as well execute everyone who might conceivably commit a murder."

3. ***Capital punishment balances the scales of justice.***

POINT: "Murder being the ultimate crime, simple justice requires that the murderer pay the ultimate penalty. After all, deterrence and prevention aren't the only purposes of punishing criminals. An equally important purpose is to see that justice is done, that moral retribution is taken. That's why we insist that the punishment must fit the crime. Furthermore, society has both the right and the obligation to express its moral outrage over the most heinous crimes committed against it. And both purposes are best served by capital punishment. Prison is just too weak a punishment for many murderers, and a prison term cannot satisfy society's moral outrage over vicious murders."

COUNTERPOINT: "You call it retribution and the expression of moral outrage, but I call it revenge. Certainly, justice requires that the guilty be punished for their crimes. It also requires that more severe crimes be met by more severe penalties. But there are moral limits to what we can inflict on even the cruelest criminals. We don't torture murderers who tortured their victims. We don't rape murderers who raped their victims. To do either wouldn't be justice but a gross perversion of justice. It would be bloodthirsty revenge, pure and simple. And that's what the death penalty is."

4. ***Society shouldn't have to pay the economic costs of life sentences for murders.***

POINT: "When you put murderers away for life, you give up all hope of reforming them. That leaves society with the heavy cost of supporting the worst criminals in maximum security prisons until they die. Why should innocent taxpayers have to foot the bill for the care of depraved criminals who've demonstrated that they have no respect for society's laws or human life?"

COUNTERPOINT: "Because the rest of us do have—or at least should have—respect for human life. But if we continue to execute our fellow human beings because it's cheaper than keeping them alive, we demonstrate that our respect for human life isn't much stronger than theirs. Besides, don't be so sure that capital punishment is cheaper than life imprisonment. The costs of executing a convict, including the costs of the lengthy appeals process and the high costs of keeping a convict on death row, are enormous."

Speech in Favor of Capital Punishment

JOHN STUART MILL

The English philosopher John Stuart Mill (1806–1873) is best known for his development of utilitarianism, as well as his sweeping defense of the importance of free speech in the development of democracies. Routinely characterized as a "liberal," he supported capital punishment on what he perceived to be humanitarian grounds drawn from his theory of utilitarianism. He delivered this speech to the English Parliament in 1868 in opposition to a bill introduced by Mr. Gilpin that would ban capital punishment.

... It would be a great satisfaction to me if I were able to support this Motion. It is always a matter of regret to me to find myself, on a public question, opposed to those who are called—sometimes in the way of honour, and sometimes in what is intended for ridicule—the philanthropists. Of all persons who take part in public affairs, they are those for whom, on the whole, I feel the greatest amount of respect; for their characteristic is, that they devote their time, their labour, and much of their money to objects purely public, with a less admixture of either personal or class selfishness, than any other class of politicians whatever.

On almost all the great questions, scarcely any politicians are so steadily and almost uniformly to be found on the side of right; and they seldom err, but by an exaggerated application of some just and highly important principle. On the very subject that is now occupying us we all know what signal service they have rendered. It is through their efforts that our criminal laws—which within my memory hanged people for stealing in a dwelling house to the value of 40s.-laws by virtue of which rows of human beings might be seen suspended in front of Newgate by those who ascended or descended Ludgate Hill—have so greatly relaxed their most revolting and most impolitic ferocity, that aggravated murder is now practically the only crime which is punished with death by any of our lawful tribunals; and we are even now deliberating whether the extreme penalty should be retained in that solitary case. This vast gain, not only to humanity, but to the ends of penal justice, we owe to the philanthropists; and if they are mistaken, as I cannot but think they are, in the present instance, it is only in not perceiving the right time and place for stopping in a career hitherto so eminently beneficial.

Sir, there is a point at which, I conceive, that career ought to stop. When there has been brought home to any one, by conclusive evidence, the greatest crime known to the law; and when the attendant circumstances suggest no palliation of the guilt, no hope that the culprit may even yet not be unworthy to live among mankind, nothing to make it probable that the crime was an exception to his general character rather than a consequence of it, then I confess it appears to me that to deprive the criminal of the life of which he has proved himself to be unworthy—solemnly to blot him out from the fellowship of mankind and from the catalogue of the living—is the most appropriate as it is certainly the most impressive, mode in which society can attach to so great a crime the penal consequences which for the security of life it is indispensable to annex to it.

I defend this penalty, when confined to atrocious cases, on the very ground on which it is commonly attacked—on that of humanity to the criminal; as beyond comparison the least cruel mode in which it is possible adequately to deter from the crime. If, in our horror of inflicting death, we endeavour to devise some punishment for the living criminal which shall act on the human mind with a deterrent force at all comparable to that of death, we are driven to inflictions less severe indeed in appearance, and therefore less efficacious, but far more cruel in reality. Few, I think, would venture to propose, as a punishment for aggravated murder, less than imprisonment with hard labor for life; that is the fate to which a murderer would be consigned by the mercy which shrinks from putting him to death.

But has it been sufficiently considered what sort of a mercy this is, and what kind of life it leaves to him? If, indeed, the punishment is not really inflicted—if it becomes the sham which a few years ago such punishments were rapidly becoming—then, indeed, its adoption would be almost tantamount to giving up the attempt to repress murder altogether. But if it really is what it professes to be, and if it is realized in all its rigour by the popular imagination, as it very probably would not be, but as it must be if it is to be efficacious, it will be so shocking that when the memory of the crime is no longer fresh, there will be almost insuperable difficulty in executing it.

What comparison can there really be, in point of severity, between consigning a man to the short pang of a rapid death, and immuring him in a living tomb, there to linger out what may be a long life in the hardest and most monotonous toil, without any of its alleviations or rewards—debarred from all pleasant sights and sounds, and cut off from all earthly hope, except a slight mitigation of bodily restraint, or a small improvement of diet? Yet even such a lot as this, because there is no one moment at which the suffering is of terrifying intensity, and, above all, because it does not contain the element, so imposing to the imagination, of the unknown, is universally reputed a milder punishment than death—stands in all codes as a mitigation of the capital penalty, and is thankfully accepted as such. For it is characteristic of all punishments which depend on duration for their efficacy—all, therefore, which are not corporal or pecuniary—that they are more rigorous than they seem; while it is, on the contrary, one of the strongest recommendations a punishment can have, that it should seem more rigorous than it is; for its practical power depends far less on what it is than on what it seems.

There is not, I should think, any human infliction which makes an impression on the imagination so entirely out of proportion to its real severity as the punishment of death. The punishment must be mild indeed which does not add more to the sum of human misery than is necessarily or directly added by the execution of a criminal. As my hon. Friend the Member for Northampton (Mr. Gilpin) has himself remarked, the most that human laws can do to anyone in the matter of death is to hasten it; the man would have died at any rate; not so very much later, and on the average, I fear, with a considerably greater amount of bodily suffering. Society is asked, then, to denude itself of an instrument of punishment which, in the grave cases to which alone it is suitable, effects its purposes at a less cost of human suffering than any other; which, while it inspires more terror, is less cruel in actual fact than any punishment that we should think of substituting for it.

My hon. Friend says that it does not inspire terror, and that experience proves it to be a failure. But the influence of a punishment is not to be estimated by its effect on hardened criminals. Those whose habitual way of life keeps them, so to speak, at all times within sight of the gallows, do grow to care less about it; as, to compare good things with bad, an old soldier is not much affected by the chance of dying in battle. I can afford to admit all that is often said about the indifference of professional criminals to the gallows. Though of that indifference one-third is probably bravado and another third confidence that they shall have the luck to escape, it is quite probable that the remaining third is real. But the efficacy of a punishment which acts principally through the imagination, is chiefly to be measured by the impression it makes on those who are still innocent; by the horror with which it surrounds the first promptings of guilt; the restraining influence it exercises over the beginning of the thought which, if indulged, would become a temptation; the check which it exerts over the graded declension towards the state—never suddenly attained—in which crime no longer revolts, and punishment no longer terrifies.

As for what is called the failure of death punishment, who is able to judge of that? We partly know who those are whom it has not deterred; but who is there who knows whom it has deterred, or how many human beings it has saved who would have lived to be murderers if that awful association had not been thrown round the idea of murder from their earliest infancy? Let us not forget that the most imposing fact loses its power over the imagination if it is made too cheap. When a punishment fit only for the most atrocious crimes is lavished on small offences until human feeling recoils from it, then, indeed, it ceases to intimidate, because it ceases to be believed in.

The failure of capital punishment in cases of theft is easily accounted for; the thief did not believe that it would be inflicted. He had learnt by experience that jurors would perjure themselves rather than find him guilty; that Judges would seize any excuse for not sentencing him to death, or for recommending him to mercy; and that if neither jurors nor Judges were merciful, there were still hopes from an authority above both. When things had come to this pass it was high time to give up the vain attempt.

When it is impossible to inflict a punishment, or when its infliction becomes a public scandal, the idle threat cannot too soon disappear from the statute book. And in the case of the host of offences which were formerly capital, I heartily rejoice that it did become impracticable to execute the law. If the same state of public feeling comes to exist in the case of murder; if the time comes when jurors refuse to find a murderer guilty; when Judges will not sentence him to death, or will recommend him to mercy; or when, if juries and Judges do not flinch from their duty, Home Secretaries, under pressure of deputations and memorials, shrink from theirs, and the threat becomes, as it became in the other cases, a mere *brutum fulmen*;[1] then, indeed, it may become necessary to do in this case what has been done in those—to abrogate the penalty.

That time may come—my hon. Friend thinks that it has nearly come. I hardly know whether he lamented it or boasted of it; but he and his Friends are entitled to the boast; for if it comes it will be their doing, and they will have gained what I cannot but call a fatal victory, for they will have achieved it by bringing about, if they will forgive me for saying so, an enervation, an effeminancy, in the general mind of the country. For what else than effeminancy is it to be so much more shocked by taking a man's life than by depriving him of all that makes life desirable or valuable? Is death, then, the greatest of all earthly ills? *Usque adeone mori miserum est?*[2] Is it, indeed, so dreadful a thing to die? Has it not been from of old one

[1] A display of force.
[2] Is it so hard a thing to die?

chief part of a manly education to make us despise death—teaching us to account it, if an evil at all, by no means high in the list of evils; at all events, as an inevitable one, and to hold, as it were, our lives in our hands, ready to be given or risked at any moment, for a sufficiently worthy object?

I am sure that my hon. Friends know all this as well, and have as much of all these feelings as any of the rest of us; possibly more. But I cannot think that this is likely to be the effect of their teaching on the general mind. I cannot think that the cultivating of a peculiar sensitiveness of conscience on this one point, over and above what results from the general cultivation of the moral sentiments, is permanently consistent with assigning in our own minds to the fact of death no more than the degree of relative importance which belongs to it among the other incidents of our humanity.

The men of old cared too little about death, and gave their own lives or took those of others with equal recklessness. Our danger is of the opposite kind, lest we should be so much shocked by death, in general and in the abstract, as to care too much about it in individual cases, both those of other people and our own, which call for its being risked. And I am not putting things at the worst, for it is proved by the experience of other countries that horror of the executioner by no means necessarily implies horror of the assassin. The stronghold, as we all know, of hired assassination in the 18th century was Italy; yet it is said that in some of the Italian populations the infliction of death by sentence of law was in the highest degree offensive and revolting to popular feeling.

Much has been said of the sanctity of human life, and the absurdity of supposing that we can teach respect for life by ourselves destroying it. But I am surprised at the employment of this argument, for it is one which might be brought against any punishment whatever. It is not human life only, not human life as such, that ought to be sacred to us, but human feelings. The human capacity of suffering is what we should cause to be respected, not the mere capacity of existing.

And we may imagine somebody asking how we can teach people not to inflict suffering by ourselves inflicting it? But to this I should answer—all of us would answer—that to deter by suffering from inflicting suffering is not only possible, but the very purpose of penal justice. Does fining a criminal show want of respect for property, or imprisoning him, for personal freedom? Just as unreasonable is it to think that to take the life of a man who has taken that of another is to show want of regard for human life. We show, on the contrary, most emphatically our regard for it, by the adoption of a rule that he who violates that right in another forfeits it for himself, and that while no other crime that he can commit deprives him of his right to live, this shall.

There is one argument against capital punishment, even in extreme cases, which I cannot deny to have weight—on which my hon. Friend justly laid great stress, and which never can be entirely got rid of. It is this—that if by an error of justice an innocent person is put to death, the mistake can never be corrected; all compensation, all reparation for the wrong is impossible. This would be indeed a serious objection if these miserable mistakes—among the most tragical occurrences in the whole round of human affairs—could not be made extremely rare.

The argument is invincible where the mode of criminal procedure is dangerous to the innocent, or where the Courts of Justice are not trusted. And this probably is the reason why the objection to an irreparable punishment began (as I believe it did) earlier, and is more intense and more widely diffused, in some parts of the Continent of Europe than it is here. There are on the Continent great and enlightened countries, in which the criminal procedure is not so favorable to innocence, does not afford the same security against erroneous conviction, as it does among us; countries where the Courts of Justice seem to think they fail in their duty unless they find somebody guilty; and in their really laudable desire to hunt guilt from its hiding places, expose themselves to a serious danger of condemning the innocent.

If our own procedure and Courts of Justice afforded ground for similar apprehension, I should be the first to join in withdrawing the power of inflicting irreparable punishment from such tribunals. But we all know that the defects of our procedure are the very opposite. Our rules of evidence are even too favorable to the prisoner; and juries and Judges carry out the maxim, "It is better that ten guilty should escape than that one innocent person should suffer," not only to the letter, but beyond the letter. Judges are most anxious to point out, and juries to allow for, the barest possibility of the prisoner's innocence. No human judgment is infallible; such sad cases as my hon. Friend cited will sometimes occur; but in so grave a case as that of murder, the accused, in our system, has always the benefit of the merest shadow of a doubt.

And this suggests another consideration very germane to the question. The very fact that death punishment is more shocking than any other to the imagination, necessarily renders the Courts of Justice more scrupulous in requiring the fullest evidence of guilt. Even that which is the greatest objection to capital punishment, the impossibility of correcting an error once committed, must make, and does make, juries and Judges more careful in forming their opinion, and more jealous in their scrutiny of the evidence. If the substitution of penal servitude for death in cases of murder should cause any declaration in this conscientious scrupulosity, there would be a great evil to set against the real, but I hope rare, advantage of being able to make reparation to a condemned person who was afterwards discovered to be innocent.

In order that the possibility of correction may be kept open wherever the chance of this sad contingency is more than infinitesimal, it is quite right that the Judge should recommend to the Crown a commutation of the sentence, not solely when the proof of guilt is open to the smallest suspicion, but whenever there remains anything unexplained and mysterious in the case, raising a desire for more light, or making it likely that further information may at some future time be obtained. I would also suggest that whenever the sentence is commuted the grounds of the commutation should, in some authentic form, be made known to the public.

Thus much I willingly concede to my hon. Friend; but on the question of total abolition I am inclined to hope that the feeling of the country is not with him, and that the limitation of death punishment to the cases referred to in the Bill of last year will be generally considered sufficient. The mania which existed a short time ago for paring down all our punishments seems to have reached its limits, and not before it was time. We were in danger of being left without any effectual punishment, except for small of offences.

What was formerly our chief secondary punishment—transportation—before it was abolished, had become almost a reward. Penal servitude, the substitute for it, was becoming, to the classes who were principally subject to it, almost nominal, so comfortable did we make our prisons, and so easy had it become to get quickly out of them. Flogging—a most objectionable punishment in ordinary cases, but a particularly appropriate one for crimes of brutality, especially crimes against women—we would not hear of, except, to be sure, in the case of garotters, for whose peculiar benefit we reestablished it in a hurry, immediately after a Member of Parliament had been garrotted. With this exception, offences, even of an atrocious kind, against the person, as my hon. and learned Friend the Member for Oxford (Mr. Neate) well remarked, not only were, but still are, visited with penalties so ludicrously inadequate, as to be almost an encouragement to the crime.

I think, Sir, that in the case of most offences, except those against property, there is more need of strengthening our punishments than of weakening them; and that severer sentences, with an apportionment of them to the different kinds of offences which shall approve itself better than at present to the moral sentiments of the community, are the kind of reform of which our penal system now stands in need. I shall therefore vote against the Amendment.

QUESTIONS FOR ANALYSIS

1. Mill defends capital punishment as the "most humane" punishment available for those who deserve severe punishment compared to the alternatives. Considering the options he weighs, is execution really the most humane? Given the punishments we typically use today, would Mill likely reach the same conclusion if he were alive now?

2. How does Mill rely on his principles of utilitarian reasoning in his consideration of capital punishment?
3. How are Mill's arguments similar to and different from contemporary debates?
4. How does he respond to concerns that innocent people might be executed? Does his answer adequately address concerns today, now that DNA testing is showing that many on death row are innocent?

The Death Sentence

SIDNEY HOOK

In this essay, professor of philosophy Sidney Hook (1902–1989) suggests that much of the debate about capital punishment suffers from vindictiveness and sentimentality. For example, abolitionists often argue that capital punishment is no more than an act of revenge, that it is the ultimate inhumanity. Hook is no more sympathetic, however, to the thrust of retentionist arguments. He points out that capital punishment has never been established as a deterrent to crime. Furthermore, he rejects as question-begging the retentionist argument that capital punishment is justified because it fulfills a community need or that it is the only appropriate punishment for certain unspeakable offenses.

So where does Hook stand on the issue? Despite his feelings that no valid case for capital punishment has thus far been made, Hook is not categorically opposed to it. Indeed, he cites two conditions under which he believes capital punishment is justified. The first is in cases where criminals facing a life imprisonment sentence request it. The second involves cases of convicted murderers who murder again. Hook regards the abolitionist objections to these exceptions as expressions of sentimentalism, even cruelty.

Is there anything new that can be said for or against capital punishment? Anyone familiar with the subject knows that unless extraneous issues are introduced, a large measure of agreement about it can be, and has been, won. For example, during the last 150 years the death penalty for criminal offenses has been abolished, or remains unenforced, in many countries; just as important, the number of crimes punishable by death has been sharply reduced in all countries. But while the progress has been encouraging, it still seems to me that greater clarity on the issues involved is desirable. Much of the continuing polemic still suffers from one or the other of the twin evils of vindictiveness and sentimentality.

Sentimentality, together with a great deal of confusion about determinism, is found in Clarence Darrow's speeches and writings on the subject. Darrow was an attractive and likable human being but a very confused thinker. He argued against capital punishment on the ground that the murderer was always a victim of heredity and environment—and therefore it was unjust to execute him. ("Back of every murder and back of every human act are sufficient causes that move the human machine beyond their control.") The crucifiers and the crucified, the lynch mob and its prey are equally moved by causes beyond their control and the relevant differences between them are therewith ignored. Although

Darrow passionately asserted that no one knows what justice is and that no one can measure it, he nonetheless was passionately convinced that capital punishment was unjust.

It should be clear that if Darrow's argument were valid, it would be an argument not only against capital punishment but against all punishment. Very few of us would be prepared to accept this. But the argument is absurd. Even if we are all victims of our heredity and environment, it is still possible to alter the environment by meting out capital punishment to deter crimes of murder. If no one can help doing what he does, if no one is responsible for his actions, then surely this holds just as much for those who advocate and administer capital punishment as for the criminal. The denunciation of capital punishment as unjust, therefore, would be senseless. The question of universal determinism is irrelevant. If capital punishment actually were a deterrent to murder, and there existed no other more effective deterrent, and none as effective but more humane, a case could be made for it.

Nor am I impressed with the argument against capital punishment on the ground of its inhumanity. Of course it is inhumane. So is murder. If it could be shown that the inhumanity of murder can be decreased in no other way than by the inhumanity of capital punishment acting as a deterrent, this would be a valid argument for such punishment.

I have stressed the hypothetical character of these arguments because it makes apparent how crucially the wisdom of our policy depends upon the alleged facts. Does capital punishment serve as the most effective deterrent we have against murder? Most people who favor its retention believe that it does. But any sober examination of the facts will show that this has never been established. It seems plausible, but not everything which is plausible or intuitively credible is true.

The experience of countries and states which have abolished capital punishment shows that there has been no perceptible increase of murders after abolition—although it would be illegitimate to infer from this that the fear of capital punishment never deterred anybody. The fact that "the state with the very lowest murder rate is Maine, which abolished capital punishment in 1870" may be explained by the hypothesis that fishermen, like fish, tend to be cold-blooded, or by some less fanciful hypothesis. The relevant question is: What objective evidence exists which would justify the conclusion that if Maine had not abolished capital punishment, its death rate would have been higher? The answer is: No evidence exists.

The opinion of many jurists and law enforcement officers from Cesare Beccaria (the eighteenth-century Italian criminologist) to the present is that swift and certain punishment of some degree of severity is a more effective deterrent of murder than the punishment of maximum severity when it is slow and uncertain. Although this opinion requires substantiation, too, it carries the weight which we normally extend to pronouncements by individuals who report on their life experience. And in the absence of convincing evidence that capital punishment is a more effective and/or humane form of punishment for murder than any other punishment, there remains no other reasonable ground for retaining it.

This is contested by those who speak of the necessity for capital punishment as an expression of the "community need of justice" or as the fulfillment of "an instinctive urge to punish injustice." Such views lie at the basis of some forms of the retributive theory. It has been alleged that the retributive theory is nothing more than a desire for revenge, but it is a great and arrogant error to assume that all who hold it are vindictive. The theory has been defended by secular saints like G. E. Moore and Immanuel Kant, whose dispassionate interest in justice cannot reasonably be challenged. Even if one accepted the retributive theory or believed in the desirability of meeting the community need of justice, it doesn't in the least follow that this justifies capital punishment. Other forms of punishment may be retributive, too.

I suppose that what one means by community need or feeling and the necessity of regarding it is that not only must justice be done, it must be seen to be done. A requirement of good law is that it must be consonant with the feeling of the community something which is sometimes called "the living law." Otherwise it is unenforceable and brings the whole system of law into disrepute. Meeting community feeling is a necessary condition for good law, but not a sufficient condition for good law. This is what Justice Holmes meant when he wrote in *The Common Law* that "The first requirement of a sound body of law is that it should correspond with the actual feelings and demands of the community, whether right or wrong." But I think he would admit that sound law is sounder still if in addition to being enforceable it is also just. Our moral obligation as citizens is to build a community feeling and demand which is right rather than wrong.

Those who wish to retain capital punishment on the ground that it fulfills a community need or feeling must believe either that community feeling *per se* is always justified, or that to disregard it in any particular situation is inexpedient because of the consequences, *viz.*, increase in murder. In either case they beg the question—in the first case, the question of justice, and in the second, the question of deterrence.

One thing is incontestable. From the standpoint of those who base the argument for retention of capital punishment on the necessity of satisfying community needs there could be no justification whatsoever for any *mandatory* death sentence. For a mandatory death sentence attempts to determine in advance what the community need and feeling will be, and closes the door to fresh inquiry about the justice as well as the deterrent consequences of any proposed punishment.

Community need and feeling are notoriously fickle. When a verdict of guilty necessarily entails a death sentence, the jury may not feel the sentence warranted and may bring in a verdict of not guilty even when some punishment seems to be legally and morally justified. Even when the death sentence is not mandatory, there is an argument, not decisive but still significant, against any death sentence. This is its incorrigibility. Our judgment of a convicted man's guilt may change. If he has been executed in the meantime, we can only do him "posthumous justice." But can justice ever really be posthumous to the victim? Rarely has evidence, even when it is beyond reasonable doubt, the same finality about its probative force as the awful finality of death. The weight of this argument against capital punishment is all the stronger if community need and feeling are taken as the prime criteria of what is just or fitting.

What about heinous political offenses? Usually when arguments fail to sustain the demand for capital punishment in ordinary murder cases, the names of Adolf Hitler, Adolf Eichmann, Joseph Stalin and Ilse Koch are introduced and flaunted before the audience to inflame their feelings. Certain distinctions are in order here. Justice, of course, requires severe punishment. But why is it assumed that capital punishment is, in these cases, the severest and most just of sentences? How can any equation be drawn between the punishment of one man and the sufferings of his numerous victims? After all, we cannot kill Eichmann six million times or Stalin twelve million times (a conservative estimate of the number of people who died by their order).

If we wish to keep alive the memory of political infamy, if we wish to use it as a political lesson to prevent its recurrence, it may be educationally far more effective to keep men like Eichmann in existence. Few people think of the dead. By the same token, it may be necessary to execute a politically monstrous figure to prevent him from becoming the object of allegiance of a restoration movement. Eichmann does not have to be executed. He is more useful alive if we wish to keep before mankind the enormity of his offense. But if Hitler had been taken alive, his death would have been required as a matter of political necessity, to prevent him from becoming a living symbol or rallying cry of Nazi diehards and irreconcilables.

There is an enormous amount of historical evidence which shows that certain political tyrants, after they lose power, become the focus of restoration movements that are a chronic source of bloodshed and civil strife. No matter how infamous a tyrant's actions, there is usually some group which has profited by it, resents being deprived of its privileges, and schemes for a return to power. In difficult situations, the dethroned tyrant also becomes a symbol of legitimacy around which discontented elements rally who might otherwise have waited for the normal processes of government to relieve their lot. A *mystique* develops around the tyrant, appeals are made to the "good old days" when his bread and circuses were used to distract attention from the myriads of his tortured victims, plots seethe around him until they boil over into violence and bloodshed again. I did not approve of the way Mussolini was killed. Even he deserved due process. But I have no doubt whatsoever that had he been sentenced merely to life imprisonment, the Fascist movement in Italy today would be a much more formidable movement, and that sooner or later, many lives would have been lost in consequence of the actions of Fascist legitimists.

Where matters of ordinary crime are concerned these political considerations are irrelevant. I conclude, therefore, that no valid case has so far been made for the retention of capital punishment, that the argument from deterrence is inconclusive and inconsistent (in the sense that we do not do other things to reinforce its deterrent effect if we believe it has such an effect), and that the argument from community feeling is invalid.

However, since I am not a fanatic or absolutist, I do not wish to go on record as being categorically opposed to the death sentence in all circumstances. I should like to recognize two exceptions. A defendant convicted of murder and sentenced to life should be permitted to choose the death sentence instead. Not so long ago a defendant sentenced to life imprisonment made this request and was rebuked by the judge for his impertinence. I can see no valid grounds for denying such a request out of hand. It may sometimes be denied, particularly if a way can be found to make the defendant labor for the benefit of the dependents of his victim, as is done in some European countries. Unless such considerations are present, I do not see on what reasonable ground the request can be denied, particularly by those who believe in capital punishment. Once they argue that life imprisonment is either a more effective deterrent or more justly punitive, they have abandoned their position.

In passing, I should state that I am in favor of permitting *any* criminal defendant, sentenced to life imprisonment, the right to choose death. I can understand why certain jurists, who believe that the defendant wants thereby to cheat the state out of its mode of punishment, should be indignant at the idea. They are usually the ones who believe that even the attempt at suicide should be deemed a crime—in effect saying to the unfortunate person that if he doesn't succeed in his act of suicide, the state will punish him for it. But I am baffled to understand why the absolute abolitionist, dripping with treacly humanitarianism, should oppose this proposal. I have heard some people actually oppose capital punishment in certain cases on the ground that: "Death is too good for the vile wretch! Let him live and suffer to the end of his days." But the absolute abolitionist should be the last person in the world to oppose the wish of the lifer, who regards this form of punishment as torture worse than death, to leave our world.

My second class of exceptions consists of those who having been sentenced once to prison for premeditated murder, murder again. In these particular cases we have evidence that imprisonment is not a sufficient deterrent for the individual in question. If the evidence shows that the prisoner is so psychologically constituted that, without being insane, the fact that he can kill again with impunity may lead to further murderous behavior, the court should have the discretionary power to pass the death sentence if the criminal is found guilty of a second murder.

In saying that the death sentence should be *discretionary* in cases where a man has killed more than once, I am *not* saying that a murderer who murders again is more deserving of death than the murderer who murders once. Bluebeard was not twelve times more deserving of death when he was finally caught. I am saying simply this: that in a sub-class of murderers, those who murder several times, there may be a special group of sane murderers who, knowing that they will not be executed, will not hesitate to kill again and again. For them the argument from deterrence is obviously valid. Those who say that there must be no exceptions to the abolition of capital punishment cannot rule out the existence of such cases on *a priori* grounds. If they admit that there is a reasonable probability that such murderers will murder again or attempt to murder again, a probability which usually grows with the number of repeated murders, and still insist they would *never* approve of capital punishment, I would conclude that they are indifferent to the lives of the human beings doomed, on their position, to be victims. What fancies itself as a humanitarian attitude is sometimes an expression of sentimentalism. The reverse coin of sentimentalism is often cruelty.

Our charity for all human beings must not deprive us of our common sense. Nor should our charity be less for the future or potential victims of the murderer than for the murderer himself. There are crimes in this world which are, like acts of nature, beyond the power of men to anticipate or control. But not all or most crimes are of this character. So long as human beings are responsible and educable, they will respond to praise and blame and punishment. It is hard to imagine it, but even Hitler and Stalin were once infants. Once you can imagine them as infants, however, it is hard to believe that they were already monsters in their cradles. Every confirmed criminal was once an amateur. The existence of confirmed criminals testifies to the defects of our education—where they can be reformed—and of our penology—where they cannot. That is why we are under the moral obligation to be intelligent about crime and punishment. Intelligence should teach us that the best educational and penological system is the one which prevents crimes rather than punishes them; the next best is one which punishes crime in such a way as to prevent it from happening again.

QUESTIONS FOR ANALYSIS

1. Why does Hook say that if Darrow's argument were valid, it would be an argument not against capital punishment but against all punishment?
2. Why is Hook not impressed by the claim that capital punishment is inhumane? Do you agree with him?
3. Why does Hook feel that those who justify capital punishment by appeal to community feeling beg the question? Do you accept his argument?
4. How does Hook respond to the retentionist claim that capital punishment is justified for politically heinous offenses?
5. Do you agree that a "lifer's" request for capital punishment ought to be honored? Is Hook's justification for his position utilitarian or nonutilitarian? Explain.
6. Why does Hook believe capital punishment is justified when a convicted murderer murders again? Is his defense utilitarian? Explain.
7. Do you agree with Hook that what are called "humanitarian" objections to his two exceptions are really expressions of sentimentalism, even cruelty?

On Deterrence and the Death Penalty

ERNEST VAN DEN HAAG

Ernest van den Haag (1914–2002) was a professor of jurisprudence and social philosophy at several universities. He begins his essay by conceding that capital punishment cannot be defended on grounds of rehabilitation or protection of society from unrehabilitated

Reprinted by special permission of the *Journal of Criminal Law, Criminology, and Police Science*, © 1969 by Northwestern University School of Law, vol. 60, no. 2.

offenders. But he does believe that the ultimate punishment can be justified on grounds of deterrence.

To make his point, van den Haag at some length provides a psychological basis for deterrence. He associates deterrence with human responses to danger. Law functions to change social dangers into individual ones: Legal threats are designed to deter individuals from actions that threaten society. Most of us, van den Haag argues, transfer these external penalty dangers into internal ones; that is, we each develop a conscience that threatens us if we do wrong. But this conscience is and needs to be reinforced by external authority, which imposes penalties for antisocial behavior.

Van den Haag then critically examines the reason punishment has fallen into disrepute as a deterrent to crime: the claim that slums, ghettos, and personality disorders are the real causes of crime. He dismisses these as spurious explanations and insists that only punishment can deter crime. In van den Haag's view, whether individuals will commit crimes depends exclusively on whether they perceive the penalty risks as worth it.

While he concedes that the death penalty cannot be proven to deter crime, van den Haag observes that this in no way means capital punishment lacks a deterrent value. Indeed, it is this very uncertainty about its deterrence that impels van den Haag to argue for its retention. In the last analysis, he believes that retaining capital punishment leads to a net gain for society, notwithstanding the occasional abuse of it. In arguing for capital punishment, then, van den Haag takes a utilitarian viewpoint.

I

If rehabilitation and the protection of society from unrehabilitated offenders were the only purposes of legal punishment, the death penalty could be abolished: It cannot attain the first end, and is not needed for the second. No case for the death penalty can be made unless "doing justice" or "deterring others" is among our penal aims.[1] Each of these purposes can justify capital punishment by itself; opponents, therefore, must show that neither actually does, while proponents can rest their case on either.

Although the argument from justice is intellectually more interesting, and, in my view, decisive enough, utilitarian arguments have more appeal: The claim that capital punishment is useless because it does not deter others is most persuasive. I shall, therefore, focus on this claim. Lest the argument be thought to be unduly narrow, I shall show, nonetheless, that some claims of injustice rest on premises which the claimants reject when arguments for capital punishment are derived therefrom; while other claims of injustice have independent standing: Their weight depends on the weight given to deterrence.

II

Capital punishment is regarded as unjust because it may lead to the execution of innocents, or because the guilty poor (or disadvantaged) are more likely to be executed than the guilty rich.

Regardless of merit, these claims are relevant only if "doing justice" is one purpose of punishment. Unless one regards it as good, or, at least, better, that the guilty be punished rather than the innocent, and that the equally guilty be punished equally,[2] unless, that is, one wants penalties to be just, one cannot object to them because they are not. However, if one does include justice among the purposes of punishment, it becomes possible to justify any one punishment—even death—on grounds of justice. Yet, those who object to the death penalty because of its alleged injustice usually deny not only the merits, or the sufficiency, of specific arguments based on justice, but the propriety of justice as an argument: They exclude "doing justice" as a purpose of legal punishment. If justice is not a purpose of penalties, injustice cannot be an objection to the death penalty, or to any other; if it is, justice cannot be ruled out as an argument for any penalty.

Consider the claim of injustice on its merits now. A convicted man may be found to have been innocent; if he was executed, the penalty cannot be reversed. Except for fines, penalties never can be reversed. Time spent in prison cannot be returned. However, a prison sentence may be remitted once the prisoner serving it is found innocent; and he can be compensated for the time served (although compensation ordinarily cannot repair the harm). Thus, though (nearly) all penalties are irreversible, the death penalty, unlike others, is irrevocable as well.

Despite all precautions, errors will occur in judicial proceedings: The innocent may be found guilty,[3] or the guilty rich may more easily escape conviction, or receive lesser penalties than the guilty poor. However, these injustices do not reside in the penalties inflicted but in their maldistribution. It is not the penalty—whether death or prison—which is unjust when inflicted on the innocent, but its imposition on the innocent. Inequity between poor and rich also involves distribution, not the penalty distributed.[4] Thus injustice is not an objection to the death penalty but to the distributive process—the trial. Trials are more likely to be fair when life is at stake—the death penalty is probably less often unjustly inflicted than others. It requires special consideration not because it is more, or more often, unjust than other penalties, but because it is always irrevocable.

Can any amount of deterrence justify the possibility of irrevocable injustice? Surely injustice is unjustifiable in each actual individual case; it must be objected to whenever it occurs. But we are concerned here with the process that may produce injustice, and with the penalty that would make it irrevocable—not with the actual individual cases produced, but with the general rules which may produce them. To consider objections to a general rule (the provision of any penalties by law) we must compare the likely net result of alternative rules and select the rule (or penalty) likely to produce the least injustice. For however one defines justice, to support it cannot mean less than to favor the least injustice. If the death of innocents because of judicial error is unjust, so is the death of innocents by murder. If some murders could be avoided by a penalty conceivably more deterrent than others—such as the death penalty—then the question becomes: Which penalty will minimize the number of innocents killed (by crime and by punishment)? It follows that the irrevocable injustice sometimes inflicted by the death penalty would not significantly militate against it, if capital punishment deters enough murders to reduce the total number of innocents killed so that fewer are lost than would be lost without it.

In general, the possibility of injustice argues against penalization of any kind only if the expected usefulness of penalization is less important than the probable harm (particularly to innocents) and the probable inequities. The possibility of injustice argues against the death penalty only inasmuch as the added usefulness (deterrence) expected from irrevocability is thought less important than the added harm. (Were my argument specifically concerned with justice, I could compare the injustice inflicted by the courts with the injustice—outside the courts—avoided by the judicial process. "Iimportant" here may be used to include everything to which importance is attached.)

We must briefly examine now the general use and effectiveness of deterrence to decide whether the death penalty could add enough deterrence to be warranted.

III

Does any punishment "deter others" at all? Doubts have been thrown on this effect because it is thought to depend on the incorrect rationalistic psychology of some of its 18th- and 19th-century proponents. Actually deterrence does not depend on rational calculation, on rationality or even on capacity for it; nor do arguments for it depend on rationalistic psychology. Deterrence depends on the likelihood and on the regularity—not on the rationality—of human responses to danger; and further on the possibility of reinforcing internal controls by vicarious external experiences.

Responsiveness to danger is generally found in human behavior; the danger can, but need not, come from the law or from society; nor need it be explicitly verbalized. Unless intent on suicide, people do not jump from high mountain cliffs, however tempted to fly through the air; and they take precautions against falling. The mere risk of injury often restrains us from doing what is otherwise attractive; we refrain even when we have no direct experience, and usually without explicit computation of probabilities, let alone conscious weighing of expected pleasure against possible pain. One abstains from dangerous acts because of vague, inchoate, habitual and, above all, preconscious fears. Risks and rewards are more often felt than calculated; one abstains without accounting to oneself, because "it isn't done," or because one literally does not conceive of the action one refrains from. Animals as well refrain from painful or injurious experiences presumably without calculation; and the threat of punishment can be used to regulate their conduct.

Unlike natural dangers, legal threats are constructed deliberately by legislators to restrain actions which may impair the social order. Thus legislation transforms social into individual dangers. Most people further transform external into internal danger: They acquire a sense of moral obligation, a conscience, which threatens them, should they do what is wrong. Arising originally from the external authority of rulers and rules, conscience is internalized and becomes independent of external forces. However, conscience is constantly reinforced in those whom it controls by the coercive imposition of external authority on recalcitrants and on those who have not acquired it. Most people refrain from offenses because they feel an obligation to behave lawfully. But this obligation would scarcely be felt if those who do not feel or follow it were not to suffer punishment.

Although the legislators may calculate their threats and the responses to be produced, the effectiveness of the threats neither requires nor depends on calculations by those responding. The predictor (or producer) of effects must calculate; those whose responses are predicted (or produced) need not. Hence, although legislation (and legislators) should be rational, subjects, to be deterred as intended, need not be: They need only be responsive.

Punishments deter those who have not violated the law for the same reasons—and in the same degrees (apart from internalization: moral obligation) as do natural dangers. Often natural dangers—all dangers not deliberately created by legislation (*e.g.*, injury of the criminal inflicted by the crime victim) are insufficient. Thus, the fear of injury (natural danger) does not suffice to control city traffic; it must be reinforced by the legal punishment meted out to those who violate the rules. These punishments keep most people observing the regulations. However, where (in the absence of natural danger) the threatened punishment is so light that the advantage of violating rules tends to exceed the disadvantage of being punished (divided by the risk), the rule is violated (*i.e.*, parking fines are too light). In this case the feeling of obligation tends to vanish as well. Elsewhere punishment deters.

To be sure, not everybody responds to threatened punishment. Non-responsive persons may be (a) self-destructive or (b) incapable of responding to threats, or even of grasping them. Increases in the size, or certainty, of penalties would not affect these two groups. A third group (c) might respond to more certain or more severe penalties.[5] If the punishment threatened for burglary, robbery, or rape were a $5 fine in North Carolina, and 5 years in prison in South Carolina, I have no doubt that the North Carolina treasury would become quite opulent until vigilante justice would provide the deterrence not provided by law. Whether to increase penalties (or improve enforcement) depends on the importance of the rule to society, the size and likely reaction of the group that did not respond before, and the acceptance of the added punishment and enforcement required to deter it. Observation would have to locate the points—likely to differ in different times and places—at which diminishing, zero, and negative returns set in. There is no reason to believe that all present and future offenders belong to the *a priori* non-responsive groups, or that all penalties have reached the point of diminishing, let alone zero returns.

IV

Even though its effectiveness seems obvious, punishment as a deterrent has fallen into disrepute. Some ideas which help explain this progressive heedlessness were uttered by Lester Pearson, then Prime Minister of Canada, when, in opposing the death penalty, he proposed that instead "the state seek to eradicate the causes of crime—slums, ghettos and personality disorders."[6]

"Slums, ghettos, and personality disorders" have not been shown, singly or collectively, to be "the causes" of crime.

(1)The crime rate in the slums is indeed higher than elsewhere; but so is the death rate in hospitals. Slums are no more "causes" of crime than hospitals are of death; they are locations of crime, as hospitals are of death. Slums and hospitals attract people selectively; neither is the "cause" of the condition (disease in hospitals, poverty in slums) that leads to the selective attraction.

As for poverty which draws people into slums, and, sometimes, into crime, any relative disadvantage may lead to ambition, frustration, resentment and, if insufficiently restrained, to crime. Not all relative disadvantages can be eliminated; indeed very few can be, and their elimination increases the resentment generated by the remaining ones; not even relative poverty can be removed altogether. (Absolute poverty—whatever that may be—hardly affects crime.) However, though contributory, relative disadvantages are not a necessary or sufficient cause of crime: Most poor people do not commit crimes, and some rich people do. Hence, "eradication of poverty" would, at most, remove one (doubtful) cause of crime.

In the United States, the decline of poverty has not been associated with a reduction of crime. Poverty measured in dollars of constant purchasing power, according to present government standards and statistics, was the condition of $\frac{1}{2}$ of all our families in 1920; of $\frac{1}{5}$ in 1962; and of less than $\frac{1}{6}$ in 1966. In 1967, 5.3 million families out of 49.8 million were poor—$\frac{1}{9}$ of all families in the United States. If crime has been reduced in a similar manner, it is a well-kept secret.

Those who regard poverty as a cause of crime often draw a wrong inference from a true proposition: The rich will not commit certain crimes—Rockefeller never riots; nor does he steal. (He mugs, but only on T.V.) Yet while wealth may be the cause of not committing (certain) crimes, it does not follow that poverty (absence of wealth) is the cause of committing them. Water extinguishes or prevents fire; but its absence is not the cause of fire. Thus, if poverty could be abolished, if everybody had all "necessities" (I don't pretend to know what this would mean), crime would remain, for, in the words of Aristotle, "the greatest crimes are committed not for the sake of basic necessities but for the sake of superfluities." Superfluities cannot be provided by the government; they would be what the government does not provide.

(2) Negro ghettos have a high, Chinese ghettos have a low crime rate. Ethnic separation, voluntary or forced, obviously has little to do with crime; I can think of no reason why it should.[7]

(3) I cannot see how the state could "eradicate" personality disorders even if all causes and cures were known and available. (They are not.) Further, the known incidence of personality disorders within the prison population does not exceed the known incidence outside—though our knowledge of both is tenuous. Nor are personality disorders necessary or sufficient causes for criminal offenses, unless these be identified by means of (moral, not clinical) definition with personality disorders. In this case, Mr. Pearson would have proposed to "eradicate" crime by eradicating crime—certainly a sound, but not a helpful idea.

Mr. Pearson's views are part as well of the mental furniture of the former U.S. Attorney General Ramsey Clark, who told a congressional committee that ". . . only the elimination of the causes of crime can make a significant and lasting difference in the incidence of crime." Uncharitably interpreted, Mr. Clark revealed that only the elimination of causes eliminates effects—a sleazy cliché and wrong to boot. Given the benefit of the doubt, Mr. Clark probably meant that the causes of crime are social; and that therefore crime can be reduced "only" by non-penal (social) measures.

This view suggests a fireman who declines firefighting apparatus by pointing out that "in the long run only the elimination of the causes" of fire "can make a significant and lasting difference in the incidence" of fire, and that fire-fighting equipment does not eliminate "the causes"—except that such a fireman would probably not rise to fire chief. Actually, whether fires are checked depends on equipment and on the efforts of the firemen using it no less than on the presence of "the causes": inflammable materials. So with crimes. Laws, courts and police actions are no less important in restraining them than "the causes" are in impelling them. If firemen (or attorneys general) pass the buck and refuse to use the means available, we may all be burned while waiting for "the long run" and "the elimination of the causes."

Whether any activity—be it lawful or unlawful—takes place depends on whether the desire for it, or for whatever is to be secured by it, is stronger than the desire to avoid the costs involved. Accordingly people work, attend college, commit crimes, go to the movies—or refrain from any of these activities. Attendance at a theatre may be high because the show is entertaining and because the price of admission is low. Obviously the attendance depends on both—on the combination of expected gratification and cost. The wish, motive or impulse for doing anything—the experienced, or expected, gratification—is the cause of doing it; the wish to avoid the cost is the cause of not doing it. One is no more and no less "cause" than the other. (Common speech supports this use of "cause" no less than logic: "Why did you go to Jamaica?" *Because* it is such a beautiful place." "Why didn't you go to Jamaica?" "*Because* it is too expensive."—"Why do you buy this?" "*Because* it is so cheap." "Why don't you buy that?" "*Because* it is too expensive.") Penalties (costs) are causes of lawfulness, or (if too low or uncertain) of unlawfulness, of crime. People do commit crimes because, given their conditions, the desire for the satisfaction sought prevails. They refrain if the desire to avoid the cost prevails. Given the desire, low cost (penalty) causes the action, and high cost restraint. Given the cost, desire becomes the causal variable. Neither is intrinsically more causal than the other. The crime rate increases if the cost is reduced or the desire raised. It can be decreased by raising the cost or by reducing the desire.

The cost of crime is more easily and swiftly changed than the conditions producing the inclination to it. Further, the costs are very largely within the power of the government to change, whereas the conditions producing propensity to crime are often only indirectly affected by government action, and some are altogether beyond the control of the government. Our unilateral emphasis on these conditions and our undue neglect of costs may contribute to an unnecessarily high crime rate.

V

The foregoing suggests the question posed by the death penalty: Is the deterrence added (return) sufficiently above zero to warrant irrevocability (or other, less clear, disadvantages)? The question is not only whether the penalty deters, but whether it deters more than alternatives and whether the difference exceeds the cost of irrevocability. (I shall assume that the alternative is actual life imprisonment so as to exclude the complication produced by the release of the unrehabilitated.)

In some fairly infrequent but important circumstances the death penalty is the only possible deterrent. Thus, in case of acute *coups d'état,* or of acute substantial attempts to overthrow the government, prospective rebels would altogether discount the threat of any prison sentence. They would not be deterred because they believe the swift victory of the revolution will invalidate a prison sentence and turn it into an advantage. Execution would be the only deterrent because, unlike prison sentences, it cannot be revoked by victorious rebels. The same reasoning applies to deterring spies or traitors in wartime. Finally, men who, by virtue of past acts, are already serving, or are threatened, by a life sentence could be deterred from further offenses only by the threat of the death penalty.[8]

What about criminals who do not fall into any of these (often ignored) classes? Prof. Thorsten Sellin has made a careful study of the available statistics: He concluded that they do not yield evidence for the deterring effect of the death penalty.[9] Somewhat surprisingly, Prof. Sellin seems to think that this lack of evidence for deterrence is evidence for the lack of deterrence. It is not. It means that deterrence has not been demonstrated statistically—not that non-deterrence has been.

It is entirely possible, indeed likely (as Prof. Sellin appears willing to concede), that the statistics used, though the best available, are nonetheless too slender a reed to rest conclusions on. They indicate that the homicide rate does not vary greatly between similar areas with or without the death penalty, and in the same area before and after abolition. However, the similar areas are not similar enough; the periods are not long enough; many social differences and changes, other than the abolition of the death penalty, may account for the variation (or lack of it) in homicide rates with and without, before and after abolition; some of these social differences and changes are likely to have affected homicide rates. I am unaware of any statistical analysis which adjusts for such changes and differences. And logically, it is quite consistent with the postulated deterrent effect of capital punishment that there be less homicide after abolition: With retention there might have been still less.

Homicide rates do not depend exclusively on penalties any more than do other crime rates. A number of conditions which influence the propensity to crime, demographic, economic or generally social changes or differences—even such matters as changes of the divorce laws or of the cotton price—may influence the homicide rate. Therefore variation or constancy cannot be attributed to variations or constancy of the penalties, unless we know that no other factor influencing the homicide rate has changed. Usually we don't. To believe the death penalty deterrent does not require one to believe that the death penalty, or any other, is the only or the decisive causal variable; this would be as absurd as the converse mistake that "social causes" are the only or always the decisive factor. To favor capital punishment, the efficacy of neither variable need be denied. It is enough to affirm that the severity of the penalty may influence some potential criminals, and that the added severity of the death penalty adds to deterrence, or may do so. It is quite possible that such a deterrent effect may be offset (or intensified) by nonpenal factors which affect propensity; its presence or absence therefore may be hard, and perhaps impossible to demonstrate.

Contrary to what Prof. Sellin *et al.* seem to presume, I doubt that offenders are aware of the absence or presence of the death penalty state by state or period by period. Such unawareness argues against the assumption of a calculating murderer. However, unawareness does not argue against the death penalty if by deterrence we mean a preconscious, general response to a severe, but not necessarily specifically and explicitly apprehended, or calculated threat. A constant homicide rate, despite abolition, may occur because of unawareness and not because of lack of deterrence: People remain deterred for a lengthy interval by the severity of the penalty in the past, or by the severity of penalties used in similar circumstances nearby.

I do not argue for a version of deterrence which would require me to believe that an individual shuns murder while in North Dakota, because of the death penalty, and merrily goes to it in South Dakota since it has been abolished there; or that he will start the murderous career from which he had hitherto refrained, after abolition. I hold that the generalized threat of the death penalty may be a deterrent, and the more so, the more generally applied. Deterrence will not cease in the particular areas of abolition or at the particular times of abolition. Rather, general deterrence will be somewhat weakened, through local (partial) abolition. Even such weakening will be hard to detect owing to changes in many offsetting, or reinforcing, factors.

For all of these reasons, I doubt that the presence or absence of a deterrent effect of the death penalty is likely to be demonstrable by statistical means. The statistics presented by Prof. Sellin *et al.* show only that there is no statistical proof for the deterrent effect of the death penalty. But they do not show that there is no deterrent effect. Not to demonstrate presence of the effect is not the same as to demonstrate its absence; certainly not when there are plausible explanations for the nondemonstrability of the effect.

It is on our uncertainty that the case for deterrence must rest.[10]

VI

If we do not know whether the death penalty will deter others, we are confronted with two uncertainties. If we impose the death penalty, and achieve no deterrent effect thereby, the life of a convicted murderer has been expended in vain (from a deterrent viewpoint). There is a net loss. If we impose the death sentence and thereby deter some future murderers, we spared the lives of some future victims (the prospective murderers gain too; they are spared punishment because they were deterred). In this case, the death penalty has led to a net gain, unless the life of a convicted murderer is valued more highly than that of the unknown victim, or victims (and the non-imprisonment of the deterred non-murderer).

The calculation can be turned around, of course. The absence of the death penalty may harm no one and therefore produce a gain—the life of the convicted murderer. Or it may kill future victims of murderers who could have been deterred, and thus produce a loss—their life.

To be sure, we must risk something certain—the death (or life) of the convicted man, for something uncertain—the death (or life) of the victims of murderers who may be deterred. This is in the nature of uncertainty—when we invest, or gamble, we risk the money we have for an uncertain gain. Many human actions, most commitments—including marriage and crime—share this characteristic with the deterrent purpose of any penalization, and with its rehabilitative purpose (and even with the protective).

More proof is demanded for the deterrent effect of the death penalty than is demanded for the deterrent effect of other penalties. This is not justified by the absence of other utilitarian purposes such as protection and rehabilitation; they involve no less uncertainty than deterrence.[11]

Irrevocability may support a demand for some reason to expect more deterrence than revocable penalties might produce, but not a demand for more proof of deterrence, as has been pointed out above. The reason for expecting more deterrence lies in the greater severity, the terrifying effect inherent in finality. Since it seems more important to spare victims than to spare murderers, the burden of proving that the greater severity inherent in irrevocability adds nothing to deterrence lies on those who oppose capital punishment. Proponents of the death penalty need show only that there is no more uncertainty about it than about greater severity in general.

The demand that the death penalty be proved more deterrent than alternatives cannot be satisfied any more than the demand that six years in prison be proved to be more deterrent than three. But the uncertainty which confronts us favors the death penalty as long as by imposing it we might save future victims of murder. This effect is as plausible as the general idea that penalties have deterrents which increase with their severity. Though we have no proof of the positive deterrence of the penalty, we also have no proof of zero or negative effectiveness. I believe we have no right to risk additional future victims of murder for the sake of sparing convicted murderers; on the contrary, our moral obligation is to risk the possible ineffectiveness of executions. However rationalized, the opposite view appears to be motivated by the simple fact that executions are more subjected to social control than murder. However, this applies to all penalties and does not argue for the abolition of any.

NOTES

1. Social solidarity of "community feeling" (here to be ignored) might be dealt with as a form of deterrence.
2. Certainly a major meaning of *suum cuique tribue.*

3. I am not concerned here with the converse injustice, *which I regard as no less grave.*
4. Such inequity, though likely, has not been demonstrated. Note that, since there are more poor than rich, there are likely to be more guilty poor; and, if poverty contributes to crime, the proportion of the poor who are criminals also should be higher than of the rich.
5. I neglect those motivated by civil disobedience or, generally, moral or political passion. Deterring them depends less on penalties than on the moral support they receive, though penalties play a role. I also neglect those who may belong to all three groups listed, some successively, some even simultaneously, such as drug addicts. Finally, I must altogether omit the far-from-negligible role that problems of apprehension and conviction play in deterrence—beyond saying that, by reducing the government's ability to apprehend and convict, courts are able to reduce the risks of offenders.
6. I quote from the *New York Times* (November 24, 1967, p. 22). The actual psychological and other factors which bear on the disrepute—as distinguished from the rationalizations—cannot be examined here.
7. Mixed areas, incidentally, have higher crime rates than segregated ones. See, e.g., R. Ross and E. van den Haag, *The Fabric of Society* (New York: Harcourt, Brace & Co., 1957), pp. 102–4. Because slums are bad (morally) and crime is, many people seem to reason that "slums spawn crime"—which confuses some sort of moral with a causal relation.
8. Cautious revolutionaries, uncertain of final victory, might be impressed by prison sentences—but not in the acute stage, when faith in victory is high. And one can increase even the severity of a life sentence in prison. Finally, harsh punishment of rebels can intensify rebellious impulses. These points, though they qualify it, hardly impair the force of the argument.
9. Sellin considered mainly homicide statistics. His work may be found in his *Capital Punishment* (New York: Harper & Row, 1967); or, most conveniently, in H. A. Bedau, *The Death Penalty in America* (Garden City, N.Y.: Doubleday & Co., 1964), which also offers other material, mainly against the death penalty.
10. In view of the strong emotions aroused (itself an indication of effectiveness to me: Might not murderers be as upset over the death penalty as those who wish to spare them?) and because I believe penalties must reflect community feeling to be effective, I oppose mandatory death sentences and favor optional, and perhaps binding, recommendations by juries after their finding of guilt. The opposite course risks the non-conviction of guilty defendants by juries who do not want to see them executed.
11. Rehabilitation or protection are of minor importance in our actual penal system (though not in our theory). We confine many people who do not need rehabilitation and against whom we do not need protection (e.g., the exasperated husband who killed his wife); we release many unrehabilitated offenders against whom protection is needed. Certainly rehabilitation and protection are not, and deterrence is, the main actual function of legal punishment if we disregard non-utilitarian ones.

QUESTIONS FOR ANALYSIS

1. Van den Haag claims that injustice is an objection not to the death penalty but to the distributive process. What does he mean? Is his distinction between penalty and distribution germane?
2. What does deterrence depend on, in van den Haag's view?
3. How does punishment differ from natural dangers?
4. What kinds of people do not respond to threatened punishment? Would you be persuaded by the anti–capital punishment argument that insists the death penalty simply does not deter certain people?
5. What determines whether penalties ought to be increased? Explain how this is a utilitarian argument.
6. Does van den Haag convince you that slums and ghettos are "no more 'causes' of crimes than hospitals are of death"?
7. In van den Haag's view, what is the sole determinant of whether people will or will not commit crimes? Do you agree?
8. Why does van den Haag not believe that the presence or absence of a deterrent effect of the death

penalty is likely to be proved statistically? Does this weaken, strengthen, or have no effect on his own retentionist position?

9. Explain why van den Haag believes there is more to be gained by retaining the death penalty than by abolishing it.

Capital Punishment and Social Defense

HUGO ADAM BEDAU

In this selection from a longer essay, abolitionist Hugo Adam Bedau, Fletcher Professor *Emeritus* of Philosophy at Tufts University, discusses the death penalty as a means of preventing convicted murderers from murdering again and as a means of deterring others from murdering. Neither, he concludes, justifies capital punishment.

When it comes to prevention, Bedau argues that few convicted murderers will murder again, and we cannot predict which ones will. Therefore, we would have to execute all convicted murderers, which is unacceptable. As for deterrence, the evidence does not show that capital punishment is a stronger deterrent than long prison terms. There are, however, significant social costs to the death penalty, including the executions of innocent people.

Bedau also argues that the courts do not apply the death penalty equitably. We do not execute the "worst of the bad," he says. Instead, we execute defendants who are put at a disadvantage by race, sex, poverty, and other unjust factors.

THE ANALOGY WITH SELF-DEFENSE

Capital punishment, it is sometimes said, is to the body politic what self-defense is to the individual. If the latter is not morally wrong, how can the former be morally wrong? In order to assess the strength of this analogy, we need first to inspect the morality of self-defense.

Except for absolute pacifists, who believe it is morally wrong to use violence even to defend themselves or others from unprovoked and undeserved aggression, most of us believe that it is not morally wrong and may even be our moral duty to use violence to prevent aggression directed either against ourselves or against innocent third parties. The law has long granted persons the right to defend themselves against the unjust aggressions of others, even to the extent of using lethal force to kill a would-be assailant. It is very difficult to think of any convincing argument that would show it is never rational to risk the death of another in order to prevent death or grave injury to oneself. Certainly self-interest dictates the legitimacy of self defense. So does concern for the well-being of others. So also does justice. If it is unfair for one person to inflict violence on another, then it is hard to see how morality could require the victim to acquiesce in the attempt by another to hurt him or her, rather than to resist it, even if that resistance involves or risks injury to the assailant.

The foregoing account assumes that the person acting in self-defense is innocent of any provocation of the assailant. It also assumes that there is no alternative to victimization except resistance. In actual life, both assumptions—especially the second—are often false, because there may be a third alternative: escape, or removing oneself from the scene of danger and imminent aggression. Hence, the law imposes on us the "duty to retreat." Before we use violence to resist aggression, must try to get out of the way, lest unnecessary violence be used to resist aggression. Now suppose that unjust aggression is imminent, and there is no path open for escape. How much violence may justifiably be used to ward off aggression? The answer is: No more violence than is necessary to prevent the aggressive assault. Violence beyond that is unnecessary and therefore unjustified. We may restate the principle governing the use of violence in self-defense in terms of the use of "deadly force" by the police in the discharge of their duties. The rule is this: Use of deadly force is justified only to prevent loss of life in immediate jeopardy where a lesser use of force cannot reasonably be expected to save the life that is threatened.

In real life, violence in self-defense in excess of the minimum necessary to prevent aggression, even though it is not justifiable, is often excusable. One cannot always tell what will suffice to deter or prevent becoming a victim, and so the law looks with a certain tolerance upon the frightened and innocent would-be victim who in self-protection turns upon a vicious assailant and inflicts a fatal injury even though a lesser injury would have been sufficient. What is not justified is deliberately using far more violence than is necessary to prevent becoming a victim. It is the deliberate, not the impulsive or the unintentional use of violence that is relevant to the death-penalty controversy, since the death penalty is enacted into law and carried out in each case only after ample time to weigh alternatives. Notice that we are assuming that the act of self-defense is to protect one's person or that of a third party. The reasoning outlined here does not extend to the defense of one's property. Shooting a thief to prevent one's automobile from being stolen cannot be excused or justified in the way that shooting an assailant charging with a knife pointed at one's face can be. In terms of the concept of "deadly force," our criterion is that deadly force is never justified to prevent crimes against property or other violent crimes not immediately threatening the life of an innocent person.

The rationale for self-defense as set out above illustrates two moral principles of great importance to our discussion. . . . One is that if a life is to be risked, then it is better that it be the life of someone who is guilty (in our context, the initial assailant) rather than the life of someone who is not (the innocent potential victim). It is not fair to expect the innocent prospective victim to run the added risk of severe injury or death in order to avoid using violence in self-defense to the extent of possibly killing his assailant. It is only fair that the guilty aggressor run the risk.

The other principle is that taking life deliberately is not justified so long as there is any feasible alternative. One does not expect miracles, of course, but in theory, if shooting a burglar through the foot will stop the burglary and enable one to call the police for help, then there is no reason to shoot to kill. Likewise, if the burglar is unarmed, there is no reason to shoot at all. In actual life, of course, burglars are likely to be shot at by aroused householders because one does not know whether they are armed, and prudence may dictate the assumption that they are. Even so, although the burglar has no right to commit a felony against a person or a person's property, the attempt to do so does not give the chosen victim the right to respond in whatever way one pleases, and then to excuse or justify such conduct on the ground that one was "only acting in self-defense." In these ways the law shows a tacit regard for the life of even a felon and discourages the use of unnecessary violence even by the innocent; morality can hardly do less.

PREVENTING VERSUS DETERRING CRIME

The analogy between capital punishment and self-defense requires us to face squarely the empirical questions surrounding the preventive and deterrent effects of the death penalty. Executing a murderer in the name of punishment can be seen as a crime-*preventive* measure just to the extent it is reasonable to believe that if the murderer had not been executed he or she would have committed other crimes (including, but not necessarily confined to, murder).

Executing a murderer can be seen as a crime *deterrent* just to the extent it is reasonable to believe that by the example of the execution other persons would be frightened off from committing murder. Any punishment can be a crime preventive without being a crime deterrent, just as it can be a deterrent without being a preventive. It can also be both or neither. Prevention and deterrence are theoretically independent because they operate by different methods. Crimes can be prevented by taking guns out of the hands of criminals, by putting criminals behind bars, by alerting the public to be less careless and less prone to victimization, and so forth. Crimes can be deterred only by making would-be criminals frightened of being arrested, convicted, and punished for crimes—that is, making persons overcome their desire to commit crimes by a stronger desire to avoid the risk of being caught and punished.

THE DEATH PENALTY AS A CRIME PREVENTIVE

Capital punishment is unusual among penalties because its preventive effects limit its deterrent effects. The death penalty can never deter the executed person from further crimes. At most, it can prevent a person from committing them. Popular discussions of the death penalty are frequently confused because they so often assume that the death penalty is a perfect and infallible deterrent so far as the executed criminal is concerned, whereas nothing of the sort is true. What is even more important, it is also wrong to think that in every execution the death penalty has proved to be an infallible crime preventive. What is obviously true is that once an offender has been executed, it is physically impossible for that person to commit any further crimes, since the punishment is totally incapacitative. But incapacitation is not identical with prevention. Prevention by means of incapacitation occurs only if the executed criminal would have committed other crimes if he or she had not been executed and had been punished only in some less incapacitative way (e.g., by imprisonment).

What evidence is there that the incapacitative effects of the death penalty are an effective crime preventive? From the study of imprisonment, parole, release records, this much is clear: If the murderers and other criminals who have been executed are like the murderers who were convicted but not executed, then (1) executing all convicted murderers would have prevented many crimes, but not many murders (less than one convicted murderer in five hundred commits another murder); and (2) convicted murderers, whether inside prison or outside after release, have at least as good a record of no further criminal activity as any other class of convicted felon.

These facts show that the general public tends to overrate the danger and threat to public safety constituted by the failure to execute every murderer who is caught and convicted. While it would be quite wrong to say that there is no risk such criminals will repeat their crimes—or similar ones—if they are not executed, it would be equally erroneous to say that by executing every convicted murderer many horrible crimes will be prevented. All we know is that a few such crimes will never be committed; we do not know how many or by whom they would have been committed. (Obviously, if we did know we would have tried to prevent them!) This is the nub of the problem. There is no way to know in advance which if any of the incarcerated or released murderers will kill again. It is useful in this connection to remember that the only way to guarantee that no horrible crimes ever occur is to execute *everyone* who might conceivably commit such a crime. Similarly, the only way to guarantee that no convicted murderer ever commits another murder is to execute them all. No modern society has ever done this, and for two hundred years ours has been moving steadily in the opposite direction.

These considerations show that our society has implicitly adopted an attitude toward the risk of murder rather like the attitude it has adopted toward the risk of fatality from other sources, such as automobile accidents, lung cancer, or drowning. Since no one knows when or where or upon whom any of these lethal events will fall, it would be too great an invasion of freedom to undertake the severe restrictions that alone would suffice to prevent any such deaths from occurring. It is better to take the risks and keep our freedom than to try to eliminate the risks altogether and lose our freedom in the process. Hence, we have lifeguards at the beach, but swimming is not totally prohibited; smokers are warned, but cigarettes are still legally sold; pedestrians may be given the right of way in a crosswalk, but marginally competent drivers are still allowed to operate motor vehicles. Some risk is therefore imposed on the innocent; in the name of our right to freedom, our other rights are not protected by society at all costs.

THE DEATH PENALTY AS A CRIME DETERRENT

Determining whether the death penalty is an effective deterrent is even more difficult than determining its effectiveness as a crime preventive. In general, our knowledge about how penalties deter crimes and whether in fact they do—whom they deter, from which crimes, and under what conditions—is distressingly inexact. Most people nevertheless are convinced that punishments do deter, and that the more severe a punishment is the better it will deter. For half a century, social scientists have studied the questions whether the death penalty is a deterrent and whether it is a better deterrent than the alternative of imprisonment. Their verdict, while not unanimous, is nearly so. Whatever may be true about the deterrence of lesser crimes by other penalties, the deterrence achieved by the death penalty for murder is not measurably any greater than the deterrence achieved by long-term imprisonment. In the nature of the case, the evidence is quite indirect. No one can identify for certain any crimes that did not occur because the would-be offender was deterred by the threat of the death penalty and could not have been deterred by a less severe threat. Likewise, no one can identify any crimes that did occur because the offender was not deterred by the threat of prison even though he would have been deterred by the threat of death. Nevertheless, such evidence as we have fails to show that the more severe penalty (death) is really a better deterrent than the less severe penalty (imprisonment) for such crimes as murder.

If the conclusion stated above is correct, and the death penalty and long-term imprisonment are equally effective (or ineffective) as deterrents to murder, then the argument for the death penalty on grounds of deterrence is seriously weakened. One of the moral principles identified earlier now comes into play. It is the principle that unless there is a good reason for choosing a more rather than a less severe punishment for a crime, the less severe penalty is to be preferred. This principle obviously commends itself to anyone who values human life and who concedes that, all other things being equal, less pain and suffering is always better than more. Human life is valued in part to the degree that it is free of pain, suffering, misery, and frustration, and in particular to the extent that it is free of such experiences when they serve no purpose. If the death penalty is not a more effective deterrent than imprisonment, then its greater severity is gratuitous, purposeless suffering and deprivation. Accordingly, we must reject it in favor of some less severe alternative, unless we can identify some more weighty moral principle that the death penalty protects better than any less severe mode of punishment does. Whether there is any such principle is unclear.

A COST/BENEFIT ANALYSIS OF THE DEATH PENALTY

A full study of the costs and benefits involved in the practice of capital punishment would not be confined solely to the question of whether it is a better deterrent or preventive of murder than imprisonment. Any thoroughgoing utilitarian approach to the death-penalty controversy would need to examine carefully other costs and benefits as well, because maximizing the balance of all the social benefits over all the social costs is the sole criterion of right and wrong according to utilitarianism. . . . Let us consider, therefore, some of the other costs and benefits to be calculated. Clinical psychologists have presented evidence to suggest that the death penalty actually incites some persons of unstable mind to murder others, either because they are afraid to take their own lives and hope that society will punish them for murder by putting them to death, or because they fancy that they, too, are killing with justification analogously to the lawful and presumably justified killing involved in capital punishment. If such evidence is sound, capital punishment can serve as a counter-preventive or even an incitement to murder; such incited murders become part of its social cost. Imprisonment, however, has not been known to incite any murders or other crimes of violence in a comparable fashion. (A possible exception might be found in the imprisonment of terrorists, which has inspired other terrorists to take hostages as part of a scheme to force the authorities to release their imprisoned comrades.) The risks of executing the innocent are also part of the social cost. The historical record is replete with innocent persons arrested, indicted, convicted, sentenced, and occasionally legally executed for crimes they did not commit. This is quite apart from the guilty persons unfairly convicted, sentenced to death, and executed on the strength of perjured testimony, fraudulent evidence, subernation of jurors, and other violations of the civil rights and liberties of the accused. Nor is this all. The high costs of a capital trial and of the inevitable appeals, the costly methods of custody most prisons adopt for convicts on "death row," are among the straightforward economic costs that the death penalty incurs. Conducting a valid cost/benefit analysis of capital punishment is extremely difficult, and it is impossible to predict exactly what such a study would show. Nevertheless, based on such evidence as we do have, it is quite possible that a study of this sort would favor abolition of all death penalties rather than their retention.

WHAT IF EXECUTIONS DID DETER?

From the moral point of view, it is quite important to determine what one should think about capital punishment if the evidence were clearly to show that the death penalty is a distinctly superior method of social defense by comparison with less severe alternatives. Kantian moralists . . . would have no use for such knowledge, because their entire case for the morality of the death penalty rests on the way it is thought to provide just retribution, not on the way it is thought to provide social defense. For a utilitarian, however, such knowledge would be conclusive. Those who follow Locke's reasoning would also be gratified, because they defend the morality of the death penalty both on the ground that it is retributively just and on the ground that it provides needed social defense.

What about the opponents of the death penalty, however? To oppose the death penalty in the face of incontestable evidence that it is an effective method of social defense violates the moral principle that where grave risks are to be run, it is better that they be run by the guilty than by the innocent. Consider in this connection an imaginary world in which by executing the murderer his victim is invariably restored to life, whole and intact, as though the murder had never occurred. In such a miraculous world, it is hard to see how anyone could oppose the death penalty on moral grounds. Why shouldn't a murderer die if that will infallibly bring the victim back to life? What could possibly be morally wrong with taking the murderer's life under such conditions? The death penalty would now be an instrument of perfect restitution, and it would give a new and better meaning to *lex talionis*, "a life for a life." The whole idea is fanciful, of course, but it shows as nothing else can how opposition to the death penalty cannot be both moral and wholly unconditional. If opposition to the death penalty is to be morally responsible, then it must be conceded that there are conditions (however unlikely) under which that opposition should cease.

But even if the death penalty were known to be a uniquely effective social defense, we could still imagine conditions under which it would be reasonable to oppose it. Suppose that in addition to being a slightly better preventive and deterrent than imprisonment, executions also have a slight incitive effect (so that for every ten murders an execution prevents or deters, it also incites another murder). Suppose also that the administration of criminal justice in capital cases is inefficient, unequal, and tends to secure convictions and death sentences only for murderers who least "deserve" to be sentenced to death (including some death sentences and a few executions of the innocent). Under such conditions, it would still be reasonable to oppose the death penalty, because on the facts supposed more (or not fewer) innocent lives are being threatened and lost by using the death penalty than would be risked by abolishing it. It is important to remember throughout our evaluation of the deterrence controversy that we cannot ever apply the principle . . . that advises us to risk the lives of the guilty in order to save the lives of the innocent. Instead, the most we can do is weigh the risk for the general public against the execution of those who are *found* guilty by an imperfect system of criminal justice. These hypothetical factual assumptions illustrate the contingencies upon which the morality of opposition to the death penalty rests. And not only the morality of opposition; the morality of any defense of the death penalty rests on the same contingencies. This should help us understand why, in resolving the morality of capital punishment one way or the other, it is so important to know, as well as we can, whether the death penalty really does deter, prevent, or incite crime, whether the innocent really are ever executed, and how likely is the occurrence of these things in the future.

HOW MANY GUILTY LIVES IS ONE INNOCENT LIFE WORTH?

The great unanswered question that utilitarians must face concerns the level of social defense that executions should be expected to achieve before it is justifiable to carry them out. Consider three possible situations: (1) At the level of a hundred executions per year, each additional execution of a convicted murderer reduces the number of murder victims by ten. (2) Executing every convicted murderer reduces the number of murders to 5,000 victims annually, whereas executing only one out of ten reduces the number to 5,001. (3) Executing every convicted murderer reduces the murder rate no more than does executing one in a hundred and no more than does a random pattern of executions.

Many people contemplating situation (1) would regard this as a reasonable trade-off: The execution of each further guilty person saves the lives of ten innocent ones. (In fact, situation [1] or something like it may be taken as a description of what most of those who defend the death penalty on grounds of social defense believe is true.) But suppose that, instead of saving 10 lives, the number dropped to 0.5, i.e, one victim avoided for each two additional executions. Would that be a reasonable price to pay? We are on the road toward the situation described in situation (2), where a drastic 90 percent reduction in the number of persons executed causes the level of social defense to drop by only 0.0002 percent. Would it be worth it to execute so many more murderers at the cost of such a slight decrease in social defense? How many guilty lives is one innocent life worth? (Only those who think that guilty lives are *worthless* can avoid facing this problem.) In situation (3), of course, there is no basis for executing all convicted murderers, since there is no gain in social defense to show for each additional execution after the first out of each hundred has been executed. How, then, should we determine which out of each hundred convicted murderers is the unlucky one to be put to death?

It may be possible, under a complete and thoroughgoing cost/benefit analysis of the death penalty, to answer such questions. But an appeal merely to the moral principle that if lives are to be risked then let it be the lives of the guilty rather than of the innocent will not suffice. (We have already noticed . . . that this abstract principle is of little use in the actual administration of criminal justice, because the police and the courts do not deal with the guilty as such but only with those *judged* guilty.) Nor will it suffice to agree that society deserves all the crime prevention and deterrence it can get as a result of inflicting severe punishments. These principles are consistent with too many different policies. They are too vague by themselves to resolve the choice on grounds of social defense when confronted with hypothetical situations like those proposed above.

Since no adequate cost/benefit analysis of the death penalty exists, there is no way to resolve these questions from that standpoint at this time. Moreover, it can be argued that we cannot have such an analysis without already establishing in some way or other the relative value of innocent lives versus guilty lives. Far from being a product of cost/benefit analysis, a comparative evaluation of lives would have to be available to us before we undertook any such analysis. Without it, no cost/benefit analysis can get off the ground. Finally, it must be noted that our knowledge at present does not approximate to anything like the situation described above in (1). On the contrary, from the evidence we do have it seems we achieve about the same deterrent and preventive effects whether we punish murder by death or by imprisonment. . . . Therefore, something like the situation in (2) or in (3) may be correct. If so, this shows that the choice between the two policies of capital punishment and life imprisonment for murder will probably have to be made on some basis other than social defense; on that basis alone, the two policies are equivalent and therefore equally acceptable. . . .

EQUAL JUSTICE AND CAPITAL PUNISHMENT

During the past generation, the strongest practical objection to the death penalty has been the inequities with which it has been applied. As the late Supreme Court Justice William O. Douglas once observed, "One searches our chronicles in vain for the execution of any member of the affluent strata of this society."[1] One does not search our chronicles in vain for the crime of murder committed by the affluent. All the sociological evidence points to the conclusion that the death penalty is the poor man's justice; hence the slogan, "Those without the capital get the punishment." The death penalty is also racially sensitive. Every study of the death penalty for rape (unconstitutional only since 1977) has confirmed that black male rapists (especially where the victim is a white female) are far more likely to be sentenced to death and executed than white male rapists. Convicted black murderers are more likely to end up on "death row" than are others, and the killers of whites (whether white or nonwhite) are more likely to be sentenced to death than are the killers of nonwhites.

Let us suppose that the factual basis for such a criticism is sound. What follows for the morality of capital punishment? Many defenders of the death penalty have been quick to point out that since there is nothing intrinsic about the crime of murder or rape dictating that only the poor or only racial-minority males will commit it, and since there is nothing overtly racist about the statutes that authorize the death penalty for murder or rape, capital punishment itself is hardly at fault if in practice it falls with unfair impact on the poor and the black. There is, in short, nothing in the death penalty that requires it to be applied unfairly and with arbitrary or discriminatory results. It is at worst a fault in the system of administering criminal justice. (Some, who dispute the facts cited above, would deny even this.) There is an adequate remedy—execute more whites, women, and affluent murderers.

Presumably, both proponents and opponents of capital punishment would concede that it is a fundamental dictate of justice that a punishment should not be unfairly—inequitably or unevenly—enforced and applied. They should also be able to agree that when the punishment in question is the extremely severe one of death, then the requirement to be fair in using such a punishment becomes even more stringent. There should be no dispute in the death penalty controversy over these principles of justice. The dispute begins as soon as one attempts to connect the principles with the actual use of this punishment.

In this country, many critics of the death penalty have argued, we would long ago have got rid of it entirely if it had been a condition of its use that it be applied equally and fairly. In the words of the attorneys who argued against the death penalty in the Supreme Court during 1972, "It is a freakish aberration, a random extreme act of violence, visibly arbitrary and discriminatory—a penalty reserved for unusual application because, if it were usually used, it would affront universally shared standards of public decency."[2] It is difficult to dispute this judgment, when one considers that there have been in the United States during the past fifty years about half a million criminal homicides but only about 3,900 executions (all but 33 of which were of men).

We can look at these statistics in another way to illustrate the same point. If we could be assured that the nearly 4,000 persons executed were the worst of the bad, repeated offenders incapable of safe incarceration, much less of rehabilitation, the most dangerous murderers in captivity—the ones who had killed more than once and were likely to kill again, and the least likely to be confined in prison without chronic danger to other inmates and the staff—then one might accept half a million murders and a few thousand executions with a sense that rough justice had been done. But the truth is otherwise. Persons are sentenced to death and executed not because they have been found to be uncontrollably violent or hopelessly poor confinement and release risks. Instead, they are executed because they have a poor defense (inexperienced or overworked counsel) at trial; they have no funds to bring sympathetic witnesses to court; they are transients or strangers in the community where they are tried; the prosecuting attorney wants the publicity that goes with "sending a killer to the chair"; there are no funds for an appeal or for a transcript of the trial record; they are members of a despised racial or political minority. In short, the actual study of why particular persons have been sentenced to death and executed does not show any careful winnowing of the worst from the bad. It shows that the executed were usually the unlucky victims of prejudice and discrimination, the losers in an arbitrary lottery that could just as well have spared them, the victims of the disadvantages that almost always go with poverty. A system like this does not enhance human life; it cheapens and degrades it. However heinous murder and other crimes are, the system of capital punishment does not compensate for or erase those crimes. It only tends to add new injuries of its own to the catalogue of human brutality.

NOTES

1. *Furman v. Georgia,* 408 U.S. 238 (1972), at pp. 251–252.
2. NAACP Legal Defense and Educational Fund, Brief for Petitioner in *Aikens v. California,* O.T. 1971, No. 68–5027, reprinted in Philip English Mackey, ed., *Voices Against Death: American Opposition to Capital Punishment, 1787–1975* (1975), p. 288.

QUESTIONS FOR ANALYSIS

1. According to Bedau, our attitude toward the risks of murder is like our attitude toward the risks of swimming. We do not outlaw swimming even though some swimmers will drown. Similarly, we do not execute all murderers even though some will murder again. In both cases, he says, the reasoning is the same: We allow some risk to the innocent in order to protect our freedoms. Do you agree with this analogy? Why or why not?
2. Bedau argues that a cost-benefit analysis of the death penalty would show that the costs outweigh the benefits. Why? What assumptions does he make? Do you accept these assumptions?
3. Even if the death penalty did deter some would-be murderers, Bedau says, there would still be good reasons to oppose it in some conditions. What conditions? Do they obtain today?
4. According to van den Haag, it is better to risk the lives of the guilty than the lives of the innocent. Bedau says that this principle will "not suffice" to justify the death penalty. Why not?
5. Bedau argues that "the strongest practical objection to the death penalty has been the inequities

with which it has been applied." What inequities? How strong do you think the objection is?

6. Does Bedau provide a convincing refutation of van den Haag? Why or why not?

CASE PRESENTATION

J. D. Autry: Death in Texas

High on booze, pot, and pills, James David (J. D.) Autry and his companion John Alton Sandifer had been bumping around Port Arthur, Texas, in a borrowed pickup one warm Sunday night in April 1980, when they stopped at a convenience store for more beer. What then happened is unclear. But a jury concluded, and a succession of appellate courts affirmed, that there had been a drunken attempt at a robbery and that Autry had shot the cashier between the eyes when she resisted. Then, fleeing the store, Autry had run into two men, both of whom he shot. One was killed, and the other was disabled for life in mind and body. Autry's net profit for the bloodshed was a $2.70 six-pack.

Before the year was out, Autry was convicted of capital murder and delivered in chains to death row—protesting his innocence all the way.

A half hour before his scheduled death by lethal injection in October 1983, Autry was plucked off the gurney. Supreme Court Justice Byron White had granted a last-minute reprieve, a chance to reexamine and re-argue the question of whether a killer should die. The reprieve meant that not only Autry but all death row inmates in Texas and California, who account for about one-quarter of the nation's condemned population, might not even be considered for execution until the spring of 1984.

In the following months, the Supreme Court heard arguments in a case from California that posed the question of a condemned prisoner's being entitled to a judicial review of his or her sentence to determine whether it is "proportional"—that is, whether like crimes typically warrant the death penalty. In the 1976 decisions that restored the death penalty, the Court noted with approval that both the Georgia and Florida courts made proportionality reviews to make sure the penalty wouldn't be imposed arbitrarily. Since then, the Court has struck down as "disproportional" death sentences for rapists and defendants who neither killed nor attempted to kill the victim. At the same time, it has upheld state statutes like that in Texas which make no mention of comparative sentence review. The Court decided that the absence of a proportionality review is not grounds to stay an execution. Shortly thereafter, on the morning of March 14, 1984, J. D. Autry was executed by lethal injection.

QUESTIONS FOR ANALYSIS

1. Do you think states should have proportionality reviews to ensure that the death penalty is not imposed arbitrarily? Do you think justice requires this?
2. Critics say proportionality review systems don't work. They point out that the state courts have failed to set standards for real comparisons, collect complete information on the sentences of all killers, and provide other judges with guidance. Discuss the implications of these charges with regard to the equitable administration of the death penalty.
3. Do you think proportionality is relevant to whether the death penalty is ever morally permissible? Explain.
4. Some say the Autry case is just another example of delay that results in a denial of justice. Both retentionists and abolitionists view such delays as support for their positions. For example, retentionists argue that the obvious difficulties in carrying out the death penalty undermine confidence in the legal system. For their part, abolitionists claim that the very tortuousness of the appeals process demonstrates there is no way to make capital punishment work. On various occasions, the Supreme Court has expressed its own concern with the delays. Justice William Rehnquist charged in 1987 that his colleagues were making a mockery of the criminal justice system by countenancing extended appeals. In 1983, Justice Lewis F. Powell, Jr., told a group of

federal judges that unless the judiciary can find a more efficient way to handle death cases, capital punishment should be abolished. And in granting Autry his last-minute stay, Justice White called for a change in the law to limit repetitive appeals. Despite the high court's impatience, it is obligated to keep reviewing death penalty cases. Do you think that delays do, in fact, result in a denial of justice? Explain. Do they make stronger the retentionist or the abolitionist position?

CASE PRESENTATION

Karla Faye Tucker and Stanley "Tookie" Williams: Rehabilitation on Death Row?

They were only two of 556 homicides recorded in Houston that year and received little initial attention, but they were surely two of the most sensational slayings in the city's history. One the night of June 14, 1983, Karla Faye Tucker and David Garrett climaxed a three-day drug binge by hacking to death Jerry Lynn Dean and Deborah Thornton. They had broken into Dean's apartment to steal motorcycle parts. Upon finding Dean at home, Garrett attacked him with a hammer. Tucker joined in with a pickax that belonged to Dean. Then she used it to kill Thornton, Dean's overnight visitor, who lay shivering in his bed. Far from feeling regret over the murders, the twenty-three-year-old former teenage prostitute boasted to friends that she felt a surge of sexual gratification with every thrust of the pickax. A year later, Tucker and Garrett were sentenced to death.

Garrett, who was Tucker's boyfriend at the time of the murders, died in prison before he could be executed. Tucker's case went on to become a worldwide controversy. While awaiting trial at the Harris County Jail, she claimed to have found God; she was now, she said, a born-again Christian who repented her crimes. At their trials, she confessed to the murders and then testified against Garrett; while on death row, she counseled her fellow inmates and married her own spiritual counselor.

Following the customary appeals through the courts, her execution was set for February 3, 1998. As the date neared, she attracted numerous supporters, including Pope John Paul II, television evangelist Pat Robertson, Jesse Jackson, the National Council of Churches, the European Parliament, and Ronald Carlson, Deborah Thornton's brother. Nearly 2,400 others sent letters to Texas Governor George W. Bush asking that her sentence be commuted to life. For many of her supporters, the issue was her religious conversion. She was not, they argued, the same woman who had committed the lurid murders. Nor was she a threat to society. Tucker argued the same point in her appeal for clemency before the Texas Board of Pardons and Parole, saying "If you decide you must carry out this execution, do it based solely on the brutality and heinousness of my crime. But please don't do it based on me being a future threat to our society, because I am definitely no longer a threat to our society, and in fact I believe I am a positive contributor to our society and helping others." Still, the board voted 16 to 0, with two abstentions, to deny her appeal.

Compounding the controversy was the fact that Tucker was a woman. Texas had not executed a woman since 1863, and the last U.S. execution of a woman—the only execution of a woman since 1976, when the Supreme Court allowed the states to resume capital punishment—had occurred in 1984 in North Carolina.

On February 3, the Supreme Court refused Tucker's last-minute appeal for a stay of execution. Governor Bush, who had the option to grant a one-time-only thirty-day stay, refused to do so, and the execution was carried out that evening by lethal injection. In her final statement, Tucker said, "I would like to say to all of you, the Thornton family and Jerry Dean's family, that I am sorry. I hope God will give you peace with this."

In 1979, four years before Tucker's crimes, Stanley "Tookie" Williams, one of the founders of the notorious Crips gang in Los Angeles, murdered a clerk at a convenience store and three people at a family-owned motel in California. He was sentenced to death but was on death row for twenty-four years while he pursued numerous appeals. He appealed for clemency from Governor Arnold Schwarzenegger, claiming that he had been transformed while in prison. He had published several books urging gang avoidance and peacemaking. But Williams, unlike Tucker, never admitted his crimes, let alone apologized for them. Prosecutors and the governor detailed the extensive evidence that he was guilty and had received a fair trial, as confirmed repeatedly during his appeals.

His case gained extensive press attention and the support of television star Mike Farrell, civil rights leader Jesse Jackson, and Sister Helen Prejean, a prominent death-penalty opponent who was the inspiration for the film *Dead Man Walking.* The governor denied his last-minute petition for clemency, and Williams was executed on December 13, 2005.

QUESTIONS FOR ANALYSIS

1. Many death row prisoners claim they have found God and been rehabilitated. If true, should their sentences be commuted? How can we decide if the claims are true?
2. Between 1976 and Tucker's execution in 1998, 432 people were executed in the United States, only one a woman. Does the enormous disparity in the numbers of executed men and women show bias in favor of women? If so, what should be done about it?
3. Given their heinous, brutal crimes, did Tucker and Williams deserve the death penalty, regardless of their later behavior on death row? Can you imagine any situations where guilty murderers on death row should have their sentences commuted because of their conduct while on death row?

CASE PRESENTATION

A Failed Experiment?

Callins v. Collins was a routine decision for the U.S. Supreme Court. With no written opinion, the Court declined to review the death sentence of Bruce Edwin Callins, who had been convicted of murder by a Texas jury. What was not routine was Justice Harry A. Blackmun's headline-making dissent. When he first joined the Court more than twenty years earlier, he had been a supporter of the death penalty. But on February 22, 1994, during his final term, Justice Blackmun announced in a lone dissent that "the death penalty experiment has failed."

In arguing that it had failed, he claimed that two constitutional requirements for imposing the death penalty are incompatible. The requirement that it must be imposed consistently (from *Furman v. Georgia*), he wrote, clashes with other precedents that require individualized sentencing. Excerpts follow:

> . . . Twenty years have passed since this Court declared that the death penalty must be imposed fairly and with reasonable consistency or not at all (see *Furman v. Georgia,* 1972), and, despite the effort of the states and courts to devise legal formulas and procedural rules to meet this daunting challenge, the death penalty remains fraught with arbitrariness, discrimination, caprice and mistakes. . . .
>
> Experience has taught us that the constitutional goal of eliminating arbitrariness and discrimination from the administration of death . . . can never be achieved without compromising an equally essential component of fundamental fairness: individualized sentencing. (See *Lockett v. Ohio,* 1978.)
>
> It is tempting, when faced with conflicting constitutional commands, to sacrifice one for the other, or to assume that an acceptable balance between them already has been struck. In the context of the death penalty, however, such jurisprudential maneuvers are wholly inappropriate. The death penalty must be imposed "fairly, and with reasonable consistency, or not at all." (*Eddings v. Oklahoma,* 1982.)
>
> To be fair, capital sentencing schemes must treat each person convicted of a capital offense with that "degree of respect for the uniqueness of the individual. . . ." That means affording the sentencer the power and discretion

to grant mercy in a particular case, and providing avenues for the consideration of any and all relevant mitigating evidence that would justify a sentence less than death.

Reasonable consistency, on the other hand, requires that the death penalty be inflicted evenhandedly, in accordance with reason and objective standards, rather than by whim, caprice or prejudice.

. . . [T]his Court, in my opinion, has engaged in a futile effort to balance these constitutional demands, and now is retreating not only from the *Furman* promise of consistency and rationality, but from the requirement of individualized sentencing as well. . . .

From this day forward, I no longer shall tinker with the machinery of death. Rather than continue to coddle the Court's delusion that the desired level of fairness be achieved and the need for regulation eviscerated, I feel morally and intellectually obligated to concede that the death penalty experiment has failed.

It seems that the decision whether a human being should live or die is so inherently subjective, rife with all of life's understandings, experiences, prejudices, and passions, that it inevitably defies the rationality and consistency required by the Constitution.

Justice Antonin Scalia, in a rebutting opinion, responded as follows:

> As Justice Blackmun describes . . . this court has attached to the imposition of the death penalty two quite incompatible sets of commands: the sentencer's discretion to impose death must be closely confined (see *Furman v. Georgia,* 1972) but the sentencer's discretion not to impose death (to extend mercy) must be unlimited (*Eddings v. Oklahoma,* 1982; *Lockett v. Ohio,* 1978). These commands were invented without benefit of any textual support; they are the product of just such "intellectual, moral and personal" perceptions as Justice Blackmun expressed today. . . .
>
> Though Justice Blackmun joins those of us who have acknowledged the incompatibility of the Court's *Furman* and *Lockett-Eddings* lines of jurisprudence . . . he unfortunately draws the wrong conclusion from the acknowledgment. . . .
>
> Surely a different conclusion commends itself to wit, that at least one of the judicially announced irreconcilable commands which cause the Constitution to prohibit what its text [the Fifth Amendment] explicitly permits must be wrong. . . .

QUESTIONS FOR ANALYSIS

1. Justices Blackmun and Scalia agree that past Supreme Court decisions regarding the death penalty are incompatible. To the former, the incompatibility shows that the death penalty cannot be imposed constitutionally. To the latter, it shows that the Court has erred. Which justice do you agree with?
2. Along with Justice Scalia, many critics have accused Justice Blackmun of reading his personal views into the Constitution. Do you agree?
3. Regardless of the constitutional issue, does Justice Blackmun have a strong moral position? That is, does justice require both evenhandedness and consideration for the uniqueness of the individual when we impose the death penalty? If so, are the two really incompatible?
4. Is the decision to impose the death penalty "inherently subjective"?

CASE PRESENTATION

Warren McClesky

Warren McClesky was black. The fatally wounded police officer was white. Their paths crossed in the Dixie Furniture Store near downtown Atlanta on May 13, 1978. McClesky was robbing the store at gunpoint; officer Frank Schlatt had responded to a silent alarm. Whether McClesky or one of his accomplices fired the bullet that killed Officer Schlatt is unknown, but in Georgia, as in many other states, McClesky could be charged with the murder nonetheless. He was tried, convicted, and sentenced to death.

On appeal, McClesky argued that his sentence was the result of racial bias. To back up the claim, the defense offered two studies by University of Iowa Professor David Baldus. These studies examined racial factors in the imposition of the death penalty in Georgia between 1973, when the state's capital punishment law took effect, and 1979. Among the results were the following:[1]

1. Although whites were victims of fewer than 40 percent of all homicides studied, they were victims in 87 percent that resulted in the death penalty for the killer.
2. Twenty-two percent of blacks convicted of killing whites received the death penalty, compared to only 8 percent of white defendants convicted of killing whites.
3. The racial disparities were greatest in cases that fell between the most heinous and least heinous murders. The death penalty was imposed in 34 percent of such cases when the victim was white, but only 14 percent when the victim was black.
4. The disparities cannot be explained by nonracial factors.

In 1987, *McClesky v. Kemp* reached the Supreme Court, which upheld the sentence. The Court accepted the studies' findings, but it ruled that they did not prove discrimination in McClesky's case. Only proof that the jury, the prosecutor, or some other decision maker in his case was influenced by racial bias could do so. Wrote Justice Lewis F. Powell in his majority opinion, "Because discretion is essential to the criminal justice process, we would demand exceptionally clear proof before we infer that the discretion has been abused."

[1]Cited in Anthony G. Amsterdam, "Race and the Death Penalty," *Criminal Justice Ethics,* Vol. 7, No 1 (1988), pp. 84–86.

QUESTIONS FOR ANALYSIS

1. One of the studies' significant implications is that a white life counts for more than a black life when it comes to imposing the death penalty. If the implication is correct, does it taint the way capital punishment is imposed in Georgia?
2. Between 1973 and 1980, seventeen defendants were charged with killing police officers in Fulton County. In only two cases did the prosecution seek the death penalty. One was McClesky's. In the other case, the slain officer was black, and his killer was sentenced to life. Is it reasonable to suspect that racial bias played a role in the decision to seek the death penalty in McClesky's case? In his being sentenced to death?
3. In 1994, the U.S. Congress passed a massive anticrime package that increased the number of federal crimes punishable by death. The Congressional Black Caucus had proposed a bill known as the Racial Justice Act, allowing convicts on death row to use statistical evidence to argue that race played a role in their sentencing. The bill was not part of the final package. Should it have been?
4. Suppose similar disparities could be found throughout the country. Would that justify the abolition of capital punishment?

CHAPTER EIGHT

War, Terrorism, and Civil Liberties

- **Just War Theory**
- **Preemptive Wars**
- **Violence and Terrorism**
- **Jihadism**
- **Pacifism**
- **Civil Liberties**
- **Arguments for Trading Civil Liberties for Safety**
- **Arguments against Trading Civil Liberties for Safety**

R. G. FREY AND CHRISTOPHER W. MORRIS **Violence, Terrorism, and Justice**
ALAN M. DERSHOWITZ **Make Torture an Option**
DAVID LUBAN **Torture and the Ticking Bomb**
DAVID COLE **National Security State**

CASE PRESENTATIONS: • *Preemptive War* • *Driving While Veiled* • *Fear of Flying* • *The Geneva Conventions and Guantanamo Bay*

DID THE TRAGIC events of 9/11 "change everything," as many have said in the years since? At a minimum, the attacks and our national response to them have led us to reexamine our views of terrorism, violence, war, and when, if ever, they can be justified. America had experienced terrorist attacks before, including the bombing of the Federal Building in Oklahoma City. But most people in this country seemed to feel largely immune from the random attacks on civilians that are all too familiar in countries such as England, which has experienced years of terrorist attacks from the Irish Republican Army over issues in Northern Ireland. The ease of international travel reminded us that broad expanses of oceans on our borders do not insulate us from violent attacks by outsiders.

Historically, we often have had to address the justifiability of military action by the nation. Few seem to doubt that the attack on American naval installations in Pearl Harbor in 1941 justified a declaration of war against Japan, but the decision to drop nuclear bombs on two Japanese cities a few years later, killing or maiming many civilians, remains controversial. The decision to intervene on the side of the Allies in Europe during World War II was controversial at the time to many

Americans who thought we should remain neutral. The American role in the Vietnam War remains perennially controversial, as do attempts by some to compare the recent invasion of Iraq to Vietnam.

In this chapter, we consider traditional and recent views on what counts as a "just war" in an age of often-frightening terrorism. We also consider a pervasive concern in our responses to terrorism, namely, the balancing of our safety and security with our tradition of freedom and civil liberties. In a well-known quotation, Benjamin Franklin said, "Those who would give up essential Liberty, to purchase a little temporary Safety, deserve neither Liberty nor Safety." Is this as true today as it was in the eighteenth century?

JUST WAR THEORY

Throughout history, people have developed justifications for their participation in war, and recent developments raise anew these issues for the American role in Afghanistan and Iraq. These theories of "just war" are often described as **jus ad bellum,** proposals to justify the use of force in a particular type of situation. Another theory, **jus in bello,** considers the justice of particular types of actions within a war, whether or not that war itself was justified. For example, a theory of *jus ad bellum* would ask whether the United States invasion of Iraq was justified. A theory of *jus in bello* would address whether it was justifiable to drop bombs on civilian areas during that war.

In the thirteenth century, St. Thomas Aquinas developed one of the most influential theories of just war in his work *Summa Theologica,* an approach which remains much debated even today. Much of Aquinas's work is rooted in that of the classic Greek philosopher Aristotle and is devoted to reconciling Aristotelian insights with Christian theology. Aquinas asked whether it is always sinful to wage war. In response, he argued, in part:

> In order for a war to be just, three things are necessary. First, the authority of the sovereign by whose command the war is to be waged. For it is not the business of a private individual to declare war, because he can seek for redress of his rights from the tribunal of his superior. Moreover it is not the business of a private individual to summon together the people, which has to be done in wartime. And as the care of the common weal is committed to those who are in authority, it is their business to watch over the common weal of the city, kingdom or province subject to them. And just as it is lawful for them to have recourse to the sword in defending that common weal against internal disturbances, when they punish evil-doers,... so too, it is their business to have recourse to the sword of war in defending the common weal against external enemies....
>
> Secondly, a just cause is required, namely that those who are attacked, should be attacked because they deserve it on account of some fault....
>
> Thirdly, it is necessary that the belligerents should have a rightful intention, so that they intend the advancement of good, or the avoidance of evil. . . . For it may happen that the war is declared by the legitimate authority, and for a just cause, and yet be rendered unlawful through a wicked intention.[1]

In summary, Aquinas believes we should first ask whether the entity declaring war is a legitimate sovereign. We might ask whether these sovereigns should include

---

[1]Literal translation by Fathers of the English Dominican Province, 1920. The complete text of the *Summa* can be found online: http://www.newadvent.org/summa/

all recognized nations, regardless of how their leaders came to power, or whether we should also consider the legitimacy of those governments and perhaps limit recognized sovereigns to democratically elected governments. In his article here, David Luban is troubled that the United Nations recognizes many nations whose leaders came to power in violent and perhaps illegitimate ways and suggests that they should not benefit from the defense of just war theory.

Second, Aquinas says that the people we attack should deserve it because of "some fault" of theirs, and we can ask what faults would legitimately support war against that country. Should we limit those faults to aggression against another nation? What if that aggression was an attempt to reclaim land that the aggressor believes was wrongfully seized centuries earlier? In the 1991 Gulf War, Iraq claimed that it was simply retaking land in Kuwait that was rightfully Iraq's anyway. In the wars in the Balkans, combatants have said they were merely reclaiming land wrongfully taken from their ancestors long ago. Who should decide who properly deserves to have this land? Should there be a statute of limitations or time limit against reclaiming land?

Are there other faults that would justify initiating war against another nation? Would knowledge of the concentration camps and the extermination of 6 million Jews in Nazi Germany have justified initiating war against that nation? If Timothy McVeigh, the Oklahoma City bomber, had been a citizen of Canada, would that alone have justified American initiation of war against Canada? If we had indisputable evidence that the Canadian government had provided McVeigh with financial assistance to carry out the bombing, would that have justified initiation of war against Canada? McVeigh, of course, was an American citizen, and there is not a shred of evidence of Canadian involvement. But it can be helpful in reasoning about a just war to imagine different hypothetical situations to test our views on the applicability of these theories.

Aquinas's third requirement for a just war is a "rightful intention," either "the advancement of good, or the avoidance of evil." How should we determine what a rightful intention is? By whose standards should we judge the advancement of "good"? Can we use the utilitarian theories of Mill or the human rights views of Kant to make these assessments? What other considerations should be brought to bear in making these decisions?

In the recent debates over the American invasion of Iraq, some argue that a well-founded belief that Saddam Hussein possessed weapons of mass destruction (WMD), which posed an imminent threat to the safety of Americans, is adequate justification for this war, even if it is later determined that those weapons did not exist. Another argument in support of the Iraq war noted that Hussein had committed genocide against his own Iraqi citizens and thus deserved to be deposed by a nation with the military power to accomplish that. How would you assess these claims using Aquinas's three requirements for a just war? Some critics of the war claim that it had a hidden agenda of gaining control over the Iraq oil fields to meet America's needs for oil. If that were true, would it constitute a violation of Aquinas's third condition?

PREEMPTIVE WARS

In 2002, President George W. Bush articulated a new theory of the justifiability of war, which has come to be known as "preemptive" war. (Excerpts from his announcement of this policy can be found in the Case Presentations.) He observes that the United States has traditionally engaged in war only in defense of aggression by other nations against us. Otherwise, we pursued a policy of deterrence from war, efforts to discourage other nations from attacking us with threats, for example, of "mutually assured destruction" from the dropping of nuclear bombs.

At the heart of the justification of preemptive war is the claim that changes in warfare and the character of our enemies throughout the world make preemption necessary in some circumstances. We can no longer wait for our adversaries to attack us, if those attacks might be nuclear bombs and other devastating attacks by terrorists that would make it impossible for us to even respond. Instead, we must strike first, the theory goes, to destroy those adversaries who pose a serious risk of attacking us first with weapons of mass destruction.

Supporters of the president's approach emphasize that the nature of warfare has changed, especially since the attacks of 9/11. The unpredictability of rogue states and the proliferation of nuclear arsenals, as well as biological weapons with enormous destructive potential, they argue, dictate that we take steps to protect ourselves that we might have found inappropriate in an earlier time. Critics are troubled by this change in longstanding national policy to become an aggressor nation. They wonder if this theory of preemptive wars will encourage other nations to initiate aggression, perhaps against us, if they suspect that we present an imminent threat to them.

VIOLENCE AND TERRORISM

Violence in the world is nothing new, and neither is terrorism. In considering these concepts, it is important to carefully scrutinize what we mean by these terms, an essential first step in good reasoning about when, if ever, they might be justifiable. Although everyone has an intuitive sense of how they understand these terms, under close scrutiny we might find that one person's justifiable aggression is another person's unjustifiable terrorism.

War itself seems necessarily to involve violence, but most people consider such violence justified, at least against military combatants, if the war itself was justified. Violence would include physical death and injury, but we also sometimes speak of "violence" to intellectual and conceptual ideas of cultural identity, economic well-being, and state of mind. Further, not all situations where physical injury might be involved seem appropriately labeled "violence."

R. G. Frey and Christopher W. Morris consider different definitions of "terrorism" in their essay in this chapter. They suggest that terrorism is included within violence but that not all violence is terrorism. One characteristic of terrorism, they suggest, is randomness or surprise. But modern warfare also depends on an element of surprise, yet that does not necessarily seem to make it terrorism. Another characteristic of terrorism is attack on nonmilitary personnel, innocent civilians, yet in war, innocent civilians often die as so-called "collateral damage," even if their deaths were not the intention of the military action. The attack of 9/11 on the Pentagon was typically called terrorism, even though most of the people killed were members or employees of the military.

If an act of violence can also be called terrorism, should this justify a change in our response to the behavior? Should we assess punishment or blame based on other factors, such as the claimed justification for the attack or the supposed involvement of the persons attacked in causing hardship to the attackers? Even if some violence can be justified—for example, violence in self-defense or violence in a justified war—can any terrorism be justified? Has the United States ever engaged in activities that others believe constituted terrorism? Are historic attacks on the United States that we considered war more appropriately reconsidered now as terrorism?

JIHADISM

Since 9/11, a concept called *jihadism* has been the source of much controversy. Some use it to describe a campaign of violence against the West by a militant, extremist form of Islam, noting that all nineteen hijackers claimed Islam as their religion. However, many scholars of Islamic religion, especially practitioners living in the West, have insisted that this is a perversion of the Islamic faith. Some people seem to use jihadism as synonymous with terrorism, even though much of the terrorism in the world has been committed by persons who had no affiliation with any version of Islam and made no claim of engaging in a religious war against the West.

A passage in the Qur'an, the sacred text of Islam, has caused special concern and debate:

> Against them make ready your strength to the utmost of your power, including steeds of war, to strike terror into (the hearts of) the enemies, of God and your enemies, and others besides, whom ye may not know, but whom God doth know.
>
> —Holy Qur'an—Sura 8:60

Taken literally, this passage might seem to authorize—indeed, to order—physical violence against anyone who does not support the Muslim religion. This might mean violence against one's own government if it does not support Islam or perhaps violence against other nations that are a threat to Islam. But many adherents of Islam insist that this passage should be considered only metaphorically and not as an authorization for physical terror against non-Muslims. They suggest that Islam cannot be forced on people and that war would be justified only in self-defense. They also cite passages in the Qur'an that prohibit suicide and the harming of innocent civilians. After 9/11, dozens of prominent Islamic world leaders and scholars criticized the attacks as contrary to the teachings of Islam. Some noted that, under Islamic law, the 9/11 terrorism constituted the crime of *hirabah* (waging war against society).

In popular literature since 9/11, the word *jihadism* has taken on a pervasive meaning of aggressive terrorism against innocent civilians for religious purposes, especially for purportedly Islamic interests. As with so many other important concepts in our understanding of these contemporary challenges, care in clarifying our understanding of terms in such a way that our dialogue is clear and not laced with fallacies of reasoning is paramount.

PACIFISM

The tradition of pacifism can be traced back thousands of years, often with religious underpinnings and sometimes as a result of philosophical and ethical views. In general, pacifists believe that violence is always wrong, although adherents might emphasize their interests in different settings. Pacifism in war promotes an absolute ban on violence among nations and urges instead peaceful, nonviolent resolution of political and social differences. A consistent pacifist would also urge that all violence is wrong, such as the killing of a human being in any setting, whether as individuals, in self-defense, or as capital punishment.

Absolutist pacifism can result in other ethical dilemmas, however. If pacifists refuse to fight to defend their country in war, are they relying instead on others to fight those wars, likely benefitting the pacifists in the end? If pacifists urge a national policy that we should never respond to any aggression against us—whether Pearl Harbor or 9/11—are they actually encouraging aggressor nations to attack us on the belief that we will not respond? Is pacifism "unilateral disarmament" that makes us vulnerable to attack by nations that do not adhere to pacifism?

Self-defense in individual situations also presents ethical dilemmas for consistent pacifists. It is one thing to believe that you should never respond to an attack on your own life in self-defense and that it is better to die consistently with your moral views than to live in violation of your pacifist convictions. But what about situations where the pacifist is in a good position to intervene to protect someone else's innocent life? If a young child is being beaten to death by an insane person and the pacifist could easily kill the attacker with a club and save the life of the child, which is the more ethical conduct—to be consistent with pacifism and watch the child murdered or to murder the wrongdoer and save the child's life? It is one thing to sacrifice your own life in the name of ethical principles, but is it equally justifiable to sacrifice the life of another in the name of those principles?

The nature of violence is important here too. We earlier discussed active, aggressive violence against the lives and health of persons. But violence might also be passive, such as in allowing someone to starve to death when we have the means to provide food or knowingly letting someone die from lack of medical attention. Does the pacifist, to be consistent, have a moral obligation to stop passive violence as well, for example, with an affirmative obligation to provide food to the starving or medicine to the sick?

Is pacifism a viable ethical alternative to just war, preemptive war, terrorism, or jihadism? In our deliberations, clarity in our understanding of these concepts is paramount, as is the avoidance of slippery language that distorts and blurs our fair consideration of these issues. One can object to preemptive war without necessarily being a pacifist. One can support preemptive war without necessarily being a terrorist. As in all areas of public dialogue, name-calling and *ad hominems* accomplish nothing.

CIVIL LIBERTIES

"The Constitution is not a suicide pact." This somewhat sarcastic remark about the role of the liberties accorded to us under the Constitution (attributed to two U.S. Supreme Court Justices, Robert Jackson and, later, Arthur Goldberg) has become a familiar refrain since 9/11. And the statistics about the terrorist dangers in the United States can be frightening. Some 300,000 foreign nationals are in this country, even though they have already been ordered deported, according to the attorney general. Even just a small number of persons could cause massive destruction in our country. The Department of Justice claims to have broken up terrorist cells in Buffalo, Detroit, Seattle, and Portland that could have caused disastrous harm to American citizens on our own soil. The popular press buzzes with accounts of thousands of "sleeper cells" in the United States, preparing to launch attacks on everything from water supplies, bridges, and tunnels to oil pipelines, nuclear power plants, and shopping centers. In the face of such uncertainty and fear, it is no wonder that many Americans have rushed to insist that everything possible be done to round up these potential terrorists, even at the expense of sacrificing their own civil liberties, guaranteed under the U.S. Constitution.

How much are people willing to give up to find the terrorists supposedly in our midst? Quite a bit it seems! David Cole, in his article here, explains that the civil liberties of legal residents who are noncitizens have been the most heavily trampled but that the risks to law-abiding citizens are also in jeopardy. In a *Newsweek* poll in November 2002, 72 percent said the restrictions on civil liberties by the Bush administration's war on terrorism were "about right."[2] In this poll 51 percent thought the Bill of Rights should apply only to U.S. citizens, excluding the many noncitizens who are in this country legally. In a poll taken two months after 9/11, Americans overwhelmingly favored restrictions on free speech if it would help the war on terrorism; 61 percent said that people who had expressed support for the terrorists should not be allowed to give a speech at a college; 40 percent would permit censorship of news reporting about war protests; and 36 percent approved of censorship of negative news reports about presidential conduct of the military.[3]

Which civil liberties are at stake? The Bill of Rights, the first ten amendments to the U.S. Constitution, is a good starting point for review of provisions that are at issue in the new anti-terrorist measures. The First Amendment protects our right of free speech, freedom of association, and academic freedom. Efforts to censor public speeches, even if supportive of terrorism in the minds of some, would be protected under this constitutional right. If a college wants to sponsor a debate on the meaning of jihadism, should restrictions be placed on how wide-ranging the debate can be? If a local school raises money to donate to a charity and later learns that it has been linked with terrorist activities, should that school lose its right of freedom of association? Freedom of religion is also protected under the First Amendment. But in the interest of protecting us against terrorism, should the government be allowed to place special restrictions on religious schools that it suspects might promote anti-American views?

The Fourth Amendment protects us against "unreasonable searches and seizures" by the government. Yet the anti-terrorism provisions make it considerably easier for the government to conduct secret searches of homes and to tap cell phones with much greater ease if it asserts a "foreign intelligence" need.

The Sixth Amendment guarantees our right to "a speedy and public trial" yet the anti-terrorist measures ordered by President Bush after 9/11 allow secret military tribunals of persons who are not American citizens. The Seventh Amendment guarantees our right to a jury trial in a criminal proceeding, yet this is also denied in the secret military tribunals of persons who are not American citizens.

The Eighth Amendment guarantees that "Excessive bail shall not be required, nor excessive fines imposed, nor cruel and unusual punishments inflicted," yet thousands of immigrants, especially those of Middle Eastern descent, are being held in detention centers without formal charges being brought against them for months, even years, at a time.

The challenge ahead is to determine how best to protect the country and its residents from future terrorist attacks without jettisoning those liberties that our forefathers and so many generations of Americans fought to preserve.

---

[2]Jennifer Barrett, "*Newsweek* Poll: Public Backs Military Tribunals; Most Americans Support New Restrictions on Civil Liberties and Expanded Government Powers—Up to a Point," December 1, 2002, *Newsweek Web Exclusive*.

[3]The survey was conducted by National Public Radio News, the Kaiser Family Foundation, and the Harvard University Kennedy School of Government. http://www.npr.org/news/specials/civillibertiespoll/011130.poll.html

ARGUMENTS FOR TRADING CIVIL LIBERTIES FOR SAFETY

1. ***Only terrorists need to worry about searches by the government, not law-abiding citizens.***

POINT: "People who have done nothing wrong have nothing to hide. If government officials want to search my house, let them. They won't find anything. If conducting a lot of searches means the government finds the terrorists and brings them to justice, then I say, let them search all of us."

COUNTERPOINT: "We all have a right to privacy in our homes. I don't want the government searching my home on a fishing expedition. I'm not a terrorist, but I don't think my life should be an open book to government officials. And what if they find things that are perfectly innocent but might be taken out of context and make me look guilty of something I didn't do?"

2. ***I'll never go on trial, as I follow the law, so the right to a public trial with a jury is irrelevant to me.***

POINT: "Most people who are arrested are probably guilty anyway. And the terrorists who aren't even American citizens don't deserve the same rights citizens have under the Bill of Rights. Most countries in the world don't even have juries, so this is a luxury that people from those countries don't deserve if they do something wrong here."

COUNTERPOINT: "Innocent people are arrested too, sometimes, and I want to know those rights will always be available to me to have a fair public trial with a jury. Further, our Bill of Rights is an important symbol we hold out to the world of our respect for human rights and human dignity. We should insist on upholding those rights, regardless of who commits a crime in our country, whether or not they are a citizen of this country."

3. ***Good citizens should not speak ill of the president and the government in a time of war anyway.***

POINT: "These are unusual times and we should all rally behind the president and the military. Publicly criticizing them is demoralizing to the nation and only encourages our enemies. Loyal Americans won't mind giving up some of their rights to free speech if it means we're more likely to defeat terrorism. Free speech is a luxury we can afford only during peacetime."

COUNTERPOINT: "Free speech is our best insurance that all viewpoints about the best way to proceed against terrorism are heard and discussed. We should never assume that one viewpoint from the government or the military is necessarily the right one. For centuries, the United States has stood for free speech and public debate on important issues, and in difficult times, we should not abandon that important debate."

4. ***Those religious schools that teach Islam are a breeding ground for terrorists and should be closed down in this country.***

POINT: "All nineteen of the hijackers on 9/11 were Muslims, and they thought they were carrying out the command of their religion. Religious schools in Saudi Arabia and Pakistan are teaching hatred of the West. I realize that most Muslims do not share those views, but while we are in danger from terrorism, we should be safe and close down the religious schools in this country that might be breeding more terrorism right here at home."

COUNTERPOINT: "Islamic leaders in the United States and around the world have denounced the teachings espoused by the hijackers. Most Muslims love peace and condemn terrorism. We should encourage more of that. Closing down religious schools because they might have some terrorists working at them is a dangerous precedent. Timothy McVeigh was raised as a Christian, but nobody thought we should close down all the Christian schools in the country because of what he did."

ARGUMENTS AGAINST TRADING CIVIL LIBERTIES FOR SAFETY

1. ***Our forefathers fought hard to give us precious civil liberties and we should value and protect them, even when times are frightening because of the threats of terrorism.***

   POINT: "Our Bill of Rights is over 200 years old and it provides a cornerstone of our country and its values. We should not so readily abandon it just because we are experiencing difficult times and fears of terrorism. Our forefathers would be disappointed to see us so readily agree to give up our liberties because we are afraid."

   COUNTERPOINT: "George Washington and the framers of the Constitution never could have envisioned a world in which we are threatened by terrorists, nuclear bombs, and hijacked airplanes flying into tall buildings. They would surely understand that we need to back away from some of their idealistic vision of liberty in the different and much more frightening world we live in today."

2. ***Our protection of civil liberties and freedom is what sets us apart from other countries. We should set an example for the world and show how a free democracy really works.***

   POINT: "If we want the rest of the world to emulate our high standards of democracy, we must be vigilant to protect the liberties of a free and open society. If we start to curtail our own liberties because we are afraid, we encourage other countries to curtail what liberties they give their citizens now or to continue to refuse to provide their citizens with any of the liberties we take for granted."

   COUNTERPOINT: "No other country provides the degree of freedom and liberty to its citizens that we do in America. Cutting back a little to keep ourselves safe from terrorism won't discourage other countries from experimenting with democracy. And even if it does, itmore important to protect our nation from total devastation than to worry about setting an example for countries who don't like us anyway."

3. ***We might think we're only hurting the terrorists and other criminals when we chip away at civil liberties, but we're putting ourselves at risk too.***

   POINT: "Innocent people are sometimes arrested wrongly. Civil liberties in the Constitution protect us in ways that innocent people are not protected in other countries. If we look the other way at the diminishment of civil liberties for some people, it's a slippery slope before they start coming after the rest of us for no good reason."

COUNTERPOINT: "As long as you stay out of trouble, the government won't waste time searching your home or throwing you into jail for no good reason. Most people who are searched by the police or arrested are probably guilty anyway. Where there's smoke, there's fire!"

4. ***Religious freedom is another hallmark of our nation, and we should continue to promote religious diversity and tolerance.***

POINT: "As a nation, we have always treasured our religious freedom, and this is no time to try to restrict some religions just because some of the terrorists belong to them. Many religions have promoted tolerance and understanding of each other, a message we desperately need in this day and age. If we have serious reason to believe terrorists plots are being developed anywhere, then go after them under the law, but don't assume an entire religion is plotting against us."

COUNTERPOINT: "Religious freedom is fine, but not when it preaches intolerance and breeds hatred against American values. We need to take whatever steps are necessary to protect us from the seething violence that is being fomented against us. Religion should not be a shield behind which terrorists can hide. Whether they are hiding in churches or charities or social groups, we need to go after them in any way we can."

Violence, Terrorism, and Justice

R. G. FREY AND CHRISTOPHER W. MORRIS

R. G. Frey is professor of philosophy at Bowling Green State University. Christopher W. Morris is professor of philosophy at the University of Maryland. Each has written extensively on social and political theory, ethical theory, and applied ethics. This essay introduces discussions of violence and terrorism from a conference they organized in 1988.

Unless one is a pacifist, one is likely to find it relatively easy to think of scenarios in which the use of force and violence against others is justified. Killing other people in self-defense, for example, seems widely condoned, but so, too does defending our citizens abroad against attack from violent regimes. Violence in these cases appears reactive, employed to defeat aggression against or violence toward vital interests. Where violence comes to be seen as much more problematic, if not simply prohibited, is in its direct use for social/political ends. It then degenerates into terrorism, many people seem to think, and terrorism, they hold is quite wrong. But what exactly is terrorism? And why is it wrong?

Most of us today believe terrorism to be a serious problem, one that raises difficult and challenging questions. The urgency of the problem, especially to North Americans and Western Europeans, may appear to be that terrorism is an issue that we confront from outside—that, as it were, it is an issue for us, not because violence for political ends is something approved of in our societies, but because we are the objects of such violence. The difficulty of the questions raised by contemporary terrorism has to do, we may suppose, with the complexity of issues having to do with the use of violence generally for political ends.

The first question, that of the proper characterization of terrorism, is difficult, in part because it is hard to separate from the second, evaluative question, that of the wrongness of terrorism. We may think of terrorism as a type of violence, that is, a kind of force that inflicts damage or harm on people and property. Terrorism thus broadly understood raises the same issues raised generally by the use of violence by individuals or groups. If we think of violence as being a kind of force, then the more general issues concern the evaluation of the use of force, coercion, and the like: When may we restrict people's options so that they have little or no choice but to do what we wish them to do? Violence may be used as one would use force, in order to obtain some end. But violence inflicts harm or damage and consequently adds a new element to the nonviolent use of force. When, then, if ever, may we inflict harm or damage on someone in the pursuit of some end? This question and the sets of issues it raises are familiar topics of moral and political philosophy.

Without preempting the varying characterizations of terrorism developed by the authors in this volume, however, we can think of it more narrowly; that is, we can think of it as a particular use of violence, typically for social/political ends, with several frequently conjoined characteristics. On this view, terrorism, as one would expect from the use of the term, usually involves creating terror or fear, even, perhaps, a sense of panic in a population. This common feature of terrorism is related to another characteristic, namely, the seemingly random or arbitrary use of violence. This in turn is related to a third feature, the targeting of the innocent of "noncombatants." This last, of course, is a more controversial feature than the others, since many terrorists attempt to justify their acts by arguing that their victims are not (wholly) innocent.

Thus characterized, terrorism raises specific questions that are at the center of contemporary philosophical debate. When, if ever, may one intentionally harm the innocent? Is the justification of terrorist violence to be based entirely on consequences, beneficial or other? Or are terrorist acts among those that are wrong independently of their consequences? What means may one use in combating people who use violence without justification? Other questions, perhaps less familiar, also arise. What does it mean for people to be innocent, that is, not responsible for the acts, say of their governments? May there not be some justification in terrorists' targeting some victims but not others? May terrorist acts be attributed to groups or to states? What sense, if any, does it make to think of a social system as terrorist?

Additionally, there are a variety of issues that specifically pertain to terrorists and their practices. What is the moral standing generally of terrorists? That is, what, if any duties do we have to them? How do their acts, and intentions, affect their standing? How does that standing affect our possible responses to them? May we, for instance, execute terrorists or inflict forms of punishment that would, in the words of the American Constitution, otherwise be "cruel and unusual"? What obligations might we, or officials of state, have in our dealings with terrorists? Is bargaining, of the sort practiced by virtually all Western governments, a justified response to terrorism? How, if at all, should our responses to terrorists be altered in the event that we admit or come to admit, to some degree, the justice of their cause?

Considered broadly, as a type of violence, or even more generally, as a type of force, terrorism is difficult to condemn out of hand. Force is a common feature of political life. We secure compliance with law by the use and threat of force. For many, this may be the sole reason for compliance. Force is used, for instance, to ensure that people pay their taxes, and force, even violence, is commonplace in the control of crime. In many such instances, there is not much controversy about the general justification of the use of force. The matter, say, of military conscription, though endorsed by many, is more controversial. In international contexts, however, the uses of force, and of violence, raise issues about which there is less agreement. Examples will come readily to mind.

More narrowly understood, involving some or all of the three elements mentioned earlier (the creation of terror, the seemingly random use of violence, and the targeting of the innocent or of noncombatants), the justification of terrorism is more problematic, as a brief glance at several competing moral theories will reveal.

Act-consequentialists, those who would have us evaluate actions solely in terms of their consequences, would presumably condone some terrorist acts. Were some such act to achieve a desirable goal, with minimal costs, the consequentialist might approve. Care, however, must be taken in characterizing the terrorists' goals and means. For contemporary consequentialists invariably are universalists; the welfare or ends of all people (and, on some accounts, all sentient beings) are to be included. Thus, terrorists cannot avail themselves of such theories to justify furthering the ends of some small group at the cost of greater damage to the interests of others. Merely to argue that the ends justify the means, without regard to the nature of the former, does not avail to one the resources of consequentialist moral theory.

Two factors will be further emphasized. First, consequentialist moral theory will focus upon effectiveness and efficiency, upon whether terrorist acts are an effective, efficient means to achieving desirable goals. The question naturally arises, then, whether there is an alternative means available, with equal or better likelihood of success in achieving the goals at a reduced cost. If resort to terrorism is a tactic, is there another tactic, just as likely to achieve the goal, at a cost more easy for us to bear? It is here, of course, that alternatives such as passive resistance and nonviolent civil disobedience will arise and need to be considered. It is here also that account must be taken of the obvious fact that terrorist acts seem often to harden the resistance of those the terrorists oppose. Indeed, the alleged justice of the terrorists' cause can easily slip into the background, as the killing and maiming come to preoccupy and outrage the target population. Second, consequentialist moral theory will focus upon the goal to be achieved: Is the goal that a specific use of terrorism is in aid of desirable enough for us to want to see it realized in society, at the terrible costs it exacts? It is no accident that terrorists usually portray their cause as concerned with the rectification and elimination of injustice; for *this* goal seems to be one the achievement of which we might just agree was desirable enough for us to tolerate significant cost. And it is here, of course, that doubts plague us, because we are often unsure where justice with respect to some issue falls. In the battle over Ireland, and the demand of the Irish Republican Army for justice, is there nothing to be said on the English side? Is the entire matter black and white? Here, too, a kind of proportionality rule may intrude itself. Is the reunification of Ireland worth all the suffering and loss the IRA inflicts? Is this a goal worth, not only members of the IRA's dying for, but also their making other people die for? For consequentialists, it typically will not be enough that members of the IRA think so; those affected by the acts of the IRA cannot be ignored.

Finally, consequentlist moral theory will stress how unsure we sometimes are about what counts as doing justice. On the one hand, we sometimes are genuinely unsure about what counts as rectifying an injustice. For instance, is allowing the Catholics of Northern Ireland greater and greater control over their lives part of the rectification process? For the fact remains that there are many more Protestants than Catholics in the North, so that *democratic* votes may well not materially change the condition of the latter, whatever their degree of participation in the process. On the other hand, we sometimes are genuinely unsure whether we can rectify or eliminate one injustice without perpetrating another. In the Arab-Israeli conflict, for example, can we remove one side's grievances without thereby causing additional grievances on the other side? Is there *any* way of rectifying an injustice in that conflict without producing another?

Thus, while consequentialist moral theory can produce a justification of terrorist acts, it typically will do so here, as in other areas, only under conditions that terrorists in the flesh will find it difficult to satisfy.

It is the seeming randomness of the violence emphasized by terrorism, understood in the narrower sense, that leads many moral theorists to question its legitimacy. Many moral traditions, especially nonconsequentialist ones, impose strict limits on the harm that may be done to the innocent. Indeed, some theories such as those associated with natural law and Kantian traditions, will impose an indefeasible prohibition on the intentional killing of the innocent, which "may not be overriden, whatever the consequences." Sometimes this prohibition is formulated in terms of the rights of the innocent not to be killed (e.g., the right to life), other times in terms merely of our duties not to take their lives. Either way the prohibition is often understood to be indefeasible.

If intentionally killing the innocent is indefeasibly wrong, that is, if it may never be done whatever the consequences, then many, if not most, contemporary terrorists stand condemned. Killing individuals who happen to find themselves in a targeted store, café, or train station may not be done, according to these traditions. Contemporary terrorists, who intend to bring about the deaths of innocent people by their acts, commit one of the most serious acts of injustice, unless, of course, they can show that these people are not innocent. Much turns on their attempts, therefore, to attack the innocence claim.

Just as natural law and Kantian moral theories constrain our behavior and limit the means we may use in the pursuit of political ends, so they constrain our responses to terrorists. We may not, for instance, intentionally kill innocent people (e.g., bystanders, hostages) while combating those who attack us. Our hands may thus be tied in responding to terrorism. Many commentators have argued that a morally motivated reluctance to use the nondiscriminating means of terrorists makes us especially vulnerable to them.

Some natural law or Kantian thinking invoke the notions of natural or of human rights to understand moral standing, where these are rights which we possess simply by virtue of our natures or of our humanity. Now if our nature or our humanity is interpreted, as it commonly is in these traditions, as something we retain throughout our lives, at least to the extent that we retain those attributes and capacities that are characteristic of humans, then even those who violate the strictest prohibitions of justice will retain their moral standing. According to this view, a killer acts wrongly without thereby ceasing to be the sort of being that possesses moral standing. Terrorists, then, retain their moral standing, and consequently, there are limits to what we may do to them, by way either of resistance or of punishment. Conversely, though there is reason to think consequentialists, including those who reject theories of rights to understand moral standing, would not deny terrorists such standing, what may be done to terrorists may not be so easily constrained. For harming those who harm the innocent seems less likely to provoke outrage and opposition and so negative consequences.

Certainly, not every member of these consequentialist traditions will agree with this analysis. John Locke, for instance, believed that a murderer has "by the unjust Violence and Slaughter he hath committed upon one, declared War against all Mankind, and therefore may be destroyed as a *Lyon* or a *Tyger*, one of those wild Savage Beasts, with whom Men can have no Society nor Security."[1] It may, however, be argued that the analysis accords with many parts of these traditions, as well as with much of ordinary, commonsense morality.

Whether we follow these theories in understanding the prohibition on the intentional killing of the innocent to be indefeasible or not, this principle figures importantly in most moral traditions. Care, however, must be taken in its interpretation and application. Even if we understand terrorism narrowly, as involving attacks on the innocent, it may not be clear here as elsewhere exactly who is innocent. As made clear in the just war and abortion literature, the term "innocent" is ambiguous. The usual sense is to designate some individual who is not guilty of moral or legal wrongdoing, a sense usually called the moral or juridical sense of the term. By contrast, in discussing what are often called "innocent threats"—for instance, an approaching infant who unwittingly is boobytrapped with explosives, a fetus whose continued growth threatens the life of the woman—it is common to distinguish a "technical" or "causal" sense of "innocence." People lack innocence in this second sense insofar as they threaten, whatever their culpability.

Determining which sense of "innocence" is relevant (and this is not to prejudge the issue of still further, different senses) is controversial. In discussions of the ethics of war, it is often thought that "noncombatants" are not legitimate targets, because of their innocence. Noncombatants, however, may share some of the responsibility for the injustice of a war or the injustice of the means used to prosecute the war, or they may threaten the adversary in certain ways. In the first case, they would not be fully innocent in the moral or juridical sense; in the second, they would lack, to some degree, causal innocence.

This distinction is relevant to the moral evaluation of terrorist acts aimed at noncombatants. Sometimes attempts are made at justification by pointing to the victims' lack of innocence, in the first sense. Perhaps this is what Emile Henry meant when he famously said, in 1894, after exploding a bomb in a Paris café, "There are no innocents." Presumably in such cases, where the relevant notion of innocence is that of nonculpability, terrorists would strike only at members of certain national or political groups. Other times it might be argued that the victims in someway (for instance, by their financial, electoral, or tacit support for a repressive regime) posed a threat. In these cases, terrorists would view themselves as justified in striking at anyone who, say, was present in a certain location. The distinction may also be of importance in discussions of the permissibility of various means that might be used in response to terrorist acts. If the relevant sense of innocence is causal, then certain means, those endangering the lives of victims, might be permissible.

Of course it is hard to understand how the victims of the Japanese Red Army attack at Israel's Lod airport in 1972 or of a bomb in a Paris department store in 1986 could be thought to lack innocence in either sense. In the first case, the victims were travelers (e.g., Puerto Rican Christians); in the second case, the store in question was frequented by indigent immigrants and, at that time of year, by mothers and children shopping for school supplies. It is this feature of some contemporary terrorism that has lead many commentators to distinguish it from earlier forms and from other political uses of violence.

The analogies here with another issue that has preoccupied moral theorists recently, that of the ethics of nuclear deterrence and conflict, are significant. The United States, of course, dropped atomic weapons on two Japanese cities at the end of the last world war. For several decades now, American policy has been to threaten the Soviet Union with a variety of kinds of nuclear strikes in the event that the latter attacked the United States or its Western allies with nuclear or, in the case of an invasion of Western Europe, merely with conventional weapons. These acts or practices involve killing or threatening to kill noncombatants in order to achieve certain ends: unconditional surrender in the case of Japan, deterrence of aggression in that of the Soviet Union. The possible analogies with terrorism have not gone unnoticed. Furthermore, just as some defenders of the atomic strikes against the Japanese have argued, those we attack, or threaten to attack, with nuclear weapons are themselves sufficiently similar to terrorists to justify our response.

A still different perspective on these issues may be obtained by turning from the usual consequentialist and natural law or Kantian theories to forms of contractarianism in ethics. Although this tradition has affinities with natural law and Kantian theories, especially with regard to the demands of justice or the content of moral principles, there are differences that are especially noteworthy in connection with the issues that are raised by terrorist violence.

According to this tradition, justice may be thought of as a set of principles and dispositions that bind people insofar as those to whom they are obligated reciprocate. In the absence of constraint by others, one has little or no duty to refrain from acting toward them in ways that normally would be unjust. Justice may be thus thought, to borrow a phrase from John Rawls, to be a sort of "cooperative venture for mutual advantage." According to this view, justice is not binding in the absence of certain conditions, one of which would be others' cooperative behavior and dispositions.

Adherents to this tradition might argue that we would be in a "state of nature," that is, a situation where few if any constraints of justice would bind us, with regard to terrorists who attack those who are innocent (in the relevant sense). As Hume argues in the *Second Enquiry*, when in "the society of ruffians, remote from the protection of laws and government," or during the "rage and violence of public war," the conventions of justice are suspended:

> The laws of war, which then succeed to those of equity and justice, are rules calculated for the advantage and utility of that particular state, in which men are now placed. And were a civilized nation engaged with barbarians, who observed no rules even of war, the former must also suspend their observance of them, where they no longer serve to any purpose; and must render every action or rencounter as bloody and pernicious as possible to the first aggressors.[2]

Unlike the earlier views, then, this view holds that terrorists who, by act or by intent, forswear the rules of justice may thereby lose the protection of those rules, and so a major part of their moral standing.

Similarly, partisans of terrorism might argue that it is the acts of their victims or of their governments that make impossible cooperative relations of fair dealing between themselves and those they attack. The acts, or intentions, of the latter remove them from the protection of the rules of justice.

In either case, the acts of terrorists and our response to them take place in a world beyond, or prior to, justice. Students of international affairs and diplomacy will recognize here certain of the implications of a family of skeptical positions called "realism."

Consequentialists, it should be noted, are likely to find this exclusive focus on the virtue of justice to be misguided, and they are likely to be less enamored of certain distinctions involving kinds of innocence or types of violence that are incorporated into contractarianism. In general, they will argue, as noted earlier, that terrorism *can* be justified by its consequences, where these must include the effects not merely on the terrorists but also on their victims (and others). As terrorist acts appear often not to produce sufficient benefits to outweigh the considerable costs they inevitably exact, there will most likely be a moral presumption, albeit defeasible, against them. But wrongful terrorism will be condemned, not because of the existence of mutually advantageous conventions of justice, but because of the overall harm or suffering caused. Consequentialists, then, will doubtless stand out as much against contractarian views here as they do against natural law or Kantian ones.

The foregoing, then, is a sketch of different ways terrorism may be understood and of different types of moral theories in which its justification may be addressed. There is serious controversy on both counts, and this fact alone, whatever other differences may exist, makes the works of philosophers and political and social scientists on terrorism contentious even among themselves....

NOTES

1. John Locke, *Second Treatise of Government*, in *Two Treatises of Government*, ed. Peter Laslett (Cambridge: Cambridge University Press, 1988), p. 274 (chap. 2, sec. 11).
2. David Hume, *An Enquiry concerning the Principles of Morals*, in *Enquiries concerning Human Understanding and the Principles of Morals*, ed. L. A. Selby-Bigge, 3d ed., ed. P. H. Nidditch (Oxford: Clarendon, 1975), pp. 187–8 (sec. 3, pt. 1).

QUESTIONS FOR ANALYSIS

1. How would you define "terrorism" using ideas from Frey and Morris? Is it "violence against innocent civilians for social and political purposes"? Is it only a particular type of violence? How is violence different from force? Does terrorism include all social and political purposes or only some? During war, innocent civilians are often killed or injured, even if that is not the intent of the attacks. How is this different from terrorism?
2. Test your definition of terrorism by considering the attacks of 9/11 on the World Trade Center and the Pentagon, the attack on the Oklahoma City Federal Building, the spread of anthrax through the U.S. mail, the attack on the American ship the U.S.S. *Cole*, and the truck bombings of the U.S. Embassy and the U.S. Marine Barracks in Beirut. Does your definition explain everything that you consider terrorism? Does it cover things you do not ordinarily consider terrorism?
3. Can terrorism ever be justified using consequentialist or utilitarian ethical reasoning? Is this a weakness of consequentialist theories or a misuse of those theories?
4. What are the advantages and disadvantages of a Kantian or a natural law approach to terrorism, under which the taking of innocent life is always wrong, whether by a terrorist or in response to a terrorist attack?

Make Torture an Option

ALAN M. DERSHOWITZ

Alan M. Dershowitz is the Felix Frankfurter Professor of Law at Harvard Law School. He has published numerous books and articles, especially on civil liberties and criminal law. In this controversial essay, he argues that torture is justified in some circumstances, but it should be authorized by judges who would issue "torture warrants."

The FBI's frustration over its inability to get material witnesses to talk has raised a disturbing question rarely debated in this country: When, if ever, is it justified to resort to unconventional techniques such as truth serum, moderate physical pressure and outright torture?

The constitutional answer to this question may surprise people who are not familiar with the current U.S. Supreme Court interpretation of the Fifth Amendment privilege against self-incrimination: Any interrogation technique, including the use of truth serum or even torture, is not prohibited. All that is prohibited is the introduction into evidence of the fruits of such techniques in a criminal trial against the person on whom the techniques were used. But the evidence could be used against that suspect in a non-criminal case—such as a deportation hearing—or against someone else.

If a suspect is given "use immunity"—a judicial decree announcing in advance that nothing the defendant says (or its fruits) can be used against him in a criminal case—he can be compelled to answer all proper questions. The issue then becomes what sorts of pressures can constitutionally be used to implement that compulsion. We know that he can be imprisoned until he talks. But what if imprisonment is insufficient to compel him to do what he has a legal obligation to do? Can other techniques of compulsion be attempted?

Let's start with truth serum. What right would be violated if an immunized suspect who

Alan M. Dershowitz, "Make Torture an Option," *Los Angeles Times* (November 8, 2001). Reprinted by permission of the author.

refused to comply with his legal obligation to answer questions truthfully were compelled to submit to an injection that made him do so? Not his privilege against self-incrimination, since he has no such privilege now that he has been given immunity.

What about his right of bodily integrity? The involuntariness of the injection itself does not pose a constitutional barrier. No less a civil libertarian than Justice William J. Brennan rendered a decision that permitted an allegedly drunken driver to be involuntarily injected to remove blood for alcohol testing. Certainly there can be no constitutional distinction between an injection that removes a liquid and one that injects a liquid.

What about the nature of the substance injected? If it is relatively benign and creates no significant health risk, the only issue would be that it compels the recipient to do something he doesn't want to do. But he has a legal obligation to do precisely what the serum compels him to do: answer all questions truthfully.

What if the truth serum doesn't work? Could the judge issue a "torture warrant," authorizing the FBI to employ specified forms of non-lethal physical pressure to compel the immunized suspect to talk?

Here we run into another provision of the Constitution—the due process clause, which may include a general "shock the conscience" test. And torture in general certainly shocks the conscience of most civilized nations.

But what if it were limited to the rare "ticking bomb" case—the situation in which a captured terrorist who knows of an imminent large-scale threat refuses to disclose it?

Would torturing one guilty terrorist to prevent the deaths of a thousand innocent civilians shock the conscience of all decent people?

To prove that it would not, consider a situation in which a kidnapped child had been buried in a box with two hours of oxygen. The kidnapper refuses to disclose its location. Should we not consider torture in that situation?

All of that said, the argument for allowing torture as an approved technique, even in a narrowly specified range of cases, is very troubling.

We know from experience that law enforcement personnel who are given limited authority to torture will expand its use. The cases that have generated the current debate over torture illustrate this problem. And, concerning the arrests made following the September 11 attacks, there is no reason to believe that the detainees know about specific future terrorist targets. Yet there have been calls to torture these detainees.

I have no doubt that if an actual ticking bomb situation were to arise, our law enforcement authorities would torture. The real debate is whether such torture should take place outside of our legal system or within it. The answer to this seems clear: If we are to have torture, it should be authorized by the law.

Judges should have to issue a "torture warrant" in each case. Thus we would not be winking an eye of quiet approval at torture while publicly condemning it.

Democracy requires accountability and transparency, especially when extraordinary steps are taken. Most important, it requires compliance with the rule of law. And such compliance is impossible when an extraordinary technique, such as torture, operates outside of the law.

QUESTIONS FOR ANALYSIS

1. Are you satisfied with Dershowitz's argument that torture is consistent with the right against self-incrimination and can be justified in certain situations, so long as a judge issues a "torture warrant"?
2. Dershowitz seems to rely on utilitarian reasoning to support his analysis justifying torture. Restate his arguments to make this utilitarianism more explicit and consider whether they sufficiently outweigh the human rights concerns.
3. Even if torture is not prohibited by the U.S. Constitution, as Dershowitz suggests, does it violate ethical standards to which we should adhere?

Torture and the Ticking Bomb

DAVID LUBAN

David J. Luban, the Frederick J. Haas Professor of Law and Philosophy at Georgetown University Law Center, has written extensively on social justice, legal ethics, and jurisprudence. In this article, he argues that the "ticking bomb" scenario to justify torture is an intellectual fraud.

Ludwig Wittgenstein once wrote that confusion arises when we become bewitched by a picture. He meant that it's easy to be seduced by simplistic examples that look compelling but actually misrepresent the world we live in.

More than a year after Abu Ghriab, we continue to confront the issues of abusive interrogation, torture, and legal positions purporting to vindicate harsh tactics in the name of national security. In this confrontation, the picture that bewitches us is the "ticking bomb" scenario. Suppose a bomb is planted somewhere in the crowded heart of an American city, and we have custody of the man who planted it. He won't talk. Surely, the scenario suggests, we shouldn't be too squeamish to torture the information out of him and save hundreds of lives. After all, abstract moral prohibitions must yield to the calculus of consequences.

To take a real-life example: in 1995, an al Qaeda plot to bomb 11 U.S. airliners was thwarted by information tortured out of a Pakistani suspect by the Philippine police. According to a report by journalists Marites Vitug and Glenda Gloria, "For weeks, agents hit him with a chair and a long piece of wood, forced water into his mouth, and crushed lighted cigarettes into his private parts. His ribs were almost totally broken and his captors were surprised he survived." Grisly, to be sure—and yet if they hadn't done it, thousands of innocent travelers might have died horrible deaths.

But look at the example again. The Philippine police were surprised he survived—in other words, they came close to torturing him to death before he talked. And they tortured him for weeks, during which time they presumably didn't know any of the details they wanted about the al Qaeda plot. What if he too hadn't known? Or what if there had been no such plot? Then they would have tortured him for weeks, possibly tortured him to death, for naught. For all they knew at the time, that is precisely what they were doing. We can't use the argument that preventing the al Qaeda attack justified the decision to torture, because at the moment the decision was made no one knew about the al Qaeda attack.

The ticking bomb scenario cheats its way around these difficulties by stipulating that the bomb is there, ticking away, and that officials know they have the man who planted it. Those conditions will seldom be met. Let's look at some more realistic scenarios and ask the questions they raise:

- The authorities know there may be a bomb plot in the offing, and they've captured a man who may know something about it, but may not. Should they torture him? How severely? For how long? For weeks? Months? The chances are considerable that they are torturing a man with nothing to tell. If he doesn't talk, is that a signal to stop, or to up the level of torture? How likely must it be that he knows something important? Fifty-fifty? Thirty-seventy? Will one out of a hundred suffice to land him on the water board?
- Do we really want to make the torture decision by running the numbers? A 1 percent chance of saving a thousand lives yields 10

David Luban, "Torture and the Ticking Bomb," *Georgetown Law* (Spring/Summer 2005), 48–51. Reprinted by permission of *Georgetown Law* and the author.

statistical lives saved. Does that mean that we will torture up to nine people on a 1 percent chance of finding crucial information?

- Suppose authorities believed that one out of a group of 50 captives at Camp X-Ray in Guantanamo Bay, Cuba might know where Osama bin Laden is hiding—but they didn't know which captive. Torture them all? That is: torture 49 captives with nothing to tell you on the uncertain chance of capturing bin Laden? For that matter, would capturing bin Laden demonstrably save a single human life? Months ago, the Bush administration stated that bin Laden had been marginalized. Maybe capturing him would save lives somehow—but how do you demonstrate it? Or doesn't it matter whether the torture was intended to save lives, as long as it furthered some goal in the War on Terror? And if the answer is that it doesn't matter, why limit the efficacy of torture to the War on Terror? Why not torture in pursuit of any worthwhile goal?
- Indeed, if we're willing to torture 49 innocent people to get information from the one person who has it, why stop there? If suspects won't break under torture, why not torture their loved ones in front of them? A moral consequentialist should be willing to accept the torture of one innocent child to save hundreds of lives. Of course, until you try, you won't know whether torturing a child will break the suspect. But that just affects the odds, not the argument.

The point of these examples is that in a world of uncertainty and imperfect knowledge, the ticking bomb scenario should not form the point of reference in the torture debate. The ticking bomb is the picture that bewitches us. The actual choice is not between one guilty man's pain and hundreds of innocent lives. It is the choice between the certainty of that anguish and the mere possibility of learning something vital and saving lives.

There is a second insidious error built into the ticking bomb hypothetical. It assumes a single ad hoc decision about whether to torture, by officials who ordinarily would do no such thing except in a desperate emergency. But in the real world of interrogations, decisions are not made that way. They are based on policies, guidelines, and directives. Officials inhabit a world of practices, not of ad hoc emergency measures. Any responsible discussion of torture therefore must address the practice of torture, not the ticking bomb hypothetical.

That means discussing other, different questions. For instance, should we create a professional cadre of torturers, of interrogators who have been trained in the techniques and who have learned to overcome their instinctive revulsion against causing pain? Medieval executioners were schooled in the arts of agony. In Louis XIV's Paris, torture was a family trade whose tricks were passed on from father to son.

Of course, in our era, higher education has replaced inheritance of family trades. Should universities create an undergraduate major in torture? Or should the major be offered only in police and military academies? Would we want federal grants for research to devise new and better torture techniques? Patents issued on high-tech torture devices? Companies competing to manufacture them? Trade conventions in Las Vegas? Should there be a medical subspecialty of torture doctors, who ensure that gasping captives don't die before they talk? Recall the chilling words of Sgt. Ivan Fredericks, one of the abusers at Abu Ghraib, who saw the body of a detainee after the interrogation went awry: "They stressed the man out so much that he passed away." Real pros wouldn't let that happen; it wastes a good source. Who should teach torture-doctoring in medical school?

The basic question is this one: Do we really want to create a torture culture and the kind of people who inhabit it? The ticking time bomb distracts us from the real issue, which is not about emergencies but about the normalization of torture. Some might argue that keeping the practice of torture secret avoids the moral corruption that might arise from creating a public culture of torture. But concealment does not reject the normalization of torture. It accepts it but layers on top of it the normalization of state secrecy. The result would be a shadow culture of torturers and those who train and support them, operating outside the public eye and accountable only to other insiders of the torture culture.

Yet a further question arises: Who can guarantee that case-hardened torturers, inured to levels of violence and pain that would sicken ordinary people, will know where to draw the line? They never have in the past. In the Argentinian Dirty War, tortures began because terrorist cells had a policy of fleeing when any of their members had disappeared for 48 hours. Authorities had just two days to wring the information out of a captive. University of Iowa law professor Mark Osiel, who has studied the Dirty War, reports that at first many in the Argentinian military had qualms about what they were doing, until their priests assured them that they were fighting God's fight. By the end of the Dirty War, the qualms were gone, and, as John Simpson and Jana Bennett have reported, hardened young officers were placing bets on who could kidnap the prettiest girl to rape and torture. Escalation is the rule, not the aberration. Abu Ghraib is the fully predictable image of what a torture culture looks like. Abu Ghraib is not a few bad apples. It is the apple tree.

That is why Harvard law professor Alan Dershowitz has argued that judges, not torturers, should oversee the permission to torture by means of warrants. The irony is that former Assistant Attorney General Jay S. Bybee, who signed a notorious, highly permissive torture memo for the Justice Department in 2002, is now a federal judge. Politicians pick judges, and if the politicians accept torture, the judges will too. Judges don't fight their culture. They reflect it. Once we create a torture culture, only the naive would suppose that judges will provide a safeguard.

The ticking bomb scenario is an intellectual fraud. In its place, we must address the real questions about torture—questions about uncertainty, questions about the morality of consequences, questions about what it does to a culture to introduce the practice of torture, questions about what torturers are like and whether we really want them walking among us.

QUESTIONS FOR ANALYSIS

1. Luban objects to consequentialist reasoning—the idea that torturing one person is justifiable if it saves the lives of hundreds. What assumptions seem to underlie his objection? Does he object to all consequentialist reasoning or only to some arguments? Can a consequentialist consistently respect a human right not to be tortured?
2. Are there any situations where Luban would find torture justifiable? Are there situations where you find torture justifiable? How might Luban object to your position and how would you respond?
3. Should we train a group of professional torturers to increase the chances of getting good information? If you find this an objectionable use of your tax money, explain why.
4. How does Luban respond to Dershowitz's proposal to have judges issue warrants to permit torture so there will be judicial oversight of this process?

National Security State

DAVID COLE

David Cole is a professor at Georgetown University Law Center and an attorney for the Center for Constitutional Rights. He is the author of numerous books and articles on civil rights, criminal justice, and constitutional law. He has been honored in recent years for his unflagging defense of civil liberties in the aftermath of 9/11. In this article, he expresses alarm about the violation of numerous civil liberties in the name of "homeland security" from terrorism.

David Cole, "National Security State," *The Nation* (December 17, 2001).

It is already a cliché that the attacks of September 11 "changed everything." One thing they do seem to have changed is liberals. Harvard law professor Laurence Tribe, a stalwart defender of civil rights and civil liberties, has condoned the use of military tribunals and the detention of more than 1,200 people, even though not a single detainee has been charged in connection with the attacks. His colleague Alan Dershowitz has suggested that torture may sometimes be justified, as long as it is authorized by a warrant. And George Washington law professor Jeff Rosen has argued that "the real story after September 11 is that America hasn't yet come close to abandoning any immutable principles of its national identity."

I cite these scholars not to single them out for criticism—all are important and courageous liberal voices—but as illustrations of a larger trend. Even liberals these days seem reluctant to criticize the government's response to the new threat of terrorism.

But a brief overview of what we've done so far in the interest of "homeland security" makes clear that we have already abandoned several of our "immutable principles" and have already begun to repeat the mistakes of the past.

Consider first the USA Patriot Act, an omnibus law of 342 pages enacted under *in terrorem*[1] threats from Attorney General John Ashcroft, who suggested that if another terrorist incident occurred before Congress passed it, the blame would rest on Congress. The nuts and bolts of the law were worked out in a couple of all-night sessions and approved by large majorities the day they were introduced, even though members could not possibly have read the bill before casting their votes.

The Patriot Act imposes guilt by association on immigrants, rendering them deportable for wholly innocent nonviolent associational activity on behalf of any organization blacklisted as terrorist by the Secretary of State. Any group of two or more that has used or threatened to use force can be designated as terrorist. This provision in effect resurrects the philosophy of McCarthyism, simply substituting "terrorist" for "communist." Perhaps not realizing the pun, the Supreme Court has condemned guilt by association as "alien to the traditions of a free society and the First Amendment itself." Yet it is now the rule for aliens in our free society.

The Patriot Act also authorizes the Attorney General to lock up aliens, potentially indefinitely, on mere suspicion, without any hearing and without any obligation to establish to a court that the detention is necessary to forestall flight or danger to the community. Moreover, most of the more than 1,200 detentions already effected have not relied upon this authority; the detainees are instead held on pretextual criminal charges, as material witnesses and under pre-Patriot Act immigration authority. The government claims that about 10 to 15 of the detained may be linked to Al Qaeda, but what about the other 1,185? We can't know the answer to that question, because the Justice Department refuses to disclose even the most basic information about most of the detainees, such as who they are, what they are being held for or where they're imprisoned. On November 27 Ashcroft reluctantly identified about 50 people in custody on federal criminal charges but refused to identify more than 500 held on immigration charges, or even to put a number on those held as material witnesses or on state charges. Never in our history has the government engaged in such a blanket practice of secret incarceration.

Secrecy has become the order of the day. Criminal proceedings are governed by gag orders—themselves secret—preventing defendants or their lawyers from saying anything to the public about their predicament. The INS has conducted secret immigration proceedings, closed to the public and even to family members. The Patriot Act authorizes never-disclosed wiretaps and secret searches in criminal investigations without probable cause of a crime, the bedrock constitutional predicate for any search. And in a federal court of appeals in Miami in November, the government renewed its defense of the use of secret evidence in immigration proceedings, arguing that it needs the authority more than ever after September 11 to detain aliens by using evidence they cannot confront or rebut.

---

[1] In Fear.

We can look forward to more secrecy still. A major impetus behind George W. Bush's presidential order authorizing the trial of suspected terrorists in military tribunals was the desire to avoid the constitutional necessity of disclosing classified evidence to the defendant in an ordinary criminal trial. In military tribunals, defendants have no right to a public trial, no right to trial by jury, no right to confront the evidence or to object to illegally obtained evidence and no right to appeal to an independent court. The military acts as prosecutor, judge, jury and executioner, and a death sentence can be imposed by a two-thirds vote of the military officers presiding.

We have used military tribunals to try our enemies in times of war before. There has been no declared war here, but perhaps that can be excused as a technicality. What cannot be excused is the extension of the tribunals to US residents who have no connection to Al Qaeda whatsoever but who are merely charged with "international terrorism," a wholly undefined offense, or of harboring someone so charged. Military tribunals have always been limited to the trial of belligerents—those fighting for the enemy, as the Supreme Court ruled in Ex Parte Milligan during the Civil War. Bush's order, however, allows the President to dispense with a criminal trial for any noncitizen accused of terrorism.

In one setting—attorney-client communications—secrecy will no longer be the rule. At the end of October, Ashcroft asserted the authority to listen in on such highly privileged discussions without a warrant.

Finally, we have succumbed to ethnic profiling. The Justice Department has instructed law enforcement agents across the country to "interview" more than 5,000 immigrants based not on any evidence that they are connected to Al Qaeda or the events of September 11 but solely on their age, gender and country of origin. The list looks suspiciously like what an enterprising lawyer would come up with if instructed to make a list of immigrant Arab men but to make it look like it wasn't based on ethnicity.

After facing some initial, albeit muted, opposition to its first antiterrorism legislative proposal to Congress, the Administration has chosen since then to bypass Congress altogether. It has also bypassed the public, instead instituting radical changes through rule-makings that go into effect the moment they are published and without notice or comment.

The Administration has made no case that its pre-existing authorities were insufficient. We have successfully tried serious terrorist crimes in open court with all the protections that customarily apply, without regard to whether the defendants were citizens or aliens. Before the Patriot Act, we could deport aliens who supported terrorist activity in any way and could detain aliens who posed a threat to national security or posed a risk of flight. And we had authority to conduct wiretaps and searches in foreign intelligence investigations without probable cause of a crime, as long as that authority was not used as an end-run around the constitutional rules that govern criminal investigations. The government has not even tried to show that the absence of any of its newfound powers contributed to its failure to identify and thwart the September 11 attacks.

Rather, what the Administration has said, time and time again, is that we are "at war." Apparently this statement renders any further argument unnecessary. Thus, Ashcroft tells us that because we are at war, "foreign terrorists who commit war crimes against the United States . . . are not entitled to and do not deserve the protections of the American Constitution." But putting aside whether we are "at war" without a declaration of war, the bigger problem is that we can't know whether someone is a "foreign terrorist" until those charges are proven in a fair proceeding. The military tribunals eliminate virtually every procedural check designed to protect the innocent and accurately identify the guilty.

These initiatives have sparked opposition from unlikely quarters. Police officers in Portland, Oregon, have refused to take part in the interviews of the 5,000 immigrant men, citing local laws against racial profiling. Spain has said it will not extradite eight men charged with complicity in the September 11 attacks unless we promise not to try them in military tribunals. Even William Safire has called the military tribunals "kangaroo courts." And on Capitol Hill,

Republican Orrin Hatch has joined Democrat Patrick Leahy in calling on Ashcroft to answer questions before the Judiciary Committee about his recent executive initiatives.

So why are so many liberals satisfied with the government's response? Why hasn't there been a louder outcry about the measures adopted? Why hasn't the Administration been asked to justify its newfound authorities on a power-by-power basis? For one thing, we are afraid, and in times of fear we crave security above all. For another, in the face of an attack we naturally and properly seek to stick together, to show a united front. But in times of fear and crisis we also panic. And panic causes us to abandon our principles.

So have we abandoned any "immutable principles," as Jeff Rosen calls them? Well, political freedom has given way to guilt by association. Due process has given way to detention on the Attorney General's say-so. Public scrutiny has given way to secret detentions and secret trials. Equal protection under law has given way to ethnic profiling. And we're only three months into this. We can't afford to let liberal vigilance give way to complacency.

QUESTIONS FOR ANALYSIS

1. Cole wrote his article a few months after the terrorists attacks of 9/11. With the passage of several years, do the alarm bells he sounded then seem more or less urgent today? Do you believe these abuses of civil liberties have made us safer from terrorists? Should we continue to take these extreme measures to protect us in the future or should we work to reinstate respect for the civil liberties that Cole argues have been taken away?
2. Before 9/11, the nation had generally come to recognize the wrongness of "racial profiling," which singles out for suspicion dark-skinned persons, especially those of African or Latino descent. Cole notes that "ethnic profiling" now seems accepted, singling out men on the basis of their age, religion, and country of origin. We all want to be safe from terrorists in our midst, but how best can we identify the real terrorists for further scrutiny? Are we safest if we focus only on young men from the Middle East? Have you or any of your friends ever been singled out for suspicion, solely on the basis of race or ethnicity?
3. The Administration claims that extraordinary measures are justified because we are "at war," yet the Congress did not make an official declaration of war after 9/11. Do you think we will always be "at war" with terrorism in general? Can you imagine a world in which we are no longer in such a war or do you expect the "war on terrorism" to be a permanent condition in the future? Would such a permanent war justify the permanent suspension of our civil liberties?
4. Cole seems to rely on appeals to basic human rights, a Kantian approach to ethical reasoning, and rejects utilitarian or consequentialist reasoning that violations of these rights are justifiable to keep us safe. What are the bases for believing such human rights exist? Is his approach to the issues persuasive in overcoming the consequentialist appeal to security?

CASE PRESENTATION

Preemptive War

President George W. Bush has articulated a new strategy of "preemptive war," a marked change from the previous U.S. policy of deterrence to war and the use of force only in self-defense. *The National Security Strategy of the United States of America,* issued by President Bush on September 17, 2002, explains preemptive war as a way to "Prevent Our Enemies from Threatening Us, Our Allies, and Our Friends with Weapons of Mass Destruction":

The nature of the Cold War threat required the United States—with our allies and friends—to emphasize deterrence of the enemy's use of force, producing a grim strategy of mutual assured destruction. With the collapse of the Soviet Union and the end of the Cold War, our security environment has undergone profound transformation. . . .

But new deadly challenges have emerged from rogue states and terrorists. None of these contemporary threats rival the sheer destructive power that was arrayed against us by the Soviet Union. However, the nature and motivations of these new adversaries, their determination to obtain destructive powers hitherto available only to the world's strongest states, and the greater likelihood that they will use weapons of mass destruction against us, make today's security environment more complex and dangerous.

In the 1990s we witnessed the emergence of a small number of rogue states that, while different in important ways, share a number of attributes. These states:

- brutalize their own people and squander their national resources for the personal gain of the rulers;
- display no regard for international law, threaten their neighbors, and callously violate international treaties to which they are party;
- are determined to acquire weapons of mass destruction, along with other advanced military technology, to be used as threats or offensively to achieve the aggressive designs of these regimes;
- sponsor terrorism around the globe; and
- reject basic human values and hate the United States and everything for which it stands.

At the time of the Gulf War, we acquired irrefutable proof that Iraq's designs were not limited to the chemical weapons it had used against Iran and its own people, but also extended to the acquisition of nuclear weapons and biological agents. In the past decade North Korea has become the world's principal purveyor of ballistic missiles, and has tested increasingly capable missiles while developing its own WMD arsenal. Other rogue regimes seek nuclear, biological, and chemical weapons as well. These states' pursuit of, and global trade in, such weapons has become a looming threat to all nations.

We must be prepared to stop rogue states and their terrorist clients before they are able to threaten or use weapons of mass destruction against the United States and our allies and friends. Our response must take full advantage of strengthened alliances, the establishment of new partnerships with former adversaries, innovation in the use of military forces, modern technologies, including the development of an effective missile defense system, and increased emphasis on intelligence collection and analysis. . . .

It has taken almost a decade for us to comprehend the true nature of this new threat. Given the goals of rogue states and terrorists, the United States can no longer solely rely on a reactive posture as we have in the past. The inability to deter a potential attacker, the immediacy of today's threats, and the magnitude of potential harm that could be caused by our adversaries' choice of weapons, do not permit that option. We cannot let our enemies strike first.

In the Cold War, especially following the Cuban missile crisis, we faced a generally status quo, risk-averse adversary. Deterrence was an effective defense. But deterrence based only upon the threat of retaliation is less likely to work against leaders of rogue states more willing to take risks, gambling with the lives of their people, and the wealth of their nations.

- In the Cold War, weapons of mass destruction were considered weapons of last resort whose use risked the destruction of those who used them. Today, our enemies see weapons of mass destruction as weapons of choice. For rogue states these weapons are tools of intimidation and military aggression against their neighbors. These weapons may also allow these states to attempt to blackmail the United States and our allies to prevent us from deterring or repelling the aggressive behavior of rogue states. Such states also see these weapons as their best means of overcoming the conventional superiority of the United States.
- Traditional concepts of deterrence will not work against a terrorist enemy whose avowed tactics are wanton destruction and the targeting of innocents; whose so-called soldiers seek martyrdom in death and whose most potent protection is statelessness. The overlap between states that sponsor terror and those that pursue WMD compels us to action.

For centuries, international law recognized that nations need not suffer an attack before they can lawfully take action to defend themselves against forces that present an imminent danger of attack. Legal scholars and international jurists often conditioned the legitimacy of preemption on the existence of an imminent threat—most often a visible mobilization of armies, navies, and air forces preparing to attack.

We must adapt the concept of imminent threat to the capabilities and objectives of today's adversaries. Rogue states and terrorists do not seek to attack us using conventional means. They know such attacks would fail. Instead, they rely on acts of terror and, potentially, the use of weapons of mass destruction—weapons that can be easily concealed, delivered covertly, and used without warning.

The targets of these attacks are our military forces and our civilian population, in direct violation of one of the principal norms of the law of warfare. As was demonstrated by the losses on September 11, 2001, mass civilian casualties is the specific objective of terrorists and these losses would be exponentially more severe if terrorists acquired and used weapons of mass destruction.

The United States has long maintained the option of preemptive actions to counter a sufficient threat to our national security. The greater the threat, the greater is the risk of inaction—and the more compelling the case for taking anticipatory action to defend ourselves, even if uncertainty remains as to the time and place of the enemy's attack. To forestall or prevent such hostile acts by our adversaries, the United States will, if necessary, act preemptively.

The United States will not use force in all cases to preempt emerging threats, nor should nations use preemption as a pretext for aggression. Yet in an age where the enemies of civilization openly and actively seek the world's most destructive technologies, the United States cannot remain idle while dangers gather. We will always proceed deliberately, weighing the consequences of our actions. To support preemptive options, we will:

- build better, more integrated intelligence capabilities to provide timely, accurate information on threats, wherever they may emerge;
- coordinate closely with allies to form a common assessment of the most dangerous threats; and
- continue to transform our military forces to ensure our ability to conduct rapid and precise operations to achieve decisive results.

The purpose of our actions will always be to eliminate a specific threat to the United States or our allies and friends. The reasons for our actions will be clear, the force measured, and the cause just.

QUESTIONS FOR ANALYSIS

1. President Bush states that preemptive war will be used only for a cause that is "just." How does he understand "just cause" from his statements here? Do his tests for when he would initiate preemptive war meet the traditional standards for just war?
2. On March 16, 2006, the president officially reaffirmed his commitment to preemptive war, even though he had previously acknowledged that no WMD were found and no real connection had been identified between Sadaam Hussein and the attacks of 9/11. Does the policy seen in light of recent events, seem to justify invasion of such countries as Iran and North Korea if the United States credibly believes they possess nuclear warheads? After our experience in invading Iraq, does the preemption doctrine today seem sound?
3. Can you think of other circumstances in our nation's history when a preemptive war would have been justified but was not initiated?
4. Are there circumstances in the world today in which preemptive war would be justified under the president's rationale? What arguments could be raised against engaging in such war?

CASE PRESENTATION

Driving While Veiled

In March 2002, an ultraorthodox Muslim woman, Sultaana Lakiana Myke Freeman, filed suit in Florida, claiming that the state's requirement that her photograph for her driver's license must be taken without her veil violated her "religious belief that her religion requires her to wear her veil in front of strangers and unrelated males." She argued that the state's revocation and cancellation of her driver's license because of her refusal to have her photograph taken without a veil violated her "religious freedom, freedom of speech, due process, equal protection and right to privacy."

After a trial in May 2003, a Florida court rejected her claim that the photographic requirement was an undue burden on the exercise of her religion: " . . . the State apparently has a practice of accommodating Muslim women holding similar beliefs on veiling. A DHSMV [Department of Highway Safety and Motor

Vehicles] manager testified that in several instances, upon appointment, DHSMV employees have escorted women to a private room, with only a female license examiner present. No males were allowed, and the room had no windows through which anyone could see. The State argued that the 'momentary' lifting of the veil in order to complete the digitalized image or photo, done in 'private circumstances' as described, does not constitute a substantial burden on Plaintiff's right to free exercise of religion. The State asserted that Plaintiff would be free to place the photo license in her pocket and never show it to anyone, except perhaps to law enforcement officers in specific situations. The Court agrees, and finds that given Plaintiff's own testimony plus the State's willingness to accommodate Plaintiff to the degree stated, the momentary raising of her veil for the purpose of the ID photo does not constitute a 'substantial burden' on her right to exercise her religion."

The court agreed with the argument of the state of Florida ". . . that when religious practices collide with public safety, public safety must prevail. . . . The State called an expert witness who has been employed in law enforcement for almost 40 years and is currently a consultant to DHSMV on security matters. He stated that a facial image is 'absolutely essential' to law enforcement officers, because without it, officers conducting traffic stops are at risk during the extra time needed to check identities to 'make sure that's the person standing in front of them.' He emphasized that it is crucial to both criminal and intelligence investigators to be able to identify possible suspects (and victims of crimes or accidents) as quickly as possible, and that this ability has a significant impact on public safety."

The court also rejected her argument ". . . that photo IDs are largely flawed and can easily be thwarted by people who change their hair, cover their foreheads and ears, wear large glasses, shave their heads, grow their beards, or alter their appearance by other means, including contact lenses and plastic surgery. She stressed that some people have aged years since their license photo was taken and for that reason alone look different from the image on the license. Plaintiff also claimed that religious hairstyles and headwear are permitted for persons of other faiths, and suggested that she is being singled out because she is Muslim." The state responded, ". . . some facial features do not change, despite changes in the individual's style or age, and that photographic images of drivers evidencing some differences are still of greater value than an image with facial features completely blocked by a mask or a veil."

The Court acknowledged ". . . that today it is a different world than it was 20–25 years ago. It would be foolish not to recognize that there are new threats to public safety, including both foreign and domestic terrorism, and increased potential for abuse' that did not exist . . ." before. But, the Court insisted, "Plaintiff is not being singled out because she is Muslim. This Court would rule the same way for anyone—Christian, Jew, Buddhist, Atheist—who wished to have his or her driver's license identification photo taken while wearing anything—ski mask, costume mask, religious veil, hood—which cloaks all facial features except the eyes. Plaintiff's veiling practices must be subordinated to society's need to identify people as quickly as possible in situations in which safety and security of others could be at risk."

QUESTIONS FOR ANALYSIS

1. The judge rejected an argument by the state of Florida that most Muslim women do not wear veils and that she was part of a very small minority. Would you agree that this should be irrelevant in this case? If the vast majority of women in Florida wanted to wear veils when obtaining their driver's licenses, do you think the state of Florida would change its position on the issues here?
2. Before 9/11, Illinois, and later Florida, had issued her a driver's license showing her wearing the veil. Only after 9/11 did the state of Florida send her a notice that if she did not agree to have her photograph taken without the veil, her license would be revoked. Does this sequence of events suggest that Florida was singling her out for discriminatory treatment because of terrorist fears? If Florida's concern was "public safety" and effective law enforcement, why wasn't it concerned before 9/11?
3. In her arguments to the court, plaintiff noted a precedent, a 1984 decision, *Quaring v. Peterson*, in which a Pentecostal Christian woman refused to have her picture taken for a Nebraska driver's

license because she believed that it would constitute making a graven image. The court found that denying the woman her license did not serve a compelling state interest. How, if at all, is this case different, and should the Florida court have followed the same reasoning?

4. Can you think of other religious or cultural forms of dress that might interfere with the full facial photograph required by Florida? Should those be allowed?
5. Using the reasoning of this Florida decision, should she also be required to provide a full facial photograph, without her veil, if she applies for a passport? An employee ID for a job? A photo ID for medical insurance coverage? If she flies on an airplane and airport security needs to compare her photo ID with her actual face, should she have to comply before boarding the airplane? How can her religious beliefs be balanced against these other societal interests in security?

CASE PRESENTATION

Fear of Flying

On the evening of September 11, 2001, then-Secretary of Transportation Norman Y. Mineta issued a statement that "In a democracy, there is always a balance between freedom and security. Our transportation systems, reflecting the values of our society, have always operated in an open and accessible manner. And, they will again." Two months later, Congress established the Transportation Security Administration (TSA) to take over all security at the nation's airports. While many members of the flying public seem to think professionalism and security have improved at the airports, others complain of what they perceive to be silly random searches of elderly grandmothers and very young children with plastic toy guns. The TSA continually announces new security problems, including ballpoint pens that hide sharp weapons and bombs made of plastic materials that are difficult to detect. Newspaper reports tell of continuing security breaches with potentially lethal weapons somehow brought past security checks onto the planes.

Despite continuing security breaches, Mineta insisted that airport screeners should not use any kind of racial profiling in identifying persons for special searches, including persons who might "appear to be of Arab, Middle Eastern or south Asian descent and/or Muslim." Mineta himself was one of the 120,000 Americans interned by the U.S. government during World War II, and he has been adamant in his public statements that this nation should not ever again practice such discrimination against anyone solely because of nationality, ancestry, or appearance. Critics of airport security complain that limited resources should be focused on the persons most likely to be 9/11 hijackers and point out that all nineteen were men of Middle Eastern descent.

QUESTIONS FOR ANALYSIS

1. If you were designing an appropriate security system for the nation's airports, how would you focus limited resources to make it most likely that you would catch persons who planned terrorist attacks on airports and airplanes? Would you single out any particular type of person for special searches to protect the flying public? On what basis would you justify these special searches? Can your security plan be criticized for engaging in such fallacies as hasty generalization or faulty analogy? What criticisms could be raised of your security plan?
2. No terrorist attacks have occurred in the United States using airplanes since 9/11. Air travel has increased after dropping off dramatically right after 9/11. Fear of flying because of concerns over terrorism has steadily declined. Do these consequences show that the current airport security system is the best approach for the nation? Are the inconveniences to ordinary citizens and the element of risk with continued security breaches outweighed by the respect for human rights in the current approach that rejects singling out men of Middle Eastern descent during security searches at airports?
3. Some of Mineta's critics charged that his personal experiences during World War II made him unable to render objective decisions on airport security after 9/11. Is this an example of an *ad hominem* argument? Is this a justifiable criticism of Mineta's approach to airport security?

CASE PRESENTATION

The Geneva Conventions and Guantanamo Bay

In late 2001 the United States Military invaded Afghanistan to root out the organizations and persons responsible for the attacks on September 11. A Yemeni national named Salim Ahmed Hamdan was captured by local militias, which turned him over to the U.S. military for transfer to its prison in Guantanamo Bay, Cuba. Over a year later, the president ruled that Hamdan was eligible for trial for unspecified crimes in a military commission. After another year passed, he was charged with "conspiracy . . . to commit . . . offenses triable by military commission." Hamdan sued in Federal court for, among other things, being tried in the absence of authority under the international law of war, the Geneva Conventions, or Congress.

The president had insisted that the persons held at Guantanamo Bay and in other prisons outside the United States were not entitled to the protections of the Geneva Conventions, because they were not from a "recognized nation," had not been wearing uniforms, and did not observe "traditional rules of war." Instead, the administration said, these "detainees" could be tried under military commissions that did not necessarily conform either to the Geneva Conventions or to requirements for justice in the United States. According to the administration, there are about 1,000 suspected terrorists being held in prisons by the United States around the world, with about 450 at Guantanamo Bay.

The Geneva Conventions do not recognize "conspiracy" as a crime in international law, nor had "conspiracy" been recognized at the Nuremberg Trials of Nazi war criminals after World War II. The Conventions also set requirements for authorized trials.

The U.S. Supreme Court held on June 29, 2006, in *Hamdan v. Rumsfeld*, that the Geneva Conventions do apply to the detainees at Guantanamo, including Hamdan. They ordered that Hamdan be tried by a "regularly constituted court affording all the judicial guarantees which are recognized as indispensable by civilized peoples." The majority opinion concluded with these words:

> Congress has not issued the Executive a "blank check." . . . Indeed, Congress has denied the President the legislative authority to create military commissions of the kind at issue here. Nothing prevents the President from returning to Congress to seek the authority he believes necessary. Where, as here, no emergency prevents consultation with Congress, judicial insistence upon that consultation does not weaken our Nation's ability to deal with danger. To the contrary, that insistence strengthens the Nation's ability to determine—through democratic means—how best to do so. The Constitution places its faith in those democratic means. Our Court today simply does the same.

A few weeks later, the President announced that the administration would henceforth comply with the Geneva Conventions and asked Congress to establish trial procedures that would meet those requirements. The Defense Department issued an order to all branches of the armed forces to review their detention procedures, including methods of interrogation, to ensure that they were in compliance with the Conventions.

QUESTIONS FOR ANALYSIS

1. Do you agree with the Court that the rights of the Geneva Conventions should be granted to persons the military suspects might be involved with terrorism, even if they have never had a trial or been charged with a specific offense recognized in international law?
2. How far should we go in granting civil liberties to possible terrorists who are being held in prisons abroad? How should they be treated?
3. Do you believe that the way we treat terrorists reflects unfavorably on our nation in the "court of world opinion"?

CHAPTER NINE

Welfare and Social Justice

- Transfer Payments
- Does Welfare Work?
- Why Have Welfare?
- Distributive Justice
- Equality, Need, and Merit
- Libertarianism, Welfare Liberalism, and Socialism
- Arguments for Welfare
- Arguments against Welfare

JOHN HOSPERS **What Libertarianism Is**
TRUDY GOVIER **The Right to Eat and the Duty to Work**
KAI NIELSEN **Radical Egalitarianism**
CHARLES MURRAY **Choosing a Future**

CASE PRESENTATIONS: • *Marta Green* • *The Poorest Place in America* • *Welfare as We've Begun to Know It* • *The Women of Project Match*

ALTHOUGH THE U.S. presidential campaign of 1992 was waged over many issues, perhaps the most memorable campaign promise came from the eventual winner, Democrat Bill Clinton, who pledged to "end welfare as we know it." By "welfare," he meant Aid to Families with Dependent Children (AFDC), a program of assistance for low-income, single parents that dates back to Franklin Roosevelt's New Deal of the 1930s. And by ending "welfare as we know it," Clinton meant changing the program rather than abolishing it. Two particular changes were key to his plan: (1) to provide job training for welfare recipients and (2) to set a two-year limit on the time they could spend on welfare. If at the end of two years the welfare recipient could not find a job in the private sector, she would have to accept a community service job from the government or be left to her own devices.

Clinton's proposal marked a sharp turnaround from the legacy of Lyndon Johnson's Great Society of the 1960s. Not only did Johnson greatly expand AFDC, but he also instituted a number of other anti-poverty programs, including Medicaid, food stamps, Head Start, and a variety of housing programs for the poor. The reasons for the turnaround are many, but they can be quickly summarized: For a small but significant portion of welfare recipients, AFDC did not seem to be working as intended.

From its inception, AFDC was always intended as a temporary helping hand to single mothers and their children. In Roosevelt's time, that meant widows and orphans in the vast majority of cases. Over the years, however, it came to mean an increasing number of women whose husbands had left them, and then, more recently, a startling rise in the number of mothers who had never been married. Many of these unwed mothers were teenaged, poor, and undereducated, and some continued to have children out of wedlock. The result in such cases came to be known as welfare dependence. Rather than serving as a temporary helping hand for these young single mothers, AFDC became a way of life.

That was the problem Clinton's proposal was meant to solve. His goal, then, was not to end welfare but to end welfare dependence. And on August 22, 1996, Clinton signed into law a bill that did abolish AFDC, replacing it with a program called Temporary Assistance for Needy Families (TANF). For the first time in six decades, the federal government would no longer guarantee welfare payments to needy families. Instead, it would supply block grants (lump-sum payments) to the states and allow them considerable freedom in setting welfare policy. The new law also placed restrictions on length of benefits, setting a five-year limit per family and requiring recipients to find work within two years. These are maximum limits. States are free to require recipients to find work in a shorter time, and they are also free to limit duration on welfare to fewer years.

Much controversy surrounds the new law. While most attention goes to critics who charge that the law is too harsh, other critics charge that the law does not go far enough. Some have called for the abolition of other anti-poverty programs. What these critics object to is a whole class of programs known as *transfer payments.*

TRANSFER PAYMENTS

AFDC was one of many federal programs that relied on transfer payments to help the needy. A **transfer payment**, as the term implies, involves the transfer of wealth from one segment of the population to another through taxation and dispersal. In the case of AFDC, the transfer payment came in the form of cash benefits. Other cash benefits included earned income tax credits, which provided generous tax refunds to the working poor, and Supplemental Security Income. But in other cases, benefits came in the form of such services as medical care (for instance, Medicaid and community health centers), low-rent public housing, food (from programs like food stamps and the School Lunch Program), job training, and education (Head Start and Pell grants, for instance).

TANF continues to provide many cash benefits, while also requiring participation in Work First programs and limiting participation to no more than five years. Comparisons with previous cash outlays under AFDC are difficult, as much of the TANF funding is provided in block grants to the states, with considerable discretion on how they use the funds. Funds are typically provided for childcare expenses, education costs, job training, transportation, housing vouchers, and food stamps. Medicaid, however, is not available to all families in TANF, but only to those who would have been eligible under the old AFDC eligibility rules. In some cases, subsidies are provided to employers who hire persons in the TANF program. The federal government also provided $100 million in bonus grants to five states with the largest decrease in the percentage of births to unwed mothers from 1995 to 1998. Bonuses also have been paid to the states with the best improvement in such measures as job entry, job retention, and earnings gains by participants in TANF.[1]

In a report to Congress in 2001, the Congressional Research Service reported that families on welfare had plunged 50 percent since TANF was enacted in 1996 but also noted that this was assisted by the strong economy in those years. In June 2000, 2.208 million families were participating in TANF, down 2.9 million (57 percent) from the record-high level in AFDC in 1994, when 5.084 million families received benefits. The number of people receiving food stamps also declined dramatically from 28 million in 1994, the peak year, to 17 million in 2000, a 39 percent drop. The percentage of women with children in the work force has also increased from 62 percent in 1994 to 75 percent in 1999, a 21 percent increase.

In extensive congressional hearings on the renewal of TANF, many positive results were reported, along with some concerns.[2] Many people have now used their entire lifetime benefits of five years provided under TANF, and critics worry that they will slip into extreme poverty without government help, especially in a period with declining employment opportunities. According to the U.S. Department of Commerce, the nation's official poverty rate rose from 11.7 percent in 2001 (32.9 million people) to 12.1 percent in 2002 (34.6 million people).[3] The Census Bureau defined poverty in 2002, for one adult and one child, as $12,400 per year, and for one adult and two children as $14,494. The poverty rate has continued to climb in the years since, to 12.7 in 2004, with the highest rates of increase among non-Hispanic whites. Critics of TANF note that, despite its success in moving people off welfare, it has not succeeded in bringing people out of poverty. In all but a few states, the rate of unwed births has increased since the passage of TANF, not decreased. It also appears that many of the people remaining in TANF have serious health problems, including mental health problems, and are unable to work at any job.

The original TANF was set to expire in 2002. For the next several years, Congress could not agree on revisions, so it simply extended the original legislation. TANF was finally passed into law on February 8, 2006, adding funds for the Healthy Marriage Initiative. New data ten years after the original passage of TANF suggest that only 60 percent of former recipients are now employed, with most earning between $6 and $8.50 an hour. Of the remaining 40 percent who lost their TANF eligibility, many suffer from mental and physical disabilities, domestic violence, learning disabilities, and poor literacy and skill levels, according to the Center on Budget and Policy Priorities.

DOES WELFARE WORK?

Franklin Roosevelt's New Deal was a response to the Great Depression, which at its depth saw as much as a third of the nation's labor force unemployed. Lyndon Johnson's Great Society, on the other hand, came during a period of national prosperity.

---

[1]Vee Burke, "IB93034: Welfare Reform: An Issue Overview," Congressional Research Service, March 15, 2001.

[2]Hearing on Welfare Reform, Subcommittee on Human Resources of the Committee on Ways and Means, House of Representatives, 107th Cong., 1st Sess., March 15, 2001.

[3]"Poverty, Income See Slight Changes; Child Poverty Rate Unchanged, Census Bureau Reports," *U.S Department of Commerce News*, September 26, 2003.

It was inspired in part by a particular book, Michael Harrington's *The Other America*. Harrington's central thesis was that certain segments of the U.S. population are so economically depressed that they constitute pockets of poverty that remain unaffected by economic growth in the country as a whole. The economy expands, new jobs are created, but people trapped in these pockets of poverty remain unemployed and poor. If they are to be lifted out of poverty, the government must help them through specific programs.

In the 1980s, another influential book came along with a conflicting message. That book was Charles Murray's *Losing Ground*, which argued that anti-poverty programs like the Great Society's actually encourage poverty rather than fight it. Part of his argument was statistical. Although the Great Society showed initial success in reducing poverty, the progress soon stopped. As benefits increased in the 1970s, the book argued, so did the number of people whose income placed them below the poverty line. The number of births to unwed mothers also rose during that time, as did the number of households headed by single women. Most disturbingly, the largest rise in single-woman households was among the poor.

Of course, such statistics lend themselves to a variety of interpretations. Why blame welfare programs for the rise in poverty and single-female households? Murray's answer is this: In certain circumstances, it is *rational* for a young, pregnant woman to keep her child and go on welfare. Suppose she is undereducated and comes from a poor family that wants her out of the house. Suppose further that she wants to leave the house as much as her family wants her out. If she aborts her pregnancy or gives the child up for adoption, she will have to support herself with a minimum-wage job. But if she keeps the child and goes on AFDC, she also gets her own apartment in addition to many other benefits. What about marrying the baby's father? That option is not always available, of course, but even when it is, she may be economically better off remaining single and accepting welfare. In either case, accepting welfare is the rational choice.

Murray's book proved to be highly controversial. For one thing, critics charge, it assumes that women bear out-of-wedlock children for economic benefit when many other factors, psychological and social, may be at work. Critics also argue that it plays down other causes of poverty, from racism to changes in the American economy, and that it also plays down the enormous good welfare accomplishes for the many women who use it as a temporary helping hand while they prepare to support themselves and their children in the workplace. In addition, many critics dispute Murray's analysis of the statistics.

Equally controversial is Murray's concluding "thought experiment," which portrays an optimistic picture of a future in which federal welfare programs have been totally eliminated. Still, the book focused attention on important questions that never quite go away: What do we want from welfare programs? Who should benefit from them? Why have welfare at all? Does welfare advance the cause of justice or hinder it?

WHY HAVE WELFARE?

Through most of U.S. history, the question of welfare rarely, if ever, arose. Help for the needy was expected to come from such private sources as charities, churches, and families. The turning point was the Great Depression, and two of the most important reasons advanced were compassion and social stability. With the economy unable to produce enough jobs, a great number of willing and able workers found themselves unemployed through no fault of their own, and private sources could not provide sufficient aid. To many Americans, the situation was intolerable. Something had to be done, both to help the victims of the Depression and to prevent unprecedented social upheaval. The only place to look, they felt, was the federal government.

Despite the widely shared sense of emergency, Roosevelt's New Deal legislation produced considerable debate. With its regulations on industry and banking as well as its social welfare programs, it greatly expanded the role of government. Critics charged that individual rights were being violated, property rights in particular, and that the New Deal amounted to "creeping socialism." (In fact, many New Deal programs had long been advocated by the American Socialist Party.) Helping people at the expense of individual rights, these critics argued, was unjust. New Deal proponents, on the other hand, argued that failing to provide the needed measures was unjust.

As with many issues in this book, the competing views turn on differing conceptions of justice. In the case of welfare and other transfer payments, it is a matter of economic justice, also called **distributive justice.** How should the wealth of society be distributed?

DISTRIBUTIVE JUSTICE

In Part 1, we looked at various principles of social justice, many of which bear on the question of distributive justice and welfare. In this section and those that follow, we will see how.

The Entitlement Conception of Justice

When discussing individual rights in Part 1, we noted the influence of the English philosopher John Locke on the U.S. Founding Fathers. According to Locke, we are born with the natural rights to life, liberty, and property, which we are free to exercise as long as we do not interfere with the natural rights of others. We are also born with the natural right to protect those three rights. In joining together to create a government, we transfer certain powers to society as a whole. That is, the government acts as our agent in exercising those powers. Because we cannot transfer to the government any powers that are not rightfully ours, the role of government is severely limited. We can transfer powers of protection—police and judicial powers, most notably—but not the power to interfere with the individual property rights of others.

How does this bear on welfare and distributive justice? According to Robert Nozick, whom we also considered in Part 1, the answer is simple: Welfare is beyond the rightful powers of government. Since no one has a natural right to force others to give to charity, we cannot transfer that power to society as a whole. However well intentioned, transfer payments are no different from ordinary theft. To demand on threat of imprisonment that individuals pay taxes to support such programs is equivalent to holding a gun to their heads and demanding that they give to our favorite charities.

On this view, then, government should not be in the business of distributing wealth at all. Wealth is not, as Nozick puts it, "manna from heaven." It does not magically appear from the sky, belonging to no one. Instead, society's wealth already belongs to particular individuals who came by it either honestly or dishonestly, through either the legitimate exercise of their natural rights or the violation of the natural rights of others. If they came by it dishonestly, they should be punished and their ill-gotten gains returned to the rightful owners. Otherwise, it is rightfully theirs. They alone are *entitled* to it, and no one, including the government, has the right to take it away from them without their consent. Thus, Nozick calls his view the **entitlement** conception of justice.

Justice as Fairness

We also looked at the views of John Rawls in Part 1. Rawls rejects the notion of natural rights. To him, social justice is a matter of fairness, in which case the just distribution of wealth is the fairest distribution. How do we decide on the fairest distribution?

Rawls's answer goes like this: Societies operate according to certain fundamental rules, and it is up to the members of society to set those rules. One such fundamental rule governs the distribution of wealth. If the rule is to be fair, it must give no member of society unfair advantage over any other members. And we can guarantee that outcome by requiring that the rule be acceptable to all members of society without knowing how the rule will work out for them. That is, they will know how wealth will be distributed among different segments of the population but not which segment they will belong to. In that case, they must be willing to accept the rule no matter what segment they will belong to.

Would an entitlement rule like Nozick's pass that test? Rawls says no because it allows for unacceptably large gaps between rich and poor. We would not know whether we will have the high-paying jobs that will make us wealthy or the low-paying jobs that will leave us unable to support our families. Nor would we know whether we will find ourselves impoverished due to a sudden loss of work or some other catastrophe. As long as we don't know where we will end up, we will demand a rule that allows every member of society a sufficient share of the wealth.

One way to accomplish this goal (Rawls's preferred way) is through transfer payments. Those nearer to the top will be taxed to supplement the incomes of the poor.

EQUALITY, NEED, AND MERIT

If we accept the justice of transfer payments, we still have to determine how generous to make the payments and under what circumstances to pay them out. That is, we will need to select a *principle* of distribution. The three most commonly cited are the principles of equality, need, and merit.

Equality

According to the **equality principle** of distribution, everyone in society ought to end up with an equal share of the wealth. Why choose this principle? Because, proponents say, when it comes to sharing the wealth, all humans deserve to be treated equally. The fact that someone is better looking than the norm (or a better athlete or musician), or lucky enough to be born into a wealthy family (or marry into one), does not make that person more deserving of wealth than others less fortunate. In that case, taxes and transfer payments should be set at rates that guarantee an equal distribution of wealth for all.

Whatever initial appeal this principle may have, at least one problem is readily apparent for those who advocate it. An equal distribution of wealth can lead to significant inequalities among individual lives. Consider healthcare, for example. To achieve real equality between a healthy person and a person with kidney failure, say, the second will need far greater benefits than the first to cover the cost of dialysis. The same consideration also applies to many other areas of life, such as education. It costs far more to educate a child with serious learning disabilities than a child without them. That's why many transfers come in the form of services rather than cash benefits, to accommodate the differing needs of different individuals. It is also why people who lean toward equal distribution usually adopt a different but related principle as well—the principle of need.

Need

According to the principle of need, everyone has an equal right to have his or her economic needs satisfied, and wealth should therefore be distributed according to the economic needs of society's members. Advocates of this principle often combine it with the principle of equality. *Basic* needs like food, housing, education, and medical care are to be taken care of according to individual need, and the remaining wealth is to be distributed equally. Other advocates demand only that everyone's basic needs be met without asking for further redistribution. In both cases, the justification of the principle of need is the same. When it comes to basic needs, everyone deserves to be treated equally. No one's basic needs should go unmet.

Opponents of both principles—need and equality—cite a variety of objections. First, of course, there are Nozick's moral arguments that government should not be in the business of redistributing wealth at all. Other objections are more practical. Rawls, for example, argues that certain inequalities ought to be allowed because they are to everyone's advantage, even those at the bottom. If we are to have an adequate supply of surgeons, for example, we must compensate them for their years spent in medical school. Many critics also argue that distribution according to need and equality discourages hard work. Why put in extra hours if we will earn no extra compensation? Indeed, why work at all if the government will take care of our basic needs and guarantee us an income equal to the income of those who do work? And even if the government guarantees our basic needs only, won't many people see that as sufficient reason not to work?

What's missing, these objectors say, is recognition of individual *merit*. Those who deserve more wealth than others—those who have earned it—should have it.

Merit

The appeal of merit as a principle of distributing wealth is more than merely practical. To many people, it is a matter of simple justice. Why should Mary, who works to support herself and her family, pay taxes on her hard-earned income so that John, a total stranger who refuses to work at all, can enjoy a standard of living equal to her own? To ask this question is to distinguish between the deserving poor and the undeserving poor, between those who can't work and those who simply won't work, between those who work hard at low wages and those who choose to freeload. To people who make this distinction, the deserving poor should be helped by transfer payments but not the undeserving poor.

Although it may be difficult to sort out the deserving poor from the undeserving poor in particular cases, at least the underlying principle seems quite clear: Freeloaders don't merit our help. But many advocates of the merit principle want to extend it to cover all members of society. In that case, matters grow far less clear. The question now becomes: How are we to rank individual merit? To see how hard it is to answer this question, ask yourself who are the most meritorious among us. Those who work the hardest? Put in the most hours every week? Shoulder the heaviest responsibility? Those who perform the most difficult tasks? The least desirable tasks? The tasks most needed by society? Or is it the best educated? The most skilled? Or those who fill the most seats at a football stadium for a concert? Or create the greatest number of jobs? Depending on how we answer these questions, the most meritorious can be a laborer, a traveling salesperson, an airline mechanic, a school bus driver, a sanitation worker, the nation's president, the founders of such enterprises as Microsoft and McDonald's, a college professor, or U2's Bono.

As matters stand in the United States, we generally let economic forces sort out such questions. The law of supply and demand is supposed to set prices and wages throughout the economy, and those who command the highest pay on the open market are said to merit it. But even if we allow that the best ballplayers, for example, make the most money in their respective sports, we might still ask if they deserve on their merits to be paid a hundred times more money than the best elementary schoolteachers. We might also ask if a nonworking mother married to a millionaire merits a standard of living considerably higher than a nonworking mother on TANF.

The answer to both questions, many would argue, is no. But if the market doesn't always reward merit, we are faced with still another question: Can society do a better job of determining the relative merits of its members? On the answer to this question, there is no clear agreement.

LIBERTARIANISM, WELFARE LIBERALISM, AND SOCIALISM

Robert Nozick's view of economic justice is often called **libertarianism** because it seeks to maximize individual liberty. In general, the libertarian view is that all forms of coercion—except to prevent harm to life, liberty, and property—are wrong, whether they come from other individuals or from the government. Because we need a police force to protect life, liberty, and property, we may be coerced into paying taxes to support one. Because transfer payments are a matter of charity, not protection, we may not be coerced into paying taxes to support them.

John Rawls's view is often called *welfare liberalism* or **welfare capitalism.** Like Nozick, Rawls recognizes many property rights—the right to own a business, the right to hire and fire workers, and the right to make economic decisions according to market forces. In other words, he supports a *capitalist* economy. But he also supports transfer payments to rectify what he considers the economic injustices of capitalism.

One way of expressing the differences between the two positions goes like this: Are we to think of the wealth in society as merely the sum of individual wealth or as society's wealth as well. Nozick gives the former answer because of his belief in natural rights. Rawls gives the latter answer because of his belief that all members of society cooperate in the creation of that wealth. Why? Because what makes it possible for individuals to earn the wealth they do are the mutually agreed upon fundamental rules of society.

There is another possible reason for giving the same answer as Rawls. This reason comes from proponents of **socialism**. Socialists ask us to consider who creates the wealth in any society. Their answer is the workers, those who turn raw materials into commodities that are sold for profit. Then they ask us to consider who, in a capitalist society, gets rich off those profits. Their answer to this question is the owners, the top executives, the bankers, the landlords, and so forth—those who don't create any wealth. The real producers of wealth, in other words, don't own the wealth they produce. They receive only a small portion of it in the form of wages. Nor do they even own a guaranteed stake in their own jobs. After investing as many as twenty years or more of their lives to create enormous wealth for others, they can be laid off or fired by the bosses they made rich.

The socialist way of achieving economic justice is to replace a capitalist economy with a socialist economy. The change involves two major steps. First, the means of production are transferred from private ownership to public ownership. Factories, mines, and other productive property will be owned by society as a whole, not by private individuals. Second, the major economic decisions—the setting of prices, wages, employment levels, and production levels—become a matter of public policy instead of being set by market forces. In a perfect socialist economy, the policy will have three crucial features: Everyone's basic needs are taken care of, everyone is guaranteed a job, and everyone receives equal pay. Welfare in such an economy becomes unnecessary.

Why adopt such sweeping measures? First, proponents argue, socialism provides true economic justice and full social equality. Second, it maximizes freedom for everyone, not just the rich. The right to liberty, they claim, like the rights to life and property, is meaningless to people who can't afford a decent standard of living. Third, socialism extends democracy from the political realm to the economic realm. Not only does everyone have an equal say in how political decisions are made, but everyone has an equal say in how major economic decisions are made as well. Fourth, it replaces the indignity of welfare with the dignity of work.

Socialism's critics raise a number of objections, many of which we have already discussed. The objections include the libertarian arguments based on liberty and natural rights, plus the moral and practical objections to the need and equality principles of distribution. Another important criticism concerns the relative merits of planned economies and market economies. Planned economies, critics say, do not work as well as market economies. As evidence, they point to the failures of Eastern Europe's planned economies, which are now being converted to market economies. They also point to the many socialist parties in Western Europe that have shifted policies in favor of a market-oriented approach.

ARGUMENTS FOR WELFARE

1. ***You can't let people starve.***

POINT: "You can't just let people starve; it's as simple as that. And you can't leave them homeless, either, or make them go without adequate healthcare and clothing. Food, housing, healthcare, and clothing are the very basics of human existence. Without them, the promise of life, liberty, and the pursuit of happiness is empty."

COUNTERPOINT: "Of course our basic needs are important, but that's not the real issue. The real issue is: Who's responsible for making sure that their needs are met? And the answer is obvious. We're all responsible for ourselves. It's up to every one of us to see that our basic needs are met. If you're out of work, get yourself a job—any job. If you can't afford children, don't have them. And most important, if you're young, stay in school."

2. ***Society is responsible for helping the unfortunate.***

POINT: "You make it sound as though it's the fault of the poor that they're poor, as though they all deserve their poverty. Maybe that's true in some cases, but look around you. If you do, you'll see people struggling to get by on inadequate incomes, people thrown out of work through no fault of their own, and people struck by disabling injuries and illnesses. And you'll also see people who never had a fair chance to begin with because they grew up in hopeless poverty or because they went to schools that couldn't give them a decent education. These unfortunates were let down by society, and it's up to all of us to give them a helping hand."

COUNTERPOINT: "Look, I'm not in favor of cutting off all kinds of help to every person who needs it. I'm not saying we should do away with unemployment compensation for people who are laid off. And I'm not saying we should cut off Social Security disability payments, either. Those programs are insurance, not welfare, and the only thing I'm talking about is welfare. If *you* want to help those 'unfortunates' who 'grew up in hopeless poverty,' go right ahead. That's what private charities are for. But don't force everyone else to help them out, especially when we see how many other people there are who grew up in poverty and turned out to be productive members of society."

3. ***Ending welfare will hurt innocent children.***

POINT: "One thing you're forgetting is the children of the poor. When you talk about cutting off welfare, you're talking about cutting off TANF, and the main recipients of TANF are innocent children. You can't blame them for their predicament, can you?"

COUNTERPOINT: "Of course not, but the answer to that problem is to stop encouraging kids to have kids, and that's exactly what TANF does—encourage kids to have kids. Have a kid, you get a place to live and a steady income. Have another one, you get a raise. I know it sounds harsh, but the only way to turn the situation around is to send poor single teenagers a message—if you have children out of wedlock, you're on your own. As for the illegitimate children already with us, there's plenty we can do. The mothers' families can take care of them, they can be put up for adoption, and private charities can give them a helping hand."

4. ***Poverty breeds other social problems.***

POINT: "Poverty is everybody's problem, not just the poor's. Where you find poverty, you find crime. Where you find poverty, you find contagious diseases. You also find drug use, fear, despair, and a terrible waste of human resources. Poverty is ruining our great cities, and the problems associated with it—street gangs, for instance—are spreading into small towns throughout the country. It's in everyone's interest to eradicate poverty."

COUNTERPOINT: "I couldn't agree with you more. It's your next step I disagree with, that welfare is the solution to all those problems. With decades of evidence staring us in the face, anyone can see that it isn't."

ARGUMENTS AGAINST WELFARE

1. ***Welfare is unjust.***

POINT: "The first thing to point out about welfare is that it's a violation of individual freedom and individual rights, pure and simple. What's mine is mine, and no one has the right to take it away from me. Don't get me wrong. I'm not in favor of selfishness. I think everyone should give to charity. I certainly do. But like everyone else, I have the right to give to the charities of my own choosing. I even have the right not to give at all if I don't want to. Selfishness may be immoral, but so are a lot of other things, like cheating at tennis. It's not government's job to outlaw either one of them. Government's job is to protect my rights, not to interfere with them."

COUNTERPOINT: "Don't we also have the right to live in dignity? The right to a decent standard of living? And don't those rights count at least as much as your property rights? Besides, where do these property rights come from? Where is it written that you're entitled to *everything* you make? After all, where would you be without the cooperation of society as a whole—without our public roads and airports, for instance, or our legal systems at the federal, state, and municipal levels, or our federal banking system? Society contributes in any number of ways. Asking you to help people who haven't benefited as much as you have isn't asking too much."

2. ***Welfare is bad social policy.***

POINT: "How much does welfare really help? There was a time when young single women didn't get pregnant, and in the rare cases that they did, they either married the father or put the baby up for adoption and went on with their lives. They finished school or they found jobs. Now they're getting pregnant in record numbers, and instead of choosing marriage or adoption, they have the baby and go on welfare. Not only that, but they stay on welfare and continue to have babies. In the old days, illegitimate births were rare, and the women who had them could salvage their lives. Now, with all the welfare benefits available, illegitimate children are all too common, and unwed mothers end up dependent on welfare."

COUNTERPOINT: "I won't deny that welfare dependence is a problem, but you have to look at the larger picture. First of all, most welfare recipients don't end up dependent on welfare. Second, you can't blame welfare alone for the rise in out-of-wedlock births. Do you really think teenage girls have future welfare benefits on their minds when they engage in sex? Do you really think the only reason they keep their children is the money? There are a lot of factors that contribute to teenage sex, from abuse in the home and the need for love to a lack of parental supervision and a general decline in values. And just as many factors contribute to a single woman's decision to keep the child if she becomes pregnant, including the same need for love and attention, the need for a feeling of self-worth, and all the satisfactions of motherhood. The way to fight welfare dependence is through welfare reform, not abolition. We have to make it easier to get off."

3. ***Welfare removes stigmas that uphold important values.***

POINT: "We both agree that it's better to work than receive welfare. We also agree that illegitimacy is a serious problem among the young and poor. But one of the biggest flaws of welfare is that it makes being a single mother on welfare an acceptable lifestyle. There used to be a stigma attached to having illegitimate children. Pregnant teenagers were sent to homes for unwed mothers and kept out of sight. There was a stigma attached to taking handouts too. People were expected to earn their own way. That's a large part of what human dignity was about, and what it should still be about. But now those stigmas are gone. We tell kids that getting pregnant when they're still in school is nothing to be ashamed of, that it's fine to set up house at taxpayer expense. Maybe they're not thinking about welfare when they become pregnant, but you can't deny that welfare produces enough role models for them in poor neighborhoods."

COUNTERPOINT: "Do you really want to make these young girls ashamed of themselves? To make them outcasts? I'd say they have enough problems already. Besides, abolishing welfare won't bring back any stigmas, especially to single motherhood. Let's face it. Single motherhood is a fact of life throughout society."

4. ***Welfare rewards fraud and freeloading.***

POINT: "What about fraud and freeloading? It's bad enough that the rest of us have to work to support the people you call unfortunate victims, but even you have to admit that a lot of cheating goes on. Will welfare reform stop people from hiding their incomes to keep the welfare checks coming in? Will it purge the welfare rolls of every freeloader who has no excuse not to be working? Will it guarantee that those of us who work for a living won't be supporting drug habits?"

COUNTERPOINT: "No, probably not. You'll find abuses in every government program. But that's no excuse to penalize honest welfare recipients, especially the children."

What Libertarianism Is

JOHN HOSPERS

In the following essay, John Hospers, professor *emeritus* of philosophy at the University of Southern California, both defines and defends the libertarian view. Central to libertarianism, he says, is the doctrine that by right every individual is in charge of his or her own life. We all have the right to live as we choose, as long as we don't infringe on the rights of others to live as they choose. In particular, we have the rights to life, liberty, and property, and each of these

---

From John Hospers, "What Libertarianism Is," in *The Libertarian Alternative,* ed. Tibor R. Machan.

rights serves as a "no trespassing" sign against interference by governments as well as other individuals. The only proper role of government is to protect those rights.

In discussing the right to property, Hospers calls it the most misunderstood and unappreciated of all rights and the right most violated by governments. It is not, he says, the right to take property but the right to obtain it without coercion. When people claim other property rights, such as the right to welfare or the right to housing at others' expense, they are claiming rights that don't exist.

The political philosophy that is called libertarianism (from the Latin *libertas,* liberty) is the doctrine that every person is the owner of his own life, and that no one is the owner of anyone else's life; and that consequently every human being has the right to act in accordance with his own choices, unless those actions infringe on the equal liberty of other human beings to act in accordance with their choices.

There are several other ways of stating the same libertarian thesis:

1. *No one is anyone else's master, and no one is anyone else's slave.* Since I am the one to decide how my life is to be conducted, just as you decide about yours, I have no right (even if I had the power) to make you my slave and be your master, nor have you the right to become the master by enslaving me. Slavery is *forced* servitude, and since no one owns the life of anyone else, no one has the right to enslave another. Political theories past and present have traditionally been concerned with who should be the master (usually the king, the dictator, or government bureaucracy) and who should be the slaves, and what the extent of the slavery should be. Libertarianism holds that no one has the right to use force to enslave the life of another, or any portion or aspect of that life.

2. *Other men's lives are not yours to dispose of.* I enjoy seeing operas; but operas are expensive to produce. Opera-lovers often say, "The state (or the city, etc.) should subsidize opera, so that we can all see it. Also it would be for people's betterment, cultural benefit, etc." But what they are advocating is nothing more or less than legalized plunder. They can't pay for the productions themselves, and yet they want to see opera, which involves a large number of people and their labor; so what they are saying in effect is, "Get the money through legalized force. Take a little bit more out of every worker's paycheck every week to pay for the operas we want to see." But I have no right to take by force from the workers' pockets to pay for what I want.

Perhaps it would be better if he *did* go to see opera—then I should try to convince him to go voluntarily. But to take the money from him forcibly, because in my opinion it would be good for *him,* is still seizure of his earnings, which is plunder.

Besides, if I have the right to force him to help pay for my pet projects, hasn't he equally the right to force me to help pay for his? Perhaps he in turn wants the government to subsidize rock-and-roll, or his new car, or a house in the country? If I have the right to milk him, why hasn't he the right to milk me? If I can be a moral cannibal, why can't he too?

We should beware of the inventors of utopias. They would remake the world according to their vision—with the lives and fruits of the labor of other human beings. Is it someone's utopian vision that others should build pyramids to beautify the landscape? Very well, then other men should provide the labor; and if he is in a position of political power, and he can't get men to do it voluntarily, then he must *compel* them to "cooperate"—i.e., he must enslave them.

A hundred men might gain great pleasure from beating up or killing just one insignificant human being; but other men's lives are not theirs to dispose of. "In order to achieve the worthy goals of the next five-year-plan, we must forcibly collectivize the peasants . . ." but other men's lives are not theirs to dispose of. Do you want to occupy, rent-free, the mansion that another man has worked for twenty years to buy? But other men's lives are not yours to dispose of. Do you want operas so badly that everyone is forced to work harder to pay for their subsidization through taxes? But other men's lives are not yours to dispose of. Do you want to have free medical care at the expense of other people, whether they wish to provide it or not? But this would require them to work longer for you whether they want to or not, and other men's lives are not yours to dispose of.

> The freedom to engage in any type of enterprise, to produce, to own and control property, to buy and sell on the free market, is derived from the rights to life, liberty, and property... which are stated in the Declaration of Independence... [but] when a government guarantees a "right" to an education or parity on farm products or a guaranteed annual income, it is staking a claim on the property of one group of citizens for the sake of another group. In short, it is violating one of the fundamental rights it was instituted to protect.[1]

3. *No human being should be a nonvoluntary mortgage on the life of another.* I cannot claim your life, your work, or the products of your effort as mine. The fruit of one man's labor should not be fair game for every freeloader who comes along and demands it as his own. The orchard that has been carefully grown, nurtured, and harvested by its owner should not be ripe for the plucking for any bypasser who has a yen for the ripe fruit. The wealth that some men have produced should not be fair game for looting by government, to be used for whatever purposes its representatives determine, no matter what their motives in so doing may be. The theft of your money by a robber is not justified by the fact that he used it to help his injured mother.

It will already be evident that libertarian doctrine is embedded in a view of the rights of man. Each human being has the right to live his life as he chooses, compatibly with the equal right of all other human beings to live their lives as they choose.

All man's rights are implicit in the above statement. Each man has the right to life: any attempt by others to take it away from him, or even to injure him, violates this right, through the use of coercion against him. Each man has the right to liberty: to conduct his life in accordance with the alternatives open to him without coercive action by others. And every man has the right to property: to work to sustain his life (and the lives of whichever others he chooses to sustain, such as his family) and to retain the fruits of his labor.

People often defend the rights of life and liberty but denigrate property rights, and yet the right to property is as basic as the other two, indeed, without property rights no other rights are possible. Depriving you of property is depriving you of the means by which you live.

> ...All that which an individual possesses by right (including his life and property) are morally his to use, dispose of and even destroy, as he sees fit. If I own my life, then it follows that I am free to associate with whom I please and not to associate with whom I please. If I own my knowledge and services it follows that I may ask any compensation I wish for providing them for another, or I may abstain from providing them at all, if I so choose. If I own my house, it follows that I may decorate it as I please and live in it with whom I please. If I control my own business, it follows that I may charge what I please for my products or services, hire whom I please and not hire whom I please. All that which I own in fact, I may dispose of as I choose to in reality. For anyone to attempt to limit my freedom to do so is to violate my rights.
>
> Where do my rights end? Where yours begin. I may do anything I wish with my own life, liberty and property without your consent; but I may do nothing with your life, liberty and property without your consent. If we recognize the principle of man's rights, it follows that the individual is sovereign of the domain of his own life and property, and is sovereign of no other domain. To attempt to interfere forcibly with another's use, disposal or destruction of his own property is to initiate force against him and to violate his rights.

I have no right to decide how you should spend your time or your money. I can make that decision for myself, but not for you, my neighbor. I may deplore your choice of life-style, and I may talk with you about it provided you are willing to listen to me. But I have no right to use force to change it. Nor have I the right to decide how you should spend the money you have earned. I may appeal to you to give it to the Red Cross, and you may prefer to go to prizefights. But that is your decision, and however much I may chafe about it I do not have the right to interfere forcibly with it, for example by robbing you in order to use the money in accordance with *my* choices. (If I have the right to rob you, have you also the right to rob me?)

When I claim a right, I carve out a niche, as it were, in my life, saying in effect, "This activity I must be able to perform without interference from others. For you and everyone else, this is off limits." And so I put up a "no trespassing" sign, which marks off the area of my right. Each individual's right is his "no trespassing" sign in relation to me and others. I may not encroach upon his domain any more than he upon mine, without my consent. Every right entails a duty, true—but the duty is only that of *forbearance*—that is, of *refraining* from violating the other person's right. If you have a right to life, I have no right to take your life; if you have a right to the products of your labor (property), I have no right to take it from you without your consent. The non-violation of these rights will not guarantee you protection against natural catastrophes such as floods and earthquakes, but it will protect you against the aggressive activities of *other men*. And rights, after all, have to do with one's relations to other human beings, not with one's relations to physical nature.

Nor were these rights created by government; governments—some governments, obviously not all—*recognize* and *protect* the rights that individuals already have. Governments regularly forbid homicide and theft; and, at a more advanced stage, protect individuals against such things as libel and breach of contract.

> It cannot be by chance that they thus agree. They agree because the alleged creating of rights [by government] was nothing else than giving formal sanction and better definition to those assertions of claims and recognitions of claims which naturally originate from the individual desires of men who have to live in presence of one another.
>
> . . . Those who hold that life is valuable, hold, by implication, that men ought not to be prevented from carrying on life-sustaining activities. . . . Clearly the conception of "natural rights" originates in recognition of the truth that if life is justifiable, there must be a justification for the performance of acts essential to its preservation; and, therefore, a justification of those liberties and claims which make such acts possible.
>
> . . . To recognize and enforce the rights of individuals, is at the same time to recognize and enforce the conditions to a normal social life.[2]

The *right to property* is the most misunderstood and unappreciated of human rights, and it is one most constantly violated by governments. "Property" of course does not mean only real estate; it includes anything you can call your own—your clothing, your car, your jewelry, your books and papers.

The right of property is not the right to just *take* it from others, for this would interfere with *their* property rights. It is rather the right to work for it, to obtain non-coercively, the money or services which you can present in voluntary exchange.

The right to property is consistently underplayed by intellectuals today, sometimes even frowned upon, as if we should feel guilty for upholding such a right in view of all the poverty in the world. But the right to property is absolutely basic. It is your hedge against the future. It is your assurance that what you have worked to earn will still be there, and be yours, when you wish or need to use it, especially when you are too old to work any longer. . . .

Indeed, only if property rights are respected is there any point to planning for the future and working to achieve one's goals. *Property rights are what makes long-range planning possible*—the kind of planning which is a distinctively human endeavor, as opposed to the day-by-day activity of the lion who hunts, who depends on the supply of game tomorrow but has no real insurance against starvation in a day or a week. Without the right to property, the right tolife itself amounts to little: how can you sustain your life if you cannot plan ahead? and how can you plan ahead if the fruits of your labor can at any moment be confiscated by government? . . .

"But why have *individual* property rights? Why not have lands and houses owned by everybody together?" Yes, this involves no violation of individual rights, as long as everybody consents to this arrangement and no one is forced to join it. The parties to it may enjoy the communal living enough (at least for a time) to overcome certain inevitable problems: that some will work and some not, that some will achieve more in an hour than others can do in a day, and still they will all get the same income. The few who do the most will in the end consider themselves "workhorses" who do the work of two or three or twelve, while the others will be "freeloaders" on the efforts of these few. But as long as they can get out of the arrangement if they no longer like it, no violation of rights is involved. They got in voluntarily, and they can get out voluntarily; no one has used force.

"But why not say that everybody owns everything? That we *all* own everything there is?"

To some this may have a pleasant ring—but let us try to analyze what it means. If everybody owns everything, then everyone has an equal right to go everywhere, do what he pleases, take what he likes, destroy if he wishes, grow crops or burn them, trample them under, and so on. Consider what it would be like in practice. Suppose you have saved money to buy a house for yourself and your family. Now suppose that the principle, "everybody owns everything," becomes adopted. Well then, why shouldn't every itinerant hippie just come in and take over, sleeping in your beds and eating in your kitchen and not bothering to replace the food supply or clean up the mess? After all, it belongs to all of us, doesn't it? So we have just as much right to it as you, the buyer, have. What happens if we *all* want to sleep in the bedroom and there's not room for all of us? Is it the strongest who wins?

What would be the result? Since no one would be responsible for anything, the property would soon be destroyed, the food used up, the facilities nonfunctional. Beginning as a house that *one* family could use, it would end up as a house that *no one* could use. And if the principle continued to be adopted, no one would build houses any more—or anything else. What for? They would only be occupied and used by others, without remuneration. . . .

GOVERNMENT

Government is the most dangerous institution known to man. Throughout history it has violated the rights of men more than any individual or group of individuals could do: it has killed people, enslaved them, sent them to forced labor and concentration camps, and regularly robbed and pillaged them of the fruits of their expended labor. Unlike individual criminals, government has the power to arrest and try; unlike individual criminals, it can surround and encompass a person totally, dominating every aspect of one's life, so that one has no recourse from it but to leave the country (and in totalitarian nations even that is prohibited). Government throughout history has a much sorrier record than any individual, even that of a ruthless mass murderer. The signs we see on bumper stickers are chillingly accurate: "Beware: the Government is Armed and Dangerous."

The only proper role of government, according to libertarians, is that of the protector of the citizen against aggression by other individuals. The government, of course, should never initiate aggression; its proper role is as the embodiment of the *retaliatory* use of force against anyone who initiates its use.

If each individual had constantly to defend himself against possible aggressors, he would have to spend a considerable portion of his life in target practice, karate exercises, and other means of self-defenses, and even so he would probably be helpless against groups of individuals who might try to kill, maim, or rob him. He would have little time for cultivating those qualities which are essential to civilized life, nor would improvements in science, medicine, and the arts be likely to occur. The function of government is to take this responsibility off his shoulders: the government undertakes to defend him against aggressors and to punish them if they attack him. When the government is effective in doing this, it enables the citizen to go about his business unmolested and without constant fear for his life. To do this, of course, government must have physical power—the police, to protect the citizen from aggression within its borders, and the armed forces, to protect him from aggressors outside. Beyond that, the government should not intrude upon his life, either to run his business, or adjust his daily activities, or prescribe his personal moral code.

Government, then, undertakes to be the individual's protector; but historically governments have gone far beyond this function. Since they already have the physical power, they have not hesitated to use it for purposes far beyond that which was entrusted to them in the first place. Undertaking initially to protect its citizens against aggression, it has often itself become an aggressor—a far greater aggressor, indeed, than the criminals against whom it was supposed to protect its citizens. Governments have done what no private citizens can do: arrest and imprison individuals without a trial and send them to slave labor camps. Government must have power in order to be effective—and yet the very means by which alone it can be effective make it vulnerable to the abuse of power, leading to managing the lives of individuals and even inflicting terror upon them.

What then should be the function of government? In a word, the *protection of human rights.*

1. *The right to life:* libertarians support all such legislation as will protect human beings against the use of force by others, for example, laws against killing, attempted killing, maiming, beating, and all kinds of physical violence.

2. *The right to liberty:* there should be no laws compromising in any way freedom of speech, of the press, and of peaceable assembly. There should be no censorship of ideas, books, films, or of anything else by government.

3. *The right to property:* libertarians support legislation that protects the property rights of individuals against confiscation, nationalization, eminent domain, robbery, trespass, fraud and misrepresentation, patent and copyright, libel and slander.

Someone has violently assaulted you. Should he be legally liable? Of course. He has violated one of your rights. He has knowingly injured you, and since he has initiated aggression against you he should be made to expiate.

Someone has negligently left his bicycle on the sidewalk where you trip over it in the dark and injure yourself. He didn't do it intentionally; he didn't mean you any harm. Should he be legally liable? Of course; he has, however unwittingly, injured you, and since the injury is caused by him and you are the victim, he should pay.

Someone across the street is unemployed. Should you be taxed extra to pay for his expenses? Not at all. You have not injured him, you are not responsible for the fact that he is unemployed (unless you are a senator or bureaucrat who agitated for further curtailing of business, which legislation passed, with the result that your neighbor was laid off by the curtailed business). You may voluntarily wish to help him out, or better still, try to get him a job to put him on his feet again; but since you have initiated no aggressive act against him, and neither purposely nor accidentally injured him in any way, you should not be legally penalized for the fact of his unemployment. (Actually, it is just such penalties that increase unemployment.)

One man, A, works hard for years and finally earns a high salary as a professional man. A second man, B, prefers not to work at all, and to spend wastefully what money he has (through inheritance), so that after a year or two he has nothing left. At the end of this time he has a long siege of illness and lots of medical bills to pay. He demands that the bills be paid by the government—that is, by the taxpayers of the land, including Mr. A.

But of course B has no such right. He chose to lead his life in a certain way—that was his voluntary decision. One consequence of that choice is that he must depend on charity in case of later need. Mr. A chose not to live that way. (And if everyone lived like Mr. B, on whom would he depend in case of later need?) Each has a right to live in the way he pleases, but each must live with the consequences of his own decision (which, as always, fall primarily on himself). He cannot, in time of need, claim A's beneficence as his right....

Laws may be classified into three types: (1) laws protecting individuals against themselves, such as laws against fornication and other sexual behavior, alcohol, and drugs; (2) laws protecting individuals against aggressions by other individuals, such as laws against murder, robbery, and fraud; (3) laws requiring people to help one another; for example, all laws which rob Peter to pay Paul, such as welfare.

Libertarians reject the first class of laws totally. Behavior which harms no one else is strictly the individual's own affair. Thus, there should be no laws against becoming intoxicated, since whether or not to become intoxicated is the individual's own decision; but there should be laws against driving while intoxicated, since the drunken driver is a threat to every other motorist on the highway (drunken driving falls into type 2). Similarly, there should be no laws against drugs (except the prohibition of sale of drugs to minors) as long as the taking of these drugs poses no threat to anyone else. Drug addiction is a psychological problem to which no present solution exists. Most of the social harm caused by addicts, other than to themselves, is the result of thefts which they perform in order to continue their habit—and then the *legal* crime is the theft, not the addiction. The actual cost of heroin is about ten cents a shot; if it were legalized, the enormous traffic in illegal sale and purchase of it would stop, as well as the accompanying proselytization to get new addicts (to make more money for the pusher) and the thefts performed by addicts who often require eighty dollars a day just to keep up the habit. Addiction would not stop, but the crimes would: it is estimated that 75 percent of the burglaries in New York City today are performed by addicts, and all these crimes could be wiped out at one stroke through the legalization of drugs. (Only when the taking of drugs could be shown to constitute a threat to *others,* should it be prohibited by law. It is only laws protecting people against *themselves* that libertarians oppose.)

Laws should be limited to the second class only: aggression by individuals against other individuals. These are laws whose function is to protect human beings against encroachment by others; and this, as we have seen, is (according to libertarianism) the sole function of government.

Libertarians also reject the third class of laws totally: no one should be forced by law to help others, not even to tell them the time of day if requested, and certainly not to give them a portion of one's weekly paycheck. Governments, in the guise of humanitarianism, have given to some by taking from others (charging a "handling fee" in the process, which, because of the government's waste and inefficiency, sometimes is several hundred percent). And in so doing they have decreased incentive, violated the rights of individuals, and lowered the standard of living of almost everyone.

All such laws constitute what libertarians call *moral cannibalism.* A cannibal in the physical sense is a person who lives off the flesh of other human beings. A *moral* cannibal is one who believes he has a right to live off the "spirit" of other human beings—who believes that he has a moral claim on the productive capacity, time, and effort expended by others.

It has become fashionable to claim virtually everything that one needs or desires as one's *right.* Thus, many people claim that they have a right to a job, the right to free medical care, to free food and clothing, to a decent home, and so on. Now if one asks, apart from any specific context, whether it would be desirable if everyone had these things, one might well say yes. But there is a gimmick attached to each of them: *At whose expense?* Jobs, medical care, education, and so on, don't grow on trees. These are goods and services *produced only by men.* Who, then, is to provide them, and under what conditions?

If you have a right to a job, who is to supply it? Must an employer supply it even if he doesn't want to hire you? What if you are unemployable, or incurably lazy? (If you say "the government must supply it," does that mean that a job must be created for you which no employer needs done, and that you must be kept in it regardless of how much or little you work?) If the employer is forced to supply it at his expense even if he doesn't need you, then isn't *he* being enslaved to that extent? What ever happened to *his* right to conduct his life and his affairs in accordance with his choices?

If you have a right to free medical care, then, since medical care doesn't exist in nature as wild apples do, some people will have to supply it to you for free: that is, they will have to spend their time and money and energy taking care of you whether they want to or not. What ever happened to *their* right to conduct their lives as they see fit? Or do you have a right to violate theirs? Can there be a right to violate rights?

All those who demand this or that as a "free service" are consciously or unconsciously evading the fact that there is in reality no such thing as free services. All man-made goods and services are the result of human expenditure of time and effort. There is no such thing as "something for nothing" in this world. If you demand something free, you are demanding that other men give their time and effort to you without compensation. If they voluntarily choose to do this, there is no problem; but if you demand that they be *forced* to do it, you are interfering with their right not to do it if they so choose. "Swimming in this pool ought to be free!" says the indignant passerby. What he means is that others should build a pool, others should provide the materials, and still others should run it and keep it in functioning order, so that *he* can use it without fee. But what right has he to the expenditure of *their* time and effort? To expect something "for free" is to expect it *to be paid for by others* whether they choose to or not.

Many questions, particularly about economic matters, will be generated by the libertarian account of human rights and the role of government. Should government have no role in assisting the needy, in providing social security, in legislating minimum wages, in fixing prices and putting a ceiling on rents, in curbing monopolies, in erecting tariffs, in guaranteeing jobs, in managing the money supply? To these and all similar questions the libertarian answers with an unequivocal no.

"But then you'd let people go hungry," comes the rejoinder. This, the libertarian insists, is precisely what would not happen; with the restrictions removed, the economy would flourish as never before. With the controls taken off business, existing enterprises would expand and new ones would spring into existence satisfying more and more consumer needs; millions more people would be gainfully employed instead of subsisting on welfare, and all kinds of research and production, released from the stranglehold of government, would proliferate, fulfilling man's needs and desires as never before. It has always been so whenever government has permitted men to be free traders on a free market. But *why* this is so, and how the free market is the best solution to all problems relating to the material aspect of man's life, is another and far longer story. It is told in detail in chapters 3 to 9 of my book, *Libertarianism*.

NOTES

1. William W. Bayes, "What Is Property?" *The Freeman,* July 1970, p. 348.
2. Herbert Spencer, *The Man vs. the State* (1884; reprinted., Caldwell, Id.: Caxton Printers, 1940), p. 191.

QUESTIONS FOR ANALYSIS

1. Hospers says that no one has the right "to enslave the life of another, or any portion or aspect of that life." Libertarians argue that the portion of their lives they spend working to earn the taxes they pay to support welfare payments amounts to a term of enslavement. Do you agree?
2. According to Hospers, property rights make all other rights possible. Why? Do you agree? If so, do property rights have to be as strong as Hospers insists to preserve our other rights?
3. Hospers says our right to property, like our rights to life and liberty, was not created by governments. Where does it come from, then?
4. Why does Hospers think that the right to property is a right to individual ownership? Why does he reject the idea that land belongs to everybody?
5. Hospers calls government "the most dangerous institution known to man." Why? Is he right?
6. How could an advocate of welfare argue against Hospers?

The Right to Eat and the Duty to Work

TRUDY GOVIER

In the following essay, philosopher Trudy Govier examines three positions on welfare rights for the needy. The first is the libertarian position, which she calls the individualist view. The second, which she calls the permissive view, holds that everyone by legal right should have his or her basic needs satisfied, regardless of behavior. The third, which she calls the puritan view, holds that the legal right to welfare benefits should be conditional on the individual's willingness to work.

After surveying these three positions, Govier evaluates them. First, she asks which has the most desirable social consequences. (This question she calls the teleological appraisal.) Second, she asks which best serves social justice. In both cases, she concludes, the permissive view is the best of the three.

Although the topic of welfare is not one with which philosophers have often concerned themselves, it is a topic which gives rise to many complex and fascinating questions—some in the area of political philosophy, some in the area of ethics, and some of a more practical kind. The variety of issues related to the subject of welfare makes it particularly necessary to be clear just which issue one is examining in a discussion of welfare. In a recent book on the subject, Nicholas Rescher asks:

> In what respects and to what extent is society, working through the instrumentality of the state, responsible for the welfare of its members? What demands for the promotion of his welfare can an individual reasonably make upon his society? These are questions to which no answer can be given in terms of some *a priori* approach with reference to universal ultimates. Whatever answer can appropriately be given will depend, in the final analysis, on what the society decides it should be.[1]

Rescher raises this question only to avoid it. His response to his own question is that a society has all and only those responsibilities for its members that it thinks it has. Although this claim is trivially true as regards legal responsibilities, it is inadequate from a moral perspective. If one imagines the case of an affluent society which leaves the blind, the disabled, and the needy to die of starvation, the incompleteness of Rescher's account becomes obvious. In this imagined case one is naturally led to raise the question as to whether those in power ought to supply those in need with the necessities of life. Though the needy have no legal right to welfare benefits of any kind, one might very well say that they ought to have such a right. It is this claim which I propose to discuss here.[2]

I shall approach this issue by examining three positions which may be adopted in response to it. These are:

1. *The Individualist Position:* Even in an affluent society, one ought not to have any legal right to state-supplied welfare benefits.
2. *The Permissive Position:* In a society with sufficient resources, one ought to have an unconditional legal right to receive state-supplied welfare benefits. (That is, one's right to receive such benefits ought not to depend on one's behaviour; it should be guaranteed.)
3. *The Puritan Position:* In a society with sufficient resources, one ought to have a legal right to state-supplied welfare benefits; this

From Trudy Govier, "The Right to Eat and the Duty to Work," in *Philosophy of the Social Sciences,* vol. 5, pp. 363–375. © 1975 by Sage Publications, Inc. Reprinted by permission of Sage Publications, Inc.

right ought to be conditional, however, on one's willingness to work.

But before we examine these positions, some preliminary clarification must be attempted....

Welfare systems are state-supported systems which supply benefits, usually in the form of cash income, to those who are in need. Welfare systems thus exist in the sort of social context where there is some private ownership of property. If no one owned anything individually (except possibly his own body), and all goods were considered to be the joint property of everyone, then this type of welfare system could not exist. A state might take on the responsibility for the welfare of its citizens, but it could not meet this responsibility by distributing a level of cash income which such citizens would spend to purchase the goods essential for life. The welfare systems which exist in the western world do exist against the background of extensive private ownership of property. It is in this context that I propose to discuss moral questions about having a right to welfare benefits. By setting out my questions in this way, I do not intend to endorse the institution of private property, but only to discuss questions which many people find real and difficult in the context of the social organization which they actually do experience. The present analysis of welfare is intended to apply to societies which (*a*) have the institution of private property, if not for means of production, at least for some basic good; and (*b*) possess sufficient resources so that it is at least possible for every member of the society to be supplied with the necessities of life.

1 The Individualist View

It might be maintained that a person in need has no legitimate moral claim on those around him and that the hypothetical inattentive society which left its blind citizens to beg or starve cannot rightly be censured for doing so. This view, which is dramatically at odds with most of contemporary social thinking, lives on in the writings of Ayn Rand and her followers.[3] The Individualist sets a high value on uncoerced personal choice. He sees each person as a responsible agent who is able to make his own decisions and to plan his own life. He insists that with the freedom to make decisions goes responsibility for the consequences of those decisions. A person has every right, for example, to spend ten years of his life studying Sanskrit—but if, as a result of this choice, he is unemployable, he ought not to expect others to labour on his behalf. No one has a proper claim on the labour of another, or on the income ensuing from that labour, unless he can repay the labourer in a way acceptable to that labourer himself. Government welfare schemes provide benefits from funds gained largely by taxing earned income. One cannot "opt out" of such schemes. To the Individualist, this means that a person is forced to work part of his time for others.

Suppose that a man works forty hours and earns two hundred dollars. Under modern-day taxation, it may well be that he can spend only two-thirds of that money as he chooses. The rest is taken by government and goes to support programmes which the working individual may not himself endorse. The beneficiaries of such programmes—those beneficiaries who do not work themselves—are as though they have slaves working for them. Backed by the force which government authorities can command, they are able to exist on the earnings of others. Those who support them do not do so voluntarily, out of charity; they do so on government command.

> Someone across the street is unemployed. Should you be taxed extra to pay for his expenses? Not at all. You have not injured him, you are not responsible for the fact that he is unemployed (unless you are a senator or bureaucrat who agitated for further curtailing of business which legislation passed, with the result that your neighbour was laid off by the curtailed business). You may voluntarily wish to help him out, or better still, try to get him a job to put him on his feet again; but since you have initiated no aggressive act against him, and neither purposefully nor accidentally injured him in any way, you should not be legally penalized for the fact of his unemployment. [4]

The Individualist need not lack concern for those in need. He may give generously to charity; he might give more generously still, if his whole income were his to use, as he would like it to be.

He may also believe that, as a matter of empirical fact, existing government programmes do not actually help the poor. They support a cumbersome bureaucracy and they use financial resources which, if untaxed, might be used by those with initiative to pursue job-creating endeavours. The thrust of the Individualist's position is that each person owns his own body and his own labour; thus each person is taken to have a virtually unconditional right to the income which that labour can earn him in a free market place.[5] For anyone to pre-empt part of a worker's earnings without that worker's voluntary consent is tantamount to robbery. And the fact that the government is the intermediary through which this deed is committed does not change its moral status one iota.

On an Individualist's view, those in need should be cared for by charities or through other schemes to which contributions are voluntary. Many people may wish to insure themselves against unforeseen calamities and they should be free to do so. But there is no justification for non-optional government schemes financed by taxpayers' money....

2 The Permissive View

Directly contrary to the Individualist view of welfare is what I have termed the Permissive view. According to this view, in a society which has sufficient resources so that everyone could be supplied with the necessities of life, every individual ought to be given the legal right to social security, and this right ought not to be conditional in any way upon an individual's behavior. *Ex hypothesi* the society which we are discussing has sufficient goods to provide everyone with food, clothing, shelter and other necessities. Someone who does without these basic goods is scarcely living at all, and a society which takes no steps to change this state of affairs implies by its inaction that the life of such a person is without value. It does not execute him; but it may allow him to die. It does not put him in prison; but it may leave him with a life of lower quality than that of some prison inmates. A society which can rectify these circumstances and does not can justly be accused of imposing upon the needy either death or lifelong deprivation. And those characteristics which make a person needy—whether they be illness, old age, insanity, feeble-mindedness, inability to find paid work, or even poor moral character—are insufficient to make him deserve the fate to which an inactive society would in effect condemn him. One would not be executed for inability or failure to find paid work; neither should one be allowed to die for this misfortune or failing.

A person who cannot or does not find his own means of social security does not thereby forfeit his status as a human being. If other human beings, with physical, mental and moral qualities different from his, are regarded as having the right to life and to the means of life, then so too should he be regarded. A society which does not accept the responsibility for supplying such a person with the basic necessities of life is, in effect, endorsing a difference between its members which is without moral justification. . . .

The adoption of a Permissive view of welfare would have significant practical implications. If there were a legal right, unconditional upon behaviour, to a specified level of state-supplied benefits, then state investigation of the prospective welfare recipient could be kept to a minimum. Why he is in need, whether he can work, whether he is willing to work, and what he does while receiving welfare benefits are on this view quite irrelevant to his right to receive those benefits. A welfare recipient is a person who claims from his society that to which he is legally entitled under a morally based welfare scheme. The fact that he makes this claim licenses no special state or societal interference with his behaviour. If the Permissive view of welfare were widely believed, then there would be no social stigma attached to being on welfare. There is such a stigma, and many long-term welfare recipients are considerably demoralized by their dependent status.[6] These facts suggest that the Permissive view of welfare is not widely held in our society.

3 The Puritan View

This view of welfare rather naturally emerges when we consider that no one can have a right to something without someone else's, or some group of other persons', having responsibilities correlative to this right. In the case in which the right in question is a legal right to social security, the correlative responsibilities may be rather extensive. They have been deemed responsibilities of "the state." The state will require resources and funds to meet these responsibilities, and these do not emerge from the sky miraculously, or zip into existence as a consequence of virtually effortless acts of will. They are taken by the state from its citizens, often in the form of taxation on earned income. The funds given to the welfare recipient and many of the goods which he purchases with these funds are produced by other members of society, many of whom give a considerable portion of their time and their energy to this end. If a state has the moral responsibility to ensure the social security of its citizens then all the citizens of that state have the responsibility to provide state agencies with the means to carry out their duties. This responsibility, in our present contingent circumstances, seems to generate an obligation to *work*.

A person who works helps to produce the goods which all use in daily living and, when paid, contributes through taxation to government endeavours. The person who does not work, even though able to work, does not make his contribution to social efforts towards obtaining the means of life. He is not entitled to a share of the goods produced by others if he chooses not to take part in their labours. Unless he can show that there is a moral justification for his not making the sacrifice of time and energy which others make, he has no legitimate claim to welfare benefits. If he is disabled or unable to obtain work, he cannot work; hence he has no need to justify his failure to work. But if he does choose not to work, he would have to justify his choice by saying "others should sacrifice their time and energy for me; I have no need to sacrifice time and energy for them." This principle, a version of what Rawls refers to as a free-rider's principle, simply will not stand up to criticism.[7] To deliberately avoid working and benefit from the labours of others is morally indefensible.

Within a welfare system erected on these principles, the right to welfare is conditional upon one's satisfactorily accounting for his failure to obtain the necessities of life by his own efforts. Someone who is severely disabled mentally or physically, or who for some other reason cannot work, is morally entitled to receive welfare benefits. Someone who chooses not to work is not. The Puritan view of welfare is a kind of compromise between the Individualist view and the Permissive view. . . .

The Puritan view of welfare, based as it is on the inter-relation between welfare and work, provides a rationale for two connected principles which those establishing welfare schemes in Canada and in the United States seem to endorse. First of all, those on welfare should never receive a higher income than the working poor. Secondly, a welfare scheme should, in some way or other, incorporate incentives to work. These principles, which presuppose that it is better to work than not to work, emerge rather naturally from the contingency which is at the basis of the Puritan view: the goods essential for social security are products of the labour of some members of society. If we wish to have a continued supply of such goods, we must encourage those who work to produce them. . . .

APPRAISAL OF POLICIES: SOCIAL CONSEQUENCES AND SOCIAL JUSTICE

In approaching the appraisal of prospective welfare policies under these two aspects I am, of course, making some assumptions about the moral appraisal of suggested social policies. Although these cannot possibly be justified here, it may be helpful to articulate them, at least in a rough way.

Appraisal of social policies is in part teleological. To the extent that a policy, P, increases the total human welfare more than does an alternative policy, P′, P is a better social policy than P′. Or, if P leaves the total human welfare as it is, while P′ diminishes it, then to that extent, P is a better social policy than P′. Even this skeletal formulation of the teleological aspect of appraisal reveals why appraisal cannot be entirely teleological. We consider total consequences—effect upon the total of "human well-being" in a society. But this total is a summation of consequences on different individuals. It includes no judgements as to how far we allow one individual's well-being to decrease while another's increases, under the same policy. Judgements relating to the latter problems are judgements about social justice.

In appraising social policies we have to weigh up considerations of total well-being against considerations of justice. Just how this is to be done, precisely, I would not pretend to know. However, the absence of precise methods does not mean that we should relinquish attempts at appraisal: some problems are already with us, and thought which is necessarily tentative and imprecise is still preferable to no thought at all.

1 Consequences of Welfare Schemes

First, let us consider the consequences of the non-scheme advocated by the Individualist. He would have us abolish all non-optional government programmes which have as their goal the improvement of anyone's personal welfare. This rejection extends to health schemes, pension plans and education, as well as to welfare and unemployment insurance. So following the Individualist would lead to very sweeping changes.

The Individualist will claim (as do Hospers and Ayn Rand) that on the whole his non-scheme will bring beneficial consequences. He will admit, as he must, that there are people who would suffer tremendously if welfare and other social security programmes were simply terminated. Some would even die as a result. We cannot assume that spontaneously developing charities would cover every case of dire need. Nevertheless the Individualist wants to point to benefits which would accrue to businessmen and to working people and their families if taxation were drastically cut. It is his claim that consumption would rise, hence production would rise, job opportunities would be extended, and there would be an economic boom, if people could only spend all their earned income as they wished. This boom would benefit both rich and poor.

There are significant omissions which are necessary in order to render the Individualist's optimism plausible. Either workers and businessmen would have insurance of various kinds, or they would be insecure in their prosperity. If they did have insurance to cover health problems, old age and possible job loss, then they would pay for it; hence they would not be spending their whole earned income on consumer goods. Those who run the insurance schemes could, of course, put this money back into the economy—but government schemes already do this. The economic boom under Individualism would not be as loud as originally expected. Furthermore the goal of increased consumption-increased productivity must be questioned from an ecological viewpoint: many necessary materials are available only in limited quantities.

Finally, a word about charity. It is not to be expected that those who are at the mercy of charities will benefit from this state, either materially or psychologically. Those who prosper will be able to choose between giving a great deal to charity and suffering from the very real insecurity and guilt which would accompany the existence of starvation and grim poverty outside their padlocked doors. It is to be hoped that they would opt for the first alternative. But, if they did, this might be every bit as expensive for them as government-supported benefit schemes are now. If they did not give generously to charity, violence might result. However one looks at it, the consequences of Individualism are unlikely to be good.

Welfare schemes operating in Canada today are almost without exception based upon the principles of the Puritan view. To see the consequences of that type of welfare scheme we have only to look at the results of our own welfare programmes. Taxation to support such schemes is high, though not so intolerably so as to have led to widescale resentment among taxpayers. Canadian welfare programmes are attended by complicated and often cumbersome bureaucracy, some of which results from the interlocking of municipal, provincial and federal governments in the administration and financing of welfare programmes. The cost of the programmes is no doubt increased by this bureaucracy; not all the tax money directed to welfare programmes goes to those in need. Puritan welfare schemes do not result in social catastrophe or in significant business stagnation—this much we know, because we already live with such schemes. Their adverse consequences, if any, are felt primarily not by society generally nor by businessmen and the working segment of the public, but rather by recipients of welfare.

Both the Special Senate Committee Report on Poverty and the Real Poverty Report criticize our present system of welfare for its demoralization of recipients, who often must deal with several levels of government and are vulnerable to arbitrary interference on the part of administering officials. Welfare officials have the power to check on welfare recipients and cut off or limit their benefits under a large number of circumstances. The dangers to welfare recipients in terms of anxiety, threats to privacy and loss of dignity are obvious. According to the Senate Report, the single aspect shared by all Canada's welfare systems is "a record of failure and insufficiency, of bureaucratic rigidities that often result in the degradation, humiliation and alienation of recipients."[8] The writers of this report cite many instances of humiliation, leaving the impression that these are too easily found to be "incidental aberrations."[9] Concern that a welfare recipient either be unable to work or be willing to work (if unemployed) can easily turn into concern about how he spends the income supplied him, what his plans for the future are, where he lives, how many children he has. And the rationale underlying the Puritan scheme makes the degradation of welfare recipients a natural consequence of welfare institutions. Work is valued and only he who works is thought to contribute to society. Welfare recipients are regarded as parasites and spongers—so when they are treated as such, this is only what we should have expected. Being on welfare in a society which thinks and acts in this fashion can be psychologically debilitating. Welfare recipients who are demoralized by their downgraded status and relative lack of personal freedom can be expected to be made less capable of self-sufficiency. To the extent that this is so, welfare systems erected on Puritan principles may defeat their own purposes.

In fairness, it must be noted here that bureaucratic checks and controls are not a feature only of Puritan welfare systems. To a limited extent, Permissive systems would have to incorporate them too. Within those systems, welfare benefits would be given only to those whose income was inadequate to meet basic needs. However, there would be no checks on "willingness to work," and there would be no need for welfare workers to evaluate the merits of the daily activities of recipients. If a Permissive guaranteed income system were administered through income tax returns, everyone receiving the basic income and those not needing it paying it back in taxes, then the special status of welfare recipients would fade. They would no longer be singled out as a special group within the population. It is to be expected that living solely on government-supplied benefits would be psychologically easier in that type of situation.

Thus it can be argued that for the recipients of welfare, a Permissive scheme has more advantages than a Puritan one. This is not a very surprising conclusion. The Puritan scheme is relatively disadvantageous to recipients, and Puritans would acknowledge this point; they will argue that the overall consequences of Permissive schemes are negative in that these schemes benefit some at too great a cost to others. (Remember, we are not yet concerned with the *justice* of welfare policies, but solely with their consequences as regards *total* human well-being within the society in question.) The concern which most people have regarding the Permissive scheme relates to its costs and its dangers to the "work ethic." It is commonly thought that people work only because they have to work to survive in a tolerable style. If a guaranteed income scheme were adopted by the government, this incentive to work would disappear. No one would be faced with the choice between a nasty and boring job and starvation. Who would do the nasty and boring jobs then? Many of them are not eliminable and they have to be done somehow, by someone. Puritans fear that a great many people—even some with relatively pleasant jobs—might simply cease to work if they could receive non-stigmatized government money to live on. If this were to happen, the Permissive society would simply grind to a halt.

In addressing these anxieties about the consequences of Permissive welfare schemes, we must recall that welfare benefits are set to ensure only that those who do not work have a bearable existence, with an income sufficient for basic needs, and that they have this income regardless of why they fail to work. Welfare benefits will not finance luxury living for a family of five! If jobs are adequately paid so that workers receive more than the minimum welfare income in an earned salary, then there will still be a financial incentive to take jobs. What guaranteed income schemes will do is to raise the salary floor. This change will benefit the many non-unionized workers in service and clerical occupations.

Furthermore it is unlikely that people work solely due to (i) the desire for money and the things it can buy and (ii) belief in the Puritan work ethic. There are many other reasons for working, some of which would persist in a society which had adopted a Permissive welfare system. Most people are happier when their time is structured in some way, when they are active outside their own homes, when they feel themselves part of an endeavour whose purposes transcend their particular egoistic ones. Women often choose to work outside the home for these reasons as much as for financial ones. With these and other factors operating I cannot see that the adoption of a Permissive welfare scheme would be followed by a level of slothfulness which would jeopardize human well-being.

Another worry about the Permissive scheme concerns cost. It is difficult to comment on this in a general way, since it would vary so much from case to case. Of Canada at the present it has been said that a guaranteed income scheme administered through income tax would cost less than social security payments administered through the present bureaucracies. It is thought that this saving would result from a drastic cut in administrative costs. The matter of the work ethic is also relevant to the question of costs. Within a Puritan framework it is very important to have a high level of employment and there is a tendency to resist any reorganization which results in there being fewer jobs available. Some of these proposed reorganizations would save money; strictly speaking we should count the cost of keeping jobs which are objectively unnecessary as part of the cost of Puritanism regarding welfare.

In summary, we can appraise Individualism, Puritanism and Permissivism with respect to their anticipated consequences, as follows: Individualism is unacceptable; Puritanism is tolerable, but has some undesirable consequences for welfare recipients; Permissivism appears to be the winner. Worries about bad effects which Permissive welfare schemes might have due to high costs and (alleged) reduced work-incentives appear to be without solid basis.

2 Social Justice under Proposed Welfare Schemes

We must now try to consider the merits of Individualism, Puritanism and Permissivism with regard to their impact on the distribution of the goods necessary for well-being. [Robert] Nozick has argued against the whole conception of a distributive justice on the grounds that it presupposes that goods are like manna from heaven: we simply get them and then have a problem—to whom to give them. According to Nozick we know where things come from and we do not have the problem of to whom to give them. There is not really a problem of distributive justice, for there is no central distributor giving out manna from heaven! It is necessary to counter Nozick on this point since his reaction to the (purported) problems of distributive justice would undercut much of what follows.[10]

There is a level at which Nozick's point is obviously valid. If A discovers a cure for cancer, then it is A and not B or C who is responsible for this discovery. On Nozick's view this is taken to imply that A should reap any monetary profits which are forthcoming; other people will benefit from the cure itself. Now although it cannot be doubted that A is a bright and hard-working person, neither can it be denied that A and his circumstances are the product of many co-operative endeavours: schools and laboratories, for instance. Because this is so, I find Nozick's claim that "we know where things come from" unconvincing at a deeper level. Since achievements like A's presuppose extensive social co-operation, it is morally permissible to regard even the monetary profits accruing from them as shareable by the "owner" and society at large.

Laws support existing income levels in many ways. Governments specify taxation so as to further determine net income. Property ownership is a legal matter. In all these ways people's incomes and possibilities for obtaining income are affected by deliberate state action. It is always possible to raise questions about the moral desirability of actual conventional arrangements. Should university professors earn less than lawyers? More than waitresses? Why? Why not? Anyone who gives an account of distributive justice is trying to specify principles which will make it possible to answer questions such as these, and nothing in Nozick's argument suffices to show that the questions are meaningless or unimportant.

Any human distribution of anything is unjust insofar as differences exist for no good reason. If goods did come like manna from heaven and the Central Distributor gave A ten times more than B, we should want to know why. The skewed distribution might be deemed a just one if A's needs were objectively ten times greater than B's, or if B refused to accept more than his small portion of goods. But if no reason at all could be given for it, or if only an irrelevant reason could be given (e.g., A is blue-eyed and B is not), then it is an unjust distribution. All the views we have expounded concerning welfare permit differences in income level. Some philosophers would say that such differences are never just, although they may be necessary, for historical or utilitarian reasons. Whether or not this is so, it is admittedly very difficult to say just what would constitute a good reason for giving A a higher income than B. Level of need, degree of responsibility, amount of training, unpleasantness of work—all these have been proposed and all have some plausibility. We do not need to tackle all this larger problem in order to consider justice under proposed welfare systems. For we can deal here solely with the question of whether everyone should receive a floor level of income; decisions on this matter are independent of decisions on overall equality or principles of variation among incomes above the floor. The Permissivist contends that all should receive at least the floor income; the Individualist and the Puritan deny this. All would claim justice for their side.

The Individualist attempts to justify extreme variations in income, with some people below the level where they can fulfill their basic needs, with reference to the fact of people's actual accomplishments. This approach to the question is open to the same objections as those which have already been raised against Nozick' s non-manna-from-heaven argument, and I shall not repeat them here. Let us move on to the Puritan account. It is because goods emerge from human efforts that the Puritan advances his view of welfare. He stresses the unfairness of a system which would permit some people to take advantage of others. A Permissive welfare system would do this, as it makes no attempt to distinguish between those who choose not to work and those who cannot work. No one should be able to take advantage of another under the auspices of a government institution. The Puritan scheme seeks to eliminate this possibility, and for that reason, Puritans would allege, it is a more just scheme than the Permissive one.

Permissivists can best reply to this contention by acknowledging that any instance of free-riding would be an instance where those working were done an injustice, but by showing that any justice which the Puritan preserves by eliminating freeriding is outweighted by *injustice* perpetrated elsewhere. Consider the children of the Puritan's freeriders. They will suffer greatly for the "sins" of their parents. Within the institution of the family, the Puritan cannot suitably hurt the guilty without cruelly depriving the innocent. There is a sense, too, in which Puritanism does injustice to the many people on welfare who are not freeriders. It perpetuates the opinion that they are non-contributors to society and this doctrine, which is oversimplified if not downright false, has a harmful effect upon welfare recipients.

Social justice is not simply a matter of the distribution of goods, or the income with which goods are to be purchased. It is also a matter of the protection of rights. Western societies claim to give their citizens equal rights in political and legal contexts; they also claim to endorse the larger conception of a right to life. Now it is possible to interpret these rights in a limited and formalistic way, so that the duties correlative to them are minimal. On the limited, or negative, interpretation, to say that A has a right to life is simply to say that others have a duty not to interfere with A's attempts to keep himself alive. This interpretation of the right to life is compatible with Individualism as well as with Puritanism. But it is an inadequate interpretation of the right to life and of other rights. A right to vote is meaningless if one is starving and unable to get to the polls; a right to equality before the law is meaningless if one cannot afford to hire a lawyer. And so on.

Even a Permissive welfare scheme will go only a very small way towards protecting people's rights. It will amount to a meaningful acknowledgment of a right to life, by ensuring income adequate to purchase food, clothing and shelter—at the very least. These minimum necessities are presupposed by all other rights a society may endorse in that their possession is a precondition of being able to exercise these other rights. Because it protects the rights of all within a society better than do Puritanism and Individualism, the Permissive view can rightly claim superiority over the others with regard to justice.

NOTES

1. Nicholas Rescher, *Welfare: Social Issues in Philosophical Perspective*, p. 114.
2. One might wish to discuss moral questions concerning welfare in the context of natural rights doctrines. Indeed, Article 22 of the United Nations Declaration of Human Rights states, "Everyone, as a member of society, has the right to social security and is entitled, through national effort and international cooperation and in accordance with the organization and resources of each State, to the economic, social and cultural rights indispensable for his dignity and the free development of his personality." I make no attempt to defend the right to welfare as a natural right. Granting that rights imply responsibilities or duties that "ought" implies "can," it would only be intelligible to regard the right to social security as a natural right if all states were able to ensure the minimum well-being of their citizens. This is not the case. And a natural right is one which is by definition supposed to belong to all human beings simply in virtue of their status as human beings. The analysis given here in the Permissive view is compatible with the claim that all human beings have a *prima facie* natural right to social security. It is not, however, compatible with the claim that all human beings have a natural right to social security if this right is regarded as one which is so absolute as to be inviolable under any and all conditions.
3. See, for example, Ayn Rand's *Atlas Shrugged, The Virtue of Selfishness,* and *Capitalism: The Unknown Ideal.*
4. John Hospers, *Libertarianism: A Political Philosophy for Tomorrow,* p. 67.
5. I say virtually unconditional, because an Individualist such as John Hospers sees a legitimate moral role for government in preventing the use of force by some citizens against others. Since this is the case, I presume that he would also regard as legitimate such taxation as was necessary to support this function. Presumably that taxation would be seen as consented to by all, on the grounds that all "really want" government protection.
6. Ian Adams, William Cameron, Brian Hill, and Peter Penz, *The Real Poverty Report,* pp. 167–187.
7. See *A Theory of Justice,* pp. 124, 136. Rawls defines the free-rider as one who relies on the principle "everyone is to act justly except for myself, if I choose not to," and says that his position is a version of egoism which is eliminated as a morally acceptable principle by formal constraints. This conclusion regarding the tenability of egoism is one which I accept and which is taken for granted in the present context.
8. *Senate Report on Poverty,* p. 73.

9. The Hamilton Public Welfare Department takes automobile license plates from recipients, making them available again only to those whose needs meet with the Department's approval. (*Real Poverty Report*, p. 186.) *The Globe and Mail* for 12 January 1974 reported that welfare recipients in the city of Toronto are to be subjected to computerized budgeting. In the summer of 1973, the two young daughters of an Alabama man on welfare were sterilized against their own wishes and without their parents' informed consent. (See *Time*, 23 July 1973.)
10. Robert Nozick, "Distributive Justice," *Philosophy and Public Affairs*, Fall 1973.

QUESTIONS FOR ANALYSIS

1. What practical advantages does the permissive view have over the puritan view according to Govier? What practical advantages does it have over the individualist view? Do you agree?
2. How does Govier respond to the charge that the permissive view discourages people from working? How convincing is her response?
3. One problem with welfare programs based on the puritan view, Govier says, is that it demoralizes welfare recipients. How does it demoralize them? How could a proponent of the puritan view respond?
4. How does Govier criticize Nozick's entitlement conception of justice? How could Nozick respond? How could Hospers respond?
5. Govier admits that the permissive view allows free-riders to sponge off others. She also admits that free-riders create an injustice to people who work to support themselves and their families. Why does she consider the permissive view to be more just than the puritan view anyway?
6. In today's United States, there are increasing calls to move closer to the individualist position and the puritan position. Why? According to Govier's discussion, the calls are misguided. Are they, or does Govier's discussion neglect important issues in the welfare debate?

Radical Egalitarianism

KAI NIELSEN

In this selection from the last chapter of *Equality and Liberty,* Kai Nielsen, professor *emeritus* of philosophy at the University of Calgary, defends a position he calls *radical egalitarianism,* which combines the principle of need and the equality principle but also recognizes limited entitlements. In a society that can afford to do so, Nielsen argues, everyone's needs should be satisfied. Then, after providing for common social and economic goods—and without violating individual entitlements—society should distribute the remaining wealth equally. He calls this view radical egalitarianism because it insists on equality of *condition* for all, not just equality of opportunity.

After setting out his position, Nielsen defends it against the charge that too much equality interferes with individual liberty. He claims we have rights to fair terms of cooperation as well as rights to noninterference. That is, we have a right not to be dominated or exploited by others. Maximizing that right, he says, results in the greatest liberty for all, even if it means limiting some rights of noninterference. He also defends his position against two other criticisms: (1) that egalitarianism penalizes the talented and (2) that no one has the authority to force egalitarianism on those who object to it. Against the first, he says money is not the only way to reward talent. Against the second, he appeals to moral authority. Anyone who considers the matter impartially, he says, and genuinely cares for humankind and is not "ideologically mystified," will see the merits of egalitarianism—at least in the abstract.

I

I have talked of equality as a right and of equality as a goal. And I have taken, as the principal thing, to be able to state what goal we are seeking when we say equality is a goal. When we are in a position actually to achieve that goal, then that same equality becomes a right. The goal we are seeking is an equality of basic condition for everyone. Let me say a bit what this is: everyone, as far as possible, should have equal life prospects, short of genetic engineering and the like and the rooting out of any form of the family and the undermining of our basic freedoms. There should, where this is possible, be an equality of access to equal resources over each person's life as a whole, though this should be qualified by people's varying needs. Where psychiatrists are in short supply only people who are in need of psychiatric help should have equal access to such help. This equal access to resources should be such that it stands as a barrier to their being the sort of differences between people that allow some to be in a position to control and to exploit others; such equal access to resources should also stand as a barrier to one adult person having power over other adult persons that does not rest on the revocable consent on the part of the persons over whom he comes to have power. Where, because of some remaining scarcity in a society of considerable productive abundance, we cannot reasonably distribute resources equally, we should first, where considerations of desert are not at issue, distribute according to stringency of need, second according to the strength of unmanipulated preferences and third, and finally, by lottery. We should, in trying to attain equality of condition, aim at a condition of autonomy (the fuller and the more rational the better) for everyone and at a condition where everyone alike, to the fullest extent possible, has his or her needs and wants satisfied. The limitations on the satisfaction of people's wants should be only where that satisfaction is incompatible with everyone getting the same treatment. Where we have conflicting wants, such as where two persons want to marry the same person, the fair thing to do will vary with the circumstances. In the marriage case, freedom of choice is obviously the fair thing. But generally, what should be aimed at is having everyone have their wants satisfied as far as possible. To achieve equality of condition would be, as well, to achieve a condition where the necessary burdens of the society are equally shared, where to do so is reasonable, and where each person has an equal voice in deciding what these burdens shall be. Moreover, everyone, as much as possible, should be in a position—and should be equally in that position—to control his own life. The goals of egalitarianism are to achieve such equalities....

II

Robert Nozick asks "How do we decide how much equality is enough?"[1] In the preceding section we gestured in the direction of an answer. I should now like to be somewhat more explicit. Too much equality, as we have been at pains to point out, would be to treat everyone identically, completely ignoring their differing needs. Various forms of "barracks equality" approximating that would also be too much. Too little equality would be to limit equality of condition, as did the old egalitarianism, to achieving equal legal and political rights, equal civil liberties, to equality of opportunity and to a redistribution of gross disparities in wealth sufficient to keep social peace, the rationale for the latter being that such gross inequalities if allowed to stand would threaten social stability. This Hobbesist stance indicates that the old egalitarianism proceeds in a very pragmatic manner. Against the old egalitarianism I would argue that we must at least aim at an equality of whole life prospects, where that is not read simply as the right to compete for scarce positions of advantage, but where there is to be brought into being the kind of equality of condition that would provide everyone equally, as far as possible, with the resources and the social conditions to satisfy their needs as fully as possible compatible with everyone else doing likewise. (Note that between people these needs will be partly the same but will still often be importantly different as well.) Ideally, as a kind of ideal limit for a society of wondrous abundance, a radical egalitarianism would go beyond that to a similar thing for wants. We should, that is, provide all people equally, as far as possible, with the resources and social conditions to satisfy their wants, as fully as possible compatible with everyone else doing likewise. (I recognize that there is a slide between wants and needs. As the wealth of a society increases and its structure changes, things that started out as wants tend to become needs, e.g., someone in the Falkland Islands might merely reasonably want an auto while someone in Los Angeles might not only want it but need it as well. But this does not collapse the distinction between wants and needs. There are things in any society people need, if they are to survive at all in anything like a commodious condition, whether they want them or not, e.g., they need food, shelter, security, companionship and the like. An egalitarian starts with basic needs, or at least with what are taken in the cultural environment in which a given person lives to be basic needs, and moves out to other needs and finally to wants as the productive power of the society increases.)

I qualified my above formulations with "as far as possible" and with "as fully as possible compatible with everyone else doing likewise." These are essential qualifications. Where, as in societies that we know, there are scarcities, even rather minimal scarcities, not everyone can have the resources or at least all the resources necessary to have their needs satisfied. Here we must first ensure that, again as far as possible, their basic needs are all satisfied and then we move on to other needs and finally to wants. But sometimes, to understate it, even in very affluent societies, everyone's needs cannot be met, or at least they cannot be equally met. In such circumstances we have to make some hard choices. I am thinking of a situation where there are not enough dialysis machines to go around so that everyone who needs one can have one. What then should we do? The thing to aim at, to try as far as possible to approximate, if only as a heuristic ideal, is the full and equal meeting of needs and wants of everyone. It is when we have that much equality that we have enough equality. But, of course, "ought implies can," and where we can't achieve it we can't achieve it. But where we reasonably can, we ought to do it. It is something that fairness requires.

The "reasonably can" is also an essential modification: we need situations of sufficient abundance so that we do not, in going for such an equality of condition, simply spread the misery around or spread very Spartan conditions around. Before we can rightly aim for the equality of condition I mentioned, we must first have the productive capacity and resource conditions to support the institutional means that would make possible the equal satisfaction of basic needs and the equal satisfaction of other needs and wants as well. . . .

In talking about how much equality is enough, I have so far talked of the benefits that equality is meant to provide. But egalitarians also speak of an equal sharing of the necessary burdens of the society as well. Fairness requires a sharing of the burdens, and for a radical egalitarian this comes to an equal sharing of the burdens where people are equally capable of sharing them. Translated into the concrete this does *not* mean that a child or an old man or a pregnant woman are to be required to work in the mines or that they be required to collect garbage, but it would involve something like requiring every able-bodied person, say from nineteen to twenty, to take his or her turn at a fair portion of the necessary unpleasant jobs in the world. In that way we all, where we are able to do it, would share equally in these burdens—in doing the things that none of us want to do but that we, if we are at all reasonable, recognize the necessity of having done. (There are all kinds of variations and complications concerning this—what do we do with the youthful wonder at the violin? But, that notwithstanding, the general idea is clear enough.) And, where we think this is reasonably feasible, it squares with our considered judgments about fairness.

I have given you, in effect appealing to my considered judgments but considered judgments I do not think are at all eccentric, a picture of what I would take to be enough equality, too little equality and not enough equality. But how can we know that my proportions are right? I do not think we can avoid or should indeed try to avoid an appeal to considered judgments here. But working with them there are some arguments we can appeal to get them in wide reflective equilibrium. Suppose we go back to the formal principle of justice, namely that we must treat like cases alike. Because it does not tell us *what* are like cases, we cannot derive substantive criteria from it. But it may, indirectly, be of some help here. We all, if we are not utterly zany, want a life in which our needs are satisfied and in which we can live as we wish and do what we want to do. Though we differ in many ways, in our abilities, capacities for pleasure, determination to keep on with a job, we do not differ about wanting our needs satisfied or being able to live as we wish. Thus, *ceterus paribus* [other things being equal], where questions of desert, entitlement and the like do not enter, it is only fair that all of us should have our needs equally considered and that we should, again *ceterus paribus,* all be able to do as we wish in a way that is compatible with others doing likewise. From the formal principle of justice and a few key facts about us, we can get to the claim that *ceterus paribus* we should go for this much equality. But this is the core content of a radical egalitarianism.

However, how do we know that *ceterus* is *paribus* here? What about our entitlements and deserts? Suppose I have built my house with my own hands, from materials I have purchased and on land that I have purchased and that I have lived in it for years and have carefully cared for it. The house is mine and I am entitled to keep it even if by dividing the house into two apartments greater and more equal satisfaction of need would obtain for everyone. Justice requires that such an entitlement be respected here. (Again, there is an implicit *ceterus paribus* clause. In extreme situations, say after a war with housing in extremely short supply, that entitlement could be rightly overridden.)

There is a response on the egalitarian' s part.... One of the things that people in fact need, or at least reflectively firmly want, is to have such entitlements respected. Where they are routinely overridden to satisfy other needs or wants, we would *not* in fact have a society in which the needs of everyone are being maximally met. To the reply, but what if more needs for everyone were met by ignoring or overriding such entitlements, the radical egalitarian should respond that that is, given the way we are, a thoroughly hypothetical situation and that theories of morality cannot be expected to give guidance for all logically possible worlds but only for worlds which are reasonably like what our actual world is or plausibly could come to be....

There are without doubt genuine entitlements and a theory of justice must take them seriously, but they are not absolute. If the need is great enough we can see the merit in overriding them, just as in law as well as morality the right of eminent domain is recognized. Finally, while I have talked of entitlements here, parallel arguments will go through for desert.

III

I want now to relate this articulation of what equality comes to my radically egalitarian principles of justice. My articulation of justice is a certain spelling out of the slogan proclaimed by Marx "From each according to his ability, to each according to his needs." The egalitarian conception of society argues for the desirability of bringing into existence a world, once the springs of social wealth flow freely, in which everyone's needs are as fully satisfied as possible and in which everyone gives according to his ability. Which means, among other things, that everyone, according to his ability, shares the burdens of society. There is an equal giving and equal responsibility here according to ability. It is here, with respect to giving according to ability and with respect to receiving according to need, that a complex equality of result, equality of condition, is being advocated by the radical egalitarian. What it comes to is this: each of us, where each is to count for one and none to count for more than one, is to give according to ability and receive according to need.

My radical egalitarian principles of justice, as we have seen, read as follows:

1. Each person is to have an equal right to the most extensive total system of equal basic liberties and opportunities (including equal opportunities for meaningful work, for self-determination and political and economic participation) compatible with a similar treatment of all. (This principle gives expression to a commitment to attain and/or sustain equal moral autonomy and equal self-respect.)
2. After provisions are made for common social (community) values, for capital overhead to preserve the society's productive capacity, allowances made for differing unmanipulated needs and preferences, and due weight is given to the just entitlements of individuals, the income and wealth (the common stock of means) is to be so divided that each person will have a right to an equal share. The necessary burdens requisite to enhance human well-being are also to be equally shared, subject, of course, to limitations by differing abilities and differing situations. (Here I refer to different natural environments and the like and not to class position and the like.)

Here we are talking about equality as a right rather than about equality as a goal as has previously been the subject matter of equality in this chapter. These principles of egalitarianism spell out rights people have and duties they have under *conditions of very considerable productive abundance.* We have a right to certain basic liberties and opportunities and we have, subject to certain limitations spelled out in the second principle, a right to an equal share of the income and wealth in the world. We also have a duty, again subject to the qualifications mentioned in the principle, to do our equal share in shouldering the burdens necessary to protect us from ills and to enhance our well-being.

What is the relation between these rights and the ideal of equality of condition discussed earlier? That is a goal for which we can struggle now to bring about conditions which will some day make its achievement possible, while these rights only become rights when the goal is actually achievable. We have no such rights in slave, feudal or capitalist societies or such duties in those societies. In that important way they are not natural rights for they depend on certain social conditions and certain social structures (socialist ones) to be realizable. What we can say is that it is always desirable that socio-economic conditions come into being which would make it possible to achieve the goal of equality of condition so that these rights and duties I speak of could obtain. But that is a far cry from saying we have such rights and duties now.

It is a corollary of this, if these radical egalitarian principles of justice are correct, that capitalist societies (even capitalist welfare state societies such as Sweden) and statist societies such as the Soviet Union or the People's Republic of China cannot be just societies or at least they must be societies, structured as they are, which are defective in justice. (This is not to say that some of these societies are not juster than others. . . .) But none of these statist or capitalist societies can satisfy these radical egalitarian principles of justice, for equal liberty, equal opportunity, equal wealth or equal sharing of burdens are not at all possible in societies having their social structure. So we do not have such rights now but we can take it as a goal that we bring such a society into being with a commitment to an equality of condition in which we would have these rights and duties. Here we require first the massive development of productive power.

The connection between equality as a goal and equality as a right spelled out in these principles of justice is this. The equality of condition appealed to in equality as a goal would, if it were actually to obtain, have to contain the rights and duties enunciated in those principles. There could be no equal life prospects between all people or anything approximating an equal satisfaction of needs if there were not in place something like the system of equal basic liberties referred to in the first principle. Furthermore, without the rough equality of wealth referred to in the second principle, there would be disparities in power and self-direction in society which would render impossible an equality of life prospects or the social conditions required for an equal satisfaction of needs. And plainly, without a roughly equal sharing of burdens, there cannot be a situation where everyone has equal life prospects or has the chance equally to satisfy his needs. The principles of radical egalitarian justice are implicated in its conception of an ideally adequate equality of condition....

[IV]

It has been repeatedly argued that equality undermines liberty. Some would say that a society in which principles like my radical egalitarian principles were adopted, or even the liberal egalitarian principles of Rawls or Dworkin were adopted, would not be a free society. My arguments have been just the reverse. I have argued that it is only in an egalitarian society that full and extensive liberty is possible.

Perhaps the egalitarian and the anti-egalitarian are arguing at cross purposes? What we need to recognize, it has been argued, is that we have two kinds of rights both of which are important to freedom but to rather different freedoms and which are freedoms which not infrequently conflict.[2] We have rights to *fair terms of cooperation* but we also have rights to *non-interference*. If a right of either kind is overridden our freedom is diminished. The reason why it might be thought that the egalitarian and the anti-egalitarian may be arguing at cross purposes is that the egalitarian is pointing to the fact that rights to fair terms of cooperation and their associated liberties require equality while the anti-egalitarian is pointing to the fact that rights to non-interference and their associated liberties conflict with equality. They focus on different liberties.

What I have said above may not be crystal clear, so let me explain. People have a right to fair terms of cooperation. In political terms this comes to the equal right of all to effective participation in government and, in more broadly social terms, and for a society of economic wealth, it means people having a right to a roughly equal distribution of the benefits and burdens of the basic social arrangements that affect their lives and for them to stand in such relations to each other such that no one has the power to dominate the life of another. By contrast, rights to non-interference come to the equal right of all to be left alone by the government and more broadly to live in a society in which people have a right peacefully to pursue their interests without interference.

The conflict between equality and liberty comes down to, very essentially, the conflicts we get in modern societies between rights to fair terms of cooperation and rights to non-interference. As Joseph Schumpeter saw and J. S. Mill before him, one could have a thoroughly democratic society (at least in conventional terms) in which rights to noninterference might still be extensively violated. A central anti-egalitarian claim is that we cannot have an egalitarian society in which the very precious liberties that go with the rights to non-interference would not be violated.

Socialism and egalitarianism plainly protect rights to fair terms of cooperation. Without the social (collective) ownership and control of the means of production, involving with this, in the initial stages of socialism at least, a workers' state, economic power will be concentrated in the hands of a few who will in turn, as a result, dominate effective participation in government. Some rightwing libertarians blind themselves to that reality, but it is about as evident as can be. Only an utter turning away from the facts of social life could lead to any doubts about this at all. But then this means that in a workers' state, if some people have capitalistic impulses, that they would have their rights peacefully to pursue their own interests interfered with. They might wish to invest, retain and bequeath in economic domains. In a workers' state these capitalist acts in many circumstances would have to be forbidden, but that would be a violation of an individual's right to non-interference and the fact, if it was a fact, that we by democratic vote, even with vast majorities, had made such capitalist acts illegal would still not make any difference because individuals' rights to non-interference would still be violated....

The proper response to this, as should be apparent from what I have argued throughout, is that to live in any society at all, capitalist, socialist or whatever, is to live in a world in which there will be some restriction or other on our rights peacefully to pursue our interests without interference. I can't lecture in Albanian or even in French in a standard philosophy class at the University of Calgary, I can't jog naked on most beaches, borrow a book from your library without your permission, fish in your trout pond without your permission, take your dog for a walk without your say so and the like. At least some of these things have been thought to be things which I might peacefully pursue in my own interests. Stopping me from doing them is plainly interfering with my peaceful pursuit of my own interests. And indeed it is an infringement on liberty, an interference with my doing what I may want to do.

However, for at least many of these activities, and particularly the ones having to do with property, even right-wing libertarians think that such interference is perfectly justified. But, justified or not, they still plainly constitute a restriction on our individual freedom. However, what we must also recognize is that there will always be some such restrictions on freedom in any society whatsoever, just in virtue of the fact that a normless society, without the restrictions that having norms imply, is a contradiction in terms.[3] Many restrictions are hardly felt as restrictions, as in the attitudes of many people toward seat-belt legislation, but they are, all the same, plainly restrictions in our liberty. It is just that they are thought to be unproblematically justified.

To the question would a socialism with a radical egalitarianism restrict some liberties, includng some liberties rooted in rights to non-interference, the answer is that it indeed would; but so would laissez-faire capitalism, aristocratic conceptions of justice, liberal conceptions or any social formations at all, with their associated conceptions of justice. The relevant question is which of these restrictions are justified.

The restrictions on liberty proffered by radical egalitarianism and socialism, I have argued, are justified for they, of the various alternatives, give us both the most extensive and the most abundant system of liberty possible in modern conditions with their thorough protection of the right to fair terms of cooperation. Radical egalitarianism will also, and this is central for us, protect our civil liberties and these liberties are, of course, our most basic liberties. These are the liberties which are the most vital for us to protect. What it will not do is to protect our unrestricted liberties to invest, retain and bequeath in the economic realm and it will not protect our unrestricted freedom to buy and sell. There is, however, no good reason to think that these restrictions are restrictions of anything like a basic liberty. Moreover, we are justified in restricting our freedom to buy and sell if such restrictions strengthen, rather than weaken, our total system of liberty. This is in this way justified, for only by such market restrictions can the rights of the vast majority of people to effective participation in government and an equal role in the control of their social lives be protected. I say this because if we let the market run free in this way, power will pass into the hands of a few who will control the lives of the many and determine the fundamental design of the society. The actual liberties that are curtailed in a radically egalitarian social order are inessential liberties whose restriction in contemporary circumstances enhances human well-being and indeed makes for a firmer entrenchment of basic liberties and for their greater extension globally. That is to say, we here restrict some liberty in order to attain more liberty and a more equally distributed pattern of liberty. More people will be able to do what they want and have a greater control over their own lives than in a capitalist world order with its at least implicit inegalitarian commitments.

However, some might say I still have not faced the most central objection to radical egalitarianism, namely its statism. (I would prefer to say its putative statism.) The picture is this. The egalitarian state must be in the redistribution business. It has to make, or make sure there is made, an equal relative contribution to the welfare of every citizen. But this in effect means that the socialist state or, for that matter, the welfare state, will be deeply interventionist in our personal lives. It will be in the business, as one right-winger emotively put it, of cutting one person down to size in order to bring about that person's equality with another person who was in a previously disadvantageous position.[4] That is said to be morally objectionable and it would indeed be deeply morally objectionable in many circumstances. But it isn't in the circumstances in which the radical egalitarian presses for redistribution. (I am not speaking of what might be mere equalizing upwards.) The circumstances are these: Capitalist A gets his productive property confiscated so that he could no longer dominate and control the lives of proletarians B, C, D, E, F, and G. But what is wrong with it where this "cutting down to size"—in reality the confiscation of productive property or the taxation of the capitalist—involves no violation of A's civil liberties or the harming of his actual well-being (health, ability to work, to cultivate the arts, to have fruitful personal relations, to live in comfort and the like) and where B, C, D, E, F, and G will have their freedom and their well-being thoroughly enhanced if such confiscation or taxation occurs? Far from being morally objectionable, it is precisely the sort of state of affairs that people ought to favor. It certainly protects more liberties and more significant liberties than it undermines.

There is another familiar anti-egalitarian argument designed to establish the liberty-undermining qualities of egalitarianism. It is an argument we have touched upon in discussing meritocracy. It turns on the fact that in any society there will be both talents and handicaps. Where they exist, what do we want to do about maintaining equal distribution? Egalitarians, radical or otherwise, certainly do not want to penalize people for talent. That being so, then surely people should be allowed to retain the benefits of superior talent. But this in some circumstances will lead to significant inequalities in resources and in the meeting of needs. To sustain equality there will have to be an ongoing redistribution in the direction of the less talented and less fortunate. But this redistribution from the more to the less talented does plainly penalize the talented for their talent. That, it will be said, is something which is both unfair and an undermining of liberty.

The following, it has been argued, makes the above evident enough.[5] If people have talents they will tend to want to use them. And if they use them they are very likely to come out ahead. Must not egalitarians say they ought not to be able to come out ahead no matter how well they use their talents and no matter how considerable these talents are? But that is intolerably restrictive and unfair.

The answer to the above anti-egalitarian argument is implicit in a number of things I have already said. But here let me confront this familiar argument directly. Part of the answer comes out in probing some of the ambiguities of "coming out ahead." Note, incidentally, that (1) not all reflective, morally sensitive people will be so concerned with that, and (2) that being very concerned with that is a mentality that capitalism inculcates. Be that as it may, to turn to the ambiguities, note that some take "coming out ahead" principally to mean "being paid well for the use of those talents" where "being paid well" is being paid sufficiently well so that it creates inequalities sufficient to disturb the preferred egalitarian patterns. (Without that, being paid well would give one no relative advantage.) But, as we have seen, "coming out ahead" need not take that form at all. Talents can be recognized and acknowledged in many ways. First, in just the respect and admiration of a fine employment of talents that would naturally come from people seeing them so displayed where these people were not twisted by envy; second, by having, because of these talents, interesting and secure work that their talents fit them for and they merit in virtue of those talents. Moreover, having more money is not going to matter much—for familiar marginal utility reasons—where what in capitalist societies would be called the welfare floors are already very high, this being made feasible by the great productive wealth of the society. Recall that in such a society of abundance everyone will be well off and secure. In such a society people are not going to be very concerned about being a little better off than someone else. The talented are in no way, in such a situation, robbed to help the untalented and handicapped or penalized for their talents. They are only prevented from amassing wealth (most particularly productive wealth), which would enable them to dominate the untalented and the handicapped and to control the social life of the world of which they are both a part....

Some anti-egalitarians would say, shifting now to another argument, that egalitarianism undermines liberty because it is in effect *authoritarian*.[6] It assumes someone, the government or an egalitarian secular mandarin, has the right to divvy up resources in such a way as maximally and equally to answer to the needs of everyone alike. But by whose *authority* are such actions taken? Egalitarians, the argument goes, just assume that someone has the authority to do this but no one has any such authority. *Perhaps* there would be such an authority if everyone had *unanimously* agreed that resources are to be divided up equally or even (though this is less likely) if they had all agreed to settle such fundamental moral issues by majority vote or a two-thirds majority vote or something of the sort. But it is perfectly evident that none of these agreements obtain in the real world or are even in the offing. There is no such consensus among our contemporaries. Moreover, it is simply not true, that as a matter of fact, everyone has an equal concern for everybody's interests. In no literal sense is it true that even in a single society every person in that society matters, and matters equally, to every other person in the society. Moreover, it is absurd to think that anything like that obtains, could obtain, or even should obtain, if it could. We typically care much more about our family, friends and close associates than we do about total strangers and it is both natural and appropriate that this should be so. But, the argument goes, to give egalitarianism the requisite moral authority, there would have to be something like this kind of consensus. But there plainly isn't and (more arguably) should not be. Moreover, we can't, even if we had such a majoritarian consensus, rely on the majority, for such fundamental issues are not vote issues. We cannot rightly railroad a dissenting minority.

I think that the moral authority for abstract egalitarianism, for the belief that the interests of everyone matter and matter equally, comes from its being the case that it is *required by the moral point of view*.[7] What I am predicting is that a person who has a good understanding of what morality is, has a good knowledge of the facts, is not ideologically mystified, takes an impartial point of view, and has an attitude of impartial caring, would, if not conceptually confused, come to accept the abstract egalitarian thesis. I see no way of arguing someone into such an egalitarianism who does not have that attitude of impartial caring, who does not in this general way have a love of humankind.[8] A hard-hearted Hobbesist is not reachable here. But given that a person has that love of humankind—that impartial and impersonal caring—together with the other qualities mentioned above, then, I predict, that that person would be an egalitarian at least to the extent of accepting the abstract egalitarian thesis. What I am claiming is that if these conditions were to obtain (if they ceased to be just counterfactuals), then there would be a consensus among moral agents about accepting the abstract egalitarian thesis.

Whether that consensus would be extendible to my specific formulations of radical egalitarian principles of justice would depend on how cogent my arguments are for them....

NOTES

1. See the debate between Robert Nozick, Daniel Bell and James Tobin, "If Inequality Is Inevitable What Can Be Done About It?" *The New York Times,* January 3, 1982, p. E5. The exchange between Bell and Nozick reveals the differences between the old egalitarianism and right-wing libertarianism. It is not only that the right and left clash but sometimes right clashes with right.
2. Richard W. Miller, "Marx and Morality," in *Marxism,* eds. J. R. Pennock and J. W. Chapman, *Nomos* 26 (New York: New York University Press, 1983), pp. 9–11.
3. This has been argued from both the liberal center and the left. Ralf Dahrendorf, *Essays in the Theory of Society* (Stanford, Cal.: Stanford University Press, 1968), pp. 151–78; and G. A. Cohen, "Capitalism, Freedom and the Proletariat" in *The Idea of Freedom: Essays in Honour of Isaiah*

Berlin, ed. Alan Ryan (Oxford: Oxford University Press, 1979).

4. The graphic language should be duly noted. Jan Narveson, "On Dworkinian Equality," *Social Philosophy and Policy* 1, no. 1 (Autumn 1983): p. 4.
5. Ibid., pp. 1–24.
6. Jan Narveson, "Reply to Dworkin," *Social Philosophy and Policy* 1, no. 1 (Autumn 1983): pp. 42–44.
7. Some will argue that there is no such thing as a moral point of view. My differences with him about the question of whether the amoralist can be argued into morality not withstanding. I think Kurt Baier, in a series of articles written subsequent to his *The Moral Point of View*, has clearly shown that there is something reasonably determinate that can, without ethnocentrism, be called "the moral point of view."
8. Richard Norman has impressively argued that this is an essential background assumption of the moral point of view. Richard Norman, "Critical Notice of Rodger Beehler's *Moral Life*," *Canadian Journal of Philosophy* 11, no. 1 (March 1981): pp. 157–83.

QUESTIONS FOR ANALYSIS

1. According to Nielsen, justice requires more than equality of opportunity. It also requires equality of "whole life prospects." What does he mean by that? Do you agree?
2. Nielsen is a socialist as well as a radical egalitarian. That is, he believes the means of production should be owned by society as a whole. Could radical egalitarianism be achieved without socialism? Why does Nielsen believe it can't?
3. Is Nielsen's egalitarianism too radical? Why or why not?
4. Nielsen gives only one example of a just entitlement, ownership of a house the owner built himself and lived in for years. What other entitlements do you think he would recognize? Are they enough?
5. Do you agree that radical egalitarianism maximizes liberty? Why or why not?
6. According to Nielsen, confiscating productive property involves no violation of civil liberties. How would a libertarian respond? Who do you think is right?

Choosing a Future

CHARLES MURRAY

Political scientist Charles Murray has been a resident scholar at the American Enterprise Institute since 1990. In this selection from the final chapter of *Losing Ground,* he engages in what he calls a **thought experiment.** What would happen, he asks, if all federal transfer payments to the poor were abolished? His answer is that society would reap large benefits, from a reduction in births to unwed teenagers to an increase in the ability of the hard-core unemployed to find work. What would happen to individuals now on welfare? Some would find jobs, some would receive help from family, local services, or private charities, and some, he admits, would "fall between the cracks." But those who would, he suggests, would be responsible for their own failures.

In defending this outcome, Murray argues that it rewards merit and increases self-respect. He also argues that it is more compassionate than our current system of transfer payments. Still, he does not call for an immediate end to welfare, which he considers politically impossible. Instead, he recommends a gradual course of radical reforms, though he doesn't say what they should be.

In the last two chapters I suggested that the kinds of help we want to provide are more limited than we commonly suppose and that, even when we want to help, the conditions under which a national program can do so without causing more harm than good are more tightly constrained than we suppose. My arguments might seem tailor-made to relieve us of responsibility for persons in need. But I believe just the contrary: that the moral imperative to do something to correct the situation of poor people and especially the minority poor is at least as powerful now as when Lyndon Johnson took office. I have for the most part used the data to make a case that the reforms flowing from the new wisdom of the 1960s were a blunder on purely pragmatic grounds. But another theme of the discussion has been that what we did was wrong on moral grounds, however admirable our intentions may have been.

It was wrong to take from the most industrious, most responsible poor—take safety, education, justice, status—so that we could cater to the least industrious, least responsible poor. It was wrong to impose rules that made it rational for adolescents to behave in ways that destroyed their futures. The changes we made were not just policy errors, not just inexpedient, but unjust. The injustice of the policies was compounded by the almost complete immunity of the elite from the price they demanded of the poor....

[I]f the behaviors of members of the underclass are founded on a rational appreciation of the rules of the game, and as long as the rules encourage dysfunctional values and behaviors, the future cannot look bright. Behaviors that work will tend to persist until they stop working. The rules will have to be changed....

A PROPOSAL FOR PUBLIC WELFARE

I begin with the proposition that it is within our resources to do enormous good for some people quickly. We have available to us a program that would convert a large proportion of the younger generation of hardcore unemployed into steady workers making a living wage. The same program would drastically reduce births to single teenage girls. It would reverse the trendline in the breakup of poor families. It would measurably increase the upward socioeconomic mobility of poor families. These improvements would affect some millions of persons.

All these are results that have eluded the efforts of the social programs installed since 1965, yet, from everything we know, there is no real question about whether they would occur under the program I propose. A wide variety of persuasive evidence from our own culture and around the world, from experimental data and longitudinal studies, from theory and practice, suggests that the program would achieve such results.

The proposed program, our final and most ambitious thought experiment, consists of scrapping the entire federal welfare and income-support structure for working-aged persons, including AFDC, Medicaid, Food Stamps, Unemployment Insurance, Worker's Compensation, subsidized housing, disability insurance, and the rest. It would leave the working-aged person with no recourse whatsoever except the job market, family members, friends, and public or private locally funded services. It is the Alexandrian solution: cut the knot, for there is no way to untie it.

It is difficult to examine such a proposal dispassionately. Those who dislike paying for welfare are for it without thinking. Others reflexively imagine bread lines and people starving in the streets. But as a means of gaining fresh perspective on the problem of effective reform, let us consider what this hypothetical society might look like.

A large majority of the population is unaffected. A surprising number of the huge American middle and working classes go from birth to grave without using any social welfare benefits until they receive their first Social Security check. Another portion of the population is technically affected, but the change in income is so small or so sporadic that it makes no difference in quality of life. A third group comprises persons who have to make new arrangements and behave in different ways. Sons and daughters who fail to find work continue to live with their parents or relatives or friends. Teenaged mothers have to rely on support from their parents or the father of the child and perhaps work as well. People laid off from work have to use their own savings or borrow from others to make do until the next job is found. All these changes involve great disruption in expectations and accustomed roles.

Along with the disruptions go other changes in behavior. Some parents do not want their young adult children continuing to live off their income, and become quite insistent about their children learning skills and getting jobs. This attitude is most prevalent among single mothers who have to depend most critically on the earning power of their offspring.

Parents tend to become upset at the prospect of a daughter's bringing home a baby that must be entirely supported on an already inadequate income. Some become so upset that they spend considerable parental energy avoiding such an eventuality. Potential fathers of such babies find themselves under more pressure not to cause such a problem, or to help with its solution if it occurs.

Adolescents who were not job-ready find they are job-ready after all. It turns out that they can work for low wages and accept the discipline of the workplace if the alternative is grim enough. After a few years, many—not all, but many—find that they have acquired salable skills, or that they are at the right place at the right time, or otherwise find that the original entry-level job has gradually been transformed into a secure job paying a decent wage. A few—not a lot, but a few—find that the process leads to affluence.

Perhaps the most rightful, deserved benefit goes to the much larger population of low-income families who have been doing things right all along and have been punished for it: the young man who has taken responsibility for his wife and child even though his friends with the same choice have called him a fool; the single mother who has worked full time and forfeited her right to welfare for very little extra money; the parents who have set an example for their children even as the rules of the game have taught their children that the example is outmoded. For these millions of people, the instantaneous result is that no one makes fun of them any longer. The longer-term result will be that they regain the status that is properly theirs. They will not only be the bedrock upon which the community is founded (which they always have been), they will be recognized as such. The process whereby they regain their position is not magical, but a matter of logic. When it becomes highly dysfunctional for a person to be dependent, status will accrue to being independent, and in fairly short order. Noneconomic rewards will once again reinforce the economic rewards of being a good parent and provider.

The prospective advantages are real and extremely plausible. In fact, if a government program of the traditional sort (one that would "do" something rather than simply get out of the way) could *as plausibly* promise these advantages, its passage would be a foregone conclusion. Congress, yearning for programs that are not retreads of failures, would be prepared to spend billions. Negative side-effects (as long as they were the traditionally acceptable negative side-effects) would be brushed aside as trivial in return for the benefits. For let me be quite clear: I am not suggesting that we dismantle income support for the working-aged to balance the budget or punish welfare cheats. I am hypothesizing, with the advantage of powerful collateral evidence, that the lives of large numbers of poor people would be radically changed for the better.

There is, however, a fourth segment of the population yet to be considered, those who are pauperized by the withdrawal of government supports and unable to make alternate arrangements: the teenaged mother who has no one to turn to; the incapacitated or the inept who are thrown out of the house; those to whom economic conditions have brought long periods in which there is no work to be had; those with illnesses not covered by insurance. What of these situations?

The first resort is the network of local services. Poor communities in our hypothetical society are still dotted with storefront health clinics, emergency relief agencies, employment services, legal services. They depend for support on local taxes or local philanthropy, and the local taxpayers and philanthropists tend to scrutinize them rather closely. But, by the same token, they also receive considerably more resources than they formerly did. The dismantling of the federal services has poured tens of billions of dollars back into the private economy. Some of that money no doubt has been spent on Mercedes and summer homes on the Cape. But some has been spent on capital investments that generate new jobs. And some has been spent on increased local services to the poor, voluntarily or as decreed by the municipality. In many cities, the coverage provided by this network of agencies is more generous, more humane, more wisely distributed, and more effective in its results than the services formerly subsidized by the federal government.

But we must expect that a large number of people will fall between the cracks. How might we go about trying to retain the advantages of a zero-level welfare system and still address the residual needs?

As we think about the nature of the population still in need, it becomes apparent that their basic problem in the vast majority of the cases is the lack of a job, and this problem is temporary. What they need is something to tide them over while finding a new place in the economy. So our first step is to re-install the Unemployment Insurance program in more or less its previous form. Properly administered, unemployment insurance makes sense. Even if it is restored with all the defects of current practice, the negative effects of Unemployment Insurance alone are relatively minor. Our objective is not to wipe out chicanery or to construct a theoretically unblemished system, but to meet legitimate human needs without doing more harm than good. Unemployment Insurance is one of the least harmful ways of contributing to such ends. Thus the system has been amended to take care of the victims of short-term swings in the economy.

Who is left? We are now down to the hardest of the hard core of the welfare-dependent. They have no jobs. They have been unable to find jobs (or have not tried to find jobs) for a longer period of time than the unemployment benefits cover. They have no families who will help. They have no friends who will help. For some reason, they cannot get help from local services or private charities except for the soup kitchen and a bed in the Salvation Army hall.

What will be the size of this population? We have never tried a zero-level federal welfare system under conditions of late-twentieth-century national wealth, so we cannot do more than speculate. But we may speculate. Let us ask of whom the population might consist and how they might fare.

For any category of "needy" we may name, we find ourselves driven to one of two lines of thought. Either the person is in a category that is going to be at the top of the list of services that localities vote for themselves, and at the top of the list of private services, or the person is in a category where help really is not all that essential or desirable. The burden of the conclusion is not that every single person will be taken care of, but that the extent of resources to deal with needs is likely to be very great—not based on wishful thinking, but on extrapolations from reality.

To illustrate, let us consider the plight of the stereotypical welfare mother—never married, no skills, small children, no steady help from a man. It is safe to say that, now as in the 1950s, there is no one who has less sympathy from the white middle class, which is to be the source of most of the money for the private and local services we envision. Yet this same white middle class is a soft touch for people trying to make it on their own, and a soft touch for "deserving" needy mothers—AFDC was one of the most widely popular of the New Deal welfare measures, intended as it was for widows with small children. Thus we may envision two quite different scenarios.

In one scenario, the woman is presenting the local or private service with this proposition: "Help me find a job and day-care for my children, and I will take care of the rest." In effect, she puts herself into the same category as the widow and the deserted wife—identifies herself as one of the most obviously deserving of the deserving poor. Welfare mothers who want to get into the labor force are likely to find a wide range of help. In the other scenario, she asks for an outright and indefinite cash grant—in effect, a private or local version of AFDC—so that she can stay with the children and not hold a job. In the latter case, it is very easy to imagine situations in which she will not be able to find a local service or a private philanthropy to provide the help she seeks. The question we must now ask is: What's so bad about that? If children were always better off being with their mother all day and if, by the act of giving birth, a mother acquired the inalienable right to be with the child, then her situation would be unjust to her and injurious to her children. Neither assertion can be defended, however—especially not in the 1980s, when more mothers of all classes work away from the home than ever before, and even more especially not in view of the empirical record for the children growing up under the current welfare system. Why should the mother be exempted by the system from the pressures that must affect everyone else's decision to work?

As we survey these prospects, important questions remain unresolved. The first of these is why, if federal social transfers are treacherous, should locally mandated transfers be less so? Why should a municipality be permitted to legislate its own AFDC or Food Stamp program if their results are so inherently bad?

Part of the answer lies in conceptions of freedom. I have deliberately avoided raising them—the discussion is about how to help the disadvantaged, not about how to help the advantaged cut their taxes, to which arguments for personal freedom somehow always get diverted. Nonetheless, the point is valid: Local or even state systems leave much more room than a federal system for everyone, donors and recipients alike, to exercise freedom of choice about the kind of system they live under. Laws are more easily made and changed, and people who find them unacceptable have much more latitude in going somewhere more to their liking.

But the freedom of choice argument, while legitimate, is not necessary. We may put the advantages of local systems in terms of the Law of Imperfect Selection. A federal system must inherently employ very crude, inaccurate rules for deciding who gets what kind of help, and the results are as I outlined them in chapter 16. At the opposite extreme—a neighbor helping a neighbor, a family member helping another family member—the law loses its validity nearly altogether. Very fine-grained judgments based on personal knowledge are being made about specific people and changing situations. In neighborhoods and small cities, the procedures can still bring much individualized information to bear on decisions. Even systems in large cities and states can do much better than a national system; a decaying industrial city in the Northeast and a booming sunbelt city of the same size can and probably should adopt much different rules about who gets what and how much.

A final and equally powerful argument for not impeding local systems is diversity. We know much more in the 1980s than we knew in the 1960s about what does not work. We have a lot to learn about what *does* work. Localities have been a rich source of experiments. Marva Collins in Chicago gives us an example of how a school can bring inner-city students up to national norms. Sister Falaka Fattah in Philadelphia shows us how homeless youths can be rescued from the streets. There are numberless such lessons waiting to be learned from the diversity of local efforts. By all means, let a hundred flowers bloom, and if the federal government can play a useful role in lending a hand and spreading the word of successes, so much the better.

The ultimate unresolved question about our proposal to abolish income maintenance for the working-aged is how many people will fall through the cracks. In whatever detail we try to foresee the consequences, the objection may always be raised: We cannot be *sure* that everyone will be taken care of in the degree to which we would wish. But this observation by no means settles the question. If one may point in objection to the child now fed by Food Stamps who would go hungry, one may also point with satisfaction to the child who would have an entirely different and better future. Hungry children should be fed; there is no argument about that. It is no less urgent that children be allowed to grow up in a system free of the forces that encourage them to remain poor and dependent. If a strategy reasonably promises to remove those forces, after so many attempts to "help the poor" have failed, it is worth thinking about.

But that rationale is too vague. Let me step outside the persona I have employed and put the issue in terms of one last intensely personal hypothetical example. Let us suppose that you, a parent, could know that tomorrow your own child would be made an orphan. You have a choice. You may put your child with an extremely poor family, so poor that your child will be badly clothed and will indeed sometimes be hungry. But you also know that the parents have worked hard all their lives, will make sure your child goes to school and studies, and will teach your child that independence is a primary value. Or you may put your child with a family with parents who have never worked, who will be incapable of overseeing your child's education—but who have plenty of food and good clothes, provided by others. If the choice about where one would put one's own child is as clear to you as it is to me, on what grounds does one justify support of a system that, indirectly but without doubt, makes the other choice for other children? The answer that "What we really want is a world where that choice is not forced upon us" is no answer. We have tried to have it that way. We failed. Everything we know about why we failed tells us that more of the same will not make the dilemma go away.

THE IDEAL OF OPPORTUNITY

Billions for equal opportunity, not one cent for equal outcome—such is the slogan to inscribe on the banner of whatever cause my proposals constitute. Their common theme is to make it possible to get as far as one can go on one's merit, hardly a new ideal in American thought.

The ideal itself has never lapsed. What did lapse was the recognition that practical merit exists. Some people are better than others. They deserve more of society's rewards, of which money is only one small part. A principal function of social policy is to make sure they have the opportunity to reap those rewards. Government cannot identify the worthy, but it can protect a society in which the worthy can identify themselves.

I am proposing triage of a sort, triage by self-selection. In triage on the battlefield, the doctor makes the decision—this one gets treatment, that one waits, the other one is made comfortable while waiting to die. In our social triage, the decision is left up to the patient. The patient always has the right to say "I can do X" and get a chance to prove it. Society always has the right to hold him to that pledge. The patient always has the right to fail. Society always has the right to let him.

There is in this stance no lack of compassion but a presumption of respect. People—all people, black or white, rich or poor—may be unequally responsible for what has happened to them in the past, but all are equally responsible for what they do next. . . . [I]n our idealized society a person can fail repeatedly and always be qualified for another chance—to try again, to try something easier, to try something different. The options are always open. Opportunity is endless. There is no punishment for failure, only a total absence of rewards. Society—or our idealized society—should be preoccupied with making sure that achievement is rewarded.

There is no shortage of people to be rewarded. Go into any inner-city school and you will find students of extraordinary talent, kept from knowing how good they are by rules we imposed in the name of fairness. Go into any poor community, and you will find people of extraordinary imagination and perseverance, energy and pride, making tortured accommodations to the strange world we created in the name of generosity. The success stories of past generations of poor in this country are waiting to be repeated.

There is no shortage of institutions to provide the rewards. Our schools know how to educate students who want to be educated. Our industries know how to find productive people and reward them. Our police know how to protect people who are ready to cooperate in their own protection. Our system of justice knows how to protect the rights of individuals who know what their rights are. Our philanthropic institutions know how to multiply the effectiveness of people who are already trying to help themselves. In short, American society is very good at reinforcing the investment of an individual in himself. For the affluent and for the middle-class, these mechanisms continue to work about as well as they ever have, and we enjoy their benefits. Not so for the poor. American government, in its recent social policy, has been ineffectual in trying to stage-manage their decision to invest, and it has been unintentionally punitive toward those who would make the decision on their own. It is time to get out of their way.

ESCAPISM

It is entertaining to indulge in speculations about solutions, but they remain only speculations. Congress will not abolish income-maintenance for the working-aged. . . . More generally, it is hard to imagine any significant reform of social policy in the near future. When one thinks of abolishing income maintenance, for example, one must recall that ours is a system that, faced with the bankruptcy of Social Security in the early 1980s, went into paroxysms of anxiety at the prospect of delaying the cost-of-living increase for six months.

But the cautiousness of the system is not in itself worrisome. Reforms should be undertaken carefully and slowly, and often not at all. What should worry us instead is a peculiar escapism that has gripped the consideration of social policy. It seems that those who legislate and administer and write about social policy can tolerate any increase in actual suffering as long as the system in place does not explicitly permit it. It is better, by the logic we have been living with, that we try to take care of 100 percent of the problem and make matters worse than that we solve 75 percent of the problem with a solution that does not try to do anything about the rest.

Escapism is a natural response. Most of us want to help. It makes us feel bad to think of neglected children and rat-infested slums, and we are happy to pay for the thought that people who are good at taking care of such things are out there. If the numbers of neglected children and numbers of rats seem to be going up instead of down, it is understandable that we choose to focus on how much we put into the effort instead of what comes out. The tax checks we write buy us, for relatively little money and no effort at all, a quieted conscience. The more we pay, the more certain we can be that we have done our part, and it is essential that we feel that way regardless of what we accomplish. A solution that would have us pay less *and* acknowledge that some would go unhelped is unacceptable.

To this extent, the barrier to radical reform of social policy is not the pain it would cause the intended beneficiaries of the present system, but the pain it would cause the donors. The real contest about the direction of social policy is not between people who want to cut budgets and people who want to help. When reforms finally do occur, they will happen not because stingy people have won, but because generous people have stopped kidding themselves.

QUESTIONS FOR ANALYSIS

1. Is Murray's picture of a future without welfare overly optimistic? How many people would "fall between the cracks"? Do you agree that they would be responsible for their failures?
2. When discussing single mothers, Murray denies that a woman has an "inalienable right" to be with her child. Do you agree? Should a woman who cannot support her children be forced to turn them over to a state-run orphanage, as some welfare opponents in Congress have advocated?
3. Do you agree with Murray's preference for local welfare programs over federal welfare programs? Will local governments find themselves overburdened if federal welfare programs are eliminated?
4. Murray asks us to imagine our own orphaned children in two different settings. In one, they are

poorly clothed and fed but their adoptive parents are hardworking. In the other, their needs are amply met but they live in a welfare family. Which would you prefer? Why?

5. Murray writes, "Government cannot identify the worthy, but it can protect a society in which the worthy can identify themselves." Would a society without federal welfare programs be such a society?
6. According to Murray, compassion, not stinginess, should lead us to make radical changes in welfare policy. Do you agree?
7. Would justice be served by the elimination of federal welfare programs?

CASE PRESENTATION

Marta Green

Marta Green was nineteen years old when she and her husband left Honduras for the United States. By her mid-twenties, broke and with little in the way of job skills, she was a divorced mother with two daughters and on welfare. In *Living on the Edge: The Realities of Welfare in America,*[1] she described to author Mark Robert Rank the impact of the divorce:

> To me my divorce and the breaking up of my house was a crisis. I had everything. Everything I needed, you know, like electrical knives. That probably doesn't sound like much to you. But I did have all my utensils in the kitchen. And then, I come to an empty place, like we came here. We didn't have a frying pan. We didn't have a plate, a cup, or anything.
>
> When you get married you get everything in the bridal shower. And in the wedding you get stuff. And then little by little, before the kids come, you get things that you need, so you're all set up. But when we moved here, I had to buy the bed for my kids because we were sleeping on the floor. That's money from the same grant, from welfare. But I could not buy that bed with the money left in one month. I had to save three-and-a-half months before I got the bed. And then there's things like the bed sheets and pillow cases. This is a crisis to me. It is. And then you come into the kitchen, and the kids want pancakes, and you don't have a frying pan (pp. 41–42).

Asked by Rank about her activities with her children, she answered:

> In the winter we don't go anywhere. Because it's very hard without a car. I always had a car until last winter. It was very hard. Because we had to wait there sometimes twenty minutes for the bus. And with the kids and the very cold days, it's very hard. I only took them out last winter once, besides the Saturday afternoons that we go to church.
>
> One Sunday, they had some free tickets to go to the circus. And I only had to buy my ticket. They both had theirs free. The circus was at seven. And it was done by ten. And we were waiting for the bus until eleven thirty that Sunday night. In the middle of the winter. And then finally we started walkin' home. We walked all the way home. We made it home by twelve thirty. They were tired and almost frozen. And then I thought, this is it, no more. So we really don't go very much anywhere (pp. 53–54).

Equally frustrating for Green is her inability to afford many things her daughters ask for, including the status symbols other parents can afford:

> Like the kids at school, they wear Nike tennis shoes. Name-brand tennis shoes. And then I go and buy them a five-dollar pair of tennis shoes. And they say, "Mom, no. We want the Nike shoes because my girlfriend, Emily, has them." And I say, "No, because for thirteen dollars I can buy shoes for both of you." And they get angry and they don't understand. But I try to talk to them. They are very good kids. They get upset for a little while and sometimes they cry, but after they get over it, I just talk to them and say, "Listen, this is the situation that we are going through. But we'll get over this. And in a couple of years, Mommy's going to buy you some nicer stuff. But right now we have to take it like it is" (p. 69).

When Rank asked her if she thought she would ever want more children, she answered:

> No. No. I don't think that I *ever* want to have another child. I think that will stop me from doing things that I want to do. And it won't be fair to me. It won't be fair for the new child. And it won't be fair at all for the two that I have (p. 77).

[1]From *Living on the Edge,* by Mark Robert Rank. © 1994 by Columbia University Press. Reprinted by permission of the publisher.

In Rank's study of Wisconsin welfare recipients from 1981 to 1986, 4 percent of the sample reported that welfare initially made them lazy and continued to make them lazy. Another 14 percent reported that they stopped feeling lazy as their sense of pride led them to seek work. Still another 8 percent reported that welfare made them feel trapped and depressed. Marta Green belongs to the 16 percent reporting that welfare makes them work harder. As she told Rank:

> It's not makin' me lazy. It's makin' me more ambitious than I was before. Because when I was livin' with my husband, I had my house and food and my part-time job. I had everything I wanted for my life. Now I am here. And I go to school in the morning. Then I come home and do something around the house. And then I look at this place empty and I say, "Welfare, is this what you're going to give me all my life?" And I do not want it. I want to get over this. It's not making me lazy. Because I do not like it. I like to be able to be free (*chooses words very carefully*) (p. 136).

Asked about her hopes, she told him:

> And the hope that I have is . . . (*sigh*) after I start workin'; I'll pay the state back somehow. I keep track of everythin' I get from them. And I already know how much I received last year from them. And this year. And if my taxes are not enough, I put in something if I am able to, to the Red Cross, Salvation Army. And this is the hope that I have. To know that I do not owe anythin'. That if ever someone ask me, "Did you ever receive welfare?" I say, "Yes. But I paid back. It was a loan that I got." That's my hope, pretty much (p. 99).

QUESTIONS FOR ANALYSIS

1. What are the most common stereotypes of a welfare mother? Does Marta Green fit them?
2. Does Marta Green seem destined for welfare dependence? Why or why not?
3. Is Marta Green one of the women who would fall through the cracks in Murray's "thought experiment"?
4. Does Marta Green's story change your opinion one way or the other about welfare? If so, how?

CASE PRESENTATION

The Poorest Place in America

"The town has no public parks or swimming pools, no movie theaters, no shopping malls, not even a McDonald's or a Wal-Mart. In fact, business in Lake Providence, Louisiana, is so bad that even the pawnshop has shut down."

So begins Jack E. White's profile of "The Poorest Place in America," which appeared in the August 15, 1994, issue of *Time*. Among the other depressing facts pointed out in the article are the following:

1. According to the 1990 census, one Census Block Number within the city, which contains three-quarters of the city's population, had the lowest median annual household income in the country, only $6,536.
2. According to a 1992 study by the Children's Defense Fund, the parish in which Lake Providence is located had the country's highest rate of children under eighteen years old living in poverty. The rate was 70.1 percent.

The article also highlights the lack of year-round work in Lake Providence, noting that jobs are "scarce, low paying and seasonal," often "back-breaking work in the nearby cotton fields," and that hundreds of families in the town of 5,500 people live on meager welfare payments most of the year. How meager? For a single mother of one, the monthly payment is $123. For a single mother of four, it amounts to only $370.

Most Lake Providence residents who can escape, the article says, do escape. Those who cannot escape have set their hopes on an application to become part of a federal empowerment zone. An empowerment zone is an area eligible for a variety of programs meant to spur economic development, including tax incentives to attract employers and jobs, federal job-training subsidies, and other grants from Washington. In the case of Lake Providence, the hopes are to attract a factory, to open a federal-loan office serving small businesses throughout the country, and to become a tourist destination. How successful the town will be remains in doubt.

QUESTIONS FOR ANALYSIS

1. Lake Providence seems a perfect example of Michael Harrington's pockets of poverty. What's the best way to deal with its problems?
2. Does Charles Murray's "thought experiment" pay sufficient attention to people like Lake Providence's poor? If not, what could Murray say about them?
3. Critics of empowerment zones say that tax breaks are not enough to bring employers to areas like Lake Providence. Employers also require a reliable work force, good schools, and a decent quality of life. Do you agree? If so, what alternatives are there for the people of Lake Providence?
4. What would Kai Nielsen say about Lake Providence? What would his solution be?
5. The total cost of proposed tax breaks and grants in the application is $100 million. Can you think of a better way of using the money to help the people of Lake Providence?

CASE PRESENTATION

Welfare as We've Begun to Know It

The 1996 welfare reform law replaced Aid to Families with Dependent Children with a program known as Temporary Assistance to Needy Families (TANF), which gives states considerable freedom in limiting benefits, cutting them off completely, and requiring recipients to work for their benefits. Many have taken advantage of this freedom.

For instance, while the law sets a lifetime limit of sixty months on benefits, many states have set even stricter limits. Some limit benefits to a specific number of months over a set period of consecutive months. In four states (Arizona, Florida, Louisiana, and Massachusetts), the limit is twenty-four months of benefits over sixty consecutive months. In Nebraska, it's twenty-four over forty-eight consecutive months; in Oregon, twenty-four over eighty-four consecutive months. Other states limit consecutive months of benefits. In four states (Illinois, Nevada, South Carolina, and Virginia), the limit is twenty-four consecutive months. In Tennessee, the limit is eighteen. Four states limit total lifetime benefits to fewer than sixty months—Connecticut to twenty-one, Delaware to forty-eight, and New Mexico and Utah to thirty-six. One state, Texas, reduces benefits every twelfth month up to the thirty-sixth month on welfare, while two others, Arizona and Indiana, reduce them after the twenty-fourth. (Not all of these limits are exceptionless. Indiana, for instance, allows an extra month of benefits for every six months of work, up to twenty-four months of extra benefits. Tennessee allows an extra six months in counties with high unemployment rates. Connecticut allows six-month extensions for victims of family violence.)

In addition to these restrictions, seventeen states deny additional benefits for a child born to a family on TANF, and two provide only partial additional benefits. Two others, Oklahoma and South Carolina, provide additional benefits only in the form of a voucher, and Maryland provides the additional benefit only to a third party.

TANF also places work requirements on recipients, who are required to seek jobs or join a work program after either twenty-four months of benefits or when the state determines that they are ready to work, whichever comes first. Here, also, the states are free to set stricter requirements, and thirty-two of them have reduced the number of months to within six. Nine require work or a job search immediately after application for benefits. Wisconsin has replaced welfare with workfare, requiring TANF families to work thirty hours a week. In thirty-five states, recipients who do not comply can lose their full cash benefits; in seven of the states, the loss of benefits can last a lifetime. (Again, there are exceptions. Twenty-four states exempt parents of children younger than one-year-old, and all states allow health exemptions.)

QUESTIONS FOR ANALYSIS

1. How would Trudy Govier and Charles Murray evaluate the changes in welfare policy?
2. Critics of the new welfare system call it an attack on the poor. Supporters call it a means of ending welfare dependence. Which side, if either, do you agree with?
3. How strict should the limits on TANF benefits be? How strict the work requirements?
4. In terms of social justice, is TANF an improvement over AFDC, a setback, or neither better nor worse? How would John Hospers and Kai Nielsen answer this question?

CASE PRESENTATION

The Women of Project Match[1]

Roslyn Hale is the thirty-year-old mother of a four-year-old son, both of them living on welfare. She had been on welfare once before but left it to take a job as a hotel maid. After being fired because of a fight with her supervisor, she began working the overnight shift at a convenience store. She left that job after a drunk from a nearby bar threatened her with a knife. Then she took a job at another convenience store, only to be laid off because of slowing business.

Alesia Watts, twenty-six, also left welfare to take a job. Hers was a telemarketing job at $5.25 an hour with no health insurance. She quit and returned to welfare after her daughter injured her foot, but she was unhappy with her job in any case. She felt sexually harassed by some of the men she called, resented the close watch by her supervisor, and considered her two bathroom breaks every five hours insufficient. Unlike Roslyn Hale, she is now back at work, this time at a race track concession. The pay is better, the job comes with health insurance, and she enjoys the work.

Vanessa Williams was less fortunate. After she left welfare, she lost a succession of jobs because of bad experiences with boyfriends. One boyfriend threw drug parties in their house when he was supposed to be babysitting, and another, after severely beating her, came to her workplace and threatened further beatings. Now, at the age of thirty-four, she is back on welfare.

All three women have been through the doors of Project Match, an employment program in the inner city of Chicago that tracks the successes and failures of the women it helps to get off welfare. They are among the increasing number of women known as welfare cyclers. According to one estimate—by LaDonna A. Pavetti of Washington's Urban Institute—about 40 percent of the women who go on welfare can be considered cyclers, which she defines as women who spend a total of twenty-four months on welfare scattered over a sixty-month period.

What causes welfare cycling? Researchers from Northwestern University who studied Project Match cite a variety of factors, including the lack of health insurance and childcare, the lack of social skills required to keep a job, resentment of supervisors, and habitual lateness. Toby Herr, the project's director, points to the frequency of Vanessa Williams's problem—resentful boyfriends. Alesia Watts, who seems to have broken the cycle, has this to say: "You have to like where you're working at. And like the money. And have the benefits. And get a babysitter. Then there's no reason for you to go on welfare."

[1]The information comes from Jason DeParle's front-page article in *The New York Times,* "Welfare Mothers Find Jobs Easy to Get but Hard to Hold," October 24, 1994.

QUESTIONS FOR ANALYSIS

1. Would ending welfare payments after two years help the women of Project Match? Would abolishing all federal transfer payments to the poor help?
2. Suppose that women who left welfare for low-paying jobs were provided with health insurance, childcare, and wage subsidies. Would that reduce welfare cycling?
3. According to project director Toby Herr, cases like Vanessa Williams's show that welfare reform cannot work until the employment rates for women are improved. Do you agree?
4. Do the women of Project Match deserve sympathy, or are they to blame for their situations?

CHAPTER TEN

Discrimination

- **Discrimination: Its Nature and Forms**
- **Evidence of Discrimination**
- **Affirmative Action: Preferential Treatment?**
- **Arguments against Affirmative Action**
- **Arguments for Affirmative Action**

TOM L. BEAUCHAMP **The Justification of Reverse Discrimination**
RICHARD WASSERSTROM **A Defense of Programs of Preferential Treatment**
WILLIAM T. BLACKSTONE **Reverse Discrimination and Compensatory Justice**
LISA NEWTON **Reverse Discrimination as Unjustified**

CASE PRESENTATIONS: ***Proposition 209*** • ***Grutter v. Bollinger: Taking Race into Account*** • ***Reparations: An Overdue Debt to African Slaves in America?*** • ***Friendly Sexual Harassment?***

ON DECEMBER 10, 1970, the Equal Employment Opportunity Commission (EEOC) petitioned the Federal Communications Commission not to back a request by American Telephone and Telegraph (AT&T) for a rate increase on the grounds that AT&T was engaging in pervasive, systemwide, and blatantly unlawful discrimination against women, blacks, Spanish-surnamed Americans, and other minorities. After nearly two years of negotiation with the EEOC, AT&T finally reached an agreement with the government on December 28, 1972, whereby it agreed, among other things, not to discriminate in the future and to set up goals and timetables for hiring women and minorities into all nonmanagement job classifications where they were underrepresented. For its part, the EEOC agreed to drop all outstanding equal-employment actions against AT&T.

Three years later, on December 8, 1975, AT&T was sued by Dan McAleer, an AT&T service representative. McAleer claimed he had lost out on a promotion to a less qualified female employee as a result of AT&T's implementation of its agreement with the EEOC. McAleer had worked for AT&T for five years and had scored thirty-four of thirty-five on the company's performance rating. Sharon Hullery, the woman who beat McAleer for the promotion, had worked at AT&T for less than five years and had scored thirty points.

On June 9, 1976, the U.S. District Court in Washington, D.C., ruled that AT&T owed McAleer monetary compensation but not the promotion. AT&T owed McAleer the money, said the court, because he was an innocent victim of an agreement intended to remedy the company's wrongdoing. But the court didn't think AT&T owed McAleer the promotion because, in the court's view, that might help perpetuate and prolong the effects of the discrimination that the AT&T–EEOC agreement was designed to eliminate.

On January 18, 1979, the agreement between AT&T and the EEOC expired. AT&T had reached 99.7 percent of the female-hiring goals it had set up in 1973.

In recent years, laws have been passed and programs formulated to ensure fair and equal treatment of all people in employment practices. Nevertheless, unequal practices still exist. To help remedy these, the federal government in the early 1970s instituted an affirmative-action program.

Before affirmative action, many institutions already followed nondiscriminatory as well as merit-hiring employment practices to equalize employment opportunities. In proposing affirmative action, the government recognized the worth of such endeavors, but said that it did not think they were enough. *Affirmative action,* therefore, refers to positive measures beyond neutral nondiscriminatory and merit-hiring employment practices. It is an aggressive program intended to identify and remedy unfair discrimination practiced against many people who are qualified for jobs. Although most of our discussion focuses on discrimination in employment, closely analogous arguments apply in debates over admission to competitive colleges and universities, especially when racial minorities or women have been admitted historically in much smaller number than their presence in the applicant pool or the general population.

Among the most controversial versions of affirmative action are preferential- and quota-hiring systems. *Preferential hiring* is an employment practice designed to give special consideration to people from groups that traditionally have been victimized by racism, sexism, or other forms of discrimination. *Quota hiring* was sometimes ordered by the courts for a specific organization that had expressly refused to hire certain groups, until some appropriate balance could be achieved. For example, companies and unions were required to provide apprentice and reapprentice training to hire, promote, and train minorities and women in specified numerical ratios, in specified job categories, until specified remedial goals were achieved. But in other situations, a less rigid "goal" is established to assess whether hiring has indeed been nondiscriminatory over a period of time. For example, if a company has hired 20 percent women for a certain type of job over a number of years, but the labor pool of persons qualified and available to work in that job was 50 percent women, then this disparity raises a presumption that discrimination against women occurred in the hiring. Although not a "quota," this use of statistical analysis has also sometimes been called "quota hiring," though supporters object that this is a misleading label for the use of statistics to analyze discrimination.

But critics charge that at least in some instances, implementing affirmative-action guidelines has led to *reverse discrimination—that is, the unfair treatment of a majority member (usually a white male).* Presumably, this was the basis for McAleer's complaint. Was he treated unfairly? Was AT&T's action moral? Would it have been fairer had the employees names been thrown into a hat from which one was drawn? Obviously, such preferential programs raise questions of social justice.

Affirmative action also has meanings other than "preferential hiring." In its mildest form, it means simply an aggressive program of recruitment of candidates to ensure that qualified women and racial minorities are appropriately represented in the applicant pool. In a somewhat stronger form, it involves a conclusion that traditional hiring criteria have masked hidden biases against certain groups, requiring a modification of those criteria to more appropriately match the actual qualifications needed for the position in a way as free of bias as possible. Ferreting out qualifications that might seem on the surface to be appropriate distinguishing criteria is a long process upon which this version of affirmative action has focused.

Undoubtedly, some will wonder: Why not focus directly on the morality of sexism? By *sexism,* we mean the unfair treatment of a person exclusively on the basis of sex. Perhaps we should focus on it, but consider that in all our discussions so far, we have made reasonable cases for at least two sides of an issue. True, perhaps one side was more flawed than another, but in all cases, reasonable people could disagree. But the fact is that few seriously argue any more that sexism, as defined, is moral. So if we focused on sexism, we would be inviting a most lopsided discussion. This would be unfortunate in the light of so many aspects of sexism that genuinely deserve moral debate. One of these aspects involves such proposed remedies as preferential treatment.

Another reason for not considering sexism exclusively is that this chapter naturally raises questions of social justice. Many discussions of social justice founder because they remain abstract, content to theorize while scrupulously avoiding practice. For example, it is easy and safe to argue that a government must remedy racial injustice. It is far more controversial to argue that a government must implement forced busing to do so. The same applies to sexism. Most would agree that the government has an obligation to correct the social injustice of sexism, but how?

It is one thing to recognize, deplore, and want to correct any injustice. It is entirely another thing to remedy the injustice fairly. Sadly, too many discussions of social justice ignore means entirely, often offering the defense that the means vary from situation to situation. This is undoubtedly true, but the debate flying around so many social justice questions today concerns proposed means. We should learn to examine every situation's means and also the common but agonizing predicament of applauding the intention and even the probable consequences of an action, but deploring the action itself. For many people, preferential treatment is just such a problem.

Although we focus on issues of race and sex discrimination in this chapter, it is worth noting the emergence in recent years of very similar issues for people with disablities, especially in the workplace. The Americans with Disabilities Act of 1990 requires that employers and educational institutions make "reasonable accommodation" so that individuals with disablities can compete to the best of their abilities in employment and education. While everyone would agree that we should not discriminate *against* people with disablities simply because of a disability, the controversy emerges over what some consider favoritism or special treatment of individuals with disablities. In a 2001 decision, the U.S. Supreme Court held that the PGA tour must allow disabled golfer Casey Martin to use a golf cart in professional tournaments, even though the other players must all walk the course. The PGA had argued that his request would "fundamentally alter the nature" of the game, but this was rejected by the Court. By considering whether this is fair to other players, we confront many of the same issues concerning justice in society that we face with discrimination by race and sex. Is society obligated to do whatever it takes to create a truly "level playing field" for everyone? Do these programs give unfair advantages to some groups but not others? Or is society obligated only to make sure we do not discriminate *against* people based on race, sex, or disability, but otherwise let people fend for themselves?

DISCRIMINATION: ITS NATURE AND FORMS

To discriminate in employment is to make an adverse decision against employees based on their membership in a certain class. Included in the preceding definition of discrimination in employment are three basic elements: (1) The decision is against employees solely because of their membership in a certain group. (2) The decision is based on the assumption that the group is in some way inferior to some other group and thus deserving of unequal treatment. (3) The decision in some way harms those it's aimed at. Since, traditionally, most of the discrimination in the American workplace has been aimed at women and minorities such as blacks and Hispanics, the following discussion focuses on these groups.[1]

On-the-job discrimination can be intentional or unintentional, practiced by a single individual or individuals in a company or by the institution itself. *Intentional* here means knowingly or consciously; *unintentional* means unthinkingly or not consciously. *Institution* refers to the business, company, corporation, profession, or even the system within which the discrimination operates. These distinctions provide a basis for identifying four forms of discrimination: (1) intentional individual, (2) unintentional individual, (3) intentional institutional, and (4) unintentional institutional.

1. ***Intentional individual*** discrimination is an isolated act of discrimination *knowingly* performed by some individual out of personal prejudice. Example: A male personnel director routinely passes over females for supervisory jobs because he believes and knowingly acts on the belief that "lady bosses mean trouble."

2. ***Unintentional individual*** discrimination is an isolated act of discrimination performed by some individual who *unthinkingly* or *unconsciously* adopts traditional practices and stereotypes. Example: If the male in the preceding case acted without being aware of the bias underlying his decisions, his action would fall into this category.

3. ***Intentional institutional*** discrimination is an act of discrimination that is part of the reactive behavior of a company or profession which knowingly discriminates out of the personal prejudices of its members. Example: The male personnel director passes over women for supervisory jobs because "the boys in the company don't like to take orders from females."

4. ***Unintentional institutional*** discrimination is an act of discrimination that is part of the routine behavior of a company or profession that has unknowingly incorporated sexually or racially prejudicial practices into its operating procedures. Example: An engineering firm routinely avoids hiring women because of the stereotypical assumption that women don't make good engineers or that its clients won't do business with women.

---

[1]Manuel G. Velasquez, *Business Ethics: Concepts and Cases* (Englewood Cliffs, N.J.: Prentice-Hall, 1982), p. 266.

In recent years, discussions of discrimination have focused on institutional forms, with special emphasis on the unintentional institutional. In fact, it's been this kind of discrimination that some believe only affirmative-action programs can root out. Others consider programs like this inherently unjust or counterproductive. They say that workplace discrimination can be corrected through strict enforcement of anti-discrimination law without resorting to preferential-treatment programs. The force of these positions depends in part on whether the body of anti-discriminatory legislation that has developed over the past twenty years has, in fact, tended to reduce discrimination in the workplace. If it has, then it would lend weight to the anti-affirmative-action positions. If it hasn't, then the proaffirmative-action position would be strengthened. So before inspecting the two positions, let's briefly examine the relative positions of whites and minorities and of males and females in the American workplace to see if they say anything about ongoing discrimination.

EVIDENCE OF DISCRIMINATION

Determining the presence of discrimination isn't easy because many factors could possibly account for the relative positions of various groups in the work world. But generally speaking, there are reasonable grounds for thinking that an institution is practicing discrimination (intentional or unintentional) when (1) statistics indicate that members of a group are being treated unequally in comparison with other groups, and (2) endemic attitudes, and formal and informal practices and policies, seem to account for the skewed statistics.

Statistical Evidence

Compelling statistical evidence points to the fact that a disproportionate number of women and minority members hold the less desirable jobs and get paid less than their white male counterparts. For example, at all occupational levels, women make less money than men—even for the same work—despite legislation forbidding discrimination on the basis of sex. According to Census Bureau statistics from 1999, women working full time earned only 75.1 percent as much as full-time male workers. Moreover, the disparity cut across all occupational categories from salaried administrators and officials (the highest paid) to farming, forestry, and fishing (the lowest paid). In the former category, the median income for men in 1998 was $55,664, while the median for women was $36,389; in the latter, the respective median incomes were $18,855 and $15,865. Even though much of the gap between men and women reflects differences among older workers, the 1999 average yearly earnings for female full-time workers under thirty years old remained lower than the average for men under thirty at every education level. For instance, the average income for male high school graduates between twenty-five and twenty-nine was $25,559 compared to $20,669 for women; among college graduates with only a bachelor's degree, the respective figures were $40,098 and $35,295; among those with a master's degree, $54,777 and $42,834.

Similar disparities show up between non-Hispanic white males and black and Hispanic males. The 1999 median income for full-time workers over twenty-five of the first group was $41,555 compared to $30,926 for their black counterparts and $25,242 for their Hispanic counterparts. Once again, the disparities applied to all educational levels. Among high school graduates, for example, the respective figures were $34,839, $27,408, and $25,291; among college graduates with only a bachelor's degree, $51,884, $40,805, and $41,467; among those with a master's degree, $61,904, $52,308, and $50,410.[2] These and other statistics indicate that women and minorities are still not treated as equals of white men.

Additional Evidence

Although some would disagree, the statistics alone don't establish discrimination, for one could always argue that other factors account for these disparities. But there are indications of widespread attitudes and formal and informal institutional practices and policies which, taken collectively, point to discrimination as the cause of these statistical differences.

One such indication is the number of job requirements that are not related to job performance but discriminate against minorities and women. Standardized intelligence tests, for example, are thought by many people to be culturally biased against blacks. Yet in many cases, standardized intelligence tests are required, and applicants scoring the highest are given the available jobs, even though lower scores do not correlate with poor job performance. Similarly, weight requirements often rule out women from jobs involving physical work even though they have the physical ability to perform well.

Then there's the commonplace practice in many trades and industries of filling positions by word-of-mouth recruitment policies. In jobs dominated by white males, the word of a job vacancy tends to reach other white males. And even when others do learn of the vacancy, they may not be in any position to be hired to fill it. The problem is particularly acute at the executive level, where many women and minorities hit "an invisible ceiling" beyond which they have difficulty rising. Part of the problem, many claim, is the existence of private white male clubs, where important business contacts are made and developed. Another, they claim, is the resistance of people at the level to those who are "not like us."

Taken together, the statistics, personal and institutional attitudes, assumptions, and practices provide powerful evidence of intractable discrimination against women and minorities in the American workplace. Recognizing the existence of such discrimination and believing that, for a variety of reasons, it's wrong, we have as a nation passed laws expressly forbidding discrimination in recruitment, screening, promotion, compensation, and firing practices. In short, specific laws have been enacted to ensure equal opportunity in employment. The aim of these policies is to prevent further discrimination, and they probably have prevented egregious instances of discrimination. But the evidence indicates that they have not had the effect of providing equal opportunity to women and minorities as groups. Furthermore, anti-discrimination laws do not address the present-day effects of past discrimination. They ignore, for example, the fact that because of past discrimination women and minorities in general lack the skills of white males and are disproportionately underrepresented in more prestigious and better paying jobs. To remedy the effects of past discrimination and seeing no other way to counteract apparently

---

[2]These figures come from the Census Bureau's Web site at Historical Income Tables—People, table P-48, and Money Income in the United States: 1999, tables 9 and 10. For more detailed information, visit the Census Bureau's web site (http://www.census.gov/) or the American FactFinder site, maintained by the Census Bureau (http://factfinder.census.gov/).

visceral racism and sexism, many people today call for specific affirmative-action programs.

AFFIRMATIVE ACTION: PREFERENTIAL TREATMENT?

As amended by the Equal Employment Opportunity Act of 1972, the Civil Rights Act of 1964 requires businesses that have substantial dealings with the federal government to undertake affirmative-action programs. *Affirmative-action programs are plans designed to correct imbalances in employment that exist directly as a result of past discrimination.* Even though these acts do not technically require companies to undertake affirmative-action programs, courts responded to acts of job discrimination by ordering the offending firms to implement such programs to combat the effects of past discrimination. In effect, then, all business institutions must adopt affirmative-action programs either in theory or in fact. They must be able to prove that they have not been practicing institutional sexism or racism, and if they cannot prove this, they must undertake programs to ensure against racism or sexism.

What do affirmative-action programs involve? The EEOC lists general guidelines as steps to affirmative action. Under these steps, firms must issue a written equal-employment policy and an affirmative-action commitment. They must appoint a top official with responsibility and authority to direct and implement their program and to publicize their policy and affirmative-action commitment. In addition, firms must survey current female and minority employment by department and job classification. Where underrepresentation of these groups is evident, firms must develop goals and timetables to improve in each area of underrepresentation. They then must develop specific programs to achieve these goals, establish an internal audit system to monitor them, and evaluate progress in each aspect of the program. Finally, companies must develop supportive in-house and community programs to combat discrimination.

In implementing such programs, some companies have adopted a policy of preferential treatment for women and minorities. *Preferential treatment refers to the practice of giving individuals favored consideration in hiring or promotions for other than job-related reasons* (such as the person is female or black). Those espousing preferential treatment argue that such a policy is the only way to remedy traditional sexism and racism or at least that it is the most expeditious and fairest way to do it. In some instances, preferential treatment for women and minorities takes the form of a quota system—that is, *an employment policy of representing women and minorities in the firm in direct proportion to their numbers in society or in the community at large.* Thus, a firm operating in a community which has a 20 percent black population might try to ensure that 20 percent of its work force be black.[3]

To unravel some of the complex moral issues affirmative-action programs can raise, let's look at a specific instance of preferential hiring. Suppose an equally

---

[3]Some institutions simply reserve a number of places for women and minority members. The University of California at Davis, for example, had such a policy in its medical school when it denied Alan Bakke admission. Bakke appealed to the Supreme Court, which—in a 5 to 4 decision in 1978—ordered that he be admitted to the medical school and struck down the set-aside quota for racial minorities that Davis had in place at the time. However, the Court also said the university may take race into account in their admissions as long as they did not establish rigid quotas for any particular group.

qualified man and woman are applying for a job. The employer, conscious of affirmative-action guidelines and realizing that the company has historically discriminated against women in its employment policies, adopts a preferential hiring system. Since males are already disproportionately well represented and females underrepresented, the preferential system gives the female applicant a decided advantage. As a result, the employer hires the female. Is this action moral? Are affirmative-action programs that operate in the preferential way moral?

Many people argue that affirmative-action programs are inherently discriminatory and therefore unjust. In this context, *discriminatory* should be understood to refer to policies that favor individuals on non-job-related grounds (for example, on the basis of sex, color, or ethnic heritage). It has been argued that preferential hiring is unjust because it involves giving preferential treatment to women and minorities over equally qualified white males, a practice that is clearly discriminatory, albeit in reverse.

Some in favor of affirmative action, however, attempt to rebut this objection by appealing to principles of *compensatory justice. Since women and minorities clearly continue to be victimized directly and indirectly by traditional discrimination in the workplace, they are entitled to some compensation.* This is one basis for preferential treatment. The soundness of this contention seems to rely on at least two factors: (1) that affirmative-action programs involving preferential treatment will in fact provide adequate compensation and (2) that they will provide compensation more fairly than any other alternative.[4] Since the justice and the morality of affirmative-action programs depend to a large degree on these assumptions, we should examine them.

The question that comes to mind in regard to the first assumption is: adequate compensation for whom? The answer seems obvious: for women and minorities. But does this mean *individual* women and minority-group members or women and minorities taken *collectively*? University of Tampa Professor Herman J. Saatkamp, Jr., has demonstrated that this question, far from being merely a technical one, bears directly on the morality of affirmative-action programs and how they are implemented.[5]

Saatkamp points out that the question of the conflict between individual and collective merit typifies the debate between government agencies and business over employment policies. On the one hand, business is ordinarily concerned with the individual merit and deserts of its employees. On the other hand, government agencies primarily focus on the relative status of groups within the population at large. To put the conflict in perspective, employment policies based solely on individual merit would try to ensure that only those individuals who could prove they deserved compensation would benefit and only those proved to be the source of discrimination would suffer. Of course, such a focus places an almost unbearable burden on the resources of an individual to provide sufficient, precise data to document employment discrimination, which is commonly acknowledged to exist at times in subtle, perhaps even imperceptible, forms at various organizational levels. Indeed, social policies recognize this difficulty by focusing on discrimination on an aggregate

---

[4]Albert W. Flores, "Reverse Discrimination: Towards a Just Society," in *Business & Professional Ethics,* a quarterly newsletter/report (Troy, N.Y.: Center for the Study of the Human Dimensions of Science & Technology, Rensselaer Polytechnic Institute, Jan. 1978), p. 4.

[5]Flores, "Reverse Discrimination," pp. 5–6.

level. Individuals, then, need not prove they themselves were discriminated against but only that they are members of groups that have traditionally suffered because of discrimination.

Taking the collective approach to remedying job discrimination is not without its own disadvantages.

1. Policies based on collective merit tend to pit one social group against another. White males face off against all nonwhite males; women find themselves jockeying with other disadvantaged groups for priority employment status; black females can end up competing with Hispanic males for preferential treatment. This factionalizing aspect of policies based on collective merit can prove detrimental to society.
2. Policies based on collective merit victimize some individuals. The individual white male who loses out on a job because of preferential treatment given a woman or a minority-group member is penalized.
3. In some cases, the women and minority members selected under preferential treatment are in fact less deserving of compensation than those women and minorities who are not selected. In short, those most in need may not benefit at all when preference by group membership is divorced from individual need.
4. Some members of majority groups may be just as deserving or more deserving of compensation than some women or members of minority groups. Many white males, for example, are more seriously limited in seeking employment than some women and minority-group members are.
5. Policies based on collective merit can be prohibitively expensive for business. To enforce such programs, businesses must hire people to collect data, process forms, deal with government agencies, and handle legal procedures. From business's viewpoint, this additional time, energy, and expense could have been channeled into more commercially productive directions.

In sum, those who argue that affirmative-action programs will provide adequate compensation for the victims of discrimination must grapple with the problems of determining the focus of the compensation: on the individual or on the group. While both focuses have merit, neither is without disadvantages. Furthermore, it seems neither approach can be implemented without first resolving a complex chain of moral concerns.

But even if we assume that affirmative-action programs will provide adequate compensation, it is still difficult to demonstrate the validity of the second assumption of those who endorse affirmative action by appealing to principles of compensatory justice: that such programs will provide compensation more fairly than any other alternative. By nature, affirmative-action programs provide compensation at the expense of the white males' right to fair and equal employment treatment. In other words, affirmative-action programs in the form of preferential treatment undermine the fundamental principle of just employment practice: that a person should be hired or promoted only on job-related grounds. Apparently, then, it is an awesome undertaking to defend the proposition that affirmative action will provide compensation more fairly than any other alternative when such a proposition makes a non-job-related factor (membership in a group) a relevant employment criterion.

Although it would appear that reverse discrimination may not be justified on grounds of compensation, we should not conclude that it cannot be justified. In fact, some people contend that a more careful examination of the principles of justice suggests an alternative defense. As we have mentioned, those who argue against affirmative-action programs do so because such programs allegedly involve unequal treatment and are therefore unjust. The clear assumption here is that whatever involves unequal treatment is in and of itself unjust. But as Professor Albert W. Flores points out, while justice would demand that equals receive equal treatment, it is likewise true that unequals should receive treatment appropriate to their differences. Hence, he concludes that "unfair or differential treatment may be required by the principles of justice."[6] In other words, unequal treatment is unfair in the absence of any characteristic difference between applicants which, from the viewpoint of justice, would constitute relevant differences. Following this line of reasoning, we must wonder whether being a female or a minority member would constitute a "relevant difference" that would justify unequal treatment.

To illustrate, let's ask how one could justify giving preferential consideration to a female job applicant over an equally qualified white male. Flores contends that while sex may be irrelevant to the job, it may be a relevant consideration as to who should be selected. In effect, he distinguishes between criteria relevant to a job and those relevant to candidate selection. He clearly bases this distinction on a concept of business's social responsibilities. As has been amply demonstrated elsewhere, business does not exist in a commercial vacuum. It is part of a social system and, as such, has obligations that relate to the welfare and integrity of society at large. Thus, Flores argues that when a firm must decide between two equally qualified applicants, say a white male and a female, it is altogether justified in introducing as a selection criterion some concept of social justice, which in this case takes cognizance of a fair distribution of society's resources amid scarcities among competing groups. From the viewpoint of justice, business may be correct in hiring the qualified female or minority member. Notice, however, that this contention is based primarily not on principles of compensatory justice but on a careful examination of the nature of justice.

The moral issues that affirmative-action programs raise in regard to justice are profound and complex. In this brief overview, we have been able to raise only a few, but these demonstrate that the morality of preferential treatment through affirmative action cuts to our basic assumptions about the nature of human beings and the principles of justice. Any moral resolution of the problem of discrimination in the workplace will not only reflect these assumptions but must justify them.

ARGUMENTS AGAINST AFFIRMATIVE ACTION

1. ***All discrimination on the basis of race and sex is inherently unfair.***

   POINT: "All human beings deserve equal treatment. No one should be denied a job because of sex or skin color. It's a simple matter of fairness that all people of good will should be able to agree on. Isn't that what the civil rights movement was originally all about? Isn't that what the feminist movement was originally all about? To discriminate against anyone on the basis of race or sex, white males included, is inherently unfair."

[6] Flores, "Reverse Discrimination," p. 4.

COUNTERPOINT: "You can't equate affirmative action with racism and sexism. The purpose of racism and sexism is to deny equal opportunity. The purpose of affirmative action is to provide it, first by ensuring that employers don't discriminate against groups that have traditionally suffered from discrimination and, second, by compensating these groups for past discrimination. Certainly, a color-blind society is the ideal, but affirmative action is necessary in today's society if we're going to achieve it someday."

2. ***Affirmative action leads to resentment and social tensions.***

POINT: "Whatever the purpose of affirmative action, the result is racial tension and increased sexism. A lot of white males justifiably feel cheated by affirmative action. Denied jobs and promotions they're qualified for because they're white males, they naturally come to resent women and minorities. Just look at the rise of racial tensions in our cities. Or look at the prevalence of racism and sexism in recent popular music and comedy acts. Affirmative action isn't bringing us to a color-blind society but to an increasingly polarized one."

COUNTERPOINT: "You could say the same thing about the original civil rights and feminist movements. Remember the name calling and rock throwing when blacks first tried to integrate public schools, buses, and lunch counters? Or all the bra-burning women's libber jokes when women began demanding equal pay for equal work? What the resentment and tensions show is pervasive racism and sexism, not the wrongness of affirmative action."

3. ***Affirmative action stigmatizes minorities and women.***

POINT: "It's not only white males who suffer from affirmative action. Minorities and women who rise to the top on their own merits also suffer. Instead of being respected for their accomplishments, they're objects of suspicion. There will always be people who believe women and minorities got where they are through preferential treatment. Not only that, but affirmative action can actually harm their careers. Given the choice between a doctor who got into medical school on his or her own merits and one who may have got in through an affirmative-action system, which would you pick? That's the stigma of affirmative action, and talented minorities and women will always have to live with it."

COUNTERPOINT: "The stigma you talk about is nothing but prejudice. Whether hired through affirmative action or not, whether admitted into medical school through affirmative action or not, people still have to prove themselves afterward. After all, the idea behind affirmative action isn't to give women and minorities a leg up through their entire careers but to give them an opportunity to prove themselves on a level playing field. And anyone who accomplishes that deserves as much respect as anyone else."

4. ***Affirmative action wastes the best human resources.***

POINT: "The real idea behind affirmative action is to make sure that the best people for the job don't get it. Places in professional schools are taken from superior students who happen to be white males. More qualified applicants who happen to be white males are denied important jobs in business and industry. No society can afford to waste its best resources like that, especially in a world as competitive as ours has become."

COUNTERPOINT: "You could just as easily say that no society can afford to waste over half its human resources by denying them the opportunity to prove themselves in areas traditionally closed to them. Remember, affirmative-action guidelines aren't designed to result in the hiring of unqualified applicants. They're designed to help less qualified applicants whose relative lack of qualifications are the product of institutional racism and sexism. By giving them that help, we give them the opportunity to overcome impediments in their background and improve their qualifications. Though there are unfortunate abuses in affirmative-action programs, in the end we still have a much larger pool of qualified workers to choose from."

ARGUMENTS FOR AFFIRMATIVE ACTION

1. ***Justice requires that we compensate for the results of past discrimination.***

POINT: "No one can deny the United States's history of racism and sexism. If the effects of that history were behind us, affirmative action would be unnecessary. But they're not behind us. Walk into any inner city neighborhood and try to tell me the children playing in the streets have the same opportunities as their white suburban counterparts. If we really believe in justice and equal opportunity, we have to compensate for the effects of our history."

COUNTERPOINT: "Compensatory justice is certainly a noble ideal, but there are two serious flaws in your argument. First, compensatory justice for one group brings harm to another, and when the harmed group isn't responsible for the plight of the others, you're punishing the innocent for the sins of their ancestors. To tell a young white male to forget about his share of the American Dream because of what happened before he was born is no kind of justice at all. Second, not all women and minorities suffer from the effects of past discrimination, whereas many white males have led truly disadvantaged lives. Take a middle-class black man or white woman who went to good schools and was always encouraged to aspire to great success. Why is that person entitled to preferential treatment over a white male from the most depressed area of Appalachia or a severely distressed manufacturing community?"

2. ***Affirmative action is the only way to overcome current racism and sexism.***

POINT: "Despite the passage of numerous civil rights laws, bias in the workplace is still with us. Women remain subject to sexual harassment. Racial and sexual stereotypes continue to take their toll. You don't even need statistics to know how bad it is. You can hear it in casual conversation and you can see it in a seemingly never-ending stream of lawsuits won by women and minorities who were denied promotions. Employers can always find a way to justify hiring or promoting a white male over a black or a woman. The only way to overcome such discrimination is through affirmative-action guidelines."

COUNTERPOINT: "The fact that women and minorities are winning their discrimination suits shows that we don't need affirmative action. The Civil Rights Act and the Equal Employment Opportunity Act give them all the legal teeth they need to fight bias, on the job or anywhere else. The just way to fight discrimination is to take the discriminators to court, not to institutionalize affirmative action."

3. ***Women and minorities need role models in all walks of life.***

POINT: "One of the most unfortunate effects of past discrimination is the lack of role models for young women and minorities. Before Sandra Day O'Connor, how many young women could aspire to be an associate justice of the U.S. Supreme Court? Before Colin Powell, how many young black men could aspire to be secretary of state? We need women and minority physics professors, architects, welders, electricians, bank presidents, and anything else you can think of to let *all* young people know that all possibilities are open to them if they have the talent and perseverance."

COUNTERPOINT: "Certainly, role models are important, but unfair discrimination against white males is too high a price to pay, especially when adequate enforcement of anti-discrimination legislation will provide them anyway. After all, Colin Powell wasn't selected for his position *because* of his race. Nor were many other talented blacks in many other kinds of work. Nor were many talented women selected for their positions because of their gender. Furthermore, many of them got where they are without any role models at all. As important as role models may be, they can't replace encouragement from parents and teachers, and they can't replace hard work."

4. ***It's just not true that all decisions in employment and education are made on the basis of pure objective merit, even leaving aside affirmative-action programs.***

POINT: "It's hypocritical to say that if it were not for affirmative action, everyone would have a fair chance to compete based strictly on merit. Many decisions are made on factors that have little to do with so-called objective merit. Many universities give preference to the children of alumni, even if they don't meet normal admissions standards. Universities seek a wide range of abilities and talents, whether athletes or musicians or artists, even if they don't meet the narrowly defined standards of grade point and SAT scores. Many corporations are notorious for hiring relatives and cronies for jobs for which those persons are less qualified. As long as we allow these other forms of unfair discrimination, we shouldn't complain about giving a break to underrepresented minorities and women."

COUNTERPOINT: "Perhaps we should insist that those other forms of discrimination be abolished too. But even if they are allowed to continue, race and gender go to core constitutional values, while those other factors don't. If you own a business, there's nothing wrong with showing favoritism to your relatives. And universities rely on their alumni for financial contributions, so why not reward them by showing a little favoritism to admissions for their children?"

The Justification of Reverse Discrimination

TOM L. BEAUCHAMP

Tom L. Beauchamp is a professor of philosophy and a senior research scholar in Georgetown University's Kennedy Institute of Ethics. In this essay, he assumes that affirmative action is reverse discrimination and that it can be morally justified. Though he concedes that reverse discrimination can create injustices, he defends the practice on two grounds. First, the eradication of pervasive discrimination in hiring and promotion requires enforced goals and quotas. Second, goals and quotas serve corporate interests as well as the public interest.

In defending his claim that discrimination in the workplace is pervasive, Beauchamp appeals to a wide range of statistical evidence. He then argues that nondiscriminatory hiring and promotion practices can be meaningfully enforced only with specified goals and timetables.

Since the 1960s, government and corporate policies that set goals for hiring women and minorities have been sharply criticized. Their opponents maintain that many policies establish indefensible quotas and discriminate in reverse against sometimes more qualified white males. In 1991 President George Bush referred to the word "quota" as the "dreaded q-word." Quotas, he said, had "finally" been eliminated from government policies.

Although it must be acknowledged that some policies with target goals or quotas do violate rules of fair and equal treatment, I believe that such policies can be justified. My objective is to defend corporate policies that set goals of representing groups in the pools from which corporations draw their employees. I argue that goals and quotas, rightly conceived, are congenial to management—not hostile as they are often depicted. Both the long-range interest of corporations and the public interest are served by carefully selected preferential policies.

TWO POLAR POSITIONS

In 1965 President Lyndon Johnson issued an executive order that announced a toughened federal initiative requiring goals and timetables for equal employment opportunity.[1] This initiative was the prevailing regulatory approach for many years. But eventually two competing schools of thought on the justifiability of preferential programs have come into sharp conflict. The first stands in opposition to quotas, accepting the view that all persons are entitled to an equal opportunity and to constitutional guarantees of equal protection in a color-blind, nonsexist society. Civil rights laws, in this approach, should offer protection only to *individuals* who have been victimized by forms of discrimination, not to *groups* (though it is controversial whether individuals can be harmed merely by virtue of a group membership[2]). Hiring goals, timetables, and quotas only work to create new victims of discrimination.

The second school supports strong affirmative action policies. The justification of affirmative action programs is viewed as the correction of discriminatory employment practices, not group compensation for prior injustice. The terms "affirmative action" and "quotas" have proved troublesome, because they have been defined in both minimal and maximal ways. The original meaning of "affirmative action" was minimalist. It referred to plans to safe-guard equal opportunity, to protect against discrimination, to advertise positions openly, and to create scholarship programs to ensure recruitment from specific groups.[3] Few now oppose open advertisement and the like, and if this were all that were meant by "affirmative action," few would oppose it. However, "affirmative action" has assumed new and expanded meanings. Today it is typically associated with quotas and preferential policies that target specific groups, especially women or minority members.

Although the meaning of "affirmative action" is inherently contestable, I will here stipulate the meaning as functionally equivalent to the following statement (in 2002) of the Hewlett-Packard Company:

> *Affirmative action* at HP means that the company extends its commitment beyond equal opportunity to proactively recruit, hire, develop and promote qualified women, minorities, people with disabilities, and Vietnam-era veterans. In addition, HP has a commitment to supporting external educational and community organizations that support these objectives.[4]

Thus, I will use "affirmative action" to refer to positive steps taken to hire persons from groups previously and presently discriminated against, leaving open what will count as a "positive step" to remove discrimination.

The supporters of affirmative action—the second school, to which I belong—view the first school as construing "equal opportunity" and "civil rights" so narrowly that persons affected by discrimination do not receive adequate aid in overcoming the effects of prejudice. This second school believes that mandated hiring protects minorities and erodes discrimination, whereas the identification of individual victims of discrimination would be, as the editors of *The New York Times* once put it, the "project of a century and [would] leave most victims of discrimination with only empty legal rights."[5]

These two schools may not be as far apart morally as they first appear. If legal enforcement of civil rights law could efficiently and comprehensively identify discriminatory treatment and could protect its victims, both schools would agree that the legal-enforcement strategy is preferable. But there are at least two reasons why this solution will not be accepted by the second school. First, there is the unresolved issue of whether those in contemporary society who have been advantaged by *past* discrimination (for example, wealthy owners of family businesses) deserve their advantages. Second, there is the issue of whether *present*, ongoing discrimination can be successfully, comprehensively, and fairly combatted by identifying and prosecuting violators without resorting to quotas. This second issue is the more pivotal one and is closely related to the justification of specific targets.

A "quota," as used here, does not mean that fixed numbers of employees should be hired regardless of an individual's qualification for a position. Quotas are simply target employment percentages. In some cases a less-qualified person may be hired or promoted; but it has never been a part of affirmative action to hire below the threshold of "basically qualified,"[6] and often significant questions exist in the employment situation about the exact qualifications needed for positions.[7] Quotas, then, are numerically expressible goals that one is obligated to pursue with good faith and due diligence. If it is impossible to hire the basically qualified persons called for by the goals in a given time frame, the schedule can be relaxed, as long as the target goals, the due diligence, and the good faith continue. The word *quota* does not mean "fixed number" in any stronger sense.

Today the language of "quotas" is almost nonexistent in corporate policy statements, but this fact should not be taken to indicate that corporations now deviate from the principles that originally gave rise to the language and use of quotas. For example, in December 2002, General Motors stated its policy on "Workplace Diversity" as follows:

> GM recognizes that it is essential for [its] work force to reflect both the marketplace and customers. . . General Motors remains committed to affirmative action. . . . GM monitors its programs to determine whether recruitment, hiring, and other personnel practices are operating in a nondiscriminatory manner. It also includes out-reach programs designed to identify and reach qualified individuals

of any race or gender that have not been fully represented in the talent pools from which GM selects and promotes employees.[8]

Similarly, ExxonMobil announced in 2002 that although its "total employment has declined in recent years, the percentage representation of women and minorities in our workforce has steadily increased." ExxonMobil announced that, by program design, among its "officials and managers," women increased 34 percent and minorities 55 percent over the previous decade; among its "professionals," women increased 9 percent and minorities 25 percent over the same period.[9]

DATA ON DISCRIMINATION

Discrimination in hiring and promotion is, of course, not present throughout American society, but it is pervasive. An impressive body of statistics constituting (prima facie) evidence of discrimination has been assembled in recent years. These data indicate that in sizable parts of American society white males continue to receive the highest entry-level salaries when compared to all other social groups; that women with similar credentials and experience to those of men are commonly hired at lower positions or earn lower starting salaries than men and are promoted at one-half the rate of their male counterparts, with the consequence that the gap between salaries and promotion rates is still growing at an increasing rate; that 70 percent or more of white-collar positions are held by women, although they hold only about 10 percent of management positions; that three out of seven U.S. employees occupy white-collar positions, whereas the ratio is but one of seven for African Americans; and, finally, that a significant racial gap in unemployment statistics is a consistent pattern in the United States, with the gap now greatest for college-educated, African-American males.[10]

Such statistics are not decisive indicators of discrimination, but additional facts also support the conclusion that racist and sexist biases powerfully influence the marketplace.

Housing. For example, studies of real estate rentals, housing sales, and home mortgage lending show a disparity in loan rejection rates between white applicants and minority applicants with comparable bank and credit histories. Wide disparities exist even after statistics are adjusted for economic differences; minority applicants are over 50 percent more likely to be denied a loan than white applicants of equivalent economic status. Other studies indicate that discrimination in sales of houses is prevalent in the United States. Race appears to be as important as socioeconomic status in failing to secure both houses and loans, and studies also show that the approval rate for African Americans increases in lending institutions with an increase in the proportion of minority employees in that institution.[11]

Jobs. A similar pattern is found in employment. In 1985 the Grier Partnership and the Urban League produced independent studies that reveal striking disparities in the employment levels of college-trained African Americans and whites in Washington, D.C., one of the best markets for African Americans. Both studies found that college-trained African Americans have much more difficulty than their white counterparts in securing employment. Both cite discrimination as the major underlying factors.[12] In a 1991 study by the Urban Institute, employment practices in Washington, D.C. and Chicago were examined. Equally qualified, identically dressed white and African American applicants for jobs were used to test for bias in the job market, as presented by newspaper-advertized positions. Whites and African Americans were matched identically for speech patterns, age, work experience, personal characteristics, and physical build. Investigators found repeated discrimination against African-American male applicants. The higher the position, the higher the level of discrimination. The white men received job offers three times more often than the equally qualified African Americans who interviewed for the same position. The authors of the study concluded that discrimination against African-American men is "widespread and entrenched."[13] Very similar results were found in other studies in the 1990s.[14]

These statistics and empirical studies help frame racial discrimination in the United States. Anyone who believes that only a narrow slice of surface discrimination exists will be unlikely to agree with what I have been and will be arguing, at least if my proposals entail strong affirmative action measures. By constrast, one who believes that discrimination is securely and almost invisibly entrenched in many sectors of society will be more likely to endorse or at least tolerate resolute affirmative action policies.

These statistics help frame the significance of racial discrimination in the United States. Although much is now known about patterns of discrimination, much remains to be discovered, in part because it is hidden and subtle.

PROBLEMS OF PROOF AND INTENTION

Although racism and sexism are commonly envisioned as intentional forms of favoritism and exclusion, intent to discriminate is not a necessary condition of discrimination. Institutional networks can unintentionally hold back or exclude persons. Hiring by personal friendships and word of mouth are common instances, as are seniority systems. Numerical targets are important remedies for these camouflaged areas, where it is particularly difficult to shatter patterns of discrimination and reconfigure the environment.[15]

The U.S. Supreme Court once held unanimously that persons may be guilty of discriminating against the handicapped when there is no "invidious animus, but rather [a discriminatory effect] of thoughtlessness and indifference—of benign neglect." The Court held that discrimination would be difficult and perhaps impossible to prove or to prevent if *intentional* discrimination alone qualified as discrimination.[16] The Court acknowledged that discrimination is often invisible to those who discriminate. This, in my judgment, is the main reason goals and quotas are an indispensable government and management tool: They may be the only way to break down patterns of discrimination and bring meaningful diversity to the workplace.

Courts in the United States have on a few occasions resorted to quotas because an employer had an intractable history and a bullheaded resistance to change that necessitated strong measures. The Supreme Court has never directly supported quotas using the term "quota,"[17] but it has upheld affirmative action programs that contain numerically expressed hiring formulas that are intended to reverse the patterns of both intentional and unintentional discrimination.[18] At the same time, the Supreme Court has suggested that some affirmative action programs using numerical formulas have gone too far.[19] Whether the formulas are excessive depends on the facts in the individual case. The case of *Adarand Constructors Inc. v. Pena* (1995) defended a standard requiring that there be a compelling governmental interest for race-based preferences in construction contracts for minority-owned companies; it continued the long line of cases that weigh and balance different interests.

I believe the Supreme Court has consistently adhered to this balancing strategy and that it is the right moral perspective as well as the proper framework for American law.[20] It allows use of race and sex as relevant bases of policies if and only if it is essential to do so in order to achieve a larger and justified social purpose.

These reasons for using race and sex in setting employment goals are far distant from the role of these properties in invidious discrimination. Racial discrimination and sexual discrimination typically spring from feelings of superiority and a sense that other groups deserve lower social status. Affirmative action entails no such attitude or intent. Its purpose is to restore to persons a status they have been unjustifiably denied, to help them escape stigmatization, and to foster relationships of interconnectedness in society.[21]

Affirmative action in pockets of vicious and visceral racism will likely be needed for another generation, after which we should have reached our goals of fair opportunity and equal consideration. Once these goals are achieved, affirmative action will no longer be justified and should be abandoned. The goal to be reached at that point is not proportional representation, which has occasionally been used as a basis for fixing target numbers in affirmative action policies, but as such is merely a means to the end of discrimination, not an end to be pursued for its own sake. The goal is simply fair opportunity and equal consideration.

Issues about the breadth and depth of discrimination may divide us as a society more than any other issue about affirmative action. Discriminatory attitudes and practices are likely to be deep-seated in some institutions, while shallow or absent in others. Society is not monolithic in the depth and breadth of discrimination. In some cases affirmative action programs are not needed; in other cases only modest good faith programs are in order; and in still others enforced quotas are necessary to break down discriminatory patterns.

Because we deeply disagree about the depth, breadth, and embeddedness of discrimination, we disagree further over the social policies that will rid us of the problem. Those who believe discrimination is relatively shallow and detectable look for formulas and remedies that center on *equal opportunity*. Those who believe discrimination is deep, camouflaged, and embedded in society look for formulas that center on *measurable outcomes*.[22]

WHY CORPORATIONS SHOULD WELCOME GOALS AND QUOTAS

Little has been said to this point about corporate policy about corporate policy. I shall discuss only *voluntary* programs that use target goals and quotas. They stand in sharp contrast to *legally enforced* goals and quotas. There are at least three reasons why it is in the interest of responsible businesses to use aggressive plans that incorporate goals and quotas: (1) an improved work force, (2) maintenance of a bias-free corporate environment, and (3) congeniality to managerial planning.

(1) First, corporations that discriminate will fail to look at the full range of qualified persons in the market and, as a result, will employ a higher percentage of second-best employees. Numerous American institutions have learned that discrimination causes the institution to lose opportunities to make contact with the full range of qualified persons who might be contacted. Their competitive position is thereby weakened, just as a state university would be weakened if it hired faculty entirely from its own state. These institutions have found that promoting diversity in the workforce is correlated with high quality employees, reductions in the costs of discrimination claims, a lowering of absenteeism, less turnover, and increased customer satisfaction.[23]

In fiscal year 2003 the Dell Computer Corporation announced that, by design, it had substantially increased its diversity recruiting and global diversity. Dell noted that "companies that diversify work force and supply bases are more successful in gaining access to multicultural markets. Mutually beneficial relationships with minority suppliers open doors for Dell to market its products and services to women and minority customers, provide growth opportunities for our suppliers, and benefit our communities."[24]

Maintaining a high-quality work force is consistent with the management style already implemented in many companies. For example, James R. Houghton, chairman of Corning Glass, established voluntary quotas to increase the quality of employees, not merely the number of women and black employees. Corning began by establishing the following increased-percentage targets for the total employment population to be met between 1988 and 1991: women professionals to increase from 17.4 percent to 23.2 percent, black professionals to increase from 5.1 percent to 7.4 percent, the number of black senior managers to increase from 1 to 5, and the number of women senior managers to increase from 4 to 10. Corning management interpreted the targets as follows: "Those numbers were not commandments set in stone. We won't hire people just to meet a number. It will be tough to meet some of [our targets]." Corning found that it could successfully recruit in accordance with these targets, but also found severe difficulty in maintaining the desired target numbers in the work force because of an attrition problem. The company continued thereafter to take the view that in an age in which the percentage of white males in the employment pool is constantly declining, a "total quality company" must vigorously recruit women and minorities using target goals.[25]

(2) Second, pulling the foundations from beneath affirmative action hiring would open old wounds in many institutions that have been developing plans through consent-decree processes with courts as well as direct negotiations with minority groups and unions. Many corporations report that they have invested heavily in eliminating managerial biases and stereotypes while training managers to hire appropriately. They are concerned that without the pressure of an affirmative action plan, which they draft internally, managers will fail to recognize their own biases and stereotypes. Removal of voluntary programs might additionally stigmatize a business by signalling to minorities that a return to older patterns of discrimination is permissible. Such stigmatization is a serious blow in today's competitive market.

(3) Third, affirmative action programs involving quotas have been successful for the corporations that have adopted them, and there is no need to try to fix what is not broken. As the editors of *Business Week* once maintained, "Over the years business and regulators have worked out rules and procedures for affirmative action, including numerical yardsticks for sizing up progress, that both sides understand. It has worked and should be left alone."[26] It has worked because of the above-mentioned improved work force and because of a business-like approach typical of managerial planning: Managers set goals and timetables for almost everything—from profits to salary bonuses. From a manager's point of view, setting goals and timetables is simply a way of measuring progress.

One survey of 200 major American corporations found that the same approach has often been taken to the management of affirmative action: Over 75 percent of these corporations already use "voluntary internal numerical objectives to assess [equal employment opportunity] performance." Another survey of 300 top corporate executives reported that 72 percent believe that minority hiring improves rather than hampers productivity, while 64 percent said there is a need for the government to help bring women and minorities into the main-stream of the work force. Many corporations have used their records in promotion and recruitment to present a positive image of corporate life in public reports and recruiting brochures.[27]

Affirmative action has also worked to increase productivity and improve consumer relationships. Corporations in consumer goods and services industries report increased respect and increased sales after achieving affirmative action results. They report that they are able to target some customers they otherwise could not reach, enjoy increased competitiveness, and better understand consumer complaints as a result of a more diverse work force. Corporations with aggressive affirmative action programs have also been shown to outperform their competitors.[28]

CONCLUSION

If the social circumstances of discrimination were to be substantially altered, my conclusions in this paper would be modified. The introduction of preferential treatment on a large scale undoubtedly runs the risk of producing economic advantages to individuals who do not deserve them, protracted court battles, congressional lobbying by power groups, a lowering of admission and work standards, reduced social and economic efficiency, increased racial and minority hostility, and the continued suspicion that well-placed minorities received their positions purely on the basis of quotas. These reasons constitute a strong case against affirmative action policies that use numerical goals and quotas. However, this powerful case is not sufficient to overcome the still stronger counterarguments.

NOTES

1. Executive Order 11246. C.F.R. 339 (1964–65). This order required all federal contractors to develop affirmative action policies. For subsequent developments, see Bernard E. Anderson, "The Ebb and Flow of Enforcing Executive Order 11246," *American Economic Review Papers and Proceedings*, 86 (1996): 298–301.

2. See J. Angelo Corlett, "Racism and Affirmative Action," *Journal of Social Philosophy* 24 (1993): 163–75; and Cass R. Sunstein, "The Limits of Compensatory Justice," *Nomos XXXIII: Compensatory Justice*, Ed. John Chapman (New York: New York University Press, 1991): 281–310.
3. See Thomas Nagel, "A Defense of Affirmative Action," Testimony before the Subcommittee on the Constitution of the Senate Judiciary Committee, June 18, 1981; and Louis Pojman, "The Moral Status of Affirmative Action," *Public Affairs Quarterly*, 6 (1992): 181–206.
4. http://www.hp.com/hpinfo/abouthp/diversity/nondisc.htm
5. "Their Right to Remedy, Affirmed," *The New York Times*, July 3, 1986, p. A30.
6. This standard has been recognized at least since *EEOC v. AT & T*, No. 73–149 (E.D. Pa. 1973). See also U.S. Department of Labor, Employment Standards Administration, Office of Federal Contract Compliance Programs. "OFCCP: Making EEO and Affirmative Action Work," January 1987 OFCCP-28.
7. See Harry Holzer and David Neumark, "Are Affirmative Action Hires Less Qualified? Evidence from Employer-Employee Data on New Hires," *Journal of Labor Economics,* 17 (1999): 534–69; Laura Purdy, "Why Do We Need Affirmative Action?" *Journal of Social Philosophy,* 25 (1994): 133–43. Holzer and Neumark make a basic distinction between educational qualifications and job performance.
8. http://www.gm.com/company/gmability/diversity/people/workforce.html
9. http://www.exxonmobil.com/news/publications/diversity/c_whyfocus.html
10. Bron Taylor, *Affirmative Action at Work: Law, Politics, and Ethics* (Pittsburgh: University of Pittsburgh Press, 1991); Morley Gunderson, "Pay and Employment Equity in the United States and Canada," *International Journal of Manpower*, 15 (1994): 26–43; Patricia Gaynor and Garey Durden, "Measuring the Extent of Earnings Discrimination: An Update," *Applied Economics*, 27August (1995): 669–76; Marjorie L. Baldwin and William G. Johnson, "The Employment Effects of Wage Discrimination Against Black Men," *Industrial & Labor Relations Review,* 49 (1996): 302–16; Franklin D. Wilson, Marta Tienda, and Lawrence Wu, "Race and Unemployment: Labor Market Experiences of Black and White Men, 1968–1988," *Women & Occupations,* 22 (1995): 245–270; Betty M. Vetter, Ed., *Professional Women and Minorities: A Manpower Data Resource Service,* 8th ed. (Washington: Commission on Science and Technology, 1989); (anonymous) "Less Discrimination for Women but Poorer Prospects at Work than Men," *Management Services,* 40 (1996): 6; Cynthia D. Anderson and Donald Tomaskovic-Devey, "Patriarchal Pressures: An Exploration of Organizational Processes that Exacerbate and Erode Gender Earnings Inequality," *Work & Occupations,* 22 (1995): 328–56; Thomas J. Bergman and G. E. Martin, "Tests for Compliance with Phased Plans to Equalize Discriminate Wages," *Journal of Applied Business Research,* 11 (1994/1995): 136–43.
11. Helen F. Ladd, "Evidence on Discrimination in Mortgage Lending," *Journal of Economic Perspectives,* 12 (1998), 41–62; Brent W. Ambrose, William T. Hughes, Jr., and Patrick Simmons, "Policy Issues concerning Racial and Ethnic Differences in Home Loan Rejection Rates," *Journal of Housing Research,* 6 (1995): 115–35; *A Common Destiny: Blacks and American Society*, Ed. Gerald D. Jaynes and Robin M. Williams, Jr., Committee on the Status of Black Americans, Commission on Behavioral and Social Sciences and Education, National Research Council (Washington: NAS Press, 1989), pp. 12–13, 138–48; Sunwoong Kim, Gregory D. Squires, "Lender Characteristics and Racial Disparities in Mortgage Lending," *Journal of Housing Research,* 6 (1995): 99–133; Glenn B. Canner and Wayne Passmore, "Home Purchase Lending in Low-Income Neighborhoods and to Low-Income Borrowers," *Federal Reserve Bulletin,* 81 February 1995): 71–103; John R. Walter, "The Fair Lending Laws and their Enforcement," *Economic Quarterly,* 81 (Fall 1995): 61–77; Stanley D. Longhofer, "Discrimination in Mortgage Lending: What Have We Learned?" *Economic Commentary* [Federal Reserve Bank of Cleveland], August 15, 1996: 1–4.
12. As reported by Rudolf A. Pyatt, Jr., "Significant Job Studies," *The Washington Post*, April 30, 1985, pp. D1–D2. See also Paul Burstein, *Discrimination, Jobs, and Politics* (Chicago: University of Chicago Press, 1985) Bureau of Labor Statistics, *Employment and Earnings* (Washington: U.S. Dept. of labor, January 1989). *A Common Destiny*, op. cit., pp. 16–18, 84–88.
13. See Margery Austin Turner, Michael Fix, and Raymond Struyk, *Opportunities Denied, Opportunities*

Diminished: Discrimination in Hiring (Washington, D.C.. The Urban Institute, 1991).

14. William A. Darity and Patrick L. Mason, "Evidence on Discrimination in Employment: Codes of Color, Codes of Gender," *Journal of Economic Perspectives*, 12 (1998), 63–90; Francine Blau, et al., *The Economics of Women, Men, and Work*, 3rd ed. Upper Saddle River, NJ: Prentice Hall, 1998.
15. See Laura Purdy, "Why Do We Need Affirmative Action?" *Journal of Social Philosophy* 25 (1994): 133–43; Farrell Bloch, *Antidiscrimination Law and Minority Employment: Recruitment Practices and Regulatory Constraints* (Chicago: University of Chicago Press, 1994); Joseph Sartorelli, "Gay Rights and Affirmative Action." In *Gay Ethics*, ed. Timothy F. Murphy (New York: Haworth Press, 1994); Taylor, *Affirmative Action at Work.*
16. *Alexander v. Choate*, 469 U.S. 287, at 295.
17. But the Court comes very close in *Local 28 of the Sheet Metal Workers' International Association v. Equal Employment Opportunity Commission*, 106 S. Ct. 3019—commonly known as *Sheet Metal Workers.*
18. *Fullilove v. Klutznick*, 448 U.S. 448 (1980); *United Steelworkers v. Weber*, 443 U.S. 193 (1979); *United States v. Paradise*, 480 U.S. 149 (1987); *Johnson v. Transportation Agency*, 480 U.S. 616 (1987).
19. *Firefighters v. Stotts*, 467 U.S. 561 (1984); *City of Richmond v. J. A. Croson Co.,* 109 S. Ct. 706 (1989); *Adarand Constructors Inc. v. Federico Pena*, 63 LW 4523 (1995); *Wygant v. Jackson Bd. of Education*, 476 U.S. 267 (1986); *Wards Cove Packing v. Atonio*, 490 U.S. 642.
20. For a very different view, stressing inconsistency, see Young S. Lee, "Affirmative Action and Judicial Standards of Review: A Search for the Elusive Consensus." *Review of Public Personnel Administration*, 12 September–December 1991): 47–69.
21. See Robert Ladenson, "Ethics in the American Workplace,“ *Business and Professional Ethics Journal*, 14 (1995): 17–31; Gertrude Ezorsky, *Racism and Justice: The Case for Affirmative Action*, op. cit.; Thomas E. Hill, Jr., "The Message of Affirmative Action," *Social Philosophy and Policy*, 8 (1991): 108–29; Jorge L. Garcia, "The Heart of Racism," *Journal of Social Philosophy*, 27 (1996): 5–46.
22. For a balanced article on this topic, see Robert K. Fullinwider, "Affirmative Action and Fairness," *Report from the Institute for Philosophy & Public Policy* 11 (University of Maryland, Winter 1991), pp. 10–13.
23. John Yinger, *Closed Doors, Opportunities Lost* (New York: Russell Sage Foundation, 1995); Jerry T. Ferguson and Wallace R. Johnston. "Managing Diversity," *Mortgage Banking*, 55 (1995); 32–36L; Joseph Semien, "Opening the Utility Door for Women and Minorities," *Public Utilities Fortnightly*, July 5, 1990, pp. 29–31.
24. http://www.dell.com/us/en/gen/corporate/vision_diversity.htm
25. Tim Loughran, "Corning Tries to Break the Glass Ceiling," *Business & Society Review* 76 (Winter 1991), pp. 52–55.
26. Editorial, "Don't Scuttle Affirmative Action," *Business Week*, April 5, 1985, p. 174.
27. "Rethinking *Weber*. The Business Response to Affirmative Action," *Harvard Law Review*, 102 January 1989), p. 661, note 18.
28. See "Rethinking *Weber*," esp. pp. 668–70; Joseph Michael Pace and Zachary Smith, "Understanding Affirmative Action: From the Practitioner's Perspective," *Public Personnel Management*, 24 (Summer 1995): 139–147.

QUESTIONS FOR ANALYSIS

1. According to Beauchamp, policies that create *injustices* are not necessarily *unjustified*. How does he support the claim? How does he apply it to reverse discrimination?
2. What statistical evidence does Beauchamp cite in support of his claim that current job discrimination is pervasive? How convincing is it?
3. Opponents of reverse discrimination argue that protection should be offered only to individuals who have suffered from discrimination, not to groups. Why does Beauchamp consider such a policy unworkable?
4. On what grounds does Beauchamp argue that reverse discrimination is required for the elimination of job discrimination?
5. Why does Beauchamp think that quotas and timetables are consistent with a businesslike approach to problems?
6. What problems does Beauchamp think businesses would face if goals and quotas were no longer allowed by law?

7. In the conclusion of his essay, Beauchamp presents the case against reverse discrimination and admits that it is a powerful one. Nevertheless, he concludes that the case in favor of reverse discrimination is even more powerful? Do you agree? Why or why not?

A Defense of Programs of Preferential Treatment

RICHARD WASSERSTROM

Richard Wasserstrom is professor *Emeritus* of philosophy at the University of California, Santa Cruz. In this essay, he provides a limited defense of preferential hiring by attacking two of the opposition's major arguments. First, opponents of preferential treatment often charge proponents with "intellectual inconsistency." They argue that those now supporting preferential treatment opposed it in the past. But Wasserstrom feels that social realities in respect to the distribution of resources and opportunities make present preferential-treatment programs enormously different from those of the past.

The second argument commonly raised is that preferential-treatment programs, by introducing sex and race, compromise what really should matter: individual qualifications. Wasserstrom counters this charge on both an operational and a theoretical level. He feels that to be decisive, this argument must appeal not to efficiency but to desert: Those who are most qualified deserve to receive the benefits. But Wasserstrom sees no necessary connection between qualifications and desert.

Many justifications of programs of preferential treatment depend upon the claim that in one respect or another such programs have good consequences or that they are effective means by which to bring about some desirable end, e.g., an integrated, equalitarian society. I mean by "programs of preferential treatment" to refer to programs such as those at issue in the *Bakke* case—programs which set aside a certain number of places (for example, in a law school) as to which members of minority groups (for example, persons who are non-white or female) who possess certain minimum qualifications (in terms of grades and test scores) may be preferred for admission to those places over some members of the majority group who possess higher qualifications (in terms of grades and test scores).

Many criticisms of programs of preferential treatment claim that such programs, even if effective, are unjustifiable because they are in some important sense unfair or unjust. In this paper I present a limited defense of such programs by showing that two of the chief arguments offered for the unfairness or injustice of these programs do not work in the way or to the degree supposed by critics of these programs.

The first argument is this. Opponents of preferential treatment programs sometimes assert that proponents of these programs are guilty of intellectual inconsistency, if not racism or sexism. For, as is readily acknowledged, at times past

From Richard Wasserstrom, "A Defense of Programs of Preferential Treatment," *Phi Kappa Phi Journal*, vol. 58 (Winter 1978); originally Part II of "Racism, Sexism, and Preferential Treatment: An Approach to the Topics," *U.C.L.A. Law Review*, vol. 24 (1977): 581. Reprinted by permission of the author.

employers, universities, and many other social institutions did have racial or sexual quotas (when they did not practice overt racial or sexual exclusion), and many of those who were most concerned to bring about the eradication of those racial quotas are now untroubled by the new programs which reinstitute them. And this, it is claimed, is inconsistent. If it was wrong to take race or sex into account when blacks and women were the objects of racial and sexual policies and practices of exclusion, then it is wrong to take race or sex into account when the objects of the policies have their race or sex reversed. Simple considerations of intellectual consistency—of what it means to give racism or sexism as a reason for condemning these social policies and practices—require that what was a good reason then is still a good reason now.

The problem with this argument is that despite appearances, there is no inconsistency involved in holding both views. Even if contemporary preferential treatment programs which contain quotas are wrong, they are not wrong for the reasons that made quotas against blacks and women pernicious. The reason why is that the social realities do make an enormous difference. The fundamental evil of programs that discriminated against blacks or women was that these programs were a part of a larger social universe which systematically maintained a network of institutions which unjustifiably concentrated power, authority, and goods in the hands of white male individuals, and which systematically consigned blacks and women to subordinate positions in the society.

Whatever may be wrong with today's affirmative action programs and quota systems, it should be clear that the evil, if any, is just not the same. Racial and sexual minorities do not constitute the dominant social group. Nor is the conception of who is a fully developed member of the moral and social community one of an individual who is either female or black. Quotas which prefer women or blacks do not add to an already relatively overabundant supply of resources and opportunities at the disposal of members of these groups in the way in which the quotas of the past did maintain and augment the overabundant supply of resources and opportunities already available to white males.

The same point can be made in a somewhat different way. Sometimes people say that what was wrong, for example, with the system of racial discrimination in the South was that it took an irrelevant characteristic, namely race, and used it systematically to allocate social benefits and burdens of various sorts. The defect was the irrelevance of the characteristic used—race—for that meant that individuals ended up being treated in a manner that was arbitrary and capricious.

I do not think that was the central flaw at all. Take, for instance, the most hideous of the practices, human slavery. The primary thing that was wrong with the institution was not that the particular individuals who were assigned the place of slaves were assigned there arbitrarily because the assignment was made in virtue of an irrelevant characteristic, their race. Rather, it seems to me that the primary thing that was and is wrong with slavery is the practice itself—the fact of some individuals being able to own other individuals and all that goes with that practice. It would not matter by what criterion individuals were assigned; human slavery would still be wrong. And the same can be said for most if not all of the other discrete practices and institutions which comprised the system of racial discrimination even after human slavery was abolished. The practices were unjustifiable—they were oppressive—and they would have been so no matter how the assignment of victims had been made. What made it worse, still, was that the institutions and the supporting ideology all interlocked to create a system of human oppression whose effects on those living under it were as devastating as they were unjustifiable.

Again, if there is anything wrong with the programs of preferential treatment that have begun to flourish within the past ten years, it should be evident that the social realities in respect to the distribution of resources and opportunities make the difference. Apart from everything else, there is simply no way in which all of these programs taken together could plausibly be viewed as capable of relegating white males to the kind of genuinely oppressive status characteristically bestowed upon women and blacks by the dominant social institutions and ideology.

The second objection is that preferential treatment programs are wrong because they take race or sex into account rather than the only thing that does matter—that is, an individual's qualification. What all such programs have in common and what makes them all objectionable, so this argument goes, is that they ignore the persons who are more qualified by bestowing a preference on those who are less qualified in virtue of their being black or female.

There are, I think, a number of things wrong with this objection based on qualifications, and not the least of them is that we do not live in a society in which there is even the serious pretense of a qualification requirement for many jobs of substantial power and authority. Would anyone claim, for example, that the persons who comprise the judiciary are there because they are the most qualified lawyers or the most qualified persons to be judges? Would anyone claim that Henry Ford II is the head of the Ford Motor Company because he is the most qualified person for the job? Part of what is wrong with even talking about qualifications and merit is that the argument derives some of its force from the erroneous notion that we would have a meritocracy were it not for programs of preferential treatment. In fact, the higher one goes in terms of prestige, power and the like, the less qualifications seem ever to be decisive. It is only for certain jobs and certain places that qualifications are used to do more than establish the possession of certain minimum competencies.

But difficulties such as these to one side, there are theoretical difficulties as well which cut much more deeply into the argument about qualifications. To begin with, it is important to see that there is a serious inconsistency present if the person who favors "pure qualifications" does so on the ground that the most qualified ought to be selected because this promotes maximum efficiency. Let us suppose that the argument is that if we have the most qualified performing the relevant tasks we will get those tasks done in the most economical and efficient manner. There is nothing wrong in principle with arguments based upon the good consequences that will flow from maintaining a social practice in a certain way. But it is inconsistent for the opponent of preferential treatment to attach much weight to qualifications on this ground, because it was an analogous appeal to the good consequences that the opponent of preferential treatment thought was wrong in the first place. That is to say, if the chief thing to be said in favor of strict qualifications and preferring the most qualified is that it is the most efficient way of getting things done, then we are right back to an assessment of the different consequences that will flow from different programs, and we are far removed from the considerations of justice or fairness that were thought to weigh so heavily against these programs.

It is important to note, too, that qualifications—at least in the educational context—are often not connected at all closely with any plausible conception of social effectiveness. To admit the most qualified students to law school, for example—given the way qualifications are now determined—is primarily to admit those who have the greatest chance of scoring the highest grades at law school. This says little about efficiency except perhaps that these students are the easiest for the faculty to teach. However, since we know so little about what constitutes being a good, or even successful lawyer, and even less about the correlation between being a very good law student and being a very good lawyer, we can hardly claim very confidently that the legal system will operate more efficiently if we admit only the most qualified students to law school.

To be at all decisive, the argument for qualifications must be that those who are the most qualified deserve to receive the benefits (the job, the place in law school, etc.) because they are the most qualified. The introduction of the concept of desert now makes it an objection as to justice or fairness of the sort promised by the original criticism of the programs. But now the problem is that there is no reason to think that there is any strong sense of "desert" in which it is correct that the most qualified deserve anything.

Let us consider more closely one case, that of preferential treatment in respect to admission to college or graduate school. There is a logical gap in the inference from the claim that a person is most qualified to perform a task, e.g., to be a good student, to the conclusion that he or she deserves to be admitted as a student. Of course, those who deserve to be admitted should be admitted. But why do the most qualified deserve anything? There is simply no necessary connection between academic merit (in the sense of being most qualified) and deserving to be a member of a student body. Suppose, for instance, that there is only one tennis court in the community. Is it clear that the two best tennis players ought to be the ones permitted to use it? Why not those who were there first? Or those who will enjoy playing the most? Or those who are the worst and, therefore, need the greatest opportunity to practice? Or those who have the chance to play least frequently?

We might, of course, have a rule that says that the best tennis players get to use the court before the others. Under such a rule the best players would deserve the court more than the poorer ones. But that is just to push the inquiry back one stage. Is there any reason to think that we ought to have a rule giving good tennis players such a preference? Indeed, the arguments that might be given for or against such a rule are many and varied. And few if any of the arguments that might support the rule would depend upon a connection between ability and desert.

Someone might reply, however, that the most able students deserve to be admitted to the university because all of their earlier schooling was a kind of competition, with university admission being the prize awarded to the winners. They deserve to be admitted because that is what the rule of the competition provides. In addition, it might be argued, it would be unfair now to exclude them in favor of others, given the reasonable expectations they developed about the way in which their industry and performance would be rewarded. Minority-admission programs, which inevitably prefer some who are less qualified over some who are more qualified, all possess this flaw.

There are several problems with this argument. The most substantial of them is that it is an empirically implausible picture of our social world. Most of what are regarded as the decisive characteristics for higher education have a great deal to do with things over which the individual has neither control nor responsibility: such things as home environment, socioeconomic class of parents, and, of course, the quality of the primary and secondary schools attended. Since individuals do not deserve having had any of these things vis-à-vis other individuals, they do not, for the most part, deserve their qualifications. And since they do not deserve their abilities they do not in any strong sense deserve to be admitted because of their abilities.

To be sure, if there has been a rule which connects, say, performance at high school with admission to college, then there is a weak sense in which those who do well at high school deserve, for that reason alone, to be admitted to college. In addition, if persons have built up or relied upon their reasonable expectations concerning performance and admission, they have a claim to be admitted on this ground as well. But it is certainly not obvious that these claims of desert are any stronger or more compelling than the competing claims based upon the needs of or advantages to women or blacks from programs of preferential treatment. And as I have indicated, all rule-based claims of desert are very weak unless and until the rule which creates the claim is itself shown to be a justified one. Unless one has a strong preference for the status quo, and unless one can defend that preference, the practice within a system of allocating places in a certain way does not go very far at all in showing that this is the right or the just way to allocate those places in the future.

A proponent of programs of preferential treatment is not at all committed to the view that qualifications ought to be wholly irrelevant. He or she can agree that, given the existing structure of any institution, there is probably some minimal set of qualifications without which one cannot participate meaningfully within the institution. In addition, it can be granted that the qualifications of those involved will affect the way the institution works and the way it affects others in the society. And the consequences will vary depending upon the particular institution. But all of this only establishes that qualifications, in this sense, are relevant, not that they are decisive. This is wholly consistent with the claim that race or sex should today also be relevant when it comes to matters such as admission to college or law school. And that is all that any preferential treatment program—even one with the kind of quota used in the *Bakke* case—has ever tried to do.

I have not attempted to establish that programs of preferential treatment are right and desirable. There are empirical issues concerning the consequences of these programs that I have not discussed, and certainly not settled. Nor, for that matter, have I considered the argument that justice may permit, if not require, these programs as a way to provide compensation or reparation for injuries suffered in the recent as well as distant past, or as a way to remove benefits that are undeservedly enjoyed by those of the dominant group. What I have tried to do is show that it is wrong to think that programs of preferential treatment are objectionable in the centrally important sense in which many past and present discriminatory features of our society have been and are racist and sexist. The social realities as to power and opportunity do make a fundamental difference. It is also wrong to think that programs of preferential treatment could, therefore, plausibly rest both on the view that such programs are not unfair to white males (except in the weak, rule-dependent sense described above) and on the view that it is unfair to continue the present set of unjust—often racist and sexist—institutions that comprise the social reality. And the case for these programs could rest as well on the proposition that, given the distribution of power and influence in the United States today, such programs may reasonably be viewed as potentially valuable, effective by which to achieve means admirable and significant social ideals of equality and integration.

QUESTIONS FOR ANALYSIS

1. What does it mean to claim that proponents of preferential treatment are guilty of "intellectual inconsistency"? Do you think that Wasserstrom convincingly refutes this charge?
2. What moral principle (or principles) underlies Wasserstrom's objection to slavery?
3. How does Wasserstrom respond to the charge that preferential-treatment programs compromise the only thing that really matters: individual qualifications?
4. Describe the inconsistency present for the person who favors "pure qualifications" on grounds of maximum efficiency.
5. Do you agree that there is no necessary connection between qualifications and desert?
6. Do you think Wasserstrom's tennis analogy is a sound one?
7. Would it be accurate to say that Wasserstrom unequivocally supports preferential-treatment programs? Explain.

Reverse Discrimination and Compensatory Justice

WILLIAM T. BLACKSTONE

William T. Blackstone (1931–1977) was a professor of philosophy at the University of Georgia. In this essay, he is concerned with a single question: Is reverse discrimination

From *Social Theory and Practice*, vol. 3, no. 3 (Spring 1975). Reprinted with permission of the publisher and Mrs. Jean T. Blackstone.

ever justified on grounds of repairing past wrongs done to women and minorities? Blackstone thinks not. In his view, reverse discrimination cannot be so justified either morally or legally.

Blackstone builds his case primarily on a utilitarian foundation. He believes that more harm than good would result from a systematic policy of reverse discrimination. (Curiously, as he points out, reverse discrimination often is justified on an appeal to utility.) Since reverse discrimination is not justified on utilitarian or justice-regarding grounds, Blackstone concludes that compensation through reverse discrimination is not justifiable. Indeed, he argues that affirmative-action programs, despite how they have sometimes been implemented, not only oppose reverse discrimination but forbid it.

Is reverse discrimination justified as a policy of compensation or of preferential treatment for women and racial minorities? That is, given the fact that women and racial minorities have been invidiously discriminated against in the past on the basis of the irrelevant characteristics of race and sex—are we now justified in discriminating in their favor on the basis of the same characteristics? This is a central ethical and legal question today and it is one which is quite unresolved. Philosophers, jurists, legal scholars, and the man-in-the-street line up on both sides of this issue. These differences are plainly reflected (in the Supreme Court's majority opinion and Justice Douglas's dissent) in *DeFunis v. Odegaard.*[1] . . .

I will argue that reverse discrimination is improper on both moral and constitutional grounds, though I focus more on moral grounds. However, I do this with considerable ambivalence, even "existential guilt." Several reasons lie behind that ambivalence. First, there are moral and constitutional arguments on both sides. The ethical waters are very muddy and I simply argue that the balance of the arguments are against a policy of reverse discrimination.[2] My ambivalence is further due not only to the fact that traditional racism is still a much larger problem than that of reverse discrimination but also because I am sympathetic to the *goals* of those who strongly believe that reverse discrimination as a policy is the means to overcome the debilitating effects of past injustice. Compensation and remedy are most definitely required both by the facts and by our value commitments. But I do not think that reverse discrimination is the proper means of remedy or compensation. . . .

I

Let us now turn to the possibility of a utilitarian justification of reverse discrimination and to the possible conflict of justice-regarding reasons and those of social utility on this issue. The category of morally relevant reasons is broader, in my opinion, than reasons related to the norm of justice. It is broader than those related to the norm of utility. Also it seems to me that the norms of justice and utility are not reducible one to the other. We cannot argue these points of ethical theory here. But, if these assumptions are correct, then it is at least possible to morally justify injustice or invidious discrimination in some contexts. A case would have to be made that such injustice, though regrettable, will produce the best consequences for society and that this fact is an overriding or weightier moral reason than the temporary injustice. Some arguments for reverse discrimination have taken this line. Professor Thomas Nagel argues that such discrimination is justifiable as long as it is "clearly contributing to the eradication of great social evils."[3] . . .

Another example of what I would call a utilitarian argument for reverse discrimination was recently set forth by Congressman Andrew Young of Georgia. Speaking specifically of reverse discrimination in the context of education, he stated: "While that may give minorities a little edge in some instances, and you may run into the danger of what we now commonly call reverse discrimination, I think the educational system needs this. Society needs this as much as the people we are trying to help . . . a society working toward affirmative action and inclusiveness is going to be a stronger and more relevant society than one that accepts the limited concepts of objectivity.... I would admit that it is perhaps an individual injustice. But it might be necessary in order to overcome an historic group injustice or series of group injustices."[4] Congressman Young's basic justifying grounds for reverse discrimination, which he recognizes as individual injustice, are the results which he thinks it will produce: a stronger and more relevant education system and society, and one which is more just overall. His argument may involve pitting some justice-regarding reasons (the right of women and racial minorities to be compensated for past injustices) against others (the right of the majority to the uniform application of the same standards of merit to all). But a major thrust of his argument also seems to be utilitarian.

Just as there are justice-regarding arguments on both sides of the issue of reverse discrimination, so also there are utilitarian arguments on both sides. In a nutshell, the utilitarian argument in favor runs like this: Our society contains large groups of persons who suffer from past institutionalized injustice. As a result, the possibilities of social discord and disorder are high indeed. If short-term reverse discrimination were to be effective in overcoming the effects of past institutionalized injustice and if this policy could alleviate the causes of disorder and bring a higher quality of life to millions of persons, then society as a whole would benefit.

There are moments in which I am nearly convinced by this argument, but the conclusion that such a policy would have negative utility on the whole wins out. For although reverse discrimination might appear to have the effect of getting more persons who have been disadvantaged by past inequities into the mainstream quicker, that is, into jobs, schools, and practices from which they have been excluded, the cost would be invidious discrimination against majority group members of society. I do not think that majority members of society would find this acceptable, i.e., the disadvantaging of themselves for past inequities which they did not control and for which they are not responsible. If such policies were put into effect by government, I would predict wholesale rejection or noncooperation, the result of which would be negative not only for those who have suffered past inequities but also for the justice-regarding institutions of society. Claims and counter-claims would obviously be raised by other ethnic or racial minorities—by Chinese, Chicanos, American Indians, Puerto Ricans—and by orphans, illegitimate children, ghetto residents, and so on. Literally thousands of types or groups could, on similar grounds as blacks or women, claim that reverse discrimination is justified on their behalf. What would happen if government attempted policies of reverse discrimination for all such groups? It would mean the arbitrary exclusion or discrimination against all others relative to a given purpose and a given group. Such a policy would itself create an injustice for which those newly excluded persons could then, themselves, properly claim the need for reverse discrimination to offset the injustice to them. The circle is plainly a vicious one. Such policies are simply self-destructive. In place of the ideal of equality and distributive justice based on relevant criteria, we would be left with the special pleading of self-interested power groups, groups who gear criteria for the distribution of goods, services, and opportunities to their special needs and situations, primarily. Such policies would be those of special privilege, not the appeal to objective criteria which apply to all.[5] They would lead to social chaos, not social justice.

Furthermore, in cases in which reverse discrimination results in a lowering of quality, the consequences for society, indeed for minority victims of injustice for which reverse discrimination is designed to help, may be quite bad. It is no easy matter to calculate this, but the recent report sponsored by the Carnegie Commission on Higher Education points to such deleterious consequences.[6] If the quality of instruction in higher education, for example, is lowered through a policy of primary attention to race or sex as opposed to ability and training, everyone—including victims of past injustice—suffers. Even if such policies are clearly seen as temporary with quite definite deadlines for termination, I am skeptical about their utilitarian value. . . .

II

The inappropriateness of reverse discrimination, both on utilitarian and justice-regarding grounds, in no way means that compensation for past injustices is inappropriate. It does not mean that those who have suffered past injustices and who have been disadvantaged by them are not entitled to compensation or that they have no moral right to remedy. It may be difficult in different contexts to translate that moral right to remedy into practice or into legislation. When has a disadvantaged person or group been compensated enough? What sort of allocation of resources will compensate without creating additional inequities or deleterious consequences? There is no easy answer to these questions. Decisions must be made in particular contexts. Furthermore, it may be the case that the effects of past injustices are so severe (poverty, malnutrition, and the denial of educational opportunities) that genuine compensation—the balancing of the scales—is impossible. The effects of malnutrition or the lack of education are often nonreversible (and would be so even under a policy of reverse discrimination). This is one of the tragedies of injustice. But if reverse discrimination is inappropriate as a means of compensation and if (as I have argued) it is unjust to make persons who are not responsible for the suffering and disadvantaging of others to suffer for those past injuries, then other means must be employed unless overriding moral considerations of another type (utilitarian) can be clearly demonstrated. That compensation must take a form which is consistent with our constitutional principles and with reasonable principles of justice. Now it seems to me that the Federal Government's Equal Opportunity and Affirmative Action programs are consistent with these principles, that they are not only not committed to reverse discrimination but rather absolutely forbid it.[7] However, it also seems to me that some officials authorized or required to implement these compensatory efforts have resorted to reverse discrimination and hence have violated the basic principles of justice embodied in these programs. I now want to argue both of these points: first, that these federal programs reject reverse discrimination in their basic principles; secondly, that some implementers of these programs have violated their own principles.

Obviously our country has not always been committed constitutionally to equality. We need no review of our social and political heritage to document this. But with the Fourteenth Amendment, equality as a principle was given constitutional status. Subsequently, social, political, and legal practices changed radically and they will continue to do so. The Fourteenth Amendment declares that states are forbidden to deny any person life, liberty, or property without due process of law or to deny to any person the equal protection of the laws. In my opinion the principles of the Equal Opportunity and Affirmative Action Programs reflect faithfully this constitutional commitment. I am more familiar with those programs as reflected in universities. In this context they require that employers "recruit, hire, train, and promote persons in all job classifications without regard to race, color, religion, sex or national origin, except where sex is a bona fide occupational qualification."[8] They state explicitly that "goals may not be rigid and inflexible quotas which must be met, but must be targets reasonably attainable by means of good faith effort."[9] They require the active recruitment of women and racial minorities where they are "underutilized," this being defined as a context in which there are "fewer minorities or women in a particular job classification than would reasonably be expected by their availability."[10] This is sometimes difficult to determine; but some relevant facts do exist and hence the meaning of a "good faith" effort is not entirely fluid. In any event the Affirmative Action Program in universities requires that "goals, timetables and affirmative action commitment, must be designed to correct any identifiable deficiencies," with separate goals and timetables for minorities and women.[11] It recognizes that there has been blatant discrimination against women and racial minorities in universities and elsewhere, and it assumes that there are "identifiable deficiencies." But it does not require that blacks be employed because they are black or women employed because they are women; that is, it does not require reverse discrimination with rigid quotas to correct the past. It requires a good faith effort in the present based on data on the availability of qualified women and racial minorities in various disciplines and other relevant facts. (Similar requirements hold, of course, for non-academic employment at colleges and universities.) It does not mandate the hiring of the unqualified or a lowering of standards; it mandates only equality of opportunity for all which, given the history of discrimination against women and racial minorities, requires affirmative action in recruitment.

Now if this affirmative action in recruitment, which is not only consistent with but required by our commitment to equality and social justice, is translated into rigid quotas and reverse discrimination by those who implement equal opportunity and affirmative action programs in the effort to get results immediately—and there is no doubt in my mind that this has occurred—then such action violates the principles of these programs.

This violation—this inconsistency of principle and practice—occurs, it seems to me, when employers hire with *priority emphasis* on race, sex, or minority-group status. This move effectively eliminates others from the competition. It is like pretending that everyone is in the game from the beginning while all the while certain persons are systematically excluded. This is exactly what happened recently when a judge declared that a certain quota or number of women were to be employed by a given agency regardless of their qualifications for the job,[12] when some public school officials fired a white coach in order to hire a black one,[13] when a DeFunis is excluded from law school on racial grounds, and when colleges or universities announce that normal academic openings will give preference to female candidates or those from racial minorities.

If reverse discrimination is prohibited by our constitutional and ethical commitments, what means of remedy and compensation are available? Obviously, those means which are consistent with those commitments. Our commitments assure the right to remedy to those who have been treated unjustly, but our government has not done enough to bring this right to meaningful fruition in practice. Sound progress has been made in recent years, especially since the Equal Employment Opportunity Act of 1972 and the establishment of the Equal Employment Opportunities Commission. This Act and other laws have extended anti-discrimination protection to over 60% of the population.[14] The Commission is now authorized to enforce anti-discrimination orders in court and, according to one report, it has negotiated out-of-court settlements which brought 44,000 minority workers over 46 million dollars in back pay.[15] Undoubtedly this merely scratches the surface. But now the framework exists for translating the right to remedy into practice, not just for sloughing off race and sex as irrelevant criteria of differential treatment but other irrelevant criteria as well—age, religion, the size of hips (I am thinking of airline stewardesses), the length of nose, and so on.

Adequate remedy to overcome the sins of the past, not to speak of the present, would require the expenditure of vast sums for compensatory programs for those disadvantaged by past injustice in order to assure equal access. Such programs should be racially and sexually neutral, benefiting the disadvantaged of *whatever sex or race*. Such neutral compensatory programs would have a high proportion of blacks and other minorities as recipients, for they as members of these groups suffer more from the injustices of the past. But the basis of the compensation would be that fact, not sex or race. Neutral compensatory policies have definite theoretical and practical advantages in contrast to policies of reverse discrimination: Theoretical advantages, in that they are consistent with our basic constitutional and ethical commitments whereas reverse discrimination is not; practical advantages, in that their consistency, indeed their requirement by our constitutional and ethical commitments, means that they can marshal united support in overcoming inequalities whereas reverse discrimination, in my opinion, can not.

NOTES

1. 94 S. Ct. 1704 (1974).
2. I hasten to add a qualification—more ambivalence!—resulting from discussion with Tom Beauchamp of Georgetown University. In cases of extreme recalcitrance to equal employment by certain institutions or businesses some quota requirements (reverse discrimination) may be justified. I regard this as distinct from a general policy of reverse discrimination.
3. "Equal Treatment and Compensatory Discrimination," *Philosophy and Public Affairs,* 2 (Summer 1974).
4. *Atlanta Journal and Constitution,* Sept. 22, 1974, p. 20-A.
5. For similar arguments see Lisa Newton, "Reverse Discrimination as Unjustified," *Ethics,* 83 (1973).
6. Richard A. Lester, *Antibias Regulation of Universities* (New York, 1974); discussed in *Newsweek,* July 15, 1974, p. 78.
7. See The Civil Rights Act of 1964, especially Title VII (which created the Equal Employment Opportunity Commission), amended by The Equal Employment Opportunity Act of 1972, found in *ABC's of The Equal Employment Opportunity Act,* prepared by the Editorial Staff of The Bureau of National Affairs, Inc., 1972. Affirmative Action Programs came into existence with Executive Order 11246. Requirements for affirmative action are found in the rules and regulations I21-CFR Part 60-2, Order #4 (Affirmative Action Programs) generally known as Executive Order #4 and Revised Order #4 41-CFT 60-2 B. For discussion see Paul Brownstein, "Affirmative Action Programs," in *Equal Employment Opportunities Compliance,* Practising Law Institute, New York City (1972), pp. 73–111.
8. See Brownstein, "Affirmative Action Programs" and, for example, *The University of Georgia Affirmative Action Plan,* Athens, Ga., 1973–74, viii, pp. 133, 67.
9. *Brownstein and The University of Georgia Affirmative Action Plan,* Athens, Ga., 1973–74, p. 71.
10. *Ibid.,* p. 69.
11. *Ibid.,* p. 71.
12. See the *Atlanta Journal and Constitution,* June 9, 1974, p. 26-D.
13. See *Atlanta Constitution,* June 7, 1974, p. 13-B.
14. *Newsweek,* June 17, 1974, p. 75.
15. *Ibid.,* p. 75.

QUESTIONS FOR ANALYSIS

1. Why does Blackstone argue his case with a certain amount of "existential guilt"?
2. State the utilitarian argument for reverse discrimination.
3. Would it be accurate to say that Blackstone rejects utility as a legitimate standard for determining the morality of reverse discrimination?
4. Consider this proposition: "Blackstone is opposed to compensating those who have suffered past injustices." Is this statement true or false? Explain.
5. What are some of the problems that compensation raises?
6. Some people would claim that it is wrong to hold people today responsible for the wrongs of their ancestors and that it is equally as wrong to compensate people today for the wrongs their ancestors may have experienced. Do you agree? Explain your answers by appeal to some concept of justice.
7. What reasons does Blackstone offer for saying that affirmative-action programs actually forbid reverse discrimination? Do you think his argument is persuasive? What objections to his interpretations might you raise?
8. Granted that reverse discrimination is prohibited by our constitution and ethical commitments, what means of redress are available? Do you agree that a vigorous and unflinching implementation of these means will satisfy the obligation to eradicate discrimination?

Reverse Discrimination as Unjustified

LISA NEWTON

Lisa Newton, a professor of philosophy at Fairfield University, delivered a version of the following essay at a meeting of the Society for Women in Philosophy in 1972. She argues that reverse discrimination cannot be justified by an appeal to the ideal of equality. Indeed, according to Newton, reverse discrimination does not advance but actually undermines equality because it violates the concept of equal justice under law for all citizens.

Specifically, Newton attacks the defense for reverse discrimination on grounds of equality. She contends that no violation of justice can be justified by an appeal to the ideal of equality, for the idea of equality is logically dependent on the notion of justice.

In addition to this theoretical objection to reverse discrimination, Newton opposes it because she believes it raises insoluble problems. Among them are determining what groups have been sufficiently discriminated against in the past to deserve preferred treatment in the present and determining the degree of reverse discrimination that will be compensatory. Newton concludes that reverse discrimination destroys justice, law, equality, and citizenship itself.

I have heard it argued that "simple justice" requires that we favor women and blacks in employment and educational opportunities, since women and blacks were "unjustly" excluded from such opportunities for so many years in the not so distant past. It is a strange argument, an example of a possible implication of a true proposition advanced to dispute the proposition itself, like an octopus absentmindedly slicing off his head with a stray tentacle. A fatal confusion underlies this argument, a confusion fundamentally relevant to our understanding of the notion of the rule of law.

Two senses of justice and equality are involved in this confusion. The root notion of justice, progenitor of the other, is the one that Aristotle (*Nicomachean Ethics* 5.6; *Politics* 1.2; 3.1) assumes to be the foundation and proper virtue of the political association. It is the conclusion which free men establish among themselves when they "share a common life in order that their association bring them self-sufficiency"—the regulation of their relationship by law, and the establishment, by law, of equality before the law. Rule of law is the name and pattern of this justice; its equality stands against the inequalities—of wealth, talent, etc.—otherwise obtaining among its participants, who by virtue of that equality are called "citizens." It is an achievement—complete, or, more frequently, partial—of certain people in certain concrete situations. It is fragile and easily disrupted by powerful individuals who discover that the blind equality of rule of law is inconvenient for their interests. Despite its obvious instability, Aristotle assumed that the establishment of justice in this sense, the creation of citizenship, was a permanent possibility for men and that the resultant association of citizens was the natural home of the species. At levels below the political association, this rule-governed equality is easily found; it is exemplified by any group of children agreeing together to play a game. At the level of the political association, the attainment of this justice is more difficult, simply because the stakes are so much higher for each participant. The equality of citizenship

From Lisa H. Newton, "Reverse Discrimination as Unjustified," *Ethics* 83 (1973): 308–12.

is not something that happens of its own accord, and without the expenditure of a fair amount of effort it will collapse into the rule of a powerful few over an apathetic many. But at least it has been achieved, at some times in some places; it is always worth trying to achieve, and eminently worth trying to maintain, wherever and to whatever degree it has been brought into being.

Aristotle's parochialism is notorious; he really did not imagine that persons other than Greeks could associate freely in justice, and the only form of association he had in mind was the Greek *polis*. With the decline of the *polis* and the shift in the center of political thought, his notion of justice underwent a sea change. To be exact, it ceased to represent a political type and became a moral ideal: the ideal of equality as we know it. This ideal demands that all men be included in citizenship—that one Law govern all equally, that all men regard all other men as fellow citizens, with the same guarantees, rights, and protections. Briefly, it demands that the circle of citizenship achieved by any group be extended to include the entire human race. Properly understood, its effect on our associations can be excellent: It congratulates us on our achievement of rule of law as a process of government but refuses to let us remain complacent until we have expanded the associations to include others within the ambit of the rules, as often and as far as possible. While one man is a slave, none of us may feel truly free. We are constantly prodded by this ideal to look for possible unjustifiable discrimination, for inequalities not absolutely required for the functioning of the society and advantageous to all. And after twenty centuries of pressure, not at all constant, from this ideal, it might be said that some progress has been made. To take the cases in point for this problem, we are now prepared to assert, as Aristotle would never have been, the equality of sexes and of persons of different colors. The ambit of American citizenship, once restricted to white males of property, has been extended to include all adult free men, then all adult males including ex-slaves, then all women. The process of acquisition of full citizenship was for these groups a sporadic trail of half-measures, even now not complete; the steps on the road to full equality are marked by legislation and judicial decisions which are only recently concluded and still often not enforced. But the fact that we can now discuss the possibility of favoring such groups in hiring shows that over the area that concerns us, at least, full equality is presupposed as a basis for discussion. To that extent, they are full citizens, fully protected by the law of the land.

It is important for my argument that the moral ideal of equality be recognized as logically distinct from the condition (or virtue) of justice in the political sense. Justice in this sense exists *among* a citizenry, irrespective of the number of the populace included in that citizenry. Further, the moral ideal is parasitic upon the political virtue, for "equality" is unspecified—it means nothing until we are told in what respect that equality is to be realized. In a political context, "equality" is specified as "equal rights"—equal access to the public realm, public goods and offices, equal treatment under the law—in brief, the equality of citizenship. If citizenship is not a possibility, political equality is unintelligible. The ideal emerges as a generalization of the real condition and refers back to that condition for its content.

Now, if justice (Aristotle's justice in the political sense) is equal treatment under law for all citizens, what is injustice? Clearly, injustice is the violation of that equality, discrimination for or against a group of citizens, favoring them with special immunities and privileges or depriving them of those guaranteed to the others. When the southern employer refuses to hire blacks in white-collar jobs, when Wall Street will only hire women as secretaries with new titles, when Mississippi high schools routinely flunk all the black boys above ninth grade, we have examples of injustice, and we work to restore the equality of the public realm by ensuring that equal opportunity will be provided in such cases in the future. But of course, when the employers and the schools *favor* women and blacks, the same injustice is done. Just as the previous discrimination did, this reverse discrimination violates the public equality which defines citizenship and destroys the rule of law for the areas in which these favors are granted. To the extent that we adopt a program of discrimination, reverse or otherwise, justice in the political sense is destroyed, and none of us, specifically affected or not, is a citizen, a bearer of rights—we are all petitioners for favors. And to the same extent, the ideal of equality is undermined, for it has content only where justice obtains, and by destroying justice we render the ideal meaningless. It is, then, an ironic paradox, if not a contradiction in terms, to assert that the ideal of equality justifies the violation of justice; it is as if one should argue, with William Buckley, that an ideal of humanity can justify the destruction of the human race.

Logically, the conclusion is simple enough: All discrimination is wrong prima facie because it violates justice, and that goes for reverse discrimination too. No violation of justice among the citizens may be justified (may overcome the prima facie objection) by appeal to the ideal of equality, for that ideal is logically dependent upon the notion of justice. Reverse discrimination, then, which attempts no other justification than an appeal to equality, is wrong. But let us try to make the conclusion more plausible by suggesting some of the implications of the suggested practice of reverse discrimination in employment and education. My argument will be that the problems raised there are insoluble, not only in practice but in principle.

We may argue, if we like, about what "discrimination" consists of. Do I discriminate against blacks if I admit none to my school when none of the black applicants are qualified by the tests I always give? How far must I go to root out cultural bias from my application forms and tests before I can say that I have not discriminated against those of different cultures? Can I assume that women are not strong enough to be roughnecks on my oil rigs, or must I test them individually? But this controversy, the most popular and well-argued aspect of the issue, is not as fatal as two others which cannot be avoided: If we are regarding the blacks as a "minority" victimized by discrimination, what is a "minority"? And for any group—blacks, women, whatever—that has been discriminated against, what amount of reverse discrimination wipes out the initial discrimination? Let us grant as true that women and blacks were discriminated against, even where laws forbade such discrimination, and grant for the sake of argument that a history of discrimination must be wiped out by reverse discrimination. What follows?

First, are there other groups which have been, discriminated against? For they should have the same right of restitution. What about American Indians, Chicanos, Appalachian Mountain whites, Puerto Ricans, Jews, Cajuns, and Orientals? And if these are to be included, the principle according to which we specify a "minority" is simply the criterion of "ethnic (sub) group," and we're stuck with every hyphenated American in the lower middle class clamoring for special privileges for *his* group—and with equal justification. For be it noted, when we run down the Harvard roster, we find not only a scarcity of blacks (in comparison with the proportion in the population) but an even more striking scarcity of those second-, third-, and fourth-generation ethnics who make up the loudest voice of Middle America. Shouldn't they demand *their* share? And eventually, the WASPs will have to form their own lobby; for they too are a minority. The point is simply this: There is no "majority" in America who will not mind giving up just a bit of their rights to make room for a favored minority. There are only other minorities, each of which is discriminated against by the favoring. The initial injustice is then repeated dozens of times, and if each minority is granted the same right of restitution as the others, an entire area of rule governance is dissolved into a pushing and shoving match between self-interested groups. Each works to catch the public eye and political popularity by whatever means of advertising and power politics lend themselves to the effort, to capitalize as much as possible on temporary popularity until the restless mob picks another group to feel sorry for. Hardly an edifying spectacle, and in the long run no one can benefit: The pie is no larger—it just that instead of setting up and enforcing rules for getting a piece, we've turned the contest into a free-for-all, requiring much more effort for no larger a reward. It would be in the interests of all the participants to reestablish an objective rule to govern the process, carefully enforced and the same for all.

Second, supposing that we do manage to agree in general that women and blacks (and all the others) have some right of restitution, some right to a privileged place in the structure of opportunities for a while, how will we know when that while is up? How much privilege is enough? When will the guilt be gone, the price paid, the balance restored? What recompense is right for centuries of exclusion? What criterion tells us when we are done? Our experience with the Civil Rights movement shows us that agreement on these terms cannot be presupposed: A process that appears to some to be going at a mad gallop into a black takeover appears to the rest of us to be at a standstill. Should a practice of reverse discrimination be adopted, we may safely predict that just as some of us begin to see "a satisfactory start toward righting the balance," others of us will see that we "have already gone too far in the other direction" and will suggest that the discrimination ought to be reversed again. And such disagreement is inevitable, for the point is that we could not *possibly* have any criteria for evaluating the kind of recompense we have in mind. The context presumed by any discussion of restitution is the context of the rule of law: Law sets the rights of men and simultaneously sets the method for remedying the violation of those rights. You may exact suffering from others and/or damage payments for yourself if and only if the others have violated your rights; the suffering you have endured is not sufficient reason for them to suffer. And remedial rights exist only where there is law: Primary human rights are useful guides to legislation but cannot stand as reasons for awarding remedies for injuries sustained. But then, the context presupposed by any discussion of restitution is the context of preexistent full citizenship. No remedial rights could exist for the excluded; neither in law nor in logic does there exist a right to *sue* for a standing to sue.

From these two considerations, then, the difficulties with reverse discrimination become evident. Restitution for a disadvantaged group whose rights under the law have been violated is possible by legal means, but restitution for a disadvantaged group whose grievance is that there was no law to protect them simply is not. First, outside of the area of justice defined by the law, no sense can be made of "the group's rights," for no law recognizes that group or the individuals in it, qua members, as bearers of rights (hence *any* group can constitute itself as a disadvantaged minority in some sense and demand similar restitution). Second, outside of the area of protection of law, no sense can be made of the violation of rights (hence the amount of the recompense cannot be decided by any objective criterion). For both reasons, the practice of reverse discrimination undermines the foundation of the very ideal in whose name it is advocated; it destroys justice, law, equality, and citizenship itself, and replaces them with power struggles and popularity contests.

QUESTIONS FOR ANALYSIS

1. What is the "fatal confusion" underlying the argument that "simple justice" requires preferential treatment?
2. Can you describe how justice under Aristotle moved from a "political type" to a "moral ideal"?
3. Why is it important for Newton's argument that she distinguish the moral ideal of equality from the condition of justice in the political sense?
4. Central to Newton's argument is her definition of justice and her assumptions about the relationship between justice and equality. Do you agree with her?
5. Do you think Rawls would agree with Newton's analysis? Explain.

6. Would you agree that in part Newton objects to reverse discrimination on utilitarian grounds? Explain.
7. Do you agree that the problems Newton says surround reverse discrimination really are "insoluble"?

CASE PRESENTATION

Proposition 209

Over the years, California voters have passed many controversial ballot initiatives that proved to be bellwethers for the rest of the nation. Among the most controversial is Proposition 209, an amendment to the state constitution that appeared on the 1996 ballot and passed by a margin of 54 percent to 45 percent. According to that measure, "The state shall not discriminate against, or grant preferential treatment to, any individual or group on the basis of race, sex, color, ethnicity, or national origin in the operation of public employment, public education, or public contracting."

These words may seem innocuous at first. In fact, they are modeled on the Civil Rights Act of 1964. But they sparked a lawsuit in federal court seeking to have the amendment declared unconstitutional. The problem, the plaintiffs argued, is that the measure puts an end to all state-sponsored affirmative-action programs, and in doing so, it places an unconstitutional hardship on minorities and women. A district court judge agreed and blocked the law with a preliminary injunction, but the Ninth Circuit Court of Appeals overruled him, and the law went into effect in August 1997. Still, the legal battle did not end until November 3 of that year, when the U.S. Supreme Court unanimously declined to hear the plaintiffs' challenge to the law.

California Governor Pete Wilson hailed the ruling. The *Los Angeles Times* quoted him as saying, "It is time for those who have resisted Prop. 209 to acknowledge that equal rights under law, not special preferences, is the law of the land. A measure that eliminates any form of discrimination based on race and gender violates no one's constitutional rights." The paper also quoted Mark Rosenbaum of the American Civil Liberties Union, the plaintiffs' chief attorney, who called the measure "mean-spirited and unjust" and "1990s-style discrimination against minorities and women, more insidious than any state-wide measure since the era of Southern resistance to *Brown v. Board of Education.*"

In the fall of 2006, only 2 percent of the incoming freshmen at UCLA were African-American, a 57 percent drop in the ten years since adoption of Prop. 209. In the ten-campus University of California system, only 3.4 percent of all freshmen offered admission were African-American for fall 2006. The UC Trustees announced that summer that they would undertake a comprehensive study of the impact of Prop. 209 on minority enrollment at the University.

A very similar measure was adopted in Washington state in 1998, promoted by the same groups that promoted Prop. 209 in California. They also succeeded in getting this measure onto the statewide ballot in Michigan for fall 2006.

QUESTIONS FOR ANALYSIS

1. Opponents of Proposition 209 charge that it targets minorities and women. Does it?
2. Proponents of Proposition 209 hail the Supreme Court decision as a major step toward a color-blind society. Do you agree?
3. According to one perspective, affirmative action leads to greater racial discord. According to another, measures like Proposition 209 do. Which view do you think is right?
4. Voters in several other states have begun movements to repeal affirmative-action laws. Is this activity a sign that affirmative action is on the way out? Should it be on the way out?

CASE PRESENTATION

Grutter v. Bollinger: *Taking Race into Account*

In June 2003, the U.S. Supreme Court announced the *Grutter v. Bollinger* decision, reaffirming a controversial element of the 1978 *Bakke* decision. In *Bakke*, the Court had said that universities may not set aside a rigid quota of places in its entering class limited to particular racial minorities but that they may "take race into account." They reasoned that diversity in college classrooms was a legitimate goal in college admissions. Just as colleges seek a diversity of athletes, musicians, artists, scholars, and scientists, so too can they legitimately pursue cultural and racial diversity in their classes of students.

The *Grutter* case challenged the policy for admission to the highly competitive University of Michigan Law School. Admissions were based on a student's academic abilities along with an assessment of a range of talents, experiences, and potential. Among the factors considered were each student's contribution to the diversity of the law school. While not limited to racial diversity, the Law School said that it was committed to including a "critical mass" of underrepresented minorities, especially African American, Hispanic, and Native American students. The majority decision, written by Justice Sandra Day O'Conner, said in part:

> . . . Today, we hold that the Law School has a compelling interest in attaining a diverse student body. The Law School's educational judgment that such diversity is essential to its educational mission is one to which we defer. . . . Our scrutiny of the interest asserted by the Law School is no less strict for taking into account complex educational judgments in an area that lies primarily within the expertise of the university. Our holding today is in keeping with our tradition of giving a degree of deference to a university's academic decisions, within constitutionally prescribed limits. . . .
>
> We have long recognized that, given the important purpose of public education and the expansive freedoms of speech and thought associated with the university environment, universities occupy a special niche in our constitutional tradition. . . . Our conclusion that the Law School has a compelling interest in a diverse student body is informed by our view that attaining a diverse student body is at the heart of the Law School's proper institutional mission, and that "good faith" on the part of a university is "presumed" absent "a showing to the contrary."
>
> As part of its goal of "assembling a class that is both exceptionally academically qualified and broadly diverse," the Law School seeks to "enroll a 'critical mass' of minority students." . . . The Law School's interest is not simply "to assure within its student body some specified percentage of a particular group merely because of its race or ethnic origin." . . . That would amount to outright racial balancing, which is patently unconstitutional. . . . Rather, the Law School's concept of critical mass is defined by reference to the educational benefits that diversity is designed to produce. . . .
>
> These benefits are not theoretical but real, as major American businesses have made clear that the skills needed in today's increasingly global marketplace can only be developed through exposure to widely diverse people, cultures, ideas, and viewpoints. . . . What is more, high-ranking retired officers and civilian leaders of the United States military assert that, "[b]ased on [their] decades of experience," a "highly qualified, racially diverse officer corps . . . is essential to the military's ability to fulfill its principle mission to provide national security." . . . The primary sources for the Nation's officer corps are the service academies and the Reserve Officers Training Corps (ROTC), the latter comprising students already admitted to participating colleges and universities. . . . At present, "the military cannot achieve an officer corps that is both highly qualified and racially diverse unless the service academies and the ROTC used limited race-conscious recruiting and admissions policies." . . . To fulfill its mission, the military "must be selective in admissions for training and education for the officer corps, and it must train and educate a highly qualified, racially diverse officer corps in a racially diverse setting." . . . We agree that "[i]t requires only a small step from this analysis to conclude that our country's other most selective institutions must remain both diverse and selective."
>
> We have repeatedly acknowledged the overriding importance of preparing students for work and citizenship, describing education as pivotal to "sustaining our political and cultural heritage" with a fundamental role in maintaining the fabric of society. . . . Effective participation by members of all racial and ethnic groups in the civic life of our Nation is essential if the dream of one Nation, indivisible, is to be realized.

Moreover, universities, and in particular, law schools, represent the training ground for a large number of our Nation's leaders. . . . Individuals with law degrees occupy roughly half the state governorships, more than half the seats in the United States Senate, and more than a third of the seats in the United States House of Representatives. . . . The pattern is even more striking when it comes to highly selective law schools. A handful of these schools accounts for 25 of the 100 United States Senators, 74 United States Courts of Appeals judges, and nearly 200 of the more than 600 United States District Court judges. . . .

In order to cultivate a set of leaders with legitimacy in the eyes of the citizenry, it is necessary that the path to leadership be visibly open to talented and qualified individuals of every race and ethnicity. All members of our heterogeneous society must have confidence in the openness and integrity of the educational institutions that provide this training. As we have recognized, law schools "cannot be effective in isolation from the individuals and institutions with which the law interacts." . . . Access to legal education (and thus the legal profession) must be inclusive of talented and qualified individuals of every race and ethnicity, so that all members of our heterogeneous society may participate in the educational institutions that provide the training and education necessary to succeed in America. . . .

QUESTIONS FOR ANALYSIS

1. Critics of the *Bakke* decision had hoped that the Court in *Grutter* would overturn the principle that it was constitutional for colleges and universities to take race into account in admission decisions, especially after a quarter of a century of continued efforts to improve opportunities for racial minorities in this country. Has the time come for a truly color-blind society in which admission decisions based solely on scholarly measures will result in a diverse student body without having to consider race during the admission process? Will such a time ever come?
2. Identify the use of consequentialist reasoning in the excerpt here. Is this persuasive? What consideration is given to the reasoning of human rights in this decision? Does the Court reason appropriately in defending its decision? Do you believe there are additional considerations that should be taken into account?
3. Can the arguments about the importance of law schools as a training ground for the nation's leaders be extended to all levels of education? Are there alternative ways of meeting that societal goal that would not involve taking race into account in law school admissions?
4. Some critics of this decision have claimed that admitting students not as well qualified academically as most entering students actually backfires because as they do not make law review or graduate at the top of the class, as they might at a less prestigious institution where their academic work would be more comparable to the other students. Is this a persuasive argument against the Michigan admissions program?
5. In California, public law schools are prohibited under Proposition 209 from taking race into account, despite this Supreme Court decision. Instead, those law schools now emphasize a variety of additional factors in their admissions, such as overcoming adversity in completing college and preparing for law school. Does this approach achieve appropriate diversity in ways that do not unfairly disadvantage white applicants?

CASE PRESENTATION

Reparations: An Overdue Debt to African Slaves in America?

Charles J. Ogletree, Jr., the Jesse Climenko Professor of Law at Harvard University, is a leading activist for the payment of reparations for the institution of slavery in the United States and co-chair and counsel for the Reparations Coordinating Committee. The RCC seeks reparations for the "contemporary victims of slavery and the century-long practice of *de jure* racial discrimination which followed slavery." The reparations movement gained recognition and momentum with the 1999 book *The Debt: What America Owes to Blacks*, by Randall Robinson, a graduate of Harvard Law School and founder of Trans-Africa, which promotes human rights in the Caribbean and Africa.

Ogletree points out that the U.S. Congress paid reparations of $20,000 each to the Japanese-Americans who had been interred during World War II. He also notes that the United Nations Conference Against Racism has defined slavery as "a crime against humanity." The call for reparations for the descendants of African slaves in America is based in part on the promise made in 1865 to give all newly freed slaves "forty acres of tillable ground," among other things. But the order was rescinded by President Andrew Johnson a few months later, after the assassination of President Abraham Lincoln, and the government seized the land that had already been allocated to 40,000 blacks in the South. The continuing discrimination against blacks, much of it mandated in the notorious "Jim Crow" laws, provides further justification of reparations.

Ogletree is not seeking payments to the individual descendants of slaves. Rather, he wants the money to go into a trust fund that would assist the poorest members of the black community to escape the grinding poverty that is one legacy of slavery and Jim Crow. His law suits are being filed against the federal government, as well as American institutions and businesses that benefitted from slavery.

Reparations also have also been sought in recent years for destruction of the property and lives of African-Americans after the abolition of slavery. In 1898, a group of white supremacists in Wilmington, North Carolina, killed 60 African-American residents and drove thousands more from the city. A North Carolina commission has urged the state government to pay damages to the descendants of that violence. A race riot in the Greenwood district of Tulsa, Oklahoma, in 1921 killed as many as 300 black residents and burned over a thousand homes, businesses, a library, and a hospital in the once-thriving black community. A lengthy report commissioned by the state legislature demonstrated in 2001 that white mob violence, assisted by the Tulsa police, was to blame. Ogletree filed suit for damages, but the case was thrown out on the grounds that the statute of limitations had expired.

In 1999, Representative John Conyers, Jr. of Michigan introduced, in the U.S. Congress, legislation

> To acknowledge the fundamental injustice, cruelty, brutality, and inhumanity of slavery in the United States and the 13 American colonies between 1619 and 1865 and to establish a commission to examine the institution of slavery, subsequently de jure and de facto racial and economic discrimination against African-Americans, and the impact of these forces on living African-Americans, to make recommendations to the Congress on appropriate remedies, and for other purposes.

Conyers has reintroduced this legislation repeatedly, but it has never been adopted or even brought up for a vote.

Critics of reparations, including such African-Americans as John H. McWhorter, a Senior Fellow at the Manhattan Institute, and Glen C. Loury, Professor of Economics at Boston University, argue that reparations have already been paid, in effect, by the government's affirmative-action programs and numerous social welfare programs, which have disproportionately benefitted persons of African descent. McWhorter complains about what he perceives as the misguided notions "that serious black achievement is impossible except under ideal conditions, that white neglect must be at the root of any black–white disparity, and that only the actions of whites can significantly improve the conditions of blacks."[1]

[1] "The Reparations Racket: America Has Already Made Amends for Slavery," *City Journal* (March 29, 2002) (http://www.city-journal.org/).

QUESTIONS FOR ANALYSIS

1. Given that all persons who were slaves and all persons who were slave-owners when President Lincoln signed the Emancipation Proclamation in 1863 are deceased, who should now have to pay reparations and who should benefit? Is it feasible to accurately identify the descendants of those slaves and slave-owners?

2. Have the government services and affirmative-action programs of the last century adequately compensated the descendants of slaves, as the critics of reparations argue? Does the government have an obligation to do more as long as significant disparities persist in the economic status of African-Americans?

3. Other immigrant groups have suffered from discrimination in this country. Should their descendants be paid reparations, too? Are there significant differences between the descendants of slaves and the descendants of other minority groups?

CASE PRESENTATION

Friendly Sexual Harassment?

In 1976, the federal courts recognized for the first time that sexual harassment in the workplace is a form of discrimination prohibited under the U.S. Civil Rights Act. The rationale was that serious and pervasive harassment makes it impossible for a woman to carry out her job responsibilities and compete fairly in the employment workplace. In the years since, additional court decisions have recognized the problem of sexual harassment of men by women and sexual harassment by men against other men perceived to be homosexual.

In 1999, Amaani Lyle was working as a comedy writers' assistant on the television show "Friends." She was fired after four months and filed suit for discrimination. Lyle complained that three male comedy writers had used sexually coarse and vulgar language and conduct, including a simulation of masturbation, during writing sessions. This, she argued, constituted sexual harassment in the workplace, making it impossible for her to carry out her job responsibilities of typing and transcribing jokes for the scripts for the show.

Warner Brothers Television argued that Lyle had been warned about the working conditions beforehand but accepted the job anyway. *Amicus curiáe* (friend of the court) briefs were filed by several organizations supporting the writers on the grounds of creative freedom and freedom of speech.

The case was decided in favor of Warner Brothers by the Supreme Court of California in April 2006. The Court noted that the vulgar language was not directed specifically at Lyle, or at any other women in the workplace, and thus did not constitute illegal harassment. Nor, the Court said, were the comments "severe enough or sufficiently pervasive to create a work environment that was hostile or abusive to" Lyle.

Supporters of the writers hailed this as a victory for free speech and creative freedom. Critics expressed concern that employers now would simply warn new employees that vulgar language might be used in the workplace and thus escape future harassment charges.

QUESTIONS FOR ANALYSIS

1. The U.S. Supreme Court has recognized that a "hostile work environment" can constitute discriminatory sexual harassment, even if there is no specific *quid pro quo* demanding sexual favors in exchange for a job or promotion. In the 1993 decision *Harris v. Forklift*, the Court found that pervasive and severe sexual innuendos and insults directed at Teresa Harris detracted from her job performance, discouraged her from remaining on the job, and kept her from advancing in her career. How should we draw the line between a discriminatory hostile work environment and one in which workers are simply exercising their right of free speech and should not be liable for harassment?
2. Should television writers for a popular show filled with sexual innuendo be held to different standards for workplace conduct than workers in

other professions? How should we balance freedom of expression with a right to freedom from harassment?

3. The Supreme Court does not require proof of psychological damage or emotional distress to demonstrate a hostile work environment, although such evidence is very relevant if it exists. Should this proof be required to help draw a workable line between innocent office joking and kidding and illegal sexual harassment?

Animal Rights and Environmental Ethics

- **What Do We Owe Nonhuman Animals?**
- **What's Wrong with Speciesism?**
- **Environmental Ethics**
- **Environmental Problems**
- **The Moral Issue**
- **Why Environmental Ethics?**
- **Arguments for Ethical Treatment of Animals and the Environment**
- **Arguments Against Ethical Treatment of Animals and the Environment**

PETER SINGER **All Animals Are Equal . . . or Why Supporters of Liberation for Blacks and Women Should Support Animal Liberation Too**

TOM REGAN **The Case for Animal Rights**

PAUL W. TAYLOR **The Ethics of Respect for Nature**

WILLIAM F. BAXTER **People or Penguins**

CASE PRESENTATIONS: ***Animal Liberators*** • ***Religious Sacrifice*** • ***A Metaphor for the Energy Debate*** • ***The Spotted Owl***

MOST OF THE ISSUES we consider in this volume involve the ethical obligations and rights of persons, but important ethical issues also arise with regard to our relationships with nonhuman animals and the entire environment itself. Whether or not it makes sense to attribute ethical rights to entities that are not persons is one issue we take up in this unit. We are used to thinking about ethics in terms of relationships among persons. We have obligations to other persons, and they have the right to expect us to treat them in certain ways. Do we have an obligation to provide a right-to-die to seriously ill patients? Do we have a right to pursue our sexual private lives in ways we choose? Does capital punishment meet our obligation to treat people convicted of serious crimes in ways that are not cruel and unusual? Do we have a right to our civil liberties, even in a time of war? These important questions all involve ethical relationships among persons.

But does it make sense to think about ethical relationships with things that are not persons and that have no ethical obligation to us in any meaningful sense? Do we have ethical obligations to lower animals, plants, trees, rocks, air, and water? Does it make sense to say those things have ethical obligations to us or even ethical rights to claim against us? Do any supposed ethical obligations of this nature really amount to obligations to other persons and concern about the impact our treatment of animals and the environment has on other persons?

In the late 1960s, the nation was preoccupied with enormous disagreements over the Vietnam war, the draft, and the burgeoning civil rights movement. By the early 1970s, attention became focused on both environmental issues and animal rights, to which we turn here.

WHAT DO WE OWE NONHUMAN ANIMALS?

In 1975, Australian philosopher Peter Singer published his landmark book, *Animal Liberation*. The title of the first chapter, like the title of the book itself, clearly announced the author's basic moral message: "All Animals Are Equal." Succeeding chapters documented another message: All animals are not treated equally. Singer's point is simple. Nonhuman animals, like human animals, can experience both pleasure and pain. And that is a morally important fact. If it is wrong to cause human suffering to achieve a good that does not outweigh that suffering, Singer argues, it is wrong to cause nonhuman suffering to achieve such a good. Given the variety of nutritious and tasty vegetarian recipes available, the suffering caused by factory farms is not justified by the human desire for meat. Given the availability of canvas shoes and leather substitutes for belts and such, human demand for leather is not worth the suffering it brings to nonhuman animals.

Historically, the weight of Western opinion has not been on Singer's side. Both our religious and philosophical traditions have been inhospitable to the notion that we have moral obligations to other animals. Let's take a brief look at both.

The Judeo-Christian Tradition

Beginning with the creation story of Genesis, Judeo-Christian thought has told us that other animals were put here for our purposes. According to that story, we are to "fill the earth and subdue it; and have dominion over the fish of the sea and over the birds of the air and over every living thing that moves upon the earth." And later in Genesis, after the flood, we are told, "Every moving thing that lives shall be food for you; and as I gave you the green plants, I give you everything."

Of course, not all Jewish and Christian thought has viewed animals as merely there for our use. St. Francis of Assisi, for example, who once preached to sparrows, is as well known for his love of animals as for founding the Franciscan order. Still, these biblical injunctions have been supported by centuries of Christian theology. Humans are created in the image of God; other animals are not. Humans have immortal souls; other animals do not. Humans belong to both the spiritual and the material worlds; other animals belong only to the material. Given these differences, plus the influence of Christian thought on Western culture, no one should be surprised by our treatment of nonhuman animals.

The Philosophical Tradition

Secular philosophers have, in the main, given nonhuman animals no greater consideration. Writing at a time when such scientists as Galileo were ushering in the era of modern science, the great French philosopher René Descartes (1596–1650) argued that nonhuman animals are no better than biological robots, incapable of feeling any sensations, even pain. The nonphysical mind is the seat of sensation, he argued, and only creatures capable of reason have nonphysical minds. Since nonhuman animals cannot reason, they are simply physical creatures. Therefore, they cannot feel pain.

Immanuel Kant had other reasons for excluding nonhuman animals from moral consideration. As we saw in Part 1, Kant put respect for *persons* at the center of morality; we are not to treat other *persons* merely as a means to our own ends. Although Kant did not deny that animals can suffer, he did deny that they are persons. To be a person, he said, is to be an autonomous being, one that has the capacity to act for reasons and to reason about its reasons. And that capacity does not belong to nonhuman animals. They are, then, beyond the pale of morality. (Kant did recommend that we be nice to animals, though—not out of moral obligation, of course, but for another reason. If we treat animals cruelly, he felt, we run the risk of developing insensitive characters.)

Another strain in moral philosophy—**social contract theory**—is equally exclusive of nonhuman animals. According to this view, morality is the product of an informal agreement among the members of society. Each of us agrees to follow certain rules on the condition that others do the same. The purpose of the agreement is to ensure that all of us act in dependable ways, providing the mutual trust necessary for social cooperation. An important aspect of social contract theory is that this informal agreement is the source of all moral obligation. We have moral obligations to others who have entered into the agreement with us. We have no such obligations to those who are not part of the agreement. Nonhuman animals, who are incapable of entering into contracts, are not part of the agreement. Therefore, we have no moral obligations to them.

In traditional Western views, then, we owe nonhuman animals nothing. We have no moral obligations to them. We may have moral obligations *concerning* them, but those obligations are *to* other people. We ought not, for example, poison somebody else's pet for the same reason that we ought not destroy somebody else's sofa. The pet and the sofa are another person's property, and our obligations to that person forbid us to destroy his or her property. The pet itself is due no more moral consideration than the sofa—none.

Utility vs. Rights

The basis of Singer's moral appeal is the principle of utility: Since we morally ought to maximize happiness and minimize suffering, and since nonhuman animals are just as capable of happiness and suffering as human animals, our calculations ought to include them as well. Against our own pleasure in eating veal, we ought to balance the suffering of veal calves. Against the benefits of research on animals, we ought to balance the suffering of laboratory animals. Their pain should matter just as much as ours.

Other animal advocates make a different moral appeal. As they see it, the principle of utility does not guarantee fit treatment of nonhuman animals. Suppose, for example, that the elimination of factory farms would create such havoc in our economy that utility is maximized by keeping them. Would that justify keeping them? If our answer is yes, we should ask ourselves an analogous question: Suppose we could maximize utility by reintroducing slavery. Would that justify doing so? Presumably, our answer to that question is no. Humans have certain rights that we morally cannot violate, regardless of utility. If we do not feel the same about at least some animals, aren't we guilty of speciesism?

Thus, philosophers like Tom Regan focus their attention on animal rights. He argues that just as respect for persons requires that we not treat other humans in certain ways, regardless of utility, so should respect for at least some nonhuman animals require that we not treat them in certain ways, regardless of utility.

Which animals? At the very least, those that, like us, are experiencing subjects of their own lives. By that phrase, Regan means the following: conscious creatures that are aware of their environment, that have desires, feelings, emotions, memories, beliefs, preferences, goals, and a sense of their own identity and future. Although we cannot be sure precisely where we can draw the line between animals that meet these criteria and animals that do not, we can be sure of one thing, he says. Adult mammals do. And because they do, their lives, like ours, have inherent value—value independent of any use they may be to us. In that case, we ought not use them merely as a means to our own ends.

WHAT'S WRONG WITH SPECIESISM?

Most of us are, undeniably, speciesists. But what, you may be wondering, is wrong with that? Most of us agree that pointless cruelty to animals should not be tolerated, but that is a far cry from agreeing that animals are our moral equals. Why should they be? Shouldn't human beings matter more than other animals?

The Conventional View Defended

Certainly, speciesism doesn't *seem* to be as bad as racism or sexism. To deny full moral equality to other people on the basis of skin color is totally arbitrary, since skin color is of no moral importance whatever. But for species? Can we really say that the differences between rabbits and humans are as trivial, morally speaking, as the differences between blacks and whites, women and men? The common-sense answer to these questions is, of course, no. The conventional view is that morality is our own—humankind's—institution, developed and maintained and improved for our own purposes, for our own individual and social good. To the extent that the good of other animals contributes to our own good, it should be of concern to us. Because our pets play unique and rewarding roles in our lives, we should treat them as more than mere things. Because sympathy, compassion, and kindness contribute in crucial ways to the human good, we should not accept needless cruelty to nonhuman animals. But we have no obligation to promote the good of nonhuman animals at humankind's own expense. To do that would be to undercut the whole purpose of morality.

The Conventional View Criticized

However reasonable the conventional view may seem, animal rights advocates attack it on two fronts. First, they claim, we do not apply the conventional view consistently. Humans who are not fully persons are protected by our morality; humans who cannot fully participate in our moral community are granted moral rights. We do not test new cosmetics on people who are severely retarded. We do not run cruel psychological experiments on infants. We do not conduct medical experiments on irreversibly comatose humans. Why not? Because they are human. Why do we test cosmetics on rabbits, experiment on dogs, raise veal calves for food? Because they are not human. And that, animal rights activists say, *is* discrimination purely on the basis of species.

Second, even if the conventional view were applied consistently, they claim, it would still be inadequate. Granted, difference of species is not the only difference between normal adult humans and farm animals, but the differences stressed by the conventional view are not morally crucial ones. What is so morally important about the fact that steers cannot enter into our social contract? Why should it matter so much that pigs can't have all the aspirations that humans have or that sheep can't develop the same virtues and talents? What the conventional view boils down to, they say, is this: Only moral *agents* can have rights.

What are moral agents? Creatures that have two closely related abilities. The first is the ability to take on moral duties toward others, to understand that they have obligations toward others that they ought to fulfill. The second is the ability to make moral claims against others, to understand that they have moral rights that others can violate. But why, critics of the conventional view ask, should those abilities be crucial?

The Conventional View Reconsidered

The foregoing criticisms show that the acceptability of our treatment of other animals turns on two points. The first is consistency. Do we apply the conventional view consistently? And if not, can we justify our inconsistency? The second strikes at the heart of the conventional view. Does it draw a morally defensible line between human and nonhuman animals? And if so, is there an even better place to draw the line between creatures with rights (or as Singer would put it, creatures whose interests matter as much as our own) and creatures without rights (or creatures whose interests do not matter as much as our own)?

Regarding the first point, defenders of current treatment of other animals can say this: If we do apply the conventional view inconsistently, we do so in a *principled* way. Moral agents—persons—stand at the center of our morality. They are the primary holders of moral rights. We grant rights to human infants because they will *become* moral agents and so deserve our respect. We grant rights to humans in comas because they *were* moral agents and so also deserve our respect. We grant rights to people who are severely retarded because they are so much like some other holders of rights that it seems almost incoherent not to.

As for second point, defenders of current practices can do little more than repeat the reasons for drawing the line where we now do and then throw the question back to their critics: Why is Singer's dividing line or Regan's any better than the one we now draw? The fact that nonhuman animals can suffer should certainly have some moral weight, but why should it lead us to put them on an equal footing with full members of our moral community? The fact that some of them are experiencing subjects of their own lives should also have some moral weight, but why should it have as much weight as other facts about ourselves?

Whether these answers are acceptable depends on two further questions. First, are at least some nonhuman animals so much like some humans that it seems almost incoherent to deny them rights? Second, assuming that morality did arise to advance the human good, should we now say that the time has come to recognize that other goods are of equal value? Critics of our treatment of other animals answer yes to both questions. Defenders answer no.

ENVIRONMENTAL ETHICS

The first Earth Day was celebrated on April 22, 1970, often considered the beginning of the modern environmental movement. Millions of Americans across the country gathered to listen to speeches and demonstrate their concern for the future of the planet. Two years later, during the presidency of Richard M. Nixon, the Federal government established the U.S. Environmental Protection Agency, underscoring the commitment of the nation to protecting the natural resources of air, water, and land from pollution.

ENVIRONMENTAL PROBLEMS

Despite expressions of concern for the environment, environmental problems continue to abound and, in many cases, worsen. Species are dying out on a daily basis; air quality is worsening in many cities; the earth's protective ozone layer is thinning; we are creating increasing amounts of trash with no place to put it; and, many scientists argue, emissions of carbon dioxide and methane gases are turning the earth's atmosphere into a greenhouse.

Ozone Depletion

Extending from approximately seven to thirty miles above the earth, the layer of the earth's atmosphere known as the stratosphere is an area of little temperature change above the earth's rain clouds. An important component of the stratosphere is ozone, which acts as a shield against the sun's ultraviolet rays. Without this shield, or even with a thinner shield, we would see a significant increase in skin cancer and diseases of the immune system. We would also see considerable damage to food crops and phytoplankton—marine plants that are a vital link in our ocean's food chain.

Although CFCs were banned in 1947 under an international agreement called the Montreal Protocol, they are very long-lived in the environment. NASA predicts that it will take fifty years for the Antarctica ozone hole to disappear.

Development of CFC alternatives has been very expensive, but the consequences to human health have been recognized as more important than these economic costs of product development, an example of consequentialist ethical reasoning.

Global Warming

Throughout the earth's history, average temperatures have changed as the atmosphere has changed, growing warmer with an increase in greenhouse gases—most notably carbon dioxide—and cooler with a decrease. The modern industrial world, chiefly through increased use of fossil fuels and through deforestation, has seen a sharp increase of greenhouse gases. Using computer models, scientists have predicted an increase in the earth's temperatures of from three to nine degrees by the middle of the twenty-first century. An increase that large would lead to severe inland droughts, resultant food shortages, coastal flooding, mass extinctions of species, and increased pollution in overheated cities.

Although most scientists agree on the dangers of global warming, the solutions are the subject of much debate. The Kyoto Protocol, an international proposal for emission reductions, was rejected by the U.S. Senate in 1997. The treaty imposed restrictions the Senate thought were unfairly burdensome on the most industrialized nations, including the United States, while allowing less well-developed nations to continue dangerous emissions. President George W. Bush has repeatedly rejected the Kyoto Protocol and insists that developing nations must also agree to emissions reductions.

Much of the current debate centers on consequentialist arguments, such as the economic cost to industry and the possible loss of jobs resulting from the proposed measures to reduce global warming.

Acid Rain

Most scientists believe that acid rain is caused primarily by pollutants from the burning of fossil fuels—carbon dioxide, sulfur dioxide, and nitrogen oxides. These pollutants, which can be carried thousands of miles by the wind, mix with other chemicals in the atmosphere to form corrosive and poisonous compounds that are washed back to earth by rainfall.

The effects of acid rain are believed to be wide ranging. They include damage to rives and lakes, ground water, soil, forests, and buildings. But because there have been relatively few studies on the subject, the extent of damage due to acid rain is difficult to gauge.

Trash

The problem of what to do with the trash of a society that throws away 16 billion disposable diapers and 2 billion disposable razors annually, yet recycles only 10 percent of its trash, is a serious one. The most common solution to the trash problem is sanitary landfills, where 80 percent of the country's solid waste ends up. But this solution is far from ideal. First, since much of our trash is non biodegradable plastic, we are quickly running out of space. Second, landfills pose risks to surface and ground water. For combustible waste, the chief alternative is incineration, which has its own problems. The ash must be treated and then disposed of, and the gases released during incineration contribute to air pollution.

Extinction of Species

Though the problems of species extinction is most acute in the Amazon, development of land by humans throughout the world is causing the loss of species at a rate estimated to be as high as one a day.

The threat of extinction is most highly publicized in cases like the tiger, blue whale, giant panda, and other animal species that humans have a particularly high regard for. But the loss of many other species—plant species as well as animal species, many of which are still unidentified—should also concern us. Species in tropical rain forests, for instance, are valuable in the development of cancer drugs and antibiotics. They also give us valuable genetic information that contributes to the raising of domestic animals and the growing of food crops.

THE MORAL ISSUE

A loss of the ozone layer and significant global warming would be disastrous for human beings. And it is because of our shared sense of impending disaster that most people now claim to be environmentalists.

In other cases of environmental damage, however, the issue is not serious danger to human life but diminishing quality of human life. We view nature as a valuable resource for recreation as well as economic development.

All such concerns are **anthropocentric** at heart; that is, they center on human well-being. We should care about the environment because it is *our* environment. We should care about the survival of various plant and animal species because they matter to *us*.

But other things matter to us as well. We want a strong economy that will produce the goods, jobs, and tax revenues we desire. We like our cars and the highways we drive them on. We like air-conditioning. We like to hold down the costs of producing consumer goods in order to hold down prices.

So when acting both as individuals and as a society, we weigh our concern for the environment against these other concerns. The result is often a compromise, such as auto emission controls that are not as strong as they otherwise might be. Because of these compromises, the most committed environmentalists have begun arguing for radical changes in our moral and legal reasoning, changes that give nature a special place in our thinking. Two proposed changes have received the most attention. Both have one thing in common. They are nonanthropocentric.

The Land Ethic

In his much discussed book, *A Sand County Almanac,* environmentalist Aldo Leopold proposed what he called the land ethic. According to Leopold's land ethic, humans are to begin thinking of themselves as part of a wider community, the biotic community, which includes not only all living things but also all members of the ecological system, including water, soil, and air. To think of ourselves in that way is to reject the view that we are masters of nature and that nature is there to be exploited by us. It is to think of ourselves as members of a team, living and working harmoniously with our teammates. It is also to recognize that the crucial moral question is not what benefits individual human beings or the human community as a whole, but what benefits the biotic community as a whole.

According to Leopold, "A thing is right when it tends to preserve the integrity, stability, and beauty of the biotic community. It is wrong when it tends otherwise."

Two things are notable about this point of view. First, of course, it is nonanthropocentric. But equally important, it is not individualistic. What is to be considered as morally fundamental is not the good of individual members of the biotic community but the good of the community itself. Thus, the land ethic is often considered to be a **holistic ethic;** that is, we have duties not just to individuals but to the whole—in this case, the biotic community.

Environmental Individualism

Others forms of environmental ethics tend to be **biocentric** but nonholistic. They stress duties to individual members of the biotic community but not to the community itself. According to this view, the good of individual plants, animals, and streams—not just the good of individual humans—must be taken into account in moral and legal reasoning.

In the moral realm, this involves balancing the interests of nonhuman members of the environment against human interests Chopping down a tree, for instance, would become a morally significant act independent of damage to its owner.

In the legal realm, it involves giving trees, lakes, and animals standing in the courts. To give them standing would be to make them interested parties in lawsuits and allow lawyers to bring suit on their behalf, not just on behalf of humans who are affected by their treatment. As matters now stand, the interests of nature are irrelevant in legal matters, unless human interests are also affected.

Holism and Individualism Compared

Although both views promote the interests of plants, animals, water, air, and soil as independent goods, their practical payoffs may be far different. To see how, we can consider the problem of endangered species.

According to the holistic point of view, a threat to an entire species is more significant than the sum total of the threats to be individual members of the species because what is morally most important is the species' contribution to the biotic community. Because species diversity contributes to ecological stability, the loss of a member of an endangered species counts more than the loss of a member of a nonendangered one. According to the nonholistic point of view, on the other hand, a threat to a species is not in itself more significant than the sum total of the threats to individual members. All other things being equal, the loss of a member of a nonendangered species is morally equivalent to the loss of a member of an endangered one.

Holists and individualists may differ on other points as well. The holistic view contains no grounds to reject hunting, for instance, unless it damages the environment. There is nothing *inherently* immoral about hunting, and when hunting contributes to the well-being of the biotic community, it is morally good. The individualistic view, however, naturally leans toward an anti-hunting position. The life of an individual deer is not to be sacrificed for the sake of the whole.

WHY ENVIRONMENTAL ETHICS?

Why, then, do environmentalists call for a radical change in our ethical thinking? The impetus toward environmental ethics has two sources. The first, as we saw, is the belief that anthropocentric ethics and law are inadequate to deal with the vast array of environmental problems that face us. The second is the belief that nature, wilderness areas, and nonhuman life have their own inherent value and therefore deserve moral consideration.

Anthropocentric Ethics

Proponents of this view deny that we need a land ethic or legal standing for trees. What we need instead, they say, are better cost-benefit analyses of decisions that affect the environment. We need to make sure that these analyses take adequate account of the harm to human interests that environmental damage can cause. In considering what limit to place on auto emissions, for example, we should take into account not only the added costs to automakers and consumers but also the costs in human disease and death from pollutants and greenhouse gases.

Critics of this approach argue that cost-benefit analyses in such cases are inadequate. The basic problem, they claim, is that cost-benefit analyses calculate only *economic* costs and benefits. But certain goods cannot be given an economic value

How much is a human life worth, for instance? How much is a beautiful view worth? How much is it worth to be able to swim or fish in a river?

Furthermore, even if we could assign economic value to such goods, is it possible to identify all the relevant costs and benefits? And even if we could identify them, why should economic costs and benefits be the only deciding factors?

Respect for Nature

A key point of environmental ethics is that nature itself or individual natural objects have their own interests and goods, which are omitted from cost-benefit analyses. We should value nature not because of its value to us but because of its inherent value.

According to this view, even if we minimize human costs and maximize human benefits, we do not act morally if we significantly harm nature. To some extent, arguments over this point can parallel animal rights disputes.

Various arguments for or against animal rights can be used as arguments for or against rights or standing for streams, species, trees, and so forth. But for many environmentalists, the issue is different. We don't have to grant nature *rights* to ensure adequate moral treatment. We only have to treat it in accordance with an attitude of proper *respect.*

ARGUMENTS FOR ETHICAL TREATMENT OF ANIMALS AND THE ENVIRONMENT

1. ***Human beings hold no special place in nature.***

   POINT: "What's so special about humans, anyway? From Mother Nature's point of view, *all* animals are equal. We all evolved from the same beginnings, we're all made of the same stuff, and we all belong to the same biosphere. The world wasn't made for any one species. It's here for all of us. And it's nothing but pure arrogance for humans to think that *we're* the pinnacle of creation, that we have the right to treat the rest of the animal kingdom any way we want. It's time we recognize that we're part of nature, not lords over it, and we ought to act accordingly."

   COUNTERPOINT: "Of course, we're part of nature. But what does that prove? Tigers, eagles, and other predators are also part of nature. What can be more natural than eating other animals? Besides, why stop at animals? Plants are part of nature too. So are rocks, rivers, and dirt. From Mother Nature's point of view, they must matter just as much as animals. Should we treat them equally too? Finally, why should we even care about Mother Nature's point of view (whatever *that* might be)? We have our own point of view—the human point of view—and if that point of view is no better than any other, it's no worse either. It's ours, and we're entitled to live our lives according to it."

2. ***Human good is not the only good.***

   POINT: "You make it sound as though human good is the only good that counts for anything. But what about the good of a species, a forest, a river, or a lake? Or even a single redwood tree? What right do we have to cut down something that's been alive for thousands of years just to make a picnic table? After all, human interests aren't the only interests. Why must our interests always come first?"

COUNTERPOINT: "To hear you tell it, someone might think a redwood tree actually cares what happens to it. But a tree has no interest in its own survival. It can't have an interest in anything. Don't get me wrong. I'm not saying we should destroy entire redwood forests just to make picnic tables. No one's saying that. I'm just as impressed by the beauty of a redwood forest as you are, and I'm just as concerned about saving that beauty for my children and grandchildren. But it's preposterous to say that our concerns don't matter more than a tree's."

3. ***The biotic community is like a human community.***

POINT: "The first principle of any community is cooperation. We have to cooperate with our family members, we have to cooperate with our fellow workers, and we have to cooperate with our fellow citizens. Not only do we have to cooperate with one another, but we also have to treat one another with respect. The same holds for the biotic community as well. Ecology has taught us that each part of an ecosystem is a member of a community, with all members working together to maintain the good of the whole. It's time that humans recognized that we're also part of the biotic community. It's time for us to work together with our fellow members and show them the respect they deserve."

COUNTERPOINT: "This notion of a biotic community is nothing but a metaphor at best. Do predators cooperate with their prey? Do members of different species resolve their differences the way people of varying interests do? Are insects and the soil members of the same team the way a pitcher and catcher are? What we've learned from ecology is certainly important, and we ignore its lessons at our own risk. But we gain nothing by sentimentalizing nature to the extent that we work against our own interests."

4. ***Nature isn't here just for human purposes.***

POINT: "When too many humans look at nature, all they see is something to be exploited. They look at forests and they see timber. They look at rivers and oceans and they see places to dump their waste. As far as they're concerned, nature is there for us, period. What they can use they take, and what they can't use they're willing to sacrifice because it's of no importance to them. But nature was here long before we were, with its own majesty and its own integrity. We're just a part of it, not its master, and we have no right to upset that integrity. To think of ourselves as nature's master is nothing but hubris."

COUNTERPOINT: "Of course we're part of nature. And like everything else in nature, we use what's useful to us. The problem isn't our tendency to look on nature as something that's there to be used by us—nothing could be more natural than that—but our tendency to use it unwisely. As long as we keep our own long-term interests clearly in mind, as long as we remember that we need trees for oxygen as well as timber, for instance, and that species of no direct use to us now can be important to us in ways we don't recognize yet, we and nature will be fine."

ARGUMENTS AGAINST ETHICAL TREATMENT OF ANIMALS AND THE ENVIRONMENT

1. ***Giving animals rights would lead to absurd interference with nature.***

POINT: "Humans aren't the only animals that eat other animals, you know. What about wolves, eagles, tigers, and other predators? If we grant rights to their prey, then we'll have to protect animals from each other, not least from ourselves. After all, if we don't have the right to violate another animal's rights, neither does a wolf. But if we do protect the prey, what happens to the predator? What, for that matter, happens to all of nature? If you follow your position to its logical conclusion, the results are absurd."

COUNTERPOINT: "The kind of interference that worries you is *not* a logical consequence of my position. What you're forgetting is that tigers and wolves aren't moral *agents*. They don't have any obligations to other animals, so there's nothing immoral about their preying on other animals. Humans are moral agents, though, so there is something immoral about our preying on other animals."

2. ***Putting our own species first is the natural thing to do.***

POINT: "It's only natural that we care more about other humans than we care about nonhumans. After all, being members of the same species is an important relationship, like being members of the same family. We care more about our parents than we do about strangers, so why shouldn't we care more about our fellow humans than we do about sheep? And just take a look at the rest of the animal kingdom. A lot of animals cooperate with members of their own species but not with other animals, and in some cases, animals will even lay down their lives for other members of their species. As the old saying goes, birds of a feather flock together. Why should humans be any different?"

COUNTERPOINT: "Humans are different. We can rise above our natural inclinations. That's what civilization and culture are all about. It's why we have laws and morality. And since you're so fond of old sayings, it's why a tiger can't change its stripes but a human can. We know the difference between right and wrong, and the point of teaching that difference is to get people to put a check on some of their natural inclinations. Selfishness is just as natural as altruism, you know—maybe even more natural—but I don't hear you saying that we shouldn't try to curb our selfishness. So even if speciesism is natural, if it's wrong we should stamp it out."

3. ***People count more than trees.***

POINT: "What environmental ethicists fail to see is that the environment matters because it's *our* environment—our water, our air, our forests. No one denies that we have to protect the environment to protect ourselves and advance our own interests. But you want to go further than that. You want to protect the environment *against* our own interests. You want to sacrifice logging jobs, wreck entire economies, to protect owls. You want to deny us badly needed power plants to protect fish.

And that's just crazy. Any way you look at it, people matter more than trees, owls, and fish."

COUNTERPOINT: "As of matter of fact, people don't matter more than trees, owls, and fish any way you look at it. To nature, all species are equal. That doesn't mean human interests *never* come first, of course, but it does mean they don't *always* come first. Job losses are unfortunate, but economies and individuals rebound. And as for your badly needed power plants, Americans rely too much on electricity as it is. Giving up some of our electric appliances is a small enough sacrifice, not only to protect an entire species but also to protect the environment as a whole."

4. ***Environmental ethics is elitist.***

POINT: "The 'small' sacrifices you call for aren't all that small to most people. When a mining, manufacturing, or logging region dies, the human costs are enormous, whether the region eventually bounces back or not. And many of them don't. Even added costs to consumer goods can be a major burden for many people. The problem with environmental ethics is that it's elitist. The well-off can easily afford the costs of putting nature on an equal footing with humans, but the rest of us can't."

COUNTERPOINT: "Nature is everyone's home, and there's nothing elitist about trying to save our home. I realize that the costs of environmentalism fall heavier on some people than others, but the answer isn't to reject environmental ethics. The answer is to adopt social policies that will compensate them for their loss—retraining, public investment, tax breaks, and other measures to help them out. If we all share the burden, it can be a small one for each of us."

All Animals Are Equal . . . or Why Supporters of Liberation for Blacks and Women Should Support Animal Liberation Too

PETER SINGER

In this selection from the first chapter of *Animal Liberation,* Peter Singer, now a professor of philosophy at Princeton Unversity, compares speciesism to sexism and racism, and he argues that the same considerations that make sexism and racism morally unjustifiable make speciesism morally unjustifiable. He bases his argument on the *principle of equal consideration,* according to which the pain that nonhuman animals feel is of equal moral importance to the pain that humans feel.

From Peter Singer, *Animal Liberation* (New York: New York Review, 1975), pp. 1–23. Reprinted with permission of the author.

While supporting the principle of equal consideration, Singer stresses that it does not always require equal treatment of all animals, since the same treatment can cause unequal amounts of suffering to different animals. He also points out that the principle does not require us to say that all lives are equal. Often, a human life is morally more important than the life of a nonhuman animal. Sometimes, though, it is not. When forced to choose between a human and nonhuman animal's life, we should base our decision on the mental capacities of the individuals involved, not on species.

"Animal Liberation" may sound more like a parody of other liberation movements than a serious objective. The idea of "The Rights of Animals" actually was once used to parody the case for women's rights. When Mary Wollstonecraft, a forerunner of today's feminists, published her *Vindication of the Rights of Women* in 1792, her views were widely regarded as absurd, and before long an anonymous publication appeared entitled *A Vindication of the Rights of Brutes.* The author of this satirical work (now known to have been Thomas Taylor, a distinguished Cambridge philosopher) tried to refute Mary Wollstonecraft's arguments by showing that they could be carried one stage further. If the argument for equality was sound when applied to women, why should it not be applied to dogs, cats, and horses? The reasoning seemed to hold for these "brutes" too; yet to hold that brutes had rights was manifestly absurd; therefore the reasoning by which this conclusion had been reached must be unsound, and if unsound when applied to brutes, it must also be unsound when applied to women, since the very same arguments had been used in each case.

In order to explain the basis of the case for the equality of animals, it will be helpful to start with an examination of the case for the equality of women. Let us assume that we wish to defend the case for women's rights against the attack by Thomas Taylor. How should we reply?

One way in which we might reply is by saying that the case for equality between men and women cannot validly be extended to nonhuman animals. Women have a right to vote, for instance, because they are just as capable of making rational decisions about the future as men are; dogs, on the other hand, are incapable of understanding the significance of voting, so they cannot have the right to vote. There are many other obvious ways in which men and women resemble each other closely, while humans and animals differ greatly. So, it might be said, men and women are similar beings and should have similar rights, while humans and nonhumans are different and should not have equal rights.

The reasoning behind this reply to Taylor's analogy is correct up to a point, but it does not go far enough. There *are* important differences between humans and other animals, and these differences must give rise to *some* differences in the rights that each have. Recognizing this obvious fact, however, is no barrier to the case for extending the basic principle of equality to nonhuman animals. The differences that exist between men and women are equally undeniable, and the supporters of Women's Liberation are aware that these differences may give rise to different rights. Many feminists hold that women have the right to an abortion on request. It does not follow that since these same feminists are campaigning for equality between men and women they must support the right of men to have abortions too. Since a man cannot have an abortion, it is meaningless to talk of his right to have one. Since a dog can't vote, it is meaningless to talk of its right to vote. There is no reason why either Women's Liberation or Animal Liberation should get involved in such nonsense. The extension of the basic principle of equality from one group to another does not imply that we must treat both groups in exactly the same way, or grant exactly the same rights to both groups. Whether we should do so will depend on the nature of the members of the two groups. The basic principle of equality does not require equal or identical *treatment;* it requires equal *consideration.* Equal consideration for different beings may lead to different treatment and different rights.

So there is a different way of replying to Taylor's attempt to parody the case for women's rights, a way that does not deny the obvious differences between humans and nonhumans but goes more deeply into the question of equality and concludes by finding nothing absurd in the idea that the basic principle of equality applies to so-called "brutes." At this point such a conclusion may appear odd; but if we examine more deeply the basis on which our opposition to discrimination on grounds of race or sex ultimately rests, we will see that we would be on shaky ground if we were to demand equality for blacks, women, and other groups of oppressed humans while denying equal consideration to nonhumans. To make this clear we need to see, first, exactly why racism and sexism are wrong.

When we say that all human beings, whatever their race, creed, or sex, are equal, what is it that we are asserting? Those who wish to defend hierarchical, inegalitarian societies have often pointed out that by whatever test we choose it simply is not true that all humans are equal. Like it or not we must face the fact that humans come in different shapes and sizes; they come with different moral capacities, different intellectual abilities, different amounts of benevolent feeling and sensitivity to the needs of others, different abilities to communicate effectively, and different capacities to experience pleasure and pain. In short, if the demand for equality were based on the actual equality of all human beings, we would have to stop demanding equality.

Still, one might cling to the view that the demand for equality among human beings is based on the actual equality of the different races and sexes. Although, it may be said, humans differ as individuals there are no differences between the races and sexes *as such*. From the mere fact that a person is black or a woman we cannot infer anything about that person's intellectual or moral capacities. This, it may be said, is why racism and sexism are wrong. The white racist claims that whites are superior to blacks, but this is false—although there are differences among individuals, some blacks are superior to some whites in all of the capacities and abilities that could conceivably be relevant. The opponent of sexism would say the same: a person's sex is no guide to his or her abilities, and this is why it is unjustifiable to discriminate on the basis of sex.

The existence of individual variations that cut across the lines of race or sex, however, provides us with no defense at all against a more sophisticated opponent of equality, one who proposes that, say, the interests of all those with IQ scores below 100 be given less consideration than the interests of those with ratings over 100. Perhaps those scoring below the mark would, in this society, be made the slaves of those scoring higher. Would a hierarchical society of this sort really be so much better than one based on race or sex? I think not. But if we tie the moral principle of equality to the factual equality of the different races or sexes, taken as a whole, our opposition to racism and sexism does not provide us with any basis for objecting to this kind of inegalitarianism.

There is a second important reason why we ought not to base our opposition to racism and sexism on any kind of actual equality, even the limited kind that asserts that variations in capacities and abilities are spread evenly between the different races and sexes: we can have no absolute guarantee that these capacities and abilities really are distributed evenly, without regard to race or sex, among human beings. So far as actual abilities are concerned there do seem to be certain measurable differences between both races and sexes. These differences do not, of course, appear in each case, but only when averages are taken. More important still, we do not yet know how much of these differences is really due to the different genetic endowments of the different races and sexes, and how much is due to poor schools, poor housing, and other factors that are the result of past and continuing discrimination. Perhaps all of the important differences will eventually prove to be environmental rather than genetic. Anyone opposed to racism and sexism will certainly hope that this will be so, for it will make the task of ending discrimination a lot easier; nevertheless it would be dangerous to rest the case against racism and sexism on the belief that all significant differences are environmental in origin. The opponent of, say, racism who takes this line will be unable to avoid conceding that *if* differences in ability do after all prove to have some genetic connection with race, racism would in some way be defensible.

Fortunately there is no need to pin the case for equality to one particular outcome of a scientific investigation. The appropriate response to those who claim to have found evidence of genetically based differences in ability between the races or sexes is not to stick to the belief that the genetic explanation must be wrong, whatever evidence to the contrary may turn up: instead we should make it quite clear that the claim to equality does not depend on intelligence, moral capacity, physical strength, or similar matters of fact. Equality is a moral idea, not an assertion of fact. There is no logically compelling reason for assuming that a factual difference in ability between two people justifies any difference in the amount of consideration we give to their needs and interests. *The principle of the equality of human beings is not a description of an alleged actual equality among humans: it is a prescription of how we should treat humans.*

Jeremy Bentham, the founder of the reforming utilitarian school of moral philosophy, incorporated the essential basis of moral equality into his system of ethics by means of the formula: "Each to count for one and none for more than one." In other words, the interests of every being affected by an action are to be taken into account and given the same weight as the like interests of any other being. A later utilitarian, Henry Sidgwick, put the point in this way: "The good of any one individual is of no more importance, from the point of view (if I may say so) of the Universe, than the good of any other." More recently the leading figures in contemporary moral philosophy have shown a great deal of agreement in specifying as a fundamental presupposition of their moral theories some similar requirement which operates so as to give everyone's interests equal consideration—although these writers generally cannot agree on how this requirement is best formulated.[1]

It is an implication of this principle of equality that our concern for others and our readiness to consider their interests ought not to depend on what they are like or on what abilities they may possess. Precisely what this concern or consideration requires us to do may vary according to the characteristics of those affected by what we do: concern for the well-being of a child growing up in America would require that we teach him to read; concern for the well-being of a pig may require no more than that we leave him alone with other pigs in a place where there is adequate food and room to run freely. But the basic element—the taking into account of the interests of the being, whatever those interests may be—must, according to the principle of equality, be extended to all beings, black or white, masculine or feminine, human or nonhuman.

Thomas Jefferson, who was responsible for writing the principle of the equality of men into the American Declaration of Independence, saw this point. It led him to oppose slavery even though he was unable to free himself fully from his slaveholding background. He wrote in a letter to the author of a book that emphasized the notable intellectual achievements of Negroes in order to refute the then common view that they had limited intellectual capacities:

> Be assured that no person living wishes more sincerely than I do, to see a complete refutation of the doubts I have myself entertained and expressed on the grade of understanding allotted to them by nature, and to find that they are on a par with ourselves . . . but whatever be their degree of talent it is no measure of their rights. Because Sir Isaac Newton was superior to others in understanding, he was not therefore lord of the property or person of others.[2]

Similarly when in the 1850s the call for women's rights was raised in the United States a remarkable black feminist named Sojourner Truth made the same point in more robust terms at a feminist convention:

> . . . they talk about this thing in the head; what do they call it? ["Intellect," whispered someone near by.] That's it. What's that got to do with women's rights or Negroes' rights? If my cup won't hold but a pint and yours holds a quart, wouldn't you be mean not to let me have my little half-measure full?[3]

It is on this basis that the case against racism and the case against sexism must both ultimately rest; and it is in accordance with this principle that the attitude that we may call "speciesism," by analogy with racism, must also be condemned. Speciesism—the word is not an attractive one, but I can think of no better term—is a prejudice or attitude of bias toward the interests of members of one's own species and against those of members of other species. It should be obvious that the fundamental objections to racism and sexism made by Thomas Jefferson and Sojourner Truth apply equally to speciesism. If possessing a higher degree of intelligence does not entitle one human to use another for his own ends, how can it entitle humans to exploit nonhumans for the same purpose?[4]

Many philosophers and other writers have proposed the principle of equal consideration of interests, in some form or other, as a basic moral principle; but not many of them have recognized that this principle applies to members of other species as well as to our own. Jeremy Bentham was one of the few who did realize this. In a forward-looking passage written at a time when black slaves had been freed by the French but in the British dominions were still being treated in the way we now treat animals, Bentham wrote:

> The day *may* come when the rest of the animal creation may acquire those rights which never could have been withholden from them but by the hand of tyranny. The French have already discovered that the blackness of the skin is no reason why a human being should be abandoned without redress to the caprice of a tormentor. It may one day come to be recognized that the number of the legs, the villosity of the skin, or the termination of the *os sacrum* are reasons equally insufficient for abandoning a sensitive being to the same fate. What else is it that should trace the insuperable line? Is it the faculty of reason, or perhaps the faculty of discourse? But a full-grown horse or dog is beyond comparison a more rational, as well as a more conversable animal, than an infant of a day or a week or even a month, old. But suppose they were otherwise, what would it avail? The question is not, Can they *reason?* nor Can they *talk?* but, *Can they suffer?*[5]

In this passage Bentham points to the capacity for suffering as the vital characteristic that gives a being the right to equal consideration. The capacity for suffering—or more strictly, for suffering and/or enjoyment or happiness—is not just another characteristic like the capacity for language or higher mathematics. Bentham is not saying that those who try to mark "the insuperable line" that determines whether the interests of a being should be considered happen to have chosen the wrong characteristic. By saying that we must consider the interests of all beings with the capacity for suffering or enjoyment Bentham does not arbitrarily exclude from consideration any interests at all—as those who draw the line with reference to the possession of reason or language do. The capacity for suffering and enjoyment is *a prerequisite for having interests at all,* a condition that must be satisfied before we can speak of interests in a meaningful way. It would be nonsense to say that it was not in the interests of a stone to be kicked along the road by a schoolboy. A stone does not have interests because it cannot suffer. Nothing that we can do to it could possibly make any difference to its welfare. A mouse, on the other hand, does have an interest in not being kicked along the road, because it will suffer if it is.

If a being suffers there can be no moral justification for refusing to take that suffering into consideration. No matter what the nature of the being, the principle of equality requires that its suffering be counted equally with the like suffering—insofar as rough comparisons can be made—of any other being. If a being is not capable of suffering, or of experiencing enjoyment or happiness, there is nothing to be taken into account. So the limit of sentience (using the term as a convenient if not strictly accurate shorthand for the capacity to suffer and/or experience enjoyment) is the only defensible boundary of concern for the interests of others. To mark this boundary by some other characteristic like intelligence or rationality would be to mark it in an arbitrary manner. Why not choose some other characteristic, like skin color?

The racist violates the principle of equality by giving greater weight to the interests of members of his own race when there is a clash between their interests and the interests of those of another race. The sexist violates the principle of equality by favoring the interests of his own sex. Similarly the speciesist allows the interests of his own species to override the greater interests of members of other species. The pattern is identical in each case.

Most human beings are speciesists. The following chapters show that ordinary human beings—not a few exceptionally cruel or heartless humans, but the overwhelming majority of humans—take an active part in, acquiesce in, and allow their taxes to pay for practices that require the sacrifice of the most important interests of members of other species in order to promote the most trivial interests of our own species.

There is, however, one general defense of the practices to be described in the next two chapters that needs to be disposed of before we discuss the practices themselves. It is a defense which, if true, would allow us to do anything at all to nonhumans for the slightest reason, or for no reason at all, without incurring any justifiable reproach. This defense claims that we are never guilty of neglecting the interests of other animals for one breathtakingly simple reason: they have no interests. Nonhuman animals have no interests, according to this view, because they are not capable of suffering. By this is not meant merely that they are not capable of suffering in all the ways that humans are—for instance, that a calf is not capable of suffering from the knowledge that it will be killed in six months time. That modest claim is, no doubt, true; but it does not clear humans of the charge of speciesism, since it allows that animals may suffer in other ways—for instance, by being given electric shocks, or being kept in small, cramped cages. The defense I am about to discuss is the much more sweeping, although correspondingly less plausible, claim that animals are incapable of suffering in any way at all; that they are, in fact, unconscious automata, possessing neither thoughts nor feelings nor a mental life of any kind.

Although, as we shall see in a later chapter, the view that animals are automata was proposed by the seventeenth-century French philosopher René Descartes, to most people, then and now, it is obvious that if, for example, we stick a sharp knife into the stomach of an unanesthetized dog, the dog will feel pain. That this is so is assumed by the laws in most civilized countries which prohibit wanton cruelty to animals. Readers whose common sense tells them that animals do suffer may prefer to skip the remainder of this section, moving straight on to page 466, since the pages in between do nothing but refute a position which they do not hold. Implausible as it is, though, for the sake of completeness this skeptical position must be discussed.

Do animals other than humans feel pain? How do we know? Well, how do we know if anyone, human or nonhuman, feels pain? We know that we ourselves can feel pain. We know this from the direct experiences of pain that we have when, for instance, somebody presses a lighted cigarette against the back of our hand. But how do we know that anyone else feels pain? We cannot directly experience anyone else's pain, whether that "anyone" is our best friend or a stray dog. Pain is a state of consciousness, a "mental event," and as such it can never be observed. Behavior like writhing, screaming, or drawing one's hand away from the lighted cigarette is not pain itself; nor are the recordings a neurologist might make of activity within the brain observations of pain itself. Pain is something that we feel, and we can only infer that others are feeling it from various external indications.

In theory, we *could* always be mistaken when we assume that other human beings feel pain. It is conceivable that our best friend is really a very cleverly constructed robot, controlled by a brilliant scientist so as to give all the signs of feeling pain, but really no more sensitive than any other machine. We can never know, with absolute certainty, that this is not the case. But while this might present a puzzle for philosophers, none of us has the slightest real doubt that our best friends feel pain just as we do. This is an inference, but a perfectly reasonable one, based on observations of their behavior in situations in which we would feel pain, and on the fact that we have every reason to assume that our friends are beings like us, with nervous systems like ours that can be assumed to function as ours do, and to produce similar feelings in similar circumstances.

If it is justifiable to assume that other humans feel pain as we do, is there any reason why a similar inference should be unjustifiable in the case of other animals?

Nearly all the external signs which lead us to infer pain in other humans can be seen in other species, especially the species most closely related to us—other species of mammals, and birds. Behavioral signs—writhing, facial contortions, moaning, yelping or other forms of calling, attempts to avoid the source of pain, appearance of fear at the prospect of its repetition, and so on—are present. In addition, we know that these animals have nervous systems very like ours, which respond physiologically as ours do when the animal is in circumstances in which we would feel pain: an initial rise of blood pressure, dilated pupils, perspiration, an increased pulse rate, and, if the stimulus continues, a fall in blood pressure. Although humans have a more developed cerebral cortex than other animals, this part of the brain is concerned with thinking functions rather than with basic impulses, emotions, and feelings. These impulses, emotions, and feelings are located in the diencephalon, which is well developed in many other species of animals, especially mammals and birds.[6]

We also know that the nervous systems of other animals were not artificially constructed to mimic the pain behavior of humans, as a robot might be artificially constructed. The nervous systems of animals evolved as our own did, and in fact the evolutionary history of humans and other animals, especially mammals, did not diverge until the central features of our nervous systems were already in existence. A capacity to feel pain obviously enhances a species' prospects of survival, since it causes members of the species to avoid sources of injury. It is surely unreasonable to suppose that nervous systems which are virtually identical physiologically have a common origin and a common evolutionary function, and result in similar forms of behavior in similar circumstances should actually operate in an entirely different manner on the level of subjective feelings.

It has long been accepted as sound policy in science to search for the simplest possible explanation of whatever it is we are trying to explain. Occasionally it has been claimed that it is for this reason "unscientific" to explain the behavior of animals by theories that refer to the animal's conscious feelings, desires, and so on—the idea being that if the behavior in question can be explained without invoking consciousness or feelings, that will be the simpler theory. Yet we can now see that such explanations, when placed in the overall context of the behavior of both human and nonhuman animals, are actually far more complex than their rivals. For we know from our own experience that explanations of our own behavior that did not refer to consciousness and the feeling of pain would be incomplete; and it is simpler to assume that the similar behavior of animals with similar nervous systems is to be explained in the same way than to try to invent some other explanation for the behavior of nonhuman animals as well as an explanation for the divergence between humans and nonhumans in this respect.

The overwhelming majority of scientists who have addressed themselves to this question agree. Lord Brain, one of the most eminent neurologists of our time, has said:

> I personally can see no reason for conceding mind to my fellow men and denying it to animals. . . . I at least cannot doubt that the interests and activities of animals are correlated with awareness and feeling in the same way as my own, and which may be, for aught I know, just as vivid.[7]

While the author of a recent book on pain writes:

> Every particle of factual evidence supports the contention that the higher mammalian vertebrates experience pain sensations at least as acute as our own. To say that they feel less because they are lower animals is an absurdity; it can easily be shown that many of their senses are far more acute than ours—visual acuity in certain birds, hearing in most wild animals, and touch in others; these animals depend more than we do today on the sharpest possible awareness of a hostile environment. Apart from the complexity of the cerebral cortex (which does not directly perceive

> pain) their nervous systems are almost identical to ours and their reactions to pain remarkably similar, though lacking (so far as we know) the philosophical and moral overtones. The emotional element is all too evident, mainly in the form of fear and anger.[8]

In Britain, three separate expert government committees on matters relating to animals have accepted the conclusion that animals feel pain. After noting the obvious behavioral evidence for this view, the Committee on Cruelty to Wild Animals said:

> . . . we believe that the physiological, and more particularly the anatomical, evidence fully justifies and reinforces the common sense belief that animals feel pain.

And after discussing the evolutionary value of pain they concluded that pain is "of clear-cut biological usefulness" and this is "a third type of evidence that animals feel pain." They then went on to consider forms of suffering other than mere physical pain, and added that they were "satisfied that animals do suffer from acute fear and terror." In 1965, reports by British government committees on experiments on animals, and on the welfare of animals under intensive farming methods, agreed with this view, concluding that animals are capable of suffering both from straightforward physical injuries and from fear, anxiety, stress, and so on.[9]

That might well be thought enough to settle the matter; but there is one more objection that needs to be considered. There is, after all, one behavioral sign that humans have when in pain which nonhumans do not have. This is a developed language. Other animals may communicate with each other, but not, it seems, in the complicated way we do. Some philosophers, including Descartes, have thought it important that while humans can tell each other about their experience of pain in great detail, other animals cannot. (Interestingly, this once neat dividing line between humans and other species has now been threatened by the discovery that chimpanzees can be taught a language.)[10] But as Bentham pointed out long ago, the ability to use language is not relevant to the question of how a being ought to be treated—unless that ability can be linked to the capacity to suffer, so that the absence of a language casts doubt on the existence of this capacity.

This link may be attempted in two ways. First, there is a hazy line of philosophical thought, stemming perhaps from some doctrines associated with the influential philosopher Ludwig Wittgenstein, which maintains that we cannot meaningfully attribute states of consciousness to beings without language. This position seems to me very implausible. Language may be necessary for abstract thought, at some level anyway; but states like pain are more primitive, and have nothing to do with language.

The second and more easily understood way of linking language and the existence of pain is to say that the best evidence that we can have that another creature is in pain is when he tells us that he is. This is a distinct line of argument, for it is not being denied that a non-language-user conceivably *could* suffer, but only that we could ever have sufficient reason to believe that he is suffering. Still, this line of argument fails too. As Jane Goodall has pointed out in her study of chimpanzees, *In the Shadow of Man*, when it comes to the expressions of feelings and emotions language is less important than in other areas. We tend to fall back on nonlinguistic modes of communication such as a cheering pat on the back, an exuberant embrace, a clasp of the hands, and so on. The basic signals we use to convey pain, fear, anger, love, joy, surprise, sexual arousal, and many other emotional states are not specific to our own species.[11]

Charles Darwin made an extensive study of this subject, and the book he wrote about it, *The Expression of the Emotions in Man and Animals,* notes countless nonlinguistic modes of expression. The statement "I am in pain" may be one piece of evidence for the conclusion that the speaker is in pain, but it is not the only possible evidence, and since people sometimes tell lies, not even the best possible evidence.

Even if there were stronger grounds for refusing to attribute pain to those who do not have a language, the consequences of this refusal might lead us to reject the conclusion. Human infants and young children are unable to use language. Are we to deny that a year-old child can suffer? If not, language cannot be crucial. Of course, most parents understand the responses of their children better than they understand the responses of other animals; but this is just a fact about the relatively greater knowledge that we have of our own species, and the greater contact we have with infants, as compared to animals. Those who have studied the behavior of other animals, and those who have pet animals, soon learn to understand their responses as well as we understand those of an infant, and sometimes better. Jane Goodall's account of the chimpanzees she watched is one instance of this, but the same can be said of those who have observed species less closely related to our own. Two among many possible examples are Konrad Lorenz's observations of geese and jackdaws, and N. Tinberger's extensive studies of herring gulls.[12] Just as we can understand infant human behavior in the light of adult human behavior, so we can understand the behavior of other species in the light of our own behavior—and sometimes we can understand our own behavior better in the light of the behavior of other species.

So to conclude: there are no good reasons, scientific or philosophical, for denying that animals feel pain. If we do not doubt that other humans feel pain we should not doubt that other animals do so too.

Animals can feel pain. As we saw earlier, there can be no moral justification for regarding the pain (or pleasure) that animals feel as less important than the same amount of pain (or pleasure) felt by humans. But what exactly does this mean, in practical terms? To prevent misunderstanding I shall spell out what I mean a little more fully.

If I give a horse a hard slap across its rump with my open hand, the horse may start, but it presumably feels little pain. Its skin is thick enough to protect it against a mere slap. If I slap a baby in the same way, however, the baby will cry and presumably does feel pain, for its skin is more sensitive. So it is worse to slap a baby than a horse, if both slaps are administered with equal force. But there must be some kind of blow—I don't know exactly what it would be, but perhaps a blow with a heavy stick—that would cause the horse as much pain as we cause a baby by slapping it with our hand. That is what I mean by "the same amount of pain" and if we consider it wrong to inflict that much pain on a baby for no good reason then we must, unless we are speciesists, consider it equally wrong to inflict the same amount of pain on a horse for no good reason.

There are other differences between humans and animals that cause other complications. Normal adult human beings have mental capacities which will, in certain circumstances, lead them to suffer more than animals would in the same circumstances. If, for instance, we decided to perform extremely painful or lethal scientific experiments on normal adult humans, kidnapped at random from public parks for this purpose, every adult who entered a park would become fearful that he would be kidnapped. The resultant terror would be a form of suffering additional to the pain of the experiment. The same experiments performed on nonhuman animals would cause less suffering since the animals would not have the anticipatory dread of being kidnapped and experimented upon. This does not mean, of course, that it would be right to perform the experiment on animals, but only that there is a reason, which is *not* speciesist, for preferring to use animals rather than normal adult humans, if the experiment is to be done at all. It should be noted, however, that this same argument gives us a reason for preferring to use human infants—orphans perhaps—or retarded humans for experiments, rather than adults, since infants and retarded humans would also have no idea of what was going to happen to them. So far as this argument is concerned nonhuman animals and infants and retarded humans are in the same category; and if we use this argument to justify experiments on nonhuman animals we have to ask ourselves whether we are also prepared to allow experiments on human infants and retarded adults; and if we make a distinction between animals and these humans, on what basis can we do it, other than a barefaced—and morally indefensible— preference for members of our own species?

There are many areas in which the superior mental powers of normal adult humans make a difference: anticipation, more detailed memory, greater knowledge of what is happening, and so on. Yet these differences do not all point to greater suffering on the part of the normal human being. Sometimes an animal may suffer more because of his more limited understanding. If, for instance, we are taking prisoners in wartime we can explain to them that while they must submit to capture, search, and confinement they will not otherwise be harmed and will be set free at the conclusion of hostilities. If we capture a wild animal, however, we cannot explain that we are not threatening its life. A wild animal cannot distinguish an attempt to overpower and confine from an attempt to kill; the one causes as much terror as the other.

It may be objected that comparisons of the sufferings of different species are impossible to make, and that for this reason when the interests of animals and humans clash the principle of equality gives no guidance. It is probably true that comparisons of suffering between members of different species cannot be made precisely, but precision is not essential. Even if we were to prevent the infliction of suffering on animals only when it is quite certain that the interests of humans will not be affected to anything like the extent that animals are affected, we would be forced to make radical changes in our treatment of animals that would involve our diet, the farming methods we use, experimental procedures in many fields of science, our approach to wildlife and to hunting, trapping and the wearing of furs, and areas of entertainment like circuses, rodeos, and zoos. As a result, a vast amount of suffering would be avoided.

So far I have said a lot about the infliction of suffering on animals, but nothing about killing them. This omission has been deliberate. The application of the principle of equality to the infliction of suffering is, in theory at least, fairly straightforward. Pain and suffering are bad and should be prevented or minimized, irrespective of the race, sex, or species of the being that suffers. How bad a pain is depends on how intense it is and how long it lasts, but pains of the same intensity and duration are equally bad, whether felt by humans or animals.

The wrongness of killing a being is more complicated. I have kept, and shall continue to keep, the question of killing in the background because in the present state of human tyranny over other species the more simple, straightforward principle of equal consideration of pain or pleasure is a sufficient basis for identifying and protesting against all the major abuses of animals that humans practice. Nevertheless, it is necessary to say something about killing.

Just as most humans are speciesists in their readiness to cause pain to animals when they would not cause a similar pain to humans for the same reason, so most humans are speciesists in their readiness to kill other animals when they would not kill humans. We need to proceed more cautiously here, however, because people hold widely differing views about when it is legitimate to kill humans, as the continuing debates over abortion and euthanasia attest. Nor have moral philosophers been able to agree on exactly what it is that makes it wrong to kill humans, and under what circumstances killing a human being may be justifiable.

Let us consider first the view that it is always wrong to take an innocent human life. We may call this the "sanctity of life" view. People who take this view oppose abortion and euthanasia. They do not usually, however, oppose the killing of nonhumans—so perhaps it would be more accurate to describe this view as the "sanctity of *human* life" view.

The belief that human life, and only human life, is sacrosanct is a form of speciesism. To see this, consider the following example.

Assume that, as sometimes happens, an infant has been born with massive and irreparable brain damage. The damage is so severe that the infant can never be any more than a "human vegetable," unable to talk, recognize other people, act independently of others, or develop a sense of self-awareness. The parents of the infant, realizing that they cannot hope for any improvement in their child's condition and being in any case unwilling to spend, or ask the state to spend, the thousands of dollars that would be needed annually for proper care of the infant, ask the doctor to kill the infant painlessly.

Should the doctor do what the parents ask? Legally, he should not, and in this respect the law reflects the sanctity of life view. The life of every human being is sacred. Yet people who would say this about the infant do not object to the killing of nonhuman animals. How can they justify their different judgments? Adult chimpanzees, dogs, pigs, and many other species far surpass the brain-damaged infant in their ability to relate to others, act independently, be self-aware, and any other capacity that could reasonably be said to give value to life. With the most intensive care possible, there are retarded infants who can never achieve the intelligence level of a dog. Nor can we appeal to the concern of the infant's parents, since they themselves, in this imaginary example (and in some actual cases), do not want the infant kept alive.

The only thing that distinguishes the infant from the animal, in the eyes of those who claim it has a "right to life," is that it is, biologically, a member of the species Homo sapiens, whereas chimpanzees, dogs, and pigs are not. But to use *this* difference as the basis for granting a right to life to the infant and not to the other animals is, of course, pure speciesism.* It is exactly the kind of arbitrary difference that the most crude and overt kind of racist uses in attempting to justify racial discrimination.

This does not mean that to avoid speciesism we must hold that it is as wrong to kill a dog as it is to kill a normal human being. The only position that is irredeemably speciesist is the one that tries to make the boundary of the right to life run exactly parallel to the boundary of our own species. Those who hold the sanctity of life view do this because while distinguishing sharply between humans and other animals they allow no distinctions to be made within our own species, objecting to the killing of the severely retarded and the hopelessly senile as strongly as they object to the killing of normal adults.

To avoid speciesism we must allow that beings which are similar in all relevant respects have a similar right to life—and mere membership in our own biological species cannot be a morally relevant criterion for this right. Within these limits we could still hold that, for instance, it is worse to kill a normal adult human, with a capacity for self-awareness, and the ability to plan for the future and have meaningful relations with others, than it is to kill a mouse, which presumably does not share all of these characteristics; or we might appeal to the close family and other personal ties which humans have but mice do not have to the same degree; or we might think that it is the consequences for other humans, who will be put in fear of their own lives, that makes the crucial difference; or we might think it is some combination of these factors, or other factors altogether.

Whatever criteria we choose, however, we will have to admit that they do not follow precisely the boundary of our own species. We may legitimately hold that there are some features of certain beings which make their lives more valuable than those of other beings; but there will surely be some nonhuman animals whose lives, by any standards, are more valuable than the lives of some humans. A chimpanzee, dog, or pig, for instance, will have a higher degree of self-awareness and a greater capacity for meaningful relations with others than a severely retarded infant or someone in a state of advanced senility. So if we base the right to

*I am here putting aside religious views, for example the doctrine that all and only humans have immortal souls, or are made in the image of God. Historically these views have been very important, and no doubt are partly responsible for the idea that human life has a special sanctity. Logically, however, these religious views are unsatisfactory, since a reasoned explanation of why it should be that all humans and no nonhumans have immortal souls is not offered. This belief too, therefore, comes under suspicion as a form of speciesism. In any case, defenders of the "sanctity of life" view are generally reluctant to base their position on purely religious doctrines, since these doctrines are no longer as widely accepted as they once were.

life on these characteristics we must grant these animals a right to life as good as, or better than, such retarded or senile humans.

Now this argument cuts both ways. It could be taken as showing that chimpanzees, dogs, and pigs, along with some other species, have a right to life and we commit a grave moral offense whenever we kill them, even when they are old and suffering and our intention is to put them out of their misery. Alternatively one could take the argument as showing that the severely retarded and hopelessly senile have no right to life and may be killed for quite trivial reasons, as we now kill animals.

Since the focus of this book is on ethical questions concerning animals and not on the morality of euthanasia I shall not attempt to settle this issue finally. I think it is reasonably clear, though, that while both of the positions just described avoid speciesism, neither is entirely satisfactory. What we need is some middle position which would avoid speciesism but would not make the lives of the retarded and senile as cheap as the lives of pigs and dogs now are, nor make the lives of pigs and dogs so sacrosanct that we think it wrong to put them out of hopeless misery. What we must do is bring nonhuman animals within our sphere of moral concern and cease to treat their lives as expendable for whatever trivial purposes we may have. At the same time, once we realize that the fact that a being is a member of our own species is not in itself enough to make it always wrong to kill that being, we may come to reconsider our policy of preserving human lives at all costs, even when there is no prospect of a meaningful life or of existence without terrible pain.

I conclude, then, that a rejection of speciesism does not imply that all lives are of equal worth. While self-awareness, intelligence, the capacity for meaningful relations with others, and so on are not relevant to the question of inflicting pain—since pain is pain, whatever other capacities, beyond the capacity to feel pain, the being may have—these capacities may be relevant to the question of taking life. It is not arbitrary to hold that the life of a self-aware being, capable of abstract thought, of planning for the future, of complex acts of communication, and so on, is more valuable than the life of a being without these capacities. To see the difference between the issues of inflicting pain and taking life, consider how we would choose within our own species. If we had to choose to save the life of a normal human or a mentally defective human, we would probably choose to save the life of the normal human; but if we had to choose between preventing pain in the normal human or the mental defective—imagine that both have received painful but superficial injuries, and we only have enough painkiller for one of them—it is not nearly so clear how we ought to choose. The same is true when we consider other species. The evil of pain is, in itself, unaffected by the other characteristics of the being that feels the pain; the value of life is affected by these other characteristics.

Normally this will mean that if we have to choose between the life of a human being and the life of another animal we should choose to save the life of the human; but there may be special cases in which the reverse holds true, because the human being in question does not have the capacities of a normal human being. So this view is not speciesist, although it may appear to be at first glance. The preference, in normal cases, for saving a human life over the life of an animal when a choice *has* to be made is a preference based on the characteristics that normal humans have, and not on the mere fact that they are members of our own species. This is why when we consider members of our own species who lack the characteristics of normal humans we can no longer say that their lives are always to be preferred to those of other animals. This issue comes up in a practical way in the following chapter. In general, though, the question of when it is wrong to kill (painlessly) an animal is one to which we need give no precise answer. As long as we remember that we should give the same respect to the lives of animals as we give to the lives of those humans at a similar mental level, we shall not go far wrong.

In any case, the conclusions that are argued for in this book flow from the principle of minimizing suffering alone. The idea that it is also wrong to kill animals painlessly gives some of these conclusions additional support which is welcome, but strictly unnecessary. Interestingly enough, this is true even of the conclusion that we ought to become vegetarians, a conclusion which in the popular mind is generally based on some kind of absolute prohibition on killing.

NOTES

1. For Bentham's moral philosophy, see his *Introduction to the Principles of Morals and Legislation,* and for Sidgwick's see *The Methods of Ethics* (the passage quoted is from the seventh edition, p. 382). As examples of leading contemporary moral philosophers who incorporate a requirement of equal consideration of interests, see R. M. Hare, *Freedom and Reason* (New York: Oxford University Press, 1963) and John Rawls, *A Theory of Justice* (Cambridge: Harvard University Press, Belknap Press, 1972). For a brief account of the essential agreement on this issue between these and other positions, see R. M. Hare, "Rules of War and Moral Reasoning," *Philosophy and Public Affairs,* vol. 1, no. 2 (1972).
2. Letter to Henri Gregoire, February 25, 1809.
3. Reminiscences by Francis D. Gage, from Susan B. Anthony, *The History of Woman Suffrage,* vol. 1; the passage is to be found in the extract in Leslie Tanner, ed., *Voices from Women's Liberation* (New York: Signet, 1970).
4. I owe the term "speciesism" to Richard Ryder.
5. *Introduction to the Principles of Morals and Legislation,* chapter 17.
6. Lord Brain, "Presidential Address" in C. A. Keele and R. Smith, eds., *The Assessment of Pain in Men and Animals* (London: Universities Federation for Animal Welfare, 1962).
7. Ibid., p. 11.
8. Richard Serjeant, *The Spectrum of Pain* (London: Hart-Davis London: , 1969), p. 72.
9. See the reports of the committee on Cruelty to Wild Animals (Command Paper 8266, 1951), paragraphs 36–42; the Departmental Committee on Experiments on Animals (Command Paper 2641, 1965), paragraphs 179–182; and the Technical Committee to Enquire into the Welfare of Animals Kept under Intensive Livestock Husbandry Systems (Command Paper 2836, 1965), paragraphs 26–28 (London: Her Majesty's Stationery Office).
10. One chimpanzee, Washoe, has been taught the sign language used by deaf people, and acquired a vocabulary of 350 signs. Another, Lana, communicates in structured sentences by pushing buttons on a special machine. For a brief account of Washoe's abilities, see Jane van Lawick-Goodall, *In the Shadow of Man* (Boston: Houghton Mifflin, 1971), pp. 252–254; and for Lana, see *Newsweek,* 7 January 1974, and *New York Times,* 4 December 1974.
11. *In the Shadow of Man,* p. 225; Michael Peters makes a similar point in "Nature and Culture," in Stanley and Roslind Godlovitch and John Harris, eds., *Animals, Men and Morals* (New York: Taplinger Publishing Co., 1972).
12. Konrad Lorenz, *King Solomon's Ring* (New York: T.Y. Crowell, 1952); N. Tinbergen, *The Herring Gull's World,* rev. ed. (New York: Basic Books, 1974).

QUESTIONS FOR ANALYSIS

1. What does Singer mean by his claim that the principle of human equality is not a description of actual equality but a prescription of how we should treat humans?
2. On what grounds does Singer equate speciesism with sexism and racism?
3. What reasons have been advanced in favor of the view that animals cannot suffer? How does Singer rebut them?
4. Singer notes certain differences between human and nonhuman capacities and the complications that follow from them. What are these differences, and what kinds of complications follow from them?
5. To reject speciesism, Singer says, is not to say that all lives are of equal worth. Why not?
6. Normally, Singer says, we should choose a human over a nonhuman life if forced to choose between them. Why? Under what circumstances should we choose the nonhuman one?
7. In what way is Singer's principle of equal consideration related to the principle of utility?

The Case for Animal Rights

TOM REGAN

In this essay, Tom Regan, now a professor *emeritus* of philosophy at North Carolina State University, offers an alternative approach to Peter Singer's. Like Singer, he opposes speciesism. Unlike Singer, he does not offer a utilitarian moral theory. He argues that the focus of our moral concern should not be to minimize suffering and maximize pleasure but to avoid treating individual animals (human and nonhuman alike) in certain ways regardless of the consequences.

All animals that are the experiencing subjects of their own lives, he says, have inherent value. They, like humans, deserve what we called in Part 1 Kantian respect. They are not to be treated as mere things, even if we can maximize happiness by doing so. What makes eating meat or experimenting on animals wrong, then, is not that the human benefit does not outweigh the animal suffering, but that such practices deny the inherent value of the animals involved.

In defending his position, Regan criticizes *contractarian* views of morality, which deny that nonhuman animals can have rights. He also disagrees with Singer's view that some lives of creatures with the right to life are more valuable than others. All lives that have inherent value, he says, are equal.

I regard myself as an advocate of animal rights — as a part of the animal rights movement. That movement, as I conceive it, is committed to a number of goals, including:

the total abolition of the use of animals in science;
the total dissolution of commercial animal agriculture;
the total elimination of commercial and sport hunting and trapping.

There are, I know, people who profess to believe in animal rights but do not avow these goals. Factory farming, they say, is wrong—it violates animals' rights—but traditional animal agriculture is all right. Toxicity tests of cosmetics on animals violates their rights, but important medical research—cancer research, for example—does not. The clubbing of baby seals is abhorrent, but not the harvesting of adult seals. I used to think I understood this reasoning. Not any more. You don't change unjust institutions by tidying them up.

What's wrong—fundamentally wrong—with the way animals are treated isn't the details that vary from case to case. It's the whole system. The forlornness of the veal calf is pathetic, heart wrenching; the pulsing pain of the chimp with electrodes planted deep in her brain is repulsive; the slow, tortuous death of the raccoon caught in the leg-hold trap is agonizing. But what is wrong isn't the pain, isn't the suffering, isn't the deprivation. These compound what's wrong. Sometimes—often—they make it much, much worse. But they are not the fundamental wrong.

The fundamental wrong is the system that allows us to view animals as *our resources,* here for *us*—to be eaten, or surgically manipulated, or exploited for sport or money. Once we accept this view of animals as our resources—the rest is as predictable as it is regrettable. Why worry about their loneliness, their pain, their death? Since animals exist for us, to benefit us in one way or another, what harms them really doesn't

From "The Case for Animal Rights," in *In Defense of Animals* edited by Peter Singer (1985), pp. 13–26. Reprinted by permission of Peter Singer and Tom Regan.

matter—or matters only if it starts to bother us, makes us feel a trifle uneasy when we eat our veal escalope, for example. So, yes, let us get veal calves out of solitary confinement, give them more space, a little straw, a few companions. But let us keep our veal escalope.

But a little straw, more space and a few companions won't eliminate—won't even touch—the basic wrong that attaches to our viewing and treating these animals as our resources. A veal calf killed to be eaten after living in close confinement is viewed and treated in this way: but so, too, is another who is raised (as they say) "more humanely." To right the wrong of our treatment of farm animals requires more than making rearing methods "more humane"; it requires the total dissolution of commercial animal agriculture.

How we do this, whether we do it or, as in the case of animals in science, whether and how we abolish their use—these are to a large extent political questions. People must change their beliefs before they change their habits. Enough people, especially those elected to public office, must believe in change—must want it—before we will have laws that protect the rights of animals. This process of change is very complicated, very demanding, very exhausting, calling for the efforts of many hands in education, publicity, political organization and activity, down to the licking of envelopes and stamps. As a trained and practising philosopher, the sort of contribution I can make is limited but, I like to think, important. The currency of philosophy is ideas—their meaning and rational foundation—not the nuts and bolts of the legislative process, say, or the mechanics of community organization. That's what I have been exploring over the past ten years or so in my essays and talks and, most recently, in my book, *The Case for Animal Rights*. I believe the major conclusions I reach in the book are true because they are supported by the weight of the best arguments. I believe the idea of animal rights has reason, not just emotion, on its side.

In the space I have at my disposal here I can only sketch, in the barest outline, some of the main features of the book. Its main themes—and we should not be surprised by this—involve asking and answering deep, foundational moral questions about what morality is, how it should be understood and what is the best moral theory, all considered. I hope I can convey something of the shape I think this theory takes. The attempt to do this will be (to use a word a friendly critic once used to describe my work) cerebral, perhaps too cerebral. But this is misleading. My feelings about how animals are sometimes treated run just as deep and just as strong as those of my more volatile compatriots. Philosophers do—to use the jargon of the day—have a right side to their brains. If it's the left side we contribute (or mainly should), that's because what talents we have reside there.

How to proceed? We begin by asking how the moral status of animals has been understood by thinkers who deny that animals have rights. Then we test the mettle of their ideas by seeing how well they stand up under the heat of fair criticism. If we start our thinking in this way, we soon find that some people believe that we have no duties directly to animals, that we owe nothing to them, that we can do nothing that wrongs them. Rather, we can do wrong acts that involve animals, and so we have duties regarding them, though none to them. Such views may be called indirect duty views. By way of illustration: suppose your neighbour kicks your dog. Then your neighbour has done something wrong. But not to your dog. The wrong that has been done is a wrong to you. After all, it is wrong to upset people, and your neighbour's kicking your dog upsets you. So you are the one who is wronged, not your dog. Or again: by kicking your dog your neighbour damages your property. And since it is wrong to damage another person's property, your neighbour has done something wrong—to you, of course, not to your dog. Your neighbour no more wrongs your dog than your car would be wronged if the windshield were smashed. Your neighbour's duties involving your dog are indirect duties to you. More generally, all of our duties regarding animals are indirect duties to one another—to humanity.

How could someone try to justify such a view? Someone might say that your dog doesn't feel anything and so isn't hurt by your neighbour's kick, doesn't care about the pain since none is felt, is as unaware of anything as is your windshield. Someone might say this, but no rational person will, since, among other considerations, such a view will commit anyone who holds it to the position that no human being feels pain either—that human beings also don't care about what happens to them. A second possibility is that though both humans and your dog are hurt when kicked, it is only human pain that matters. But, again, no rational person can believe this. Pain is pain wherever it occurs. If your neighbour's causing you pain is wrong because of the pain that is caused, we cannot rationally ignore or dismiss the moral relevance of the pain that your dog feels.

Philosophers who hold indirect duty views—and many still do—have come to understand that they must avoid the two defects just noted: that is, both the view that animals don't feel anything as well as the idea that only human pain can be morally relevant. Among such thinkers the sort of view now favoured is one or other form of what is called *contractarianism*.

Here, very crudely, is the root idea: morality consists of a set of rules that individuals voluntarily agree to abide by, as we do when we sign a contract (hence the name contractarianism). Those who understand and accept the terms of the contract are covered directly; they have rights created and recognized by, and protected in, the contract. And these contractors can also have protection spelled out for others who, though they lack the ability to understand morality and so cannot sign the contract themselves, are loved or cherished by those who can. Thus young children, for example, are unable to sign contracts and lack rights. But they are protected by the contract none the less because of the sentimental interests of others, most notably their parents. So we have, then, duties involving these children, duties regarding them, but no duties to them. Our duties in their case are indirect duties to other human beings, usually their parents.

As for animals, since they cannot understand contracts, they obviously cannot sign; and since they cannot sign, they have no rights. Like children, however, some animals are the objects of the sentimental interest of others. You, for example, love your dog or cat. So those animals that enough people care about (companion animals, whales, baby seals, the American bald eagle), though they lack rights themselves, will be protected because of the sentimental interests of people. I have, then, according to contractarianism, no duty directly to your dog or any other animal, not even the duty not to cause them pain or suffering; my duty not to hurt them is a duty I have to those people who care about what happens to them. As for other animals, where no or little sentimental interest is present—in the case of farm animals, for example, or laboratory rats—what duties we have grow weaker and weaker, perhaps to vanishing point. The pain and death they endure, though real, are not wrong if no one cares about them.

When it comes to the moral status of animals, contractarianism could be a hard view to refute if it were an adequate theoretical approach to the moral status of human beings. It is not adequate in this latter respect, however, which makes the question of its adequacy in the former case, regarding animals, utterly moot. For consider: morality, according to the (crude) contractarian position before us, consists of rules that people agree to abide by. What people? Well, enough to make a difference—enough, that is, *collectively* to have the power to enforce the rules that are drawn up in the contract. That is very well and good for the signatories but not so good for anyone who is not asked to sign. And there is nothing in contractarianism of the sort we are discussing that guarantees or requires that everyone will have a chance to participate equally in framing the rules of morality. The result is that this approach to ethics could sanction the most blatant forms of social, economic, moral and political injustice, ranging from a repressive caste system to systematic racial or sexual discrimination. Might, according to this theory, does make right. Let those who are the victims of injustice suffer as they will. It matters not so long as no one else—no contractor, or too few of them—cares about it. Such a theory takes one's moral breath away . . . as if, for example, there would be nothing wrong with apartheid in South Africa if few white South Africans were upset by it. A theory with so little to recommend it at the level of the ethics of our treatment of our fellow humans cannot have anything more to recommend it when it comes to the ethics of how we treat our fellow animals.

The version of contractarianism just examined is, as I have noted, a crude variety, and in fairness to those of a contractarian persuasion it must be noted that much more refined, subtle and ingenious varieties are possible. For example, John Rawls, in his *A Theory of Justice,* sets forth a version of contractarianism that forces contractors to ignore the accidental features of being a human being—for example, whether one is white or black, male or female, a genius or of modest intellect. Only by ignoring such features, Rawls believes, can we ensure that the principles of justice that contractors would agree upon are not based on bias or prejudice. Despite the improvement a view such as Rawls's represents over the cruder forms of contractarianism, it remains deficient: it systematically denies that we have direct duties to those human beings who do not have a sense of justice—young children, for instance, and many mentally retarded humans. And yet it seems reasonably certain that, were we to torture a young child or a retarded elder, we would be doing something that wronged him or her, not something that would be wrong if (and only if) other humans with a sense of justice were upset. And since this is true in the case of these humans, we cannot rationally deny the same in the case of animals.

Indirect duty views, then, including the best among them, fail to command our rational assent. Whatever ethical theory we should accept rationally, therefore, it must at least recognize that we have some duties directly to animals, just as we have some duties directly to each other. The next two theories I'll sketch attempt to meet this requirement.

The first I call the cruelty–kindness view. Simply stated, this says that we have a direct duty to be kind to animals and a direct duty not to be cruel to them. Despite the familiar, reassuring ring of these ideas, I do not believe that this view offers an adequate theory. To make this clearer, consider kindness. A kind person acts from a certain kind of motive—compassion or concern, for example. And that is a virtue. But there is no guarantee that a kind act is a right act. If I am a generous racist, for example, I will be inclined to act kindly towards members of my own race, favouring their interests above those of others. My kindness would be real and, so far as it goes, good. But I trust it is too obvious to require argument that my kind acts may not be above moral reproach—may, in fact, be positively wrong because rooted in injustice. So kindness, notwithstanding its status as a virtue to be encouraged, simply will not carry the weight of a theory of right action.

Cruelty fares no better. People or their acts are cruel if they display either a lack of sympathy for or, worse, the presence of enjoyment in another's suffering. Cruelty in all its guises is a bad thing, a tragic human failing. But just as a person's being motivated by kindness does not guarantee that he or she does what is right, so the absence of cruelty does not ensure that he or she avoids doing what is wrong. Many people who perform abortions, for example, are not cruel, sadistic people. But that fact alone does not settle the terribly difficult question of the morality of abortion. The case is no different when we examine the ethics of our treatment of animals. So, yes, let us be for kindness and against cruelty. But let us not suppose that being for the one and against the other answers questions about moral right and wrong.

Some people think that the theory we are looking for is utilitarianism. A utilitarian accepts two moral principles. The first is that of equality: everyone's interests count, and similar interests must be counted as having similar weight or importance. White or black, American or Iranian, human or animal—everyone's pain or frustration matters, and matters just as much as the equivalent pain or frustration of anyone else. The second principle a utilitarian accepts is that of utility: do the act that will bring about the best balance between satisfaction and frustration for everyone affected by the outcome.

As a utilitarian, then, here is how I am to approach the task of deciding what I morally ought to do: I must ask who will be affected if I choose to do one thing rather than another, how much each individual will be affected, and where the best results are most likely to lie—which option, in other words, is most likely to bring about the best results, the best balance between satisfaction and frustration. That option, whatever it may be, is the one I ought to choose. That is where my moral duty lies.

The great appeal of utilitarianism rests with its uncompromising *egalitarianism:* everyone's interests count and count as much as the like interests of everyone else. The kind of odious discrimination that some forms of contractarianism can justify—discrimination based on race or sex, for example—seems disallowed in principle by utilitarianism, as is speciesism, systematic discrimination based on species membership.

The equality we find in utilitarianism, however, is not the sort an advocate of animal or human rights should have in mind. Utilitarianism has no room for the equal moral rights of different individuals because it has no room for their equal inherent value or worth. What has value for the utilitarian is the satisfaction of an individual's interests, not the individual whose interests they are. A universe in which you satisfy your desire for water, food and warmth is, other things being equal, better than a universe in which these desires are frustrated. And the same is true in the case of an animal with similar desires. But neither you nor the animal has any value in your own right. Only your feelings do.

Here is an analogy to help make the philosophical point clearer: a cup contains different liquids, sometimes sweet, sometimes bitter, sometimes a mix of the two. What has value are the liquids: the sweeter the better, the bitterer the worse. The cup, the container, has no value. It is what goes into it, not what they go into, that has value. For the utilitarian you and I are like the cup; we have no value as individuals and thus no equal value. What has value is what goes into us, what we serve as receptacles for; our feelings of satisfaction have positive value, our feelings of frustration negative value.

Serious problems arise for utilitarianism when we remind ourselves that it enjoins us to bring about the best consequences. What does this mean? It doesn't mean the best consequences for me alone, or for my family or friends, or any other person taken individually. No, what we must do is, roughly, as follows: we must add up (somehow!) the separate satisfactions and frustrations of everyone likely to be affected by our choice, the satisfactions in one column, the frustrations in the other. We must total each column for each of the options before us. That is what it means to say the theory is aggregative. And then we must choose that option which is most likely to bring about the best balance of totaled satisfactions over totaled frustrations. Whatever act would lead to this outcome is the one we ought morally to perform—it is where our moral duty lies. And that act quite clearly might not be the same one that would bring about the best results for me personally, or for my family or friends, or for a lab animal. The best aggregated consequences for everyone concerned are not necessarily the best for each individual.

That utilitarianism is an aggregative theory—different individuals' satisfactions or frustrations are added, or summed, or totaled—is the key objection to this theory. My Aunt Bea is old, inactive, a cranky, sour person, though not physically ill. She prefers to go on living. She is also rather rich. I could make a fortune if I could get my hands on her money, money she intends to give me in any event, after she dies, but which she refuses to give me now. In order to avoid a huge tax bite, I plan to donate a handsome sum of my profits to a local children's hospital. Many, many children will benefit from my generosity, and much joy will be brought to their parents, relatives and friends. If I don't get the money rather soon, all these ambitions will come to naught. The once-in-a-lifetime opportunity to make a real killing will be gone. Why, then, not kill my Aunt Bea? Of course I *might* get caught. But I'm no fool and, besides, her doctor can be counted on to cooperate (he has an eye for the same investment and I happen to know a good deal about his shady past). The deed can be done . . . professionally, shall we say. There is *very* little chance of getting caught. And as for my conscience being guilt-ridden, I am a resourceful sort of fellow and will take more than sufficient comfort—as I lie on the beach at Acapulco—in contemplating the joy and health I have brought to so many others.

Suppose Aunt Bea is killed and the rest of the story comes out as told. Would I have done anything wrong? Anything immoral? One would have thought that I had. Not according to utilitarianism. Since what I have done has brought about the best balance between totaled satisfaction and frustration for all those affected by the outcome, my action is not wrong. Indeed, in killing Aunt Bea the physician and I did what duty required.

This same kind of argument can be repeated in all sorts of cases, illustrating, time after time, how the utilitarian's position leads to results that impartial people find morally callous. It is wrong to kill my Aunt Bea in the name of bringing about the best results for others. A good end does not justify an evil means. Any adequate moral theory will have to explain why this is so. Utilitarianism fails in this respect and so cannot be the theory we seek.

What to do? Where to begin anew? The place to begin, I think, is with the utilitarian's view of the value of the individual—or, rather, lack of value. In its place, suppose we consider that you and I, for example, do have value as individuals—what we'll call *inherent value*. To say we have such value is to say that we are something more than, something different from, mere receptacles. Moreover, to ensure that we do not pave the way for such injustices as slavery or sexual discrimination, we must believe that all who have inherent value have it equally, regardless of their sex, race, religion, birthplace and so on. Similarly to be discarded as irrelevant are one's talents or skills, intelligence and wealth, personality or pathology, whether one is loved and admired or despised and loathed. The genius and the retarded child, the prince and the pauper, the brain surgeon and the fruit vendor, Mother Teresa and the most unscrupulous used-car salesman—all have inherent value, all possess it equally, and all have an equal right to be treated with respect, to be treated in ways that do not reduce them to the status of things, as if they existed as resources for others. My value as an individual is independent of my usefulness to you. Yours is not dependent on your usefulness to me. For either of us to treat the other in ways that fail to show respect for the other's independent value is to act immorally, to violate the individual's rights.

Some of the rational virtues of this view—what I call the rights view—should be evident. Unlike (crude) contractarianism, for example, the rights view in *principle* denies the moral tolerability of any and all forms of racial, sexual or social discrimination; and unlike utilitarianism, this view *in principle* denies that we can justify good results by using evil means that violate an individual's rights—denies, for example, that it could be moral to kill my Aunt Bea to harvest beneficial consequences for others. That would be to sanction the disrespectful treatment of the individual in the name of the social good, something the rights view will not—categorically will not—ever allow.

The rights view, I believe, is rationally the most satisfactory moral theory. It surpasses all other theories in the degree to which it illuminates and explains the foundation of our duties to one another—the domain of human morality. On this score it has the best reasons, the best arguments, on its side. Of course, if it were possible to show that only human beings are included within its scope, then a person like myself, who believes in animal rights, would be obliged to look elsewhere.

But attempts to limit its scope to humans only can be shown to be rationally defective. Animals, it is true, lack many of the abilities humans possess. They can't read, do higher mathematics, build a bookcase or make *baba ghanoush*. Neither can many human beings, however, and yet we don't (and shouldn't) say that they (these humans) therefore have less inherent value, less of a right to be treated with respect, than do others. It is the *similarities* between those human beings who most clearly, most noncontroversially have such value (the people reading this, for example), not our differences, that matter most. And the really crucial, the basic similarity is simply this: we are each of us the experiencing subject of a life, a conscious creature having an individual welfare that has importance to us whatever our usefulness to others. We want and prefer things, believe and feel things, recall and expect things. And all these dimensions of our life, including our pleasure and pain, our enjoyment and suffering, our satisfaction and frustration, our continued existence or our untimely death—all make a difference to the quality of our life as lived, as experienced, by us as individuals. As the same is true of those animals that concern us (the ones that are eaten and trapped, for example), they too must be viewed as the experiencing subjects of a life, with inherent value of their own.

Some there are who resist the idea that animals have inherent value. "Only humans have such value," they profess. How might this narrow view be defended? Shall we say that only humans have the requisite intelligence, or autonomy, or reason? But there are many, many humans who fail to meet these standards and yet are reasonably viewed as having value above and beyond their usefulness to others. Shall we claim that only humans belong to the right species, the species *Homo sapiens*? But this is blatant speciesism. Will it be said, then, that all and only—humans have immortal souls? Then our opponents have their work cut out for them. I am myself not ill-disposed to the proposition that there are immortal souls. Personally, I profoundly hope I have one. But I would not want to rest my position on a controversial ethical issue on the even more controversial question about who or what has an immortal soul. That is to dig one's hole deeper, not to climb out. Rationally, it is better to resolve moral issues without making more controversial assumptions than are needed. The question of who has inherent value is such a question, one that is resolved more rationally without the introduction of the idea of immortal souls than by its use.

Well, perhaps some will say that animals have some inherent value, only less than we have. Once again, however, attempts to defend this view can be shown to lack rational justification. What could be the basis of our having more inherent value than animals? Their lack of reason, or autonomy, or intellect? Only if we are willing to make the same judgment in the case of humans who are similarly deficient. But it is not true that such humans—the retarded child, for example, or the mentally deranged—have less inherent value than you or I. Neither, then, can we rationally sustain the view that animals like them in being the experiencing subjects of a life have less inherent value. All who have inherent value have it *equally*, whether they be human animals or not.

Inherent value, then, belongs equally to those who are the experiencing subjects of a life. Whether it belongs to others—to rocks and rivers, trees and glaciers, for example—we do not know and may never know. But neither do we need to know, if we are to make the case for animal rights. We do not need to know, for example, how many people are eligible to vote in the next presidential election before we can know whether I am. Similarly, we do not need to know how many individuals have inherent value before we can know that some do. When it comes to the case for animal rights, then, what we need to know is whether the animals that, in our culture, are routinely eaten, hunted and used in our laboratories, for example, are like us in being subjects of a life. And we do know this. We do know that many—literally, billions and billions—of these animals are the subjects of a life in the sense explained and so have inherent value if we do. And since, in order to arrive at the best theory of our duties to one another, we must recognize our equal inherent value as individuals, reason—not sentiment, not emotion—reason compels us to recognize the equal inherent value of these animals and, with this, their equal right to be treated with respect.

That, *very* roughly, is the shape and feel of the case for animal rights. Most of the details of the supporting argument are missing. They are to be found in the book to which I alluded earlier. Here, the details go begging, and I must, in closing, limit myself to four final points.

The first is how the theory that underlies the case for animal rights shows that the animal rights movement is a part of, not antagonistic to, the human rights movement. The theory that rationally grounds the rights of animals also grounds the rights of humans. Thus those involved in the animal rights movement are partners in the struggle to secure respect for human rights—the rights of women, for example, or minorities, or workers. The animal rights movement is cut from the same moral cloth as these.

Second, having set out the broad outlines of the rights view, I can now say why its implications for farming and science, among other fields, are both clear and uncompromising. In the case of the use of animals in science, the rights view is categorically abolitionist. Lab animals are not our tasters; we are not their kings. Because these animals are treated routinely, systematically as if their value were reducible to their usefulness to others, they are routinely, systematically treated with a lack of respect, and thus are their rights routinely, systematically violated. This is just as true when they are used in trivial, duplicative, unnecessary or unwise research as it is when they are used in studies that hold out real promise of human benefits. We can't justify harming or killing a human being (my Aunt Bea, for example) just for these sorts of reason. Neither can we do so even in the case of so lowly a creature as a laboratory rat. It is not just refinement or reduction that is called for, not just larger, cleaner cages, not just more generous use of anaesthetic or the elimination of multiple surgery, not just tidying up the system. It is complete replacement. The best we can do when it comes to using animals in science is—not to use them. That is where our duty lies, according to the rights view.

As for commercial animal agriculture, the rights view takes a similar abolitionist position. The fundamental moral wrong here is not that animals are kept in stressful close confinement or in isolation, or that their pain and suffering, their needs and preferences are ignored or discounted. All these *are* wrong, of course, but they are not the fundamental wrong. They are symptoms and effects of the deeper, systematic wrong that allows these animals to be viewed and treated as lacking independent value, as resources for us—as, indeed, a renewable resource. Giving farm animals more space, more natural environments, more companions does not right the fundamental wrong, any more than giving lab animals more anaesthesia or bigger, cleaner cages would right the fundamental wrong in their case. Nothing less than the total dissolution of commercial animal agriculture will do this, just as, for similar reasons I won't develop at length here, morality requires nothing less than the total elimination of hunting and trapping for commercial and sporting ends. The rights view's implications, then, as I have said, are clear and uncompromising.

My last two points are about philosophy, my profession. It is, most obviously, no substitute for political action. The words I have written here and in other places by themselves don't change a thing. It is what we do with the thoughts that the words express—our acts, our deeds—that changes things. All that philosophy can do, and all I have attempted, is to offer a vision of what our deeds should aim at. And the why. But not the how.

Finally, I am reminded of my thoughtful critic, the one I mentioned earlier, who chastised me for being too cerebral. Well, cerebral I have been: indirect duty views, utilitarianism, contractarianism—hardly the stuff deep passions are made of. I am also reminded, however, of the image another friend once set before me—the image of the ballerina as expressive of disciplined passion. Long hours of sweat and toil, of loneliness and practice, of doubt and fatigue: those are the discipline of her craft. But the passion is there too, the fierce drive to excel, to speak through her body, to do it right, to pierce our minds. That is the image of philosophy I would leave with you, not "too cerebral" but *disciplined passion*. Of the discipline enough has been seen. As for the passion: there are times, and these not infrequent, when tears come to my eyes when I see, or read, or hear of the wretched plight of animals in the hands of humans. Their pain, their suffering, their loneliness, their innocence, their death. Anger. Rage. Pity. Sorrow. Disgust. The whole creation groans under the weight of the evil we humans visit upon these mute, powerless creatures. It is our hearts, not just our heads, that call for an end to it all, that demand of us that we overcome, for them, the habits and forces behind their systematic oppression. All great movements, it is written, go through three stages: ridicule, discussion, adoption. It is the realization of this third stage, adoption, that requires both our passion and our discipline, our hearts and our heads. The fate of animals is in our hands. God grant we are equal to the task.

QUESTIONS FOR ANALYSIS

1. What is the difference between direct and indirect duties? Why does Regan reject the view that we can have only indirect duties to nonhuman animals?
2. On what grounds does Regan reject contractarian views of moral obligations?
3. What is the cruelty–kindness view of morality? Why does Regan find it inadequate?
4. What does Regan find appealing about utilitarian thinking? What does he find objectionable about it?
5. What does Regan mean by inherent value? What traits must a creature possess to have it?
6. What objections to the view that some animals have inherent value does Regan consider? How does he rebut them?
7. What practical differences can you see between Regan's view and Singer's?

The Ethics of Respect for Nature

PAUL W. TAYLOR

The following essay by Paul W. Taylor, professor *emeritus* of philosophy, Brooklyn College, presents an alternative theory of environmental ethics to Aldo Leopold's land ethic. Though nonanthropocentric and sensitive to ecological issues, it is individualistic rather than holistic. According to Taylor, the principal moral concern of environmental ethics is individual organisms, not the biotic community. Ecological relationships provide us with important knowledge that help us in our dealings with individual organisms, he says, but they do not provide us with moral norms.

In developing his view of respect for nature, Taylor emphasizes that the respect he means is an ultimate attitude, one that is not derived from some other moral norm but is fundamental, like Kantian respect for persons. We should adopt that attitude, he says, because of a recognition that all living things, not just humans, have inherent worth.

I. HUMAN-CENTERED AND LIFE-CENTERED SYSTEMS OF ENVIRONMENTAL ETHICS

In this paper I show how the taking of a certain ultimate moral attitude toward nature, which I call "respect for nature," has a central place in the foundations of a life-centered system of environmental ethics. . . .

In designating the theory to be set forth as life-centered, I intend to contrast it with all anthropocentric views. According to the latter, human actions affecting the natural environment and its nonhuman inhabitants are right (or wrong) by either of two criteria: they have consequences which are favorable (or unfavorable) to human well-being, or they are consistent (or inconsistent) with the system of norms that

From *Environmental Ethics*, vol. 3 (Fall 1981), pp. 197–218. Reprinted by permission of the author.

protect and implement human rights. From this human-centered standpoint it is to humans and only to humans that all duties are ultimately owed. We may have responsibilities *with regard to* the natural ecosystems and biotic communities of our planet, but these responsibilities are in every case based on the contingent fact that our treatment of those ecosystems and communities of life can further the realization of human values and/or human rights. We have no obligation to promote or protect the good of nonhuman living things, independently of this contingent fact.

A life-centered system of environmental ethics is opposed to human-centered ones precisely on this point. From the perspective of a life-centered theory, we have prima facie moral obligations that are owed to wild plants and animals themselves as members of the Earth's biotic community. We are morally bound (other things being equal) to protect or promote their good for *their* sake. Our duties to respect the integrity of natural ecosystems, to preserve endangered species, and to avoid environmental pollution stem from the fact that these are ways in which we can help make it possible for wild species populations to achieve and maintain a healthy existence in a natural state. Such obligations are due those living things out of recognition of their inherent worth. They are entirely additional to and independent of the obligations we owe to our fellow humans. Although many of the actions that fulfill one set of obligations will also fulfill the other, two different grounds of obligation are involved. Their well-being, as well as human well-being, is something to be realized *as an end in itself.*

If we were to accept a life-centered theory of environmental ethics, a profound reordering of our moral universe would take place. We would begin to look at the whole of the Earth's biosphere in a new light. Our duties with respect to the "world" of nature would be seen as making prima facie claims upon us to be balanced against our duties with respect to the "world" of human civilization. We could no longer simply take the human point of view and consider the effects of our actions exclusively from the perspective of our own good.

II. THE GOOD OF A BEING AND THE CONCEPT OF INHERENT WORTH

. . . Two concepts are essential to the taking of a moral attitude of the sort in question. A being which does not "have" these concepts, that is, which is unable to grasp their meaning and conditions of applicability, cannot be said to have the attitude as part of its moral outlook. These concepts are, first, that of the good (well-being, welfare) of a living thing, and second, the idea of an entity possessing inherent worth. I examine each concept in turn.

1. Every organism, species population, and community of life has a good of its own which moral agents can intentionally further or damage by their actions. To say that an entity has a good of its own is simply to say that, without reference to any other entity, it can be benefited or harmed. One can act in its overall interest or contrary to its overall interest, and environmental conditions can be good for it (advantageous to it) or bad for it (disadvantageous to it). What is good for an entity is what "does it good" in the sense of enhancing or preserving its life and well-being. What is bad for an entity is something that is detrimental to its life and well-being.[1]

We can think of the good of an individual nonhuman organism as consisting in the full development of its biological powers. Its good is realized to the extent that it is strong and healthy. It possesses whatever capacities it needs for successfully coping with its environment and so preserving its existence throughout the various stages of the normal life cycle of its species. The good of a population or community of such individuals consists in the population or community maintaining itself from generation to generation as a coherent system of genetically and ecologically related organisms whose average good is at an optimum level for the given environment. (Here *average good* means that the degree of realization of the good of *individual organisms* in the population or community is, on average, greater than would be the case under any other ecologically functioning order of interrelations among those species populations in the given ecosystem.)

The idea of a being having a good of its own, as I understand it, does not entail that the being must have interests or take an interest in what affects its life for better or for worse. We can act in a being's interest or contrary to its interest without its being interested in what we are doing to it in the sense of wanting or not wanting us to do it. It may, indeed, be wholly unaware that favorable and unfavorable events are taking place in its life. I take it that trees, for example, have no knowledge or desires or feelings. Yet it is undoubtedly the case that trees can be harmed or benefited by our actions. We can crush their roots by running a bulldozer too close to them. We can see to it that they get adequate nourishment and moisture by fertilizing and watering the soil around them. Thus we can help or hinder them in the realization of their good. It is the good of trees themselves that is thereby affected. We can similarly act so as to further the good of an entire tree population of a certain species (say, all the redwood trees in a California valley) or the good of a whole community of plant life in a given wilderness area, just as we can do harm to such a population or community. . . .

2. The second concept essential to the moral attitude of respect for nature is the idea of inherent worth. We take that attitude toward wild living things (individuals, species populations, or whole biotic communities) when and only when we regard them as entities possessing inherent worth. . . .

What does it mean to regard an entity that has a good of its own as possessing inherent worth? Two general principles are involved: the principle of moral consideration and the principle of intrinsic value.

According to the principle of moral consideration, wild living things are deserving of the concern and consideration of all moral agents simply in virtue of their being members of the Earth's community of life. From the moral point of view their good must be taken into account whenever it is affected for better or worse by the conduct of rational agents. This holds no matter what species the creature belongs to. The good of each is to be accorded some value and so acknowledged as having some weight in the deliberations of all rational agents. Of course, it may be necessary for such agents to act in ways contrary to the good of this or that particular organism or group of organisms in order to further the good of others, including the good of humans. But the principle of moral consideration prescribes that, with respect to each being an entity having its own good, every individual is deserving of consideration.

The principle of intrinsic value states that, regardless of what kind of entity it is in other respects, if it is a member of the Earth's community of life, the realization of its good is something *intrinsically* valuable. This means that its good is prima facie worthy of being preserved or promoted as an end in itself and for the sake of the entity whose good it is. Insofar as we regard any organism, species population, or life community as an entity having inherent worth, we believe that it must never be treated as if it were a mere object or thing whose entire value lies in being instrumental to the good of some other entity. The well-being of each is judged to have value in and of itself.

Combining these two principles, we can now define what it means for a living thing or group of living things to possess inherent worth. To say that it possesses inherent worth is to say that its good is deserving of the concern and consideration of all moral agents, and that the realization of its good has intrinsic value, to be pursued as an end in itself and for the sake of the entity whose good it is. . . .

III. THE ATTITUDE OF RESPECT FOR NATURE

Why should moral agents regard wild living things in the natural world as possessing inherent worth? To answer this question we must first take into account the fact that, when rational, autonomous agents subscribe to the principles of moral consideration and intrinsic value and so conceive of wild living things as having that kind of worth, such agents are *adopting a certain ultimate moral attitude toward the natural world*. This is the attitude I call "respect for nature." It parallels the attitude of respect for persons in human ethics. When we adopt the attitude of respect for persons as the proper (fitting, appropriate) attitude to take toward all persons as persons, we consider the fulfillment of the basic interests of each individual to have intrinsic value. We thereby make a moral commitment to live a certain kind of life in relation to other persons. We place ourselves under the direction of a system of standards and rules that we consider validly binding on all moral agents as such.[2]

Similarly, when we adopt the attitude of respect for nature as an ultimate moral attitude we make a commitment to live by certain normative principles. These principles constitute the rules of conduct and standards of character that are to govern our treatment of the natural world. This is, first, an *ultimate* commitment because it is not derived from any higher norm. The attitude of respect for nature is not grounded on some other, more general, or more fundamental attitude. It sets the total framework for our responsibilities toward the natural world. It can be justified, as I show below, but its justification cannot consist in referring to a more general attitude or a more basic normative principle.

Second, the commitment is a *moral* one because it is understood to be a disinterested matter of principle. It is this feature that distinguishes the attitude of respect for nature from the set of feelings and dispositions that comprise the love of nature. The latter stems from one's personal interest in and response to the natural world. Like the affectionate feelings we have toward certain individual human beings, one's love of nature is nothing more than the particular way one feels about the natural environment and its wild inhabitants. And just as our love for an individual person differs from our respect for all persons as such (whether we happen to love them or not), so love of nature differs from respect for nature. Respect for nature is an attitude we believe all moral agents ought to have simply as moral agents, regardless of whether or not they also love nature. Indeed, we have not truly taken the attitude of respect for nature ourselves unless we believe this. . . .

Although the attitude of respect for nature is in this sense a disinterested and universalizable attitude, anyone who does adopt it has certain steady, more or less permanent dispositions. These dispositions, which are themselves to be considered disinterested and universalizable, comprise three interlocking sets: dispositions to seek certain ends, dispositions to carry on one's practical reasoning and deliberation in a certain way, and dispositions to have certain feelings. We may accordingly analyze the attitude of respect for nature into the following components. (a) The disposition to aim at, and to take steps to bring about, as final and disinterested ends, the promoting and protecting of the good of organisms, species populations, and life communities in natural ecosystems. (These ends are "final" in not being pursued as means to further ends. They are "disinterested" in being independent of the self-interest of the agent.) (b) The disposition to consider actions that tend to realize those ends to be prima facie obligatory *because* they have that tendency. (c) The disposition to experience positive and negative feelings toward states of affairs in the world *because* they are favorable or unfavorable to the good of organisms, species populations, and life communities in natural ecosystems.

IV. THE JUSTIFIABILITY OF THE ATTITUDE OF RESPECT FOR NATURE

I return to the question posed earlier, which has not yet been answered: why *should* moral agents regard wild living things as possessing inherent worth? . . .

We must keep in mind that inherent worth is not some mysterious sort of objective property belonging to living things that can be discovered by empirical observation or scientific investigation. To ascribe inherent worth to an entity is not to describe it by citing some feature discernible by sense perception or inferable by inductive reasoning. Nor is there a logically necessary connection between the concept of a being having a good of its own and the concept of inherent worth. We do not contradict ourselves by asserting that an entity that has a good of its own lacks inherent worth. In order to show that such an entity "has" inherent worth we must give good reasons for ascribing that kind of value to it (placing that kind of value upon it, conceiving of it to be valuable in that way). Although it is humans (persons, valuers) who must do the valuing, for the ethics of respect for nature, the value so ascribed is not a human value. That is to say, it is not a value derived from considerations regarding human well-being or human rights. It is a value that is ascribed to nonhuman animals and plants themselves, independently of their relationship to what humans judge to be conducive to their own good.

Whatever reasons, then, justify our taking the attitude of respect for nature as defined above are also reasons that show why we *should* regard the living things of the natural world as possessing inherent worth. We saw earlier that, since the attitude is an ultimate one, it cannot be derived from a more fundamental attitude nor shown to be a special case of a more general one. On what sort of grounds, then, can it be established?

The attitude we take toward living things in the natural world depends on the way we look at them, on what kind of beings we conceive them to be, and on how we understand the relations we bear to them. Underlying and supporting our attitude is a certain *belief system* that constitutes a particular world view or outlook on nature and the place of human life in it. To give good reasons for adopting the attitude of respect for nature, then, we must first articulate the belief system which underlies and supports that attitude. If it appears that the belief system is internally coherent and well-ordered, and if, as far as we can now tell, it is consistent with all known scientific truths relevant to our knowledge of the object of the attitude (which in this case includes the whole set of the Earth's natural ecosystems and their communities of life), then there remains the task of indicating why scientifically informed and rational thinkers with a developed capacity of reality awareness can find it acceptable as a way of conceiving of the natural world and our place in it. To the extent we can do this we provide at least a reasonable argument for accepting the belief system and the ultimate moral attitude it supports.

I do not hold that such a belief system can be *proven* to be true, either inductively or deductively. As we shall see, not all of its components can be stated in the form of empirically verifiable propositions. Nor is its internal order governed by purely logical relationships. But the system as a whole, I contend, constitutes a coherent, unified, and rationally acceptable "picture" or "map" of a total world. By examining each of its main components and seeing how they fit together, we obtain a scientifically informed and well-ordered conception of nature and the place of humans in it.

This belief system underlying the attitude of respect for nature I call (for want of a better name) "the biocentric outlook on nature." . . . It might best be described as a philosophical world view, to distinguish it from a scientific theory or explanatory system. However, one of its major tenets is the great lesson we have learned from the science of ecology: the interdependence of all living things in an organically unified order whose balance and stability are necessary conditions for the realization of the good of its constituent biotic communities.

Before turning to an account of the main components of the biocentric outlook, it is convenient here to set forth the overall structure of my theory of environmental ethics as it has now emerged. The ethics of respect for nature is made up of three basic elements: a belief system, an ultimate moral attitude, and a set of rules of duty and standards of character. These elements are connected with each other in the following manner. The belief system provides a certain outlook on nature which supports and makes intelligible an autonomous agent's adopting, as an ultimate moral attitude, the attitude of respect for nature. It supports and makes intelligible the attitude in the sense that, when an autonomous agent understands its moral relations to the natural world in terms of this outlook, it recognizes the attitude of respect to be the only *suitable* or *fitting* attitude to take toward all wild forms of life in the Earth's biosphere. Living things are now viewed as *the appropriate objects of the attitude of respect* and are accordingly regarded as entities possessing inherent worth. One then places intrinsic value on the promotion and protection of their good. As a consequence of this, one makes a moral commitment to abide by a set of rules of duty and to fulfill (as far as one can by one's own efforts) certain standards of good character. Given one's adoption of the attitude of respect, one makes that moral commitment because one considers those rules and standards to be validly binding on all moral agents. They are seen as embodying forms of conduct and character structures in which the attitude of respect for nature is manifested.

This three-part complex which internally orders the ethics of respect for nature is symmetrical with a theory of human ethics grounded on respect for persons. Such a theory includes, first, a conception of oneself and others as persons, that is, as centers of autonomous choice. Second, there is the attitude of respect for persons as persons. When this is adopted as an ultimate moral attitude it involves the disposition to treat every person as having inherent worth or "human dignity." Every human being, just in virtue of her or his humanity, is understood to be worthy of moral consideration, and intrinsic value is placed on the autonomy and well-being of each. This is what Kant meant by conceiving of persons as ends in themselves. Third, there is an ethical system of duties which are acknowledged to be owed by everyone to everyone. These duties are forms of conduct in which public recognition is given to each individual's inherent worth as a person. . . .

V. THE BIOCENTRIC OUTLOOK ON NATURE

The biocentric outlook on nature has four main components. (1) Humans are thought of as members of the Earth's community of life, holding that membership on the same terms as apply to all the nonhuman members. (2) The Earth's natural ecosystems as a totality are seen as a complex web of interconnected elements, with the sound biological functioning of each being dependent on the sound biological functioning of the others. (This is the component referred to above as the great lesson that the science of ecology has taught us.) (3) Each individual organism is conceived of as a teleological center of life, pursuing its own good in its own way. (4) Whether we are concerned with standards of merit or with the concept of inherent worth, the claim that humans by their very nature are superior to other species is a groundless claim and, in the light of elements (1), (2), and (3) above, must be rejected as nothing more than an irrational bias in our own favor.

The conjunction of these four ideas constitutes the biocentric outlook on nature. In the remainder of this paper I give a brief account of the first three components, followed by a more detailed analysis of the fourth. I then conclude by indicating how this outlook provides a way of justifying the attitude of respect for nature.

VI. HUMANS AS MEMBERS OF THE EARTH'S COMMUNITY OF LIFE

We share with other species a common relationship to the Earth. In accepting the biocentric outlook we take the fact of our being an animal species to be a fundamental feature of our existence. We consider it an essential aspect of "the human condition." We do not deny the differences between ourselves and other species, but we keep in the forefront of our consciousness the fact that in relation to our planet's natural ecosystems we are but one species population among many. Thus we acknowledge our origin in the very same evolutionary process that gave rise to all other species and we recognize ourselves to be confronted with similar environmental challenges to those that confront them. The laws of genetics, of natural selection, and of adaptation apply equally to all of us as biological creatures. In this light we consider ourselves as one with them, not set apart from them. We, as well as they, must face certain basic conditions of existence that impose requirements on us for our survival and well-being. Each animal and plant is like us in having a good of its own. Although our human good (what is of true value in human life, including the exercise of individual autonomy in choosing our own particular value systems) is not like the good of a nonhuman animal or plant, it can no more be realized than their good can without the biological necessities for survival and physical health.

When we look at ourselves from the evolutionary point of view, we see that not only are we very recent arrivals on Earth, but that our emergence as a new species on the planet was originally an event of no particular importance to the entire scheme of things. The Earth was teeming with life long before we appeared. Putting the point metaphorically, we are relative newcomers, entering a home that has been the residence of others for hundreds of millions of years, a home that must now be shared by all of us together.

The comparative brevity of human life on Earth may be vividly depicted by imagining the geological time scale in spatial terms. Suppose we start with algae, which have been around for at least 600 million years. (The earliest protozoa actually predated this by several *billion* years.) If the time that algae have been here were represented by the length of a football field (300 feet), then the period during which sharks have been swimming in the world's oceans and spiders have been spinning their webs would occupy three quarters of the length of the field; reptiles would show up at about the center of the field; mammals would cover the last third of the field; hominids (mammals of the family *Hominidae*) the last two feet; and the species *Homo sapiens* the last six inches.

Whether this newcomer is able to survive as long as other species remains to be seen. But there is surely something presumptuous about the way humans look down on the "lower" animals, especially those that have become extinct. We consider the dinosaurs, for example, to be biological failures, though they existed on our planet for 65 million years. One writer has made the point with beautiful simplicity:

> We sometimes speak of the dinosaurs as failures; there will be time enough for that judgment when we have lasted even for one tenth as long. . . .[3]

The possibility of the extinction of the human species, a possibility which starkly confronts us in the contemporary world, makes us aware of another respect in which we should not consider ourselves privileged beings in relation to other species. This is the fact that the well-being of humans is dependent upon the ecological soundness and health of many plant and animal communities, while their soundness and health does not in the least depend upon human well-being. Indeed, from their standpoint the very existence of humans is quite unnecessary. Every last man, woman, and child could disappear from the face of the Earth without any significant detrimental consequence for the good of wild animals and plants. On the contrary, many of them would be greatly benefited. The destruction of their habitats by human "developments" would cease. The poisoning and polluting of their environment would come to an end. The Earth's land, air, and water would no longer be subject to the degradation they are now undergoing as the result of large-scale technology and uncontrolled population growth. Life communities in natural ecosystems would gradually return to their former healthy state. Tropical forests, for example, would again be able to make their full contribution to a life-sustaining atmosphere for the whole planet. The rivers, lakes, and oceans of the world would (perhaps) eventually become clean again. Spilled oil, plastic trash, and even radioactive waste might finally, after many centuries, cease doing their terrible work. Ecosystems would return to their proper balance, suffering only the disruptions of natural events such as volcanic eruptions and glaciation. From these the community of life could recover, as it has so often done in the past. But the ecological disasters now perpetrated on it by humans—disasters from which it might never recover—these it would no longer have to endure.

If, then, the total, final, absolute extermination of our species (by our own hands?) should take place and if we should not carry all the others with us into oblivion, not only would the Earth's community of life continue to exist, but in all probability its well-being would be enhanced. Our presence, in short, is not needed. If we were to take the standpoint of the community and give voice to its true interest, the ending of our six-inch epoch would most likely be greeted with a hearty "Good riddance!"

VII. THE NATURAL WORLD AS AN ORGANIC SYSTEM

To accept the biocentric outlook and regard ourselves and our place in the world from its perspective is to see the whole natural order of the Earth's biosphere as a complex but unified web of interconnected organisms, objects, and events. The ecological relationships between any community of living things and their environment form an organic whole of functionally interdependent parts. Each ecosystem is a small universe itself in which the interactions of its various species populations comprise an intricately woven network of cause–effect relations. Such dynamic but at the same time relatively stable structures as food chains, predator–prey relations, and plant succession in a forest are self-regulating, energy-recycling mechanisms that preserve the equilibrium of the whole.

As far as the well-being of wild animals and plants is concerned, this ecological equilibrium must not be destroyed. The same holds true of the well-being of humans. When one views the realm of nature from the perspective of the biocentric outlook, one never forgets that in the long run the integrity of the entire biosphere of our planet is essential to the realization of the good of its constituent communities of life, both human and nonhuman.

Although the importance of this idea cannot be overemphasized, it is by now so familiar and so widely acknowledged that I shall not further elaborate on it here. However, I do wish to point out that this "holistic" view of the Earth's ecological systems does not itself constitute a moral norm. It is a factual aspect of biological reality, to be understood as a set of causal connections in ordinary empirical terms. Its significance for humans is the same as its significance for nonhumans, namely, in setting basic conditions for the realization of the good of living things. Its ethical implications for our treatment of the natural environment lie entirely in the fact that our *knowledge* of these causal connections is an essential *means* to fulfilling the aims we set for ourselves in adopting the attitude of respect for nature. In addition, its theoretical implications for the ethics of respect for nature lie in the fact that it (along with the other elements of the biocentric outlook) makes the adopting of that attitude a rational and intelligible thing to do.

VIII. INDIVIDUAL ORGANISMS AS TELEOLOGICAL CENTERS OF LIFE

As our knowledge of living things increases, as we come to a deeper understanding of their life cycles, their interactions with other organisms, and the manifold ways in which they adjust to the environment, we become more fully aware of how each of them is carrying out its biological functions according to the laws of its species-specific nature. But besides this, our increasing knowledge and understanding also develop in us a sharpened awareness of the uniqueness of each individual organism. Scientists who have made careful studies of particular plants and animals, whether in the field or in laboratories, have often acquired a knowledge of their subjects as identifiable individuals. Close observation over extended periods of time has led them to an appreciation of the unique "personalities" of their subjects. Sometimes a scientist may come to take a special interest in a particular animal or plant, all the while remaining strictly objective in the gathering and recording of data. Nonscientists may likewise experience this development of interest when, as amateur naturalists, they make accurate observations over sustained periods of close acquaintance with an individual organism. As one becomes more and more familiar with the organism and its behavior, one becomes fully sensitive to the particular way it is living out its life cycle. One may become fascinated by it and even experience some involvement with its good and bad fortunes (that is, with the occurrence of environmental conditions favorable or unfavorable to the realization of its good). The organism comes to mean something to one as a unique, irreplaceable individual. The final culmination of this process is the achievement of a genuine understanding of its point of view and, with that understanding, an ability to "take" that point of view. *Conceiving of it as a center of life, one is able to look at the world from its perspective.*

This development from objective knowledge to the recognition of individuality, and from the recognition of individuality to full awareness of an organism's standpoint, is a process of heightening our consciousness of what it means to be an individual living thing. We grasp the particularity of the organism as a teleological center of life, striving to preserve itself and to realize its own good in its own unique way.

It is to be noted that we need not be falsely anthropomorphizing when we conceive of individual plants and animals in this manner. Understanding them as teleological centers of life does not necessitate "reading into" them human characteristics. We need not, for example, consider them to have consciousness. Some of them may be aware of the world around them and others may not. Nor need we deny that different kinds and levels of awareness are exemplified when consciousness in some form is present. But conscious or not, all are equally teleological centers of life in the sense that each is a unified system of goal-oriented activities directed toward their preservation and well-being.

When considered from an ethical point of view, a teleological center of life is an entity whose "world" can be viewed from the perspective of *its* life. In looking at the world from that perspective we recognize objects and events occurring in its life as being beneficent, maleficent, or indifferent. The first are occurrences which increase its powers to preserve its existence and realize its good. The second decrease or destroy those powers. The third have neither of these effects on the entity. With regard to our human role as moral agents, we can conceive of a teleological center of life as a being whose standpoint we can take in making judgments about what events in the world are good or evil, desirable or undesirable. In making those judgments it is what promotes or protects the being's own good, not what benefits moral agents themselves, that sets the standard of evaluation. Such judgments can be made about anything that happens to the entity which is favorable or unfavorable in relation to its good. As was pointed out earlier, the entity itself need not have any (conscious) interest in what is happening to it for such judgments to be meaningful and true.

It is precisely judgments of this sort that we are disposed to make when we take the attitude of respect for nature. In adopting that attitude those judgments are given weight as reasons for action in our practical deliberation. They become morally relevant facts in the guidance of our conduct.

IX. THE DENIAL OF HUMAN SUPERIORITY

This fourth component of the biocentric outlook on nature is the single most important idea in establishing the justifiability of the attitude of respect for nature. Its central role is due to the special relationship it bears to the first three components of the outlook. This relationship will be brought out after the concept of human superiority is examined and analyzed.[4]

In what sense are humans alleged to be superior to other animals? We are different from them in having certain capacities that they lack. But why should these capacities be a mark of superiority? From what point of view are they judged to be signs of superiority and what sense of superiority is meant? After all, various nonhuman species have capacities that humans lack. There is the speed of a cheetah, the vision of an eagle, the agility of a monkey. Why should not these be taken as signs of *their* superiority over humans?

One answer that comes immediately to mind is that these capacities are not as *valuable* as the human capacities that are claimed to make us superior. Such uniquely human characteristics as rational thought, aesthetic creativity, autonomy and self-determination, and moral freedom, it might be held, have a higher value than the capacities found in other species. Yet we must ask: valuable to whom, and on what grounds?

The human characteristics mentioned are all valuable to humans. They are essential to the preservation and enrichment of our civilization and culture. Clearly it is from the human standpoint that they are being judged to be desirable and good. It is not difficult here to recognize a begging of the question. Humans are claiming human superiority from a strictly human point of view, that is, from a point of view in which the good of humans is taken as the standard of judgment. All we need to do is to look at the capacities of nonhuman animals (or plants, for that matter) from the standpoint of *their* good to find a contrary judgment of superiority. The speed of the cheetah, for example, is a sign of its superiority to humans when considered from the standpoint of the good of its species. If it were as slow a runner as a human, it would not be able to survive. And so for all the other abilities of nonhumans which further their good but which are lacking in humans. In each case the claim to human superiority would be rejected from a nonhuman standpoint.

. . . There is, however, another way of understanding the idea of human superiority. According to this interpretation, humans are superior to nonhumans not as regards their merits but as regards their inherent worth. Thus the claim of human superiority is to be understood as asserting that all humans, simply in virtue of their humanity, have *a greater inherent worth* than other living things.

The inherent worth of an entity does not depend on its merits.[5] To consider something as possessing inherent worth, we have seen, is to place intrinsic value on the realization of its good. This is done regardless of whatever particular merits it might have or might lack, as judged by a set of grading or ranking standards. In human affairs, we are all familiar with the principle that one's worth as a person does not vary with one's merits or lack of merits. The same can hold true of animals and plants. To regard such entities as possessing inherent worth entails disregarding their merits and deficiencies, whether they are being judged from a human standpoint or from the standpoint of their own species.

The idea of one entity having more merit than another, and so being superior to it in merit, makes perfectly good sense. Merit is a grading or ranking concept, and judgments of comparative merit are based on the different degrees to which things satisfy a given standard. But what can it mean to talk about one thing being superior to another in inherent worth? In order to get at what is being asserted in such a claim it is helpful first to look at the social origin of the concept of degrees of inherent worth.

The idea that humans can possess different degrees of inherent worth originated in societies having rigid class structures. Before the rise of modern democracies with their egalitarian outlook, one's membership in a hereditary class determined one's social status. People in the upper classes were looked up to, while those in the lower classes were looked down upon. In such a society, one's social superiors and social inferiors were clearly defined and easily recognized.

Two aspects of these class-structured societies are especially relevant to the idea of degrees of inherent worth. First, those born into the upper classes were deemed more worthy of respect than those born into the lower orders. Second, the superior worth of upper class people had nothing to do with their merits nor did the inferior worth of those in the lower classes rest on their lack of merits. One's superiority or inferiority entirely derived from a social position one was born into. The modern concept of a meritocracy simply did not apply. One could not advance into a higher class by any sort of moral or nonmoral achievement. Similarly, an aristocrat held his title and all the privileges that went with it just because he was the eldest son of a titled nobleman. Unlike the bestowing of knighthood in contemporary Great Britain, one did not earn membership in the nobility by meritorious conduct.

We who live in modern democracies no longer believe in such hereditary social distinctions.

Indeed, we would wholeheartedly condemn them on moral grounds as being fundamentally unjust. We have come to think of class systems as a paradigm of social injustice, it being a central principle of the democratic way of life that among humans there are no superiors and no inferiors. . . . That idea is incompatible with our notion of human equality based on the doctrine that all humans, simply in virtue of their humanity, have the same inherent worth. (The belief in universal human rights is one form that this egalitarianism takes.)

The vast majority of people in modern democracies, however, do not maintain an egalitarian outlook when it comes to comparing human beings with other living things. Most people consider our own species to be superior to all other species and this superiority is understood to be a matter of inherent worth, not merit. There may exist thoroughly vicious and depraved humans who lack all merit. Yet because they are human they are thought to belong to a higher class of entities than any plant or animal. That one is born into the species *Homo sapiens* entitles one to have lordship over those who are one's inferiors, namely, those born into other species. The parallel with hereditary social classes is very close. Implicit in this view is a hierarchical conception of nature according to which an organism has a position of superiority or inferiority in the Earth's community of life simply on the basis of its genetic background. The "lower" orders of life are looked down upon and it is considered perfectly proper that they serve the interests of those belonging to the highest order, namely humans. The intrinsic value we place on the well-being of our fellow humans reflects our recognition of their rightful position as our equals. No such intrinsic value is to be placed on the good of other animals, unless we choose to do so out of fondness or affection for them. But their well-being imposes no moral requirement on us. In this respect there is an absolute difference in moral status between ourselves and them.

This is the structure of concepts and beliefs that people are committed to insofar as they regard humans to be superior in inherent worth to all other species. . . . This structure of concepts and beliefs is completely groundless. If we accept the first three components of the biocentric outlook and from that perspective look at the major philosophical traditions which have supported that structure, we find it to be at bottom nothing more than the expression of an irrational bias in our own favor.

. . . That [it] is nothing more than a deep-seated prejudice is brought home to us when we look at our relation to other species in the light of the first three elements of the biocentric outlook. Those elements taken conjointly give us a certain overall view of the natural world and of the place of humans in it. When we take this view we come to understand other living things, their environmental conditions, and their ecological relationships in such a way as to awake in us a deep sense of our kinship with them as fellow members of the Earth's community of life. Humans and nonhumans alike are viewed together as integral parts of one unified whole in which all living things are functionally interrelated. Finally, when our awareness focuses on the individual lives of plants and animals, each is seen to share with us the characteristic of being a teleological center of life striving to realize its own good in its own unique way.

. . . Rejecting the notion of human superiority entails its positive counterpart: the doctrine of species impartiality. One who accepts that doctrine regards all living things as possessing inherent worth—the *same* inherent worth, since no one species has been shown to be either "higher" or "lower" than any other. Now we saw earlier that, insofar as one thinks of a living thing as possessing inherent worth, one considers it to be the appropriate object of the attitude of respect and believes that attitude to be the only fitting or suitable one for all moral agents to take toward it. . . .

X. MORAL RIGHTS AND THE MATTER OF COMPETING CLAIMS

I have not asserted anywhere in the foregoing account that animals or plants have moral rights. This omission was deliberate. I do not think that the reference class of the concept, bearer of moral rights, should be extended to include nonhuman living things. My reasons for taking this position, however, go beyond the scope of this paper. I believe I have been able to accomplish many of the same ends which those who ascribe rights to animals or plants wish to accomplish. There is no reason, moreover, why plants and animals, including whole species populations and life communities, cannot be accorded *legal* rights under my theory. To grant them legal protection could be interpreted as giving them legal entitlement to be protected, and this, in fact, would be a means by which a society that subscribed to the ethics of respect for nature could give public recognition to their inherent worth.

There remains the problem of competing claims, even when wild plants and animals are not thought of as bearers of moral rights. If we accept the biocentric outlook and accordingly adopt the attitude of respect for nature as our ultimate moral attitude, how do we resolve conflicts that arise from our respect for persons in the domain of human ethics and our respect for nature in the domain of environmental ethics? This is a question that cannot adequately be dealt with here. My main purpose in this paper has been to try to establish a base point from which we can start working toward a solution to the problem. I have shown why we cannot just begin with an initial presumption in favor of the interests of our own species. It is after all within our power as moral beings to place limits on human population and technology with the deliberate intention of sharing the Earth's bounty with other species. That such sharing is an ideal difficult to realize even in an approximate way does not take away its claim to our deepest moral commitment.

NOTES

1. The conceptual links between an entity *having* a good, something being good *for* it, and events doing good to it are examined by G. H. Von Wright in *The Varieties of Goodness* (New York: Humanities Press, 1963), chaps. 3 and 5.
2. I have analyzed the nature of this commitment of human ethics in "On Taking the Moral Point of View," *Midwest Studies in Philosophy*, vol. 3, *Studies in Ethical Theory* (1978), pp. 35–61.
3. Stephen R. L. Clark, *The Moral Status of Animals* (Oxford: Clarendon Press, 1977), p. 112.
4. My criticisms of the dogma of human superiority gain independent support from a carefully reasoned essay by R. and V. Routley showing the many logical weaknesses in arguments for human-centered theories of environmental ethics. R. and V. Routley, "Against the Inevitability of Human Chauvinism," in K. E. Goodpaster and K. M. Sayre, eds., *Ethics and Problems of the 21st Century* (Notre Dame: University of Notre Dame Press, 1979), pp. 36–59.
5. For this way of distinguishing between merit and inherent worth, I am indebted to Gregory Vlastos, "Justice and Equality," in R. Brandt, ed., *Social Justice* (Englewood Cliffs, N.J.: Prentice-Hall, 1962), pp. 31–72.

QUESTIONS FOR ANALYSIS

1. According to Taylor, every "organism, species population, and community of life has a good of its own." What does he mean by that claim? What importance does it have for environmental ethics?
2. Taylor says that inherent worth is not an objective property. He also says that the attitude of ultimate respect for nature is supported by a belief system that cannot be proven true. Why, then, should we adopt that attitude?
3. In discussing individual organisms as teleological centers of life, Taylor says that we can look at the world from a plant's point of view without engaging in "false anthropomorphizing." What does he mean by that? How is it possible?
4. Much of Taylor's argument against human superiority rests on the claim that inherent worth does not admit of degrees. Do you agree? Why or why not?
5. Though Taylor does not advocate giving nonhuman organisms moral rights, he does advocate giving them *legal* rights. What might his justification be for denying one but granting the other?
6. Is Taylor's individualistic view preferable to Leopold's holistic view?

People or Penguins

WILLIAM F. BAXTER

The following selection by William F. Baxter (1929–1998) presents an anthropocentric view of environmental issues. In contrast to Taylor, Baxter argues that Kantian respect should not be extended to nonhuman organisms. In contrast to Leopold, he argues that an economic approach to environmental issues is the correct one. Thus, he favors a cost-benefit analysis of environmental impact, where the economic costs and benefits involved are applicable to humans only. Baxter was a professor of law at Stanford University.

I start with the modest proposition that, in dealing with pollution, or indeed with any problem, it is helpful to know what one is attempting to accomplish. Agreement on how and whether to pursue a particular objective, such as pollution control, is not possible unless some more general objective has been identified and stated with reasonable precision. We talk loosely of having clean air and clean water, of preserving our wilderness areas, and so forth. But none of these is a sufficiently general objective: each is more accurately viewed as a means rather than as an end.

With regard to clean air, for example, one may ask, "how clean?" and "what does clean mean?" It is even reasonable to ask, "why have clean air?" Each of these questions is an implicit demand that a more general community goal be stated—a goal sufficiently general in its scope and enjoying sufficiently general assent among the community of actors that such "why" questions no longer seem admissible with respect to that goal.

If, for example, one states as a goal the proposition that "every person should be free to do whatever he wishes in contexts where his actions do not interfere with the interests of other human beings," the speaker is unlikely to be met with a response of "why." The goal may be criticized as uncertain in its implications or difficult to implement, but it is so basic a tenet of our civilization—it reflects a cultural value so broadly shared, at least in the abstract—that the question "why" is seen as impertinent or imponderable or both.

I do not mean to suggest that everyone would agree with the "spheres of freedom" objective just stated. Still less do I mean to suggest that a society could subscribe to four or five such general objectives that would be adequate in their coverage to serve as testing criteria by which all other disagreements might be measured. One difficulty in the attempt to construct such a list is that each new goal added will conflict, in certain applications, with each prior goal listed; and thus each goal serves as a limited qualification on prior goals.

Without any expectation of obtaining unanimous consent to them, let me set forth four goals that I generally use as ultimate testing criteria in attempting to frame solutions to problems of human organization. My position regarding pollution stems from these four criteria. If the criteria appeal to you and any part of what appears hereafter does not, our disagreement will have a helpful focus: which of us is correct, analytically, in supposing that his position on pollution would better serve these general goals. If the criteria do not seem acceptable to you, then it is to be expected that our more particular judgments will differ, and the task will then be yours to identify the basic set of criteria upon which your particular judgments rest.

My criteria are as follows:

1. The spheres of freedom criterion stated above.
2. Waste is a bad thing. The dominant feature of human existence is scarcity—our available resources, our aggregate labors, and our skill in employing both have always been, and will continue for some time to be, inadequate to yield to every man all the tangible and intangible satisfactions he would like to have. Hence, none of those resources, or labors, or skills, should be wasted—that is, employed so as to yield less than they might yield in human satisfactions.
3. Every human being should be regarded as an end rather than as a means to be used for the betterment of another. Each should be afforded dignity and regarded as having an absolute claim to an evenhanded application of such rules as the community may adopt for its governance.
4. Both the incentive and the opportunity to improve his share of satisfactions should be preserved to every individual. Preservation of incentive is dictated by the "no-waste" criterion and enjoins against the continuous, totally egalitarian redistribution of satisfactions, or wealth; but subject to that constraint, everyone should receive, by continuous redistribution if necessary, some minimal share of aggregate wealth so as to avoid a level of privation from which the opportunity to improve his situation becomes illusory.

The relationship of these highly general goals to the more specific environmental issues at hand may not be readily apparent, and I am not yet ready to demonstrate their pervasive implications. But let me give one indication of their implications. Recently scientists have informed us that use of DDT in food production is causing damage to the penguin population. For the present purposes let us accept that assertion as an indisputable scientific fact. The scientific fact is often asserted as if the correct implication—that we must stop agricultural use of DDT—followed from the mere statement of the fact of penguin damage. But plainly it does not follow if my criteria are employed.

My criteria are oriented to people, not penguins. Damage to penguins, or sugar pines, or geological marvels is, without more, simply irrelevant. One must go further, by my criteria, and say: Penguins are important because people enjoy seeing them walk about rocks; and furthermore, the well-being of people would be less impaired by halting use of DDT than by giving up penguins. In short, my observations about environmental problems will be people-oriented, as are my criteria. I have no interest in preserving penguins for their own sake.

It may be said by way of objection to this position, that it is very selfish of people to act as if each person represented one unit of importance and nothing else was of any importance. It is undeniably selfish. Nevertheless I think it is the only tenable starting place for analysis for several reasons. First, no other position corresponds to the way most people really think and act—i.e., corresponds to reality.

Second, this attitude does not portend any massive destruction of nonhuman flora and fauna, for people depend on them in many obvious ways, and they will be preserved because and to the degree that humans do depend on them.

Third, what is good for humans is, in many respects, good for penguins and pine trees—clean air for example. So that humans are, in these respects, surrogates for plant and animal life.

Fourth, I do not know how we could administer any other system. Our decisions are either private or collective. Insofar as Mr. Jones is free to act privately, he may give such preferences as he wishes to other forms of life: he may feed birds in winter and do with less himself, and he may even decline to resist an advancing polar bear on the ground that the bear's appetite is more important than those portions of himself that the bear may choose to eat. In short my basic premise does not rule out private altruism to competing life-forms. It does rule out, however, Mr. Jones' inclination to feed Mr. Smith to the bear, however hungry the bear, however despicable Mr. Smith.

Insofar as we act collectively, on the other hand, only humans can be afforded an opportunity to participate in the collective decisions. Penguins cannot vote now and are unlikely subjects for the franchise—pine trees more unlikely still. Again each individual is free to cast his vote so as to benefit sugar pines if that is his inclination. But many of the more extreme assertions that one hears from some conservationists amount to tacit assertions that they are specially appointed representatives of sugar pines, and hence that their preferences should be weighted more heavily than the preferences of other humans who do not enjoy equal rapport with "nature." The simplistic assertion that agricultural use of DDT must stop at once because it is harmful to penguins is of that type.

Fifth, if polar bears or pine trees or penguins, like men, are to be regarded as ends rather than means, if they are to count in our calculus of social organization, someone must tell me how much each one counts, and someone must tell me how these life-forms are to be permitted to express their preferences, for I do not know either answer. If the answer is that certain people are to hold their proxies, then I want to know how those proxy-holders are to be selected: self-appointment does not seem workable to me.

Sixth, and by way of summary of all the foregoing, let me point out that the set of environmental issues under discussion—although they raise very complex technical questions of how to achieve any objective—ultimately raise a normative question: what *ought* we to do. Questions of *ought* are unique to the human mind and world—they are meaningless as applied to a nonhuman situation.

I reject the proposition that we *ought* to respect the "balance of nature" or to "preserve the environment" unless the reason for doing so, express or implied, is the benefit of man.

I reject the idea that there is a "right" or "morally correct" state of nature to which we should return. The word "nature" has no normative connotation. Was it "right" or "wrong" for the earth's crust to heave in contortion and create mountains and seas? Was it "right" for the first amphibian to crawl up out of the primordial ooze? Was it "wrong" for plants to reproduce themselves and alter the atmospheric composition in favor of oxygen? For animals to alter the atmosphere in favor of carbon dioxide both by breathing oxygen and eating plants? No answers can be given to these questions because they are meaningless questions.

All this may seem obvious to the point of being tedious, but much of the present controversy over environment and pollution rests on tacit normative assumptions about just such nonnormative phenomena: that it is "wrong" to impair penguins with DDT, but not to slaughter cattle for prime rib roasts. That it is wrong to kill stands of sugar pines with industrial fumes, but not to cut sugar pines and build housing for the poor. Every man is entitled to his own preferred definition of Walden Pond, but there is no definition that has any moral superiority over another, except by reference to the selfish needs of the human race.

From the fact that there is no normative definition of the natural state, it follows that there is no normative definition of clean air or pure water—hence no definition of polluted air—or of pollution—except by reference to the needs of man. The "right" composition of the atmosphere is one which has some dust in it and some lead in it and some hydrogen sulfide in it—just those amounts that attend a sensibly organized society thoughtfully and knowledgeably pursuing the greatest possible satisfaction for its human members.

The first and most fundamental step toward solution of our environmental problems is a clear recognition that our objective is not pure air or water but rather some optimal state of pollution. That step immediately suggests the question: How do we define and attain the level of pollution that will yield the maximum possible amount of human satisfaction?

Low levels of pollution contribute to human satisfaction but so do food and shelter and education and music. To attain ever lower levels of pollution, we must pay the cost of having less of these other things. I contrast that view of the cost of pollution control with the more popular statement that pollution control will "cost" very large numbers of dollars. The popular statement is true in some senses, false in others; sorting out the true and false senses is of some importance. The first step in that sorting process is to achieve a clear understanding of the difference between dollars and resources. Resources are the wealth of our nation; dollars are merely claim checks upon those resources. Resources are of vital importance; dollars are comparatively trivial.

Four categories of resources are sufficient for our purposes: At any given time a nation, or a planet if you prefer, has a stock of labor, of technological skill, of capital goods, and of natural resources (such as mineral deposits, timber, water, land, etc.). These resources can be used in various combinations to yield goods and services of all kinds—in some limited quantity. The quantity will be larger if they are combined efficiently, smaller if combined inefficiently. But in either event the resource stock is limited, the goods and services that they can be made to yield are limited; even the most efficient use of them will yield less than our population, in the aggregate, would like to have.

If one considers building a new dam, it is appropriate to say that it will be costly in the sense that it will require *x* hours of labor, *y* tons of steel and concrete, and *z* amount of capital goods. If these resources are devoted to the dam, then they cannot be used to build hospitals, fishing rods, schools, or electric can openers. That is the meaningful sense in which the dam is costly.

Quite apart from the very important question of how wisely we can combine our resources to produce goods and services, is the very different question of how they get distributed—who gets how many goods? Dollars constitute the claim checks which are distributed among people and which control their share of national output. Dollars are nearly valueless pieces of paper except to the extent that they do represent claim checks to some fraction of the output of goods and services. Viewed as claim checks, all the dollars outstanding during any period of time are worth, in the aggregate, the goods and services that are available to be claimed with them during that period—neither more nor less.

It is far easier to increase the supply of dollars than to increase the production of goods and services—printing dollars is easy. But printing more dollars doesn't help because each dollar then simply becomes a claim to fewer goods, i.e., becomes worth less.

The point is this: many people fall into error upon hearing the statement that the decision to build a dam, or to clean up a river, will cost $X million. It is regrettably easy to say: "It's only money. This is a wealthy country, and we have lots of money." But you cannot build a dam or clean a river with $X million—unless you also have a match, you can't even make a fire. One builds a dam or cleans a river by diverting labor and steel and trucks and factories from making one kind of goods to making another. The cost in dollars is merely a shorthand way of describing the extent of the diversion necessary. If we build a dam for $X million, then we must recognize that we will have $X million less housing and food and medical care and electric can openers as a result.

Similarly, the costs of controlling pollution are best expressed in terms of the other goods we will have to give up to do the job. This is not to say the job should not be done. Badly as we need more housing, more medical care, and more can openers, and more symphony orchestras, we could do with somewhat less of them, in my judgment at least, in exchange for somewhat cleaner air and rivers. But that is the nature of the tradeoff, and analysis of the problem is advanced if that unpleasant reality is kept in mind. Once the trade-off relationship is clearly perceived, it is possible to state in a very general way what the optimal level of pollution is. I would state it as follows:

People enjoy watching penguins. They enjoy relatively clean air and smog-free vistas. Their health is improved by relatively clean water and air. Each of these benefits is a type of good or service. As a society we would be well advised to give up one washing machine if the resources that would have gone into that washing machine can yield greater human satisfaction when diverted into pollution control. We should give up one hospital if the resources thereby freed would yield more human satisfaction when devoted to elimination of noise in our cities. And so on, trade-off by trade-off, we should divert our productive capacities from the production of existing goods and services to the production of a cleaner, quieter, more pastoral nation up to—and no further than—the point at which we value more highly the next washing machine or hospital that we would have to do without than we value the next unit of environmental improvement that the diverted resources would create.

Now this proposition seems to me unassailable but so general and abstract as to be unhelpful—at least unadministerable in the form stated. It assumes we can measure in some way the incremental units of human satisfaction yielded by very different types of goods. The proposition must remain a pious abstraction until I can explain how this measurement process can occur. In subsequent chapters I will attempt to show that we can do this—in some contexts with great precision and in other contexts only by rough approximation. But I insist that the proposition stated describes the result for which we should be striving—and again, that it is always useful to know what your target is even if your weapons are too crude to score a bull's eye.

QUESTIONS FOR ANALYSIS

1. According to Baxter, there is no right or wrong level of pollution independent of human needs. How does he support his claim? How would Taylor and Leopold respond?
2. Baxter argues that "the costs of controlling pollution are best expressed in terms of the other goods we will have to give up to do the job." What kinds of other goods does he include?
3. In viewing environmental decisions as trade-offs between environmental goals and other goods, Baxter argues that we should divert our resources to improve the environment until we value the next improvement less than "the next washing machine or hospital that we would have to do without." If the value we assign to each is based on adequate information, would this approach make for a sound environmental policy?
4. Baxter admits that there are serious difficulties in assigning economic values to all human satisfactions. Do those difficulties damage his argument?

CASE PRESENTATION

Animal Liberators

On May 24, 1984, five members of the Animal Liberation Front (ALF) raided the University of Pennsylvania's Experimental Head Injury Lab, located in the subbasement of the Anatomy-Chemistry Building. Although the purpose of most ALF raids is to liberate laboratory animals, this raid was different. This time, the goal was to "liberate" videotapes of the experiments being conducted in the lab, experiments that included using a hydraulic jack to compress the heads of monkeys. They found what they came for, and along the way, they ransacked the lab—destroying equipment and removing files.

What the videotapes showed was gruesome. There were images of pistons piercing the heads of baboons and of unanesthetized primates crawling in pain from operating tables. There were also images that showed clear violations of standard research procedures, such as operations performed without surgical masks while workers were smoking cigarettes.

A great controversy followed the release of the tapes. Dr. Thomas Gennarelli, head of the lab, defended his research and decried the raid. All animals were anesthetized and felt no pain, he insisted, and the raid had seriously set back important medical research. The university also defended Dr. Gennarelli's research, as did the National Institutes of Health (NIH), which, despite protests from People for the Ethical Treatment of Animals, gave the lab a new grant of $500,000.

The raiders, in an interview that appeared in the November 1986 issue of *Omni* ("Inhuman Bondage" by Robert Well), likened the research to the cruel medical experiments that Nazi Dr. Josef Mengele conducted on humans. (Indeed, one of the raiders was himself a survivor of a Nazi concentration camp.)

As the controversy continued, protesters demonstrated at the Penn campus, and animal rights activists staged a sit-in at the NIH until Secretary of Health and Human Services Margaret Heckler ordered a halt to all federal funding of the Head Injury Lab. That was July 18, 1985. Four months later, Penn agreed to pay a $4,000 fine for violating the Animal Welfare Act. The university also agreed to improve its use of pain-relieving drugs, its care of injured animals, and its training of research workers who handle laboratory animals.

And the raiders? Despite a grand jury investigation, no indictments were handed down. ALF members, invoking their Fifth Amendment rights, refused to testify against themselves.

QUESTIONS FOR ANALYSIS

1. Is the comparison between Drs. Gennarelli and Mengele justified?
2. Dr. Gennarelli and the NIH obviously believed that his research would bring significant medical benefit. If his research workers had not violated standard research procedures, would that benefit have justified it?
3. Suppose that ALF and Tom Regan are right about such experiments violating animals' rights. Does that justify ALF's tactics?
4. Which is the more important moral issue—the research itself or the violations of the Animal Welfare Act? Why?
5. If similar research was done on mice, would your reaction to it be any different?

CASE PRESENTATION

Religious Sacrifice

Of the many Cubans who have come to southern Florida in recent decades, some 70,000 practice the religion of Santería. Santería is a distinctively Afro-Cuban religion. It combines the Roman Catholicism of Cuba's Spanish settlers and the traditional Yoruba religion of West Africa, which came to the Caribbean island on the slave ships. Among Santería's traditional Yoruba rituals is animal sacrifice. Turtles, pigeons, chickens, goats, and sheep are slaughtered to appease the Santería gods, after which they are usually eaten by adherents in attendance.

Like other cities in southern Florida, Hialeah has its share of Cuban immigrants. In 1987, the Church of Lukumi Babalu Aye announced its plans to build a Santería church and community center in Hialeah. The city responded with a series of ordinances banning the ritual sacrifice of animals, with one of the ordinances defining the outlawed practice this way: To perform a ritual animal sacrifice is to "unnecessarily kill, torment, torture or mutilate an animal in a public or private ritual or ceremony not for the primary purpose of food consumption."

The church went to court, charging that the ordinances violated the religious freedom of its members. Hialeah defended the ordinances as a public health measure. In a unanimous decision announced in June of 1993, the U.S. Supreme Court ruled in favor of the church. Santería's adherents were jubilant, but opponents of cruelty to animals worried about the fate of animal cruelty laws throughout the country.

QUESTIONS FOR ANALYSIS

1. The Court saw the case as a matter of religious freedom, not as a matter of cruelty to animals. Hialeah claimed to see the case as a matter of public health rather than a matter of cruelty to animals. How do you think Singer and Regan would feel about that?
2. In an earlier case, Native Americans who use peyote in religious rituals sought exemption from drug laws that ban peyote's use. The Court ruled against them because the drug laws were not designed to interfere with religion. But the Hialeah ordinances were so designed, according to the

Court, because they singled out only one reason for killing animals. Should Hialeah have broadened them to include other reasons? If so, how?

3. Should animal sacrifices be permitted? How would Singer and Regan answer?
4. If you agree that at least some animals have rights, how would you balance them against human rights to practice religion?

CASE PRESENTATION

A Metaphor for the Energy Debate

In the worst oil spill in U.S. history, the *Exxon Valdez* tanker spilled 11 million gallons of crude oil into Alaska's Prince William Sound. The March 24, 1989, spill affected more than 1,000 miles of shoreline, including three national wildlife refuges, and left many thousands of animals dead, including an estimated 100,000 birds and 1,000 sea otters.

At the time of the spill, the oil industry had been hoping that the federal government would open the coastal plain of Alaska's Arctic National Wildlife Refuge to drilling. Two hundred and fifty miles north of the Arctic Circle, this tundra area is inhabited by caribou and musk oxen. Since only a few hundred Eskimos also live there, its 19 million acres are practically untouched by humans. The coastal plain area of the preserve, which covers 1.5 million acres, may also be home to the largest untapped oil reserve in the country. A five-year study by the Department of the Interior had reported in 1987 that the plain presented "the best single opportunity to increase significantly domestic oil production." But after the massive public outrage sparked by the *Exxon Valdez* spill, opening the plain to drilling was politically unthinkable.

A year and a half later, the unthinkable suddenly became thinkable when Iraq invaded Kuwait and the flow of oil from the two Persian Gulf countries was halted. Public attention quickly focused on U.S. dependence on foreign oil, and with the renewed attention came a renewal of the drilling debate. In the words of Alaska's Governor Steve Cowper, who noted that Alaska was both the country's wilderness and major source of energy, "This is a metaphor for the energy debate."

That debate, and the refuge's centrality to it, continues to this day, reaching another peak in the year 2000. After years of decline, energy prices suddenly soared to near record levels, and the Clinton administration, bowing to public pressure, released oil from the strategic oil reserve in an effort to lower fuel prices. Once again, concern grew over U.S. dependence on foreign oil, and the question of drilling in the refuge became a major issue in that year's presidential election campaign. George W. Bush, the eventual winner of the election in a very close race, campaigned in favor of drilling. Gale Norton, his selection to head the Department of the Interior, had also voiced support for it.

To those who favor drilling, the plain is a frozen desert with significant potential to strengthen national security and improve the economy of the northern part of the state. To those who oppose drilling, the plain is a magnificent wilderness that must be protected from aesthetic and ecological damage. And while drilling proponents point to the Department of the Interior's conclusion that development of the plain would have no significant environmental impact, opponents continue to challenge the report in the courts.

QUESTIONS FOR ANALYSIS

1. Many people consider reliance on foreign oil a threat to national security. Options for reducing U.S. reliance include energy conservation, alternative fuels, and increased domestic drilling. Should drilling be allowed in areas currently protected by federal law?
2. Oil companies and the Department of the Interior claim that drilling in the coastal plain will not harm the environment. The environmentalists dispute the claim but also argue that aesthetic damage will occur in any case. How much weight should aesthetics be given when balanced against energy needs and economic concerns?
3. The Arctic National Wildlife Refuge is isolated, generally considered less attractive than many

other protected areas, and rarely visited by outsiders. Do those factors improve the case of drilling proponents, or are they irrelevant to the dispute?

4. Debate also surrounds the issue of new drilling off the coasts of California and Florida. Given our dependence on foreign oil, should offshore drilling be increased in those areas?

CASE PRESENTATION

The Spotted Owl

On June 22, 1990, the U.S. Fish and Wildlife Service declared the northern spotted owl a threatened species. Under the Endangered Species Act of 1973, the declaration made it illegal to harm the owl or its habitat, the Pacific Northwest forests.

Though environmentalists hailed the declaration, other groups, most notably the timber industry, objected. The Pacific Northwest forests are home to giant cedars, Douglas firs, and redwood trees, and the timber industry constituted a large portion of the economies of Washington, Oregon, and northern California. Of the seventeen national forests involved, the timber industry cleared 70,000 acres annually. Under a plan proposed by federal biologists, 4 million acres were to be added to the 1.5 million acres already off limits to logging.

Like many such disputes, this one pitted environmental concerns against economic ones. On the one side was not only the future of the spotted owls—which were down to 3,000 mating pairs—but the future of the forests, which had already lost 90 percent of their ancient trees. On the other side was the future of the area's economy. According to government estimates, 28,000 jobs would be lost over a ten-year period. According to industry officials' estimates, the number could be as high as 50,000.

Four days later, the Bush administration, which initially said it would not interfere with plans to protect the owl's habitat, reversed itself. Instead of going ahead with the original plans, it decided to delay protection of the forests while it set up a commission to study ways of balancing the interests of the logging industry and the owls. It also decided to seek changes in the Endangered Species Act to make it easier to permit some species to diminish in order to avoid severe economic consequences. As the law stood at the time (and still does), such permission could be given only by a committee of federal agency heads, informally known as the "God Committee." Because of the difficulties involved in convening a meeting of the committee and the time involved in coming to a decision, the procedure is rarely used.

Neither side was pleased by the administration's plan to delay a solution to the problem. Environmentalists claimed that the administration was declaring war on the Endangered Species Act, while the timber industry argued that the delay would aggravate the region's economic uncertainty. Then, in 1991, a federal judge in Seattle ordered an end to the logging, ruling that the Bush administration was in violation of federal laws. Judge William Dryer also ordered the government to devise an environmental plan for the region. Until an acceptable plan was presented to him, the ban on logging would remain.

The issue wasn't settled until December 1994, when the same judge gave final approval to a plan proposed fifteen months earlier by the newly inaugurated Clinton administration. Under that plan, which the administration hailed as a way to protect the region's economy as well as its natural habitats, logging resumed at a reduced level. The plan also included restoration projects for damaged forests and streams in addition to other forms of economic aid to the region. Once again, neither side was satisfied, especially the timber industry, which vowed to continue its battle over the Endangered Species Act in Congress.

QUESTIONS FOR ANALYSIS

1. To what extent should economic impact be considered when seeking a plan to protect an endangered species or a forest area?
2. Since most of the timber harvested in the seventeen northwestern forests is exported to other countries, closing an additional 4 million acres to

foresting will not affect lumber supplies or building costs in the United States. Is that a relevant factor in deciding whether to close off the acres to logging?

3. Environmental groups had been trying to save the Pacific Northwest forests long before the spotted owl was declared a threatened species. What economic costs should we be willing to allow to protect our forests, even when diminishing them does not affect a threatened species?
4. Should it be easier or more difficult to allow a species to become extinct in order to prevent severe economic harm?

CHAPTER TWELVE

Computer Ethics and the Internet

- **What Is Computer Ethics?**
- **Issues in Computer Ethics**
- **Arguments in Favor of Ethical Conduct with Computers and the Internet**
- **Arguments Against Ethical Conduct with Computers and the Internet**

LAURENCE H. TRIBE **The Constitution in Cyberspace: Law and Liberty Beyond the Electronic Frontier**

RICHARD A. SPINELLO **Free Speech in Cyberspace**

BERNARD GERT **Is It Moral to Make Copies of Software for My Friends?**

HERMAN T. TAVANI AND FRANCES S. GRODZINSKY **Cyberstalking, Personal Privacy, and Moral Responsibility**

CASE PRESENTATIONS: *Ticketed for Obscenity on the Information Superhighway* • *A Chill in Cyberspace* • *Censoring Political Speech* • *Pirates of the Campuses*

AUGUST 12, 2006 marked the twenty-fifth anniversary of the first IBM personal computers, which made the use of computing seem acceptable for ordinary people. Although the Apple II computer was introduced in 1977 and some small computer kits had been available before this for what we might now call "geeks," the PC brought computing into the mainstream and revolutionized the way we live, work, and play.

What we now call the Internet began as something called ARPAnet, which in 1969 linked computers at universities and the U.S. Defense Department. The goal at the time was to develop a communications system that could withstand military attack. Because there is no central switching physical location, bombing the location of one computer in the system would not disable the communications among the others. The earliest e-mail programs can be traced to 1971. But it was not until development of the international HTML protocols for the World Wide Web in the early 1990s and recognition of the enormous potential for commercial and private use of the web and e-mail that most people even heard about these electronic methods for communication and information exchange. Now, it is difficult to imagine a college or business or public library that is not connected to the Internet. As the prices of personal computers and laptops fell, they became increasingly ubiquitous in society, although the technological "divide" attributable to economic realities also became an issue.

With these new technologies, however, also came a burgeoning range of ethical issues. Do the rights we take for granted elsewhere also apply on the Internet? Should we be able to exercise the rights of free speech under the First Amendment online, especially when so many young children have easy access to the Internet? Should we be as respectful of the intellectual property rights of software owners and artists online as we are expected to be in the world of hard-copy books and paintings on canvas? Can we expect the same right to privacy in our e-mail communications as we demand in our telephone calls? With the rapid-fire communication possible online, has defamation of the character of persons become much more serious than when we merely utter some defamatory remarks in the physical presence of a few friends?

Computer ethics long predates personal computers, however. In 1950, Norbert Wiener, a mathematics professor at the Massachusetts Institute of Technology, published what many experts consider the first systematic consideration of computer ethics, *The Human Use of Human Beings.* In this chapter, we will consider some of these ethical problems, as we encounter them today in our use of computers and the Internet. We also will chart some things to consider in identifying and addressing ethical issues that present themselves as technologies evolve in ways we cannot yet imagine in these early years of the twenty-first century. Can we identify long-standing ethical principles from Kantian and utilitarian perspectives that will assist us in responding to these newly emerging ethical problems?

WHAT IS COMPUTER ETHICS?

In 1985, James H. Moor, a professor at Dartmouth College, published the seminal article "What Is Computer Ethics?"[1] that has defined the issues in recent decades. He proposed defining **computer ethics** as "the analysis of the nature and social impact of computer technology and the corresponding formulation and justification of policies for the ethical use of such technology." It seems consistent with his definition to recognize the Internet, which emerged into general use a decade later, as an element or application of that technology. Moor noted that we are provided with "new capabilities" and "new choices for action" because of computers, but no policies or guidelines for how to behave ethically in that environment.

We are faced with two challenges. First, studying computer ethics should help us identify specific issues in this area in such a way that we can clearly and systematically consider them. Second, we can then consider whether ethical-reasoning methods will help us chart a well-reasoned path to decision making in what Moor considers uncharted terrain.

ISSUES IN COMPUTER ETHICS

We here identify a sampling of the issues we face in computer ethics. This is intended not as a comprehensive or exhaustive list but, rather, as representative of the issues we face today.

---

[1]James H. Moor, "What Is Computer Ethics"? *Metaphilosophy* 16:4 (1985).

Freedom of Expression

Freedom of expression is guaranteed in the First Amendment to the U.S. Constitution and hence is one of the ten amendments known as the Bill of Rights. It is also guaranteed in Article 19 of the Universal Declaration of Human Rights of the United Nations:

> Everyone has the right to freedom of opinion and expression; this right includes freedom to hold opinions without interference and to seek, receive and impart information and ideas through any media and regardless of frontiers.

We recognize this right in our ability to speak freely in a public square or publish a newspaper or deliver a speech. But even though mass communication long predates computers and the Internet, the speed with which speech can be disseminated worldwide to untold millions of people renews our focus on these rights.

Defamation is one of several exceptions to our right of free speech, which is not absolute. It consists of a factual claim that is false and is damaging to someone's reputation. Spoken defamation is **slander,** and written defamation is **libel.** If a television reporter publicly claimed that a certain famous singer was a child molester, it would be defamation, but only if that statement were false, because truth is an absolute defense to defamation.

Although this legal wrong has been recognized for centuries in Anglo-American law, it can cause massive damage with the speed of communication of the Internet. A defamatory statement made in front of a few people in the same physical location might not cause too much damage, especially if it were followed by a sincere apology. But a defamatory statement posted on the Web or blasted out via a listserv e-mail to thousands of people can cause irreparable harm to someone's career or financial investments or professional standing. And once something is out there in cyberspace, it never really disappears, magnifying the damage. Defaming another person's reputation is not just a legal issue. It also is an ethical problem, because one person can cause serious harm to another person—a wrong whether viewed from a Kantian respect for persons or from a utilitarian concern for maximizing pleasure and minimizing pain.

Another exception to freedom of expression is **obscenity.** Philosopher J. S. Mill, as he stated in his book *On Liberty* (1859), and many civil libertarians believe that obscenity should enjoy the same free-speech protections as all other speech. However, in the United States, the Supreme Court has never recognized this right. Defining obscenity is particularly difficult. In the landmark decision *Miller v. California,*[2] the Court said that something is obscene only if it meets all elements of this three-pronged test:

> (A) whether "the average person, applying contemporary community standards" would find that the work, taken as a whole, appeals to the prurient interest, (b) whether the work depicts or describes, in a patently offensive way, sexual conduct specifically defined by the applicable state law, and (c) whether the work, taken as a whole, lacks serious literary, artistic, political, or scientific value.

---

[2]413 U.S. 15 (1973).

But almost every word and phrase in this definition is fraught with interpretive difficulties and disagreement. What are "contemporary community standards," especially with the worldwide reach of the Internet? Should the standards be those of a rural community in the South or those of an urban neighborhood in New York or Los Angeles? What is a "prurient interest"? Who decides what is "patently offensive"? How do we determine whether a painting has serious "artistic" value?

But the new worldwide community isn't the only problem we face in making sense of the issue of sexually explicit material. It has long been recognized by the courts that material that is pornographic or offensive in any way *is* protected by the First Amendment, so long as it is not "obscene." But even then, it is legitimate to restrict access to this material to minors. Municipalities can legitimately enact zoning rules that restrict "adult bookstores" to certain neighborhoods and require that persons buying that material be at least eighteen years of age. Municipalities also can legitimately, without infringing on First Amendment protection, restrict public displays of pornography, as on billboards or outdoor stages. These restrictions balance the right of adults to see such materials, if they choose, against the right of others not to be forced to look at them, while denying minors access to them.

The Web complicates this long-standing balance enormously. Children who cannot gain admittance to an adult movie theater or bookstore can find it easy to access the same material on the Web. Rules that only those with credit cards can see such pages are difficult to enforce, if children know the credit card numbers of their parents. In the landmark 1997 case *Reno v. ACLU,*[3] the U.S. Supreme Court struck down, as excessively broad, federal legislation that attempted to ban all such material. The goal of blocking access to children resulted in a suppression of protected free-speech material to adults, the Court reasoned, and it encouraged better use of screening tools by parents to restrict access to content they found objectionable. It also is often noted that a substantial portion of the controversial content available on the Web is being sent from locations outside the United States, where U.S. laws could not be enforced anyway.

Privacy

The use of computers to gather and store information has been hailed as a huge achievement in most sectors of life. In just the last few years, our lives have been transformed by the ease with which we can access data online and perform tasks once limited to the U.S. mail or telephone calls or personal office visits. We can renew our driver's license, pay our taxes, buy books, and check whether a package was delivered by FedEx or UPS or the United States Postal Service, all on the Internet. We can search databases of newspapers, magazines, court cases, and even books in a matter of minutes to do research that used to require hours and days in a traditional print library. Some medical services, especially the Veterans Administration and some large HMOs (such as Kaiser Permanente in California and other states), now maintain all of our medical records on electronic databases, so doctors at any location can quickly and efficiently see our entire medical history.

But this massive data storage and access have created huge problems with violation of our privacy. Regular news reports in recent years reveal numerous breaches of

---

[3]521 U.S. 844 (1997).

security of these databases. Lost laptops containing confidential employment information, health data, and other records place thousands of private citizens at risk of identity theft. Hackers frequently find ways to access these confidential data and misuse them in many different ways.

Although some laws are in place to prosecute misuse of confidential data, it can be very difficult to identify the persons who found the data or to correct the damage. Identity theft can victimize innocent persons for many years while they try to clear their credit records.

As with so many issues involving computers and the Internet, these problems are not new. A clerk in a doctor's office might have misused confidential information in a private medical file in the past. A dishonest employee at a government agency might look at tax returns or driver's license records or other government documents and misuse that information. But computerized databases make that information far more accessible and easier to obtain and misuse by many more people.

The ethical obligations extend not only to those persons who might steal and misuse this private information, but also to the organizations that collect the data and fail to put in place appropriate security to protect our privacy.

Intellectual Property

Copyright protects the expression of ideas, whether in words, symbols, or other forms of expression. The founding fathers provided for copyright protection in the U.S. Constitution, because granting a limited monopoly on this work so it could be exploited financially was thought to be a good way to encourage creativity that would benefit the entire nation. Issues of intellectual property, which includes patent and trademark as well as copyright, have existed for centuries. Once again, though, computers and the Internet have magnified the potential abuse and the possibilities for theft of other people's work.

Stealing someone else's words and passing them off as your own has been possible as long as students have been in school. This is likely not only to violate someone's copyright but also to constitute plagiarism prohibited at schools, colleges, and universities. Computers and the Internet make this theft much easier, because so much material is available and easy to "copy and paste" into any document on any topic. But just as it is easy for students to steal other people's work, it is equally easy for professors to find the source, using such search tools as Google.com. Commercial products such as Turnitin.org, now widely used at colleges and universities, enable professors to submit an entire document in digitized form and have it compared in minutes with a massive database. This database includes not only the entire contents of the Web but also the contents of "term paper mills" where some students buy papers *and* all previous papers submitted by all instructors using the service around the country.

Plagiarism can have serious consequences for a student, including a failing grade or suspension from a university. It also raises serious ethical issues, because it consists of stealing someone else's work and falsifying its source by turning it in as one's own.

Intellectual-property violations of other kinds also are now rampant on the Internet. Words and images are easily retrieved and saved in digitized files. Graphics software can be used to modify images, violating yet another right of copyright owners. Posting the text of a copyrighted book can damage the commercial potential of that print book irretrievably.

Intellectual-property issues also arise with the sharing of copyrighted files for music and film. Although many Internet users seem to have a "Wild West" mentality, believing that everything should be free, that attitude overlooks the fact that most of this material is actually property owned by somebody who worked hard to produce it and wants a fair return in exchange. Copying copyrighted software in violation of the terms of the purchase of that software is another violation of intellectual property.

All of these violations raise legal issues. The copyright owners can sue for damages for misuse—and they often do. But these are also ethical issues. They involve behavior that we routinely recognize as unethical, even if we are never caught by legal officials: theft, violations of another person's autonomy, and dishonesty.

Computer Crime

Computers and the Internet have spawned all sorts of crimes that interfere with the peaceable enjoyment of those technologies by everyone. Hackers steal confidential data online. Sending "viruses" through e-mail interferes with the regular access of thousands of Internet users, destroying a valuable property interest in our computers and Internet services. Spam messages clog our e-mail, slow down services, and might constitute harassment that interferes with our daily lives and work.

All of this behavior is not only illegal but also unethical. These crimes existed in various forms before computers and the Internet. But, like the other issues we are considering, they are magnified exponentially by the capabilities of the technology.

Access to the Internet and the Technological "Divide"

For all the new opportunities presented by computers and the Internet, they depend on the economic capability of accessing these technologies. Many schools have tried to ensure that all students have access, regardless of their economic means. Public libraries provide free access to all residents, at least in industrialized nations. But access to these technologies in developing and impoverished nations can be very restricted, further exacerbating the divide in economic development between the "haves" and the "have-nots." If wealthy nations have an ethical obligation to help provide basic nourishment and healthcare to impoverished nations, do they also have an ethical obligation to assist those nations in gaining access to these increasingly vital technologies?

Moral and Legal Issues

Most of the issues here have a legal dimension and a moral dimension as well. One method for analysis is to identify the underlying ethical issue and ask how and whether it can be extended to the dimensions of computers and the Internet. Some of these ethical issues can be extended without difficulty. Others might demand fresh approaches, as the magnitude of the problems forces serious reconsideration.

Our right to protect our privacy is fundamental to our basic autonomy as persons. Not only is it a crime to violate that privacy by stealing confidential information from a computerized database, but it also violates our ethical rights to privacy and autonomy.

Our right to freedom of expression also might require re-examination, especially if our expression exposes minors to inappropriate material. We might want to protect our own rights, but don't we have an ethical obligation not to cause emotional harm to minors who have easy access to material we might be posting?

Our ethical obligation not to steal seems to extend not only to our neighbor's car or watch but also to the intellectual property we find on the Internet—the writing, visual images, software, and music files. Those who believe the ethical obligation not to steal does not apply on the Internet have the burden of coming up with a plausible justification for such a view.

ARGUMENTS IN FAVOR OF ETHICAL CONDUCT WITH COMPUTERS AND THE INTERNET

1. ***I strive to be ethical whether or not other people know about it because it makes me a better person overall.***

   POINT: "Behaving ethically is something I strive for, regardless of whether anybody knows it. I just feel better about myself knowing that I am doing my best to be a better person. Although it might be easier to misbehave in the privacy of my study logged onto the Internet, I still know what I'm doing and it's important to me to respect myself. And there's always the chance that somebody will find out what I am doing anyway. With all the tracking systems on the Internet, I'm not confident that anything I do there will not someday become known to other people."

   COUNTERPOINT: "It's a tough world out there, and if you can get away with something in private, go for it. Everybody else is out for themselves, and that's the only way to get ahead in this cut-throat world we live in. Besides, if you're careful, you can stay anonymous on the Internet, at least for things you don't want others to know about. Your chances of getting caught doing something unethical are pretty slim, and most of your friends are probably doing the same thing anyway.

2. ***I don't post pornography on the web or look at it because I consider it degrading to women.***

   POINT: "Every piece of pornography shares at least one thing with every other piece of pornography—it degrades human beings. By separating sex from love, by concentrating on impersonal lust at the expense of our more human emotions, by appealing to and arousing the lust of its readers and viewers, even the mildest pornography reduces humanity to the level of animals. And much of today's pornography goes even further, portraying the most disgusting and dehumanizing acts of sexual sadomasochism imaginable."

   COUNTERPOINT: "You might find pornography degrading, but many other people don't. In fact, they actually enjoy it. And there's no reason why they shouldn't. After all, lust is as human as any other emotion, and there isn't anything inherently immoral about being 'turned on' by erotic pictures and writings. Nor is there anything inherently immoral about portraying sex without love. Even if most people consider sex with love the ideal, why must everything we see and read portray ideal situations only, sexual or nonsexual? And even though much of today's pornography disgusts me as much as it disgusts you, the fact that we're disgusted by it doesn't make it immoral or dehumanizing, any more than the fact that we find certain foods or clothing styles disgusting makes them immoral or dehumanizing."

3. ***I don't download music or movies or share files for those with my friends, because stealing is always wrong.***

POINT: "I wouldn't dream of trying to shoplift in a record store or movie rental store, because if I got caught, having a criminal record would really wreck my career plans. In just the same way, I don't want to take a chance that I'd get caught illegally downloading music or movie files on the Internet. The entertainment industry is after college students nowadays, and my campus is also cracking down on these illegal downloads. Even if I don't get caught today, I'll always worry that they'll track me down in the future, with all the capabilities they have now for tracing computer records. And whether or not I get caught, I'll always know that I behaved unethically by stealing something that didn't belong to me."

COUNTERPOINT: "There are millions of college students in this country. What are the odds that the entertainment industry will come after me? I wouldn't shoplift either, but the changes of getting caught in illegal downloading from the Internet are just very slim to almost nonexistent. Besides, the industry is wealthy beyond belief. They've made plenty of money off me already when I buy CDs and DVDs, and it's only fair that I get a little free 'bonus' now and then from the Internet. Ordinarily, stealing is wrong, but it can be justified in circumstances like this."

4. ***If I see something on the web that looks like a criminal might be threatening another person, I'll report it to the proper authorities.***

POINT: "We all have to watch out for each other in this world. If somebody were threatening me on the Web, I'd want to know about it and would want others to do what they could to tell the authorities. It takes a little time to do these things and get involved, but we'd all be in a better world if more people would take the time and effort to do this."

COUNTERPOINT: "Turning somebody else in could jeopardize my own life. And the authorities will insist that I testify and spend my own precious time pursuing whatever case they think they might have. It's risky to get involved. Everybody needs to watch out for themselves and not assume some do-gooders will get involved."

ARGUMENTS AGAINST ETHICAL CONDUCT WITH COMPUTERS AND THE INTERNET

1. ***I can be anonymous on the Internet, so nobody will know if I spam or send out viruses or steal music off the web.***

POINT: "The great thing about the Internet is that it's so easy to do things I could never get away with in person. I can look up all kinds of confidential information about people I don't like. I can blast spam and viruses out to let the world know how much power ordinary people have, thanks to computers and the Internet. Huge multinational corporations need to be reminded that they don't control everything, and stealing music or sending out viruses or spam is a good way to protest."

COUNTERPOINT: "You're really not anonymous on the Internet. People who steal music or movies on the web are being sued by the big entertainment companies. The police and FBI are finding ways to track down spammers and those who send viruses. The consequences if you are caught at any of this stuff could be very severe, and a criminal record could ruin your future plans for education and career. If you want to protest the control of huge corporations, find a different way to do it that doesn't jeopardize your own future. It would be a brutish world if all we cared about in ethical decisions was whether or not we might get caught. We should be following good ethical standards regardless."

2. ***Everybody cheats on the Internet and hardly anybody ever gets caught.***

POINT: "I have lots of friends who find material on the Internet that they take without change and submit in their classes as their own work. I hear them brag all the time about how they got away with it, and the professors don't seem to notice. I'm working part-time to put myself through college and I don't have time to go to the library and write everything from scratch. Plagiarism is so rampant nowadays that I don't see how it could hurt me, even if I do get caught. Some famous authors, professors, and even university presidents have been found to be plagiarizing. If it's okay for them, it ought to be okay for students to do the same thing."

COUNTERPOINT: "It's gotten very easy for professors to find plagiarism when you turn in your papers, especially with new search tools that can find it almost instantaneously. I don't hear my friends bragging when they get caught and flunk a course or get suspended from school, so I don't believe nobody gets caught nowadays. Computers make it easy to steal, but they also make it easy for professors to find plagiarism. It's just not worth the risk. My professors try to play fair with me, so I owe it to them to try my best in my work for class, idealistic as that might sound."

3. ***The Internet is the new Wild West. I can say or do whatever I want and nobody has any grounds for complaining.***

POINT: "At last, ordinary people like me have a place where we can speak our mind, whether by creating a website or posting comments to a chatroom or blasting out e-mail that speaks the truth about people or corporations I don't like. Isn't that what free speech is all about? If they don't like what I'm saying, they can post their own stuff on the web to respond, but at least I have a chance to vent in a public place where people can hear me."

COUNTERPOINT: "We do have a lot of freedom of expression, but it's not absolute. Whether in person or on the web, we have to respect some limits. We should not defame innocent people by spreading falsehoods that hurt their reputations. We should not incite crime against other people. If we all respect a few reasonable limits on free speech, we as a society will all be better off."

4. ***Posting pornography on the web or looking at pornography that others have posted is my right under the principle of free speech. Pornography can actually be beneficial.***

POINT: "Despite all your talk of the harmful effects of pornography, it actually has many beneficial effects. It can aid normal sexual development, invigorate flagging sexual relationships, encourage openness about sex between sexual partners, and provide a release for people who, for one reason or another, are unable to find sexual fulfillment in other ways. It's even been used successfully in sex therapy to treat various sexual disorders. Finally, there's reason to believe that pornography prevents sex crimes by providing catharsis for people who would otherwise behave harmfully."

COUNTERPOINT: "Reliable scientific studies refute your catharsis argument. Studies show that the group reporting the highest rate of excitation to masturbation by pornography were rapists. Obviously, pornography didn't provide these possible rapists with an adequate outlet. As for the rest, much of it is just speculation. And even if some of it is true, it hardly justifies pornography, which remains degrading to all humans, most of all to women. When something is inherently immoral, as pornography is, a few beneficial effects can't make it moral, especially when we have evidence that it has harmful effects as well."

The Constitution in Cyberspace: Law and Liberty Beyond the Electronic Frontier

LAURENCE H. TRIBE

Laurence H. Tribe is the Carl M. Loeb University Professor at Harvard Law School and a well-known expert on constitutional law. In these excerpts from his pioneering keynote address at the First Conference on Computers, Freedom and Privacy, March 26, 1991, he outlines a range of basic principles that frame not only our understanding of legal problems presented by the Internet, but also ethical issues of continuing concern.

His central focus is whether a document written in the eighteenth century to address the realities of the world at that point in history can appropriately be applied to the world of cyberspace and virtual reality that we now inhabit. He believes the core values of the Constitution will best endure if we recognize that it protects people, not places.

My topic is how to "map" the text and structure of our Constitution onto the texture and topology of "cyberspace." That's the term coined by cyberpunk novelist William Gibson, which many now use to describe the "place"—a place without physical walls or even physical dimensions—where ordinary telephone conversations "happen," where voice-mail and e-mail messages are stored and sent back and forth, and where computer-generated graphics are transmitted and transformed, all in the form of interactions, some real-time and some delayed, among countless users, and between users and the computer itself.

. . . My topic, broadly put, is the implications of that rapidly expanding array for our constitutional order.... When the lines along which our Constitution is drawn warp or vanish, what happens to the Constitution itself?

SETTING THE STAGE

To set the stage with a perhaps unfamiliar example, consider a decision handed down nine months ago, *Maryland v. Craig*, where the U.S. Supreme Court upheld the power of a state to put an alleged child abuser on trial with the defendant's accuser testifying not in the defendant's presence but by one-way, closed-circuit television. The Sixth Amendment, which of course antedated television by a century and a half, says: "In all criminal prosecutions, the accused shall enjoy the right . . . to be confronted with the witnesses against him." Justice O'Connor wrote for a bare majority of five Justices that the state's procedures nonetheless struck a fair balance between costs to the accused and benefits to the victim and to society as a whole. . . .

But new technological possibilities for seeing your accuser clearly without having your accuser see you at all—possibilities for sparing the accuser any discomfort in ways that the accuser couldn't be spared before one-way mirrors [and] closed-circuit TVs were developed—*should* lead us at least to ask ourselves whether *two*-way confrontation, in which your accuser is supposed to be made uncomfortable, and thus less likely to lie, really *is* the core value of the Confrontation Clause. If so, "virtual" confrontation should be held constitutionally insufficient. If not—if the core value served by the Confrontation Clause is just the ability to *watch* your accuser say that you did it—then "virtual" confrontation should suffice. New technologies should lead us to look more closely at just *what values* the Constitution seeks to preserve. New technologies should *not* lead us to react reflexively *either way*—either by assuming that technologies the Framers didn't know about make their concerns and values obsolete, or by assuming that those new technologies couldn't possibly provide new ways out of old dilemmas and therefore should be ignored altogether.

. . . The world in which the Sixth Amendment's Confrontation Clause was written and ratified was a world in which "being confronted with" your accuser *necessarily* meant a simultaneous physical confrontation so that your accuser had to *perceive* you being accused by him. Closed-circuit television and one-way mirrors changed all that by *decoupling* those two dimensions of confrontation, marking a shift in the conditions of information-transfer that is in many ways typical of cyberspace.

What does that sort of shift mean for constitutional analysis? A common way to react is to treat the pattern as it existed *prior* to the new technology (the pattern in which doing "A" necessarily *included* doing "B") as essentially arbitrary or accidental. Taking this approach, once the technological change makes it possible to do "A" *without* "B"—to see your accuser without having him or her see you, or to read someone's mail without her knowing it, to switch examples—one concludes that the "old" Constitution's inclusion of "B" is irrelevant; one concludes that it is enough for the government to guarantee "A" alone. Sometimes that will be the case; but it's vital to understand that, sometimes, it won't be.

A characteristic feature of modernity is the subordination of purpose to accident—an acute appreciation of just how contingent and coincidental the connections we are taught to make often are. We understand, as moderns, that many of the ways we carve up and organize the world reflect what our social history and cultural heritage, and perhaps our neurological wiring, bring to the world, and not some irreducible "way things are." . . .

The Constitution's core values, I'm convinced, need not be transmogrified, or metamorphosed into oblivion, in the dim recesses of cyberspace. But to say that they *need* not be lost there is hardly to predict that they *will* not be. On the contrary, without further thought and awareness of the kind this conference might provide, the danger is clear and present that they *will* be.

The "event horizon" against which this transformation might occur is already plainly visible. Electronic trespassers like Kevin Mitnik don't stop with cracking pay phones, but break into NORAD—the North American Defense Command computer in Colorado Springs—not in a *WarGames* movie, but in real life.

Less challenging to national security but more ubiquitously threatening, computer crackers download everyman's credit history from institutions like TRW; start charging phone calls (and more) to everyman's number; set loose "worm" programs that shut down thousands of linked computers; and spread "computer viruses" through everyman's work or home PC.

It is not only the government that feels threatened by "computer crime"; both the owners and the users of private information services, computer bulletin boards, gateways, and networks feel equally vulnerable to this new breed of invisible trespasser. . . .

THE PROBLEM

The Constitution's architecture can too easily come to seem quaintly irrelevant, or at least impossible to take very seriously, in the world as reconstituted by the microchip. I propose today to canvass five axioms of our constitutional law—five basic assumptions that I believe shape the way American constitutional scholars and judges view legal issues—and to examine how they can adapt to the cyberspace age. My conclusion (and I will try not to give away too much of the punch line here) is that the Framers of our Constitution were very wise indeed. They bequeathed us a framework for all seasons, a truly astonishing document whose principles are suitable for all times and all technological landscapes.

Axiom 1: There is a Vital Difference Between Government and Private Action

The first axiom I will discuss is the proposition that the Constitution, with the sole exception of the Thirteenth Amendment prohibiting slavery, regulates action by the *government* rather than the conduct of *private* individuals and groups.

. . . [A]s a general proposition it is only what *governments* do, either through such rules or through the actions of public officials, that the United States Constitution constrains. And nothing about any new technology suddenly erases the Constitution's enduring value of restraining *government* above all else, and of protecting all private groups, large and small, from government.

It's true that certain technologies may become socially indispensable—so that equal or at least minimal access to basic computer power, for example, might be as significant a constitutional goal as equal or at least minimal access to the franchise, or to dispute resolution through the judicial system, or to elementary and secondary education. But all this means (or should mean) is that the Constitution's constraints on government must at times take the form of imposing *affirmative duties* to ensure access rather than merely enforcing *negative prohibitions* against designated sorts of invasion or intrusion.

Today, for example, the government is under an affirmative obligation to open up criminal trials to the press and the public, at least where there has not been a particularized finding that such openness would disrupt the proceedings. The government is also under an affirmative obligation to provide free legal assistance for indigent criminal defendants, to ensure speedy trials, to underwrite the cost of counting ballots at election time, and to desegregate previously segregated school systems. But these occasional affirmative obligations don't, or shouldn't, mean that the Constitution's axiomatic division between the realm of public power and the realm of private life should be jettisoned.

Nor would the "indispensability" of information technologies provide a license for government to impose strict content, access, pricing, and other types of regulation. *Books* are indispensable to most of us, for example—but it doesn't follow that government should therefore be able to regulate the content of what goes onto the shelves of *bookstores*. The right of a private bookstore owner to decide which books to stock and which to discard, which books to display openly and which to store in limited access areas, should remain inviolate. And note, incidentally, that this needn't make the bookstore owner a "publisher" who is liable for the words printed in the books on her shelves. It's a common fallacy to imagine that the moment a computer gateway or bulletin board begins to exercise powers of selection to control who may be on line, it must automatically assume the responsibilities of a newscaster, a broadcaster, or an author. For computer gateways and bulletin boards are really the "bookstores" of cyberspace; most of them organize and present information in a computer format, rather than generating more information content of their own.

Axiom 2: The Constitutional Boundaries of Private Property and Personality Depend on Variables Deeper Than Social Utility and Technological Feasibility

The second constitutional axiom, one closely related to the private–public distinction of the first axiom, is that a person's mind, body, and property belong *to that person* and not to the public as a whole. Some believe that cyberspace challenges that axiom because its entire premise lies in the existence of computers tied to electronic transmission networks that process digital information. Because such information can be easily replicated in series of "1"s and "0"s, anything that anyone has come up with in virtual reality can be infinitely reproduced. I can log on to a computer library, copy a "virtual book" to my computer disk, and send a copy to your computer without creating a gap on anyone's bookshelf. The same is true of valuable computer programs, costing hundreds of dollars, creating serious piracy problems. This feature leads some, like Richard Stallman of the Free Software Foundation, to argue that in cyberspace everything should be free—that information can't be owned. Others, of course, argue that copyright and patent protections of various kinds are needed in order for there to be incentives to create "cyberspace property" in the first place.

Needless to say, there are lively debates about what the optimal incentive package should be as a matter of legislative and social policy. But the only *constitutional issue,* at bottom, isn't the utilitarian or instrumental selection of an optimal policy. Social judgments about what ought to be subject to individual appropriation, in the sense used by John Locke and Robert Nozick, and what ought to remain in the open public domain, are first and foremost *political* decisions.

To be sure, there are some constitutional constraints on these political decisions. The Constitution does not permit anything and everything to be made into a *private commodity.* Votes, for example, theoretically cannot be bought and sold. Whether the Constitution itself should be read (or amended) so as to permit all basic medical care, shelter, nutrition, legal assistance and, indeed, computerized information services, to be treated as mere commodities, available only to the highest bidder, are all terribly hard questions—as the Eastern Europeans are now discovering as they attempt to draft their own constitutions. But these are not questions that should ever be confused with issues of what is technologically possible, about what is realistically enforceable, or about what is socially desirable.

Similarly, the Constitution does not permit anything and everything to be *socialized* and made into a public good available to whoever needs or "deserves" it most. I would hope, for example, that the government could not use its powers of eminent domain to "take" live body parts like eyes or kidneys or brain tissue for those who need transplants and would be expected to lead particularly productive lives. In any event, I feel certain that whatever constitutional right each of us has to inhabit his or her own body and to hold on to his or her own thoughts and creations should not depend solely on cost–benefit calculations, or on the availability of technological methods for painlessly effecting transfers or for creating good artificial substitutes.

Axiom 3: Government May Not Control Information Content

A third constitutional axiom, like the first two, reflects a deep respect for the integrity of each individual and a healthy skepticism toward government. The axiom is that, although information and ideas have real effects in the social world, it's not up to government to pick and choose for us in terms of the *content* of that information or the *value* of those ideas.

This notion is sometimes mistakenly reduced to the naive child's ditty that "sticks and stones may break my bones, but words can never hurt me." Anybody who's ever been called something awful by children in a schoolyard knows better than to believe any such thing. The real basis for First Amendment values isn't the false premise that information and ideas have no real impact, but the belief that information and ideas are *too important* to entrust to any government censor or overseer.

If we keep that in mind, and *only* if we keep that in mind, will we be able to see through the tempting argument that, in the Information Age, free speech is a luxury we can no longer afford. That argument becomes especially tempting in the context of cyberspace, where sequences of "0"s and "1"s may become virtual life forms. Computer "viruses" roam the information nets, attaching themselves to various programs and screwing up computer facilities. Creation of a computer virus involves writing a program; the program then replicates itself and mutates. The electronic code involved is very much like DNA. If information content is "speech," and if the First Amendment is to apply in cyberspace, then mustn't these viruses be "speech"—and mustn't their writing and dissemination be constitutionally protected? To avoid that nightmarish outcome, mustn't we say that the First Amendment is *inapplicable* to cyberspace?

The answer is no. Speech is protected, but deliberately yelling "Boo!" at a cardiac patient may still be prosecuted as murder. Free speech is a constitutional right, but handing a bank teller a hold-up note that says, "Your money or your life," may still be punished as robbery. Stealing someone's diary may be punished as theft—even if you intend to publish it in book form. And the Supreme Court, over the past fifteen years, has gradually brought advertising within the ambit of protected expression without preventing the government from protecting consumers from deceptive advertising. The lesson, in short, is that constitutional principles are subtle enough to bend to such concerns. They needn't be broken or tossed out.

Axiom 4: The Constitution Is Founded on Normative Conceptions of Humanity That Advances in Science and Technology Cannot "Disprove"

A fourth constitutional axiom is that the human spirit is something beyond a physical information processor. That axiom, which regards human thought processes as not fully reducible to the operations of a computer program, however complex, must not be confused with the silly view that, because computer operations involve nothing more than the manipulation of "on" and "off" states of myriad microchips, it somehow follows that government control or outright seizure of computers and computer programs threatens no First Amendment rights because human thought processes are not directly involved. To say that would be like saying that government confiscation of a newspaper's printing press and tomorrow morning's copy has nothing to do with speech but involves only a taking of metal, paper, and ink. Particularly if the seizure or the regulation is triggered by the content of the information being processed or transmitted, the First Amendment is of course fully involved. Yet this recognition that information processing by computer entails something far beyond the mere sequencing of mechanical or chemical steps still leaves a potential gap between what computers can do internally and in communication with one another—and what goes on within and between human minds. It is that gap to which this fourth axiom is addressed; the very existence of any such gap is, as I'm sure you know, a matter of considerable controversy.

What if people like the mathematician and physicist Roger Penrose, author of *The Emperor's New Mind,* are wrong about human minds? In that provocative recent book, Penrose disagrees with those Artificial Intelligence, or AI, gurus who insist that it's only a matter of time until human thought and feeling can be perfectly simulated or even replicated by a series of purely physical operations—that it's all just neurons firing and neurotransmitters flowing, all subject to perfect modeling in suitable computer systems. Would an adherent of that AI orthodoxy, someone whom

Penrose fails to persuade, have to reject as irrelevant for cyberspace those constitutional protections that rest on the anti-AI premise that minds are *not* reducible to really fancy computers?

Consider, for example, the Fifth Amendment, which provides that "no person shall be . . . compelled in any criminal case to be a witness against himself." The Supreme Court has long held that suspects may be required, despite this protection, to provide evidence that is not "testimonial" in nature—blood samples, for instance, or even exemplars of one's handwriting or voice. Last year, in a case called *Pennsylvania v. Muniz*, the Supreme Court held that answers to even simple questions like "When was your sixth birthday?" are testimonial because such a question, however straightforward, nevertheless calls for the product of mental activity and therefore uses the suspect's mind against him. But what if science could eventually describe thinking as a process no more complex than, say, riding a bike or digesting a meal? Might the progress of neurobiology and computer science eventually overthrow the premises of the *Muniz* decision?

I would hope not. For the Constitution's premises, properly understood, are *normative* rather than *descriptive*. The philosopher David Hume was right in teaching that no "ought" can ever be logically derived from an "is." If we should ever abandon the Constitution's protection for the distinctively and universally human, it won't be because robotics or genetic engineering or computer science have led us to deeper truths, but rather because they have seduced us into more profound confusions. Science and technology open options, create possibilities, suggest incompatibilities, generate threats. They do not alter what is "right" or what is "wrong." The fact that those notions are elusive and subject to endless debate need not make them totally contingent on contemporary technology.

Axiom 5: Constitutional Principles Should Not Vary with Accidents of Technology

In a sense, that's the fifth and final constitutional axiom I would urge upon this gathering: that the Constitution's norms, at their deepest level, must be invariant under merely *technological* transformations. Our constitutional law evolves through judicial interpretation, case by case, in a process of reasoning by analogy from precedent. At its best, that process is ideally suited to seeing beneath the surface and extracting deeper principles from prior decisions. At its worst, though, the same process can get bogged down in superficial aspects of preexisting examples, fixating upon unessential features while overlooking underlying principles and values.

When the Supreme Court in 1928 first confronted wiretapping and held in *Olmstead v. United States* that such wiretapping involved no "search" or "seizure" within the meaning of the Fourth Amendment's prohibition of "unreasonable searches and seizures," the majority of the Court reasoned that the Fourth Amendment "itself shows that the search is to be of material things—the person, the house, his papers or his effects," and said that "there was no searching" when a suspect's phone was tapped because the Constitution's language "cannot be extended and expanded to include telephone wires reaching to the whole world from the defendant's house or office." After all, said the Court, the intervening wires "are not part of his house or office any more than are the highways along which they are stretched." . . .

It is easy to be pessimistic about the way in which the Supreme Court has reacted to technological change. . . . For example, when movies were invented, and for several decades thereafter, the Court held that movie exhibitions were not entitled to First Amendment protection. When community access cable TV was born, the Court hindered municipal attempts to provide it at low cost by holding that rules requiring landlords to install small cable boxes on their apartment buildings amounted to a compensable taking of property. And in *Red Lion v. FCC*, decided twenty-two years ago but still not repudiated today, the Court ratified government control of TV and radio broadcast content with the dubious logic that the scarcity of the electromagnetic spectrum justified not merely government policies to auction off, randomly allocate, or otherwise ration the spectrum according to neutral rules, but also much more intrusive and content-based government regulation in the form of the so-called "fairness doctrine."

Although the Supreme Court and the lower federal courts have taken a somewhat more enlightened approach in dealing with cable television, these decisions for the most part reveal a curious judicial blindness, as if the Constitution had to be reinvented with the birth of each new technology. Judges interpreting a late 18th century Bill of Rights tend to forget that, unless its *terms* are read in an evolving and dynamic way, its *values* will lose even the *static* protection they once enjoyed. Ironically, *fidelity* to original values requires *flexibility* of textual interpretation. . . .

Judicial error in this field tends to take the form of saying that, by using modern technology ranging from the telephone to the television to computers, we "assume the risk." But that typically begs the question. Justice Harlan, in a dissent penned two decades ago, wrote: "Since it is the task of the law to form and project, as well as mirror and reflect, we should not . . . merely recite . . . risks without examining the *desirability* of saddling them upon society." (*United States v. White*, 401 U.S. at 786). And, I would add, we should not merely recite risks without examining how imposing those risks comports with the Constitution's fundamental values of *freedom, privacy,* and *equality.*

Failing to examine just that issue is the basic error I believe federal courts and Congress have made:

- in regulating radio and TV broadcasting without adequate sensitivity to First Amendment values;
- in supposing that the selection and editing of video programs by cable operators might be less than a form of expression;
- in excluding telephone companies from cable and other information markets;
- in assuming that the processing of "O"s and "1"s by computers as they exchange data with one another is something less than "speech"; and
- in generally treating information processed electronically as though it were somehow less entitled to protection for that reason.

The lesson to be learned is that these choices and these mistakes are not dictated by the Constitution. They are decisions for us to make in interpreting that majestic charter, and in implementing the principles that the Constitution establishes.

CONCLUSION

If my own life as a lawyer and legal scholar could leave just one legacy, I'd like it to be the recognition that the Constitution *as a whole* "protects people, not places." If that is to come about, the Constitution as a whole must be read through a technologically transparent lens. That is, we must embrace, as a rule of construction or interpretation, a principle one might call the "cyberspace corollary." It would make a suitable Twenty-seventh Amendment to the Constitution, one befitting the 200th anniversary of the Bill of Rights. Whether adopted all at once as a constitutional amendment, or accepted gradually as a principle of interpretation that I believe should obtain even without any formal change in the Constitution's language, the corollary I would propose would do for *technology* in 1991 what I believe the Constitution's Ninth Amendment, adopted in 1791, was meant to do for *text.*

The Ninth Amendment says: "The enumeration in the Constitution, of certain rights, shall not be construed to deny or disparage others retained by the people." That amendment provides added support for the long-debated, but now largely accepted, "right of privacy" that the Supreme Court recognized in such decisions as the famous birth control case of 1965, *Griswold v. Connecticut.* The Ninth Amendment's simple message is: The *text* used by the Constitution's authors and ratifiers does not exhaust the values our Constitution recognizes. Perhaps a Twenty-seventh Amendment could convey a parallel and equally simple message: The *technologies* familiar to the Constitution's authors and ratifiers similarly do not exhaust the *threats* against which the Constitution's core values must be protected.

The most recent amendment, the Twenty-sixth, adopted in 1971, extended the vote to 18-year-olds. It would be fitting, in a world where youth has been enfranchised, for a Twenty-seventh amendment to spell a kind of "childhood's end" for constitutional law. The Twenty-seventh Amendment, to be proposed for at least serious debate in 1991, would read simply:

This Constitution's protections for the freedoms of speech, press, petition, and assembly, and its protections against unreasonable searches and seizures and the deprivation of life, liberty, or property without due process of law, shall be construed as fully applicable without regard to the technological method or medium through which information content is generated, stored, altered, transmitted, or controlled.

QUESTIONS FOR ANALYSIS

1. Tribe details several ways in which the courts have had difficulty grasping technological changes to adapt legal principles. Are there parallel problems in our development of ethical principles?
2. Tribe identifies several political decisions we face in society in the recognition of technological change, and he appeals to political philosophers we considered in Part I, especially John Locke and Robert Nozick. How should we proceed in developing those policies? Should we recognize a right of access to technology by all citizens in order to participate fully in our democracy? Should we expand the recognition of the public domain and fair use of intellectual property, so people would not have to pay so much money in royalties for the software, recordings, and writings of others?
3. In Axiom 4, Tribe appeals to the philosopher David Hume in arguing that new *descriptive* information, knowledge, or technology can never transform our *normative* standards. What does Tribe mean by that? Do you agree that new scientific or technological information does not force us to change our normative views, whether in the law or in ethics?
4. Assess Tribe's proposed Twenty-seventh Amendment to the Constitution. Is it written in such a way as to protect our core constitutional values, regardless of what technologies emerge in the future that we cannot today even imagine? Do you anticipate that some of those values will have to be relinquished in the face of new technologies?

Free Speech in Cyberspace

RICHARD A. SPINELLO

Richard A. Spinello, a research professor at the Carroll School of Management, Boston College, has published extensively on issues of ethics and law related to the Internet and cyberspace. In this excerpt from his book *Cyberethics: Morality and Law in Cyberspace,* he reviews a wide range of problematic free-speech issues, including pornography, filtering mechanisms to restrict content, hate speech, anonymous speech, and spam.

INTRODUCTION

The Internet has clearly expanded the potential for individuals to exercise their First Amendment right to freedom of expression. The 'net gives all of its users a vast expressive power if they choose to take advantage of it. For example, users can operate their own bulletin boards, public

From Richard Spinello, *Cyberethics: Morality and Law in Cyberspace* (Sudbury, Mass.: Jones and Bartlett Publishers, 2000).

electronic newsletters, or establish a home page on the Web. According to Michael Godwin, the net "puts the full power of 'freedom of the press' into each individual's hands."[1] Or as the Supreme Court eloquently wrote in its *Reno v. ACLU* decision, the Internet enables an ordinary citizen to become "a pamphleteer,. . . a town crier with a voice that resonates farther than it could from any soapbox."[2]

As a result, the issue of free speech and content control in cyberspace has emerged as arguably the most contentious moral problem of the nascent Information Age. Human rights such as free speech have taken a place of special prominence in this century. In some respects, these basic rights now collide with the state's inclination to reign in this revolutionary power enjoyed by Internet users. Although the United States has sought to suppress on-line pornography, the target of some European countries, such as France and Germany, has been hate speech.

In addition, speech is at the root of most other major ethical and public policy problems in cyberspace, including privacy, intellectual property, and security....

Those who pioneered Internet technology have consistently asserted that the right to free expression in cyberspace should have as broad a scope as possible. For many years, the government was reluctant to restrict or filter any form of information on the network for fear of stifling an atmosphere that thrives on the free and open exchange of ideas.

However, the increased use of the Internet, especially among more vulnerable segments of the population (such as young children), forced some public policy makers to rethink this laissez-faire approach. In the United States, the result has been several futile attempts to control Internet content through poorly crafted legislation. An unfortunate byproduct of this has been publicity and attention to this matter that is probably out of proportion to the depth or gravity of the problem.

Despite the calls for regulation, there is a powerful sentiment among many Internet stakeholders to maintain this status quo. The strongest voices continue to come from those who want to preserve the Internet's libertarian spirit and who insist that the surest way to endanger the vitality of this global network are onerous regulations and rules, which would stifle the creative impulses of its users and imperil this one last bastion of free, uninhibited expression. . . .

PORNOGRAPHY IN CYBERSPACE

Before we discuss the U.S. Congress' recent efforts to regulate speech on the net we should be clear about what constitutes pornographic speech. There are two broad classes of such speech: (1) obscene speech, which is completely unprotected by the First Amendment, and (2) "indecent" speech, which is not obscene for adults but should be kept out of the hands of children under the age of seventeen. In *Miller v. California* (1973), the Supreme Court established a three-part test to determine whether or not speech fell in the first category and was obscene for everyone. To meet this test, speech had to satisfy the following conditions: (1) it depicts sexual (or excretory) acts explicitly prohibited by state law; (2) it appeals to prurient interests as judged by a reasonable person using community standards; and (3) it has no serious literary, artistic, social, political, or scientific value. Child pornography is an unambiguous example of obscene speech.

The second class of speech, often called *indecent* speech, is obscene for children but not for adults. The relevant legal case is *Ginsberg v. New York,* which upheld New York's law banning the sale of speech "harmful to minors" to anyone under the age of seventeen. The law in dispute in the Ginsberg case defined *harmful to minors* as follows: "that quality of any description or representation, in whatever from, of nudity, sexual conduct, sexual excitement, or sado-masochistic abuse, when it: (1) predominantly appeals to the prurient, shameful, or morbid interests of minors, and (2) is patently offensive to prevailing standards in the adult community as a whole with respect to what is suitable for minors, and (3) is utterly without redeeming social importance for minors." Although state legislatures have applied this case differently to their statutes prohibiting the sale of obscene material to minors, these criteria can serve as a general guide to what we classify as "Ginsberg" speech, which should be off limits to children under the age of seventeen.

PUBLIC POLICY OVERVIEW

The Communications Decency Act (or CDA 1)

The ubiquity of both forms of pornography on the Internet is a challenge for lawmakers. As the quantity of communications grows in the realm of cyberspace, there is a much greater likelihood that people will become exposed to forms of speech or images that are offensive and potentially harmful. If you are seeking to send an e-mail to the President of the United States and accidentally retrieve the Web site www.whitehouse.com instead of www.whitehouse.gov, you will see what we mean. By some estimates, the Internet currently has about 280,000 sites that cater to various forms or pornography, and some sources report that there is an average of an additional 500 sites coming on-line everyday, hence the understandable temptation of governments to regulate and control free expression on the Internet to contain the negative effects of unfettered free speech on this medium. The Communications Decency Act (CDA), recently ruled unconstitutional by the U.S. Supreme Court, represented one such futile, and some say misguided, attempt at such regulation. . . .

The CDA included several key provisions that restricted the distribution of sexually explicit material to children. It imposed criminal penalties on anyone who "initiates the transmission of any communication which is . . . indecent, knowing that the recipient of the communication is under 18 years of age." It also criminalized the display of patently offensive sexual material "in a manner available to a person under 18 years of age"[3]. . .

A panel of federal judges in Philadelphia ruled unanimously that the CDA was a violation of the First and Fifth Amendments. The Justice Department appealed the case, which now became known as *Reno v. ACLU,* but to no avail. The Supreme Court agreed with the lower court's ruling, and in June 1997, it declared that this federal law was unconstitutional. The Court was especially concerned about the vagueness of this content-based regulation of speech. According to the majority opinion written by Justice Stevens, "We are persuaded that the CDA lacks the precision that the First Amendment requires when a statue regulates the content of speech. In order to deny minors access to potentially harmful speech, the CDA effectively suppresses a large amount of speech that adults have a constitutional right to receive and to address to one another."[4] Stevens also held that the free expression on the Internet is entitled to the highest level of First Amendment protection. This is in contrast to the more limited protections for other more pervasive media such as radio and broadcast and cable television, where the Court has allowed many government-imposed restrictions. In making this important distinction, the Court assumes that computer users have to actively seek offensive material, whereas they are more likely to encounter it accidentally on television or radio if it were so available.

CDA II

Most of those involved in the defeat of the CDA realized that the issue would not soon go away. Congress, still supported by public opinion, was sure to try again. In October 1998, they did try again, passing an omnibus budget package that included the Child Online Protection Act (COPA), a successor to the original CDA, which has become known as CDA II. The law was signed by President Clinton, and like its predecessor, it was immediately challenged by the ACLU. CDA II would make it illegal for the operators of commercial Web sites to make sexually explicit materials harmful to minors available to those younger than seventeen years of age. Commercial Web site operators would be required to collect an identification code, such as a credit card number, as proof of age before allowing viewers access to such material.

The ACLU and other opponents claimed that the law would lead to excessive self-censorship. CDA II would have a negative impact on the ability of these commercial Web sites to reach an adult audience. According to Max Hailperin, "There is no question that the COPA impairs commercial speakers' ability to cheaply, easily, and broadly communicate material to adults that is constitutionally protected as to the adults (non-obscene), though harmful to minors."[5] The law is more narrowly focused than CDA I because it attempts to define objectionable sexual content more carefully. Such content would lack "serious literary, artistic, political or scientific value" for those younger than seventeen years of age. However, the law's critics contend that it is still worded too broadly. Those critics also worry about what will happen if the law is arbitrarily or carelessly applied. For example, would some sites offering sexual education information violate the law?

In February 1999, a Philadelphia federal judge issued a preliminary injunction against CDA II, preventing it from going into effect. This judge accepted the argument that the law would lead to self-censorship and that "such a chilling effect could result in the censoring of constitutionally protected speech, which constitutes an irreparable harm to the plaintiffs." An appeal is considered likely, meaning that the ultimate resolution will have to await the Supreme Court's decision.

At the heart of the debate about the CDA and content regulation is the basic question . . . about how the Internet should be controlled. Should government impose the kind of central controls embodied in this legislation? Or should the Internet be managed and controlled through a more bottoms-up, user-oriented approach, with users empowered to develop their own solutions tailored to their own needs and value systems? One advantage of the latter approach is that such controls are more consistent with the Internet's decentralized network architecture. For many users, decentralism in the area of content control seems preferable to formal state regulations. It respects civil liberties and leaves the opportunity for content control in the hands of those most capable of exercising it.

However, reliance on a decentralized solution is certainly not without opposition and controversy. If we empower users to control Internet content in some ways, we are still left with many questions. If we assert that the purpose of censoring the Internet is the preservation of the community's values, how do we define *community*? Also, how do we ascertain what the community's values really are? Finally, can we trust technology to help solve the problem or will it make matters even worse?

AUTOMATING CONTENT CONTROLS

Nonetheless, thanks to the rulings against CDA I and II, the burden of content control is now shifting to parents and local organizations. This communal power has raised some concerns. To what extent should local communities and institutions (such as schools, prisons, libraries, and so on) assume direct responsibility for controlling content on the Internet? Libraries, for example, must consider whether it is appropriate to use filtering software to protect young patrons from pornography on the Internet. Is this a useful and prudent way to uphold local community or institutional standards? Or does this sort of censorship compromise a library's traditional commitment to the free flow of ideas?

There are two broad areas of concern about the use of content controls that need elaboration. The first area concerns the ethical probity of censorship itself, even when it is directed at the young. There is a growing tendency to recognize a broad spectrum of rights, even for children, and to criticize parents, educators, and politicians who are more interested in imposing their value systems on others than in protecting vulnerable children. . . .

Lurking in the background of this debate is the question of whether children have a First Amendment right to access indecent materials. Legal scholars have not reached a consensus about this, but if children do have such a right, it would be much more difficult to justify filtering out indecent materials in libraries or educational institutions. One school of thought about this issue is that a child's free speech rights should be proportionate to his or her age. The older the child, the more problematic are restrictions on indecent material.

The second area of concern pertains to the suitability of the blocking methods and other automated controls used to accomplish this censorship. Two basic problems arise with the use of blocking software. The first problem is the unreliability and lack of precision that typifies most of these products; there are no perfect or foolproof devices for filtering out obscene material. Programs like the popular SurfWatch operate by comparing Web site addresses to a list of prohibited sites that are known to contain pornographic material. SurfWatch currently prohibits more than 30,000 Web sites. However, this filtering program is less effective with Usenet newsgroups (electronic bulletin boards or chat rooms). SurfWatch depends on the name of the newsgroup to decide whether it should be banned; thus, an earlier version missed a chat room that displays pornographic material but goes under the name alt.kids-talk.penpals.

Another problem is that these blocking programs can be used to enforce a code of political correctness unbeknownst to parents or librarians who choose to install them. Sites that discuss AIDS, homosexuality, and related topics are routinely blocked by certain filtering programs. Often, these programs are not explicit or forthright about their blocking criteria, which greatly compounds this problem. . . .

It is never easy to advocate censorship at any level of society precisely because the right to free expression is so valuable and cherished. However, proponents of automated content controls argue that all human rights, including the right to free expression, are limited by each other and by other aspects of the common good, which can be called *public morality*. According to this perspective, parents and schools are acting prudently when they choose to *responsibly* implement filtering technologies to help preserve and promote the values of respect for others and appropriate sexual conduct that are part of our public morality. Preserving free speech and dealing with sexually explicit material will always be a problem in a free and pluralistic society, and this is one way of achieving a proper balance when the psychological health of young children is at stake.

HATE SPEECH

The rapid expansion of hate speech on the Web raises similar problems and controversies. Many groups, such as white supremacists and anarchists, have Web sites that advocate their particular point of view. Some of these sites are blatantly anti-Semitic, whereas others are dominated by Holocaust revisionists who claim that the Holocaust never happened. On occasion, these sites can be especially virulent and outrageous, such as the Web site of the Charlemagne Hammerskins. The first scene reveals a man disguised in a ski mask who is bearing a gun and standing next to a swastika. The site has this ominous warning for its visitor: "Be assured, we still have one-way tickets to Auschwitz."

Some hate Web sites take the form of computer games, such as Doom and Castle Wolfenstein, which have been constructed to include African Americans, Jews, or homosexuals as targets of violence. In one animated game, the Dancing Baby, which became a popular television phenomenon, has been depicted as the "white power baby."

In the United States, the most widely publicized of these hate speech sites are those that attack doctors who perform abortions. Some of these sites are especially menacing and venomous, such as "The Nuremberg Files," which features a "Wanted" list of abortion doctors. The site's authors contend that they are not advocating violence but only expressing their opinion, albeit in a graphic format.

What can be done about this growing subculture of hate on the Internet? The great danger is that the message of hate and bigotry, once confined to reclusive, powerless groups, can now be spread more efficiently in cyberspace. Unlike obscenity and libel, hate speech is not illegal under U.S. federal law and is fully protected by the First Amendment. Even speech that incites hated of a particular group is legally acceptable. The only exception to this is the use of "fighting words," which were declared beyond the purview of the First Amendment by the Supreme Court. Such speech, however, must threaten a clear and present danger. In the controversial case of the antiabortion Web sites, a federal court recently ruled that the site's content was too intimidating and hence was not protected by the First Amendment. But in general, censorship of on-line hate speech is inconsistent with the First Amendment.

On the other hand, in European countries like Germany and France, anti-Semitic, Nazi-oriented Web sites are illegal. In Germany, the government has required ISPs to eliminate these sites under the threat of prosecution. Critics of this approach argue that it is beyond the capability of ISPs to control content in such a vast region as the World Wide Web. It is also illegal for Internet companies to ship Nazi materials into Germany. This means that Amazon.com should not be selling books like Hitler's *Mein Kampf* to its German customers, although this restriction too will be difficult to enforce.

Although government regulation and explicit laws about hate speech are suitable for some countries, an alternative to government regulation is once again reliance on user empowerment and *responsible* filtering that does not erroneously exclude legitimate political speech. Parents and certain private and religious institutions might want to seize the initiative to shield young children and sensitive individuals from some of this material such as virulent anti-Semitism.

However, even more caution must be exercised in this case because the distinction between hate speech and unpopular or unorthodox political opinion is sometimes difficult to make. A rule of thumb is that hate speech Web sites are those that attack, insult, and demean whole segments of the population, such as Jews, Italians, African-Americans, whites, homosexuals, and so forth. Many sites will fall in a nebulous gray area, and this will call for conscientiousness and discretion on the part of those charged with labeling those sites.

ANONYMOUS SPEECH

Anonymous communication in cyberspace is enabled largely through the use of anonymous remailers, which strip off the identifying information on an e-mail message and substitute an anonymous code or a random number. By encrypting a message and then routing that message through a series of anonymous remailers, a user can rest assured that his or her message will remain anonymous and confidential. This process is called *chained remailing*. The process is effective because none of the remailers will have the key to read the encrypted message; neither the recipient nor any remailers (except the first) in the chain can identify the sender; the recipient cannot connect the sender to the message unless every single remailer in the chain cooperates. This would assume that each remailer kept a log of their incoming and outgoing mail, which is highly unlikely....

Do we really need to ensure that digital anonymity is preserved, especially since it is so often a shield for subversive activities? It would be difficult to argue convincingly that anonymity is a core human good, utterly indispensable for human flourishing and happiness. One can surely conceive of people and societies where anonymity is not a factor for their happiness. However, although anonymity may not be a primary good, it is surely a secondary one because *for some people in some circumstances,* a measure of anonymity is important for the exercise of their rational life plan and for human flourishing. The proper exercise of freedom, and especially free expression, requires the support of anonymity in some situations. Unless the speaker or author can choose to remain anonymous, opportunities for free expression become limited for various reasons and that individual may be forced to remain mute on critical matters. Thus, without the benefit of anonymity, the value of freedom is constrained.

We can point to many specific examples in support of the argument that *anonymous free expression* deserves protection. Social intolerance may require some individuals to rely on anonymity to communicate openly about an embarrassing medical condition or an awkward disability. Whistleblowers may be understandably reluctant to come forward with valuable information unless they can remain anonymous. And political dissent even in a democratic society that prizes free speech may be impeded unless it can be done anonymously. Anonymity then has an incontestable value in the struggle against repression and even against more routine corporate and government abuses of power. In the conflict in Kosovo, for example, some individuals relied on anonymous programs (such as anonymizer.com) to describe atrocities perpetrated against ethnic Albanians. If the Serbians were able to trace the identity of these individuals, their lives would have been in grave danger.

Thus, although there is a cost to preserving anonymity, its central importance in human affairs is certainly beyond dispute. It is a positive good; that is, it possesses positive qualities that render it worthy to be valued. At a minimum, it is valued as an instrumental good, as a means of achieving the full actualization of free expression.

Anonymous communication, of course, whether facilitated by remailers or by other means, does have its drawbacks. It can be abused by criminals or terrorists seeking to communicate anonymously to plot their crimes. It also permits cowardly users to communicate without civility or to libel someone without accountability and with little likelihood of apprehension by law enforcement authorities. Anonymity can also be useful for revealing trade secrets or violating other intellectual property laws. In general, secrecy and anonymity are not beneficial for society if they are overused or used improperly. . . .

Although we admit that too much secrecy is problematic, the answer is not to eliminate all secrecy and make everything public and transparent, which could be the inevitable result of this loss of digital anonymity. Nonetheless, it cannot be denied that anonymity has its disadvantages and that digital anonymity and an unfettered Internet can be exploited for many forms of mischief. Therefore, governments are tempted to sanction the deployment of architectures that will make Internet users more accountable and less able to hide behind the shield of anonymity.

Despite the potential for abuse, however, there are cogent reasons for eschewing the adoption of those architectures and protecting the right to anonymous free speech. A strong case can be put forth that the costs of banning anonymous speech in cyberspace are simply too high in an open and democratic society. The loss of anonymity may very well diminish the power of that voice that now resonates so loudly in cyberspace. As a result, regulators must proceed with great caution in this area. . . .

SPAM AS COMMERCIAL FREE SPEECH

Spam refers to unsolicited, promotional e-mail, usually sent in bulk to thousands or millions of Internet users. Quite simply, it is junk e-mail that is usually a significant annoyance to its recipients. The major difference between electronic junk mail and paper junk mail is that the per copy cost of sending the former is so much lower. There are paper, printing, and postage charges for each piece of regular junk mail, but the marginal cost of sending an additional piece of junk e-mail is negligible. For example, some direct marketers who specializes in spam charge their clients a fee as low as $400 to send out several million messages.

But spam is not cost free. The problem is that the lion's share of these costs are externalities, that is, they are costs borne involuntarily by others. As Robert Raisch has observed, spam is "postage-due marketing."[6] The biggest cost associated with spam is the consumption of computer resources. For example, when someone sends out spam the messages must sit on a disk somewhere, and this means that valuable disk space is being filled with unwanted mail. Also, many users must pay for each message received or for each disk block used. Others pay for the time they are connected to the Internet, time that can be wasted downloading and deleting spam. As the volume of spam grows and commercial use of the Internet expands, these costs will continue their steady increase. Furthermore, when spam is sent through ISPs they must bear the costs of delivery. This amounts to wasted network bandwidth and the use of system resources such as disk storage space along with the servers and transfer networks involved in the transmission process. . . .

Should all bulk e-mail, even noncommerical communications, be considered spam? If the Internet is to realize its full potential as a "democratizing force," shouldn't some forms of bulk e-mail be permitted, both morally and legally? What should be the decisive factors in determining when bulk e-mail is intrusive spam or a legitimate form of communication? . . .

POSTSCRIPT

Spam, pornography, libel, hate speech—all are problematic forms of free expression that pose formidable challenges to cyberspace jurisprudence, which seeks to balance individual rights with the public good. Ideally, of course, individuals and organizations should regulate their own expression by refraining from hate speech, refusing to disseminate pornography to children, and repressing the temptation to use spam as a means of advertising goods or services. In the absence of such self-restraint, Internet stakeholders must make difficult decisions about whether to shield themselves from unwanted speech, whether it be crude obscenities or irksome junk e-mail.

Top-down government regulations such as the CDA II or laws that ban junk e-mail represent one method for solving this problem. Sophisticated filtering devices, which will undoubtedly continue to improve in their precision and accuracy, offer a different, but more chaotic, alternative. As we have been at pains to insist here, whatever combination of constraints are used—code, law, market, or norms—full respect must be accorded to key moral values such as personal autonomy; hence the need for nuanced ethical reflection about how these universal moral standards can best be preserved as we develop effective constraints for aberrant behavior in cyberspace. Otherwise, our worst apprehensions about the tyranny of the code *or* the laws of cyberspace may be realized.

Another option, of course, is to refrain from the temptation to take *any* action against these controversial forms of speech in cyberspace. Some civil libertarians convincingly argue that Internet stakeholders should eschew regulations and filtering and leave the Internet as unfettered as possible. We should tolerate nuisance speech on the Internet just as we tolerate it in the physical world.

NOTES

1. Godwin, M. 1998. *CyberRights.* New York: Random House, p. 16.
2. *ACLU v. Reno,* 521 U.S. p. 870 (1997).
3. See *Communications Decency Act,* 47 U.S.C. p. 223 (d)(1)(B).
4. *ACLU v. Reno,* p. 882.
5. Halperin, M. 1999. The COPA BATTLE AND THE FUTURE OF FREE SPEECH. *Communications of the ACM* p. 42(1): 25.
6. Raisch, R. *Postage due marketing: An Internet company white paper.* Available http://www.internet.com:2010/marketing/postage.html

QUESTIONS FOR ANALYSIS

1. How would you propose to restrict access by children to pornography in cyberspace without interfering with the rights of adults to access this material? Do you support the approach taken by Congress or the emphasis on free speech upheld by the courts with regard to the Communications Decency Acts I and II? Or do you support unrestricted access by children to all material?
2. Should hate speech be protected by the First Amendment? If we can prove that it provokes illegal activity against certain groups, should we restrict or prohibit it?
3. Should anonymous speech be protected, especially if we learn that it is being used by terrorists and other criminals? Would prohibiting it for them infringe on the rights of others with legitimate noncriminal reasons for communicating anonymously?
4. Should spam be protected as commercial free speech?

Is it Moral to Make Copies of Software for My Friends?

BERNARD GERT

In this brief excerpt from a longer article on "common morality and computing," Bernard Gert, professor of philosophy at Dartmouth College, argues that common morality provides a clear answer to the question raised above—namely, that it is not moral to make copies of software for friends. For a more extended account of his influential moral theory, which is strongly influenced by Kant, see Bernard Gert, *Morality: Its Nature and Justification* (Oxford University Press, 1998).

. . . It might be rational to favour allowing a person to illegally copy software for a friend. It might even be rational to favour allowing everyone to know that they can illegally copy software for a friend. But in order to have the kind of impartiality required by morality, one can not limit the subject matter of the law to a particular law one dislikes. This would be like people saying that it is justified to violate the law prohibiting smoking by minors, but not justified to violate the law prohibiting drinking by minors. Or that it is justified to violate the law prohibiting one's favourite illegal drug, but not justified to violate the law prohibiting other illegal drugs. In order to justify illegally copying software, one has to hold either that the law is clearly an unjust one, or that it is morally justifiable to break morally acceptable laws with which one disagrees for the benefit of oneself or one's friends. A seemingly controversial case is one in which the law is morally unacceptable, in the sense that no fully informed impartial rational person would favour that law over other alternatives, but the law is not unjust in any clear or straightforward sense.

No one holds that it is morally justifiable to break morally acceptable laws concerning computing with which one disagrees for the benefit of oneself or one's friends. Present copying laws are not clearly unjust, so that it seems that the only way to justify violating the law prohibiting copying software is to show that the law is morally unacceptable. However, if some fully informed impartial rational persons would publicly allow the restrictions imposed by the present law, that is, if they would be willing for everyone to know that such restrictions are allowed, then the law is morally acceptable and it is not morally justified to violate that law under normal circumstances. Similarly, if the speed limit that is adopted for certain roads in one state, is such that some fully informed, impartial rational persons would favor such a law, then under normal circumstances, it is not morally justified to exceed that speed limit. One can only justifiably violate a morally acceptable law in circumstances where one would be willing to publicly allow any morally acceptable law to be violated. To publicly allow a violation of a rule is to propose that this kind of violation be allowed by the public system that is morality. That is why the impartiality required by morality does not allow one to break a law when one cannot describe the situation by means of the morally relevant features that all moral agents can understand.

From Bernard Gert, "Common Morality and Computing," *Ethics and Information Technology* 1 (1999): 57–64. Published by Kluwer Academic Publishers.

This means that one cannot justifiably pick some special class of morally acceptable laws, e.g., speeding laws, and claim that one would favour everyone knowing that they are allowed to violate those particular morally acceptable laws. In order to justify the violation of a morally acceptable law, one must be able to describe the circumstances in terms of morally relevant features that everyone can understand. It is not justifiable to violate a law simply because one believes, even justifiably believes, some other law would be better. To publicly allow violations in such circumstances, that is, to favour everyone knowing that they are allowed to violate the law in such circumstances, would lead to anarchy and no impartial rational person would publicly allow it.

Only the requirement that the violation be publicly allowed, which requires that it be formulated in terms of the morally relevant features that all rational persons can understand, guarantees the kind of impartially required by morality. When one is impartial in the way required by morality, it is clear that, except to prevent serious harms, one is not justified in breaking a morally acceptable law. In the situation described by Helen Nissenbaum, it is clear that serious harms are not being prevented, rather one is simply doing a favour for a friend.

Even if the law is not a morally acceptable one, e.g., if there are better laws, that is, laws that all fully informed impartial rational persons would prefer to the present law, it is still not clear that it is justifiable to violate the law.[1] It would have to be obvious that the present law is morally unacceptable before it would be clear that it is justifiable to violate it. Whether some other law would be a better law than the present law is a difficult question, and I do not know enough about the law to claim that there might not be several better laws. It might be that a more liberal copying law would be preferable to the restrictive one now in place, but that is certainly not obvious. If, as is most likely, fully informed, impartial rational persons disagree, and some favour the present law, it should be clear to all that it is not morally justifiable to violate the law simply to benefit a friend.

Two people, both fully informed, impartial and rational, who agree that two actions count as the same kind of violation, need not always agree on whether or not to advocate that this kind of violation be publicly allowed. They may rank the benefits and harms involved differently or they may differ in their estimate of the consequences of publicly allowing this kind of violation. But sometimes this disagreement may be due to one of them having too narrow a description of the kind of violation in question. For example, two persons may agree that one particular act of illegally copying a software program to benefit a friend will have no significant harmful consequences. However, they may disagree about the consequences of publicly allowing that kind of violation, one holding that everyone knowing that this kind of violation is allowed will result in a very significant harm to software companies, and the other holding that it will result in only an insignificant harm, which will be more than justified by the benefits gained by one's friends from such copying. Thus it may seem that there is an unresolvable moral disagreement.

However, 'illegally copying a software program' does not describe the act solely in terms of the morally relevant features. It brings in one's biases with regard to software; it allows one not to be impartial without even realizing it. Especially when one also bring in other irrelevant factors, such as, that the benefit of the illegal act is not oneself, but one's friend; as if whether it is oneself or a friend who benefits from the illegal act is a morally relevant feature. Doing something for a friend may be a good motive, but motives do not determine the morality of an action. If they did then all genuinely paternalistic deception by doctors would be morally acceptable. As discussed early, it seems that the proper description of the act is "violating a morally acceptable law to gain some benefit." Described in this way, no impartial rational person would publicly allow the act, hence it is an unjustified violation.

This consideration of this particular case, which at first seems controversial, shows the usefulness of a clear, comprehensive, and precise formulation of the moral system. Note that, unlike the discussion of what would be the best law concerning the copying of software, the discussion of whether it is justifiable to illegally copy software does not require an intimate knowledge of the nature of software, and the relations between the producers and users of software. If some impartial rational person could favour such a law, it is clear that it is unjustifiable to violate that law in order to do a favor for a friend. However, most morally problematic cases, e.g., those that involve the making of laws or policies concerning copying software, their ownership, etc. are very unlikely to have such clear answers. Nor is it likely that one will be able to provide even plausible answers without an intimate knowledge of the nature of software, and the relations between the producers and users of software. Induction on the basis of a single example is always very risky....

NOTES

1. See Le Droit de Nature. *Le Pouvoir et le Droit: Hobbes et les fondements de la Loi,* Textes réunis par by Louis Roux et François Triçaud, Publications de l'Université de Saint-Étienne, pp. 27–48, 1992. That paper explains and supports Hobbes's argument that it is better for every person to obey a law rather than follow their own rule, even if each of the rules that a person wants to follow is such that it if it were the law it would be a better law than the present law.

QUESTIONS FOR ANALYSIS

1. Gert claims that the laws against copying software are "not clearly unjust." Yet some argue that software companies with very dominant monopolies, such as Microsoft, have been able to inflate prices unfairly and that, accordingly, it is not unfair to sometimes make copies of their software to fight back against such monopolies. Do you find those arguments persuasive? How would Gert respond?
2. Gert considers "impartiality" essential in any moral system. What ideas in Kant seem to have inspired this focus on "impartiality" in Gert's contemporary work on moral theory?
3. Could a utilitarian justify copying software for one's friends?

Cyberstalking, Personal Privacy, and Moral Responsibility[1]

HERMAN T. TAVANI AND FRANCES S. GRODZINSKY

In this excerpt from a longer article, some of the moral issues presented by the more dangerous aspects of cyberspace are explored. Herman T. Tavani is a professor of philosophy at Rivier College, and Frances S. Grodzinsky is a professor of computer science and information technology at Sacred Heart University. The easy availability of personal information about all of us on the Internet also makes it easier for criminals who stalk and sometimes murder their prey. Tavani and Grodzinsky ask whether so much private information should be

From Herman T. Tavani and Frances S. Grodzinsky, "Cyberstalking, Personal Privacy, and Moral Responsibility," *Ethics and Information Technology* 4 (2002): 123–132. Published by Kluwer Academic publishers.

available on the Internet and whether all Internet users have a moral obligation to assist victims of cyberstalking.

CYBERSTALKING: AN INTRODUCTION AND OVERVIEW

What exactly is cyberstalking, and how do stalking incidents in cyberspace raise concerns for ethics? In answering these questions, we begin with a definition of stalking in general. According to *Webster's New World Dictionary of the American Language*, to engage in stalking is 'to pursue or approach game, an enemy, etc. stealthily, as from cover.' In the context of criminal activities involving human beings, a stalking crime is generally considered to be one in which an individual ('the stalker') clandestinely tracks the movements of an another individual or individuals ('the stalkee[s]'). Cyberstalking can be understood as a form of behavior in which certain types of stalking related activities, which in the past have occurred in physical space, are extended to the on-line world. On the one hand, we do not claim that cyberstalking is a new kind of crime.[2] On the other hand, we believe that the Internet has made a relevant difference with respect to stalking-related crimes because of the ways in which stalking activities can now be carried out. For example, Internet stalkers can operate anonymously or pseudononymously while on-line. In addition, a cyberstalker can stalk one or more individuals from the comfort of his or her home, and thus not have to venture out into the physical world to stalk someone. So Internet technology has provided stalkers with a certain mode of stalking that was not possible in the pre-Internet era.

Many people have become concerned about the kind of stalking-related activities that have recently occurred in cyberspace, and there are several reasons why these individuals would seem justified in their concern. Because stalking crimes in general are not fully understood in terms of their conceptual boundaries and their implications, it is that much more difficult to comprehend exactly what it would mean to commit a stalking crime in the cyber-realm. . . .

SOME ETHICAL REFLECTIONS ON THE AMY BOYER CASE

On October 15, 1999, Amy Boyer, a twenty-year-old resident of Nashua, NH, was murdered by a young man who had stalked her via the Internet. Her stalker, Liam Youens, was able to carry out many of the stalking activities that eventually led to Boyer's death by using a variety of on-line tools available to him. Through the use of standard Internet search facilities, and related on-line tools, Youens was able to find out where Boyer lived, where she worked, what kind of vehicle she drove, and so forth. In addition to using Internet search-related tools to acquire personal information about Boyer, Youens was also able to take advantage of other kinds of online facilities, such as those provided by Internet service providers (ISPs), to construct two Web sites. On one site, he posted personal information about Boyer, including a picture of her; and on another site, Youens described, in explicit detail, his plans to murder Boyer.

The Amy Boyer case has raised some controversial questions, many of which would seem to have significant moral implications for cyberspace. But is there anything special about the Amy Boyer case from an ethical perspective? One might be inclined to answer *no*. For example, one could argue that 'murder is murder', and that whether a murderer uses a computing device that included Internet tools to assist in carrying out a particular murder is irrelevant from an ethical point of view. One could further argue that there is nothing special about cyberstalking incidents in general—irrespective of whether or not those incidents result in the death of the victims—since stalking activities have had a long history of occurrence in the 'off-line' world. According to this line of reasoning, the use of Internet technology could be seen simply as the latest in a series of tools or techniques that have become available to stalkers to assist them in carrying out their criminal activities. However, it could also be argued that certain aspects of cyberstalking raise special problems that challenge our conventional moral and legal frameworks. For example, one could point out that a cyberstalker can stalk multiple victims simultaneously through the use of multiple 'windows' on his or her computer. The stalker can also stalk victims who happen to live in states and countries that are geographically distant from the stalker. We leave open the question whether any of the ethical issues involving cyberstalking are new or unique.[3] Instead, we focus on some ways in which cyberstalking challenges our existing moral framework.

We have argued elsewhere (see Grodzinsky and Tavani, 2002) that cyberstalking activities have significant implications for a range of ethical and social issues, including security, free speech, and censorship. In this essay, we argue that cyberstalking also raises questions involving personal privacy, moral responsibility and legal liability. Our primary focus, however, is on some of the ways that these particular ethical issues impact the Amy Boyer case. For example, was Boyer's right to (or at least her expectations about) privacy violated because of the personal information about her that was made available so easily to Internet users such as Liam Youens? Did Youens have a 'right' to set up a dedicated Web site about Amy Boyer without Boyer's knowledge and express consent; and did Youens have a right to post on that Web site any kind of information about Boyer—regardless of whether that information about her was psychologically harmful, offensive, or defamatory? If so, is such a right one that is—or ought to be—protected by free speech? Should the two ISPs that permitted Youens to post such information to Web sites that reside in their Internet 'space' be held legally liable, especially when information contained on those sites can easily lead to someone being physically harmed or, as in the case of Amy Boyer, murdered? Furthermore, do ordinary users who happen to come across a web site that contains a positing of a death threat directed at an individual or group of individuals have a moral responsibility to inform those individuals whose lives are threatened? . . .

INTERNET SEARCH ENGINES, PUBLIC RECORDS, AND PERSONAL PRIVACY

Consider the useful, and arguably important, function that Internet search engines provide in directing us to online resources involving academic research, commerce, recreation, and so forth. Hence, some might be surprised by the suggestion that search-engine technology itself could be controversial in some way. However, search engines can also be used to locate personal information about individuals. Sometimes that personal information resides in the form of public records that are available to Internet users, as in the case of information acquired about Amy Boyer by Liam Youens. Other types of personal information about individuals can also be acquired easily because of certain kinds of personal data that have been made accessible to Internet search engines without the knowledge and consent of the person or persons on whom an on-line search is conducted. But one might still ask why exactly the use of search-engine technology is controversial with respect to the privacy of individuals. Consider that an individual may be unaware that his or her name is among those included in one or more databases accessible to search engines. Because of this, individuals have little, if any, control over how information about them can be made available and be disseminated across the Internet.[4] This was certainly the case in the incident involving Amy Boyer, who had no knowledge about or control over the ways in which certain kinds of personal information about her was accessible to Youens through Internet search engines. It should be noted that Boyer neither placed any personal information about herself on the Internet, nor was she aware that such information about her had been so listed.

It could be argued that all information currently available on the Internet, including information about individual persons such as Amy Boyer, is, by virtue of the fact that it resides on the Internet, public information. Traditionally, information about persons that is available to the general public has not been protected by privacy laws and policies. We can, of course, question whether all of the information currently available on the Internet should be treated as 'public information' that deserves no normative protection.

Because of concerns related to the easy flow of personal information between and across databases, certain laws have been enacted to set limits on the ways in which electronic records containing *confidential* or *intimate* data can be exchanged. However, these laws and policies typically apply only to the exchange of electronic information such as that contained in medical records and financial records. Helen Nissenbaum (1998) has pointed out that such protection does not apply to personal information in the public sphere or in what she describes as 'spheres other than the intimate.'[5] Unfortunately for Amy Boyer, the kind of information that was gathered about her by Youens would be considered non-intimate and non-confidential in nature and thus would likely be viewed, by default, as information that does not warrant normative protection. Is this presumption about non-intimate personal information that is publicly available on the Internet one that it is either reasonable or fair? Was it fair to Amy Boyer?

The Commodification of Personal Information in Public Records

With respect to privacy policies and laws in the Internet age, what status should be accorded to personal information that resides in public sources, such as in public records? Consider that in the era preceding the Internet, information of this particular kind could be acquired by individuals who were willing to travel to municipal buildings and, where applicable, pay a small fee for a copy of the desired records. If this kind of information was already available to the general public before the advent of cyber-technology, why should its status necessarily change because of the new technology? Perhaps an equally important question is: Why were such records made public in the first place? For example, were they made public so that on-line entrepreneurs like Docusearch.com could collect this information, combine it with other kinds of personal information, and then sell it for a profit? Of course, it could be argued that entrepreneurs who were so motivated could have engaged in this activity—and some, no doubt, did—in the era preceding the Internet. But we could respond by asking how profitable and how practical such an enterprise would have been.

First, consider that 'information merchants' would have had to purchase copies of the physical records (that were publicly available). These merchants would then have had to hire legions of clerks to convert the purchased data into electronic form, sort the data according to some scheme, and finally prepare it for sale. This process, in addition to being highly impractical in terms of certain physical requirements, would hardly have been a profitable venture given the amount of labor and cost involved. So, most likely, it would not have occurred to entrepreneurs to engage in such a business venture prior to the advent of sophisticated information technology. But again, we should ask why public records were made 'public' in the first place.

In order for governmental agencies at the local, state, and federal levels to operate efficiently, records of certain kinds of personal information were needed to be readily available for access. For example, municipal governments needed certain information for tax-assessment purposes, such as assessing tax rates for houses and commercial real estate. State governments needed information about motor vehicles registered in a particular state as well as information about the residents of that state who are licensed to drive those vehicles. And federal governments needed relevant information as well. Those records had to be accessible to governmental agencies at various levels and had to be able to be transferred and exchanged relatively easily. Since the records in question contained personal information that was generally considered to be neither confidential nor intimate, there were good reasons to declare them 'public records.' It was assumed that no harm could come to individuals because of the availability of those public records, and it was believed that communities would be better served because of the access and flow of those records for purposes that seemed to be legitimate. But certain factors have changed significantly. Information-gathering companies now access those public records, manipulate the records in certain ways, and then sell that information to third parties.[6] Was this the original intent for making such information accessible to the public?

A Questionable Inference

Many information merchants seem to believe that because: (a) *public records have always been available in a public space;* and (b) *the Internet is a public space;* it follows that (c) *all public records ought to be made available online.* According to this line of reasoning, it is not only a good thing that many public records have, in fact, been placed on-line; rather it is assumed that municipal governments should be required to make *all* public records available online. Defenders of this view often proceed on the reasoning that, as citizens, we have a right to know what the government is up to (based on the notion of freedom of information). Placing public records on-line, they further assume, will ensure that such information flows freely. However, there have now been several cases in which operating on such a presumption has caused outrage on the part of many citizens,[7] as well as harm to some, which in the case of Amy Boyer resulted in death. So perhaps we should rethink our policies regarding access to on-line public records. We should also perhaps develop specific policies and guidelines regarding which kinds of personal information should be made available to search engines.

If Youens [had] had to track down Amy Boyer without the aid of Internet search facilities, would it have made a difference? Would he have gone to the relevant municipal building to acquire information about Boyer (or would he possibly have hired a private detective to do so)? If Youens himself had gone to the municipal building, would it have been possible that someone, for example a clerk in one of the offices, might have noticed that Youens was behaving strangely? If so, would such an observation have promoted the clerk to notify his or her supervisor or possibly even the police? And would such an action, in turn, possibly have helped to avoid the tragic outcome of the Boyer case? Of course, each of these questions is speculative in nature.[8] And because we are focusing here on the Boyer incident, it is difficult do say what the answers to these questions would mean in a broader sense with regard to cyberstalking and to the easy access of public records. But these questions do give us some pause, and they may force us to reconsider our current beliefs about the public vs. private realm of personal information. These questions also cause us to consider the need for implementing explicit policies with regard to use of Internet search engines in the retrieval of personal information.

What can we conclude so far with respect to Amy Boyer's rights and expectations regarding privacy? Was her privacy violated; and if so, in what sense? Amy Boyer's stepfather, Tim Remsberg, believes that his stepdaughter's privacy was indeed violated. He has appeared before congressional groups and has influenced those in the U.S. Congress to sponsor legislation that would make it illegal to sell the social security numbers of one or more individuals as a part of online commercial transactions. Remsberg has also sued Docusearch.com, the online company that provided Youens with information about where Boyer lived and worked. Additionally, Remsberg has filed a wrongful death suit against Tripod and Geocities, the two ISPs that hosted the Web sites that Youens set up about Boyer....

MORAL OBLIGATION AT THE LEVEL OF INDIVIDUALS

We now consider the question of individual moral obligation, by asking what kinds of responsibilities Internet users have to inform 'would-be victims' of their immanent danger to online stalkers. For example, if an Internet user had been aware of Boyer's situation, should that user have notified Boyer that she was being stalked? In other words, is that user under a moral obligation to do so? If we want to be responsible, or at least caring citizens, in cyberspace, the answer would seem to be *yes*. In this case, it would not be morally permissible to wait for stalking activities to move into physical space before we took any action.

Various proposals for controlling individual behavior in on-line society have resulted in a conflict between those who wish to regulate by law and those who wish to preserve the practice of self-regulation. Of course, this dispute is sometimes also at the base of arguments involving claims having to do with a 'safe' social space vs. 'restrictive' one. In the case of cyberstalking, should our duty, if we have one, to assist others be based on legal regulations or should it rest on grounds of individual moral obligation to assist others?

What exactly is meant by 'moral obligation'? Historically, philosophers have offered diverse, and sometimes competing, definitions of what is meant by this expression. An Internet user consulting a dictionary to locate a colloquial definition would likely discover one similar to the following: '[moral obligation is] founded on the fundamental principles of right conduct rather than on legalities enactment of custom' (*Random House Dictionary*). Of course, philosophers have attempted to give us far more rigorous definitions of 'moral obligation.' An interesting question is whether our notion of moral obligation is one that is derived from our concept of justice, or whether instead our sense of 'justice' derives from moral obligation. This, obviously, is a complex question and is one that cannot be satisfactorily discussed and answered in this paper. Of course, the question of which moral notion—obligation or justice—is more fundamental could help us to get a clearer sense of exactly what is at stake in disputes involving individual moral responsibility. Contemporary philosophers and ethicists as diverse as Josef Peiper (1966), Carol Gilligan (1982), and Anton Vedder (2001) have explored this question. Unfortunately, we are not able to examine the three positions in the depth that each deserves. Nonetheless, we sketch out some general themes in their respective arguments.

Three Views of Moral Obligation: The Peiper, Gilligan, and Vedder Models

Josef Peiper (1966) has argued that the concept of moral obligation is one that is not only 'personal' but also linked to one's community. For Peiper, 'doing good' is more than obeying some abstract norm (i.e., some Kantian abstract notion of duty and universality). Rather, it is about the individual's relationship to other individuals and to the community itself. Carol Gilligan (1982), in her work in feminist ethics, first proposed a position similar to Peiper's. Both Peiper and Gilligan suggest that moral obligation goes far beyond the notion of an individual simply obeying laws. For them, moral obligation is closely tied with a more complex concept of justice. As such, justice involves the *relationship* of individuals, including their individual moral obligations to one another. In the writings of both Peiper and Gilligan, despite their very different objectives, can be found the basis for the thesis that individuals are interconnected and that these individual relationships play a primary role in the development of the concept of moral responsibility.

The notion of moral obligation is seen as extending beyond the self to others, both in Pieper's concept of 'commutative justice' and Gilligan's 'ethic of care.' This 'ethic of care,' as it is labeled in feminist ethics, is more than a mere 'non-interference ethic.' Based on that belief that care and justice are part of the same moral framework, it has been argued that individuals have a moral obligation to assist others and to prevent harm. From this perspective, individuals would be compelled to act from a basis of moral obligation, even though there may be no specific laws or rules to prescribe such actions.[9]

Anton Vedder (2001) has recently put forth a theory of moral obligation that also has implications at the level of the individual. From Vedder's view, it would seem to follow that we cannot excuse ourselves from our moral responsibility to inform the victim of a threat to his/her life simply because there is no specific law obligating us to do so. Vedder asserts that 'the sheer ability and opportunity to act in order to avoid or prevent harm, danger, and offense from taking place' puts an obligation on the agent. We saw in the preceding section how Vedder's argument can be applied to issues of moral responsibility involving organisations. He also points out that in cases 'when harm, danger or offense would be considerable while the appropriate action would not present significant risks, costs or burdens to the agent,' the same notion of moral responsibility applies, regardless of whether the *agent* is a natural person or an organization (Vedder, 2001).

A Minimalist Notion of Moral Obligation

Some have argued that, while morality can demand of an agent that he or she 'do no harm' to others, it cannot *require* the agent to actively 'prevent harm' or 'do good.' In one sense, to do no harm is to act in accordance with moral obligation. But is doing so always sufficient for complying with what is required of us as moral agents? In other words, if it is in our power to prevent harm and to do good, *should* we always be required to do so? And, if the answer to this question is *yes,* what are the grounds for such a theory of obligation.

A number of theoretical perspectives support the view that individuals should prevent harm (and other wise do good) whenever it is in their power to do so. For example, if one believes, as some natural law theorists assert, that the purpose of morality is to alleviate human suffering and to promote human flourishing whenever possible, then clearly we would seem obligated to prevent harm in cyberspace. For an interesting account of this type of moral theory, see Louis Pojman (2001). Unfortunately, we are not able to present Pojman's argument here in the detail that it deserves, since doing so would take us beyond the scope of this paper. But we can at least now see how, based on a model like Pojman's, one might develop a fuller theory in which individuals have an obligation to prevent harm or a 'duty to assist.' Of course, we recognize the difficulties of defending a natural law theory and we are not prepared to do so here. However, we also believe that the kind of limited or 'moderate' natural law theories that can be found in Pojman, and to some extent in James Moor (1988), can be very useful in making the case for individual moral obligation.

Expanding the Sphere of Moral Obligation: The Duty to Assist

Questions concerning whether individuals have a 'duty to assist' others often arise in the aftermath of highly publicized crimes, such as the one involving in the Kitty Genovese case in 1964. A young woman, Genovese was murdered on the street outside her apartment building in Queens, New York, as thirty-eight of her neighbors watched. None of her neighbors called the police during the 35-minute period of repeated stabbings. Some have since referred to this refusal to assist a neighbor in critical need as 'the Genovese syndrome.' Police involved in the Genovese case believe that the witnesses were morally obligated to notify the police, even though there may have been no formal law or specific statute requiring them to do so.

Drawing an analogy between the Genovese and Boyer cases, we can ask whether users who might have been able to assist Boyer should have done so (i.e., morally obligated to assist). We can also ask what kind of place cyberspace will become, if people refuse to assist users who may be at risk to predators and murderers. Is our obligation to our fellow users one in which we are required merely to do no harm? Peiper, Gilligan and Vedder would each answer *no.* Consider the potential harm that could come from doing nothing vs. the level of inconvenience caused to self, which would be minimal, by coming to the assistance of others who may be in danger in cyberspace. In the cyberstalking case involving Barber and Dellapenta, Barber's father, with the cooperation of the men who were soliciting her, provided evidence that led to Dellapenta's arrest. In the case of Amy Boyer, however, the sense of individual moral responsibility was not apparent, since certain online users had indeed viewed the Youens'

Web site and did not inform Amy Boyer that she was being stalked. As in the case of Kitty Genovese, Boyer was also murdered. Was Boyer's death an on-line manifestation of the 'Genovese syndrome?'

In light of what happened to Amy Boyer, we suggest that on-line users adopt a notion of individual responsibility to assist others. Doing so would help to keep cyberspace a safer place for everyone, but especially for women and children who are particularly vulnerable groups. Some might be inclined to argue that the threat to Boyer was merely virtual, since the threat itself did not occur in physical space.[10] Such an argument, however, ignores the fact that threats in virtual space have, in fact, resulted in physical harm to individuals. In addition to the harm resulting in cyberstalking cases, consider the physical harm that has resulted to some victims of Internet pedophilia. In avoiding our individual duty to assist, individual users disconnect themselves from their responsibility towards fellow human beings. When they accept the duty to assist, they are acknowledging their moral obligation to help prevent others from being harmed.

CONCLUSION

We have examined some ethical aspects of cyberstalking in general, and the Amy Boyer case in particular. We saw that the cyberstalking case involving Boyer raised privacy concerns that cause us to reconsider the kinds of protections currently accorded to on-line public records. We also saw that cyberstalking issues have raised questions for ISPs having to do with legal liability and moral responsibility. It was argued that issues of moral responsibility involving cyberstalking span two spheres: the collective (e.g., ISPs) and the individual (i.e., ordinary Internet users). We believe that both ISPs and individual users, each in different ways, should assume some moral responsibility for preventing harm from coming to individuals targeted by cyberstalkers. Although we recognise the difficulties inherent in defending arguments involving moral responsibility at both the collective and individual levels, we nonetheless offer some preliminary suggestions for why both organisations (such as ISPs) and individuals should act to prevent harm from coming to their fellow Internet users, whenever it is in their power to do so.

ACKNOWLEDGMENTS

We are grateful to Anton Vedder for some very helpful comments on an earlier version of this paper. We also wish to thank Detective Sergeant Frank Paison of the Nashua, NH Police Department, who was the chief investigator in the Amy Boyer cyberstalking case, for some helpful information that he provided during an interview with him.

BIBLIOGRAPHY

Alison Adam. Cyberstalking: Gender and Computer Ethics. In Eileen Green and Alison Adam, Editors, *Virtual Gender: Technology, Consumption, and Identity,* Pages 209–234. Routledge, London, 2001.

Alison Adam. Cyberstalking and Internet Pornography: Gender and Gaze. *Ethics and Information Technology,* 4(2): 133–142, 2002.

Richard T. De George. Law and Ethics in the Information Age. A paper presented at River College, Nashua, NH, April 3, 2001.

Carol Gilligan. *In a Different Voice.* Harvard University Press, Cambridge, 1982.

Frances S. Grodzinsky and Herman. T. Tavani. Is Cyberstalking a Special Type of Computer Crime? In Terrell Ward Bynum, et al. editors. *Proceedings of ETHICPMP 2001: The Fifth International Conference on the Social and Ethical Impacts of Information and Communication Technology,* Vol. 2, pages 72–81. Wydawnicktwo Mikom Publishers, Gdańsk, Poland, 2001.

Frances S. Grodzinsky and Herman T. Tavani. Cyberstalking, Moral Responsibility, and Legal Liability Issues for Internet Service Providers. In Joseph Herkert, editor, *Proceedings of ISTAS 2002: The International Symposium on Technology and Society.* pages 331–339. IEEE Computer Society Press, Los Alamitos, CA, 2002.

Deborah G. Johnson. *Computer Ethics,* 3rd ed. Prentice Hall, Upper Saddle River, NJ, 2001.

James H. Moor. Reason, Relativity, and Responsibility in Computer Ethics. *Computers and Society,* 28(1): 14–21, 1998.

James H. Moor. Just Consequentialism. A paper presented at the 2000–2001 River College Humanities Lecture Series, Nashua, NH, February 20, 2001.

Helen Nissenbaum. Computing and Accountability. In Deborah Y. Johnson and Helen Nissenbaum, Editors, *Computing, Ethics and Social Values,* pages 526–538. Englewood Cliffs, NJ, Prentice Hall, 1995.

Helen Nissenbaum. Toward an Approach to Privacy in Public: Challenges of Information Technology. *Ethics & Behavior,* 7(3): 207–219, 1997.

Helen Nissenbaum. Protecting Privacy in an Information Age: The Problem of Privacy in Public. *Law and Philosophy,* 17: 559–496. 1998.

Josef Peiper: *The Four Cardinal Virtues.* University of Notre Dame Press, Indiana, 1966.

Louis P. Pojman, *Ethics: Discovering Right and Wrong,* 4th ed. Wadsworth, Belmont, CA, 2001.

Michael Scanlan. Informational Privacy and Moral Values. *Ethics and Information Technology,* 3(1): 3–12, 2001.

Richard A. Spinello. Internet Service Providers and Defamation: New Standards of Liability. In Richard A. Spinello and Herman T. Tavanii, Editors, *Reading in CyberEthics,* pages 198–209. Sudbury, MA, Jones and Bartlett, 2001.

Herman T. Tavani. Internet Search Engines and Personal Privacy. In Jeroen van den Hoven, Editor, *Proceedings of CEPE '97: Conference on Computer Ethics—Philosophical Enquiry,* pages 214–223. Erasmus University Press, Rotterdam, The Netherlands, 1998.

Herman T. Tavani, Defining the Boundaries of Computer Crime: Piracy, Break-ins and Sabotage in Cyberspace. *Computers and Society,* 30(4): 3–9, 2000.

Herman T. Tavani. The Uniqueness Debate in Computer Ethics: What Exactly Is at Issue, and Why Does It Matter? *Ethics and Information Technology,* 4(1): 37–54, 2002.

Anton H. Vedder. Accountability of Internet Access and Service Providers: Strict Liability entering Ethics. *Ethics and Information Technology,* 3(1): 67–74, 2001.

NOTES

1. An earlier version of this paper was presented at the CEPE 2001 Conference, Lancaster University, UK, December 14–16, 2001. The present paper expands on two earlier works (Grodzinsky and Tavani, 2001, 2002). Portions of this article are extracted from H.T. Tavani, *Ethics in an Age of Information and Communication Technology* (forthcoming from John Wiley & Sons Publishers). We are grateful to Wiley for permission to use that material in this paper.
2. Nor do we argue that cyberstalking is a 'genuine computer crime.' See Tavani (2000) for some distinctions that can be drawn between genuine computer crimes and computer-related crimes.
3. For an in-depth discussion of the question whether cyberstalking has introduced any unique ethical issues, see Tavani (2002).
4. For a more detailed discussion of privacy problems that can arise from certain uses of Internet search engines, see Tavani (1998).
5. See also Nissenbaum (1997) for a discussion of some of the challenges that information technology poses for the 'problem of privacy in public.'
6. Richard De George (2001) has suggested that because Internet and computing technology has made it possible for organisations and individuals to gather information in ways that were not possible in the pre-Internet era, we need to reconsider why societies have public records and how those records should be protected.
7. For example, Michael Scanlan(2001) describes a controversial case involving the state of Oregon, which sold records in its Motor Vehicle Registry database to an on-line consulting business. The citizens of Oregon complained and the state eventually reversed its policy regarding the sale of information about its licensed drivers.
8. Richard De George (2001) points out that when public records were accessible only in public buildings, there was a much easier way of tracing the acquisition of those records in the event that some 'misuse' had been made of the information contained in them.
9. For a discussion of some ways in which Gilligan's system of ethics can be applied to issues involving cyberstalking, as well as to issues in computer ethics in general, see Alison Adam (2001, 2002).
10. This type of reasoning is a variation of what James Moor (2001) refers to as the 'virtuality fallacy.' According to this particular line of fallacious reasoning: *X* exists in cyberspace; cyberspace is not in the real world; therefore, *X* is exempt from the demands of the real world.

QUESTIONS FOR ANALYSIS

1. Does the sad fact of cyberstalking and the murder of innocent victims like Amy Boyer justify more serious efforts to restrict access to our private data on the Internet? Has our demand for easy access to information gone too far, resulting in these crimes? What kind of legislation do you believe would be appropriate to curtail such activities, balancing freedom of expression of non-criminals with the threatening behavior of people like Boyer's murderer?
2. Should the freedom of expression to post threatening web sites, as Boyer's murder did, be restricted? Who should police such sites? Should the Internet service providers be responsible for monitoring such web sites and taking them offline?
3. Would you, as a user of the Internet, feel a moral obligation to contact people like Amy Boyer if you saw something on the Web that seemed threatening? Or would you be reluctant to "get involved," as people were in the Kitty Genovese case many years ago in New York?

CASE PRESENTATION

Ticketed for Obscenity on the Information Superhighway

Robert and Carleen Thomas ran a computer bulletin board for members only from their home in Milpitas, California. What bound the members of Amateur Action Bulletin Board System was an interest in kinky pornography, which the married couple provided for a fee. The operation ran smoothly until a postal inspector in Memphis, Tennessee, joined the bulletin board under an assumed name and began receiving sexually explicit photographs on his computer. As a result, the Thomases were charged with violating federal obscenity laws. In July of 1994 they were tried and convicted of eleven counts of transmitting obscenity through interstate phone lines. They were sentenced to 37 and 30 months of incarceration, respectively.

Theirs was not the first case of a bulletin board operator being tried for violating federal obscenity laws, but in all previous cases the trials were held in the area where the material originated. The Thomas trial was held in Memphis, where the photographs were received. A federal appeals court in Cincinnati upheld their convictions and sentences in January 1996.

The U.S. Supreme Court, in 1997, declined to hear the case. The issue that free-speech supporters had hoped the Court would address was the obscenity test from *Miller v. California,* which appeals to "contemporary community standards," where *community* means "local community." Memphis is a very conservative community when it comes to pornography and censorship; its standards are stricter than California's. For the Thomases, it was a question of fairness. Did the prosecutors shop around for a trial venue that would guarantee a conviction? Should the defendants be judged by the standards of a community other than their own? For the nation's freedom of speech on the information superhighway, the questions are much broader: What constitutes a community on computer networks? Should the standards of the most conservative communities govern the free-speech rights of the rest of the country? The Appeals Court had rejected the arguments of the Thomases' lawyers that new technology had wiped out traditional concepts of community. Instead, it ruled that *Miller* applies to the Internet.

Civil libertarians consider the Thomas case an alarming reminder of the problems in applying traditional concepts of free speech to the Internet. Electronic Internet communications do not always have a clear counterpart in traditional print formats, and new principles are needed to guarantee traditional rights.

QUESTIONS FOR ANALYSIS

1. How would you answer the four questions posed in the third paragraph?
2. Does the notion of a local community make sense in the context of a computer network available to individuals throughout the nation and much of the world?
3. *Miller v. California*'s obscenity test was designed in part to let residents control their own communities. Let the standards of New Yorkers determine what bookstores and movie theaters are acceptable in New York City, and let those of Memphis residents determine the same for their city. Is that purpose applicable to international computer networks?
4. What kind of obscenity test do you think is appropriate for computer networks?
5. Should minors be protected from indecent material on the Internet? If so, how?

CASE PRESENTATION

A Chill in Cyberspace

When John Osborne and his roommate moved from Florida to Georgia in 1997, their U-Haul rental truck broke down repeatedly, and their trip turned into a 27-hour nightmare. After U-Haul seized their property and made them pay to fix the truck, Osborne filed complaints with U-Haul and the Better Business Bureau. When those approaches failed to resolve the matter to Osborne's satisfaction, he turned to the Internet, posting a site called "The U-Hell Website: Misadventures in Moving," and he encouraged disgruntled U-Haul customers to post their own stories.

U-Haul filed suit in Arizona for libel and trademark infringement, claiming that Arizona Internet users would be able to see the site, but also knowing that Osborne could not afford to defend himself in a distant state. The Electronic Frontier Foundation and the Arizona ACLU provided free legal assistance to Osborne and got the case dismissed, but U-Haul is now threatening to sue him in Georgia.

QUESTIONS FOR ANALYSIS

1. Osborne successfully argued that the Internet's availability in Arizona was not sufficient to warrant filing a lawsuit against him in that state. Yet the Thomases, in the previous case presentation, were not able to succeed with such an argument. Do the courts seem clear on the nature of the Internet in making what seem to be contradictory rulings about the "location" of the Internet? Where do you think "virtual reality" is located? Should wrong-doers be able to escape the reach of the law entirely?
2. Aggressive lawsuits by such companies as U-Haul have had a chilling effect on individual persons with complaints about those companies, creating a *David v. Goliath* scenario that most ordinary people cannot afford to fight. Defamation is not protected under the free-speech guarantees of the first amendment, but should the courts participate in this apparent attempt by large corporations to suppress legitimate free speech by disgruntled consumers? Knowing Osborne's legal nightmare with U-Haul, would you be less likely to post angry web sites or comments to a chatroom criticizing a big company by name? Should the courts attempt to level the playing field by refusing to hear such defamation cases?
3. In the early years of the Internet, some supporters saw it as the Wild West, with no rules or laws, and reveled in this freedom. Should we try to return to that environment, or should all the laws and ethical principles that apply in non-cyberspace apply to our interactions online?
4. Have you ever posted comments that might be defamatory on a site like Ratemyprofessors.com? Should professors be able to sue for defamatory statements posted on such sites on the Internet?

CASE PRESENTATION

Censoring Political Speech

Although the Internet has been proclaimed an extraordinary mechanism for worldwide communication, free of government interference, political speech is encountering censorship after all, to the dismay of many Internet users.

The German government bans the publication and sale of Adolf Hitler's *Mein Kampf*, a ban originally ordered by the Allies at the end of World War II. That ban was easier to enforce when the book was available only at physical book stores and libraries in a physical form. The Allies and later the German government defended the ban as necessary to prevent the rise of neo-Nazism in the country responsible for the horrors of the Holocaust. With the easy availability of texts online, however, German Internet users can now access the banned book on several Internet sites. Amazon.com ran afoul of the German government when German patrons started ordering the book from the American site, even though the German version of Amazon.com refused to sell the book. Bans on the sale of *Mein Kampf* are widespread in other countries in Europe. It cannot be sold in France, except in scholarly editions with commentaries and discussions.The Netherlands prohibits sale of the book, but not owning or lending it. The state of Bavaria has attempted to prohibit sales on the grounds that it owns the copyright on the book, but the English version has not been copyrighted in Bavaria and is freely available in the United States and the United Kingdom.

Another form of censorship of political speech on the Internet recently emerged in China. The huge Internet search engine Google.com agreed to censor its search engine in the Chinese language, at the insistence of the Chinese government. Searches in that language do not report sites that present candid information about the democracy protests at Tiananmen Square in 1989 or the protest group Falun Gong, for example. In its defense, Google argues that it does not block access to the actual web sites, but only removes them from the search results. Some staunch supporters of free speech are trying to protest by refusing to use Google or dropping Google ads from their own web sites. Other well-known search engines, including Yahoo and MSN, have also entered into censorship agreements with the Chinese government.

QUESTIONS FOR ANALYSIS

1. Do these attempts at government censorship reduce the value of the Internet as a medium for international education and free speech? Should world governments—or perhaps the United Nations—attempt to intervene and insist on free speech and unfettered access to information?
2. Do you agree with the European governments that fear that being able to read *Mein Kampf* might encourage a resurgence of neo-Nazism? Or would you agree with J. S. Mill and civil libertarians that the best way to learn what is wrong with those benighted ideas is to expose them to the light of day and encourage free and open debate?
3. Is there anything we can do to protest the censorship of the Google.com search engine in China? Or is this a matter of national autonomy that should not concern us? If the U.S. government demanded that Google.com censor its search engine to eliminate access to controversial political speech that the government deemed inappropriate, would you support this censorship?

CASE PRESENTATION

Pirates of the Campuses

In 2004, the Recording Industry Association of America filed lawsuits against 532 individuals for illegally swapping songs. Eighty-nine of those users were students using 21 different university networks across the country. For years, the RIAA had pressured university administrators to crack down on students who were using campus broadband Internet capabilities to swap music using technologies like Napster, in violation of copyright law.

Universities complain that they are trying to get students to behave in compliance with the law by running educational programs about the illegality of file-sharing of copyrighted music. The RIAA complains that these efforts have been ineffective and that they are losing huge revenues from the sale of CDs or legal downloads on the Internet, for which one must pay a fee.

Two much-publicized lawsuits have sided with the industry. In *A&M Records v. Napster,* the Federal Court of Appeals for the Ninth Circuit in 2001 sided with the recording industry in ruling that the Napster technology for sharing music files online encouraged users to violate copyright. The site for free downloads was essentially put out of business, but it has re-emerged along with several other sites to sell the downloads, with a portion of the royalties going to the record industry.

In 2005, the U.S. Supreme Court unanimously sided with Metro-Goldwyn-Mayer Studios in a lawsuit against Grokster Ltd., which developed and promoted a program that facilitated downloads on the Internet of movies, as well as songs. As Justice David Souter wrote in the court's opinion, "We hold that one who distributes a device with the object of promoting its use to infringe copyright . . . is liable for the resulting acts of infringement by third parties."

QUESTIONS FOR ANALYSIS

1. Many students believe that downloading free music and movies from the Internet is their best way of protesting what they consider excessively high prices charged by unfair monopolies in the entertainment industry. Do you believe this provides an ethical justification for downloading, in violation of copyright law and the property rights of the movie and recording industries? Are there additional considerations here that provide ethical support for this file-sharing?
2. Deterrence is one major theory of punishment in the criminal law. Now that the recording industry is aggressively filing suit against college students for these downloads, does this reduce the likelihood that you yourself will engage in this practice, whether or not you have in the past? What other considerations would make you less likely to continue to engage in illegal downloading?
3. Say you are a struggling artist, filmmaker, or musician hoping to earn income from your artistic work and support yourself in a career. Do you think it would be fair for future college students to download your work without paying you copyright royalties?
4. Say you are a computer software engineering student. Do you think it will be fair for you to be held responsible if someone misuses the software you design to violate the law? (This is essentially what the courts did in the *Napster* and *Grokster* decisions.)

AFTERWORD

MORE THAN ONE CYNIC has claimed that logical arguments are nothing but rationalizations of our prejudices. And there is, unfortunately, some truth to that claim, at least when it comes to people who spout reason but refuse to listen to reason. But when we are truly open to the arguments of others, the claim clearly misses, especially when we allow ourselves to be convinced by compelling arguments and consequently change our minds.

Now that your course in applied ethics is finished, it might be wise to ask yourself a few questions about it. Did the arguments you came across, either in class or in this book, cause you to reevaluate your positions on some topics? Did any one of them cause you to soften a given position? Cause you to change your mind completely? If you can answer yes to any or all of these questions, the course has served you well, regardless of your grade. If you cannot, you might want to ask yourself another question. Why can't you? And if your quick answer is that you were right all along, you might want to search for a not-so-quick one.

That's one point worth making at the end of your course. Another concerns all the topics you didn't cover, including some in this book (no single-semester course can cover them all) and those not in this book. (For reasons of space and format, we could not include every possible issue in applied ethics.) The latter include questions about "political correctness," for example; about the extent of our obligations to starving peoples throughout the world; about healthcare, scientific experimentation, and genetic engineering; and about all the many issues that we can't anticipate but that are sure to arise over the years. Like the issues you did cover, each of them is difficult, involving complex matters of fact, morality, and often law. We hope your experiences in this course have prepared you to deal with them in a thorough, dispassionate way and maybe to reevaluate your views on some of them.

Finally, we hope the course has been a real eye-opener for you. Even if you changed your mind about nothing, we hope you at least were struck by the complexities of the issues you studied, the many ingenious approaches to them you encountered, and the reasonableness of your opponents' positions.

GLOSSARY

Abolitionist Someone who advocates doing away with a particular practice, such as the death penalty.

Active euthanasia The act of painlessly putting to death persons suffering from incurable conditions or diseases.

***Ad hominem* argument** An **argument** that relies on attacking the opponent rather than the opponent's argument. When the attack is irrelevant to whether we should accept the opponent's argument, it is considered a **fallacy.**

Anthropocentric Centering on human beings, or regarding human beings as central to any larger group. In ethics, it means centering on human welfare or regarding the environment as important only as it affects human welfare.

Argument A collection of statements containing a conclusion and supporting statements (also called *evidence, reasons, grounds,* or *premises*) whose purpose is to show that the conclusion is true or likely to be true.

Argument by analogy An **argument** that concludes that two different things are alike in some ways because they are alike in some other ways. When such an argument fails to make its case, it is considered both a **faulty analogy** and a **fallacy.**

Assisted suicide Suicide by a patient, with assistance from a physician, usually by prescribing a lethal dose of drugs.

Autonomy Independence, particularly from the control of outside forces. In philosophy, it refers to the capacity to act on our choices, where these choices are the product of our own goals, desires, and reasoning powers. To have this capacity is to be an autonomous being.

Biocentric Centering on the *biosphere,* or the earth's ecological system. In ethics, it means regarding the health of the ecological system as central rather than the welfare of humans.

Biotic community In the philosophy of Aldo Leopold and his followers, a community made up of all members of the ecological system, including water, soil, and air as well as living things.

Capitalism An economic system in which the means of production are in private hands and economic decisions are made by private individuals in response to market forces.

Casuistic Determining what is right and wrong by appeal to principles in ethics.

Categorical imperative In the philosophy of Kant, a command that applies to all rational beings independent of their desires; a command they ought to follow whether they want to or not.

Causal generalization The conclusion that one thing causes another because of observations that the first has been followed by the other.

Certiorari Agreement by an appeals court to review the decision of a lower court.

Charity, principle of Understanding the arguments of opponents in the most reasonable or plausible way possible to give them a fair hearing.

Civil union A formal partnership between two people with some, but not necessarily all, of the rights of a married couple, as recognized by a governmental authority.

Clone An exact genetic copy of a cell, plant, or animal.

Consequentialist Ethical reasoning that looks to the consequences of alternative actions to determine which is right.

Contractarianism An ethical theory based on appeal to a social contract entered into voluntarily.

Counterexample An example that shows a generalization to be false or a rule of reasoning to be invalid.

Cultural relativism In ethics, the view that moral truths are not absolutely true but are relative to a particular society, that whether an act is right or wrong depends on the moral norms of society and not on an absolute standard.

Deductive argument An **argument** that claims to follow **truth-preserving** rules.

Deductive logic The area of logic that deals with **deductive arguments.**

Defamation Words communicating claims that are false and that damage the reputation of another person.

Deterrence The preventing or discouraging of an act, often by fear or doubt.

Difference principle In the philosophy of John Rawls, the principle that determines what kinds of inequalities can exist in a just society.

Distributive justice The area of justice that deals with how society's wealth should be distributed among its members.

Ecocentric Centering on the ecological health of the environment. See **biocentric.**

Egalitarianism The belief in equal rights for all people, including political, economic, and social rights.

Entitlement A right or a claim to something.

Equality principle In the philosophy of John Rawls, the principle that every person has a right to the greatest basic freedom compatible with equal freedom for all.

Equivocation Implicitly relying on two or more meanings of the same word. When an **argument** relies on the premise to reach a conclusion, it is a **fallacy.**

Ethical relativism The view that moral truths are not absolutely true but true relative to some particular standards.

Eudaimonia Happiness, or total well-being.

Euthanasia Literally, "good death." The term is usually applied to the act of ending the life of someone suffering from a fatal or incurable disease or, most commonly in the case of nonhuman animals, ending a life painlessly.

Ex parte Done for one party only, in the absence of the other party in a legal proceeding.

Ex post facto law A law passed after the fact; a retroactive law.

Fallacy An unreliable way of reasoning that does not provide good reason for accepting an **argument**'s conclusion.

Faulty analogy An **argument by analogy** that fails to make its case.

Formal fallacy A rule of reasoning that appears to be **truth preserving** but isn't.

Germ cell A sperm or an egg.

Greatest happiness principle See **principle of utility.**

Hegemony Predominance, or predominant influence, of one state over others.

Holistic ethics Ethical views that focus on duties to some particular whole, such as the **biotic community** or the state.

Hypothetical imperative In the philosophy of Kant, a command we have reason to follow only if it serves a desire of ours.

Idealist Someone who has high ideals, even if unrealistic and visionary; a philosophical theory that ideas are more real than external objects of perception.

In camera In private; in the chambers of the judge in a legal proceeding.

Individual relativism In ethics, the view that moral truths are not absolute but relative to individuals, that whether an act is right or wrong depends on the convictions of the person performing it and not on an absolute standard.

Inductive argument An **argument** in which the supporting statements, or evidence, aim to show that it is reasonable to accept that the conclusion is true.

Informal fallacy A common but unreliable reasoning strategy that generally relies on hidden **premises** that are false, irrelevant, or otherwise suspect.

Involuntary euthanasia Termination of a life when decision is made by someone else, and the patient has never made preferences known to anyone.

Jus ad bellum The justice of war; the law on the use of force.

Jus cogens Overriding principles of general international law.

Jus in bello The law or justice within a war, regardless of the justifiability of the war itself.

Libel Written defamation.

Libertarianism In political thought, the view that all forms of coercion—except to prevent harm to life, liberty, and property—are wrong, whether they come from individuals or from the government.

Living will A document executed by a competent adult directing physicians not to use artificial or extraordinary measures to prolong the person's life.

Maxim In the philosophy of Kant, a general principle of behavior; for example, whenever someone hurts me, I will hurt him back.

Moral agent A being capable of making moral claims and accepting moral duties.

Moral intuition A moral conviction arrived at after careful consideration of the relevant facts.

Natural law Any law of nature, as opposed to a state law or federal law. In ethics, moral laws that are embedded in nature as scientific laws are.

Natural rights Rights that all persons are born with. Rights that all persons have by virtue of being persons.

Nonvoluntary euthanasia Ending the life of a person suffering a fatal or incurable disease, in which the decision is made by someone other than the patient.

Obscenity In U.S. law, pornography that is not protected by the First Amendment.

Ontological Relating to the theory and nature of being and existence.

Ontology The theory and nature of being and existence.

Passive euthanasia Any act of allowing a patient to die.

Paternalism The practice of treating others as a father would. In political thought, government policies that limit individual rights to protect individuals from harming themselves.

Person In ethics, either an **autonomous** being or a being who is a full-fledged member of the moral community.

Pluralism The existence of many independent centers of power within a society.

Pornography Erotic material that is intended primarily to cause sexual arousal or in fact does have that primary effect.

Practical imperative In Kant's philosophy, respect for persons as ends, never as means.

Premise A supporting statement in an **argument.** A statement that aims to show that the conclusion is true or likely to be true.

***Prima facie* duty or obligation** An obligation that may or may not be binding at a given time depending on whether some other obligation takes precedence at that time.

Principle of utility The moral principle that we should produce the greatest balance of happiness over unhappiness, giving equal consideration to the happiness and unhappiness of everyone who will be affected by our actions.

Procrustes' bed In Greek mythology, cutting off one's feet to fit the size of the bed; in reasoning, altering important facts to meet an arbitrary or inappropriate standard or rule.

Question-begging argument A form of **fallacy** in which you assume as a **premise** what you want to prove.

Realism A political theory favoring pragmatism and literal truth; a philosophical position that universal principles are more real than sensory objects.

Red herring A form of **fallacy** in which an irrelevant issue is introduced to distract attention from the issue at hand.

Respect for persons The moral principle that we should never use another person merely as a means to our own ends.

Retentionist Someone who advocates keeping in place a particular practice, such as the death penalty.

Retribution Punishment for wrongdoing.

Sexual libertarianism The view that sex is morally no different from any other activity, that there are no special moral rules that apply only to sexual behavior.

Si vis pacem, para bellum If you wish for peace, prepare for war.

Sine qua non Without which not; something essential or indispensable.

Slander Spoken defamation.

Slippery slope argument Assuming that an action will lead to an unwanted outcome as a result of many small steps that will inevitably follow. If the assumption is not sufficiently justified, it is a **fallacy.**

Social contract theory Ethical or political thought that views morality or the state as the product of an agreement (a social contract) among individuals.

Socialism An economic system in which the means of production are collectively owned and the major economic decisions are made by society rather than private individuals.

Somatic cell Any cell that is not a **germ cell.**

Sound deductive argument An argument that is valid *and* in which all premises are true.

Speciesism The position that it is ethically justifiable to give preference to members of the species *Homo sapiens* over other animal species.

Stare decisis The tradition in English common law of following the precedent of previous decisions.

Straw man A form of **fallacy** in which the opponent's position is distorted.

Teleological Pertaining to design or ultimate purpose.

Thought experiment A mental exercise in which someone imagines a set of circumstances to try to discover what would follow from it. In ethics, the purpose is usually to test moral principles or rules.

Transfer payment A payment that involves the transfer of wealth from one segment of the population to another—for example, welfare payments.

Truth-preserving rule A valid rule of **deductive logic;** a rule of reasoning that guarantees that the conclusion is true if the **premises** are true.

Utilitarianism The moral philosophy that considers the **principle of utility** to be the one basic moral principle.

Valid deductive argument An **argument** that follows **truth-preserving rules** only.

Veil of ignorance In the philosophy of John Rawls, a condition for deciding if the basic structures of society are just. To decide from behind a veil of ignorance is to decide without knowing how any one individual will be affected by these structures.

Virtue A habit, tendency, or disposition that helps us to achieve our goals.

Voluntary euthanasia Ending the life of someone who is a competent adult patient requesting or giving informed consent to a particular course of medical treatment or nontreatment.

Warranted argument An **inductive argument** in which the supporting statements, or evidence, show that it is reasonable to accept the conclusion.

Welfare capitalism An economic system that follows most tenets of **capitalism** but also includes **transfer payments.**

INDEX